SHAKESPEARE'S TRAGIC ART

Shakespeare's Tragic Art

Rhodri Lewis

PRINCETON UNIVERSITY PRESS

PRINCETON & OXFORD

Published by Princeton University Press
41 William Street, Princeton, New Jersey 08540
99 Banbury Road, Oxford OX2 6JX

press.princeton.edu

Library of Congress Cataloging-in-Publication Data

Names: Lewis, Rhodri, 1976– author.
Title: Shakespeare's tragic art / Rhodri Lewis.
Description: Princeton: Princeton University Press, 2024. | Includes bibliographical
    references and index.
Identifiers: LCCN 2023051754 (print) | LCCN 2023051755 (ebook) | ISBN 9780691246697
    (hardcover; acid-free paper) | ISBN 9780691246710 (ebook)
Subjects: LCSH: Shakespeare, William, 1564–1616—Tragedies. | Shakespeare, William,
    1564–1616—Philosophy. | Shakespeare, William, 1564–1616—Criticism and
    interpretation. | Tragedy. | LCGFT: Literary criticism.
Classification: LCC PR2983 .L46 2024 (print) | LCC PR2983 (ebook) |
    DDC 822.3/3—dc23/eng/20231102
LC record available at https://lccn.loc.gov/2023051754
LC ebook record available at https://lccn.loc.gov/2023051755

British Library Cataloging-in-Publication Data is available

Editorial: Anne Savarese and James Collier
Production Editorial: Kathleen Cioffi
Jacket Design: Katie Osborne
Production: Erin Suydam
Publicity: Alyssa Sanford and Carmen Jimenez
Copyeditor: Lachlan Brooks

Jacket image: Alexkava / Adobe Stock

This book has been composed in Miller

Printed on acid-free paper. ∞

Printed in the United States of America

10 9 8 7 6 5 4 3 2 1

In memory of Katherine Duncan-Jones

CONTENTS

ILLUSTRATIONS

I BY AND LARGE MAKE USE of the Shakespeare texts in the Arden
Third Series, occasionally emending readings that seem to me in error.
When quoting from non-Shakespearean early modern sources, I refer to
modern scholarly editions wherever possible. Where these do not exist,
I cite and quote from early modern printed works—highlighting textual
plurality, difficulty, or ambiguity where necessary. (While cleaving to the
particularities of early modern punctuation and orthography, I have mod-
ernized u/v and i/j, normalized the long s, and expanded the remnant of
the scribal thorn—initial "y"—to the digraph "th.") Though by no means
all of my readers will have access to the rare books collection of a major
research library, the wide availability of accurate facsimiles on Google
Books, *Early English Books Online*, *Gallica*, and similar databases means
that those with a mind to do so can investigate my readings with comparative ease. When citing or quoting from the Bible and from classical works,
I use the standard reference numbers (chapter and verse, section and line,
etc.). Unless otherwise stated, all translations from languages other than
English are my own.

SHAKESPEARE'S TRAGIC ART

Introduction

SEVERAL YEARS AGO, I wrote a book. In it, I offered an analysis of Shakespeare's *Hamlet* as a work first written and performed in or around the year 1600, and took issue with many of the critical orthodoxies through which the play has usually been regarded. One of these orthodoxies concerns itself with the characteristics of tragedy as Shakespeare wrote it, and I put the case that *Hamlet*, understood as a work of early seventeenth-century art, prompts us to think again about what Shakespearean tragedy might be said to comprise.

Although I had imagined that departure from Elsinore would serve as a temporary farewell to Shakespeare studies, it soon became apparent that things were going to take a different course. Writing is hard. I began to see that I had failed to communicate, even to those who had read and liked my book, that which I thought I had set out plainly; I also began to see that I had more to say. As another study of *Hamlet* was out of the question, I found myself thinking about Shakespearean tragedy in the round—sometimes, about whether there is any such thing, rather than a cluster of individual tragedies that happen to have been written, singly or collaboratively, by William Shakespeare.

It was thus in a spirit of something between curiosity and exploratory inquiry that I set out to write two essays. One on Roman attitudes to Egypt in *Antony and Cleopatra*; the other on time, temporality, and prophecy in *Macbeth*. Doing so convinced me that, despite persistent rumors to the contrary, many features of Shakespeare's tragic plays have passed unremarked. It also helped me to understand that there is more than enough in them to define "Shakespearean tragedy" as a tool for critical thinking, if not quite as a literary kind. Both essays are folded into the chapters that follow.

So much for how this book came about. The version of it before you has two goals. First, it aims to let readers see for themselves how Shakespeare's tragedies work, or at least to let them see how I see them working—from *Titus Andronicus* at some point around 1590 through to *Coriolanus* nearly twenty years later. These plays are, I suggest, preoccupied from first to last with the inscrutability of human life, the indeterminacy of the universe to which human life belongs, the unacknowledged fictions through which human beings attempt to make their existences feel meaningful, and the unhappy consequences to which these fictions generally give rise. Second, this book is an attempt to explain *why* Shakespeare wrote his tragedies the way he did, and to get at something of what—beyond gratifying patrons and getting people to buy theater tickets or printed books—he hoped to achieve by putting them out there in the world. My claim is that he did so to affirm the status of dramatic art as a medium—perhaps the *best* medium—through which to explore the truth of human experience in a world that is not fully susceptible to rational analysis.

When thinking about comedies like *A Midsummer Night's Dream* or *Love's Labour's Lost* or *As You Like It*, it is straightforward enough to establish that Shakespeare was aware of the degree to which human affairs depend on delusionality of one kind or another; that delusion frequently becomes belief; that belief frequently becomes identity. Here, although delusion threatens chaos and destruction, it is ultimately tamed or rendered benign by the comic-harmonic resolutions of the plot. In Shakespeare's tragedies, delusion takes on a very different aspect, and not only because it aims to generate pathos rather than eye-rolling or laughter. As we shall see, it becomes causal—an animating force of plots in which contrivance is precisely the problem, and where the endings are anything but clearly ordered or resolved.

The difficulty faced by Shakespeare was to find a way of writing about a world framed and characterized by delusions of one sort or another without surrendering his works to expediency, opportunism, deceit, self-deceit, and despair. The challenge was the more acute for a playwright who came to the view that conventionally received models of drama were themselves a part of the problem—not only encouraging misconceptions about the human condition, but providing society at large with a treasure house of metaphors through which to legitimate or otherwise to dignify the delusions it lives by. If writing plays risks making things worse, why bother at all? Why not embrace the misanthropy and dogmatic pessimism of a Thersites or a Timon, and retire to Stratford to hoard more grain?

In what follows, I propose that Shakespeare never settled on a single answer to this series of questions, and that he neither elaborates nor implies a theory of tragedy along the lines of those we can find in, for example, Aristotle and Hegel. But his tragedies are by no means a collection of improvisatory one-offs. They are instead a series of experiments in which he pulls his art this way and that in the conjoined attempts to represent the particularities of the world as they appear to him, and to discover how far tragic representation can be stretched in order accommodate the darker aspects of this vision. What is more, Shakespeare wants us to infer that dramatic art might help us to understand our place within the miserably compromised situations that it depicts. Tentatively, perhaps, to contemplate the possibility of moving beyond it.

In responding to a line from the first part of *Henry IV*, James Baldwin captures something vitally important about the Shakespeare in whom I am interested: "Art is here to prove, and to help one bear, the fact that all safety is an illusion."[1] Baldwin frequently writes of illusion (the convenient fictions, whether fashioned by others or oneself, by which one is taken in) and delusion (the distortion of things or events so that they cohere with our prior beliefs and opinions) when thinking his way inside the difficulty many Americans have in acknowledging the significance of slavery and segregation in the history of their nation. But he is just as concerned to delineate the role of the artist or poet (for him, the two terms are interchangeable) more generally. Which, as he puts it in his superlative essay on how and why he came to admire Shakespeare, is to overturn the belief that the evil of the world "can be laid at the door of Another," and to help us understand that we "feed" this evil "by failing so often in our private lives to deal with our private truth—our own experience."[2] For Baldwin, two of the most valuable functions of art are to reveal the unexamined fictions through which we divert our gaze from the reality of our lives, and to suggest as much as it can of what that reality might be said to consist. By doing so, by "correct[ing] the delusions to which we fall prey" when handling the common currency of "birth, suffering, love, and death," it might have the capacity to "make the world a more human dwelling place."

> It goes without saying, I believe, that if we understood ourselves better, we would damage ourselves less. But the barrier between oneself and one's knowledge of oneself is high indeed. There are so many things one would rather not know! We become social creatures because we cannot live any other way. But in order to become social, there are a great many other things that we must not become, and we are frightened, all of us, of these forces within us that perpetually menace our precarious security. Yet the forces are there: we cannot will them away. All we can

do is learn to live with them. And we cannot learn this unless we are willing to tell the truth about ourselves, and the truth about us is always at variance with what we wish to be. The human effort is to bring these two realities into a relationship resembling reconciliation.[3]

In exposing the delusionality to which every human being is prone, Shakespeare's tragedies kindle something adjacent to Baldwin's acts of effortful reconciliation—howsoever fragile, contingent, or disappointing these reconciliations might sometimes seem to be. *Shakespeare's Tragic Art*, I suppose, seeks to evangelize on their behalf.

———

A word or two on my approach to the Shakespearean text.

At all times, my intention has been to reconstruct as cogently and coherently as possible what I take Shakespeare to have been doing in writing his tragedies as he did—and to offer such reconstructions with an intelligently and sympathetically open mind. I do not have a critical credo as such, but I am bound to Frank Kermode's doctrine that the primary and indispensable quality of good literary criticism is "a scepticism, an interest in things as they are, in inhuman reality as well as in human justice."[4] Another governing assumption has been the belief that Shakespeare's plays are carefully constructed works of art: that although the plays demand of their performers and readers and spectators that they figure things out for themselves, this freedom of interpretation finds expression within the boundaries set by the design of the work. As Joel Altman phrases it in his indispensable *The Tudor Play of Mind*, the drama that Shakespeare learned to write "functioned as a medium of intellectual and emotional exploration" for individuals who had been taught to think in the rhetorical tradition, and who "were accustomed to examine many sides of a given theme." Meaning "could be discerned only through the total action of the drama."[5] Even though Shakespeare is famous for tragic characters that seem to transcend the plays to which they belong—Brutus, Hamlet, Lear, Macbeth, Iago, Cleopatra—I have tried to keep in mind that the "total action of the drama" is the thing.

It follows that I am a historicist of sorts. Necessarily so: to understand what Shakespeare wrote and to explain why he wrote it, one needs the patience and scholarly curiosity required to identify and then sift the various contexts with which his writing intersects. I believe that anyone proposing to read his plays closely (there are, to be clear, many other ways of approaching them) needs to do so alongside fine-grained analyses of the discursive traditions with which they are in contact, and in which they sometimes have a considerable share. The challenge is to do so without losing sight of the primary object of inquiry. That is, not to use—in general practice, to excerpt from—Shakespeare's tragedies to support a thesis about the history of literature, literary theory, politics, political theory, society, social theory, religion, theology, rhetoric, ideas, the theater, or anything else, but to use different sorts of history to illuminate Shakespeare's tragedies as they are available to us. In the introduction to her edition of Shakespeare's sonnets, Helen Vendler makes the point well:

> Aesthetically speaking, it is what a lyric *does with* its borrowed social languages—i.e., how it casts them into permutational and combinatorial forms—that is important. Shakespeare is unusually rich in his borrowings of diction and formulas from patronage, from religion, from law, from courtship, from diplomacy, from astronomy, and so on; but he tends to be a blasphemer in all of these realms. He was a master subverter of the languages he borrowed, and the point of *literary* interest is not the fact of his borrowings but how he turned them inside out.[6]

Without long hours of reading, note-taking, and thinking in the library, no recognition of the "social languages" that Shakespeare subverts would be possible; without an awareness that these labors are only of use to the extent that they help us explain and interpret the poems and plays, it is hard not to mistake the scale and the nature of Shakespeare's achievement.

All of which is to say that the criteria through which I decide whether one set of contextual data or another passes the "so what?" test are critical. Do they or don't they help us to understand Shakespeare's tragedies as works of art? Everything beyond the particular Shakespearean tragedy under discussion is contextual, and each of the contexts to which I turn— some indisputable, others at first blush tenuous—has been admitted only in the service of my efforts at exegesis and interpretation. I thus employ the term "context" broadly and sometimes anachronistically: to cover not only the social, political, historical, religious, intellectual, educational, cultural, or biographical-prosopographical topics that we usually think of in this connection, but also questions such as the origins and nature of tragedy, and the status of poetic and material form; if the likes of Kierkegaard, Heidegger, or Barthes help me to make a point with more nuance or exactitude than would otherwise be the case, then they are in.

That said, my most frequent contextual concern has been to imagine my way inside Shakespeare's complicated and ultimately conflicted engagements with humanism—with the body of doctrine centered on the *studia humanitatis* that dominated the cultural life of sixteenth-century England. *Studia humanitatis* literally means "studies of humanity," but has a more specific sense here as the imitative study of ancient literature and of the arts associated with it. (The phrase is itself borrowed from Cicero.) Humanists believed that attending to ancient texts and ideas would inculcate a model of virtue and virtuosity that, they claimed, had been lost to pious obscurantism in the centuries after the fall of the Roman Empire in the West; humanistic learning would as such translate—in the sense both of carrying over and adapting—the glories of the ancient past so that they could answer and ameliorate the exigencies of the present. Humanism was native to the Italian lands of the 1300s, and was a later import to England and Northern Europe; furthermore, when it took root in the north in the later fifteenth and early sixteenth centuries, it was as an elite phenomenon—a token with which to assert one's place within the international cognoscenti. It remains the case that for Shakespeare as for all of those who completed a grammar school education in the later sixteenth and earlier seventeenth centuries, the *studia humanitatis* was simply how one learned to read, think, speak, write, and behave. (To avoid confusion, let me add before moving on that my uses of "humanism" and the related term "humanist," both as a noun and an adjective, belong exclusively within this early modern semantic field. At no point do I identify, or seek to identify, the *studia humanitatis* with the ideals of human freedom, agency, and self-sufficiency that became articles of faith for anti-religious "humanists" from the nineteenth century onward.)[7]

If this attention to humanism smells a little too much like erudition to account for plays written by a man who grew up in the provinces and made his living in the theater, it shouldn't. Although reconstructing the practices and assumptions of humanism costs the twenty-first-century scholar a sizable outlay of time and energy, versions of it were the bread and butter of all early modern writers. Shakespeare was not particularly learned, and had smaller Latin and less Greek than his near contemporaries Ben Jonson and George Chapman (neither of whom, incidentally, went to university). But he was more than learned enough. As a schoolboy, he had been immersed in humanistic culture, and, as a professional writer from his mid-twenties to his late forties, he returned to what we now call the classics as often, and with as much attention, as he needed to.[8] In brief, Shakespeare drew on all aspects of life as he experienced it in completing his work. Everything was copy, and he was content to leave to others the task of policing the barriers between high and low, learned and vernacular.

We do not need to recognize every quotation, allusion, pastiche, or *hommage* in a film by the Coen Brothers or Quentin Tarantino, in a play by Tony Kushner or Martin McDonagh or Annie Baker, or in an episode of *The Sopranos* (or *Doctor Who*) in order to appreciate the experience of viewing them—any more than we need to be familiar with the intricacies of the *Odyssey* to appreciate Joyce's *Ulysses* or *King Lear* to appreciate Kurosawa's *Ran*. But if we do notice that an artist is in some way—which is to say, deliberately or inadvertently—nodding to another artist or work or technique or tradition or formula, we experience the work differently. As the actors John Heminges and Henry Condell phrase it in their prefatory remarks to the 1623 Folio, Shakespeare's works addressed everyone "from the most able, to him that can but spell." The patterns of artifice through which a dramatist creates the illusion of reality lend themselves, more perhaps than any other verbal art form, to being interpreted on a variety of levels. Shakespeare knew this, and never worried that every audience member or reader should be able to "get" every resonance of his writing. Consider his use of Latin in *Titus Andronicus*, his use of macaronic Latin (Latin deliberately jumbled up with English to comic effect) in *Love's Labour's Lost* and *The Merry Wives of Windsor*, his jokes about the Pythagorean transmigration of souls in *As You Like It* and *Twelfth Night*, or his later and occasionally downright risky experiments with what Stephen Orgel calls the "poetics of incomprehensibility."[9] If the play is good enough, Shakespeare seems to have concluded, then a little obscurity can serve to draw its audience members in by flattering them both for what they recognize, and for what they don't. The bigger danger, which Shakespeare saw with the clarity of one who had scrambled to obtain much of his cultural capital for himself, was the snobbery of talking down to the groundlings. He avoids it with an audacity that is quicksilver and steadfast. In considering his tragedies afresh, this audacity is one of the things that I seek better to understand.

This might be the point at which to stress that Shakespeare's writings do not embody the soul or spirit or anything else of his age. For the most part, this is because "ages," or historical periods, have such limited value as analytical tools: despite the gallons of ink that continue to be spilled over and around them, they are no more than the approximate categories through which we seek to make stretches of the past more readily digestible. This is not to say that notions like the medieval, the Renaissance, the Elizabethan, the Jacobean, the modern, the early modern, the baroque, or even "the age of Shakespeare" do not have value as a form of shorthand— and in the case of the Renaissance, as more than a shorthand (it was an artistic movement before it came to denote a period of time). Instead, it is to remind ourselves that, as such notions are fictions, we should be wary of reifying or essentializing them; the history of any given "age" encompasses a plurality of voices and perspectives that cannot be unified without distortion.[10] In the latter part of the sixteenth century and early part of the seventeenth, one of those voices belonged to Shakespeare. As it had to, this voice emerged from the cultural, social, and intellectual orthodoxies that informed its historical moment—but so did those of countless others, the vast majority of whom were not distinguished writers. What makes Shakespeare distinctive is not his refusal to be constrained by these orthodoxies (again, the same is true of many others), but the extraordinary appropriations, transformations, and analyses to which he subjects them in his art. He was not a representative man, never the shuttle to anyone else's loom.

————

One of the most salutary features of Shakespeare criticism over the past four decades has been the renewed interest in his plays as theatrical artifacts—as works intended not to be read in a library or classroom, but to be performed, heard, and viewed in a playhouse or theater. As will be apparent at numerous points below, I am in debt to this work, and am moreover grateful to it for helping to disentangle Shakespeare's tragedies from the totalizing idealism in which they have too often been bundled up. The emphasis on performance has been complemented by the research of Lukas Erne and others on Shakespeare's cultivation of a print readership—in the literary marketplace of Elizabethan and Jacobean England, and in posterity.[11] When, in the late 1630s, the great portraitist Anthony van Dyck painted the Cavalier poet Sir John Suckling and wanted to show that Suckling was a Shakespearean, he didn't depict him holding a stage prop like a skull, but a copy of the First or Second Folio, open at the beginning of *Hamlet*. The obvious position for once seems to be the right one: Shakespeare wrote for the stage, for the page, and for the innumerable spaces between. Both/and, not either/or. In Claire Bourne's apt summary, for the early moderns, the theater and the book were "mutually constitutive sites of dramatic action."[12]

A good index of this complementary relationship is that almost all of what little we know about the circumstances in which Shakespeare's plays were first performed comes not from living theatrical tradition, but from documents. These mostly take the form of printed play-texts, but also

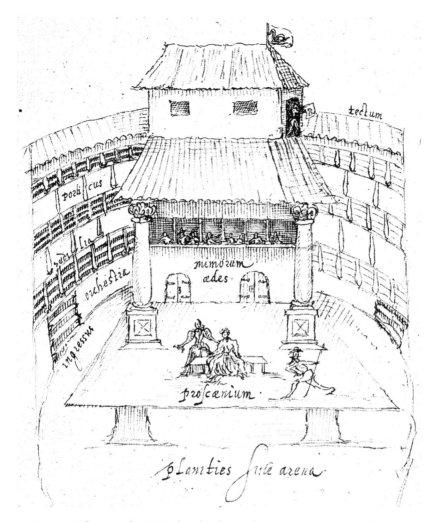

FIGURE 1. Johannes de Witt, sketch of a performance in progress at
The Swan theater in 1596, as copied in Aernout van Buchell's *Adversaria*.
Universiteitsbibliotheek Utrecht, Ms. 842, fol. 132r.

include manuscripts like Henslowe's diary, and—exceptionally—visual evidence like Johannes de Witt's 1596 drawing of a performance in progress
at The Swan theater (see figure 1), or Henry Peacham's ambiguously-dated
sketch of *Titus Andronicus* (see figure 4). ("Almost all" because archae-
ological excavations at the sites of The Rose and The Curtain have also
had important things to tell.) Unfortunately, these documentary sources
are not always reliable. To take one famous example, the title page of the
apparently unauthorized edition of *Hamlet* published in 1603 advertises

that it had been performed "diverse times . . . in the two Universities of Cambridge and Oxford." Maybe. But the absence of corroborative evidence means that there is no way of gauging whether the claim is accurate, or an advertising ploy designed to lure recent graduates—or those who merely wished they were—into making a purchase. The truth is that the destruction of The Globe in 1613 and the effacement of the theaters altogether in 1642 leave us with a dearth of records from which to piece together the history of the English theater's golden age. In a few lucky cases, there are enough data for us to infer some detail or other of the way in which Shakespearean tragedies were staged—gorily, affectingly, with frenetic actorly energy, on a stage draped in black, perhaps with a dance once the main action of the play was over. More frequently, our ignorance of the conditions and norms that shaped theatrical production from 1580 to 1642 means that such detail can only be conjectured. The late sixteenth- and early seventeenth-century English theater is no Stonehenge, but it is in various important senses pre-historic—an institution that we know existed, but whose modalities for the most part lie beyond the surviving record.[13]

So it was that someone, most likely the learned fabulist John Payne Collier, decided to forge a document witnessing the earliest known performances of *Hamlet*, alongside one of *Richard II*: on a boat, in 1607, off the coast of Sierra Leone.[14] I hope to have resisted less serious versions of the same temptation—that is, to have kept my conjectures both conjectural and to a minimum. Like the actors and directors who, in the decades after 1660, adapted Shakespeare for the Restoration stage and began—that is, invented—the tradition of Shakespeare-in-performance as we know it, I use the printed and manuscript record to reconstruct what I can of the circumstances in which Shakespeare's works were first staged.[15] But the task I have set myself is at once freer and more constrained than theirs: to understand as fully as I can what Shakespeare wrote, and why he wrote it when he wrote it. A more complete archive of his tragedies' early performance histories would be of the utmost assistance to this end. Alas, it does not exist.

Disheartening though this state of affairs can sometimes feel, it permits us one marginal gain: the obligation to remember a distinction that was central to early modern concepts of drama. On one side, stagecraft and acting as mechanical rather than liberal arts; on the other, the more elevated business of "dramatic poetry," with "poetry" here doing duty for all forms of imaginative writing (what we might call "literature") rather than just those forms of it written in verse. The line between the two was policed by university-educated rivals of Shakespeare like Robert Greene (for whom, only the elite should write dramatic poetry; upstart mechanicals like Shakespeare should stick to performing), by writers like Philip Sidney's exact but much longer-lived contemporary Fulke Greville (who fastidiously declared that his own tragedies were "no plays for the stage"), and by many opponents of the theater (dramatic poetry, when read inwardly or aloud to a select few, was acceptable; dramatic poetry when performed for paying audiences through the artifice of stagecraft was the work of the devil).[16]

As we shall see, there are good reasons for concluding that Shakespeare was impatient with this distinction, and not only because his career—like that of Ben Jonson—did much to change the status of the dramatic poet in the early seventeenth century.[17] All I would like to stress for the moment is that Shakespeare's first two publications were heavily classicizing exercises in the stylized mini-epic that would become known as the epyllion: *Venus and Adonis* and *The Rape of Lucrece.* Both were extremely popular and helped him to establish himself as a "name" in the Elizabethan cultural marketplace. Likewise, several of Shakespeare's sonnets were in scribal circulation by the late 1590s, and an entire sequence of them was printed in 1609. Put simply, a key part of Shakespeare's repudiation of the split between dramatic poetry and stagecraft was that he, a theatrical professional, wanted his dramatic language to be enjoyed on the page just as much as in the performances of the Lord Chamberlain's (later, the King's) Men. By the time the first quarto edition of *Troilus and Cressida* emerged in 1609, its publisher could blurb it by telling Shakespeare's readers that they "have here a new play, never staled with the stage, never clapper-clawed with the palms of the vulgar." The pitch is a contestable and remarkably un-Shakespearean one, but it is striking even so.[18]

In his great humanistic commentary on Aristotle's *Poetics,* the Italian scholar and controversialist Francesco Robortello observed that tragedy

> may be considered in two ways, either insofar as it is theatrical and performed by the actors, or insofar as it is made by the poet as he writes. If you think of it in terms of the poet as he writes, then we may say that the principal end of tragedy is to imitate the dispositions of souls and the moral characters (*mores*) of human beings through written words, through which description it is possible to discern whether men are fortunate or unfortunate. If you assume it to refer to the actor as he performs, then we may say that the greatest and most powerful end [of tragedy] is that very action as the result of which people are judged to be fortunate or unfortunate.[19]

I suspect that Robortello would have struggled with Shakespeare, but to anyone contemplating Shakespeare's tragic output, his formulation functions as a reassurance and a challenge. The fact that we cannot say much about the plays in their earliest performances is undeniably frustrating. The fact that there is still a lot to say about the plays as dramatic poems—as intelligently assembled works of writerly art that attempt to "imitate" the features of the human condition that lead us to feel the ways we feel and do the things we do—gives rise to headaches of a very different sort. Oftentimes, to vertigo.

CHAPTER ONE

Tragedy, History, Irony

FOR THE PAST TWO AND A HALF CENTURIES, Shakespeare's tragedies have enjoyed unrivaled prominence as a staple of theatrical repertories, school and university classrooms, and most corners of the literary imagination. Although this prominence has much to recommend it, at least one of its features should give us pause: the plays themselves have remarkably little in common with the convictions that lifted them up to greatness in the later eighteenth century, and that have helped to keep them there since. It is with these convictions—and with the stimuli from which they arose—that we need to begin.

In the hundred years after the British theaters reopened in 1660, Shakespeare's tragedies were celebrated for their psychological insight and poetic abundance, but were often a theme of regret. Shakespeare failed to conform to the doctrines of tragic structure and decorum propagated by neoclassical theorists like René Rapin and Nicolas Boileau, and modeled by playwrights like Boileau's friend, Jean Racine. This is why John Dryden tidied up *Antony and Cleopatra* into *All for Love* and *Troilus and Cressida* into *Truth Found Too Late*, why Thomas Rymer mocked *Othello* as a play whose lesson is "a warning to all good Wives that they look well to their Linnen," and why Nahum Tate "rectifie[d] what was wanting in the Regularity and Probability" of *King Lear*—excising the Fool, and furnishing the plot with a happy ending in which Lear regains his throne and Cordelia survives to marry Edgar.[1] Samuel Johnson was no slave to neoclassical nicety, but even he could do no more than give Shakespeare a pass for having lived at a time when "the rules of the ancients were known to so few," "the publick judgment was unformed," and there was "no example of such fame as might force him upon imitation, nor criticks of such authority as might restrain his extravagance." Instead, Shakespeare relied on—and "indulged"—his "natural disposition." For Johnson, this disposition was comic rather than tragic: comedy came to Shakespeare easily, but in tragedy his "performance seems constantly to be worse, as his labour is more. The effusions of passion . . . are for the most part striking and energetick: but whenever he solicits his invention, or strains his faculties, the offspring of his throes is tumour [i.e., bombast], meanness, tediousness, and obscurity." In Johnson's estimation, the art and moral dignity of tragic drama require more than native talent and a fluid way with words.[2]

Fashions change, and it was a combination of Shakespeare's expansiveness and indifference to classically derived tragic norms that made him so attractive to a later generation of critics—principally those with German or English as a mother tongue, and who found in him an antidote to the universalizing and putatively hegemonic rationalism that they identified with French literary culture.[3] For the Romantics and Idealists—starting with Herder, and arriving at A. C. Bradley via Goethe, the Schlegels, Coleridge, Hazlitt, and above all Hegel—the freedom that Shakespeare permitted himself in writing his tragedies enabled him to capture the spirit of a distinctively modern age. On their account, the ancient Greeks (principally Aeschylus and Sophocles) established that the stuff of tragedy was the conflict of goods (such as a collision between the duties imposed by love for one's family and the need to obey the law), and that its purpose was to arrive at a synthesis through which these conflicts could to some degree be resolved. In their turn, these resolutions showed the dialectic of history moving forward. Shakespeare, by contrast, marks the point in history at which an older order of being (public, communal, external, possibly even sacred) gives way to the individualism of the modern age; he breaks from the classical model by writing tragedies in which conflicting goods are features of his characters' psychological, emotional, and spiritual existences. Hamlet's nobly contemplative soul disdains the compromises and corruptions demanded by action in the world, but the situation in which he finds himself requires decisively worldly action. His inability to choose one or other of these ways forward leads to his demise—apparently as a result of external events, in reality because his character has preordained it. Thus, the birth of modern individuality, and the pains with which modern individuality is unavoidably tangled up, can be observed. Acknowledging this situation invests the death of tragic protagonists like Hamlet, and even of obvious evildoers like Macbeth, with a powerfully redemptive force.

In case the previous paragraph too much resembles caricature, I should emphasize that although the Romantic Shakespeareans run too freely to abstraction, any student of Shakespearean tragedy owes them a great deal. For one thing, they affirmed the seriousness of Shakespeare's tragic vision: its unflinching concern with questions of suffering, determinism (whether historical, providential, psychological, or some combination of the three), freedom, mortality, and moral ambiguity, along with its willingness to wonder both at the meaning of life and at the nature of historical change. We can also be grateful for the informed, inventive, sympathetic, and astute readings of the plays offered by Coleridge, Hazlitt, and Bradley. It is just that the Romantic-Idealist approach to tragedy, and therefore to Shakespeare, is essentially theological. More precisely, one of semi-secularized theology, in which giving a coherent description of a work of tragic art is of less significance than validating a hypostatized notion of "the tragic"—an ideology whose origins are found not in the writings of Sophocles or Shakespeare or any other playwright, but within the dialectic of history. Truth is historical-spiritual-philosophical, and comes first. Tragic drama, now a vehicle for "the tragic," is brought into line to the best of the critic's ability.

There is of course much to be gained from studying works of tragedy or of any other literary kind alongside history, philosophy, and theology. Moreover, there need not be a problem with writing history, philosophy, and theology through the medium of literary history or criticism: although critics of Shakespeare have long broken with Idealist theories of history, of character criticism, and of tragedy's redemptive force, the practice of reading the plays as representations of historically defined value conflicts continues to the present day. We only get into difficulty when it comes to a *Macbeth*, a *King Lear*, or a *Hamlet*, all of which weave topics like history, philosophy, and theology into the fabric of their tragic art, and all of which admit these topics only in the service of that tragic art. I hope it won't sound banal if I insist that in studying Shakespeare's tragedies, the art has to come first. Not only because to do otherwise would be to risk mistaking a play for a theoretical dialogue (all plays are dialogic; not all dialogues are plays), but because it would be fundamentally to distort the ways in which Shakespeare's tragic vision responds to the push and pull of history, and to the charge of many other phenomena besides. To put it another way, in diminishing the status of plot and structure, and by sidelining the experience of the plays as dramatic wholes, Romantic and post-Romantic approaches to Shakespeare's tragedies risk doing them as much of a disservice as the neoclassical cultural cringe.

This is not a plea for keeping things simple or for literary-critical purity. Rather, the design of this book is to demonstrate that by attending as closely as possible to Shakespeare's tragedies as works of dramatic art, we are able to behold an engagement with questions of history, philosophy, theology, politics, and the rest that is both more sustained and more unsettling than is commonly understood.

Writing about ancient Greek tragedy, Jean-Pierre Vernant and Pierre Vidal-Naquet argue that in "the development of what may be called a tragic consciousness, man and his action were presented, in tragedy's own peculiar perspective, not as stable realities that could be placed, defined, and judged, but as problems, unanswerable questions, riddles whose double meanings remain enigmatic however often decoded."[4] On a similar tack, Bernard Williams observes that for minds like those of "Plato, Aristotle, Kant, [and] Hegel . . . the universe or history or the structure of human reason can, when properly understood, yield a pattern that make sense of human life and human aspirations." From the tragic perspective (as also, he notes, from that of a historian like Thucydides), we are left with no such sense, and are instead confronted by representations of human beings "dealing sensibly, foolishly, sometimes catastrophically, sometimes nobly, with a world that is only partially intelligible to human agency and in itself not necessarily well adjusted to ethical aspirations."[5]

Although Shakespeare wrote in a context that had very little in common with the Athens inhabited by Aeschylus, Sophocles, and Euripides, he too believed that human beings struggle fully to comprehend the world of which they are a part. Unlike the ancient Athenians, the Elizabethans had access to Christianity as a totalizing account of the cosmos and of the place occupied by humankind within it; but as we shall see, within Shakespeare's tragedies Christianity is granted little special significance. Rather than confronting his tragic protagonists with conflicting goods or forcing them to recognize conflicting impulses to the good within themselves, Shakespeare presents us with a world in which indeterminacy and ambiguity take on a starkly different cast. To adapt a line from V. S. Naipaul, it is not that Shakespeare's tragic landscape is a space in which there is no right and no wrong, but that it is one in which, if right exists, it is all but indistinguishable—certainly, one with no kind of right that can be thought of as natural, divinely ordained, or metaphysically fixed.[6] We need to tread carefully.

———

As we do when referring to "tragedy": despite several shelves of books arguing otherwise, it has always resisted settled definition.[7] Even if, as we must, we narrow our field of inquiry by excluding wars, plagues, and natural disasters (in Erasmus's helpful analysis, "tragedies are different: in real disasters we do not need a character to grieve with us and join his tears with ours"), tragedy emerges as profoundly unstable—both as a practice and an idea.[8] Aristotle's precepts differ from those that can be abstracted from the surviving corpus of Greek tragedies; Greek tragedies differ from Roman ones, which in their turn differ from tragedy as understood by an author like Chaucer; all differ from the kinds of tragedies written for the Elizabethan and Jacobean stage, which themselves differ—sometimes radically—from one another and from the early modern tragedies produced in Spain, France, Italy, the Low Countries, and the German-speaking lands. What happens to tragedy after the Romantic invention of "the tragic," even at the fairly basic level of its growth to embrace the novel and other nondramatic forms of writing? Can tragedy have a place in capitalist, liberal, egalitarian, or otherwise modern societies? Did the abomination of the Holocaust leave tragedy dead in its wake? Do Artaud and Beckett and Miller and Pinter and Ionesco count? How does tragedy translate to music, opera, film, television, the new media, and the visual arts—if, indeed, it does? In one of the best books about Shakespearean tragedy written in the past half century, Stephen Booth puts it well. Given that works of tragic art are concerned with what happens beyond the rationally drawn boundaries and categories through which we seek to measure our lives, trying to reduce tragedy to one rational definition or another is destined to fail—and is positively dangerous for those seeking to interpret works of tragic art. Too often, "theories of tragedy keep us from facing tragedy itself."[9] Similar dangers afflict those who would write unified histories of tragedy as an idea or practice. As I see it, the best we can say is that tragedy, since first appearing circa 500 BCE, has meant many things to many different people. Although these meanings generally stand in discernable historical relation to one another, these historical relationships cannot be constrained to an orderly pattern, be it linear or stadial or cyclical. Before turning to Shakespeare's own engagements with the tragic, my goal over the next several pages is simpler, if far from straightforward: better to understand "tragedy" as Shakespeare and his contemporaries encountered it.

———

The "Induction" to the anonymous *A Warning for Fair Women* is a good place to start.[10] This play dramatizes a murder that took place in London in 1573: a wife conducts an affair, somewhat against her better judgment;

her lover kills her husband; the wife comes to regret her part in the murder; the guilty parties are caught and punished. If the printed version of the text is to be believed, it was performed by Shakespeare's acting company, the Lord Chamberlain's Men, at some point in or before 1599. The play begins with the personifications of Tragedy, History, and Comedy squabbling over their mutual standing. History and Comedy attack Tragedy as a "common executioner" and "common hangman unto Tyrannie," whose sense of her own importance was belied by the preference of playgoers for lighter and more readily digestible works. Audiences only bothered with tragedies for the entertainment offered by the display of sensationalism and moralistic guignol: "Some damned tyrant, to obtaine a crowne, / Stabs, hands, impoysons, smothers, cutteth throats," before being pursued to his demise by Choruses, "filthie whining ghost[s]," and the forces of overwritten retribution more generally. The essence of tragedy, Comedy concludes—adroitly splicing Horace's *purpurei panni* ("purple patches") with the excesses of sanguinary spectacle—is "Pure purple Buskin, blood and murther right."[11]

Tragedy is having none of it. In due course she will "scourge and lash" her frivolous interlocutors from the stage, but she first shares her thoughts about why hers is the preeminent dramatic kind:

> I must have passions that must move the soule,
> Make the heart heave, and throb within the bosome,
> Extorting tears out of the strictest eyes,
> To racke a thought and straine it to his forme,
> Untill I rap the sences from their course,
> This is my office.

Much could be said about this "Induction," the more so as it may have been performed at the newly opened Globe theater—with Shakespeare himself plausibly taking the role of Tragedy, which features prominently for the remainder of the play (Comedy addresses her as "Madam *Melpomine*," and wonders "whose mare is dead / That you are going to take off her skin?": Melpomene was the muse of tragedy, and "whose mare is dead" appears to riff a line of Falstaff from *Henry IV*).[12] Our focus here must nonetheless remain on the question of genre.

Although we are familiar with the categories of comedy, tragedy, and history from the 1623 folio edition of Shakespeare's complete works, this division was uncommon within works of early modern literary theory and criticism. Rather, the emphasis was on comedy and tragedy alone: the two were defined in opposition to one another, and were as such kept carefully apart.[13] So it was that when Francis Meres praised Shakespeare in 1598, he claimed that "As *Plautus* and *Seneca* are accounted the best for Comedy and Tragedy among the Latines: so *Shakespeare* among the English is the most excellent in both kinds for the stage."[14] But the inclusion of History alongside Comedy and Tragedy in the "Induction" to *A Warning for Fair Women* is more valuable than simply offering a generic category to fit the likes of Shakespeare's *Henry VI* and *Henry IV* plays. It also discloses something that theoretical accounts of genre in general and tragic genre in particular tend to obscure: like historical drama, and like comedy, the early moderns primarily identified tragedy not by its form, but by its subject matter. History is concerned with stories of warfare and conflict (she enters bearing "Drum and Ensigne"), and Comedy with stories of love and ingenuity and subterfuge (she has, according to Tragedy, "some sparkes of wit . . . To tickle shallow injudiciall eares, / Perhaps some puling [i.e., feeble] passion of a lover"). Tragedy, as we have already seen, is on this reckoning concerned with crimes committed by those in great place, and by the sufferings and punishments—sometimes, by the acts of vengeance—to which these crimes lead. The anti-theatricalist Philip Stubbes would have been dismayed by Tragedy's insistence that the power of tragedy to "move the soule" and "Make the heart heave" was something to celebrate, but he would otherwise have found little from which to dissent. According to his *Anatomy of Abuses*, tragedy is defined by "Anger, Wrath, immunity, Cruelty, injurie, incest, murther, and such like."[15]

Of the many other supporting examples that could be drawn from the English theater of the years around 1600, two bookends to Shakespeare's writing career might suffice. In Thomas Kyd's *The Spanish Tragedy*, Hieronimo pursues his vengeance against the killers of his son by inviting them to play parts in the tragedy of "Soliman and Perseda" that, he says, he had written as a student. When Balthazar cools on the idea and suggests that "a comedy might be better," Hieronimo responds with as much fire as art: "A comedy? / Fie, comedies are fit for common wits: / But to present a kingly troop withal, / Give me a stately-written tragedy; / *Tragedia Cothurnata*, fitting kings, / Containing matter, and not common things." A *tragedia cothurnata* is a Latin play with a Greek subject, such as the Medea plays by Seneca and Ovid (the Latin *cothurnus* denotes a buskin): weighty "matter" presented in a style of appropriate grandeur. About twenty-five years later, John Webster prefaced his tragedy of intrigue, *The White Devil*, with some preemptively ironized reflections on his writerly lot. He asks his readers to imagine that even "*the most sententious Tragedy that ever was written, observing all the crittical lawes, as heighth of stile;*

and gravety of person" might not win popular acclaim.[16] Sententiousness, or the higher quotability, is a tragic attribute to which I return at greater length below, but the other characteristics with which Webster associates tragedy were the stuff of commonplace.

The concentration on subject matter as the foundational dividing line between genres has a long pedigree. From the perspective of the early moderns, its origins lay in two works that survived the fall of ancient Rome: Horace's *Ars poetica*, and the commentaries on the work of the comic playwright Terence that were compiled by the fourth-century grammarians Evanthius and Donatus. As usual, Horace is concerned with how to put the right words in the right places:

> A comic subject will not be set out in tragic verse; likewise, the Banquet of Thyestes disdains being told in poetry of the private kind, that borders on the comic stage. Everything must keep the appropriate place to which it was allotted. Nevertheless, comedy does sometimes raise her voice, and angry Chremes perorates with swelling eloquence. Often too Telephus and Peleus in tragedy lament in prosaic language, when they are both poor exiles, and throw away their bombast and words half a yard long, if they are anxious to touch the spectator's heart with their complaint. It is not enough for poetry to be beautiful; it must also be pleasing and lead the hearer's mind wherever it will.[17]

The subject (*res*) of a play will determine whether it is a comedy or a tragedy, and the status of a play as a comedy or tragedy will determine the style and quality of the language to be used within it. Except when the particular play demands the inclusion of language that breaches the rules of decorum, such as in the comedies of Terence (Chremes is a character in *Andria*) and the tragedies of Euripides (*Telephus* is preserved only in fragments, but Peleus is a character in *Andromache*). Crucially, Horace insists that poetry should not merely touch the heart or present the eye with a beautiful spectacle, but that it must move the mind.

We get a better-defined idea of what comic and tragic subjects were taken to comprise from Evanthius, who prefaces Donatus's commentary on Terence:

> Many things distinguish comedy from tragedy. In comedy, people are of mediocre fortune, perils trifling, actions have happy outcomes. In tragedy, all is inverted: persons are mighty, fears are great, outcomes lethally destructive. The first begins in turbulence, but concludes in tranquility; in tragedy things take place in the opposite order. Whereas

tragedy presents the kind of life from which one seeks to flee, in comedy life is readily to be embraced. Finally, all comedies are based on fictional stories, whereas tragedy often strives for the verisimilitude of history (*historia fide*).[18]

Comedy deals with the middling crises of the middling sort, proceeds from turbulence to tranquility, and is always based on fictional rather than historical sources. Tragedy deals with the deadly crises of the most socially elevated and powerful sort (i.e., those whose private actions have public ramifications), proceeds from tranquility to turbulence, and is frequently based on historical sources. But as the medieval and early modern readers of these commentaries understood, Evanthius offers no explicit distinction between the comic and tragic forms. Indeed, the next portion of his commentary shows that it was through comedy that tragedy and all other sorts of drama were comprehended. Comedy provides the origins of the doctrine that drama is "an imitation of life, a mirror of custom, and an image of truth."[19] Likewise, it reveals the three-part structure of all dramatic plots (*fabulae*): the *protasis* (the beginning, in which the story is outlined and the audience's attention caught), the *epitasis* (the middle, in which the story is expanded to its full complexity), and the *catastrophe* (the end, in which the story is unraveled or resolved). No matter the character of the story that the playwright invents or adapts, the shape of the drama stays the same.[20]

Despite the hostility of many church fathers to pagan distractions from the serious business of Christian salvation, tragedy—and the idea of tragedy—would gradually find itself baptized. The fontal text was Boethius's *Consolation of Philosophy*. Early on, Lady Philosophy disparages the Muses as the "whores" of the stage (*scenicas meretriculas*), but a little later she propounds the idea that "the clamor of tragedies" (*tragoediarum clamor*) represents the "overthrow," by Fortuna, of "happy kingdoms with an unexpected blow" (*Fortunam felicia regna vertentem*). Fortuna was the personification of "fortune," the category of "chance" (*casus*) that raises people up but that—as in the case of the imprisoned Boethius—just as readily and just as inscrutably casts them down. In Boethius's philosophical theology, however, fortune only seems to be random or capricious. In reality, it belongs to the hierarchy of order: providence proposes, fate (an intermediate category between providence and fortune) disposes; chance and fortune obey; philosophy helps humankind to understand, and is that to which the *Consolation* directs our attention. But not just philosophy. Tragedy, too, has its place, and Lady Philosophy approvingly quotes the

Andromache of Euripides (described simply as *tragicus*, or a "tragic poet") on the transience of glory. Later, she also cites "my Euripides" (*Euripidis mei*) in noting the emotional demands of parenthood.[21]

It is a short step from here to the belief the tragedies do not represent a collision between individual ambition and inscrutable fortune, but the consequences of a failure, or refusal, to acknowledge the limitations of human agency within a divinely ordained cosmos. Although such a step had already been taken by Sophocles, Euripides, and Seneca, it does not seem to have been followed by Boethius himself; many later students of the *Consolation* would nevertheless make it their own. In the so-called *de casibus* (hard to translate, but "downfall" comes close) tradition, tragedy (in this version by no means an exclusively or even primarily dramatic form of writing) tracked the fall from greatness of princes and other prominent figures who had misunderstood or otherwise abused their position. The change is striking: the calamities that overcome tragic protagonists are not simply aspects of a providence that can never fully be apprehended, but are the consequences of human action and character. Tragedies could thus warn against excess or neglect in those holding positions of prominence or power.[22]

In England, this tradition passed from Chaucer and Lydgate to the mid-sixteenth-century compilation *A Mirror for Magistrates*, where it mingled with the examples of Greek (for instance, in Erasmus's Latin translation of Euripides) and above all Senecan tragedy to become a staple of the Elizabethan theater, and of the politically minded beyond.[23] Thomas Elyot viewed "readyng tragoedies" as a way to "execrate and abhore the intollerable life of tyrantes," Thomas Lodge imagined Greek tragedy depicting "the sower fortune of many exiles, the miserable fal of haples princes, the reuinous decay of many countryes," and William Webbe described the lamentable stuff of "gods and goddesses, kings and queens, and great states," suffering "miserable calamities and dreadful chances, which increased worse and worse, till the came to the most woeful plight that might be devised." By the 1610s, Fulke Greville felt able to suggest that the purpose of his own, late Elizabethan, tragic experiments had been "to trace out the highways of ambitious governors, and to show in the practice of life that the more audacity, advantage and good success such sovereignties have, the more they hasten to their own desolation and ruin." Even so, that a play like Greville's *Mustapha* answers only imperfectly to these ideals offers us an additional clue in piecing together tragedy as the early moderns understood it: most tragic playwrights (Shakespeare, for once, is a good exemplar) eschewed the moral didacticism of tragic theory in their writings. To the extent that they examined collisions between individual freedom and cosmic necessity, they seem to have been content with positions closer to that of Boethius, rather than those of the Boethian tradition. Marlowe's Tamburlaine, who dies peacefully with his conquests and succession intact, is only the most extreme example of this anti-didactic strain: "View but his picture in this tragicke glasse, / And then applaud his fortunes as you please."[24]

By this point in my sketch of the history of tragedy, you could be forgiven for the suspicion that I am ignoring the elephant—or, rather, the Stagyrite—in the room. Aristotle's *Poetics*, though frequently hard to digest, remains the most powerful and comprehensive attempt to describe and to theorize the art of ancient tragedy. Writing seventy years after the deaths of Sophocles and Euripides, and more than a century after the death of Aeschylus, Aristotle analyzed tragic writing in order to defend it from the censures of Plato's Socrates. In the famous formulation of his sixth chapter, "a tragedy is a *mimēsis* [an imitative representation] of a high, complete action, in speech pleasurably enhanced, the different kinds of enhancement occurring in separate sections, in dramatic, not narrative form, effecting through pity and fear the *catharsis* of such emotions."[25] Aristotle continues that tragedies consist of six distinct elements—plot (*muthos*), character (*ethos*), thought (*dianoia*), diction (appropriate meter and rhythm), songwriting, and stagecraft. Of these, the first three elements are presented as essential to tragedy, the second three inessential (and, in the case of stagecraft, actually extrinsic). Because tragedy imitates action—that is, people *doing* things—plot is the most important element, and offers the "principle of life" in virtue of which character and thought, respectively the second and third most important elements of tragedy, are conceived and arranged.[26]

In chapters 7–9, Aristotle delineates the characteristics of a tragic plot (it should be whole, orderly, unified, and governed by the laws of probability and necessity), and in chapter 11, he outlines its three key "elements": change of fortune (*peripeteia*), recognition (*anagnorisis*), and an act involving destruction or pain (*pathos*). *Peripeteia* and *anagnorisis* can only take place within the "complex" tragic plots that Aristotle prefers, but *pathos* is a feature of all tragic plots, no matter how simple. Finally, in chapters 13–15 and 19–22, Aristotle expounds the "most excellent" kinds of tragic composition: for instance, the place of *hamartia*—often conceived of as a tragic protagonist's fatal flaw (such as pride, indecision, or quickness to anger), but better translated as the sort of error committed by a tragic protagonist on account of his or her ignorance or mistaken judgment.[27]

For all its brilliance, the *Poetics* demands a lot of its readers. What are we supposed to do with the fact that many of Aristotle's examples of successful tragic plotting and characterization are drawn from Homer's *Iliad* and *Odyssey*, works that are written in narrative, not dramatic, form? Granted that a tragedy need not have a disastrous ending to be called a tragedy (any conclusion that conduces to the arousal of fear and pity will do), are happy endings to be condemned, tolerated, or praised in the right circumstances? Chapters 13 and 14 take contradictory positions. Other challenges are not hard to come by. In confronting them, readers of the *Poetics* have tended to follow well-trodden interpretative paths. That is, in attempting to explain a work that is sometimes obscure and self-contradictory, they have either replicated its confusions, or overdetermined parts of it in order to remake the whole of it in the image of their own preoccupations. The latter path has generally proven to be the more enticing.[28] Thus the twelfth-century Cordovan polymath Averroës (Abū al-Walīd Ibn Rushd) followed Arabic tradition in maintaining that the *Poetics* comprises two complementary treatises: one on the rhetoric of praising virtue, the other on syllogistic logic. His commentary was translated from Arabic to Latin by Herman the German (Hermannus Alemannus) in the middle of the thirteenth century, and remained current for the next three hundred years—a period in which Aristotle's *Poetics* did not have a lot to do with tragedy as an idea or a literary practice. By the mid-sixteenth century, this situation had begun to change. Through the efforts of scholars like Robortello, Scaliger, Antonio Minturno, and Lodovico Castelvetro, Aristotle's text (by this point available in various Latin translations and paraphrases) was massaged and dragged into harmony with the theories of tragedy espoused by Horace, Evanthius, Boethius, and their commentators; such is the eclectic Aristotelianism that we find in English works like Sidney's *Defence* and Scott's *Model*.[29]

Over the past decade or so, some fine studies have turned to Aristotle in rescuing early modern tragic poetics from the ante-neoclassical blancmange to which they have too often been consigned by Hegelian posterity. Among other things, these studies have suggested that early modern tragic theory was an important tool for teaching and thinking within the Protestant churches, and that the neoclassical tragic ideals of the later seventeenth century have a longer, more complex, and more revealing genealogy than has often been allowed.[30]

What has proved harder to establish is that these early modern tragic poetics resonate in the tragedies that were produced in the sixteenth and early seventeenth centuries. Even playwrights as keen to burnish their humanistic credentials as Thomas Watson and George Buchanan are a long way from the exactingly decorous *ancienneté* to which Dryden would look with approbation. Writing in 1570, Roger Ascham could praise Watson's *Absalom* and Buchanan's *Jephtha*—both examples of the post-Reformation vogue for *tragoedia sacra*, or Latin-language tragedies on biblical themes—for coming close to "Aristotle's precepts and Euripides' examples." But, as the purpose of sacred tragedies was theological and pedagogic, and as neither Aristotle nor Euripides conceived of tragedy as a vehicle for theology or for teaching, then proximity to the tragic was as close as Watson and Buchanan could get. Ascham goes on to criticize another, unnamed, writer at the University of Cambridge who, "well liked of many, but best liked of himself," brought "matters upon stages which he called tragedies." The stated fault of this writer was to have used, in the *protasis*, the kind of verse that belongs only to the *epistasis*—but we are invited to infer that his shortcomings were more fundamental than this.[31] Philip Sidney, normally untroubled by fantasies of generic hygiene, made a different sort of complaint about the failure of Thomas Norton and Thomas Sackville's *Gorboduc* to observe the Aristotelian unities of "place and time." The fault was even more grievous in lesser tragedies "where you shall have Asia of the one side, and Afric of the other, and so many other under-kingdoms, that the player, when he cometh in, must ever begin with telling where he is, or else the tale will not be conceived." A Spanish musket ball meant that Sidney was not obliged to confront Marlowe's *Tamburlaine* or *Doctor Faustus*, but he was not vexed by disunity alone. Violations of tragic decorum also caught his attention: "clowns" have no legitimate place in plays concerned with "kings." Such interpolations are not only a distraction from the "admiration and commiseration" with which tragedies should be regarded, but give comedy a bad name. In that "comical part" of tragedy, there is "nothing but scurrility, unworthy of any chaste ears, or some extreme show of doltishness, indeed fit to lift up a loud laughter, and nothing else."[32]

It is likely that Shakespeare read and learned from the hybrid Aristotelianism of the *Defence*, and we might also conjecture that Sidney would have been an astute enough observer to have concluded that the graveyard scene in *Hamlet* or Lear's exchanges with the Fool should be treated as exceptions to his dramatic rules. It remains the case that the *Defence*, like the theoretical tradition of which it is an intelligently witty representative, is not the right lens through which to regard Shakespeare's tragic art. The tragic essentialism of many neo-Aristotelian poetic theorists means that their writings, though frequently works of deft and imaginative synthesis, can offer the student of Shakespeare little more than an assemblage of counterpoints: they help us to discern what Shakespeare, like most of those writing tragedies for the London stage in the 1590s and 1600s, chose *not* to do. By contrast, and although I can find no reason to conclude that Shakespeare had direct knowledge of the *Poetics*, Aristotle himself bequeaths us a series of powerful heuristics with which to approach Shakespeare's plays. Reading Seneca and writing comedies informed by the examples of Terence and Plautus taught Shakespeare all that he needed to know about crafting recognition scenes, but *anagnorisis* as described by Aristotle teaches us to appreciate their function in *Hamlet* and *Othello* and *King Lear*.[33]

———————

If Shakespeare's tragic plays are not greatly illuminated by neo-Aristotelianism, how do they relate to the bigger picture of early modern tragic theory? Shakespeare's most well-known account of genre falls from Polonius's lips as he vies with Hamlet for control over the company of players who have just arrived at Elsinore. According to Polonius, these visitors are:

> The best actors in the world, either for tragedy, comedy, history, pastoral, pastoral-comical, historical-pastoral, tragical-historical, tragical-comical-historical-pastoral, scene indivisible, or poem unlimited. Seneca cannot be too heavy, nor Plautus too light. For the law of writ, and the liberty, these are the only men. (2.2.392–98)

Although Polonius succeeds in presenting himself as a more up-to-date man of the theater than Hamlet, we are of course supposed to laugh at the ways in which he undoes himself through his bumptious hair-splitting.[34] We are also nudged toward a skeptical perspective: as the scene develops, the energies that have gone into Polonius's generic categorizing come to seem beside the point—ostensibly of the players' art, but also of Shakespeare's purpose in writing *Hamlet*.

If the "passionate speech" in the person of Hecuba and Hamlet's adaptation of *The Murder of Gonzago* are anything to go by, it was not only genre theory that Shakespeare viewed with something between skepticism and ironic detachment. Despite Hamlet's claims on their behalf, their style and subject matter closely match those criticized by Comedy in *A Warning for Fair Women*: "Pure purple Buskin, blood and murther right." In a similar vein, we might also adduce "Pyramus and Thisbe" in *A*

Midsummer Night's Dream or Falstaff's parody of "King Cambyses' vein" in *Henry IV, Part 1*.[35] The high tragic manner that the Elizabethans had begun to invent for themselves provided Shakespeare with some useful material, but was not something to which he turned with much in the way of reverence.

Still, when Shakespeare began his career as a playwright, "tragedy," "tragic," and "tragedian" were important parts of his lexicon.[36] Take *Henry VI, Part 2*, where Warwick tells Queen Margaret that the untimely death of Duke Humphrey is a "tragedy," or *Richard III*, where the now aged Queen Margaret hopes that her flight to France will prove "bitter, black and tragical" for her Plantagenet enemies. Tragedy here is used in an approximation of its *de casibus* sense, denoting any fall or misfortune afflicting one of great place.[37] More commonly, early Shakespeare employs tragedy and its cognates within a purposely dramatic field of reference—specifically, as a meta-dramatic metaphor through which to represent a turn in human affairs that is grave, affecting, and violently executed. Returning to *Henry VI, Part 2*, we find Gloucester condemning those who have conspired to kill him: "If my death might make this island happy / And prove the period of their tyranny, I would expend it with all willingness. / But mine is made the prologue to their play; / For thousands more that yet suspect no peril / Will not conclude their plotted tragedy" (3.1.148–53). When, in *Richard III*, the Duchess of York encounters a distracted Queen Elizabeth and asks, "What means this scene of rude impatience?," the Queen responds, "To make an act of tragic violence" (2.2.38–39): after the death of her husband, she considers suicide in the fashion of Seneca's Phaedra, Antigone, Jocasta, or Medea. It is exactly this affecting quality that Richard Gloucester and his sidekick Buckingham plan to exploit in seeking to "counterfeit the deep tragedian" (3.5.5). Counterfeit, that is, the professional counterfeiters. Buckingham's words echo another example, drawn from *Henry VI, Part 3*. Warwick rages self-accusingly after Richard has told him that his brother has been killed by Lancastrian forces: "Why stand we like soft-hearted women here, / Wailing our losses whiles the foe doth rage, / And look upon, as if the tragedy / Were played in jest by counterfeiting actors?"[38] He promptly returns to the battlefield.

Warwick lays bare the impossibility of placing oneself outside the action when participating in a civil war, but of greater moment here is that he hints at a theme that Shakespeare will often revisit: if all the world is a stage, then everyone in it is, wittingly or unwittingly, a player; if the world is a theater, then there is the possibility of spectatorship, reflection, and more.[39] For instance, in *Richard III*, Hastings imagines himself, "twelve-month hence," laughing "to look upon their [his adversaries'] tragedy" (3.2.56, 58). As it happens, his adversaries will end up laughing at him: his actions help to advance a plot that will see him decapitated, and his head turned into a stage prop.

A more involved example of the same dynamic comes from *Titus Andronicus*. After hearing that Lavinia was raped and mutilated in the hunting grounds that he and his brother had previously visited for sport, Marcus wonders "why should nature build so foul a den, / Unless the gods delight in tragedies?" (4.1.59–60). In so doing, he gestures toward a conventional understanding of the *theatrum mundi* (theater of the world) in which human life comprises a comedy or a tragedy performed before God and his angels. But what catches the eye is the way in which Shakespeare— perhaps revising or in collaboration with George Peele—handles the topos. The *theatrum mundi* is not presented as a master metaphor through which to comprehend the situation of humanity within the divinely regulated cosmos, but as a fiction to which a character turns in confronting the horror of the moment: the events in which he has been caught up are so terrible that they must have been devised by the gods. It is a fiction, moreover, that Marcus will later abandon for another, opting for the "commiseration" of tragic spectatorship (recall that Sidney's "commiseration" does duty for Aristotle's "pity") over admitting any possibility that he might have been an agent in the main action of the play. Let someone else "tell the tale / While I stand by and weep." The someone else in question is Marcus's nephew, Lucius— Titus's son, Lavinia's brother, and on Marcus's reckoning "Rome's young captain" (5.3.92–94). Once Lucius has narrated a version of what we in the audience have seen unfold, Marcus is anything but overcome: "Now it is my turn to speak" (5.3.118). He does so, and quickly wins support for vengeance against Aaron and the acclamation of Lucius as Emperor. As such, Marcus furthers his dynastic ends with consummate rhetorical finesse. The rub is that rather than leading to *catharsis* or even serving as an end in itself, tragic commiseration is made into a tool for political manipulation. By the time Aaron is buried in his comeuppance, the only tragic frame left standing belongs to what the title page of its 1594 first printing calls *The Most Lamentable Romaine Tragedie of Titus Andronicus*.

"Tragedy," then, makes for a dramatic metaphor with a certain heft. But by the time Shakespeare finished his work on *Titus Andronicus*, he seems to have realized that its effectiveness was diminished by repetition: implied, rather than explicit, self-reflexivity could more powerfully draw his tragic audiences in. With a couple of exceptions (single instances in *Henry V* and *Othello*), Shakespeare's drama never again employs tragedy or its cognates to signify anything other than a tragic play or matters related to it.[40] Even so, and as *Pyramus and Thisbe* and *The Murder of Gonzago* are on their own enough to remind us, the orbit of Shakespeare's dramatic intelligence would continue to show the influence—the gravitational pull—exerted by tragic convention.

Consider Albany's response as the corpses of Goneril and Regan are brought on stage in act 5 of *King Lear*: "This judgement of the heavens that makes us tremble / Touches us not with pity."[41] Albany uses a distinction borrowed directly or indirectly from chapter 13 of Aristotle's *Poetics* to declare that although these deaths are terrible, they are not tragic. Observing the dead bodies of his wife and her sister frightens him, but because their fates are so thoroughly deserved, it does not generate pity. Far from feeling moved to compassion, he elevates himself in moral judgment.

The obvious point of comparison is Albany's response to the first portion of Edgar's "woeful" tale, where the Scottish nobleman declares himself "almost ready to dissolve" (5.3.201–2). In feeling himself thus moved, Albany's sense of propriety is unimpeachable. The only problem is that this propriety—like the idea of tragedy that underlies it—cannot accommodate the tragic action of *King Lear*. Just as Albany's response to the blinding of Gloucester is that of the moralist (Cornwall's death at the hands of an unnamed servant proves that divine "justicers . . . these our nether crimes / So speedily can venge" [4.2.80–81]), so he cannot reconcile his belief that all get their just desserts with the fates that engulf Lear and Cordelia. Edgar, who believes both that he has an unusually refined tragic sensibility (he is one who, "by the art of known and feeling sorrows," is "pregnant to good pity" [4.6.218–19]) and that his father's eye-gouging is just retribution for the extramarital sex that led to Edmund's birth ("The gods are just and of our pleasant vices / Make instruments to plague us" [5.3.168–69]), finds himself in a similar position.[42]

After Kent returns to the stage to remind Albany of the "Great thing of us forgot!" (5.3.235), the whereabouts of Lear and Cordelia are determined and their reprieve is sent with all haste. It gets there too late. Lear arrives on stage bearing Cordelia's hanged body, and delivers himself of his intermingled grief, desperation, anger, and despair. Albany, Kent, and Edgar cannot acknowledge the significance of the tragic scene before them, and—like Nahum Tate and many others—find excuses to look away. First, they collectively wonder whether it heralds, or perhaps only represents, the end of the world (5.3.261–62); rather as Gloucester had averted his attention from Lear's fallen condition by reflecting that "this great world / Shall so wear out to naught" (4.6.130–31).[43] Then Kent seeks validation from

Lear for what he has endured on his behalf. When this is not forthcoming, Albany reassures Kent that he shouldn't take it personally: Lear "knows not what he says [or, in the quarto version of the text, 'sees'] and vain is it / That we present us to him" (5.3.291–92). Edgar agrees. Now, Albany none-theless fantasizes a return to the *ancien régime*, in which Lear is invested with "our absolute power," and in which "All friends shall taste / The wages of their virtue and all foes / The cup of their deservings" (5.3.299, 301–3). Insensible with pain, Lear dies. Once Kent has suggested that the length of Lear's life (not, that is, the agonized desolation of its final passage, or even having "overlived" himself by abdicating the office of monarchy) makes the old king's death a mercy, Albany moves things on to the division of the kingdom.[44] In a culminating irony, either Albany or Edgar (the quarto and folio texts do not agree on who speaks the play's final lines) assumes the majestic plural to unburden himself of the sententious couplet that "The weight of this sad time we must obey, / Speak what we feel, not what we ought to say" (5.3.322–23). As if a sense of "what we ought to say"—of how the relationship between suffering, tragedy, and moral-political order ought to be conceived—had not served to moderate their pain while Lear, cradling Cordelia's mortal remains, unraveled before them. As if a sense of "what we ought to say" is not that which licenses the platitudes through which the ship of state will sail on with Edgar and Albany at the helm. As if Cordelia and then Lear speaking as they really "feel" did not set the tragedy in motion back in act 1.

Something comparable takes place in *Hamlet*. As Fortinbras advances with the English ambassadors to greet Horatio amid the corpses of Ham-let, Gertrude, Claudius, and Laertes, he asks, "Where [i.e., whence, from where] is this sight?" Horatio—working hard to balance the demands of self-preservation, doing justice to the dead, assessing Fortinbras's inten-tions, and preventing any more bloodshed—responds, "What is it you would see? / If aught of woe or wonder, cease your search" (5.2.366–67). "Woe or wonder" recalls Sidney's "admiration and commiseration": "woe" generalizes the effect of "commiseration," and "wonder" is the common-place sixteenth-century substitute for Aristotle's "fear" (the Latin term for "wonder," borrowed from the rhetoric handbooks and Englished by Sidney, is *admiratio*).[45] Horatio's goal is to make Fortinbras view the scene as the affecting culmination of a tragedy that is now over—not, that is, one in which he as the incoming Danish monarch should feel the need to participate.

The problematic first quarto edition of *Hamlet* throws this moment into even sharper relief. Here, in response to Fortinbras's question, Hora-tio declares that "If aught of woe or wonder you'd behold / Then look upon this tragic spectacle." The impact is cruder than that of Horatio's lines in the second quarto and folio texts, but leaves us in little doubt as to what is going on. As, in a different way, does the first quarto's rendition of what Horatio says next. He addresses the English ambassadors, and perhaps also Fortinbras: "Content yourselves. I'll show to all the ground, / The first beginning of this tragedy."[46] Compare his words in the two most authoritative versions of the text:

> And let me speak to th'yet unknowing world
> How these things came about. So shall you hear
> Of carnal, bloody and unnatural acts,
> Of accidental judgments, casual slaughters,
> Of deaths put on by cunning and forc'd cause,
> And, in this upshot, purposes mistook
> Fall'n on th'inventors' heads. All this can I
> Truly deliver. (5.2.384–91)

Whether one prefers the folio's "cunning and forced cause" (a cause whose truthfulness has been distorted into falsehood) or the second quarto's "cunning and for no cause" (which speaks for itself), Horatio invites us to think again about what, other than the spectacle of death encountered by Fortinbras, might be the occasion of "woe or wonder."[47] As such, *Hamlet* for once coalesces with the inset play, "The Mousetrap," that sits at its center. Here, the Player King gently suggests to his wife that her avowals of unending love might be misconceived: *"Our wills and fates do so contrary run / That our devices still are overthrown: / Our thoughts are ours, their ends none of our own"* (3.2.206–8). The tragic "things" that Horatio has to relate are shaped not by probability or necessity or unity of action—or by providential oversight—but by aleatory happenstance; by accidents, errors, and misapprehensions; by the collision of competing plots, schemes, and stratagems. Against the grain of tragic expectation, Horatio insists that it didn't have to be this way. Nothing has taken place that should be bracketed as inevitable, or inexorably determined by the laws of causation once Claudius had killed his brother and married his sister-in-law. What is more, he allows us to infer that as Fortinbras (who does not know that Hamlet has nominated him for the kingship with his dying breath) arrives to seize power with his army, the consequences of the tragedy that he would now narrate are far from over: Denmark is about to be taken over by a youthful warlord who thinks nothing of killing thousands "to gain a little patch of ground / That hath in it no profit but the name" (4.4.18–19). So much for actions that are whole unto themselves.[48]

Let's look at this from a slightly different angle. Ostensibly, the action of *Hamlet* is resolved in the form of a closing frame, not unlike that provided by the return of Malcolm in *Macbeth*. The problem, attested by the frequency with which Fortinbras's return is cut from performances of the play, is that the agents of that resolution can feel like they are intruding from outside the main thrust of the plot. The resolutions themselves can thus feel contrived, and awkwardly proximate to the *deus ex machina* devices belittled by Aristotle, Horace, and their innumerable later followers.[49] Perhaps this sort of thing is what drove Johnson to complain of Shakespeare's tragedies that "terrour and pity, as they are rising in the mind, are checked and blasted by sudden frigidity."[50] Certainly, it is what led George Steiner to assert "a radical split between true tragedy and Shakespearean 'tragedy.'" For Steiner, although *King Lear* and *Timon of Athens* attain tragic authenticity, "Shakespeare's other mature tragic plays have in them strong, very nearly decisive, counter-currents of repair, of human radiance, of public and communal restoration. Danemark [*sic*] under Fortinbras, Scotland under Malcolm, will be eminently better realms to live in." As he explains later, "Any realistic notion of tragic drama must start from the fact of catastrophe. Tragedies end badly."[51]

Steiner deserves credit for noticing that there is something unexpected about Shakespeare's tragic endings, but aside from the fact that plays like Aeschylus's *Eumenides*, Sophocles's *Philoctetes*, and Euripides's *Alcestis* seem not, on his account, to qualify as "true" tragedies, what he misses is the self-conscious intelligence that animates Shakespeare's structural art. Shakespeare knew well that he could have ended *Hamlet* and *Macbeth* with the deaths of their protagonists, as he does *Othello* and *Coriolanus*. But in *Hamlet* and *Macbeth*, he advances a bolder gambit by prompting his audience to consider their expectations of how a tragedy ought to conclude—going as far as to flirt with the possibility of bathos. It is not simply that he makes time to allow the consequences of a tragic death to become apparent (as in *Julius Caesar* and *Antony and Cleopatra*), or that some participant or other in the main part of the action will (as in *Romeo and Juliet* and *King Lear*) unsettle our attempts to make sense of what we have seen by mouthing bromides of which not even they sound fully convinced. Rather, Shakespeare adapts the tragic examples found in works like Euripides's *Medea* and Seneca's *Phaedra*. He wants not to present us with a reassertion of order that is bound to seem as cosmetic as that avowed by Edgar and Albany, but to make us aware that all such reassertions of moral and political order are in themselves cosmetic, contrived, deluded—that the human sufferings and perplexities depicted in tragic art are inscrutable, and cannot therefore be reduced to neatly rational representations. He wants, in the fullest sense of the term, to make us "wonder."

———

Terence Cave has written of Shakespeare's plays that they "advertise the force of ways of knowing and understanding that ordered discourse is accustomed to reject." For Cave, the plays' "frequent moments of self-consciousness . . . are not signs of formalistic inbreeding, a narcissistic self-mirroring of the text. They seem rather an assertion of mastery, pre-empting our right to intervene and judge the fictions presented to us as anything other than an autonomous form of life."[52] This judgment is surely right. Shakespeare depicted conventional theories and practices of tragedy neither to identify his own tragic works with them, nor merely to set his own tragic works apart. Instead, by acknowledging tragic convention but positioning himself deliberately outside it, he sought to encompass tragedy as his peers wrote and understood it—before putting it to work for him in the creation of something new.

In trying to discern where this novelty lies, Horatio again makes for an illuminating focal point. It is true that his emphasis on contingency, inadvertency, and happenstance can make his vision of tragedy sound like that of Boethianism: fortune and chance are incomprehensible, and their operations bring down even the mightiest seemingly at random; in the more moralistic key of *de casibus* storytelling, wrongdoers become the authors of their own misfortune. One might also recall Auden's distinction between the tragedies of "necessity" ("what a pity it had to be this way") found in ancient Greece, and those of "possibility" ("what a pity it was this way when it might have been otherwise") that are more characteristic of the Christian era.[53] But the most conspicuous feature of Horatio's account of events in and around Elsinore is that it finds no place for reason, nature, or providence as the author of the tragic plot that has claimed so many lives. He instead presents the "things" that have come inadvertently to pass as the results of human agency, and human agency alone. J.G.A. Pocock has written powerfully of a Greek tradition in historiography, in which history is regarded as "an exercise in political ironies," and in which historical writing is concerned to tell "an intelligible story of how men's actions produce results other than those they intended."[54] I would like to suggest that, in Shakespeare's tragic writing, he sets himself a similar task—one in which history and the contingency of historical events are allowed to transform the philosophical plotting of tragedy.

We have seen Evanthius conclude that "tragedy often strives for the verisimilitude of history," but it is to chapter 9 of Aristotle's *Poetics* (1451a–1452a) that we must turn for the most probing discussion of the relationship between tragedy and historicity. Its outlines are familiar to anyone who has tried to justify the study of literature to skeptical parents or classmates: history is bound to particulars, and to those events that happen to have happened; poetry is concerned with the concepts of things derived from the common, and cumulative, human experience of the world, and takes as its subject everything that might possibly happen or have happened. History deals in facts. Poetry deals in truth, and is as such akin to philosophy. Unlike comedy, however, whose plots are exclusively fictional, tragedy draws from the historical record. Sometimes, historical events lend themselves directly to tragic art, but on most occasions the poet-dramatist must remake them in accordance with the criteria of probability and necessity through which Aristotle measures unity of action. On this model, history comprises a catalogue of events, with no readily discernable beginning, middle, or end—in which y follows x, but is not caused by x. By contrast, the events depicted in a drama, and especially a tragic drama, should stand in clear causal relation to one another.[55] In the beginning of the play, to their consequences; in the middle, to their antecedents and consequences; at the end, to their antecedents alone.

For Aristotle, then, unity of action is dual. It includes the form of a play (i.e., its plot, or "principle of life"), and the actions that its plot seeks to imitate. Underpinning both aspects of this unitary vision is the belief that all parts of the human experience are intelligible to reason. This is fine as far as it goes, but Aristotle was too observant to overlook the element of surprise in tragic plots, especially as embodied in the moments of *peripeteia* and *anagnorisis* that he valued so highly, in leading an audience to feelings of pity, fear, and wonder. Something surprising is, by definition, beyond the limits of what one might reasonably expect to happen, and if not exactly trying to have his cake while eating it, Aristotle shows his greatness through his willingness to sacrifice discursive coherence to the claims of veracity. Tragic surprises should occur "unexpectedly but because of each other . . . even chance events arouse more wonder when they look as if they were meant to happen."[56] *As if* they were meant to happen: with this qualification, Aristotle admits a discrepancy between unity of action in the plot (which remains governed by probability and necessity) and the events that the plot represents through mimesis (which elude rational explanation). In other words, he reveals a tension between the theoretical and descriptive aspirations of the *Poetics*—between aesthetic order and events in the world, wrought as they are by contingency and chance. This tension returns in chapter 18: as "it is likely that many things should happen contrary to likelihood," then it is only right for some of the surprises to which *peripeteia* leads to seem a little improbable.[57] Then, in chapter 24, we are told that "the irrational" lies behind most manifestations of wonder and surprise, and that such irrationality belongs more to epic than to tragedy. In composing a tragic plot, "one ought to prefer likely impossibilities to unconvincing possibilities" and should therefore cast aside all "irrational parts."[58] Aristotle settles on the view that if the events to be represented in the play—whether their origins lie in history, the playwright's own ingenuity, or somewhere between—are stranger than the rules of tragic fiction can allow, then they should in all but the most exceptional instances be struck out. The competing claims of chance on one side and probability and necessity on the other remain unresolved.

Shortly after this discussion, in the notoriously knotty chapter 25, Aristotle endorses Sophocles's claim that "he represented people as they should be, and Euripides as they are."[59] Although Aristotle had a high opinion of Euripides, Sophocles's assent to the primacy of tragic propriety and rationality (along, it must be said, with his show of playful humility) makes Aristotle's approval easy to understand. But from the perspective of Shakespeare's tragedies, it is the Euripidean example that counts. Had Euripides responded to Sophocles, he might have said that he only represented people as they seemed to him, and that in its fidelity to his worldview—to history as he saw it—his drama was no less inventively poetic than that of Aeschylus or of Sophocles himself. Had somebody put something of the kind to Shakespeare, and had Shakespeare had the advantage of someone to record his table talk like Drummond of Hawthornden did for Ben Jonson (or Boswell did for Samuel Johnson), it would be unsurprising to learn that he thought in cognate terms.

Although recent work by Lorna Hutson and Quentin Skinner has made plain Shakespeare's use of likelihood and inference as features of humanist rhetoric, such concerns had little impact on the fundamental structure of his tragic designs.[60] Put simply, Shakespeare had no time for unitary action as defined by Aristotle: as he did not believe that events as they play out in the world proceed in an orderly fashion from soup to nuts, he did not believe that the mimetic object of a tragedy ought to be shaped by unity and wholeness of action. When things happen in a way that is surprising or otherwise beyond the province of what human reason deems probable or necessary, as for Shakespeare they often do, tragedy should be able account for them rather than burying or dissembling them in the service of a predetermined moral, political, philosophical, theological, or even poetic agenda.[61] To borrow a narratological distinction from Roland Barthes, we might say that Shakespeare's tragic plots proceed along hermeneutic rather than proairetic lines; that the propulsive force with which he imbues them—the suspenseful quality that keeps us watching and reading—comes not from the anticipation of an action's resolution according to the canons of probability and necessity, but from unanswered questions. What Joel Altman relatedly calls "questions of fiction."[62] For Shakespeare as for Euripides and Seneca, the cynosure of tragic drama is precisely those aspects of human experience that exceed rational expectation, but that nevertheless need to be examined and in some measure understood.

And because Shakespeare took the doctrine of unitary action to be a form of rationalizing make-believe, he saw no need to respect it in the fictional but verisimilar plots through which he sought to achieve tragic mimesis. Cue the ready availability of narcotics in Verona, the gullibility of Othello, Gloucester's blinding, the flamboyantly stagy tiffs between Antony and Cleopatra, the quasi-supernatural apparatus that frames the plots of *Hamlet* and *Macbeth*—and so on to the laundry list of complaints leveled against Shakespeare from Dryden and Rymer to Johnson's declaration that his "plots are often so loosely formed that a very slight consideration may improve them, and so carelessly pursued that he seems not always fully to comprehend his own design."[63] By imputing carelessness to Shakespeare's plotting, Johnson does not suggest loose ends, or even apparent slips like furnishing Bohemia with a coastline in *The Winter's Tale*. Rather, he has in mind what he regards as Shakespeare's tendency to display an excessive historicity born of cleaving too closely to his sources. As the pithily Aristotelian Rymer had suggested several decades earlier, it was incumbent on those who would write tragedies to remember that "*History*, grosly taken, was neither proper to *instruct*, nor apt to *please*." Tragic authors should refine their historical reading, thereby "contriv[ing] something more *philosophical*, and more *accurate*" than an episodic mélange of things as they happen to have happened. Rymer judged that Shakespeare and the other English tragic playwrights of the early seventeenth century had failed to take such pains, and concluded that it was at best an open question whether they "had any *design* in their *designs*, and whether it was to *prudence* or to *chance* that they sacrificed."[64]

Notwithstanding the fact that Shakespeare's basic unit of composition was the scene rather than the acts into which his plays would later be organized, it is hard not to regard Rymer's strictures as an exercise in critical perversity. Despite his disparagement of Shakespeare's plots, one index of Johnson's superiority as a critic is that he was too sharp and honest to overlook that Shakespeare's "plan has commonly what *Aristotle* requires, a beginning, a middle, and an end; one event is concatenated with another, and the conclusion follows by easy consequence."[65] If there is a contradiction between this position and his insistence that Shakespeare "seems not always fully to comprehend his own design," then it is not one that Johnson himself would have recognized. He had scant regard for the unities as upheld by Rymer, but his steadfast moralism made him as much of a teleological thinker as any Aristotelian. A true tragedy must give rise to "terrour and pity," and advance the causes of what Johnson took to be virtue and right. Shakespeare's tragedies do not do so, and for Johnson it follows that their plots must be desultory—"loosely formed," "carelessly pursued"—even if they do have basic dramatic coherence to recommend them.

One burden of this book is to establish that, in their different ways, Rymer and Johnson both miss the point. To establish, that is, that Shakespeare's tragedies are more than merely coherent, and that they have a deliberate and carefully elaborated "design." This may have been denied them by neoclassical critics and adaptors, as also by those who have seen in them an expression of "the tragic" consonant with the onset of modernity; but these denials tell us less about Shakespeare than they do the need to rethink our theories of tragedy such that they might keep up with Shakespeare's tragic art. As we shall see, it is just not the case that the tragedies regurgitate the material Shakespeare found in Holinshed, Plutarch, and collections of prose fiction like Cinthio's *Gli Hecatommithi* and Belleforest's *Histoires tragiques*. Rather, the sense of history to which his reading led him prevented him from accepting conventional notions of providential or tragic order in formulating the plots that animate his tragedies.[66] There is no question of his abandoning or neglecting the plasticity of art in favor of a ploddingly incoherent historicism: his focus is not on *whether* to reshape events into an object worthy of mimetic endeavor, but *how* to do so without sacrificing the complexity of the world as he has experienced it to one kind or other of tragic decorum. Disorder, discontinuity, contingency, chaos, and even history are *concepts* after all—ways in which the human mind gives shape to realities (human and nonhuman) that would otherwise seem formless. *A fortiori* works of art that seek to represent the experience of disorder, discontinuity, or chaos. The experience, that is, of historically contingent living.[67]

In attending to the historicity of the tragedies as a carefully patterned simulacrum of historical existence, we can begin to understand one of their subtlest and most confounding elements: over and again, they resist the suggestibility of their own topical-historical allusions. Yes, they gesture toward the domain of succession crises, religious conflict, social discord, and imperial ambition. In one rather limited sense, they thereby put history on the stage while exploring the ways in which human individuals and societies relate themselves to it; it may even be that they can illuminate that history more fully than would otherwise be the case. But such gestures only signify within a dramatic framework that at once incorporates and places itself beyond other forms of discourse. Within it, the vicissitudes and conflicts of late Elizabethan and early Jacobean history are treated not as the focus of the action, much less as a source of truth or essential value conflict, but as another object for the seriously mimetic attention of tragic art. The tensions that would erupt in the Essex Revolt and the near calamity of the Gunpowder Plot are hugely important contexts for reading, respectively, *Hamlet* and *Macbeth*. But these events, climactic though they must have been to those caught up in them, were little more than starting points for works of art that transcend historical-political allegory or commentary, and that strive in their own way for the analytical universality that the Aristotelians saw as the true province of poetry.

But this is to get too far ahead of ourselves. Suffice it to say that behind Shakespeare's rejection of rationally ordered Aristotelian plots lies the conviction that as nothing other than death is inevitable, tragedies should not pretend otherwise. Romeo and Juliet may be young and in love, foolish, and frustrated by uncooperative parents, but their deaths are caused by a letter that goes undelivered in the midst of a plague lockdown; similar predicaments are brought to comic resolution in *A Midsummer Night's Dream*, *As You Like It*, and *Much Ado About Nothing*. Cordelia's slightly truculent rectitude at the start of *King Lear* may or may not warrant retribution, but her death comes about because Edgar enjoys talking about himself and because Albany is happier listening to him than probing Edmund on the whereabouts of the king and his daughter. It could easily have been avoided. Lear's abdication at the start of the play has dire consequences but is not obviously more unwise than that of Charles V, who divided the Habsburg Empire into Spanish and Austrian branches when retiring from public life in 1556. Lear endures a lot for what turns out to be his poor judgment, but dies on account of Cordelia's needless execution.

One might go on. The key point is that, for Shakespeare, although suffering is a universal of the human condition, its occurrences are invariably circumstantial. It always arises from a concatenation of accidents, contingencies, passions, misapprehensions, noble deeds and aspirations, ignoble deeds and aspirations, and sheer bad timing. No less than appeals to voices from above, the doctrine of inevitability—of suffering brought inexorably about through the laws of probability and necessity—is a way of averting our gaze, of denying our agency, of shirking responsibility for the consequences of the decisions we make. Even in the special case of revenge tragedy, where the revenger must be punished for his transgressions of morality and the law in achieving his wild kind of justice, Shakespeare leaves us with a sense of arbitrariness and ambiguity, of mystery and force majeure: "accidental judgments," "casual slaughters," and "purposes mistook." In pretending otherwise, whether in devising events to imitate or in devising the plots through which to imitate those events, Aristotelian theories of tragedy distort the truth. In their turn, these distortions lead to delusions about how human suffering comes about and about how, in some measure and at some point, it might be ameliorated. Shakespeare's tragedies are as short on didacticism as they are on the clutching of pearls, but it seems to me that they present this state of affairs as a problem.

———————

I want now to turn, more briefly, to the other two chief objects of tragic imitation in the Aristotelian tradition: character (*ethos*) and thought (*dianoia*). Again, not because I take Shakespeare to have been a student of the *Poetics*, but because they make a fine heuristic through which to approach his plays.

Although there was extensive discussion as to whether plot or character should be regarded as the most important object of tragic imitation (Castelvetro, for example, turns the question over at length), plot invariably prevailed. Perhaps the biggest single difference between the idea of tragedy as articulated in early modern and Romantic-Idealist theories of poetry is that, for the early moderns, character was ancillary to the design of the drama as a whole. It is not that characters are servants of the plot, but that they only exist to the extent that they do or say things within it. As Aristotle insists, you can have a tragedy (a bad one) without vividly individuated characters, but you cannot have one without a plot in which things take place:

> If you put down one after another speeches that depicted *ethos*, finely expressed and brilliant in *dianoia*, that would not do the job that, by definition, tragedy does do . . . a tragedy with a plot, that is, an ordered series of particular actions, though deficient in these other points [i.e., the mimesis of character and thought], would do its job much better.

So it is that within the Shakespearean hierarchy of consciousness, characters only have childhoods and earlier lives when they or some other member of the dramatis personae tell us about them, or prompt us to infer
their existence. When, that is, such depth of characterization is deemed
necessary by Shakespeare. To put that in Aristotelian terms, not every
character in Shakespeare's tragic plays demonstrates *ethos*, and even those
who do should not be mistaken for autonomous moral agents. Still, the
reaction against Bradleyan character criticism often goes too far. We experience Edgar and Juliet and Troilus and Lady Macbeth *as if* they were real
people, even though they have no more external reality than the particular configurations of paint spread against particular support media that
we recognize as Vermeer's Delft or Magritte's pipe. Our focus should be
less on pointing out that the most vivid or naturalistic representations of
things are illusions than on exploring 1) how this illusory effect has been
accomplished, and 2) where its force and purpose can be said to reside.[68]

In reading Shakespeare or the *Poetics*, the English "character" can be
a slippery term with which to work. Aristotle's *ethos* was usually translated into Latin as *mos* (the plural of which is the more familiar *mores*);
although this certainly bears translation into English as "character," it does
so carrying the sense of dispositions that reveal themselves through our
actions and moral behaviors, and that have no status when not shaping
those actions and behaviors. Or, as Thomas Cooper translated it in the
1560s, *mos* represents character as "a condition." It was in this sense that
the Theophrastan "characters" sketched by Joseph Hall and Thomas Over-
bury in the early seventeenth century were quasi-satirical types, illustrating
the traits or dispositions that—if allowed to impress themselves too arkedly
on our actions—would lead to vice. It is also the case that the early moderns thought about the "persons" of a drama (preserved in the notion of
dramatis personae) rather than its characters. A *persona* (like the Greek
prosopon) was the mask worn by actors while on stage to make their stage
roles known, and in time came to denote both stage roles as a category and
the actors who played them. Why not resuscitate this usage, and use "person" to denote the members of the dramatis personae? Because, like so
much else about the discourse of selfhood, things are complicated. The
persona was also a crucial element of the Ciceronian moral philosophy that
shaped so much of the humanist world view. Here, one only gets to attain
one's true self by inhabiting *personae* consonant both with one's innate
dispositions and abilities (the hard-to-translate Latin *ingenium*) and the
demands of one's social context. As *persona* is a term that reveals much
about the ways in which the human individual was conceived in the early

modern period, and as it is one to which I return frequently in the chapters that follow, I designate parts in plays as "characters"—irrespective of whether these characters can lay claim to tragic *ethos* in the Aristotelian manner.[69]

The ancillary status of Shakespeare's characters is straightforward enough to lay out in theory, but can be hard to square with the experience of reading or watching the tragedies to which these characters belong. Shakespeare is so good at the work of characterization (that is, at the deep characterization of Aristotelian *ethos*) that it can threaten to occlude the mastery and significance of his plotting, as can the affective force of the actorly virtuosity (modeled, it would seem, by Richard Burbage) required to bring his characters to life on the stage.[70] Shakespeare's version of tragedy, particularly as it plays upon our emotions as playgoers and readers, can thus seem like a matter of intensely individual significance; the kinds of things that happen in tragedies only become tragic because they happen to a Lear or a Cordelia, not to an Edmund or a Goneril. The difficulty is exacerbated because, as we shall see, Shakespeare takes pains to depict the historical fortune, fate, and happenstance in which his principals become caught up as the products of exclusively human forms of agency; because, that is, Shakespeare understands the force of Aristotle's belief that the moral choices made by dramatic characters simultaneously reveal their *ethos* and drive forward the action of the plot.[71] In saying so, I don't mean to resuscitate the old critical standby that character is fate. Instead, I have something Jamesian in mind: "What is character but the determination of incident? What is incident but the illustration of character?"[72] I want to suggest Shakespeare's preoccupation with the hugely complicated relationships of causation that arise from the collisions between individual characters' actions, utterances, feelings, beliefs, and desires. To suggest that, at all times, the relationship between Shakespearean plot and *ethos* is thoroughly, and disorientingly, interpenetrative. And that it remains so even when a character or group of characters attempts to comprehend the forces shaping the world as a matter of fate, fortune, nature, destiny, or providence.

Discussing Othello's final speech, T. S. Eliot proposed that no writer "has ever exposed . . . the human will to see things as they are not" more clearly than Shakespeare.[73] I suspect that others have in fact come close (Chekhov, say, or Euripides; Stendhal or Tolstoy or Flaubert), but Eliot's insight is valuable. It indexes a further difficulty in trying to comprehend the deep characterization of the tragedies. Shakespeare's brilliance is not simply to make us sympathize with portraits of transgressive villainy

alongside suffering virtue, but is to present Edmund and Claudius alongside Edgar and Hamlet, and to show how all of them are prey to the most
basic delusions about who they are, what they are, and what they can
know. At some level, this is standard tragic fare: as the action unfolds,
tragic heroes like Oedipus come to recognize aspects of themselves to
which they had previously been blind. It is a sort of self-*anagnorisis*. But
for Shakespeare such recognition is never more than a gesture—another
way to show his characters telling themselves stories, and in which to
scramble the tragic expectations of his audiences. In their different ways,
Octavius Caesar and perhaps Cleopatra attain and hold onto a share of
self-knowledge, but it is King Lear who speaks for the special kind of lone-
liness endured by the remainder of Shakespeare's tragic protagonists:
"Who is it that can tell me who I am?" (1.4.221). He never discovers a way
of knowing that does not demand the affirmation of others.[74]

Behind the frustrations of self-knowledge lies the problem of language
and self-representation. Because Shakespeare recognizes that we can only
analyze ourselves through the medium of language, and because language
(especially the poetic, religious, philosophical, and literary kinds of language through which we most often conduct self-analysis) imposes its own
order on the phenomena it represents, his characters are unable fully to
examine themselves as they are or might be. Even the soliloquies of Hamlet and Macbeth are exercises in failed privacy, thwarted immediacy, and
deliberate or inadvertent self-distortion.

Ralph Waldo Emerson's essay "Experience" captures something vital
here. Looking back on the devastation of his son's death two years earlier,
Emerson notes that

> There are moods in which we court suffering, in the hope that here
> at least we shall find reality, sharp peaks and edges of truth. But it
> turns out to be scene-painting and counterfeit. The only thing grief
> has taught me is to know how shallow it is. That, like all the rest, plays
> about the surface, and never introduces me into the reality, for contact
> with which we would even pay the costly price of sons and lovers.

Emerson, part-rueful and part-sorrowful, regrets that he can only grieve
for the loss of the son he loved through the narratives and formulae—the
fictions—that his intellect has constructed. He cannot grieve, that is, without narrating to himself and to others the fact that he is grieving, and
cannot narrate without employing the languages of discursive convention.
As to narrate in these terms would be to simplify and distort, to allow
the sign to smother the referent and the signified to become lost amongst

unmoored signifiers, to sacrifice the exactitude of his suffering to the taste-lessness of generality, he backs away—as many of us have felt the urge to do when struggling to resist the tug of cliché in articulating grief. But the problem Emerson faces goes further than how to respond to the death of a loved one, or how to sidestep the automaticity of the language through which we habitually mourn. If our experiences are one of the things that make us who we are and if the memory of them shapes the way in which we encounter the future, what are we to do if these memories are dis-tortions and these experiences are inaccessible to our thinking faculties? How do we ensure the privacy of our most intimate feelings and reflec-tions? Other than fashioning a self as the point of view from which to write creative nonfiction, Emerson's answer was that one should seek out mystical kinds of experience, so that one might transcend the limits of language and commune directly with the universe.[75] Shakespeare could never be mistaken for a Transcendentalist along Emersonian lines, but Emerson's account of conventional living, and of the "scene-painting and counterfeit" on which it depends, reveals much about the force of Shake-speare's tragic characterization.

Another way of approaching the question is to say that Shakespeare's tragic characters reflect a deeply un-Aristotelian view of the world, and a concomitantly un-Aristotelian choice of objects to imitate. On the evi-dence of his tragedies, Shakespeare did not believe human beings to have stable forms, purposes, or essences—much less ones that can be rationally understood. People as he sees them are not fixed entities, but events; not things, but processes; not merely mortal beings, but *temporal* ones. They are always moving, changing, growing, growing old, learning, forgetting. Like the actorly selves performed in the theater, the self as Shakespeare's characters represent it is something that continually *happens*, and that continues evolving unto death under the pressure of experience.

And as Emerson reminds us, experience is complicated. It is common-place to talk about one's current preoccupations distorting and displac-ing one's memories (after Romeo sees Juliet, he is tormented no longer by thoughts of Rosaline), but in Shakespeare's rendering it is not just the memory that is pliable. Like hope, expectation, and desire, remember-ing the past or one's experiences of the past can distort, and ultimately threaten to displace, the experience of the present. Just as we cannot see ourselves without the aid of a mirror, so not even something as basic as grief can be experienced in an unmediated form. Selfhood here exists as an approximation—a working fiction that plays an essential role in enabling us to stand easily with our portion of human nature, and as a placeholder for a phenomenon (i.e., human life as each of us lives it) that we do not fully understand. It is simpler and more demanding than Aristotelian or Hegelian poetics would have one believe. The plots in which Shakespeare's protagonists have been involved have made them different people. It is the recognition of this difference, and of the inescapability of always differing from themselves, with which Shakespeare shows them sometimes struggling, sometimes fighting—and from which they sometimes flee. The reason that Hamlet, Macbeth, Othello, Lear, Cleopatra, and the others do not experience self-discovery at the end of the plays of which they are a part is that there is no stable or autonomous "self" there for them to discover.

Shakespeare is uninterested in what we are, at least in the a priori sense demanded by most philosophers and theologians. He sees that we are unusually intelligent animals—and that the common features of humanity are as much the products of our animal natures as of our intelligence—and is content to leave it at that. Instead, he commits his energies to recreating as best he can the contingency, flux, and uncertainty at the core of the human condition, and to exploring the costs and benefits of the ways in which human beings look for the security of meaning in notions like the soul, the self, the family, the nation, the crown, the church, or that within which passes show. There is ambition here: Shakespeare positions his tragedies as being better able to make sense of human affairs than works of history, philosophy, or theology. But there is also a deep circumspection, an epistemic humility about what can and can't meaningfully be understood. Not a Cavellian petition to forgo the pursuit of knowledges that we already intuit, but an insistent exploration of what it is possible for us to recognize of ourselves, and of the ways—learned and intuitive, public and private—through which we might come to recognize it.[76]

Shakespeare's imitation of thought, or *dianoia*, requires less exposition. In chapter 19 of his *Poetics*, Aristotle explains that the kind of thinking he has in mind comprises "every effect to be produced by speech. Its sections are proof and disproof, rousing emotion (pity, fear, anger, and so on), making a thing look important or unimportant." Not the kind of demonstrative reasoning that Aristotle's logical writings seek to advance, and Aristotle directs the reader to his treatise on *Rhetoric* for further discussion.[77]

This emphasis on rhetoric helps to disentangle an apparent anomaly in early modern theories of tragedy: in all the Latin translations and discussions of the *Poetics* that I have read, *dianoia* is translated not as *ratio* (reason), but as *sententia*.[78] In the Roman rhetorical tradition, *sententia* denotes a thought expressed in words, particularly in the form of an aphorism, maxim, adage, axiom, proverb, commonplace, or saying—and so it does here. *Sententiae* were taken to represent a kind of general truth (as opposed to the specific examples with which the historian was bound to work), and confirmed one's arguments by investing them with the gravity and wisdom of commonly acknowledged authority. That they were often models of felicitous expression was an additional lure for those seeking to create the impression of eloquence. Accordingly, sixteenth-century school-boys were urged by their humanist teachers to collect *sententiae* in the course of their reading, and to record them in their commonplace books. If they did so, they would have ready access to a rich supply of materials with and around which to compose their own writings or orations. As a work like William Cornwallis's *Discourses Upon Seneca the Tragedian* and the example of that astutely compendious reader Gabriel Harvey tend to confirm, tragedies were identified as an especially rich source of *sententiae*; their printed versions often highlighted the parts of the text that the aspiring rhetorician might want to make his own.[79]

So, if the Senecan example was not on its own enough to impress on Shakespeare the force of having his tragic characters express themselves in mightily eloquent terms, his grammar school education would have emphasized the point. Certainly, it was not lost on him: consider the vast range of ends into which quotations from the plays continue to be pressed, or the fact that when the first quarto of *Hamlet* was printed in 1603, the *sententiae* within it were marked off for the convenience of those reading with their commonplace books or writing tablets to hand.[80] Shakespeare was, in short, a maestro of reading for what Erasmus called the *insigne verbum* (distinctive expression)—not for guidance or instruction as such, but for the striking word, image, or *sententia* that could be jotted down before being put to work within his own compositions. Like the learned bee imagined by Seneca (which gathers up nectar from a range of different sources before transforming it into discursive honey of its own), or like Montaigne (who declared that "I only quote others the better to quote myself"), there is a sense that Shakespeare is at his most unique when he is at his most assimilative.[81]

But if quotability was necessary, Shakespeare by no means thought it suf-ficient: Aristotle's insistence that *dianoia* and *ethos* are not inherently tragic finds ample affirmation within the plays. Think of Hamlet and Polonius savoring the obscurely impressive phrase "the mobbled queen" as spoken by the lead player in the person of Aeneas (2.2.498–500). Irrespective of whether they grasp its meaning more fully than we do, they see it as an *insigne verbum*, something that they can repurpose to their own rhetorical ends. The image of Polonius doing so, no doubt with a self-consciousness balanced awkwardly between the preening and the preposterous, springs readily to mind. It might be harder to imagine Hamlet similarly engaged, but his speech—whether addressed to himself or to others—is just as reflexively full of topoi, commonplaces, *sententiae*, appeals to authority, and rhetorical patterning as that of the old counselor he disdains. It is just that Hamlet is better at concealing his art.[82] Although Shakespeare experiments with the display of *dianoia* and sententiousness to suggest the ways in which his dramatic characters differ from one another, these differences are in the last analysis of degree rather than kind—as are those between the languages of the early tragedy *Titus Andronicus* (weighed down by sententious Latinity) and those of *Hamlet, Lear,* or *Macbeth* (which are not).

By the same token, Shakespeare's investiture of his tragic protagonists with the capacity for moving or persuasive speech hints at a preoccupation that endures from his first tragedy to his last: the instrumentality of humanistic learning, and its indifference to the moral virtues that it was supposed to inculcate in the young. In this instance, he follows Marlowe's Senecan lead in juxtaposing the practice of humanist tragedy with the ideology of humanist rhetoric. For humanist ideologues, it was a given that only the good and wise man (*vir bonus*) could hope fully to praise virtue and censure vice, and therefore to attain true eloquence. But, in writing Claudius, Iago, Edmund, and Macbeth, Shakespeare had in mind the examples of Tamburlaine and his own Richard III. They speak as intimately, as engagingly, as defiantly, and with as much muscular flair as Hamlet, Othello, and Lear. They do so not to usurp the prerogatives of tragic heroism as such, but to make us think again about where the substance of heroism—tragic and otherwise—might be said to reside. The correlations between virtue and eloquence, eloquence and *ethos*, become even murkier when we venture into the Roman plays. For Shakespeare, rhetoric not only works to stir the passions of its listeners or readers, but reflects the appetites and desires of those who deploy it—and, by giving those appetites and desires the appearance of dignity, often serves to lead those who would deploy it astray. The typically Shakespearean paradox is that he puts this case through a form of poetic writing that, not least in its reliance on *sententiae*, is itself profoundly rhetorical.[83]

———

In the concluding chapter of my book on *Hamlet,* I tried to come to an understanding of the ends at which Shakespearean tragedy aims. I suggested that, rather than analyzing the play through the lens of Aristotelian *catharsis*, we should look to the notion of *ekstasis* elaborated in the treatise *On the Sublime* usually attributed to the Roman-Greek author Longinus. *Ekstasis* connotes the condition of being transported beyond oneself, of experiencing an exalted level of feeling that captures one's consciousness and elevates it above rational thought. (Note that Longinan sublimity simply connotes heightened language, not the notions of the "the sublime" found in the aesthetic theories of Burke, Kant, Lyotard, and others.) The goal of tragic *ekstasis* is to raise our everyday expectations to a loftier pitch—thereby to expand our horizons—by generating states of heightened feeling like pity and fear.[84]

I stand by much of this judgment. In considering the "Induction" to *A Warning for Fair Women*, it is no stretch to find something Longinan about the claim made by Tragedy that her "office" is to "rap the sences from their course." Thinking about what Patrick Cheney calls the "early modern sublime" also helps us to move away from the idea that Shakespearean tragedy should give rise to *catharsis*, and that this *catharsis* should lead to a kind of purgation or purification (whether of the spirit, the soul, or the body) in which the readers or spectators of a play are left less prone to emotional disturbance.[85] After all, despite the prominence given to *catharsis* in the tragic theories of the later seventeenth to nineteenth centuries (echoed in Brecht's dismissal of *catharsis* as insipidly bourgeois fare), it was not that prominent a feature of tragedy as the early moderns conceived it. Scaliger views it as unduly restrictive and excludes it from his definition of the tragic, and Castelvetro sees it as something akin to the desensitization to death experienced during outbreaks of plague and by soldiers in time of war: by exposing ourselves to the imitation of piteous or fearful events in tragedies, we will be able to handle the experience of the real thing with greater equanimity. When a version of *catharsis* appears in Webster's *Duchess of Malfi* (the title character assures her maid that she would like to hear of "some dismall Tragedy" because "To hear of greater griefe, would lessen mine"), it is as an index of a mind already weakened by the apprehension of its own (in the *de casibus* sense) "tragic" fate.[86] None of this does anything like the cathartic work demanded by later traditions.

Even so, I am not completely sure that in concentrating on sublimity I didn't mistake a *what* question for a *why* question. Yes, Shakespearean tragedy seeks to arouse states of heightened feeling, and yes, these states of heightened feeling can be construed as a more elevated perspective from which to regard our everyday lives. And? Climbing the local church tower may give us a different perspective on the tenement in which we live, but we still need a reason to believe that this perspective has value—in itself, and when viewed retrospectively on our return home.

We can find the lineaments of such a reason in recent work exploring less vaulting senses of Aristotelian *catharsis*. In particular, Martha Nussbaum's discussion of *catharsis* as a kind of clarification, rather than purgation or purification, sheds important light on why Shakespeare troubled himself with the arousal of fear and pity. For Nussbaum, *catharsis* enables us to see and to comprehend our human status more distinctly than would otherwise be the case: "It is a recognition of practical values, and therefore of ourselves, that is no less important than the recognitions and perceptions of the intellect. Pity and fear are themselves elements in an appropriate practical perception of our situation." Here, *catharsis* clarifies the emotional experiences that are an ineradicable part of our lives, and helps us better to understand the circumstances within which we are at once free and constrained to exist. What is more, it illuminates the experiences of pity and fear to help us see more clearly that the emotions, always conjoined with the activities of the intellect, are themselves a part of the mechanism through which we are able understand our condition. Like the activities of the intellect, they need to be cultivated through the acquisition of good habits.[87]

In most respects, this account of *catharsis* fits Shakespearean tragedy perfectly. Shakespeare wants to prompt us into better envisioning the nature of our emotional lives, just as he wants to jolt us into recognizing the ways in which we attempt to disguise or theorize away the messier portions of human existence. In writing tragedies rather than, say, rigorously argued works of theology or moral philosophy, Shakespeare also endorses the view that our emotional responses are indispensable in recognizing who and what we are. Shakespeare only parts company from Nussbaum's Aristotle in his belief that although such recognition may not be impossible, humankind has not thus far been able to attain it. Further, that in striving to attain such recognition, humankind has frequently fallen victim to delusions of the most fundamental sort, and has thereby failed to arrive at any comprehensive or coherent notion of what the good life—Aristotle's *eudaimonia*—should entail. Shakespeare, as I have already suggested, is closer to Bernard Williams's judgment that tragedy concerns itself "with a world that is only partially intelligible to human agency," and to Robert Pippin's assessment that "tragedy, understood broadly, deeply, and rightly, is foreign to philosophy as traditionally conceived."[88] It is easy to lose Samuel Johnson's claim that "Shakespeare seems to write without moral purpose" in the noise of his revulsion at the death of Cordelia, but as usual Johnson has an important point. Shakespeare *does* fail to make a "just distribution of good or evil"; it *is* the case that he "carries his persons indifferently through right and wrong, and at the close dismisses them without further care, and leaves their examples to operate by chance." Because Johnson believed that "it is always a writer's duty to make the world better," to bring it into concord with his notions of the good, he is appalled by these omissions.[89] But for the Shakespeare of the tragedies, the duty of the writer is to tell the truth as best he can (not least about the fact that the good is astonishingly hard to identify) while keeping his playing company in business. Life as Shakespeare sees it is vastly more disorderly and ambiguous than even the most disorderly and ambiguous—or apparently disorderly and ambiguous—products of his art. What to Johnson looked like omissions are, in fact, integral parts of Shakespeare's tragic design.

———————

Irony might not seem like a helpful category through which to proceed. In mentioning it, I do not have in mind instances of verbal legerdemain in which one thing is said but the opposite is meant (from simple examples like the litotes in "Madness in great ones must not unwatched go," to complex ones like Antony's repeated declarations that "Brutus is an honorable man"), and in which Shakespeare invites his audiences to share the joke. Nor am I thinking of the phenomenon of "dramatic irony" (in which an onstage character says things that we in the audience know to be erroneous or likely to precipitate a crisis), the "structural irony" that William Elton finds in *King Lear*, the Socratic irony (or mode of irony often imputed to Socrates) of affecting ignorance in order to confute your opponent in a debate, or the so-called Romantic irony of an authorial voice affecting detachment—sometimes, a dismissive skepticism—toward the work of which it is a part.[90] Instead, the irony in which I am interested has a more existential cast. Working from the assumption that the innocent or otherwise untutored eye sees nothing, it provides a space in which to negotiate the collisions that occur between our attempts to understand ourselves in all our emotional complexity, and an awareness that such acts of understanding can only be arrived at through a cognitive process in which our emotional dispositions have a crucial role to play.

As a graduate student, the Danish philosopher Søren Kierkegaard wrote a dissertation under the sway of Hegel's aesthetic theories, subsequently published as *The Concept of Irony*. In it, he explored the notion of irony as "infinite absolute negativity." That is, as the key to something not unlike the theological *via negativa*: an intellectual posture that defines all things and concepts, and not just the Christian God, by saying what they are not. But in his mature writing, Kierkegaard had moved on ("What a Hegelian fool I was!"), and explored irony in a more capacious sense. It became a source not of absolute negativity, but of provisional affirmation. In his *Concluding Unscientific Postscript* (written under the pseudonym of Johannes Climacus), he treats irony as an expression of life lived in the twin beliefs that one must *learn* to become fully human, and that such learning comes neither easily nor certainly. Irony here is "an existence-determination," the "cultivation of spirit" through which we can apprehend the contradictions between our inward existences and the ways in which we express ourselves to the world—even as we cannot reliably apprehend what those inward existences might be, and even as attempting any such apprehension is itself to act in conformity with our own and other people's expectations of what we ought to be doing. Or, as Jonathan Lear puts it, Kierkegaard understood that irony (when "done well") is

> a manifestation of a practical understanding of one aspect of the finiteness of human life: that the concepts with which we understand ourselves and live our lives have a certain vulnerability built into them. Ironic existence thus has a claim to be a human excellence because it is a form of truthfulness. It is also a form of self-knowledge: a practical acknowledgement of the kind of knowing that is available to creatures like us.

Irony can thus be more than wordplay, the simulations and dissimulations of political and courtly speech, a shield behind which to hide one's true opinions from others, a way of offering decorously veiled criticism, or a mode of showing off one's dryly humorous virtuosity. Rather than being another part of the discursive repertory, it is a way of disrupting that repertory—a disruption that enables us to grasp the limitations both of the repertory itself, and of the repertorial thinking to which it leads. Put differently, irony is a way of moving beyond the habits of imitation and pretense through which we understand ourselves and the world around us, while acknowledging that it is only through these habits of imitation and pretense that we are able to think, and to think critically, at all.[91]

Shakespearean tragedy, I would like to suggest, functions in a similar way. It demonstrates that the ideas and identities through which its protagonists navigate their lives are not the fixedly or transcendently meaningful entities that they are supposed to be. They are instead situational and vulnerable in roughly equal measure; expressions of the desire for a security and an integrity and an authenticity that can never fully be realized. But like Kierkegaard's irony, the irony of Shakespeare's tragic vision is not intended to provoke despair: it is instead a part of the *catharsis-as-clarification* into which he seeks to raise his audiences. The studied fictionality and artificiality of Shakespearean tragedy allows it to represent, to interrogate, and finally to integrate the fictions and artifices through which humankind seeks to make sense of itself. Precisely because Shakespeare disavowed didacticism and all kinds of moral or hortatory uplift—because his tragedies reside in the experiential—he was able to tell the truth as he saw it of what it is to be alive. To be sure, some of our idées reçues should be cast aside. (I am confident of very little about the beliefs of Shakespeare the man. One exception is that he regarded the heroic ideal of martial-masculine valor as a toxic mess.) But the gift of the irony that emerges from Shakespeare's tragedies is a recognition that we can retain our beliefs and identities while simultaneously acknowledging their approximate or contingent character. We see that the value of that which we hold dear inheres in its importance to us in our practical lives, and that we only usually get into trouble when—as is often the case, most of all at moments of crisis—we seek to deny this.

So, in addition to generating fear and pity, Shakespeare follows the advice of Horace's *Ars poetica*, and tries to make us think. When the young John Milton paid elegantly agonistic tribute to a great predecessor, he claimed that it was "too much conceiving" that turned the wits of Shakespeare's readers to "marble"—not an excess of passionate grandeur.[92] To anyone far enough gone on *pathos* or purgation, such cerebral concerns may not seem compatible with what George Steiner calls "true tragedy." But in the words of the ancient rhetorician and sophist Gorgias of Leontini, we can find an inkling that in tragedy it has ever been thus. According to Gorgias, the peculiar quality of tragic drama is that "the deceiver is more just than the non-deceiver, and the deceived is wiser than the undeceived."[93] Because tragic mimesis pretends to historicity, it is a kind of deception; but it is an alethic kind of deception—one through which it is possible to tell the truth. This truth-telling makes the tragic poet more committed to justice, order, and good judgment (the Greek *dike* of Plutarch's original exceeds simple "justice") than one wedded to plainspoken history, and makes the members of the audience wiser about themselves and the world around them. If you are only interested in being made to wince or cry or shudder, then this version of tragedy is a nonstarter.

Still, although Shakespeare was clearly drawn to the idea that the truest poetry is the most feigning, it is the nature of the truths that his tragedies seek to tell that most demands our attention here—not least because it differs so markedly from the Christian conviction to which Kierkegaard's irony leads. (Rowan Williams sums up well the distinction between tragic and Christian mentalities: "Tragedy typically leaves questions painfully open, religious language aspires to some kinds of—if not closure, then at least the promise of sense or of reconciliation.")[94] A good point of reference comes from *Measure for Measure*, as Isabella and Angelo duel for Claudio's life. Isabella, working hard to jolt Angelo out of his faux-pious dogmatizing, conjures an image of

> man, proud man,
> Dressed in a little brief authority,
> Most ignorant of what he's most assured,
> His glassy essence, like an angry ape
> Plays such fantastic tricks before high heaven
> As makes the angels weep, who with our spleens
> Would all themselves laugh mortal.[95]

She thus employs the *theatrum mundi* topos to imagine human affairs being played out as the angels watch on. "Glassy essence" relates to the belief that the human intellect is able, in some versions on account of its manufacture in the image of God, accurately to reflect the nature of the created world. But for Isabella, as for many of those who took "carnal reason" to be of limited utility, this is a delusion supported by pride and worldly authority—a delusion, furthermore, that leads to tragic outcomes. Angelo should check himself while he still has the chance.[96]

Isabella plays her hand well—better perhaps than she intends to. She arouses Angelo's desire along with his interest, and he invites her back to press her suit again the following day. But even assuming that Isabella is sincere in these lines (as I think she is), and not saying what needs to be said to pique the conscience of a moralistic authoritarian, Shakespeare wants us to notice something odd here. The frame of *Measure for Measure* is not provided by spectating angels or ghosts, but by something altogether more of this world: a Duke who has temporarily abdicated his power in order to observe his subjects from beneath the anonymity of a friar's habit. Other than Shakespeare himself, the only beings able to regard the "fantastic tricks" of the play as a whole are those of us who encounter it through the stage or the printed page. Many of these tricks involve the religious rituals, doctrines, institutions, and habits of mind that Christianity offers as a reassurance that its version of the human condition is the true one.

If we stick with the idea that all the world is merely a stage, it can be hard to contemplate *Measure for Measure* while escaping some version or other of Macbeth's gloomy verdict that life is no more than "a walking shadow."[97] If, however, we are prepared to countenance the notion of the world as the theater to which Shakespeare's Warwick and Hastings allude—with spectators *within* rather than beyond it—then things start to look different. In doing so, and implausible though it might seem, Martin Heidegger can help.

His 1938 essay on "The Age of the World Picture [*Weltbild*]" contends that modernity came into being when humankind began to apprehend itself in relation to a picture in which it is both the object that is observed, and the subject that does the painting and observing. The possibility of humankind objectifying itself had, in Heidegger's telling, been impossible in the Middle Ages because the world and its human inhabitants were then conceived of as expressions of God the creator: "The world picture does not change from an earlier medieval to a modern one; rather, that the world becomes a picture at all distinguishes the essence of modernity." Although religious belief had previously given meaning to existence, in the modern age it becomes just another feature of the human experience as represented in the *Weltbild*.[98]

Heidegger was no more a historian than he was an exponent of plain and perspicuous prose; nor was he, it seems safe to assume, a reader of Boccaccio or Chaucer. But when employed with due restraint, his *Weltbild* offers more than an extreme iteration of the conceit that the poet or artist is a second creator. For instance, it provides us with a boldly illuminating perspective on a painting like Bruegel the Elder's *The Triumph of Death*, produced in 1562 or 1563 (see figure 2). Here, Bruegel transforms the pictorial conventions of themes including the danse macabre and Triumph of Death to depict a desolate coastal landscape in which the living are overwhelmed by the forces of the dead. Moving from left to right along the lower part of the painting, we might note a king being attacked, a cardinal being abducted, a dog picking at the corpses of a mother and baby, another dead mother and baby being carted along in an open coffin, a pilgrim having his throat cut, the corpse of a fully armored solider face down in the dirt, a terrified gallant drawing his sword against he knows not what, and a skeleton disrupting the music-making of two young lovers by joining them with his viola da braccio. Raising our eyes to the middle right, we find dozens of people being driven into a gigantic mousetrap decorated with crosses, alongside which the armies of the dead are arrayed behind coffin lids (again, marked with the sign of the cross) used as shields. Those

FIGURE 2. Pieter Bruegel the Elder, *The Triumph of Death*. Museo Nacional del Prado, Madrid.

trying to escape are being hunted down. On the horizon, smoke drifts up from burning ships and buildings; from over the horizon, there is the orange-black glow of huge fires burning. We infer that the horror is more than local.[99]

The detail is remarkable, but Bruegel's greatest innovation is what he leaves out. This is a scene of the last days, as prophesied in the Book of Revelation: "And the sea gave up her dead, which were in her, and death and hell delivered up the dead, which were in them: and they were judged every man according to their works." But in Bruegel's version, there is no judgment, no figure of Christ as judge, and no suggestion that any of the still living or already dead will proceed to heaven or hell. It is not even apparent where one is supposed to look for narrative guidance: what story, exactly, are we being asked to observe? (Compare figure 3: Bruegel's own design for the Last Judgment, in which the figure of Christ is central.) The dead come, in well-organized military formation, to claim the still living for their number; nobody, not even those holding fast to the church (the Cardinal) or to the simplicity of holy living (the pilgrim) is saved. In Walter Gibson's apt phrase, what Bruegel presents us with is a "secular apocalypse." For Christian theologians of all denominations, the apocalypse is the moment at which divine eternity explodes into the temporal order of the created world (in Latin, the *saeculum*), before subsuming it entirely. What Bruegel offers in place of this is a Heideggerian version of the end times defined by human suffering, by the exposure of the delusion that wealth or love or valor or religious observance might allow us to elude our mortality, by the belief that human life is an end unto itself—and not a destination to be passed through en route to a for-ever-and-ever of one kind or another. In other words, Bruegel looks at the worst that can happen and uses his art not to redeem it, but to help us acknowledge that dying is as much a part of the human experience as hope, fear, bravery, love, sexual desire, violence, ambition, religiosity, culture, technical advancement, or any of the other phenomena depicted in *The Triumph of Death*.[100]

In bringing this chapter to a close, I want to suggest that the *theatrum mundi* can do for Shakespearean tragedy what the *Weltbild* does for Bruegel. As Frank Kermode remarks, in Shakespeare the apocalypse is transposed from its place at the end point of historical time to the cultivated sempiternity of art. "Tragedy assumes the figurations of apocalypse, of death and judgment, heaven and hell," and as such absorbs the terror of living both in medias res and in the knowledge of one's mortal finitude.[101] More generally, Shakespearean tragedy does not regard human existence

FIGURE 3. Pieter Bruegel the Elder, *The Last Judgement*. Albertina, Vienna.

as surrounded by mysteries that can only be made to cohere by revelation or within a system of religious belief, but allows us to infer that human life—in all its inscrutability and indeterminacy—is itself the mystery. For Shakespeare, the struggle is to find a vantage from which to plot the scope of the human while at the same time affirming that the human is, for us (if only for us), the measure of all things. The object of the theater of the world remains the same, but its subject is no longer God and his angels. Rather, it is book-buying readers and playgoing spectators who now get to see the action unfold (recall that the Greek *theatron* is simply "a place for beholding"), albeit only in the special sense that they get to observe fictional-heuristic imitations of worldly deeds.[102] In Shakespeare's restless hands, tragic drama allows us to discover versions of ourselves, and to discover versions of ourselves struggling to find security and identity with the discursive resources available to them; these include different kinds of religion, history, and philosophy, of course, but also the tragic as commonly understood. It is not, as is so often the case with Romantic and Idealist versions of "the tragic," that tragedy does the work of secularized religion. Rather, Shakespeare offers a secular and necessarily circumscribed alternative to the totalizing accounts of the cosmos, and of the place occupied by humankind within it, offered by Christian theology: not redemption or even consolation, but the promise to delineate and invigorate through art.

Put another way, tragedy as Shakespeare approaches it not only becomes the representative object of human experience—the one which, in its mixture of artifice, emotion, and commitment to truth, best stands for human endeavor tout ensemble—but emerges as the medium through which we are able to observe the fullest and most truthful representations of ourselves. The theater of the world is no longer a capacious metaphor through which to regulate human affairs, but encapsulates the means through which those affairs can least imperfectly be apprehended. Tragedy is not a mirror held up to nature, but is a window—or just a frame—through which to behold the most uncomfortable aspects of what being human involves. Through which to arrive at a perspective on the peculiar situation of being an animal with the intelligence to have arrived at self-consciousness, and at an awareness of its place in a universe to which it is, or seems to be, a matter indifferent.

CHAPTER TWO

Early Experiments

*TITUS ANDRONICUS, ROMEO AND
JULIET, AND JULIUS CAESAR*

REFLECTING ON TRAGEDY as it appeared in the Italian states of the 1300s and 1400s, Gary Grund observes that it "proved to be a much less popular and stable literary form than its sister genre, humanist comedy." Although tragedy, drawing almost exclusively on the Senecan example, made the earlier start (Albertino Mussato's *Ecerinis* was written in 1314), it had largely run its course by the end of the fifteenth century because "the chamber pots of comedy were more easily adaptable to daily life than the ill-starred misfortunes of kings." If this seems a little peremptory in sidelining the tragic drama of the cinquecento, there can be little argument that tragedy was a comparatively minor feature of the sixteenth-century Italian stage—or that when it did feature prominently, it was as the *tragedia di fin lieto* ("tragedy with a happy ending") pioneered by Cinthio and refined by Guarini and Tasso. That is, as what in English is usually referred to as tragicomedy.[1] Tragedy never came close to dominating the English stage (consider Shakespeare himself: of the approximately forty-five plays that he wrote singly or in which he is likely to have had a hand, less than a third are tragedies), but England might have been at an advantage in coming to tragic drama comparatively late in the piece. Its tragic playwrights were able to learn from the Italian example—consciously and unconsciously, directly (via the plays themselves) and indirectly (via Chaucer, Lydgate, and the *Mirror for Magistrates*).[2]

Whether written for the universities, the court, the Inns of Court, or the professional playhouses that began to emerge in the 1560s and 70s, the first wave of English tragic drama did much to translate Seneca's seriousness and sententiousness to the modern stage. But from the perspective of a book concerned with Shakespearean tragedy, even the most impressive of these early Elizabethan works, such as Sackville and Norton's *Gorboduc* or Preston's *Cambyses*, are of value less for themselves than for the perspective they offer on what would happen next. Which, to adapt Hemingway on bankruptcy, came about in two ways. Gradually, and suddenly. When Christopher Marlowe and Thomas Kyd thrust themselves onto the scene in 1587, they not only changed English tragedy for good, but began to realize the potential of the tragic forms with which the generation before them had wrestled.

Much can be said about the ways in which they did so, but the headlines are these: both adapted the example of Italian *versi sciolti* to write in robustly flexible blank verse iambics, rather than the rhyming couplets and stiff or cumbersome meters that had previously been current; both eschewed the idea that tragic drama should be didactic or homiletic or morally improving; Marlowe's characterization exploited the possibilities of Aristotelian *ethos* with a flair, an energy, and a sophistication hitherto unseen on the English stage; Kyd breathed intelligent new life into the tightly wrought, and often self-ironic, forms of dramatic plotting that he found in Seneca's tragedies.[3] Shakespeare learned from both masters, in whose plays he may well have performed as a young actor. His line and characterization are as mighty as Marlowe's. His plotting and embrace of open-endedness—his willingness to pay his audiences the compliment of putting the interpretative ball in their court—are the equal of Kyd's. His genius lay in being able to identify the strengths that made Marlowe and Kyd great, before assimilating and surpassing these strengths within his own tragic output.

As Madeline Doran long ago suggested, the tragedies produced in England in the period from the late 1580s to the early 1630s can usefully be comprehended under three headings.[4] First, tragedies of ambition and high place in something like the *de casibus* style; second, revenge tragedies, often involving elements of Italianate intrigue; third, domestic tragedies, sometimes involving elements of Italianate intrigue. The works gathered under the first and second headings can easily be reconciled with the traditions of tragedy that we have heard articulated by Aristotle, Horace, Donatus-Evanthius, Boethius, and their innumerable later expositors and adaptors. By contrast, because it involved characters drawn from everyday life rather than those of high status such as kings, princes, or aristocrats, domestic tragedy was something new. The anonymous *A Warning for Fair Women* discussed in the previous chapter is a good example, but it was *Arden of Faversham* (printed anonymously in 1592 and sometimes attributed to Marlowe, Kyd, or Shakespeare—or to some combination of the three) that broke the mold.

In examining Shakespeare's early experiments with tragic drama, I want to use these headings as a way of interrogating three plays from the first half of Shakespeare's playwrighting career: *Titus Andronicus*, a revenge tragedy written at some point in the late 1580s or early 1590s; *Romeo and Juliet*, written circa 1595 and treated here as a domestic tragedy; and *Julius Caesar*, written in 1599 and on any reckoning a tragedy concerned with ambition and high place. When examining the development of Shakespeare's tragic technique over the course of a decade in which he went from obscurity to fame, what becomes apparent is his preoccupation with a problem that Aristotle would have recognized: how to weave together the demands of plot and of affective characterization to form a compelling tragic whole. If we consider the third of the three most important objects of tragic mimesis mentioned in the *Poetics*, we find Shakespeare learning how to handle the expression of thought in eloquent speech (*dianoia*) without lapsing into sententiousness or thick-fingered bombast.

———

Titus Andronicus is difficult to love. Its compound of murder and countermurder, revenge and counter-revenge, cruelty and counter-cruelty generate plenty of fear, but precious little pity—and combine to make it feel uncomfortably like a slasher movie. A slasher movie that acknowledges itself as such, to be sure, but a slasher movie nevertheless.[5] In Edward Ravenscroft's frequently-quoted dismissal, originally part of the preface to his 1686 adaptation of the play, "'tis the most incorrect and indigested piece in all his Works; It seems rather a heap of Rubbish than a Structure."[6] At best, the ardent Shakespearean might admit to a version of Keats's reckoning that although a quarrel in the streets is a hateful thing, the energies displayed in it are fine.

And yet *Titus Andronicus* was an indisputably successful work. It went through three printed editions by 1611, and when in 1614 Ben Jonson wrote the "Induction" to his *Bartholomew Fair*, he saw the affective potential of rolling his eyes at those who "will swear *Jeronimo* [i.e., Kyd's *Spanish Tragedy*] or *Andronicus* are the best plays."[7] The force of Jonson's critique is not that *Titus* is beyond the pale on the grounds of dramatic crudity or overly sanguinary bad taste, but that it was still popular when it should not have been—that, twenty-five years or so after it was first staged, the playgoing public ought to have moved on. Perhaps so, but although the

FIGURE 4. Henry Peacham, sketch of *Titus Andronicus* in performance.
Longleat Archives Portland Papers, vol. 1, fol. 159^b. Image reproduced by kind
permission of the Marquess of Bath, Longleat.

obsessively citational sententiousness of *Titus* was a little shopworn by the
early 1610s, other features of the play were anything but old-fashioned.
Unlovely though *Titus* may be, much of that which we esteem in Shakespeare's later tragedies is present within it in embryonic form.

In developing this case, Henry Peacham's famous sketch of—or after—a
performance of *Titus* (see figure 4) is an excellent point of reference. We
do not know when he drew it, but it hints at one of the play's greatest but
least appreciated strengths: a tragic plot that is structured just as tightly
as that of the roughly contemporaneous *Comedy of Errors*.[8]

The scene Peacham depicts does not appear within the texts of the
play as they survive, but nonetheless reflects the central moment of act 1.
Titus has returned to Rome in triumph after his victory over the Goths, and
parades the Gothic Queen, Tamora, and her sons as his captives. Tamora
pleads for the life of her eldest son, Alarbus, whom Titus has chosen to
sacrifice as an offering to the ghost of his son (the twenty-first of Titus's
male children to die fighting for Rome), recently killed in the conflict
against the Goths. Behind Tamora kneel the bound figures of her two
other sons, Chiron and Demetrius, and behind them her confederate and
lover, Aaron, raises a sword and points his index finger in a threatening
but unintelligible manner. Behind Titus are two figures dressed, somewhat incongruously, in Elizabethan doublets; most likely, these represent
two of Titus's four surviving sons—if so, Quintus and Martius rather than
Mutius or Lucius. The difference in dress between Titus and his children is
presumably designed to emphasize the distance—part generational, part

moral-cultural—that will emerge between Titus and his children as Titus tries to force Lavinia to marry the new emperor, kills Mutius for opposing him, and then tries to deny Mutius a place in their family tomb.[9]

Although it is peculiar that Aaron is not bound with Chiron and Demetrius, the sketch offers us a tableau of the forces arranged at the beginning of the play. On the one side, Titus lives his ideal of martial and patriarchal honor, embodying the Romans' self-image of unflinchingly vigorous autonomy. Here, it is not that honor is maintained despite human cost, but that human cost—pain, whether inflicted or endured—vouchsafes the honor and integrity of one's deeds. On the other, Tamora cleaves in defeat to the love she feels for her children, and does all she can to provoke compassion (and with it mercy) in her Roman captor. This denied her, and Alarbus murdered on a whim of cruel superstition, she and her family (aided by Aaron's clear-sighted wiles) are consumed with the desire for vengeance—against Titus and his family, and against the Rome they represent. So, although the action of *Titus* as a whole can make it very hard to discern either cause and effect or right and wrong, there is no ambiguity about how the plot is set in motion: Alarbus, whose only stated crime is that he is the eldest son of Queen Tamora, is ritually slaughtered by Titus and his sons. Whenever it was that he sat down to make his sketch, Henry Peacham understood.

It is often observed that because human sacrifice was condemned as abhorrent by Roman law and custom, Titus's killing of Alarbus to honor the ghost of his dead son is a transgressive act that invites the horrors that follow. True enough, but Alarbus's death is even more resonant than this. As Heather James notes, it echoes Aeneas's response to the death of his adoptive son Pallas: first in the ideas of compensatory human sacrifice that shape Pallas's funeral rites in book 11 of the *Aeneid*, and then in Aeneas's retributive murder of Turnus (without returning Turnus's body to his father so that it could be buried with the proper funeral rites) at the end of book 12. Just as Aeneas's devoted *pietas* leads him into a kind of barbarism, so Titus's rigidly upright attachment to the cult of the noble warrior—to a fundamentalist version of *Romanitas*—drags him into a moral quagmire that calls into question both the virtue of Roman civilization and its distinctiveness from those of the peoples that it seeks to subjugate within what, elsewhere in the *Aeneid*, is imagined as "empire without end."[10]

In the *Henry VI* plays, Shakespeare explores the ways in which people will embrace almost any principle or ideology in the attempt to convince themselves and others that what they and their faction want is not just desirable, but right—and believe themselves to be virtuous in so doing. In its fixation on the discrepancies between the appearance and reality of life in Rome, *Titus Andronicus* draws from the same well. The play opens with Saturninus's plea to his fellow patricians as "patrons of my right." They should, he suggests, "Defend the justice of my cause with arms" (1.1.1–2)—irrespective of the facts 1) that the Rome over which he proposes to rule is an elective rather than primogeniture monarchy, and 2) that his "right," like the "justice" of his cause, resides in being the eldest son of the recently deceased Emperor. When Bassianus responds by addressing his peers as "favourers of *my* right" (emphasis mine), he does so by implying that his elder brother is wanting in "virtue," "justice," and "continence," and by making himself the candidate of "freedom in your choice"—the candidate of patrician rather than monarchical-imperial sovereignty (1.1.10–17). Marcus Andronicus, as tribune of the people, now intervenes by affecting to rise above a squabble between "factions" and "friends" vying for power (1.1.18), and instead makes the case for the emperor being elected by popular acclamation—whether directly or through the recommendation of one nominated by the populace to speak for them. The candidate Marcus has in mind is Titus Andronicus: a military hero "surnamed Pius" (1.1.23) for embodying the heroic virtues of Aeneas, but also Marcus's own brother. At no point does Marcus acknowledge their fraternal relation. Beneath the facade of rectitude carefully cultivated by each of Saturninus, Bassianus, and Marcus lies a common appetite for power, and a determination to use whatever means are available to satisfy it.

The notion that the roles one is obliged to adopt by social mores and convention have only a superficial integrity is a staple of literary and moral discourse from Plato, Juvenal, and Seneca down to Augustine, Rousseau, and Holden Caulfield. The distinctively Shakespearean twist is that these facades are not hypocritical deceptions of the sort employed by Aaron. They are instead the means through which his Romans seek to rationalize the desires and habits and anxieties that shape their lives. In fact, it might be better not to call them facades at all. As performed by Shakespeare's Romans, social roles (or *personae*) measured by honor, rectitude, and decorous virtue comprise one's truest identity.[11] Viewed from a Gothic perspective, this might look like self-serving nonsense: an expression of no more than the resolve to legitimate, thereby to obscure, a way of living that rests on having a better army than your neighbors. But to the Romans it is who they *are*, the story they tell themselves in order to get through the day. One often reads that Titus—honorable, upright, and dignified even in his imprecatory excess—stands outside the order evinced at the start of the play, in which self-interest defines ideological conviction. In reality, his approach to who and what he is makes him its cardinal embodiment: imperceptive, thuggish, unerringly self-righteous.

That such an understanding of Rome owes more to Ovid than to Virgil is by now standard in discussions of *Titus*. Chiron and Demetrius learn from Tereus's rape of Philomela in premeditating their crimes against Lavinia, and the younger Lucius appears on stage holding the copy of the *Metamorphoses* that had been given to him by his mother. This may have been one of the collections of "Sweet poetry" (4.1.14) that, along with Cicero's *Orator*, his aunt Lavinia had been wont to read to him; in any case, it is her nephew's copy of the *Metamorphoses* that Lavinia uses to disclose what was done to her in the "vast and gloomy woods" (4.1.53). More broadly, we see that in the Rome of *Titus*, *pietas* of one kind or another is supplanted by the violence and carnality of the *Amores*, where "Mars doth rage abroad without all pitty, / And Venus rules in her Aeneas Citty." Whether expressed through martial or sexual activity, the governing force here is appetite, not grandly impersonal virtue.[12]

It would nevertheless be misguided to pin down *Titus* as an exclusively Ovidian endeavor. Without doubt, Ovid helped Shakespeare to realize that the *Aeneid* is less imperial propaganda than a meditation on the power of such propaganda, and on the related distortions to which the conviction of a nation's manifest destiny—its imperial telos—must lead. But so, in a slightly different way, did Seneca's bloody post-republican tragedies of revenge and self-deceit, alongside which we might also place Euripides, who was freely available in Latin translation and whose *Iphigenia* had been translated into English by Shakespeare's collaborator Peele. Better to say that the vision of Rome we find in *Titus* is an exercise in the poetics of "contamination" (*contaminatio*), according to which humanistic writers made a show of blending together different classical texts to create something new of their own. In offering such a novelty, however, Shakespeare does more than affirm his learned virtuosity. Recall that after Chiron finds some Latin verse inscribed on a scroll attached to an arrow he has been sent by Titus, he recognizes it as a line from Horace's *Odes* (1.22). Not because he is a devotee of lyric poetry (unlike Aaron, he fails to grasp its significance), but because he remembers it from the Latin textbooks of his schooldays: "I read it in the grammar long ago" (4.2.23). In *Titus*, what Shakespeare creates is not a Virgilian, Ovidian, Senecan, Horatian, Livian, or Ciceronian likeness of Rome, but an image of the humanistic culture that fused these and other traditions together into a fetish for the linguistic arts as they had flourished in the millennium or so after the foundation of the Roman Republic in 509 BCE. For Shakespeare, in *Titus* as in all of his tragedies, this picture is neither a pretty nor a straightforward one.[13]

As the long first scene comes to an end, and it is agreed that the dual marriages of Saturninus and Tamora and Bassianus and Lavinia should be celebrated with a "solemn hunting" (1.1.612), the status of *Titus Androni-cus* as a revenge tragedy starts to become apparent. With the assistance of Tamora and Aaron, Chiron and Demetrius contrive to murder Bassianus and rape Lavinia as acts of retributive violence: "We hunt not, we, with horse nor hound, / But hope to pluck a dainty doe to ground" (2.1.25–26). The woods in which they do so owe much to Ovid and Seneca—also perhaps to *Arden of Faversham*—and once Lavinia has been raped, they lop off her hands and cut out her tongue in a grotesque parody of the ceremonial "unmaking" or "breaking up" that took place at the end of a successful deer hunt. Lavinia's uncle, Marcus, later describes to Titus how he found her "straying in the park, / Seeking to hide herself, as doth the deer / That hath received some unrecuring wound." Titus responds that "It was my dear, and he that wounded her / Hath hurt me more than he had killed me dead" (3.9.89–91)—not because he values his daughter's well-being more than his own, but because he has been dishonored by the violation of something over which he, by virtue of his name and lineage, has proprietary rights. Once he discovers the identity of Lavinia's attackers, he seeks vengeance, and assumes a camouflage of "feigned ecstasies" (4.4.21) to beat the Gothic interlopers at their own game: "I knew them all, though they supposed me mad, / And will o'erreach them in their own devices—/ A pair of cursed hellhounds and their dam" (5.2.142–44). For Titus, the hunters thus become the righteously hunted, and embody a sort of dramaturgic symmetry—one that reflects the biblical injunction that "He who diggeth a pit, shall fall into it." Aaron baits a "guileful hole" (5.1.104) with the corpse of Bassianus to entrap Quintus and Martius, but will himself die buried "breast-deep in earth" (5.3.178).[14]

The rub is that this symmetry works, as it were, both ways. Throughout *Titus*, the lines of demarcation between hunter and prey or between criminal and victim—in the final analysis, between Roman civilization and Afro-Gothic barbarism—become indistinguishable. Here is Lucius, the character who will be installed as Emperor at the end of act 5, informing Titus that Alarbus has been put to death:

> See, lord and father, how we have perform'd
> Our Roman rites. Alarbus' limbs are lopp'd,
> And entrails feed the sacrificing fire,
> Whose smoke like incense doth perfume the sky. (1.1.142–45;
>   cf. 1.1.130–32)

Lucius's words are more than just disconcertingly eager to please. Like the description of Lavinia's mutilation by Chiron and Demetrius, they parody the ceremonial language of the "breaking up" at the end of a deer hunt. In the case of hunting, this ritual works hard to dignify a pastime that might, by transforming the hunter into a simulacrum of a predatory beast, blur the distinction between human and animal forms of life. But in the case of Alarbus's murder, motivated as it is by a desire for vengeance dressed up as religious piety, the hunting language serves a different purpose. It affirms that, for all their civilizational amour propre, for all their mutually corroborative talk of honorable conduct, Titus and his children treat the eldest son of the Gothic queen as if he were a nonhuman animal.[15]

It was from Seneca that Shakespeare learned the potential of these unsettling symmetries. In particular, from Seneca's *Phaedra*: as one recent study of the play has summarized, hunting is "used to structurally pervasive and ironic effect" throughout it.[16] Hippolytus is an ardent hunter who imagines himself above the animals he pursues just as he imagines himself beyond the passions of his fellow human beings. His problem is that he fails to grasp that the nature he so reveres is far from being the force of rationality, constancy, order, and justice to which he has committed himself—and that, on account of this, he is as vulnerable as any other human being. Whether understood through the violence of the wild (qua the goddess Diana) or that of the bedroom (qua the goddess Venus), nature is *itself* a hunter whose motives are as passionately appetitive as those of any human being, and whose prerogatives will not be denied. Once Theseus returns from the underworld and hears Phaedra's false claim to have been raped by the stepson she had insistently sought to seduce, Hippolytus is ripped apart in his own hunting equipment, and in the landscape over which his equipment had helped him to assert dominion. Phaedra comes to understand something of her predicament in desiring as illicitly she does, but Hippolytus perishes in the precise equivalent of the uncomprehending terror in which the countless deer and boar he has hunted met their ends. As the play concludes, this incomprehension—this delusionality about the scope of human agency and about the nature of a "nature" not constrained by human notions of the right—is echoed by Theseus and by the Chorus. In Seneca's Athenian playworld, things will carry on as they did before. His Roman audiences were supposed to take note, and to monitor their own tendencies toward self-deceiving arrogance accordingly. In *Titus*, the conditions of human existence are no better understood than they are in the *Phaedra*, but they are not governed by nature or any other voice from above. They are instead an expression of the intensely complicated relationships of causation that arise from the collisions between the different protagonists' words, deeds, and "devices."

This is why Aaron, once he has been captured, makes out that he has been responsible for all the ills that have taken place over the previous four and a half acts, and only regrets that he cannot now engineer more wrong-doing or mischief: "I have done a thousand dreadful things . . . / And nothing grieves me heartily indeed / But that I cannot do ten thousand more" (5.1.142–44; cf. 5.3.183–89). On one level, he is trying to ensure that he goes out in style, the more so as he has gone against his apparent credo by sacrificing himself and selling out his cause to ensure the life of his child. (There is an obvious contrast here with Titus—who values the lives of the two sons he kills less than his sense of honor.) On another, Shakespeare subverts the conventions of the medieval Vice character that Aaron in many respects resembles: banish him from the playworld, or so the theory goes, and harmonious virtue will reassert itself. Marcus is keen to echo this line, and declares that this "irreligious Moor," dark-skinned and dark-hearted, has been the "Chief architect and plotter of these woes" (5.3.120–21).[17] But Marcus is scapegoating. Just as Aaron overlooks the crimes that, whether by sins of omission or commission, were perpetrated by Titus, Saturninus, Tamora, and even Lavinia, so the action of the play in the round—its plot—reminds us of the contingency, confusions, and unintended consequences on which it depends. Aaron no more envisaged being buried and left to die than Tamora thought Titus would see through her ruse in appearing as the personification of Revenge. Similarly, when Titus acclaimed the corruptible Saturninus emperor after killing Alarbus, he failed to suspect that Saturninus might turn his affections to Tamora, and that he might thereby give the Goths the chance to exact vengeance on him and his family. (Remarkably, once Saturninus and Tamora are betrothed, it still does not occur to Titus that he might have a problem.) In *Titus Andronicus*, virtue and villainy both depend on delusions of control—on a belief in the competence of human agency to define the moral terrain within which it is constrained to act.

As this book will go on to suggest on more than one occasion, the gap between rhetoric and reality is central to Shakespeare's conceptions of Rome and of the heavily Romanizing notions of humanism that shaped, though did not always delimit, the cultural and political horizons of late Elizabethan and early Jacobean England. In *Titus*, a gap opens up between *verba* (words, or language in general) and *res* (the subject matter that language is supposed to represent) that goes beyond the dissonance between things said and things done that is a hallmark of Senecan tragedy. Even the most eloquent and rhetorically skilled—the most sententious, the most authoritative—forms of speech are unable to persuade, unable to gain traction in the worlds that they seek to influence.[18] Pleas for compassion, no matter how elaborate and no matter whether they are uttered by Tamora or Lavinia or Titus, go unanswered. Grief, as articulated by Marcus and Titus after they encounter the mutilated and unavoidably mute Lavinia (2.3.13–37, 3.1.67–81), relies on prefabricated formulae and narrative models; a coping mechanism, indubitably, but one that is indistinguishable from the copiously ornamental speech on display elsewhere in the play. Both the senior Andronici are so detached from the scene before them that neither of them evinces the least concern to offer Lavinia comfort, to ensure her wellbeing, or to ameliorate her suffering. By the time Titus has followed the Senecan maxim *scelera non ulcisceris, nisi vincis* ("you do not avenge crimes unless you surpass them") in having Tamora "daintily" eat the remains of her own children, there are no words left with which even to go through the motions of outrage or grief.[19] Perpetrator and victim (and victim and perpetrator) die immediately. Marcus and Lucius set about the task of winning the imperial purple for the Andronici.

In his *Scholemaster*, Roger Ascham cautioned that "you know not what hurt you do to learning that care not for words but for matter and so make a divorce betwixt the tongue and the heart [i.e., the capacity for understanding and thought, as well as that for feeling and emotion]." On his account, as it is impossible to speak well unless one has a virtuous and well-ordered mind (recall the discussion of the *vir bonus* in chapter 1), so learning to speak well will necessarily inculcate the right kind of discursive and moral qualities. Although this reads like theoretical boilerplate, Ascham in fact says something revealing. He agrees with Cicero in asserting that *res* and *verba* must be wedded together, but there is a crucial difference between their positions: for Cicero, *res* must come first; for Ascham the sixteenth-century educationalist, the priority goes to *verba*. So it was that Shakespeare, like every other Elizabethan grammar school pupil, was obliged to learn and remember, translate and retranslate page after page of Latin literature with a view to preparing himself for a positive contribution to the active life—whether in the church or in some civic-legal-political function. *Titus* though tells a very different story, one that Marlowe's deliberately impious manifestations of humanist virtuosity had already begun to disclose. Here, the facility with words ensured by immersion in the humanist educational curriculum is just that—a facility with words. A necessary skill (had Lavinia not found a way to communicate, her assailants would have triumphed), but by no means a sufficient one, nor one that confers powers of judgment or ratiocination. Eloquence, howsoever hard-won, guarantees nothing beyond sounding good. Further, by being mistaken for an end in itself, it impedes our ability to understand or represent our own existences—just as it impedes our ability to understand, and to communicate with, those around us.[20]

Over the past two decades, there has been a good deal of work on *Titus* as an intervention in the English politics of the early 1590s—specifically, an intervention in the debates around the succession of Elizabeth I. As she was by then certain to die without having given birth to an heir, should the next monarch be chosen by election, by the nearest approximation of primogeniture succession, or by some blend of the two? There is much of value here: indubitably, *Titus* maps on to aspects of the politico-dynastic anxiety that marked the last years of Elizabeth's long reign. But if we are to understand *Titus* as a tragedy, and as the point at which the arc of Shakespeare's tragic writing begins, then our concern must be less with the minutiae of political history than with the underlying cultural, moral, and political beliefs through which this historical moment regarded itself. With, that is, the ideology that on the account of Henry Peacham (he who produced that sketch of the pleading Tamora) allowed William Cecil, Lord Burghley and the long-serving chief advisor to Elizabeth I, to claim that he owed it all to Cicero's *De officiis*—to a treatise written in the desperate attempt to preserve republican government in the face of a rush to monarchical imperialism: "to his dying day," Cecil would "always carry it about him, either in his bosome or pocket, beeing sufficient . . . to make both a Scholler and an honest man." Perhaps so, but Cecil's indifference to the substance of Cicero's treatise runs deep. In asserting that the *De officiis* is enough to fashion perfect specimens of civic virtue, he was, as a skilled rhetorician, telling his listeners what he knew they wanted to hear, and doing so with an example that he knew they would recognize. In this case, by repeating a commonplace about the value of the *De officiis* that was frequently repeated by the likes of Erasmus, and that has its origins in Pliny's *Natural History*. Less a book recommendation than an exercise in semi-citational performance art—incidentally confirming the humanist weakness for *verba* over *res*, impact over resonance, and persuasiveness over truth-telling.[21]

Throughout, *Titus* is preoccupied with the logic and implications of the humanist project. Even the gore for which it is notorious is stylized, and thereby effaced. Yes, we witness seven murders by stabbing and two by throat-cutting, and also see Titus voluntarily having his hand cut off. But, like the executions of Quintus, Martius, and the Clown, the more sensational acts of violence happen by report and evocation. Alarbus is killed and dismembered offstage; Lavinia is raped and mutilated offstage; Chiron and Demetrius are butchered and cooked up offstage; Aaron's protracted death awaits him once the action is over. This matters not simply as an index of Shakespeare's skill in evocation, of what he thought would exceed the kind of theatrical decorum recommended by Horace, or of how far he had to travel before he could devise a tragic action like that of *King Lear* (in which we see Gloucester's eyes being gouged out but only behold Cordelia's hanging through the medium of Lear's anguished testimony).[22] Conceiving of Alarbus's death as a hunting ritual, Lavinia's violation in terms of Ovidian poetry, the treatment of Chiron and Demetrius as a specimen of Senecan pastiche, and Aaron's demise as a sort of biblical retribution are ways of averting our gaze while affecting to focus it, of translating brutally sanguinary reality into a prearranged pattern of words. It is a mode of representation through which one is able to entertain the most terrible things without becoming sullied with that terror oneself. What is more, it is a way of permitting forms of conduct that, on the face of it, exceed moral reckoning. By imagining themselves as ceremonial huntsmen, agents of Ovidian transgression, or ministers of vengeance, the protagonists of *Titus* license themselves to depravity, much as many an imperialist has turned to the example of Aeneas in rationalizing that one cannot make an omelet without breaking eggs.

Still, Shakespeare's alertness to the calcified aspirations of humanist rhetoric presented him with an obstacle that it would take him a lot of time and effort to clear. According to the theory of Aristotelian *dianoia* as *sententia*, tragic protagonists are supposed to show themselves thinking in a grand style—whether through the sententiousness of the humanist classroom, or through the language of condensed, and densely patterned, artifice that is the Senecan stock-in-trade. How to square the circle of writing tragedies in which the propensity for speaking in this manner is at the root of human delusionality? Shakespeare hit upon a preliminary answer in *Titus*: by investing his characters' modes of expression with as much classical heft as possible—quite aside from the Ovidian, Senecan, and Virgilian intertexts, no other play by Shakespeare has such a high proportion of Latin—it was possible for him to make a point about the unacknowledged distance between *res* and *verba*, and with it to critique the complacencies of humanist cultural and educational orthodoxy. But doing so merely replaces one conundrum with another. By using his characters' language to subvert his audience's understandings of eloquent speech and those who are able to use it, the Shakespeare of *Titus* makes it very hard for himself to develop character (*ethos*) in anything like the depth that, on

Aristotle's account, is required by the most accomplished tragic art. Not necessarily a problem if writing comedy or satire or a morality play. But, as *Titus* and its checkered reception history make plain, a definite short-coming when attempting to arouse fear, pity, or wonder—or when trying to devise plots that use the unintended consequences of characters' actions as a way in which to represent, or rather to imitate, that which was usually ascribed to fate, fortune, or providence. If an audience only regards a character as a type or cartoon, it is difficult for them to see his or her actions as anything other than servants of a preordained plot; in the case of *Titus*, the servants of a determination to fashion a revenge play that was as sensationally bloody as possible.

Shakespeare needed to do something more fundamental if he was going to reconcile tragedy with the necessity of having his characters speak in eloquent and moving language. He needed, in short, to find other ways in which to represent the experience of human thought, and to find other forms of human experience—not just the travails of kings, princes, and leaders—to make the object of his tragic attention. *Romeo and Juliet*, written somewhere between three and five years after *Titus Andronicus*, attempts to realize both of these goals.

———

Romeo and Juliet begins with a chorus declaiming a Prologue. It takes the form of a sonnet, and offers a condensed account of what is about to happen:

> Two households, both alike in dignity
> In fair Verona, where we lay our scene,
> From ancient grudge break to new mutiny,
> Where civil blood makes civil hands unclean.
> From forth the fatal loins of these two foes
> A pair of star-crossed lovers take their life,
> Whose misadventured piteous overthrows
> Doth with their death bury their parents' strife.
> The fearful passage of their death-marked love,
> And the continuance of their parents' rage,
> Which but their children's end naught could remove,
> Is now the two hours' traffic of our stage;
> The which, if you with patient ears attend,
> What here shall miss, our toil shall strive to mend. (1.0.1–14)

The plot is mapped out accurately, and its substance—mutually hostile families, illicit love, death by misadventure, final reconciliation—is presented as the very model of tragic probability and necessity. One thing leads to, and causes, another. Moreover, in being imagined as born of "fatal loins" and as becoming "star-crossed lovers," the two as yet unnamed principals seem to embody another kind of necessity: "fatal" here means "condemned by fate," or perhaps just "doomed." We are left to surmise that beholding such "death-marked" love will generate feelings of pity and fear.

Compare the "Argument," also in the form of a sonnet, with which Arthur Brooke prefaced his *Tragicall Historye of Romeus and Juliet*. This long narrative poem was Shakespeare's source in writing *Romeo and Juliet*, and adapts a story most fully elaborated in Matteo Bandello's celebrated *Novelle*—mediated in this case through the French of Pierre Boaistuau's *Histoires tragiques*. Thus Brooke:

> Love hath inflamed twayne by sodayn sight.
>> And both do graunt the thing that both desyre.
>> They wed in shrift by counsell of a frier.
>> Yong Romeus clymes fayre Juliets bower by night.
> Three monthes he doth enjoy his cheefe delight.
>> By Tybalts rage, provoked unto yre,
>> He payeth death to Tybalt for his hyre.
>> A banisht man he scapes by secret flight.
> New mariage is offred to his wyfe:
>> She drinks a drink that seemes to reve her breath.
>> They bury her, that sleping yet hath lyfe.
> Her husband heares the tydings of her death.
>> He drinks his bane. And she with Romeus knyfe,
> When she awakes, her selfe (alas) she sleath.

Shakespeare manifestly took the idea of beginning *Romeo and Juliet* with a sonnet from Brooke, but his version sketches a tragedy that differs radically from Brooke's "tragicall historye." Brooke's summary, right down to the short paratactic sentences in which it is written, is granular. The action it describes proceeds by a series of contingencies: sexual hunger at first sight, the mutual decision to submit to this hunger before contracting a secret wedding with the assistance of a corrupt friar (tellingly rhymed with "desyre"), Tybalt's factional rage leading to a killing from which Romeus has to flee, Juliet's plan to feign her death to escape a second marriage, Romeus's misapprehension that she is actually dead, his subsequent suicide by poison, and—finally—Juliet's resolution to kill herself with

Romeus's knife once she awakes to find him dead beside her. There is no sense of necessity here, whether of plot or of preordination: things happen on account of the bad decisions taken by over-sexed young lovers. If Brooke's poem has more to offer than a sensational story, it is the moral lesson that the young should learn to keep their desires under control—just as they should take care to obey their parents and to steer clear of the mendicant orders.[23]

The irony is that Brooke's poem has more in common with the action of *Romeo and Juliet* than does Shakespeare's Prologue. Indeed, if the Prologue did not tell us otherwise, the first two acts of *Romeo and Juliet* might lead one to conclude that it is a comedy of love. Romantic passion impeded by a family feud that nobody (other than Tybalt) takes that seriously, and overcome through ingenious-ingenuous subterfuge; toothlessly meddling patriarchs restrained by their wives and ruler; the sparkling contrivance—a festive adaptation of stichomythia—of having the lovers' first exchange take the form of a coauthored sonnet (1.5.92–105), concluded with a kiss;[24] witty but ultimately indulgent commentary on the folly of young lovers, mainly provided by Mercutio; in general, the comedic world described by Evanthius, in which "people are of mediocre fortune, perils trifling, [and] actions have happy outcomes."

Even when the play turns darker, events proceed by accidents rather than necessity. Although Mercutio's Queen Mab speech at 1.4.53–94 hints at depths that go beyond the scope of comedic convention (and has the further effect of making him sound like Hamlet to Romeo's Osric), and although Tybalt is full of violently expressed tragic tenacity, it remains the case that Tybalt is only able to kill Mercutio because Romeo comes between them—justifying himself to his dying and incredulously angry friend by saying that "I thought it all for the best" (3.1.106). Likewise, the plan hatched by Juliet and Friar Laurence might have worked but for the fact that the letter informing Romeo of it cannot be delivered due to an outbreak of plague preventing the intended messenger, Friar John, from leaving the monastery he had been visiting. This is tragedy as broken comedy. As Susan Snyder puts it, in the tragic space of Shakespeare's Verona "there is no villain, only chance and bad timing." Should we then conclude that the Prologue is an exercise in fine-sounding strategic misdirection? That Shakespeare failed to notice the distance he had placed between the *verba* of his introductory sonnet and the *res* of the play it represents, between what the rhetoricians called the *thesis* of the case (what happens) and its *hypothesis* (how it happens)? That we should follow the example of the 1623 folio edition of Shakespeare's complete works and strike out the

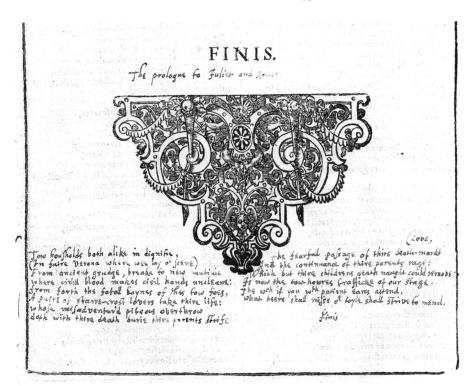

FIGURE 5. *Mr. William Shakespeares Comedies, Histories, & Tragedies* (London, 1623), sig. ee2v. Rare Book Department, Free Library of Philadelphia (RBD EL SH15M 1623).

introductory sonnet altogether? A clue that the Prologue matters and that it was a part of Shakespeare's design comes from the hand of John Milton, who took the trouble to inscribe it from a quarto edition of the text (probably the fifth quarto of 1637) in his copy of the 1623 folio (see figure 5). But fully to grasp the significance of the Prologue, we need to take a couple of steps backward.[25]

One characteristic feature of Senecan tragedy is the ironic interplay between the choral framing and the main action of the drama. In particular, the prologues—as in, say, *Medea*—set up an order of causal determinism that Seneca's plotting and characterization work to undermine. Tragedy, especially if directed by the whims of the gods, would seem to take away the possibility of moral responsibility. Seneca, while paying due respect to tragic expectations and the beliefs with which they often cohere, wants his audience to reconsider where such responsibility can be said to lie—along with the various ideologies to which human beings turn in seeking to evade it. As Joel Altman has suggested, Thomas Kyd was the first playwright to translate this aspect of Seneca's art to the English stage. *The Spanish Tragedy* presents us with a Prologue spoken by the ghost of the recently deceased Andrea, alongside a personified Revenge. They lay out a pattern of retributive justice, only for its validity to be cast into doubt by the dilemmas, uncertainties, duplicities, and cruelties to which Hieronimo and Bel-imperia, both of whom regard themselves as good and just, are driven in serving Balthazar and Lorenzo their due. In Altman's judgment, "the play invites us to respond in several different ways: to enjoy the visceral pleasures of a well-deserved blood revenge, to ponder more carefully the problematic situation of the man who would be just, *and to reflect upon the simplistic judgment of the frame as an aspect of his problem.*"[26]

In *Romeo and Juliet*, Shakespeare reveals himself as Kyd's student. Against the necessity of a tragic plot measured by unity of action (and against the suggestion that such plots might imitate everyday events that are themselves preordained), Shakespeare sets the causal agency of individuals doing the things they feel they have to, with unintentionally and unpredictably lethal consequences. The ironic relation between the Prologue and the main action of the play further prompts us to reflect on the Prince's confidence that the deaths of Romeo and Juliet (like those of Mercutio and Paris) were a "scourge" sent from "heaven" to punish the needless enmity between Montagues and Capulets (5.2.292–93)—as also on Romeo's invocation of "black fate" after the death of Mercutio (3.1.121), Juliet's hyperbolical complaint that "heaven should practise stratagems" on her (3.5.210), and Friar Laurence's gestures to the role of "unhappy fortune" and "lamentable chance" in upsetting his plans (5.2.17, 5.3.146). Glancing for a moment beyond *Romeo and Juliet* itself, the Prologue is just as important for allowing us to discern Shakespeare's continued experimentation with the things that he might be able to make tragedy do—the ways in which he might bend it to his own design. Yes, "fatal loins" and suchlike invest tragic plots with a sort of elemental force, but they do so at the cost of the moral agency that invests the things that tragic characters say and do with emotional and intellectual significance. They moreover do away with the aleatory features that, for Shakespeare, are crucial to fully realized tragic art. Shakespeare avoids the difficulty by integrating it into the fabric of his drama: despite the claim of its Prologue, *Romeo and Juliet* is not a work of tragic inevitability, but one that takes tragic inevitability as one of its subjects.[27] We will almost certainly never know who was responsible for the title-page of the 1597 first quarto edition, in which *Romeo and Juliet* is described as "An Excellent conceited Tragedie."

But whoever it was had a point. Shakespeare is thinking very hard indeed. After feeling compassion for the sufferings of the young lovers, and perhaps also anger at the circumstances that bring these sufferings about, he wants his audiences to do the same.

———

Tragedy as personified in the "Induction" to *A Warning for Fair Women* might say otherwise, but love was not an unusual subject for tragic drama: take Mary Sidney Herbert's translation of Robert Garnier's *Marc Antoine*, first printed in 1592, then again in 1595. What makes *Romeo and Juliet* stand out is that, although the relationship between the two title characters goes against their parents' wishes, it is not transgressive in the manner of the affair between Clytemnestra and Aegisthus, Phaedra's desire for Hippolytus, or the marriage between Oedipus and Jocasta. Nor are Romeo and Juliet inheritors of great place, and their marriage has none of the political implications attendant on Jason's abandonment of Medusa for Creusa, or of a union such as that between Saturninus and Tamora. In Ovid's *Amores* 3.1, Tragedy attacks Elegy for wasting her poetic talent on the frivolities of romantic love: "Tis time to move grave things in lofty stile, / Long hast thou loyterd, greater workes compile. / The subject hides thy wit, mens acts resound, / This thou wilt say to be a worthy ground."[28] Ovid's Elegy goes on to refute her assailant with forceful elegance, but in *Romeo and Juliet*, Shakespeare goes further: the business of falling in love, quotidian and shrouded in bad verse though it might be, offers one basis on which to set about saving tragedy from itself—by taking it past sententiousness and stagy grandeur, past ritual bloodletting, past the compulsions of revenge plotting, and past the troubled lives of princes.

After Romeo is banished, his young wife and her family household become the center of the action. This social space, allowing as it does for intermingling between the middling sort and the lower orders, is the terrain of the domestic tragedies that the English stage had just begun to make its own. In *Arden of Faversham* and the tradition to which it gave rise, the novelty and based-on-a-true-story sensationalism of the material is offset by a moralism that, ostensibly, is only just this side of homiletic: in conferring tragic stature on characters—notably, on female characters— who are far removed from royalty or great place, care needed to be taken not to be seen too brazenly disrupting the codes of moral, legal, and social convention that bound the late Elizabethan world to order.[29] In any case, and whether or not Shakespeare contributed to *Arden*, the playworld in the second half of *Romeo and Juliet* is a markedly different affair. Even here, however, tragedy is not obvious. Juliet deals with the departure of Romeo, and then the prospect of marriage to Paris, as if the play were still a love comedy—first, in discussion with her confidant-cum-helpmeet, the Nurse, whose counsel to forget Romeo and marry Paris she dismisses; then, in conspiratorial mode with Friar Laurence. If it is not quite true to say that nobody here is conscious of doing the wrong thing, then all take the view that the rules they are proposing to break are insignificant.

Why then do the comedic accommodations of the Nurse and the Friar fail? How is it that *Romeo and Juliet* concludes as a tragedy and not a dark-edged but ultimately celebratory comedy like *Much Ado About Nothing* (another work that leans on Bandello's *novellieri* and their translations)? One answer might be that the Nurse underestimates the degree of passionate conviction with which Juliet regards her identity as Romeo's wife, and that this underestimation reflects a Capulet household whose social preoccupations make no space for the realities of human emotion. But the truth of the matter is, I think, simpler than this. *Romeo and Juliet* is a tragedy because Shakespeare wants it to be. Because he wants us to see how fine are the lines between tragic and comedic endings, how much depends on details like the expeditious delivery of the mail—by extension, how much we miss by cleaving to the doctrines of tragic inevitability sketched in the Prologue. Friar Laurence's plan is risky but could easily have worked as well as the one hatched by Friar Francis in *Much Ado*. For the tragic denouement of *Romeo and Juliet* to come about, for it to engender feelings of woe and wonder in its audiences, all it takes is the wrong things happening at the wrong time.

But rather than its plot, its subject matter, or the social status of its protagonists, the most far-reaching experiment of *Romeo and Juliet* the tragedy might be the way in which Shakespeare has his characters speak. Not so much Romeo (in whose mouth Petrarchan love conceits do duty for the *sententiae* declaimed by the Roman cast of *Titus Andronicus*), or even Mercutio (despite his Queen Mab speech, and striking though his habitual drollery must have sounded within a work self-described as a tragedy).[30] Instead, the domestic setting of the play frees Shakespeare to develop, in Juliet, a kind of *dianoia* that moves decisively away from the mannered or the bombastic, and that allows him better to create the illusion of a mind thinking through the challenges of its moment.

From the first time we encounter her, Juliet shows that, despite her youth, she is wise to the reflexive citationality of humanist discourse: she teases Romeo that he "kiss[es] by th' book" (1.5.109)—as if he were in a courtly romance rather than before a flesh-and-blood woman. She likewise understands that language signifies conventionally rather than naturally ("That which we call a rose / By any other word would smell as sweet" [2.2.43–44]), and that these conventions, irrespective of their truth content, can be manipulated to play on the emotions of one's intended audience ("Dost thou love me? I know thou wilt say 'Ay,' / And I will take thy word . . . At lovers' perjuries, / They say, Jove laughs" [2.2.90–93]). The skill with which Juliet appropriates Ovid's laughing Jove to maneuver Romeo into confirming his amatory boldness reminds us that her own speech is far from unsophisticated, as does her insistence that the morning lark is a nightingale (3.5.1–5); indeed, her soliloquy at 3.2.1–33 suggests that when the mood takes her, she can be her husband's equal in breathless artifice.[31] But as the plot closes in around her after Romeo's departure, she becomes plainer and more affecting than anyone else in either Verona or the Rome of *Titus Andronicus*. Once she has negotiated her parents' cloddish authoritarianism and tactfully but firmly shrugged off the Nurse, she articulates exactly what is at stake: either Friar Laurence will provide her with a "remedy" for her ills, or she will take her own life (3.5.242–43). She does so without quoting from, for instance, Ovid's tale of Pyramus and Thisbe, or comparing her predicament to that of Dido when facing up to an unwanted marriage after Aeneas's sudden departure from Carthage. When she says she will stab herself rather than exchange vows with Paris, we are to infer that she means it.

After another expert show of simulation and dissimulation for the benefit of her parents and the Nurse, she again finds herself alone. The sensation is not one of relief: "I have a faint cold fear thrills through my veins, / That almost freezes up the heat of life. / I'll call them back again to comfort me. / Nurse!—What should she do here? / My dismal scene I needs must act alone" (4.3.15–19). Frightened but resolute, Shakespeare shows her determined to act but worried at what might come. What if the potion does not work, and she awakes the next morning? What if, to hide his guilt at having married her to Romeo in secret, the Friar has substituted a lethal poison? What if she wakes in her family tomb before Romeo comes to her, and suffocates? What if she doesn't suffocate, and is obliged to live on in "the horrible conceit of death and night" (4.3.37)? She worries that the experience will drive her mad:

> O, if I wake, shall I not be distraught,
> Environed with all these hideous fears,
> And madly play with my forefathers' joints,

And pluck the mangled Tybalt from his shroud
And, in this rage, with some great kinsman's bone,
As with a club, dash out my desperate brains?
O, look, methinks I see my cousin's ghost
Seeking out Romeo that did spit his body
Upon a rapier's point. Stay, Tybalt, stay!
Romeo, Romeo, Romeo, here's drink. I drink to thee. (4.3.49–58)

Conflicted, anxious, courageous, intelligent, self-questioning, nightmar-ishly vivid, and—as we know from the Prologue, and might in any case surmise from the desperately unmetrical final line—doomed. I am not sure whether Juliet is Shakespeare's first great tragic character, but this is his first great tragic speech. Granted that the problem for Juliet is how she can hold onto that which she believes is best for her, and that many of Shakespeare's later tragic protagonists are more complicated creations, in whom the struggle is not to hold onto that which they cherish the most, but to discover who and what they are—and, much more tentatively, to find a way of living with the knowledge that they exist beyond their own cognizance and control. The fact remains that as Juliet confronts the mor-tal risks ahead of her, she does so in a form of words whose paratactic affect shows Shakespeare the tragedian, for the first time, offering an imi-tation of thought with serious claims not merely to eloquence, but to an eloquence that permits verisimilitude and psychological insight.[32]

When Juliet is found the next morning, apparently dead, her family's grieving encapsulates the "scene-painting and counterfeit" from which Emerson would recoil. Beholding the carefully staged illusion of her death, they react as if watching a melodrama. Their loss is real enough, but even now Juliet is to them a token—or, better, an actor bred to play the part of the daughter they had in mind. The Nurse and Juliet's mother repeat ever more clamorous versions of "Alack the day" and "O lamentable day," and although Capulet professes himself dumbstruck, he quickly recovers with a series of grotesqueries about personified Death having deflowered his daughter by marrying her in Paris's stead, before—after being upbraided by Friar Laurence for forgetting that death is but the beginning of the life eternal—settling into a series of platitudes that offer a leaden inver-sion of the lines with which *Richard III* bursts into life: "All things that we ordained festival / Turn from their office to black funeral" (4.5.84–85).[33] Once Juliet really is dead, things are quieter. The emphasis now is less on the display of grief than on resolving what the Prince calls "these ambi-guities" (5.3.217). That is, on a forensic inquiry into that which we in the audience have already seen unfold: how Romeo, Juliet, and Paris came to die.[34] This inquiry serves as a reminder that there was nothing necessary or preordained about their ends. They instead came about through a concatenation of accidents, contingencies, and misfiring schemes. As this situation precludes any faction or individual party from being held responsible, we are left with the crestfallen Montague and Capulet elders making peace with one another. Finally, the play concludes with the Prince attempting to restore order: "Go hence, to have more talk of these sad things. / Some shall be pardoned and some punished, / For never was a story of more woe / Than this of Juliet and her Romeo" (5.3.308–10). He is right to speak of woe, as he is to place Juliet in the tragic foreground. Beyond this, however, he is winging it—hoping that the appearance of authority will suffice.

One sign of Shakespeare's growing confidence in his own tragic vision is found in the very title of *Julius Caesar*. According to Scaliger, for instance, the greatest care should be taken to ensure that the title (*inscriptio*) of a tragedy reflects the most essential event or character within the play.[35] In *Titus Andronicus* and *Romeo and Juliet*, the rule was one that Shakespeare was content to follow—as he would in most of his tragic plays. But in *Julius Caesar*, he disregards it utterly. The title character appears in only three scenes, speaks only 130 lines, and is assassinated at the beginning of act 3; his corpse then becomes an oratorical prop before his spectral or fantastical form flickers briefly in act 4. It is as if the Scottish play were known as *Duncan* and not *Macbeth*.

William Hazlitt is rarely juxtaposed with Scaliger, but his censure of *Julius Caesar* calls for it. Although the play "abounds in admirable and affecting passages and is remarkable for the profound knowledge of character," there is one crucial exception: "the hero of the piece himself . . . we do not much admire the representation given here of Julius Caesar." Rather than acting with suitable grandeur and purpose, this Caesar "makes several vapouring and rather pedantic speeches, and does nothing. Indeed, he has nothing to do."[36] Others have shared Hazlitt's concerns, and in the first half of the twentieth century it was seriously suggested that *Julius Caesar* (the text of which is witnessed in the 1623 folio alone) was a coauthored and/or mutilated text. Only such a compromised situation could account for the discrepancy between a tragedy titled *Julius Caesar* and Caesar as the play neglectfully depicts him.[37]

There is a sense in which the play's critics are correct: despite its title, *Julius Caesar* takes remarkably little interest in Julius Caesar. Instead, its focus is twofold. In the first place, the conspirators and their determination to protect their power and status from the threat posed by Caesar and his party. In the second, the collision between the conspirators and the Caesarian party as they battle for mastery of events after the extrajudicial murder on the steps of the capitol. The essential character in all of this is not Caesar, but Brutus. Although Shakespeare gives Brutus nearly six hundred lines more than Caesar, the difference between them is qualitative rather than merely quantitative: Brutus reveals the motions of his thought in a way that Caesar does not so much as approximate.

What makes *Julius Caesar* so interesting is not that Shakespeare uses Brutus to put flesh on the bones of his plot, or that Shakespeare transforms his approach to tragic *dianoia* by having Brutus speak in a muscular, spare, and transparent style that could hardly be further removed than it is from the sententious excesses of *Titus*.[38] Rather, this "noblest Roman of them all" (5.5.69) marks Shakespeare's first experimentation with a technique that would hold his attention for as long as he wrote tragedies. Plot still exerts control, and is still animated by the carefully contrived appearance of contingency and misadventure—not the burnished chains of cause and effect demanded by tragic necessity.[39] Where *Julius Caesar* diverges from *Titus Andronicus* and *Romeo and Juliet* is that these contingencies are no longer the property of external events like plague lockdowns, missed connections, or familial rites of vengeance. They emerge instead from Brutus's *ethos* and from the actions to which Brutus's *ethos* gives rise. From his fears, delusions, ambitions, and qualities of mind—from his conviction that he must move against Caesar to be true to himself, from the languages in which he conceives of that necessity and that self, and from the ways in which his decision to murder Caesar exposes the difficult truth that his identity (like that of Caesar) is a matter not of *res*, but of *verba*.

So, why did Shakespeare title Brutus's play *Julius Caesar*? In part, to toy with his audience's expectations of what they had paid to see. Perhaps a work like Marc-Antoine Muret's *Julius Caesar*, Robert Garnier's *Cornélie* (adapted into English by Kyd in 1594), or the anonymous *Caesar's Revenge* (likely written and staged in the early to mid-1590s), all of which show a dominant Caesar, speechifying in the grand style. Perhaps a tragedy of the *de casibus* sort, in which Caesar's vices of pride and (to borrow an adjective from Shakespeare's Rosalind) "thrasonical" arrogance lead to his fall from fortune's favors—as is the case in the life of Caesar added by

John Higgins to the *Mirror for Magistrates* in 1587.[40] But by the end of the first act, it is hard not to notice that *Julius Caesar* is tragedy of great place with a very different sort of complexion—and to pay closer attention on account of it.

We should also note that in naming his tragedy *Julius Caesar*, Shakespeare set up a mutually ironic relationship between the dramatic frame and that which the frame encloses. In other words, the title does the work of the prefatory sonnet in *Romeo and Juliet*, inviting the audience to imagine something not unlike the two parts of Marlowe's *Tamburlaine*, where the title character's qualities of eloquence and martial force enable him to conquer all before him. Marlowe undermines the *de casibus* tradition by neglecting to judge or to punish Tamburlaine for his pride, ambition, and cruelty, but in *Julius Caesar* Shakespeare subverts it altogether. It is not that great figures bend fortune to their will and thereby operate on a moral plane of their own creation, but that they are not ostensibly great at all. Their power lies in maintaining their status as the figureheads for, or representatives of, the oligarchic factions to which they belong. Not what they are, but what they are seen to be by their supporters and opponents alike. In this moral and dramatic economy, Caesar is not only not the powerfully autonomous force of nature familiar from the history books, but is not even the character most worthy of tragic imitation. The earliest known spectator of *Julius Caesar*, a Swiss-German tourist who visited the Globe in the company of his brother on September 21, 1599, did not speak English and could not grasp the subtleties of Shakespeare's plot or characterization. It nevertheless seems appropriate that, in recording his impressions of "the tragedy of the first emperor Julius Caesar," what struck him was not any display of histrionic virtuosity from the actor playing Caesar, but the ensemble qualities of the performance put on by the Lord Chamberlain's Men as a whole.[41]

For those of us who are able to engage with Shakespeare's English (and for whom the stagecraft of the Lord Chamberlain's Men can only be conjectured), the question is one of how to bring the relationship between the play's plotting and characterization into sharper focus. As with *Titus Andronicus*, one answer comes from the language and assumptions of hunting. The most obvious manifestation of this comes in the murder of Caesar himself, which—like the killing of Alarbus and the attack on Lavinia—Shakespeare depicts through the rituals of "unmaking" or "breaking up" at the end of a successful deer hunt.

It falls to Brutus fully to elaborate the logic and self-deceiving ceremonialism of what the conspirators plan to do. He begins by insisting that in killing Caesar, they should "be sacrificers, not butchers," and think of themselves as extinguishing Caesar's "spirit," not his body. At the same time, he acknowledges that "Caesar must bleed for it." This being the case, the killing should be dignified rather than wrathful or frenzied: "Let's carve him as a dish fit for the gods, / Not hew him as a carcass fit for hounds" (2.1.165–73). The enormity of what the conspirators envisage is suggested by the very fact of imagining Caesar as a deer: Caesar's association with deer hunting was long standing, but he was on the side of the hunters rather than the prey. Triumphant huntsmen, as attested by Jaques in *As You Like It* (4.2.3–4), were often garlanded with Caesar's crown, while the long-lived deer wearing a collar bearing Caesar's writ is a topos most famously attested in Petrarch's canzone 190 and Wyatt's "Whoso List to Hunt."[42] All of this is turned on its head. But what captures Brutus's imagination is the distinction between sacrificial carving and the kind of butchery fit only for hounds:

> The meticulous, almost religious, precision with which the dead hart [a mature male deer and the most prestigious game animal] was reduced to joints of meat and pieces of offal was a tribute to the qualities of the animal; it was not simply handed over to a butcher for dismembering, but was dissected in a ritual sequence, often by the king or the most distinguished person present, his sleeves turned back to the elbows to keep them out of the blood.[43]

On the one hand, there was an elaborate hierarchy dictating who got particular cuts of the venison. On the other, the hounds were rewarded for their efforts with the "quarry" (from the French *curée*), consisting of what was left behind: chopped up parts of the hart's stomach, intestines, lungs, heart, and liver, mixed with bread and blood and presented in the hart's hide.[44]

Compared to the elaborately sanguinary account of it in Plutarch (where, in North's translation, Caesar was "hacked and mangeled amonge them, as a wilde beaste taken of hunters") or its dramatic reconstruction in the anonymous *Caesar's Revenge*, the killing when it comes is brisk and almost clinical, notably unaccompanied by displays of passionate excess from the conspirators: the stage direction *They stab Caesar*, the famous "*Et tu, Brute?*—Then fall, Caesar," and the business is done (3.1.76–77).[45] That the conspirators become covered in Caesar's blood occurs not on account of their attack itself, but because—Caesar now lying dead before them—Brutus exhorts them to "bathe" their hands in his blood "Up to the elbows" (3.1.106–7); doing so echoes the rite of "blooding" (in which huntsmen are daubed with the blood of the vanquished hart) that seems to have had a

place in the rituals of the early modern hunt.[46] The spectacle is too much
for Antony:

> Here was thou bayed, brave hart.
> Here didst thou fall. And here thy hunters stand
> Signed in thy spoil and crimsoned in thy lethe.
> O world, thou wast the forest to this hart,
> And this indeed, O world, the heart of thee.
> How like a deer, strucken by many princes,
> Dost thou here lie? (3.1.204–10)

Far from being all-powerful or a tyrant, Antony sees Caesar as a courageous, noble, and peaceable beast of the sort brought low in Gascoigne's
"Wofull Words of the Hart to the Hunter" (a translation of Guillaume
Bouchet's "Complainte du cerf"), one done to his death by a collection of
"princes" keen to sport with the prerogatives of their worldly power. Not
only this. By informing Caesar's corpse that the conspirators are "signed
in thy spoil and crimsoned in thy lethe," Antony underlines that which
Brutus would rather not acknowledge: Caesar's blood has turned them
into marked men.[47]

Unlike Cassius, Brutus does not hear anything amiss in Antony's words,
and he permits Antony to speak at Caesar's funeral. His error of judgment
soon becomes plain. Once Antony is alone on the stage, he reveals the
nature and intensity of his true feelings:

> All pity choked with custom of fell deeds,
> And Caesar's spirit, ranging for revenge,
> With Ate by his side come hot from hell,
> Shall in these confines, with a monarch's voice,
> Cry havoc and let slip the dogs of war,
> That this foul deed shall smell above the earth
> With carrion men, groaning for burial. (3.1.269–75)

Caesar and Atè (the Greek goddess of blind infatuation) recall Seneca's
Atreus: they are two hunting dogs working together to find the traces
of their intended prey, thereafter single-mindedly to run them to their
deaths. "Havoc" was originally a military term for the order licensing an
army to spoil and pillage, but had long taken on a secondary sense as a
haphazard and senselessly destructive form of hunting. In retaliation
for the killing of Caesar, Antony resolves to unleash a mob that will lay
waste to everything that Brutus and his patrician cohort—the *optimates*—
hold dear. The *optimates* may not know it yet, but they are no longer the

decorously idealized hunters of their imagining; they have instead turned themselves into the prey of a group of hunters with little interest in disguising their bloodlust beneath ceremonial brocade.[48]

In *Titus*, hunting is an index of the unconstrained (though generally occluded) appetites that lie behind even the most apparently virtuous actions, and with the ways in which these appetites hollow out the ideas of virtue and vice as the Romans understood them. The inhabitants of late republican Rome as Shakespeare recreates it from Plutarch are nothing if not appetitive. But, in *Julius Caesar*, this perspective on human motives is only the starting point for a drama that has more in common with Erasmus's *Praise of Folly* than a treatise on proto-Hobbesian Realpolitik. The real reason that Shakespeare focuses on the rituals of the hunt is that they are a kind of magical thinking—the willful distortion of a pastime whose reality would, if fully acknowledged, shatter the conspirators' decorous self-image as paradigm cases of Roman virtue.[49]

Although Cicero was tolerant of hunting in certain circumstances, he took the view that the guileful qualities required of it—the deception and pretense involved in the successful use of camouflage, lures and bait, hidden traps and snares, and so forth—were inimical to the civic good: crimes of deceit were more dangerous than those of mere violence.[50] He was right to be wary, because the dividing line between the practice of animalistic guile that he deplored and the performance of moral virtue as he conceived of it could easily seem indistinct. The key here is the notion of the *persona*, which lies at the center both of Cicero's *De officiis* and of the Ciceronian ideology on which humanist moral philosophy depended. *Personae*, as discussed in the previous chapter, were the masks worn by Roman actors to make their characters known on stage. For Cicero, they were a powerful metaphor through which to represent the parts to be played by individual citizens within the well-ordered drama of civic life. These parts were defined by the social-rational virtues of honor (*honestas*) and seemliness or propriety (*decorum*); self-knowledge entailed the capacity to cultivate the public good by understanding which of these parts one had been fitted to play by nature. In addition to seeking guidance from parents and teachers, this understanding was to be arrived at by observing the likenesses of oneself reflected back by others. Directly, from interpersonal observation, especially of one's friends; indirectly, by studying examples (good and bad) from history and literature. Although *personae* comprise our truest selves, it follows that they are fundamentally public, fundamentally representational, and fundamentally concerned with the *performance* of a particular identity: a matter of doing rather than simply of being. It is also the case that *personae* are far from singular. *Decorum* demands that one speak and behave differently in different situations, making it necessary to adopt identities that reflect the contexts in which one has to operate. If one is a magistrate, for instance, one must set aside one's amiable *persona* if a friend appears on trial in one's court.[51]

Shakespeare found this Ciceronian account of human identity unsatisfactory, but—along with later attempts to critique or supplant it, be they Christian, Aristotelian, Platonic, Stoic, Epicurean, Machiavellian, or Montaignian—it is everywhere present in his tragedies.[52] Sticking for the moment with *Julius Caesar*, consider Cassius getting Brutus where he wants him by making him see his "face" through the eyes of others ("for the eye sees not itself / But by reflection")—purportedly understanding himself better, but in reality falling into line with what Cassius and the other conspirators would like him to do (1.2.48–70).[53] A little later in the action, Brutus bids his fellow republicans to steel themselves for the task ahead, and invokes the doctrine of the *personae* directly: "Let not our looks put on our purposes, / But bear it as our Roman actors do, / With untired spirits and formal constancy" (2.1.224–26). For Brutus, as for Cicero in some moods, the supreme virtue is the ability to remain in character.[54]

Brutus forgets that just as actors play different characters in different plays, so the civic *personae* are plural. But let that pass. Of greater moment is the possibility of error: if our true selves are the offices that society views us as best able to fill—if, that is, we *are* what society views us as best able to *do*—then our identity is defined by the way in which we stand in relation to those around us. Once the *persona* has been admitted as the currency of moral virtue, then public recognition or acceptance determines how that virtue should be estimated. It might even seem possible to attain a virtue that is not fully, or even partially, one's own—whether by fraud, or by having it imposed by the judgments of others. Cicero sees no problem here. Because the creation and recognition of *personae* depends on reason (*ratio*)—the power of mind that grants humankind dominion over other forms of animal life—they are not to be understood as fictions at all, and are quite unlike the disguises or facades through which acts of deception (criminal or otherwise) take place.[55] That Antony pretends to plainspoken simplicity while working the mourners at Caesar's funeral into a vindictive mob is an example of rhetorical proficiency—an oratorical ruse de guerre— quite in keeping both with the *persona* of the passionately valorous general that he otherwise projects, and with the rhetorical-political goal of attaining victory by moving the emotions of one's audience. But elsewhere in *Julius Caesar* matters are more complicated. The unfortunate Cinna the poet, for instance, is brutally done to death by a mob for whom it is enough that he shares a name with Cinna the conspirator (3.3.1–38). To which I suppose a Ciceronian might respond that, rather like the common soldiers who believe that Lucilius is Brutus (5.4.7–19), the plebeians who make up the Cinna-killing mob are not the kind of mirror in which the *personae* can be clearly discerned.[56]

It is harder to explain away the discrepancy between Caesar as he appears to us in the play, and the light in which Brutus, Cassius, and the other conspirators are determined to regard him. For them, he is tyrant, a would-be monarch, and a threat to the liberty of the republic. In most iterations, such views arose from Caesar's overwhelming strength and virtuosity. Lucan's *Pharsalia*, book 1 of which was translated into English by Marlowe, is a good case in point; another can be found in the divinity that, in Kyd's translation of Robert Garnier's *Cornèlie*, Caesar is allowed to assume. The selfsame qualities were what Caesar's supporters understood not as a threat, but as the promise of deliverance from bad government and republican cant—a promise that would be cruelly sawn off by the envy of lesser men on the Ides of March. Whether feared or revered, this Caesar spoke as decisively as he acted. In George Puttenham's summary of Caesar's most famous proclamation—*veni, vidi, vici*—the "tenor" of his language was "no less swift and speedy" than his mode of conquest.

Whenever Shakespeare referred to Caesar before *Julius Caesar*, it was in this vein; and, given the proverbial nature of Caesar's speech and accomplishments, it was usually turned to comic effect. In *Julius Caesar*, his Caesar is a study in magnificently perverse dissimilarity. Not only does the great man repeatedly refuse the crown on having it pressed upon him after defeating Pompey at Pharsalus, but his character is measured by physical and mental decrepitude. His speech is prolix, bombastic, transparently self-mythologizing; he is imperceptive, hesitant, and superstitious; he is an epileptic, who "swooned and fell down" (1.2.247) when presented with the kingship—Plutarch is the source of Caesar's epilepsy, but rather than having Caesar foam at the mouth while losing the power of speech, his life of Caesar at this point suggests that Caesar "rose out of his chayer" and "commanded" that the crown be taken elsewhere. In two other Shakespearean inventions, Caesar is a weak swimmer and deaf in one ear. Simply put, Shakespeare's Caesar more closely resembles Lucan's Pompey—an old soldier living on former glories—than the force of nature so vividly, and fearfully, conjured in the republican imagination. None of which is to suggest that Caesar's physical incapacity excludes the possibility of him turning tyrannical; it is merely to note the care with which Shakespeare undermines the basis on which *divus Julius* is cast as a tyrant by Cassius, Brutus, and the others.[57]

The main reason Shakespeare wrote the character of Caesar as he did was to emphasize that the *optimates* see in him what they need to in their quest to defend the privileges and prerogatives of their faction. However inaccurate their perception of Caesar as a tyrant might be, accuracy has little significance in a world defined by *honestas* and *decorum*. Soliloquizing in his orchard, Brutus has the nous to recognize some of the problem, only then to dismiss it through sophistry. It is a given that Caesar is a tyrant and that he must die on account of it; so, if the case against him as yet "bear[s] no colour for the thing he is, / Fashion it thus: that what he is, augmented, / Would run to these and these extremities" (2.1.28–30).[58] On the other hand, Cassius and the other assassins are content to condemn Caesar as a tyrant without going through the deliberative motions. His *persona* seems like a threat to the patriciate to them, and is ipso facto tyrannical. That is enough. The irony is that this *persona* (absent the urge to tyranny) is Caesar's own creation: he unabashedly refers to himself in the third person, and elevates himself as a kind of deity—a being greater by far than those who populate the rest of the Roman scene. As he insists to his wife, "The things that threatened me / Ne'er looked by on my back: when they shall see / The face of Caesar, they are vanished" (2.2.10–12). Presumably not after he has swooned and fallen to the floor. Likewise, when he makes himself as big as possible to frighten off the clamorous senators in the capitol ("I am as constant as the Northern Star," "Wilt thou lift up Olympus?" [3.1.60, 74]), it only affirms the conspirators' determination to act. The *persona* that he uses to intimidate his rivals, and that—as his rivals reflected it back at him—helps in warding off his own anxieties, becomes the pretext for his violent death.

Still, it is Brutus rather than Caesar who serves as the focal point in Shakespeare's exploration of Ciceronian-humanist *personae* as the embodiment and reflection of self-knowledge. What makes his tragic character so remarkable is that, in him, Shakespeare hits upon the truth that just as we are constrained to representations in seeking knowledge of others, so in seeking knowledge of ourselves we are constrained to representative *personae*—to expressions of ourselves *doing* the kinds of things that we expect ourselves to be able to do. Aristotle's *Nicomachean Ethics* suggests that the superficiality of honor and of the *personae* makes them unsuitable as criteria for virtuous living, but Shakespeare's Brutus identifies a phenomenon more unsettling than Aristotle can allow.[59] A phenomenon, furthermore, that will become a touchstone of Shakespeare's tragic

characterization. The *personae* and the culture of *honestas* may be superficial, but they express something essential about the human condition
that philosophical (and, in postclassical Western Europe, religious)
approaches to it tend to obscure: however sincere or intelligent or clear-
sighted our attempts at self-examination might be, our innermost *res* can
only be inferred from the *verba* of self-presentations that are, as they must
be, shaped by that of which we have come to hope or fear or believe our
innermost *res* must consist. For better or worse, these hopes and fears
and beliefs are shaped by the languages of the cultural, social, and moral
worlds to which we belong.

How does this play out in practice? We have already seen Cassius
manipulating Brutus's contemplative and morally upright *persona* while
suborning him into the anti-Caesarian conspiracy, and Brutus himself
using the same *persona* as a fig leaf with which to make his deeply felt
conviction that Caesar must die look more respectable. It would be easy
to criticize Brutus for priggish bad faith here, perhaps even hypocrisy. But
I don't think that this is what Shakespeare wants us to notice. Consider
the quarrel scene, in which Brutus is affronted by Cassius's refusal to send
him the gold he needs to keep his legions fighting. Brutus intones that he
"can raise no money by vile means," and that he cannot "wring / From the
hard hands of peasants their vile trash / By any indirection" (4.3.71–75).
It simply does not occur to Brutus that such tawdry deeds are exactly
what he expects, and needs, Cassius to accomplish on his behalf. This is
because, under pressure from his consciousness of what happened when
he and Cassius "made great Julius bleed for justice' sake" (4.3.19)—and
of the outcomes (civil war, proscriptions, the suicide of his wife) to which
this deed has given rise—he clings more and more fervently to his self-
image of Stoic constancy, honesty, seemliness, and probity. This, he needs
to believe, is who he really is. If it is who he really is, and if he at all times
behaved in a fashion consonant with this self-image, things could not be
otherwise than they are; nor should he feel too badly about the course that
things have taken, and might yet take. The gospel of absolute self-control
paradoxically allows him to abdicate responsibility for the consequences
of his actions, if not quite for his actions themselves.[60]

One of the standard early modern critiques of Stoicism, derived from
book 14 of Augustine's *Of the City of God* but most prominently articulated in Erasmus's *Praise of Folly*, is that Stoics are arrogantly delusional.
Kidding themselves about the reality of their emotional dispositions, and
abusing their powers of reasoning to deny the appetites and desires common to all human beings, including God the Son in his incarnated form.

Stoic constancy and self-control are on this account not an alternative to the social currency of the Ciceronian *personae*, but are its logical end point.[61] And yet it is not, or not just, Stoicism that Shakespeare has in his sights in the character of Brutus—rather, it is the *personae*, the pretense on which they depend, and the extreme difficulty of doing without them when trying and almost certainly failing to make sense of oneself. Brutus does not present himself as something other than he knows himself to be so as to put one over on Cassius, but because he is straining every sinew to hold together what he takes to be his identity and self-image—his *persona*. The challenge is that this *persona* is not of his own creation. It is instead a collaborative fiction, coauthored by Brutus and his peers with reference to the doctrines of *honestas* and *decorum*, and which Brutus has internalized to the degree that his sense of his own integrity depends on it. The pressure of staying in character leads to the confounding appearance of Caesar's ghost ("art thou any thing?" [4.3.276]), and the slackening of the bonds that held his selfhood together. After the disaster of Philippi, he seeks to maintain—or perhaps restore—his dignity through suicide. But he is unable to accomplish this alone, and is reduced to pleading with his confederates for assistance. Eventually, Strato agrees to hold Brutus's sword for him to run onto. Straying like Cassius before him from the ideal of terminal autonomy, Brutus instructs Strato to "turn away" his "face" (5.5.48). If nobody can see it happen, then it cannot be dishonorable; he can meet his end with equanimity.[62] Suffice it to say that Shakespeare's Brutus is a long way away from the idealized model of republican virtue sculpted by Michelangelo.

Once the victorious Octavius and Antony arrive, Strato does the decent thing and lies ("Brutus only overcame himself" [5.5.57]), only for Messala to expose the untruth by asking for details. Nobody minds. As Antony was at pains to stress when rabble-rousing at Caesar's funeral, Brutus's *persona* is that of an "honorable man." Now that he is dead and his cause has been safely vanquished, Antony returns to the theme in the hope of displaying his magnanimity—thereby to nudge Brutus's followers into joining the cause of the triumvirate. He praises Brutus as "the noblest Roman of them all," the only one of the conspirators to have acted from principle rather than "envy of great Caesar," and of whom "nature might stand up / And say to all the world, 'This was a man!'" (5.5.69–76). Although Antony earlier on made no distinction between the motives of those who had stabbed Caesar to death, he is not being entirely disingenuous. He believes in the value of the *personae* (most particularly, in his own), and is trying to square Brutus's much-vaunted nobility with the reality of his conduct in conspiring against Caesar. As Brutus himself had come to discover, when a Roman finds himself "with himself at war" (1.2.46) or struggles to harmonize his "genius" and his "mortal instruments," the alternative to suffering the "nature of an insurrection" within (2.1.66–69) is to commit more fully to the *persona* that he thinks of as his own. The play comes to an end with Antony brazening things out on behalf of both his dead rival and the ideals that they share: true *Romanitas* is mastery over oneself and over a world within which Roman dominion is the guarantor of virtuous living.

There is, of course, a rich comic vein in drawing attention to the discrepancy between what people are and the way in which they see themselves, or imagine themselves to be seen. Erasmus, for instance, has Folly joke that without her gift of self-love to delude people about their qualities—she lists orators, musicians, poets, painters, actors, doctors, the civilized (*urbanus*) in general—*decorum* would be as nothing. In his copy of the *Praise of Folly*, the young Hans Holbein wittily illustrated the point with a drawing of a man whose reflection does not correspond to his self-image (see figure 6).[63] The problem is that such comedy only becomes possible when there is a clear sense of what a character really is, so that the pretense and pretension are readily identifiable. As in Malvolio, say, or pretty much any male character in *Love's Labour's Lost*. Without that clarity, the door is open to the kind of tragedy that Shakespeare would make his own. Brutus glimpses this opacity in his "phantasma or hideous dream" of self-insurrection, but turns away from it. Only the lethally dispassionate Octavius can embrace himself for what he is, and work with the fact that his essence—like that of the Rome that he will go on to dominate as *princeps*—is not virtue but the fusion of strength, strategic insight, and political guile required to keep on winning; all of which is prudently shrouded beneath the social-moral fictions of *honestas, decorum, pietas,* magnanimity, fellow-feeling, and the rest. What Shakespeare leaves unresolved is that, for all his perceptiveness and laconic brilliance, Octavius is a monster.

In *Titus Andronicus*, hunting helped Shakespeare to frame a plot in which Romans and barbarians were all but indistinguishable from one another. In *Julius Caesar*, the *optimates* and the Caesarian faction are likewise bound together by ties of appetite and duplicity that only one side is able to acknowledge: just as the ritualism and ceremonies of the early modern hunt served to conceal the bloodily guileful compulsion to hunt and kill, so Brutus and his cohort transform their determination to preserve their power and prestige into a defense of freedom against tyranny.

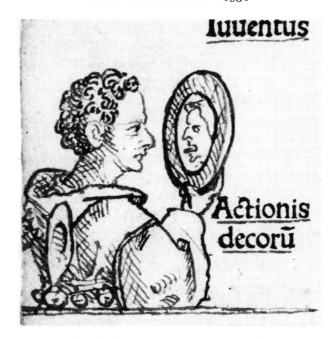

FIGURE 6. Desiderius Erasmus, *Erasmi Roterodami*
μωρίας ἐγκώμιον. *i.[e.] Stulticiae laus* (Basel, 1515), sig. E2v.
Kunstmuseum Basel, Kupferstichkabinett, Inv. 1662.166,
no. 13.

And yet Brutus's problem is not just that he only thinks he knows who
he is on account of his ideological commitments. Nor is it that his fixation
with the surfaces of things gets in the way of true self-recognition, in a version of the charge laid against secular *Romanitas* by figures like Augustine.
It is that he is unable to countenance uncertainty about himself, unable to
live without hard-and-fast knowledge of who and what he is—unable to view
himself, and everyone else, as a work in progress. Instead, high on principle, he insists that his *persona* is not a reflection of his standing and self-
positioning in Roman society, but something fixed and more fundamental. A metaphor through which to make human identity more intelligible
is mistaken for who and what human beings really are; a useful fiction
is transformed into a myth. This misprision makes Brutus as abysmal a
judge of other people and their motives as he is of himself. To take just
a handful of examples, he insists that Antony is no threat and should be
spared; he allows Antony to speak at Caesar's funeral; his own funeral
oration fails to anticipate the emotions of the mourning populace, or the
ways in which Antony might seek to work on them; he fails to imagine
the ramifications of keeping Portia, despite her protests, in the "suburbs"

of his affections (2.1.284), presumably because he fears allowing his emotions into his decision-making process; he insists on abandoning a strong military position in the "hills and upper regions" (5.1.3) to confront Octavius and Antony at Philippi—and, once there, is a dismally confused general. Although he will eventually echo Cassius's turn to fatalism in claiming that his defeat was the doing of Caesar's "spirit" (which "walks abroad and turns our swords / In our own proper entrails" [5.3.95–96]), the events that we see transpire demand no supernatural explanation. In a line that surely caught Shakespeare's attention, Plutarch gets straight to the point: "For nothing undid them, but that Brutus went not to helpe Cassius, thinking he had overcome them, as him selfe had done: and Cassius on the other side taried not for Brutus, thinking he had bene overthrowen, as him selfe was."[64] If Brutus had been better organized and if Cassius had possessed more belief in Brutus's ability to lead, then the outcome would have been different. There was nothing preordained about it, however consoling it might be to pretend otherwise after the fact. Cassius got it right earlier on: "The fault, dear Brutus, is not in our stars / But in ourselves" (1.2.139–40).

Errors of judgment are, of course, nothing new for tragic protagonists. *Julius Caesar* is nonetheless a watershed in two respects. First, in the character of Brutus, we get to see the whys and wherefores of these errors. Brutus moves forward in ignorance of himself and of the world around him, and does so because he believes in the rectitude of viewing things through the lens of *honestas* and *decorum*. Because the world best reveals itself through its "face," there is no need for the discerning Roman to look anywhere else. If this leads to a dangerous complacency, then that is in many respects the least of it: the performative nature of virtue also gives rise to a version of moral vanity, in which Brutus craves the reflection of his own virtuous *persona* as mirrored back at him by others. (There is a critique of humanist moral philosophy here, no less thoroughgoing for being advanced en passant.) Second, it is these errors-as-aspects-of-character that drive forward the plot as it is presented to us. This approach not only knits together *ethos* and *muthos* more tightly than Marlowe, Kyd, or Shakespeare himself had previously been able to contrive, but enables Shakespeare to continue his experimentation with tragedy as the kind of writing that is best able to explore the areas beyond rational comprehension; beyond systems of moral, philosophical, and theological order; beyond the fictive constructs with which human beings seek to make sense of themselves. In *Julius Caesar*, Shakespeare begins his exploration of a world whose inhabitants are determined to understand, but whose efforts toward this end lead them further and further into the dark.

It is one of Shakespeare's crowningly dry ironies that a fictionalized version of Cicero comes nearer than anyone—other than Octavius—to acknowledging this state of affairs: "Indeed it is a strange-disposed time. / But men may construe things after their fashion / Clean from the purposes of the things themselves" (1.3.33–35). In speaking thus, Cicero shrugs at Caska's enthusiastic recounting of the prodigies that he claims to have witnessed. When Shakespeare next turned to tragedy after finishing *Julius Caesar*, these prodigies stayed with him; they were an excellent way in which to think about, and to dramatize, the experience of living in a world in which "things" indubitably exist, but in which they are rendered indeterminate by the obscurity of their purposes. That play was *Hamlet*.

CHAPTER THREE

Things, Things, Things

HAMLET

ONE DISTINGUISHING FEATURE of literary and cultural history as it has been written over the past two or three decades is the attention paid to things over words and images: clothing (and textiles in general), furniture, effigies, buildings, ruins, toys, clocks, jewelry, ornaments, stage props, vehicles, cabinets of curiosities, food, kitchen utensils, weapons, and—of course—books and manuscripts as physical objects. No doubt some of this should be seen as a retreat from the grandiosities of Theory as it reached its apogee a few years either side of 1990; or, in a formulation that made me laugh the first few times I heard it, the sad decline of Marxism into antiquarianism. The turn toward material culture nevertheless bespeaks more than a loss of confidence or ideological conviction: there is a deep coherence in the belief that, if the conditions of materiality have done so much to shape the development of human affairs, then attention must be paid to material objects in and of themselves. Consider Bill Brown's "thing theory," where the physicality of the objects with which we surround ourselves is afforded a "vitality" of its own. The crucial distinction here originates with Heidegger, and maintains that an object (*Gegenstand*) becomes a thing (*Ding*) when it ceases to inhabit the identity through which a particular subject apprehends it—when a clock or an automobile stops working, we no longer see its objecthood, but rather are confronted with the inscrutable materiality, the thingness, that its objecthood has hidden from view. We may think of ourselves as surrounded by "things" in the items with which we fill up the spaces around us, but this is another of the fictions through which we seek to impose order on our lives; in reality, the ways in which we comprehend—that is, objectify—these items obscure what is really there. For

Brown, one purpose of art (be it literary, visual, or plastic) is to help us discern that which exists behind the inventory of everyday existence.[1]

Brown is concerned with the twentieth century: with cinema, photography, sculpture, and the novel. In writing about a stage tragedy written in or around the year 1600, I do not want to push my luck. The fact remains that *Hamlet* is a play obsessed with "things"—which is to say, with entities and phenomena that demonstrably exist, but that resist definition or comprehension in the object representations through which we are bound to think about them. The most obvious of these entities is the Ghost. According to the three characters we first hear discussing it, it is a "thing" the status of which defies explanation (1.1.24, 1.1.153, 1.2.210), and that should be regarded with a mixture of skepticism and wariness. Textbook stuff, to which Hamlet, after his interview with the Ghost, counters that "there are more things in heaven and earth" (1.5.174) than received wisdom can dream of. In the second quarto version of the text, Hamlet speaks to Horatio of the shortcomings in "your philosophy"; in the 1623 folio, of "our philosophy." But the distinction between the two pronouns is unimportant, and not just because the second quarto's "your" is almost certainly generic-deictic rather than possessive (i.e., it denotes philosophy in general, not Horatio's philosophy in particular). The "things" that Hamlet refers to are indeterminate entities—that for which philosophy of all sorts has failed to provide a rational account. His point is that neither he nor Horatio can make sense of the Ghost as it has just appeared to their eyes and ears.[2]

As *Hamlet* will go on to suggest, Hamlet is importantly right: there *is* much in human affairs that defies philosophical (or theological, or historical, or forensic) explanation. But alongside his diminution of philosophy sits his conviction that he, Hamlet, somehow or other understands—and that Horatio and the others should therefore do as he tells them. This conviction, along with his need to be able to tell himself that he is someone who sees the world as it really is, are amongst the play's foremost difficulties. Like Brutus before him, Hamlet cannot own that at the heart of his mystery lies an emergent awareness that human beings, to whose number he indisputably belongs, have not been able to comprehend themselves—despite straining their ingenuity to the utmost in the attempt to convince themselves that they do. One burden of this chapter is to suggest that human beings are another of the "things standing thus unknown" (5.2.350) that litter the moral and epistemological topographies of Shakespeare's Denmark.

Before going any further, we should acknowledge something that, until the 2007 publication of Margreta de Grazia's powerfully intelligent study, *"Hamlet" without Hamlet*, Hamlet criticism had too often been prepared to overlook: the play's center of gravity is a royal prince with a highly-developed sense of his own cultural, social, political, and emotional entitlements; he can only be cast as an everyman figure by ignoring the majority of the work that bears his name. Still, William Empson gives a good account of why such concerns need not detain us for long. Talking himself out of his feelings of annoyance at the sociopolitical complacencies of Gray's "Elegy Written in a Country Churchyard," Empson remarks that "the waste even in a fortunate life, the isolation even of a life rich in intimacy, cannot but be felt deeply, and is the central feeling of tragedy."[3] Just so. In the unmistakably privileged character of Hamlet, Shakespeare continues his exploration of how it is to live with the first stirrings of a consciousness that one does not know who or what one is, as also with the suspicion that one's cultural, spiritual, and intellectual resources can do nothing to help. Such feelings are not the province of royalty or the leisured classes alone.

———————

The action begins with an armed man groping his way along the castle walls of Elsinore. It is the dead of the Baltic night, and visibility is all but zero. Hearing a noise, he calls out: "Who's there?" His question is met not with an answer, but with a challenge from a second armed man: "Nay, answer me. Stand and unfold yourself." The two men still cannot see one another. Rather than doing as he has been instructed, the first man shouts, "Long live the King!"—which may or may not be a countersign, or prearranged military password. The second man now changes tone. "Barnardo?" (1.1.1–4). It is, and although any clear sense of interrogative hierarchy is withheld (who is asking the questions here? Who is answering them?), we learn that this Barnardo has come to relieve the other man, named Francisco, from sentry duty.

It turns out that Barnardo is expecting company. Once pleasantries are out of the way and Francisco has staggered off to the warmth of his bed, we find out why. Marcellus (or, if the second quarto edition of the text is to be credited, Horatio) wonders, "What, has this thing appear'd again tonight?" The "thing" in question, Marcellus tells Barnardo, is on Horatio's account no more than "our fantasy." He continues that he has asked Horatio to join them in the attempt to dispel his doubts: "If again this apparition come, / He may approve our eyes and speak to it." Horatio remains dubious, so Barnardo entreats him to "Sit down awhile, / And let us once again assail your ears, / That are so fortified against our story, / What we have two nights seen" (1.1.24–36). Horatio agrees, and Barnardo takes a deep breath before launching into an evocative and self-consciously poetic set-piece of the sort that the rhetoricians recommended to accomplish *enargeia,* or the condition of evocative intensity in which the listeners (or readers) "see," in their mind's eye, just what the orator (or writer) wants them to. There can be very few twenty-first-century readers and playgoers who do not know what is coming, but as the same was by no means true for those in the play's initial audiences, Barnardo's words are as much for our benefit as Horatio's:

> Last night of all,
> When yond same star that's westward from the pole,
> Had made his course t'illume that part of heaven
> Where now it burns, Marcellus and myself,
> The bell then beating one—   (1.1.38–42)

As the language of the preceding thirty-seven lines has been so simple, not to say homely, the shift to a more elevated register (evincing the kind of grandeur that one might *expect* to find in a tragic play) is striking. Then, suddenly, Barnardo has to stop. That which he has been trying to conjure with his eloquence suddenly appears on stage: *Enter* GHOST. What is more, it (in "the same figure like the King that's dead") remains magisterially silent, quite unlike the revenants that seem to have been a feature of tragic drama in the London of the 1590s. Urged on by his two associates, Horatio addresses it with what he takes to be the requisite gravity:

> What art thou that usurp'st this time of night,
> Together with that fair and warlike form
> In which the majesty of buried Denmark
> Did sometimes march? By heaven, I charge thee speak. (1.1.49–52)

It ignores him, and departs the scene—maybe offended at the charge of usurpation and at the presumption inherent in being asked a direct question, maybe not. In a spectacularly mute coup de théâtre, the well-chosen words of Barnardo and Horatio are overwhelmed by dramatic reality. No one is any the wiser, and Horatio—previously confident in dismissing the "thing" as the product of a mental disturbance—finds himself perplexed: "'Tis strange" (1.1.67).[4]

His reaction is one that the audience shares. The puzzlement is compounded by what comes next. By a good deal of background information on the state in which Denmark finds itself (wary of Norwegian invasion; defended by sentries who have not been told why they are on "strict and most observant watch" [1.1.74]), but by nothing more to the point than Horatio's guess that the Ghost might be a kind of ill omen ("some strange eruption to our state" [1.1.72]) with which to comprehend what has just taken place.[5] It is hard to avoid the inference that by narrating how it was that the conflict with Norway came to pass, Horatio attempts to frame the events in which he is caught up, thereby to exert a measure of control over them—or at least to convince himself that he is in a position so to do. When this framing is itself made redundant by the reappearance of the "thing" after forty-four lines, Horatio abandons his formal mode of address to plead, "Stay, illusion . . . stay, and speak" (1.1.130, 142). Unmoved, the Ghost disappears again: still obscure, still silent, still resembling the recently deceased king. Horatio and Barnardo theorize that it might be the sort of spirit that flees the sunrise, before Horatio once more ascends the stylistic register to remark that "the morning russet mantle clad / Walks o'er the dew of yon high eastward hill" (1.1.171–72). As so often in this play of verbal amplification, *copia* emerges not as the pleasure-giving adornment prescribed by the rhetorical handbooks, but as a coping mechanism. The group as a whole finally agrees "to impart what we have seen tonight" to a character of whom we in the audience have thus far heard nothing: "young Hamlet" (1.1.174–75).

If there is a tragedy with a better, more audacious, or more efficient opening scene than *Hamlet*, I do not know it. Plunging us in medias res, Shakespeare opens up a playworld in which the protagonists do not know either what is happening or what to do with their bafflement. In its turn, the audience is obliged to grapple with the appearance of phenomena— things, *res*—whose significance is unclear and possibly unknowable, along with the difficulty of finding the words through which to discuss these "things" without distortion or make-believe.

When Hamlet—who turns out 1) to be the son of the recently deceased king in whose likeness the Ghost has appeared, and 2) to be suffering from feelings of extreme disenchantment with his lot—joins Horatio and the others on the castle walls the next night, the Ghost reappears. Hamlet turns declarative: "Be thou a spirit of health or goblin damn'd . . . Thou com'st in such a questionable shape / That I will speak to thee" (1.4.40, 43–44). Which is to say that he takes the apparition to be either a good angel ("a spirit of health") or a fallen one (a devil, or "goblin damn'd") that has assumed the appearance of his dead father, and not his father's spirit itself. In response, the Ghost beckons Hamlet to go with it, but remains silent. Horatio and Marcellus urge Hamlet not to follow on the basis that, as the Ghost is likely to be a devil, it may lure Hamlet to his doom. Regardless, Hamlet resolves to follow: "My fate cries out / And makes each petty artire [i.e., artery] in this body / As hardy as the Nemean lion's nerve" (1.4.81–83). The Nemean lion is the legendarily fierce beast killed by Hercules as the first of his seven labors, and provides the amatory *persona* assumed by the ludicrous Don Armado in *Love's Labour's Lost*. Horatio concludes that Hamlet "waxes desperate with imagination" (1.4.87).[6]

Finally alone with Hamlet, the Ghost speaks: "I am thy father's spirit, / Doom'd for a certain time to walk the night, / And for the day confin'd to fast in fires, / Till the foul crimes done in my days of nature / Are burnt and purg'd away" (1.5.9–13). So, not an angel or a devil, but a roaming inmate of Purgatory—and one determined to seek redress for the terminal wrong that had been done to its mortal self. Initially, Hamlet seems convinced: "Touching this vision here, / It is an honest ghost, that let me tell you" (1.5.143–44). Before Horatio can do any more than reflect that the business at hand is "wondrous strange," Hamlet insists that there are more things in heaven and earth and changes the subject—with subterranean backing vocals from "old mole" (1.5.173, 170).

The next time that Hamlet mentions the Ghost, at the end of his third soliloquy, he strikes a different note. Now, he has decided to have a visiting troupe of players act out "something like the murder of my father / Before mine uncle" in order to establish his uncle's guilt or innocence. After all, "The spirit that I have seen / May be a devil, and the devil hath power / T'assume a pleasing shape, yea, and perhaps, / Out of my weakness and my melancholy, / As he is very potent with such spirits, / Abuses me to damn me. I'll have grounds / More relative than this" (2.2.591–92, 594–600). We are not told what might have intervened to make him change his mind about the Ghost, but his worries are consonant with those expressed by his companions back on the castle walls. He repeats himself when explaining his plan to Horatio: if his adaptation of *The Murder of Gonzago* does not "unkennel" Claudius's "occulted guilt," then "It is a damned ghost that we have seen, / And my imaginations are as foul / As Vulcan's stithy" (3.2.80–84). (Note that as Hamlet here regards Claudius's guilt as a given—it is "occulted," and needs merely to be dragged into the open—it is not clear how Claudius's response to the play can have any bearing on the nature of the Ghost.) But after Claudius's hasty departure from the inset play has confirmed his offense to Hamlet's satisfaction, any doubts disappear: "O good Horatio, I'll take the ghost's word for a thousand pound" (3.2.280–81). As a demon could easily have spoken the truth with malicious intent, this conclusion might seem overhasty—but the topic is not one with which Hamlet, despite the circumspection with which Horatio hears him out, appears to be concerned.

When the Ghost returns for the third and final time during the closet scene, it is only visible to Hamlet. Peremptory but apparently unaware that Hamlet has just stabbed Polonius to death in the mistaken belief that he was Claudius, the Ghost bids him not to "forget": "This visitation / Is but to whet thy almost blunted purpose" (3.4.110–11). Gertrude thinks that Hamlet has gone mad. In terms closely related to those in which Horatio dismissed that which Barnardo and Marcellus had seen as a "fantasy," she tells him that the apparition to which he has tried to direct her attention "is the very coinage of your brain" (3.4.139). In his determination to make her confess her wrongdoing, Hamlet does not press the point. The closet scene over, neither Hamlet nor anyone else so much as allude to the Ghost in the remaining two acts of the play.

Like Horatio's claim that the Ghost is a "mote . . . to trouble the mind's eye" (1.1.115), Gertrude's inability to see her dead husband's spectral form is telling. To the early moderns, spiritual beings were substances without bodies; these "sightless substances" (the phrase is Lady Macbeth's) could instigate visions of themselves in human subjects by seizing control of their imaginations, and could accordingly appear in whatever form they chose. This power also meant that they could instigate visions of themselves in one person, and not in another—even if both these people were present in the same place at the same time. Nobody, in other words, believed that ghosts as they appeared were "real": they were instead understood as figments of the beholder's imagination. Disagreement only came about with attempts to say what caused such imaginary visions. For Protestants, hostile to the idea of Purgatory as a power-grabbing ruse dreamed up by the medieval church, they could only be the work of devils (usually) or angels (exceptionally). For Roman Catholics, devils and angels were also in play, but so were the restless spirits of those confined in Purgatory and seeking assistance—in the form of prayer, almsgiving, or other pious deeds—with which to reduce the length of their penitential term. Even those who disputed the existence of spiritual beings like ghosts, such as the magnificently outspoken Reginald Scot, agreed with the standard account of the mechanisms through which they were "seen." It is just that, for Scot, these visions were not instigated by angels, devils, or the spirits of the wandering dead. They were instead hallucinations: symptoms of mental illness.[7]

Much scholarly-critical attention has been paid to the confessional significance of the Ghost. What does it mean that a Protestant prince (attending university at Wittenberg, the seat of Lutheranism) sees a distinctly Roman Catholic vision? For all its diligence, most of this work misses the point. As Peter McCullough observes, "the impulse to define the play as either broadly Catholic or broadly Protestant flies in the face of its own relentless effort to assert both possibilities in a dramaturgical process that cancels the signifying power of each." *Hamlet* deliberately subverts the "promised conventional meaning" of ghosts, prayer, sparrows, and any number of other religious topoi.[8] What the Ghost presents us with is a study in inescapable subjectivity: apparitions are something that one sees differently depending on the nature of one's religious beliefs. The different forms of objecthood through which apparitions were conceived of by Protestants, Roman Catholics, and skeptics like Reginald Scot are an index not only of a gulf between *verba* and *res*, but of the broader failure to find a language equal to the comprehension of the things that human beings encounter in the world. In other words, by dramatizing disagreements about the reality of spiritual beings in the figure of the Ghost, Shakespeare transforms them into a stunningly original metaphor through which to apprehend a moral order in which people, in Elsinore as in London, see what they need to. If the way things seem to be has no firm connection with the way they are, and if things seem different to those with different but comparably rational systems of belief, then the Ciceronian-humanist model of moral philosophy—in which the world is a well-ordered stage play and in which self-knowledge is the ability to recognize the *personae* that one should assume within it—begins to look insupportable.

Perhaps the one forum in which supernatural beings like ghosts or fairies could be apprehended unambiguously was the theater. Take the Senecan revenant framing *The Spanish Tragedy*; Oberon, Titania, and the other fairies in *A Midsummer Night's Dream*; the practices of staging Hell and Purgatory in the medieval mystery plays. Each of them has a reality that does not depend on verisimilitude or any other kind of mimesis, and that can be apprehended by even the least experienced theatergoer without difficulty. Understanding this well, one Protestant polemicist, John Gee, went as far as to deadpan that Roman Catholic priests *"make their spectators pay to deare for their Income. Representations and Apparitions from the dead might be seene farre cheaper at other Play-houses. As for example, the Ghost in Hamblet, Don Andreas Ghost in Hieronimo."*[9] In *Hamlet*, however, Shakespeare subverts the generic categories through which even these theatrical objects can be agreed to signify. They too are things unknown to which form and meaning can only be assigned tentatively, if at all. We in the audience are left with work to do.

So it is that whether considered through the lenses of plot (*muthos*), character (*ethos*), or thought (*dianoia*), *Hamlet* emerges as a play preoccupied with the difficulty of drawing conclusions—more particularly, of doing so without falling prey to the dangers of erroneous inference and interpretation. Some of this is comparatively uncomplicated. Polonius misreads Hamlet's disaffection as a response to Ophelia breaking off their relationship, and aids her path to destruction by making her complicit in his attempt to prove Hamlet's love for the benefit of Claudius and Gertrude: rather than being provoked into declaring his passion by her pre-scripted coquetries, the jilted lover is angry, hurt, and keen to lash out.[10] Some of it is more complicated. After Hamlet intervenes in the players' staging of *The Murder of Gonzago* with the choric announcement that that the murderer is "one Lucianus, *nephew* to the King" (my emphasis) rather than the king's brother, Claudius rises in disgruntlement before Polonius calls, "Lights, lights, lights," and everyone other than Hamlet and Horatio exits the stage (3.2.239, 264). Does Claudius rise because he recognizes the likeness of his crime in poisoning Old Hamlet in his orchard? Or does he do so because his nephew, still profoundly discontented with his lot, has just issued a thinly veiled threat to kill him? Viewed as a sign, his action in walking out is ambiguous. Once we hear Claudius confess to a version of his crimes in his chapel (a privilege not enjoyed by Hamlet or anyone else onstage), we are in a position to confirm his guilt. But as our only details of the killing depend on the word of the Ghost, even we are in no position to judge whether Claudius rises in offense at Hamlet's implied threat to his life, in shocked recognition of his crime, in mock-offense to cover up the shocked recognition of his crime, or simply in vexation at the discovery that—somehow or other—Hamlet is on his case. What we can say with near certainty is that to anyone who has not had the benefit of the Ghost's testimony, it can only look like Claudius has risen because his nephew has committed an act of outrageous lèse-majesté: staging a dramatically crude fantasy of his uncle's murder before the assembled royal court. Even Horatio, who has presumably been told what the Ghost had to relate, is studiously noncommittal in the face of Hamlet's forensic euphoria: "Very well, my lord . . . I did very well note him" (3.2.282, 284).[11]

What of the Ghost's testimony? Are we supposed to take it at face value, or should we regard it as a carefully worked exercise in rhetorical *enargeia*, designed to work Hamlet into the frenzy of condign rage required for acts of vengeance, especially those that are to be prosecuted against a reigning monarch—hedged as he is, if not by divinity, then by the well-armed apparatus of his security services? Designed, perhaps, to lure him into damnation (murder is a mortal sin) thereby? If so, perhaps the killing of Old Hamlet by Claudius is itself a fabrication, an elaborately evocative fiction intended to rouse the emotions and warp the judgment of the troubled young prince? There was a celebrated disagreement on the subject between W. W. Greg and John Dover Wilson. Although this has more recently been resuscitated by Stanley Cavell, it can safely be put to one side. If, as we must, we aim for an account that can accommodate the dramatic facts of the Ghost's narration, the action surrounding *The Murder of Gonzago*, and Claudius's chapel scene confession, the best we can say is that although Old Hamlet was killed by his brother, we are in no position to judge *how* the murder took place. It may be that the Ghost's narrative is accurate (though as Hamlet's father was apparently sleeping when he was killed, some of the details must have been arrived at through conjecture—or perhaps the testimony of unmentioned chthonic others), it may be that it reflects a greater or lesser degree of embellishment, or it may be that the whole story is a verisimilar fiction. Anything more than this is special pleading.[12]

The audience's predicament does not differ significantly elsewhere in the play. We are constrained to questions that have no clear answers when worrying about the dividing lines between Hamlet's antic disposition and his discourse with himself; about Old Hamlet's failure to nominate his son as his designated successor; about the nature of the relationship between Hamlet and Ophelia; about the presence in Denmark of a professional acting company normally resident in Wittenberg; about the existence of a professional acting company in Wittenberg; about Gertrude's knowledge of (and possible complicity in) her second husband's crimes; about the sudden disappearance of the Ghost; about the speed with which Laertes raises and then abandons his rebellion against Claudius's rule; about the circumstances of Ophelia's death; about the circumstances of Hamlet's adventures in the North Sea; about the identity of the bones lying exposed in the graveyard; about Hamlet's age; about Hamlet's failure to tell Claudius that he is, at least in part, killing him in revenge for Old Hamlet's murder; about the proximity of Fortinbras and his army to the catastrophe that overwhelms the Danish royal family; about the absence of clergymen at the Danish court; about a host of other topics large and small.

With such questions in mind, it is often remarked that the clouds in which Hamlet makes Polonius say that he sees a weasel, a camel, and a whale serve as a motif for *Hamlet* as a whole, and that the play is a sort of Rorschach inkblot within which we are invited to identify whatever forms we can.[13] Or, to recast this thought in Heideggerian language, these mutable-metamorphic clouds can be said to draw attention to the status of *Hamlet* as a work of art within which we are extended the freedom to transform an indeterminate "thing" into an "object" of our choosing.

Perhaps so. But a better way of thinking about this moment in the play is to observe that, within it, Shakespeare takes two of the received ways in which the ability to discern images in the clouds were regarded, and subverts them through conflation. In the first place, claiming to see images in the clouds had, since Erasmus's colloquy "The Exorcism" at the latest, been understood as an emblem of posturing superstition. In the second, the imaginative capacity to detect images and shapes in the clouds—instances of what the art historian H. W. Janson called "the image made by chance"—was a sign of the transformative imaginative powers through which the true artist was able to imitate the world. Hamlet has both of these traditions in mind when toying with Polonius, but in the immediate aftermath of what he takes to have been his forensic triumph in the play-within-the-play, the second of them is probably foremost in his thoughts: his artist's imagination has snared his duplicitous uncle, and his uncle's factotum is too obtuse to notice. But the moment is more complex than Hamlet can allow. Polonius, after all, has a job to do in persuading Hamlet to visit his mother the queen, and is bound to humor the young prince's whims, no matter how humiliating it might feel to do so. Hamlet gets to think that he is putting an odious yes-man in his place, and to affirm his sense of his own imaginative-poetic integrity. Shakespeare wants his audiences to look more closely.[14]

As discussed above, the outcome of *The Murder of Gonzago / Mousetrap* is irreducibly ambiguous: Hamlet seems convinced that Claudius has given a sign of his guilt, but to those unfamiliar with the Ghost's claims, it looks like Claudius has responded to another outburst of his nephew's intemperate hostility. So, rather than nudging us to celebrate the sovereignty of the creative imagination or the free play of its interpretative cousin, the exchange on the clouds puts us further on our guard. What are the limitations of mimetic art? How should we comprehend the limitations of audience response? Can we avoid the conclusion that, in beholding a work of art, what you see and how you understand it depends on your perspective and your presuppositions? This is not tragedy holding "the mirror up to nature" in the humanistic fashion suggested by Hamlet himself (3.2.22). Shakespeare instead indicates that, in a stage-play world like that espoused by Ciceronian humanism, the special status of tragedy is that it can reveal to its audiences their tendency, when confronted by utterances that do not fit into prearranged discursive categories, to "botch the words up fit to their own thoughts" (4.5.10). And if that is the case for words, so much the worse for the subject matter that these words are intended to represent. Gertrude teases Polonius by demanding "More matter with less art" (2.2.95), but what she says could just as well be applied to the utterances of any other character in the play. Strive though Shakespeare's Danes might for matter (*res*), whether understood as things-in-the-world or as concepts, they are unable to pass beyond the enticements—the illusions, the evasions, the pleasures, the performativity—of verbal artifice. Everyone is left to plaster over this reality with the one discursive resource left available to them: words, words, words. The adequacy of the objects that frame and populate their conceptual worlds suffers accordingly.[15]

The object with which the play is most fully preoccupied is that of human identity. After we have waited some 170 lines to hear of Hamlet's existence in the play's first scene, he has been on stage for sixty-four lines before we hear him speak in the second. He does so to deflect the suggestions made by his mother and uncle that it is time to move on from the grief he feels for his dead father. As grief is the standard reaction to the loss of a loved one, his mother wonders "Why it seems so particular with thee?" Hamlet's irate response takes us to the core of the dilemma with which *Hamlet* struggles from beginning to end: "Seems, madam? Nay, it is. I know not 'seems.'" He proceeds to disparage "the fruitful river in the eye," along with "the dejected haviour of the visage, / Together with all forms, moods, shapes of grief." These commonly received signs of mourning cannot "denote me truly" because "they are actions that a man might play." His own feelings and identity are, he claims, things of much greater integrity: "I have that within which passes show, / These but the trappings and the suits of woe" (1.2.76–86). We infer that he regards the humanist conception of selfhood (*personae* governed by *honestas* and *decorum*, reason and virtue) as an exercise in glib plausibility—something with no more claim to authenticity than an actor feigning to be someone other than himself while on stage. By so openly professing an inner life that is resistant to public scrutiny, he also distances himself from his mother, his uncle, and the rest of the Danish court—who are, in Hamlet's reckoning, unduly content to perform a poor imitation of Denmark under the rule of his dead father.

So much is uncontroversial. But the dilemma revealed by Hamlet's response to Claudius and Gertrude is real. Once he is alone on the stage, its nature becomes clear. Now, in his first soliloquy, he concedes that he is at a loss to penetrate the surface of human affairs: "How weary, stale, flat, and unprofitable / *Seem* to me all the uses of this world!" (1.2.133–34;

emphasis mine): he does not know whether the worldly phenomena that he despises really are superficial, or whether he is missing something. And as the ostentation with which he insists on shunning the compromised decorum of the court might already imply, he is not perplexed by the "uses of this world" alone: he has very little sense either of what his "that within" might be said to be, or of how he might go about understanding it. What Shakespeare depicts so forcefully, here and in Hamlet's next three soliloquies, are exercises in failed privacy. It is one thing for the dynamics of social exchange, not the least part of which is the need to remember that you are addressing not just your interlocutors but those to whom they will relay what you have to say, to prevent you from establishing a meaningful connection with those to whom you are bound. But in his characterization of Hamlet, Shakespeare hits on something more disconcerting—something potentially more terrifying—by far: that we talk to ourselves just as we talk to others, and that in doing so we are just as prone to being led astray as we are in conversation.

Hamlet's most famous soliloquy, probably the most famous dramatic speech of all, captures this predicament especially well. "To be, or not to be" is "the question" (3.1.56), but the fact that Hamlet poses it while Claudius and Polonius are surreptitiously observing him indicates that nothing here can be taken for granted. For instance, if the stage direction of the first quarto edition of the text is to be credited, as I think it is, Hamlet enters while "poring upon a book." He breaks off from whatever he is reading, and only then begins to speak: "to be, or not to be," on this reckoning, is a quotation.[16] By turning it into a "question," Hamlet does not lay out a problem demanding an answer, but a *quaestio*—a subject of contention in rhetorical debate or disputation. Compare Barnardo's "That was and is the question of these wars" (1.1.114), Rosencrantz's "the poet and the player went to cuffs in the question" (2.2.353–54), or Hamlet's "some necessary question of the play" (3.2.42–43) and "Two thousand souls and twenty thousand ducats / Will not debate the question of this straw!" (4.4.25–26)—to say nothing of his assertion that the Ghost "com'st in such a questionable shape" (1.4.43). In the early modern university, a student would be assessed for his ability to argue persuasively on either side of the question (*in utramque partem quaestionis*), irrespective of where truth or received wisdom were said to lie. In proposing to address a "question," Hamlet the student lets it be known that he is going to turn over his subject matter in something akin to an academic exercise. To give, or to appear to give, both sides of the question their due before arriving at a judicious, or apparently judicious, conclusion.[17]

What of that question itself? What might Hamlet have been reading and how does it relate to the rest of his soliloquy? It is hard to say. The liberties of the inkblot test notwithstanding, one reason for this is that nobody could claim that what Hamlet has to say comprises a successful academic oration. For all the dramatic affect with which it is invested—and despite its totemic status as a benchmark of actorly virtuosity on the modern stage—it remains singularly difficult to say what Hamlet is talking about. Critical opinion has been various, and has tended to seize upon one part or other of the speech to the diminution of the rest. Some of the more prominent candidates have included suicide, murder, mortality (general), mortality (particular), and revenge.[18] What I want to suggest is that resistance to argument and topical analysis is exactly Shakespeare's point. Rather than a disquisition on life and death or living and dying, we are presented with a depiction of a young mind—an intelligent young mind trained up in and straining against the humanist tradition—doing everything it can to reassure itself that it understands, and can in some measure thereby control, the circumstances in which it has been caught up; to reassure itself that, in a repudiation of Schopenhauer's famous phrase, it can not only do what it wills, but that it can also will what it wills.[19]

The first clue that something is amiss comes with "to be, or not to be" itself. In ruminating on it, we can usefully turn a text that was as familiar to early modern university students as it is obscure to us: Aristotle's *On Interpretation*, his treatise on the fundamentals of language and logic. Aristotle lays down that although the copula is implied in all verbs, it cannot signify by itself: "For not even 'to be' or 'not to be' [*tò eînai ē mē eînai*] is a sign of the thing . . . for by itself it is nothing." (In the Latin through which Aristotle was read and studied in the long sixteenth century, the key phrase is rendered as *esse aut non esse*.)[20] The claim is made clearer by an observation offered a little earlier in *On Interpretation*. Here, Aristotle proposes that an imaginary creature like the hybrid of a goat and a stag may be a legitimate sign in that it represents something that can be thought, but that it cannot be "anything true or false—unless 'is' or 'is not' [*tò eînai ē mē eînai; esse aut non esse*] is added."[21]

Another useful point of reference is the first book of Cicero's *Tusculan Disputations*, within which Cicero is concerned to inculcate a philosophically elevated contempt for death. It takes the form of a dialog between M. and A., and one of M.'s first undertakings is to dispense with A.'s assertion that being dead is wretched. In so doing, M. refers directly to the passage of Aristotle's *On Interpretation* discussed above. As, on A.'s own account, the dead have ceased to be, M. insists that they cannot be wretched or anything else. To claim otherwise would be "as though whatsoever you do so pronounce must not cither be or not he [*esse aut non esse*]. Are you nothing skilfull in Logicke? Emonges the verye principles of that arte, this is taught. That every proposition . . . is eyther true or false."[22] For Cicero's M., as for Cicero's humanist readers, *esse aut non esse* is not a question but the logical precondition of any significant statement, or of any rhetorical or philosophical inquiry. In framing a question for a disputation, the canons of logic insist that "to be, or not to be" can only be considered in relation to a particular set of circumstances: "to be, or not to be" an entity like a sheep, a goat, an angel, or a human being; "to be, or not to be" in a given condition, such as dead or alive.

What interests me here is not what text Hamlet was reading or had in mind. Nor is it that his solecism misconstrues the same Aristotelian text that had been forgotten by that other great Wittenberger of the late Elizabethan stage, Marlowe's Faustus—who, in his opening soliloquy, takes his leave of Aristotle's works by declaring that "A greater subject fitteth Faustus' wit. / Bid *on kai me on* farewell." The Greek *on kai me on* translates as "being or not being," but appears nowhere in Aristotle; instead, Faustus the professedly supreme scholar has attributed to Aristotle words that belong to Gorgias of Leontini, as reported in Sextus Empiricus's *Against the Logicians*. The juxtaposition between the two fictional Wittenbergers is striking. Hamlet is no Faustus, but there is a concord in the distance between the ways in which the two men regard their philosophical acuity, and the nature of that acuity as their creators have them manifest it in their speech.[23]

Instead, the most revealing line of inquiry centers on Hamlet's resemblance to "moral philosophers" as imagined in Sidney's *Defence*. Sidney has them stepping forth "with a sullen gravity, as though they could not abide vice by daylight, rudely clothed for to witness outwardly their contempt of outward things, with books in their hands against glory." Furthermore, they "with a scornful interrogative do soberly ask whether it be possible to find any paths so ready to lead a man to virtue as that which teacheth what virtue is." As such, says Sidney, they are much less effective at propagating the goals of virtuous living than the poets, who are able to make abstract philosophical doctrines not only plain, but emotionally immersive. Poetry, declares Sidney, far exceeds moral philosophy in furthering "the knowledge of a man's self, in the ethic and politic consideration, with the end of well-doing and not of well knowing only." (Note that Sidney here thinks of self-knowledge in Ciceronian terms as the knack of adopting the most fitting *persona* for civic life.) Hamlet enters reading a book, dressed in the academic black; he poses an academic question of apparently moral import; he expends a lot of time and sophisticated verbosity in seeking to determine the principles according to which he should behave. And yet he is no caricature of the sort with which Sidney makes do. He speaks with the *sententiae* and plangent density that are the tragic hero's staple, and makes good use of the vivid examples that Sidney the poet and rhetorician valued so highly.[24]

To take just a few instances from the first half of the soliloquy, the "slings and arrows" of *Fortuna* the huntress are a topos—against which, according to Seneca, the philosophically fortified soul should be able to defend itself.[25] The image of Fortune as a turbulent and unpredictable "sea" is no less resonant.[26] And yet this is anything but commonplace writing: through the device of transposing a response to one standard Fortune-metaphor (the ballistic huntress or assailant) onto another (the sea), Shakespeare has Hamlet imply something about both the futility of attempting to shape one's own destiny, and of the difficulty in thinking about the fact. Next, Hamlet turns to another corner of his rhetorical store-house to imagine death as a kind of sleep. This has its origins in a famous passage from book 1 of Cicero's *Tusculan Disputations*, where Cicero quotes Plato quoting Socrates facing down his persecutors, and where Socrates concludes by declaring himself unafraid of journeying into the indeterminate landscape of the afterlife. There is no need to labor the point: Cicero lends the central portion of Hamlet's speech both its starting point and the structure of its journey from death-as-sleep to the "undiscover'd country, from whose bourn / No traveller returns" (3.1.79–80). Shakespeare knew that a sizeable portion of his audience would have recognized the Ciceronian material with which he makes Hamlet work. He also knew that, in "the undiscover'd country," some of them would have recognized Hamlet's Ciceronian source text being spliced with borrowings from Seneca's *Phaedra* and Marlowe's *Edward II*.[27]

At one level then, this is copy-book humanism: an inventively assembled bricolage of authorities and poetic eloquence. But together with Hamlet's other soliloquies, it also represents a new approach to tragic *dianoia*—one in which Shakespeare does away not only with the showy citationality of a play like *Titus*, but with the kinds of deliberation that preoccupy tragic heroes in Seneca, Kyd, and Marlowe. (We can be grateful that Shakespeare disregarded Aristotle's warning that "when character and intellect are being represented, too brilliant a style often conceals them.")[28] Against the grain of Sidneyan convention, Shakespeare does not have Hamlet use his heightened and sententious language to meditate on a moral dilemma or on the ways he has been wronged or misunderstood, but to show him struggling with the matrices of discursive thought itself—with the limits of what language can be asked to do. The unifying thread is provided not by a *quaestio* or even a text like Cicero's *Tusculan Disputations*, but by a reflex of the speaker's mind. Specifically, by the habit of what Aristotle calls paralogism (*paralogismos*): a tendency toward unwittingly false or erroneous reasoning. Examples include confused understandings of the relationship between the general and the particular; confused understandings of what a "cause" is; begging the question; errors of logical progression; ambiguous or otherwise unintelligible word choice or expressions; and the all-encompassing vice of *ignoratio elenchi*—of arguing irrelevantly or beside the point. Although Aristotle remarks that paralogism is a particular threat in discussion or debate with others, he notes that "even when inquiring alone, a man is prone to error when he uses words as the medium of his inquiry."[29]

In making Hamlet speak as he does, Shakespeare does not want us to infer that the young man has been a refractory student. Hamlet's paralogism arises not from any indiscipline or inattentiveness of the sort that Aristotle seems to have had in mind, and nor is it akin to the calculatingly fallacious speech deployed by Edmund and Macbeth, Iago and Iachimo, or the tribunes and Aufidius in *Coriolanus*. Rather, it is the work of what, in every Shakespearean tragedy, is an inalienable but distinctly un-Aristotelian feature of the human condition: reason always panders will, even when—as is the case with Brutus—a particular character has become attached to a notion of his rationally analytical sovereignty. In Hamlet's case, the difficulty is exacerbated by absorption in a rhetorical-humanist culture that, on Shakespeare's reckoning, prioritized suasive force over veracity; victory over truth; affective power and the *performance* of authority over orderly exposition and authority itself.

The lines with which Hamlet draws his great speech to a close are a good case in point:

Thus conscience does make cowards of us all,
And thus the native hue of resolution
Is sicklied o'er with the pale cast of thought,
And enterprises of great pitch and moment
With this regard their currents turn awry
And lose the name of action. (3.1.84–88)

His conclusion that "conscience makes cowards of us all" is a commonplace—as Zachary Lesser has shown, an occasionally disputed commonplace—arising from the "puzzled will" that itself arises from "the dread of something after death."[30] It is of course perfectly possible that Hamlet's uncertainties about the afterlife have made him think twice about his implied desire to commit suicide, as also about putting his life in jeopardy by killing Claudius. As death may not be either an end or a terminal somnolence, and as perdition of one kind or another is not a desirable outcome, neither self-harm nor vengeance seem worth the risk. But even assuming that his uncertainty about the afterlife is in earnest and not simply an echo of his reading in Cicero and Seneca and Marlowe, it in no sense follows that such doubts could cause him to become cowardly in all particulars, or that they do the same for the rest of humankind. Nor is it the case that uncertainty in the face of death can be equated with "conscience," which in its turn is no guarantor of cowardice in either its general or particular manifestations.

Hamlet, though, is only concerned with two things. First, to cast his particular problems as the general ills of the human condition, whether as a way of escaping responsibility for them, or as a sort of enabling fiction through which to contemplate them at all; an incidental benefit of doing so is that he can spare himself the task of acknowledging the reality of other people, each with his or her own share of woes and difficulties—all belong to a type of which he is the supreme representative. Second, to help him hide from an awareness that his "native hue of resolution" (whether understood as a will to suicide, or as a will to the kind of brisk vengeance that he imagined would engulf him as the Ghost began to narrate the circumstances of his father's death) has never existed. As a result of this dual focus, his paralogisms shade into sophistry: the repeated adverb "thus" is a mode of speaking that recalls nothing so much as Polonius's clumsily pharisaical efforts to sound the part. After losing the thread he is attempting to spin for Claudius and Gertrude about Hamlet's purported lovesickness, the old counselor struggles to make what he is saying sound consequential, or perhaps just consecutive: "Thus it remains; and the remainder thus" (2.2.104). The reality of the situation is that however many times Polonius might say "thus" (or therefore or accordingly), the illusion is transparent. He has no notion of what he has been saying, and has no way of connecting it to what he would like to say next—much less of showing that what he says next proceeds from that which has gone before it. We laugh at his attempts to pretend otherwise. We are not supposed to laugh at Hamlet's use of "thus," but it plays an identically cosmetic role. It strains to conceal paratactic affect beneath a mask of hypotactic, and hierarchically ordered, discourse—to give the impression of control and of considered authority where neither exists.

So, rather than a deliberation on both sides of a question, or even a digressive circumambulation in the fashion of Montaigne's *Essais*, the pattern underlying the soliloquy is strictly associationist. One commonplace or topos or term or image makes Hamlet think of another, which makes him think of another, and so on. The *verba* through which he articulates what he is thinking are as grandly metrical as they are sententious, but the thoughts and things—the thoughts *as* things, the *res*—with which his language seeks to engage are confused, murky, and ill-defined. Contra Sidney, the stylistic and linguistic wherewithal required to speak like a poet (with which Hamlet's tragic *dianoia* equips him in abundance) provides no guarantee of being able to acquire "knowledge of a man's self," much less of being able to employ that knowledge more usefully than in treatises of moral philosophy.

Crucially though, we are not supposed to condemn Hamlet for these shortcomings, any more than we are supposed to point the finger at him for generating the impression of depth without the encumbrance of content. There is another sense in which Aristotle discusses paralogism, and it is essential to an appreciation of the work that Hamlet's sonorous fallacies do within the play as a whole.

Chapters 16 and 24 of the *Poetics* present paralogistic writing as one of the tools at the disposal of the poet (tragic or otherwise) in attaining fictional verisimilitude. The relevant lines of chapter 16 are obscure, and relate to an apparently lost play called *Odysseus the False Messenger* (or, perhaps, simply to a part of Homer's *Odyssey*). In them, Aristotle describes how on- and offstage audiences draw technically false but dramatically valid inferences about the identity of the fictionalized Odysseus. Such false inferences, Aristotle suggests, lend themselves to a species of *anagnorisis*, or recognition. He is slightly more forthcoming in chapter 24: "Now it was Homer who taught other poets the proper way to tell lies, that is, by using paralogism. For people think that if, whenever one thing is true or happens, another thing is true or happens, then if the second is true, the first is true or happens; but this is not so. That is why, if the first is false, but if it were true something else must be true or happen, one should add the second; for because we know that the second is true, our soul falsely infers that the first is also true." It is unclear whether Aristotle means to discuss paralogistic language passing between characters or between the writer and his audience, but at the most basic level, paralogism (which for these purposes is indistinguishable from sophistry) is one of the ways in which to make fictions seem real. That is, to invest them with causal verisimilitude: to help with creating the impression of probability and necessity by which Aristotle sets such store. In due course, it is the *impression* of probability and necessity that will be overturned by the instant of *anagnorisis* in which it becomes apparent that things are not as they have seemed to be—and in virtue of which the tragic denouement takes its course, for protagonists and audience alike.[31]

Viewed from here, the place and status of paralogism in Hamlet's fourth soliloquy start to look different. We might say that Shakespeare has Hamlet himself make use of paralogism (or fail to avoid it) in fashioning a version of his troubled self; or, rather, a *persona* through which he can observe himself contemplating the difficult circumstances in which he has become ensnared. And as far as this goes, we would be right. But we are also equipped to discern something more fundamental about the novelty and power of Shakespeare's tragic characterization.

It should by now be clear enough that Shakespeare's tragic plotting in *Hamlet* prompts us to make inferences before undercutting what we have inferred and the way in which we have inferred it. We may or may not satisfy ourselves that we've figured out who's there as the play begins, but "what happens in *Hamlet*?" remains a very pertinent question. It is a very Shakespearean one too. As Lorna Hutson has shown, Shakespeare's dramaturgical preference was not to spell out how, where, when, or why the action is unfolding, but to confront his audiences with the circumstantial data required for them to deduce its causes for themselves.[32] His audiences thereby learn to recognize their own potential for error, sometimes for catastrophic error, within even the most apparently clear-cut acts of interpretation.

Moving focus from *muthos* to *ethos* and *dianoia*, Shakespeare achieves something very similar in the paralogistic language through which he dramatizes Hamlet's processes and patterns of thought. In the soliloquies, we are prompted to recognize that despite the charismatic heft of the performance, Hamlet presents himself to himself through a series of *personae*. Or, as he puts it when wondering at the player's lachrymose Aeneas at the start of his third soliloquy, "in a fiction" (2.2.546). We *want* to have access to Hamlet's "that within" just as much as he does, and we experience the seductive force of his attempts to realize it—but these insights are denied us by a Shakespeare fixated on the artifice, the contingency, and the emotional imperatives through which human beings are bound to interpret themselves. It is not that artifice gets in the way of philosophical and personal integrity, but that philosophical and personal integrity is a form of artifice. Another fiction through which to cleave to the belief, or the ghost of the belief, that we can understand who and what we are. Through which to translate the unaccommodated reality of "things" into the conceptual "objects" through which we can at once think about them and aspire to control them.

One index of the extraordinary power with which Hamlet's soliloquies are invested is that what would be the centerpiece of another play is often passed over without comment: Claudius's performance in the chapel scene. Beleaguered with an awareness of his wrongdoing after witnessing *The Murder of Gonzago*, and almost certainly concerned that Hamlet suspects his secret (though giving no direct sign that this is the case, and not yet having resolved to order his nephew's death), he looks upward:

> May one be pardon'd and retain th'offence?
> In the corrupted currents of this world
> Offence's gilded hand may shove by justice,
> And oft 'tis seen the wicked prize itself
> Buys out the law. But 'tis not so above . . .
> O wretched state! O bosom black as death!
> O limed soul, that struggling to be free
> Art more engag'd! Help, angels! Make assay. (3.3.56–69)

Although Claudius does not scruple to exploit the contingency of human law, morality, and custom in his everyday affairs, he fears that things might be different in the court of the almighty. And yet he is no ordinary penitent. As answering to the dictates of an all-seeing God would involve him giving up his "crown," "ambition," and "queen" (3.3.55)—giving up that which he now *is*, or takes himself to be—he casts around for an alternative. He settles on a boldly unusual prayer, or what he calls an "assay." That is, an experiment or trial on grounds similar to Pascal's wager. If God or his angels are willing to look mercifully on the bind in which he finds himself, then "All may be well" (3.3.72). If not, then he will not be significantly worse off than he already is.[33]

When no sign from above is forthcoming, the "assay" ostensibly fails. It may or may not be appropriate to think of prayer as George Herbert's "soul in paraphrase," but Claudius's words are a study in the dangers of separating *verba* from *res*, of allowing paraphrase to slide into imitation, imitation into counterfeit.[34] We do not get to hear it (the prayer was presumably silent), but Claudius certainly seems to think so, and reflects in a couplet of Polonian sententiousness that "My words fly up, my thoughts remain below. / Words without thoughts never to heaven go" (3.3.97–98). As befits one who long ago learned not to worry about the strict veracity of his utterances, Claudius is untroubled. We might even wonder whether his prayer was really intended for God, or whether it was an act of camou-flaged self-*catharsis*; certainly, performing it restores his equanimity, and once he has finished he carries on about his business.

But assuming that Claudius's prayer is meant in earnest and is not a ritual of elaborately disguised self-care, what he hopes is that God and his angels will infer his sincerity from the fact that he *seems* to be sincerely at prayer. That, in other words, God and his angels will lapse into the paralogistic fallacy of the false cause. Although Claudius as such aims high, he does little more than adapt his standard mode of behavior—in which he exploits the common belief that a person cannot perform well-tempered and eloquent persuasiveness unless he is, in fact, a *vir bonus*. And for a worldly audience, the posture of penitence is enough: Hamlet can hardly be counted as one of those likely to take his uncle's word for it, and his failure even to suspect that Claudius's show of piety might be bogus reveals how powerful paralogism can be in the mind of the beholder. People infer the causes of things and events according to the concepts through which they are disposed to make sense of the world, whether those things and events are spectral (the Ghost), religious (Claudius at prayer, Ophelia at her deceptively solitary devotions), forensic (the causes of Hamlet's disaffection in the first two acts of the play; of Claudius's hasty departure from *The Murder of Gonzago*; of Ophelia's death), or political (the ease with which the Danish court accepts the carefully scripted legiti-macy of Claudius's rule).

Claudius and Hamlet both recognize this state of affairs, and both are inclined to pat themselves on the back for doing so. Claudius, for his abil-ity to see things as they are rather than as they ought to be, and willing-ness to immerse himself in the murkiest of historical byways; Hamlet, for his posture of resistance and commitment to the way things really are. So it is that as the play's last movement begins, Hamlet tells Horatio that he thinks of himself and his uncle as "mighty opposites" (5.2.62). Shake-speare, though, wants us to see things differently: the two characters are just one of *Hamlet*'s many instances of deliberate pairing, or doubling. Each of them casts the other into more revealing relief; each is unaware of the dramatic reality that his most distinctive features stand in continuous rather than contiguous relation to those of the other.[35]

Despite his manifestly shrewd intelligence, Claudius fails to grasp that although his brand of quasi-Machiavellian subtlety makes hay with the artifice of the moral orders on which Ciceronian humanism, Christianity, and divinely hedged monarchical rule insist, it is itself a flawed attempt to impose order on a world of things that it does not fully comprehend. And one of those things is Claudius himself. He is not a squeamish or sentimental man, much less a weak or vacillating one, but he feels "guilt" for what he has done to obtain the throne and the woman he loves. After giving voice to this feeling, he tidies it away with his prayerful "assay." But he does not understand, or care to explore, *why* it is that he should feel this way when he had merely done what he had to do to get what he wanted, and when what he wanted was very likely in the best interests of Denmark (war with Norway averted, a clear line of succession established, etc.). As this sense of his own wrongdoing is not the work of his rational faculties, where exactly does it come from? The text gives us no clues. And yet despite the art with which Claudius contrives to distract himself from his guilt and its causes, they are not going anywhere. It is this blind spot, this conviction that his supremely rational plotting is able to encompass both his own motives and the motives and deeds of others, that will lead to his downfall. Although Machiavelli would have us believe otherwise, Shakespeare suggests that the doctrine of the truly virtuous prince being able to subdue fortune to the dictates of his will is just another politically expedient fiction—a more lifelike fiction than those propagated within the moral-political mainstream, maybe, but a fiction even so.[36]

Hamlet is in many ways a simpler case. His sense of grievance at having been wronged by his mother, his uncle, and the Danish court (all of whom had a share in the election of Claudius after Old Hamlet's death) not only sets him apart, but leads him to the belief that he, and he alone, can see Elsinore as it really is. The Ghost does little more than bring this belief into focus by revealing the ulcerous truth, or what Hamlet is content to accept as the ulcerous truth, that the paralogisms of the new regime have been organized to occlude.

Things become more complicated because, after learning a version of the circumstances in which his father was killed, Hamlet does not experience the condign intensity that he feels should be his as the son of a cruelly murdered father. It is not that he has forgotten his father the old king, but that he is only able to remember him through the idealizations of the myth-kitty: "So excellent a king, that was to this / Hyperion to a satyr . . ." (1.2.39–40). We are not told why this should be the case, but might surmise that Old Hamlet's failure to designate his son as his heir has something to do with it. By contrast, Hamlet regards his mother and uncle with nightmarish intensity: "Why, she would hang on him / As if

increase of appetite had grown / By what it fed on" (1.2.143–45). These idealized images of his father—dutiful, impersonal, oddly hygienic—are not
enough to fuel vengeance; Hamlet is dissatisfied and perhaps dismayed
that this should be the case, but collides with the reality that one cannot
will what one wills. Even as he vows to raze "all forms, all pressures past"
in favor of the command issued by his father's spectral form to "Remember me," the Claudian tug proves irresistible: "Meet it is I set it down /
That one may smile, and smile, and be a villain" (1.5.100, 107–8).[37]

And so, just as Claudius hides away from his sense of guilt, Hamlet
works discursive overtime to prevent himself from having to confront
either the reality of his emotional disposition or the reasons for its existence. Not through the polished disingenuousness of prayer-assays, but
by the extension of his *personae* and "antic disposition." Through, that is,
what the early moderns often called "passionating": *performing* the role
of the avenger, the poet, the conflicted philosopher, and so on. By the final
third of the play, he has realized that he can make none of these *personae*
his own. But rather than turn his attention to himself, to the nature of his
feelings for his father, and to the situation in which he has become entan-
gled, he has one last performative heave. No longer a man self-defined by
the prerogatives of his virtue, Hamlet transforms himself into an agent
of providence. He is the "scourge and minister" of heaven while inadvertently murdering Polonius (3.4.177), and after deciding on a whim to have
Rosencrantz and Guildenstern executed by the King of England, reflects
that "There's a divinity that shapes our ends, / Rough-hew them how we
will" (5.2.7–11). Lest Horatio should think this second deed cruel, he adds
that the circumstances in which it was possible were in "heaven ordinant"
(5.2.50). This is the mindset of Marlowe's Tamburlaine, dubbing himself
"the Scourge of God and the terrour of the world" as a way of making the
extremities of his career easier for him, and those close to him, to live
with.[38]

Like Brutus before them, Hamlet and Claudius believe that they exist
outside the Ciceronian hall of mirrors. One in virtue of his hardheaded
rationality, the other through the conviction of his emotional integrity. Or,
to put this slightly differently, Claudius and Hamlet each believe themselves to possess the sovereign subjectivity through which to transform
things into objects. Accordingly, they refuse any suggestion that they
might themselves be the objects of anyone else's attention. To recognize
such a predicament would, after all, be to admit the existence of other
subjects, other perspectives from which to formulate meaningful definitions of the way things are.

Much of the tragic force with which *Hamlet* is imbued resides in the inability of anyone to attain such exclusive subjectivity—even monarchs or would-be monarchs. As striving to attain it must depend on a state of denial about the sort of being one is, doing so must result in privation. More often than not, in death. A case might therefore be made that, for Shakespeare, the rhetorical, imitative, political, and emotional points of focus that occupy the quadrants of the humanist's compass lead people astray—by filling up their heads with well-written and elaborately patterned fictions of human nature, and by depriving them of the chance and the means to learn more about themselves and the world around them. Up to a point, yes. But as with dutifully historicist excavations of the political contexts to which Shakespeare's writings respond, there is a risk of misprision if we push this line too far. Of confusing the tulips and the dung. Topical concerns unquestionably helped to fertilize Shakespeare's artistic imagination, but it did not bloom in sentiments such as those in which Francis Bacon deprecated the tendency of Ciceronian humanists "to hunt more after wordes, than matter, and more after the choisenesse of the Phrase . . . then after the weight of matter, worth of subject, soundnesse of argument, life of invention, or depth of judgment."[39] Rather, Shakespeare was interested in the way that his tragic characters speak—in their *dianoia*—because he knew well that human beings have no need of the *studia humanitatis* to elevate the gratifications of eloquence and affective impact above soundness of argument, depth of judgment, and the rest. Consider the Gravedigger (whose education stopped some distance short of the grammar school) or Claudius (who leaves humanist nostrums of one kind or another far behind him): neither of them is remotely interested in the distinction between truth and lies, or that between coherence and incoherence, as anything more than an impediment to their efforts to make their listeners respond to them as they desire. Precisely because reason panders will, *everyone* tends to make *res* subservient to *verba*—consciously or unconsciously to describe things (to themselves and to others) as they need or would like them to be.

Seen from here, the genius and the threat of humanism in the Roman-Ciceronian guise of the sixteenth-century English is that it gets so much of human nature so very right. It understands the indispensable centrality of the emotions to human thought and communication, and likewise understands that although reason and logic and the pursuit of truth can have roles in moving the emotions, they are less important to this end than *seeming* reasonable and logical and committed to veracity. This, of course, is where Cicero, Quintilian, Erasmus, and—say—Thomas Wilson would draw attention to the Aristotelian distinction between an enthymeme and a syllogism; likewise to the doctrine that unless the orator seeks to articulate the claims of truth and virtue (both of which are conceived of in rational rather than affective terms), he cannot hope to speak effectively any more than one could effectively assume a *persona* to which one was not suited by nature. Shakespeare takes a different view, but is fascinated by the implications of the humanist approach to language and performance. And although he decouples this approach from its governing ideologies as early as *Titus*, fascinated by it he remains: its cultivated paralogism is an exceptionally responsive medium through which to depict and to explore the native paralogism of human thought and speech, even at its most rational or apparently heartfelt.

———

Let me conclude this chapter by saying something about what, in *Hamlet*, Shakespeare began to see tragedy as having the capacity to accomplish.

In the first place, *Hamlet* exemplifies Martha Nussbaum's notion of *catharsis* as clarification, and not as purgation or purification. It helps us to recognize not only the difficulty of translating the world and our experience of it into the representations (concepts, words, "objects") through which we are bound to think and judge, but the skill, tenacity, and occasional desperation with which we tend to hide this difficulty from ourselves. Whether we like it or not, our emotions—ambition, envy, resentment, anger, appetite, fear, pity, hope, love, the need to feel appreciated—are as much a part of our attempts to understand ourselves and the world around us as our aptitude for intelligent thought. They moreover mean that our attempts to understand ourselves and the world around us are always imperfect, always contingent, always works in progress: in a word, opinions. And as should become clearer in the discussions of *Troilus and Cressida* and *Othello* in my next chapter, a moral and epistemological economy of this sort not only makes it very hard to profess something as a fact, a truth, or a virtue. It is also one in which suffering is the coin of the realm. In Susan Snyder's typically penetrating analysis, *Hamlet* transmutes the comedic world of multiplicity and mistaken identity "into an existential nightmare of competing perceptions of reality."[40]

And yet despite its emphasis on the indeterminacy of things (and of things like us), the clarification offered by *Hamlet* is no prompt to resignation or despair. In their different ways, theology and philosophy both offer totalizing accounts of what things are, and the way they are: one in virtue of a deity standing outside, and regulating, the constituent parts of his creation; the other in virtue of reason being able to detach itself from, and thereby to analyze, the conditions of existence. These accounts offer stability and fixity. They also provide their adherents with the meaning of life, or as much of it as they are prepared to allow (here, needless to add, there is a difference between the claims of philosophy and those of theological doctrines whose basis is suprarational). In *Hamlet*, by contrast, philosophy and theology are presented as fictions to which people commit themselves to ward off their fear of the unknown, or of that which they might find within. Even Claudius's ruthlessly wily stratagems are cast as an attempt to impose a kind of order on events that, in Shakespeare's carefully crafted plotting, seem to be the province of arbitrariness, ambiguity, and chance—of Horatio's "accidental judgments," "casual slaughters," and "purposes mistook." The unacknowledged fictions that shape life in Elsinore also extend to the characters' discourses with themselves. By presenting himself to himself as Aeneas, Pyrrhus, a Senecan hunting dog, a morally deliberative philosopher, the scourge of God, and a casebook melancholic, Hamlet reveals the conditions of fictionality on which his engagements with himself depend. These engagements take the form of a process in which Hamlet employs his subjective powers of will and intellect to make himself comprehensible to himself: an attempted self-objectification. The fictions to which he is drawn are thus in one sense empowering. Without them, he would be constrained to the discourse of humanistic propriety. The problem is that they—like the fictions through which Claudius, Polonius, Laertes, Ophelia, and a host of less prominent characters seek to fit themselves out—are ultimately distorting, alienating, hostile to the convolutions and ambiguities that lie at the heart of the human mystery.

It is in so astutely representing this condition that the brilliance of *Hamlet* lies. The play is itself a fictional contrivance, a work of dramatic artifice, that details how and why we are bound to fictional contrivances when contemplating ourselves, our relationships with other people, and our place in the cosmos: because despite the power of our rational faculties, the way in which we encounter the world and one another is essentially animalistic, essentially dependent on our emotions. Some of these emotions are elevated, like the compassion that we feel when beholding the suffering of another, or a successful work of tragedy; others are baser, like ambition, envy, and appetite. All are contingent (I might not feel later that which I feel, and am proud of feeling, now), all are fundamental to the kinds of knowing that are available to human beings, and all militate against the totalizing worldviews to which we are led by our ratiocinative flair and by ideas like the immortality of the soul. For Shakespeare, that which we can know is made most fully available not through philosophical or theological rigor, or through supernatural-mystical vision. It is glimpsed instead through the experience of a form of art in which our emotional and analytical responses are tested to their utmost. By the time Fortinbras marches onstage, it is too late for Hamlet, Laertes, Claudius, Gertrude, Polonius, Ophelia, Rosencrantz, and Guildenstern. One sign that little other than the nationality of their monarch will change for Horatio and the other survivors is that they will never be able to see, or to read, the tragedy in which they have participated; they are stuck with the forensic-didactic delusions of early modern tragic theory, with plays like *The Murder of Gonzago*, and with the incongruity of Hamlet's military funeral.

Toward the end of chapter 1, I described these features of Shakespearean tragedy with reference to Kierkegaard's notion of irony. Like Kierkegaardian irony, Shakespearean tragedy is a way of moving beyond the habits of pretense through which we understand ourselves and the world around us, while acknowledging that it is only through pretense that we are able to think, and to think critically, at all.

But in bringing to a close a reading of *Hamlet* in which I have frequently employed the Heideggerian distinction between things and objects to make sense of Shakespeare's preoccupation with entities that defy comprehension, Heidegger's use of the term *Dasein* in his *Being and Time* makes for an equally germane point of reference. Dasein literally means "being there," but in Heidegger's reckoning it takes on a special significance as the only space in which human subjectivity and agency can meaningfully be understood. Not, that is, in sources like consciousness, the immortal and/or immaterial soul, the mind, or the ego—and certainly not in the *personae* of humanist moral philosophy. Dasein instead connotes a sort of being practically engaged with the operations of the world. Indeed, it suggests that being in its fullest sense *is* the inescapably mutual engagement between self and world. Being, that is, as the condition of existing with some awareness of the material and mortal finitude of human existence; of the fallibility and limitations of the cognitive powers with which it is possible to understand the world, and of having the wherewithal to understand something of what being in the world might entail; of the truth that human beings are at root occurrences rather than things or objects; of the truth that such occurrences are fraught with possibility, and are measured as much by the anticipation of their potential futures as by an awareness of their pasts.[41]

How Shakespeare would have read Heidegger is anyone's guess. With difficulty, I suppose, but also with interest and the increasing suspicion that he might be the sort of specimen about whom a play could be written. What I want to suggest here is that within *Hamlet* and Shakespearean tragedy more generally, the kind of clarification made possible through *catharsis* has much in common with Heidegger's Dasein. Shakespeare provides us with a frame through which to view versions of ourselves trying and failing to find understanding, and doing so by employing the fictions to which all human beings are drawn in the search for meaning or identity or consolation. In looking through this frame, we behold selfhood—and humanity itself—as entities that can only find expression, howsoever imperfectly, on account of their place within the contingent realm of historical living. As Heidegger himself puts it when deliberating on the ways in which Dasein might be realized, "the communication of the existential possibilities of attunement [to the states of mind in which we engage the world], that is, the disclosing of existence, can become the true aim of 'poetic' speech."[42]

I do not mean to intimate that Shakespeare has a philosophical theory to sell. He is no teacher, and his writing is distinctly post-philosophical: tragedy as he sees it is not a conduit for another order of truth, but an emancipation from the dead hands of philosophy and theology. Rather, my hope is that Heidegger's Dasein can function as a heuristic through which to cast Shakespeare's achievement into sharper and more revealing relief. In *Hamlet*, Shakespeare makes the case—one he will make over and again in the first decade of the seventeenth century—for tragedy as the best and perhaps only medium through which one might discern what it is to be human. This is because tragic art of the sort that Shakespeare attempted in *Hamlet* insists on two things. First, the fundamental unity of human reason and emotion. This unity is affirmed both in the language through which the inhabitants of his Elsinore shape their thoughts, and in their commitment to fictions of one sort or another through which to make sense of their world—fictions that frequently lead them into error, misprision, and suffering. Second, that we in the audience recognize our responses to the play as the products of the same intellectual and emotional unity, and as prone to the same errors of interpretation, conviction, and belief. Tragedy yields up the horizon within which we are most fully able to examine who and what we are; thinking through dramatic fiction frees us from the pretense of understanding more than we do, and allows us to discern why this pretense is so stubbornly widespread. Even if we don't regard Hamlet's "to be, or not to be" as the solecism that its humanistic contexts imply, from this perspective it begs the question. For *Hamlet*, the real topic of inquiry is whether we are able to arrive at an understanding of human being at all. As Fortinbras's soldiers fire off their pseudo-commemorative "peal of ordnance" for the dead of the Danish royal family, Shakespeare's answer is an exhilaratingly circumscribed, not to say wary, "yes."

CHAPTER FOUR

Being, Wrought

TROILUS AND CRESSIDA AND OTHELLO

> *The heart is deceitful above all things, and desperately wicked:*
> *who can know it?*
>
> —JEREMIAH 17:9

WHAT DO YOU DO AFTER WRITING SOMETHING LIKE *Hamlet*? A play in which you revisit a hoary old piece about a prince, his uncle, and his father the ghost not merely to shatter generic notions of what tragedy can do, but to make contingency and indeterminacy—and the attempts of human beings to deny the matrices of contingency and indeterminacy within which they exist—the true subjects of tragic art. A play in which you have sacrificed theatrical practicality to other imperatives (there is no way that *Hamlet*, in either the folio or second quarto versions of the text, can be performed within what the Prologue to *Romeo and Juliet* calls "the two hours' traffic of our stage" [1.0.12]). Perhaps the most obvious answer is that you might spend some time trying to figure out what, in *Hamlet*, you had done. But as your livelihood and professional status depend on turning out plays for your company to perform, you cannot do so at your leisure: you have to write.

There are so many unknowns (known and unknown) that any chronology of Shakespeare's writings is bound to be a work of creative nonfiction: a heuristic that has its uses, and that retains them for only as long as we do not mistake it for hard fact. But assuming as on balance we can that Shakespeare wrote *Hamlet* in 1599–1600 and that *Othello* was written in 1603–1604, it would—after Fortinbras's peal of ordnance had first been fired off—take between three and four years for Shakespeare to complete another incontestably tragic drama. The interim was occupied with experiments and exploration. With the question of how most effectively to dramatize a world in which all judgments seem to be opinions unmoored, wittingly or unwittingly, from truth. A world in which honor and virtue (whether understood in social or individual terms) seem to function as a fig leaf for appetite; in which humankind is unable, despite its most strenuous efforts, to abstract itself from the flux and the compromises of history and historicity; in which human vanity and weakness and ingenuity make human beings strangers to themselves, to those around them, and to the affective-political-natural worlds to which they for better or worse belong.

The works in which Shakespeare most directly addressed the legacies of *Hamlet* are *Troilus and Cressida, All's Well That Ends Well,* and *Measure for Measure*—though one can also trace their presence in the sonnets, the perplexing allegories of "The Phoenix and the Turtle," and in *Twelfth Night* (which goes further than any of his earlier comedies in exposing the fear and cruelty that lurk behind Plautine festivity). *Troilus, All's Well,* and *Measure for Measure* are usually discussed as "problem" plays on the grounds that none of them fit neatly into the categories of comedy, history, and tragedy within which the contents of the 1623 first folio were arranged. Saying so makes Shakespearean comedy, history, and tragedy sound narrower and more stable than is actually the case, but it can help us to understand these plays as a space in which Shakespeare worked through his evolving senses of tragic possibility.

In other words, after the astonishing achievement of *Hamlet*, Shakespeare presented himself with a problem. It ran roughly as follows: how, without being able to rely on his audience's knowledge of an earlier play like the *Ur-Hamlet*, was he to write tragedy while 1) disavowing the paraphernalia of Aristotelian tragic unity, and 2) maintaining artistic control over plot, characterization, and the kinds of language in which his characters speak? How, as he had done in *Hamlet*, was he to find a mode of writing tragic drama that simultaneously engaged the emotions and intellect of his audiences—that made them see how emotive even the most intellectually abstract forms of thought must be—while taking as his raw materials the words and deeds of dramatis personae whose emotions lead them into error, and whose errors lead them into forms of suffering that do not occasion much in the way of recognition or acknowledgment? It would have been relatively easy to write satire with such concerns in mind, and there are certainly satiric elements in all of the so-called "problem" plays. What was harder by far was to treat this sort of subject matter while aspiring to the tragic goals of fear, pity, wonder, and *catharsis*. *Othello,* swiftly followed by *Macbeth* and *King Lear*, would not have been possible without a great deal of preparatory labor.

Other than *Othello* itself, my focus in this chapter is on *Troilus and Cressida*. The reasons for this are several, and go beyond considerations of verbal economy. *Troilus* is the play that Shakespeare most likely wrote straight after *Hamlet*. Although the title pages of its 1609 first printed editions proclaim it as a history, and although the publisher's preface to the second of these 1609 editions describes it a comedy, it is the only one of the three "problem" plays that John Heminges and Henry Condell, the compilers of the first folio, seem to have bracketed as a tragedy. Most importantly, in its preoccupation with the gap between the ideals and something like the reality of romantic love, of warfare, of conquest, of honor, and of self-knowledge—in its determination to literalize the Ovidian topos, a staple for Petrarch and his heirs, that *militat omnis amans* ("all lovers are soldiers")—*Troilus and Cressida* shares more than the Eastern Mediterranean with the story of Iago, Othello, and Desdemona.[1] Dryden is right to observe that the play falls short when measured against conventional critical theory: although "the Author seems to have begun it with some fire . . . the latter part of the Tragedy is nothing but a confusion of Drums and Trumpets, Excursions and Alarms. The chief persons, who give name to the Tragedy, are left alive; *Cressida* is false, and is not punish'd."[2] What seems not to have occurred to Dryden is that these imputed flaws are a part of Shakespeare's design, and that—as in *Othello* and all the other plays treated in this book—this design answers to Shakespeare's emergent and never-settled notions of what tragedy can and cannot, should and should not, seek to accomplish.

———

Troilus and Cressida opens with a Prologue gesturing to the stage around him. He addresses the audience in the stateliest and most heightened manner:

> In Troy there lies the scene. From isles of Greece
> The princes orgulous, their high blood chafed,
> Have to the port of Athens sent their ships
> Fraught with the ministers and instruments
> Of cruel war. (1.0.1–5)

One imagines a certain kind of humanist sounding his approval of "princes orgulous," just as Shakespeare has Polonius and Hamlet do over "mobbled queen." The Prologue goes on to rehearse the familiar tale of the Trojan war: Helen (wife of the Spartan King Menelaus) has eloped with Paris (son of the Trojan King Priam), and a coalition of Greek states have waged war to get her back. The Greeks are now laying siege to Troy:

> And hither am I come,
> A Prologue armed, but not in confidence
> Of author's pen or actor's voice, but suited
> In like conditions as our argument,
> To tell you, fair beholders, that our play
> Leaps o'er the vaunt and firstlings of those broils,
> Beginning in the middle, starting thence away
> To what may be digested in a play. (1.0.22–29)

The audience is informed that the play it is about to witness will begin in medias res—like most ancient tragedies, like Homeric and Virgilian epic, and just as Horace's *Ars poetica* recommends. Which is to say, in the thick of the action, and not ab ovo, or from the actual beginning of the story it seeks to represent.[3] A copybook formulation, but one that is shot through with paradox: a play that begins with a prologue declaring that it is about to begin in medias res does not in fact begin in medias res. (Compare the opening scene of *Hamlet*, or those of *Othello*, *Macbeth*, and *King Lear*.) What soon becomes apparent is that, in *Troilus and Cressida*, Shakespeare has established another ironic relationship between a dramatic frame and the action that it encloses. The matter, or *res*, that is "digested" within the main body of the play has only the most fleeting resemblance to the *verba*—the stylized evocation of heroic conflict—through which it has been introduced. It follows that when the action gets under way, we notice with more of a jolt than might otherwise have been the case that in this Troy, heroism exists as something between a chimera and a sham. We are also alerted to one of the play's primary concerns: the discrepancy between, on the one hand, the ways in which we might think about and discuss the world and, on the other, the dynamics of that world as, within Shakespeare's tragic vision, it appears to exist.

Once the Prologue has left the stage, we are introduced to two men— one several years younger than the other. The younger man is Troilus, and believes himself to be unworthy of the battlefield on account of being weakened by the "cruel battle" (1.1.4) taking place within his heart. The older man, Pandarus, is the uncle of "fair Cressid" (1.1.28); that is, the woman who is the cause of Troilus's embattled heart. Pandarus counsels patience, before growing irritated with Troilus's lovestruck verbiage and his failure to acknowledge the pains that he, Pandarus, has already taken to go "between and between" (1.1.69) in the attempt to bring Troilus and Cressida together. He departs, leaving Troilus to soliloquize on his miserable plight: "O gods, how you do plague me! / I cannot come to Cressid but by Pandar, / And he's as tetchy to be wooed to woo / As she is stubborn-chaste against all suit" (1.1.90–93). He is cut short by a call to arms and the arrival of his kinsman and commander Aeneas, who demands to know why he is not "afield"—that is, out fighting the Greeks in a suitably valorous fashion. Troilus responds simply "because not there," before condemning himself as "womanish" for saying so. Aeneas then informs him that Paris has been injured on the field of battle by Menelaus—the Spartan king to whom Helen had been married before her elopement. Troilus jokes that this wound from a cuckold's horn can be no more than "a scar to scorn," and the two nobles resolve to transport themselves "in all swift haste" to where the action is (1.1.101–12). There is little heroic about this exchange (Troilus lost in amorous self-pity, Aeneas absent for unstated reasons of his own), or about the conflict with which it is concerned. The rivalry between Paris and Menelaus for the affections of Helen—that is, the casus belli—is a subject for awkwardly sardonic humor rather than respect or reverence. And yet, the awkwardness does not detain them for long; the only thing that matters is the chance provided by the war to make a show of their masculine virtue. Whatever else these voices articulate, it is not *pietas* or nobly purposive duty. If there is muddled thinking in asserting romantic love as the enemy of masculine heroism while simultaneously embracing the chance to display that masculine heroism in a conflict arising from the vagaries of romantic love, then Troilus and Aeneas pay it no heed.

It is easy to see in *Troilus and Cressida* a critique of the ideals that have often been found within Homer's *Iliad*—a critique that is likely to reflect Shakespeare's engagement with the "ironic" Homer presented in George Chapman's translation of the *Iliad*, the first instalment of which was published in 1598. We might also compare the pointedly agnostic account of heroic valor given in Ariosto's *Orlando furioso*, where the English knight Astolfo, after making a successful voyage to the moon, questions a fictionalized version of St. John the Apostle about the ways of the world. John tells him that although he admired poets (and counted himself one of their number), they tended to overdo it when memorializing their subjects: "Perhapps *Eneas* was not so devout, / Nor *Hector* nor *Achilles* were so brave, / But thousands have as honest been and stout / And worthie by desert more prayse to have." And as Ariosto's list of heroes suggests (Aeneas has a not insignificant part in the *Iliad*, but becomes the central figure of Rome's poetic self-image), such doubts about the virtues of hero-ism, and of the heroic models depicted in ancient literature, were by no means confined to the Homeric tradition.[4]

But by sharing in such skepticism, *Troilus and Cressida* does more than assert the currency of weakness, and wishful thinking, through the ages. It also calls into question the origin myths of Rome and, more significantly for a work written in London at the beginning of the seventeenth century, Brit-ain. On one frequently repeated account, derived from Geoffrey of Mon-mouth's pseudo-historical *History of the Kings of Britain* and enshrined in Holinshed's *Chronicle*, Britain was founded by Aeneas's grandson or great-grandson, Brutus. Who, in the words of Spenser's *Faerie Queene*, redeemed Albion from the offspring of its "native slime," renamed it Brit-ain, and "raigned long in great felicity, / Lov'd of his freends, and of his foes eschewed." Half a century after Henry VIII had severed connections with the papacy, the time had come—or so the story went—for Britain to reclaim its true status as the deutero-Rome. Unlike several of his contemporaries, Shakespeare does not trouble the historicity of this argument. Instead, he offers something more incisive by far: the implication that such origins are nothing to be proud of. In *Troilus and Cressida*, the "roiall stock" (Spenser again) of ancient Troy is no more or less upstanding than anyone else, then or now. It is just that, when they put their minds to it, the Trojans were very good at fighting—not unlike the Romans, Angles, Saxons, Jutes, Vikings, and Normans who would later subdue parts of the British Isles.[5]

In brief, the Homeric scene of *Troilus and Cressida* is at all times a palimpsest—and not one in which either Homer or the virtuous Trojan exiles of the *Aeneid* are the main source of the overwriting. The love story of Troilus and Cressida was devised not in antiquity, but by the twelfth-century French poet Benoît de Sainte-Maure as a vehicle through which to meditate on the ideals of chivalry and courtly love. It was later reworked by Boccaccio in his *Il filostrato*, and from there became the basis of Chaucer's courtly romance, *Troilus and Criseyde*—described by Chaucer himself as "litel mine tragedie." Although the fact that *Troilus and Cressida* may have been a response to a lost 1599 play of the same title by Thomas Dekker and Henry Chettle means that it is impossible to be sure, Chaucer seems to have been one of Shakespeare's two principal sources. William Caxton's transla-tion of Raoul Lefèvre's *Recueil des histoires de Troie* is the other.[6]

However it was that Shakespeare encountered the fiction originally conceived by Benoît, he found in it the freedom not just to complicate ancient source material as he had done in *Julius Caesar*, but to imagine the Homeric moment to his own ends. In particular, Benoît allowed him to imagine this setting through ruthlessly subverted versions of (1) chivalry (the author of *Richard II* and the two cycles of the *Henriad* knew well the discrepancy between chivalric ideals and human reality), (2) romantic love, and (3) the humanist moral philosophy that made so much of its borrowings from Greco-Roman tradition.

The distinctiveness of Shakespeare's vision becomes clearer once Aeneas and Troilus rouse themselves to depart. In their absence, we meet Cressida. She is far from being the Petrarchan cipher of whom Troilus has so breathlessly held forth. Her aide, Alexander, describes Ajax to her: "They say he is a very man *per se*, / And stands alone." She immediately shoots back, in prose, that "So do all men, unless they are drunk, sick, or have no legs" (1.2.15–18). Pandarus arrives and does his best to draw out a declaration of his niece's affections—by praising Troilus over Hector, by suggesting that Troilus has caught Helen's eye, and so on. Cressida is wise to his maneuvers, and outwits him with ease. Once Pandarus leaves her—summoned by Troilus, whose martial exertions are now over for the day—she speaks her mind:

> Words, vows, gifts, tears and love's full sacrifice
> He offers in another's enterprise;
> But more in Troilus thousandfold I see
> Than in the glass of Pandar's praise may be.
> Yet hold I off. Women are angels, wooing;
> Things won are done; joy's soul lies in the doing.
> That she beloved knows naught that knows not this:
> Men prize the thing ungained more than it is.
> That she was never yet that ever knew
> Love got so sweet as when desire did sue.
> Therefore this maxim out of love I teach:
> 'Achievement is command; ungained, beseech.' (1.2.273–84)

She is as enamored of Troilus as Troilus himself might wish, and has a far fuller picture of his virtues than that available in "Pandar's praise." She has nevertheless determined to keep her feelings hidden. Not from adherence to a policy of playing hard to get, but because she believes that once she gives herself to Troilus, he will come to view her as she "is." Not, that is, with the eyes of love—not as the intentional object of his desire.

A maxim out of Shakespearean tragedy is that when a character speaks in rhyming couplets, he or she is attempting to create the impression of order, authority, or understanding where it does not exist. (A just about arguable exception: the Fool in *King Lear*.) For all her keenness of perception,

Cressida is trying to convince herself that she has successfully marshaled a cluster of feelings that will, as her obscure syntax already suggests, soon get the better of her good judgment. She is correct to observe that a "she beloved" will fail to understand her position if she fails to understand the nature of the feelings of the one who desires her. But as Cressida speaks, it is what she fails to perceive of herself that is the defining point: her feelings for Troilus have already begun to exceed her ability to govern them. Throughout Shakespeare's comedies, the condition of being in love leads to delusionality, and to the exposure of delusionality in those not ostensibly in love: consider the way in which Theseus's authoritarian rationalism is undercut both by the action of *A Midsummer Night's Dream* and by Hippolyta's rejoinders to his dogmatism. None of this troubles a comic plot. The mania of the lover or the hubris of a Theseus are aberrations from an order that is capacious enough both to harmonize them, and to show awareness of its own artificiality in so doing; this can happen because the plot, howsoever contrived or fanciful it might seem, rests on foundations of moral and cognitive stability. In the tragedies, things are almost exactly reversed. People's beliefs—about love, about heroism, about honor, about virtue, about politics, about blood, about their own emotional and intellectual dispositions—are not only shown to be confused and contingent, cut off from any possibility of extra-dramatic order; they are also the warp and weft from which the plot is woven. These plots may be the only viable principles of order to be found within Shakespeare's tragic playworlds, but their design is to juxtapose and illuminate, not to harmonize or resolve. Sticking for now with *Troilus and Cressida*, Cressida's speech encapsulates a central preoccupation of the play. Even as delusionality and the conditions in which it can arise are acknowledged, the act of acknowledgment involves unacknowledged delusions of its own.

Shakespeare's Ulysses is much too skilled an operator to be caught rhyming, but he too is bound to versions of the delusionality that he would, as he deems fit, expose or exploit. We are introduced to him during the Greek council scene that begins immediately after Cressida has unburdened herself of her thoughts. The Greek commander, Agamemnon, argues against despair at the lack of progress being made against the Trojans, and suggests that—rather than being signs of military ineptitude—they are "naught else / But the protractive trials of great Jove / To find persistive constancy in men" (1.3.19–21). Agamemnon thus appeals to the Senecan and neo-Senecan ideals of *constantia* by which Shakespeare's Brutus had previously set such store: we must show our mettle by bearing the slings and arrows of outrageous fortune with dignity, patience, and philosophical equanimity. And yet Agamemnon's altogether un-Stoic prolixity ("persistive constancy" may not quite be a tautology, but *is* glaringly pleonastic) suggests that we should look more closely. After the elderly Nestor has agreed at length that patience is a good thing, Ulysses is invited to speak. He replies with perhaps the greatest set-piece oration of a play that, as preoccupied with the conditions of rhetorical debate as anything Shakespeare wrote (*King John* strikes me as its only rival), is full to the brim with them.[7]

In it, Ulysses elaborates at length on the ideology of hierarchical order, or what he calls "degree."[8]

> Take but degree away, untune that string,
> And hark what discord follows. . . .
> Force should be right; or rather, right and wrong,
> Between whose endless jar justice resides,
> Should lose their names, and so should justice too.
> Then everything includes itself in power,
> Power into will, will into appetite;
> And appetite, an universal wolf,
> So doubly seconded with will and power,
> Must make perforce an universal prey
> And last eat himself up. (1.3.109–24)

There is little more commonplace in early modern political thought than the belief that without hierarchy of one kind or another, human society would descend into anarchic horror: the "Chain of Being" was a Platonic idea that was readily Christianized and was the principle of order that held the natural and political worlds together. Ulysses works artfully with it, just as he does in pointing to the monarchical commonwealth of bees imagined in book 4 of Virgil's *Georgics* (1.3.81–83) and in elaborating on a version of the Ptolemaic cosmos in which harmony is maintained by the sun as regnant "planet" (1.3.85–94); the latter passage is derived from Cicero's *Dream of Scipio*, well-known in its own right but also the sixth and final book of Cicero's treatise *On the Republic*.[9] (We might observe one benefit conferred by rewriting the Homeric past through the adaptation of a medieval love story: the freedom to put ostensibly anachronistic words in the mouths of one's protagonists. Because the *Dream of Scipio* was known to Chaucer et al., it is known to Shakespeare's Trojans.) So much so humanistic: Ulysses knows how to put his reading to judicious use, and his oration claims further authority by employing so many recognizable topoi and *sententiae* without drawing attention to them. What is more, in the "universal wolf," Ulysses is furnished with a distinctly Shakespearean coup de grâce, an arresting image with which he not only makes his case more vividly, but darkens its moral horizon. By giving in to its animal appetites, humankind will not be destroyed by the wrath of a disappointed deity, but by itself. Not through the duplicity and brute force of a world shaped either by the hunt or the principle of dog-eat-dog, but through a kind of self-consumption. All told, Ulysses speaks well.

But he speaks as he does to the particular end of persuasion. Not to tell the truth as he sees it about the world as it is, but to find the best form of words in which to bend Agamemnon, his ruler and general, to his will. He speaks, that is, against the grain of his argument that those even "one step below" (1.3.130) should simply obey. So it is that if Ulysses muddles the intermediary position of justice within Aristotelian and Ciceronian moral philosophy (it emerges not at the midpoint between "right" and "wrong," but at that between excess and deficiency), it is no great concern. As long as Agamemnon keeps nodding along, all may still be well.[10]

What does Ulysses wish Agamemnon to do? To abandon his Stoic passivity and assert his authority—command Achilles and his Myrmidons back to the battlefield, and take the fight to the Trojans. Troy only endures because "the speciality of rule hath been neglected" (1.3.78). Unfortunately for Ulysses, Agamemnon fails to get the point. Rather than being provoked into asserting himself, he agrees that "this neglection of degree" is indeed a problem, and asks Ulysses to tell him what the "remedy" for it might be (1.3.141). Ulysses continues on the theme of Achilles, going as far as to describe how Achilles's companion Patroclus "pageants us" with "ridiculous and awkward action—/ Which, slanderer, he imitation calls." Patroclus's Agamemnon, on Ulysses's account, involves much strutting around and grandiloquent speechifying: "fusty stuff" (1.3.161). Still, Agamemnon is unmoved. Ulysses and Nestor proceed further to dissect Achilles's disregard for the Greek war council, when the already lengthy scene is interrupted by the arrival of an outsider. Aeneas, no less, come to inform the Greeks that Hector volunteers single combat to anyone brave enough to meet his challenge. Aeneas begins with a question whose elevated tone is at once necessary and utterly incongruous: "Is this great Agamemnon's tent, I pray you?" Agamemnon (without yet revealing his identity) affirms that it is, and adds that Aeneas could feel confident delivering his message to him, because "all the Greekish lords . . . with one voice / Call Agamemnon head and general." Aeneas, not recognizing Agamemnon as the man in charge, demands to know which of the characters before him "is that god in office, guiding men" (1.3.216, 221–22, 231). Despite the courtly language through which it is asserted, Agamemnon's greatness and capacity to lead—let alone his quasi-divinity—are anything other than obvious.

Lest we should miss the charge, Shakespeare quickly reinforces it. After Agamemnon and Aeneas depart amid much chivalric self-congratulation, Ulysses and Nestor confer. Something has to be done about Achilles, and, as Agamemnon is unable to do it, Ulysses maneuvers himself into the breach. By flattering Ajax and putting him into combat with Hector, he will pique Achilles's pride such that he will return to action and bolster the Greek cause: "Ajax employed plucks down Achilles' plumes" (1.3.387). Never mind that this stratagem is at odds with the ideals of order and obedience and harmony advanced in his great oration—these were just words. Powerfully elegant ones, to be sure, but ones that failed to achieve their purpose.

The new plan, to which Agamemnon will reportedly sign up after being briefed by Nestor, works as Ulysses intends. In act 3 scene 1, the Greek leaders visit Achilles's tent in the company of Ajax, and when Achilles refuses to come out, they make a lot of noise in praise of Ajax. A little later, they again walk past Achilles's tent. This time, Achilles stands outside it, and Ulysses arranges things so that they affect not to pay attention to him—in Agamemnon's words, they "put on / A form of strangeness" (3.3.51) as they pass by. Ulysses himself hangs back, occupied with a book or some papers. Stung, Achilles seeks Ulysses's counsel. In response, Ulysses shares with him the substance of his reading, which just so happens to describe the socially-politically situated self that humanist moral philosophers elaborated from Cicero: "Man, how dearly ever parted, / How much in having, or without or in, / Cannot make boast to have that which he hath / Nor feels what he owes, but by reflection" (3.3.97–100). Ulysses continues to praise the "drift" of his anonymous author in making so clear the truth that "no man is the lord of anything, / Though in and of him there by much consisting, / Till he communicate his parts to others, / Nor doth he of himself know them [i.e., his 'parts'] for aught / Till he behold them formed in th' applause" (3.3.116–20).

Unlike Achilles, we in the audience are able to appreciate the irony of Ulysses once again putting the commonplaces of humanist moral philosophy to work. He does so in order to make someone over whom he has no ostensible power do what he wants; not, that is, because he thinks that the *res* of what he is saying is true or valuable, but because the *verba* with which he purports to express this *res* have affective force. And, as luck would have it, Achilles proves himself a better listener than Agamemnon. He quickly grasps that these ideas relate to his predicament ("What, are my deeds forgot?" [3.3.145]; "I see that my reputation is at stake. / My fame is shrewdly gored" [3.3.228–29]), and resolves to reengage—to displace Ajax as the champion of the Greeks. Ulysses's rhetorical performance appears to have been consummate, his psychological insight vindicated by positive results.

While this strand of the plot is working itself out, Shakespeare cuts to Troy. In so doing, he reveals that the Trojans are also humanist moral philosophers of a sort, and that their attitude to their governing philosophy is indistinguishable from that of their Greek foes: a matter of expediency, to be pushed aside when it fails to serve. The most important case in point comes when Hector puts Troilus and Paris in their place for their impolitic rashness—their willingness to allow blood and pride and hunger for glory to cloud their strategic judgment. Troilus and Paris argue that Helen should not be handed back to the Greeks: "What treason it were to the ransacked queen, / Disgrace to your great worths, and shame to me, / Now to deliver her possession up / On terms of base compulsion!" (2.2.150–53). Unimpressed, Hector counters that, for all their chivalric ardor, they have discussed the "question" (again, and as so often in *Hamlet*, a *quaestio*—the subject of a disputation) "but superficially, not much / Unlike young men, whom Aristotle thought / Unfit to hear moral philosophy. / The reasons you allege do more conduce / To the hot passion of distempered blood / Than to make up a free determination / 'Twixt right and wrong" (2.2.164–71).

Although there is something coruscating in the inverted parallelism of Trojans citing Greeks immediately after Greeks have been quoting Romans, my interest does not lie in the anachronism of Hector seeking to make some of Aristotle's authority his own. Nor does it lie in Aristotle's conviction that, as politics was the exclusive province of mature males, only they could achieve mastery of moral philosophy as a whole (the three constituent parts of which were ethics, oeconomics, and politics), central though this belief was to early modern education and gender relations alike. Rather, the force of the dramatic charge that manifests itself as Hector talks on is that his words, considered though they seem to be, are a beard for sentiments that he would prefer not directly to confront. Beginning his peroration, he switches briefly to the third person and declares that "Hector's opinion / Is this [i.e., that Helen should be returned to the Greeks] in way of truth; yet, ne'ertheless, / My sprightly bretheren, I propend to you / In resolution to keep Helen still; / For 'tis a cause that hath no mean dependence / Upon our joint and several dignities" (2.2.188–93). He *propends*, no less: an inkhorn Latinism that beautifully captures the solemnity with which he would like to be heard. "No mean dependence" is likewise a fine example of litotes (the figure of speech that affirms something by denying its contrary) being used in the sense recommended by the rhetorical handbooks: to give the impression of authoritative calmness and disinterest. And yet for all Hector's loftiness, his "resolution" turns out to be coextensive with that of Troilus and Paris. Helen is to be kept and fought for because returning her to the Greeks would involve a loss of face. Against the reality of this "opinion," "the way of truth" calls for elaborately honorific language, but can command no obedience.[11]

It is this commitment to his eloquently chivalric self-image that will, in due course, lead to Hector's demise. Determined to engage in single combat with the best of the Greeks—and in lieu of this, to fight and kill lesser Greeks in a manner of his own choosing—he fails to observe the dynamics of the battlefield on which he seeks to present himself, is surprised by Achilles and his Myrmidons, and is hacked unceremoniously to death. But *Troilus and Cressida* is concerned with more than the unworldly worldliness of those who seek dignity or glory in military confrontation. Ulysses's sophisticated exercises in pretense and quasi-Machiavellian statecraft, like those of Claudius and Richard III before him, fare little better. Despite Ulysses's demonstrable intelligence, they comprise an attempt to impose order on the hugely complicated relationships of causation that are the *res* of events as they play out in history—relationships that he does not, in fact, comprehend. Yes, Ulysses successfully manipulates Achilles, but when Achilles joins the fray it is because Hector has killed Patroclus; what is more, Achilles does so in a way that cannot but disfigure the plots of Ulysses's strategic imagination. Even before the play's denouement, Thersites is moved to observe that "the policy of those crafty swearing rascals—that stale old mouse-eaten dry cheese, Nestor, and that same dog-fox, Ulysses—is proved not worth a blackberry." The Greeks may or may not win their fight against the Trojans, but they have begun to "proclaim barbarism"—to prefer ignorant noise over peaceably civilized wisdom (5.4.8–15).

In this light, it is tempting to view *Troilus and Cressida* as a satire on human folly, arrogance, and delusionality. On the belief of these purportedly heroic characters that their misconceived notions of themselves and of the moral world around them reflect things as they really are. This idea has much to recommend it. To paraphrase a famous line from Juvenal's first *Satire*, in a place like Shakespeare's Troy it is very hard *not* to write satire. The play is shot through with satiric *contaminatio*, and other than the rebarbative figure of Thersites, the only people to show the slightest awareness of the compromised situation in which both Trojans and Greeks find

themselves are women. Not unlike Portia in *Julius Caesar*, they are therefore ignored or traduced on the basis that, like the "young men . . . unfit to
hear moral philosophy," they have not yet learned to govern their emotions.
Cassandra's prophetic visions do not correspond with what her family wish
to hear; Andromache's concern for Hector's safety is dismissed as tremulous
nonsense; and Cressida's refusal to paper over the gap between the rhetoric
and the reality of romantic love is enough to have her written off as a mer-
etricious piece of work—by Ulysses, by Thersites, and eventually by Troilus.
Everyone else carries on regardless. As Thersites puts it, taking his cue from
a line in which Horace uses the Trojan war to reflect on the barbarity of the
human condition before civilization had come to pass, "All the argument is
a whore and a cuckold; a good quarrel to draw emulous factions and bleed
to death upon" (2.3.69–71). All the argument *is* a whore and a cuckold, note:
Helen and Menelaus, appraised according to the values of their peers, are
transformed into the symbolic objects over which so many others will dispute, fight, die, and strive to make themselves into symbols of honor, valor,
bravery, and so on. Like everyone else, Helen and Menelaus matter on
account of their status within the *theatrum mundi*; as devices within a
plot scripted by an author or authors unknown.[12]

But a narrowly satirical reading will not do. Thersites, the verbally
dexterous embodiment of the satirist as angry outsider, is a railing nui-
sance rather than a scourge of vice or a physician restoring the body politic
to health with his scalpel and harsh medicines. One, in short, reduced to
playing the part of the satirist, and whose offensiveness is so much less
than truly shocking that, as in Erasmus's *Adages*, he becomes a commonplace or a type. As the play finishes, he is nowhere to be seen. His part is
taken by Pandarus, now scorned by Troilus as a "broker-lackey" (5.11.33).
Rather than speaking an epilogue infused with satiric ire, he laments the
hypocrisy of those—including his "brethren and sisters" in the audience
(5.11.51)—who would enjoin the services of amatory or sexual go-betweens
before, their usefulness gone, moralizing them to shame. For Philip Sidney, Juvenalian satire (which he calls "iambic") is "bitter but wholesome,"
and "rubs the galled mind in making shame the trumpet of villainy, with
bold and open crying out against naughtiness." In place of remedies, Pandarus promises their antithesis: contagion, and contagion alone. Departing for now to "sweat and seek about for eases," he taunts his audience
that he will return to "bequeath you my diseases" (5.11.55–56). More often
than not, satire is written from a conservative standpoint: the decadence
of the present is revealed through its juxtaposition with a vision of some
more upright past; less frequently, satire is the medium of the idealistic

reformer, damning the decadent present by measuring it against a prospective future of greater justice, equity, grace, or honor. Even a Menippean satire like Erasmus's *Praise of Folly*, relentless in its seriously playful exposition of human weakness, rests on a clear sense of what humankind *is*, the better to prescribe the Christlike humility through which it should comprehend and perhaps redeem itself. In Shakespeare's depiction of Troy, there is no such fixity of moral and political vision. In its absence, Shakespeare presents a grotesquely ironized parody of satire, perhaps even of satire as written by rival playwrights like John Marston and Ben Jonson.[13]

It is not only satire that Pandarus's final words undercut. On one influential reading of Aristotle's *Poetics*, the arousal of fear and pity in tragic drama creates the conditions for *catharsis* as a kind of purgation (or purification) of the emotions and soul. Or, in Sidney's vivid phrase, it is tragedy "that openeth the greatest wounds, and showeth forth the ulcers that are covered with tissue"—the better to set about treating and healing them.[14] As I argued in chapter 1, Shakespeare did not have much time for these theories; the threat of contagion rather than purgation at the end of *Troilus and Cressida* tends strongly to confirm the point. But I also proposed that Shakespeare was concerned to generate tragic *catharsis* in another sense. One in which, after Martha Nussbaum, the end of tragedy is clarification, and not purgation or purification. Shakespeare wants us not only to see ourselves, but to see the ways in which we see ourselves: to acknowledge our status as beings whose emotional dispositions are inherent to the ways in which they can know or understand, and whose knowledge and understanding (of themselves, of other people, of the world) is on this account always imperfect.[15] Troilus is not drawn on a scale comparable to those of Brutus and Hamlet, but in the great scene outside Calchas's tent—where the headstrong, anxious lover disintegrates before our eyes— Shakespeare limns the possibilities of tragic clarification in fine miniature.

When it becomes clear that Troilus and Cressida will have to part from one another if the Greeks are to release Antenor from his imprisonment, they exchange vows and tokens of their mutual and heavily idealized love. Cressida leaves for the Greek camp, to which her father (a Trojan priest) has defected after having a premonitory vision of Trojan defeat. Shortly afterward, Troilus finds himself with the opportunity to test her fidelity. In the company of Ulysses, and with Thersites trailing a little behind, he follows Diomedes to Calchas's tent. Things do not turn out as Troilus might have hoped. Cressida, flattered by Diomedes's interest, enjoys flirting with him while putting up a show of resistance—before abandoning her vows to Troilus, handing Diomedes the token that Troilus had given to her to mark his devotion, and entreating Diomedes to come again to her tent. (It is also possible that they kiss: at one point Cressida says that "I kiss thee" [5.2.87], but she is probably addressing the token—a sleeve—that Troilus gave to her and that she passes on to Diomedes.)

The scene is refracted through a series of dramatic frames. We watch Thersites watching Troilus and Ulysses watching Diomedes and Cressida. Each of them, in their turn, performs for and carefully watches the another. The primary frame belongs to Thersites's acerbic commentary, and as so often in the satiric tradition, he maintains that sexual appetite lies at the root of all corruption. And, as women are the embodiment of sexual appetite (both as objects to be desired and as beings less able to control their sexual urges), so they bear particular responsibility for the corruptions of the world. After Cressida reflects with an insight that is part-rueful, part-resigned on her inability to deny the force of her feelings for Diomedes ("the error of our eye directs our mind. / What error leads must err" [5.2.116–17]), Thersites hears only one thing: "A proof of strength she could not publish more, / Unless she said, 'My mind is now turned whore'" (5.2.119–20). By contrast, when he condemns Diomedes, it is as no more than a habitually dishonest "rogue" (5.1.86, 5.2.197). Meanwhile, when Troilus tries and fails to make sense of what he is seeing—to reconcile the Cressida from whom he parted with the Cressida before him—Thersites is incredulous. "Will 'a swagger [i.e., bluster] himself out on's own eyes?" (5.2.142–43): he is a dupe in the making. The entire episode serves to confirm Thersites's estimation of the low motives that, for the most part unacknowledged, animate the chivalric mode: "Lechery, lechery, still wars and lechery; nothing else holds fashion" (5.2.201–3).

But rather than stripping things down to their essentials, Thersites's satirical preoccupations get in the way. Putting to one side his censorious verdict on Cressida (one shared by many later critics of the play—who, like Dryden, seem aggrieved that Shakespeare doesn't kill her off for the sin of moving on), he fails to grasp what happens to Troilus. Let me try to sketch what that is. On one level, he becomes aware that the idealized Petrarchanism through which he has conceived of his relationship with Cressida is a fiction. Pleasant as far as it goes, but unequal to the situation in which he finds himself. The kind of bookish enthusiasm out of which, in a comedy, a Rosalind would gently but firmly educate her lover. But Troilus's pain is not simply a matter of having to figure things out for himself, any more than it is one of having been unlucky in love: he undergoes a cognitive-psychological breakdown. This matters to *Troilus and Cressida* because it illuminates the ways in which almost everybody in the play tries, and ultimately fails, to bring their worlds to order.

The scene is Shakespearean tragedy in the raw, though as Colin Burrow has observed, it has a distinctly non-tragic point of origin: the Roman comedy of Plautus's *The Braggart Soldier*.[16] Here, Sceledrus the slave catches sight of his master's unwilling partner (Philocomasium) kissing her true love, but because the cunning Philocomasium gaslights him so effectively, he comes to doubt the evidence of his eyes: "I didn't see her and yet I did see her," "this is and is not her." Always alert to the *insigne verbum* that could serve as the germ for writing of his own, Shakespeare sees the potential in having a more textured character—more textured, that is, than a gullible fool like Sceledrus—experience similar doubts. In *Hamlet*, he began to explore the propensity of human beings to behold "things" in accordance with their beliefs and needs: I say spirit of health, you say goblin damned; he says my father's spirit, she says the very coinage of my brain. In Troilus's response to what he sees in Calchas's tent, Shakespeare takes this a stage further. To the point at which a character becomes conscious of the reality that he may not, in fact, be equipped to experience the world in anything other than a distortion.

Troilus's first burden is that he must not speak. He is present where he shouldn't be, and not even Ulysses would be able to save him from lethal danger if he were to be discovered. "I will not speak a word," he twice declares as Ulysses urges him to leave before his anguish "break[s] out": "There is between my will and all offences / A guard of patience" (5.2.46–56). A little later, as Cressida departs to fetch Diomedes a token of her affection for him, Ulysses reminds Troilus of his promise. Troilus reassures him that there is nothing to fear ("I will not be myself, nor have cognition / Of what I feel. I am all patience" [5.2.64–66]), only to blurt, "O beauty, where is thy faith?" when Cressida returns with his sleeve (5.2.69). Ulysses remonstrates again, and Troilus reaffirms that "I will be patient; outwardly I will" (5.2.71). From this point onward, he is as good as his word—but, as his "outwardly" suggests, doing so comes at a cost. Constrained to silence, he cannot remonstrate, distract himself, or rationalize the pain away, cannot evade or mitigate an experience that rips apart the fabric of who and what he takes himself to be.

Once Cressida and Diomedes have parted, Troilus asks Ulysses if they can stay awhile. Ulysses is perplexed, so Troilus explains that he wants

To make a recordation to my soul
Of every syllable that here was spoke.

But if I tell how these two did co-act,
Shall I not lie in publishing a truth?
Sith yet there is a credence in my heart,
An esperance so obstinately strong,
That doth invert th'attest of eyes and ears,
As if those organs had deceptious functions,
Created only to caluminate.
Was Cressid here? (5.2.122–31)

This opening sentiment is uncomplicated. As Troilus distrusts the ability of his memory (one of the so-called "internal senses") to retain an impression of what he has beheld, he turns to the practice of recollection (the two standard Latin terms for which are *recordatio* and *reminiscentia*) as a rational and therefore less vulnerable way of fixing the past in his mind. This idea mirrors the conceptual basis on which the so-called "art of memory" depends; Troilus's deployment of it is akin to Hamlet asserting control over the "book and volume" of his brain while processing the revelations that had just been shared with him by the Ghost.[17]

From here onward, things get disorienting. Troilus worries that if he were to use his powers of reasoning to make an accurate mental note of what he has seen, he would simultaneously "lie" by betraying the "credence in [his] heart"—his conviction that the woman he takes himself to love could never behave in such a manner. What is more, it soon becomes apparent that the "credence" that makes him doubt the evidence of his eyes and ears is not, or not only, the result of his grand passion for Cressida. Instead, it arises from his solicitousness to protect his notion of "womanhood" from Cressida's behavior. That is, to protect "the general sex"—virtuous, simple, loyal, loving, and obedient creatures (this is one of the few scenes in *Troilus and Cressida* that makes no mention of dogs)—from the taint of guilt by association. And this image is itself the product of his rational faculties, of his reading in Petrarchan romance and humanist moral philosophy. As he continues:

O, madness of discourse,
That cause set up with and against itself!
Bifold authority, where reason can revolt
Without perdition, and loss assume all reason
Without revolt! This is and is not Cressid. (5.2.149–53)

The "madness" of the first line ironically echoes his earlier insistence that there was "no taste of madness" in his suspicion that Cressida had not been present before him. "Discourse" requires a little more work. Troilus does not just speak of his capacity for speaking or for communicating through language, but of the power of mind that—in almost all early modern accounts of the subject—made possible the higher kinds of linguistic activity, such as the pursuit and recognition of truth, the discovery of the causes of things, self-governance and the governance of the polity, and so on. What, in a more formal locution, was called "discourse of reason." Accordingly, when Hector upbraids Troilus for his passionate determination to defend Helen's honor whatever the cost, he wonders whether Troilus's "blood" is "so madly hot that no discourse of reason" can "qualify" it (2.2.115–17). Preaching the gospel of rational self-mastery that he will presently disavow in the name of the Trojans' "joint and several dignities," Hector asserts the capacity of a particular segment of society (well-educated males) to regulate their own emotions and enhance their understandings. Such was the dividing line between higher (elite male) and lower (everyone else, but especially women and children) forms of human existence, as also between human and animal forms of life: recall Hamlet's criticism of Gertrude's over-hasty remarriage: "A beast that wants discourse of reason / Would have mourn'd longer" (1.5.103).[18]

In contrast with Hector, the most striking feature of Troilus's attitude to reason is not that he is worried about its overthrow by his passions, but that he sees it as self-conflicted and thus as no guide. Having vouchsafed his apprehensions with "recordation" rather than simple memory, he *knows* what he has seen, but what he has seen conflicts fundamentally with what he *knows* of Cressida and womankind in general. In short, the pain of beholding Cressida and Diomedes leaves him floundering because it takes from him the capacity to arbitrate truth or knowledge. If both the positions he wants to hold are rational, then reason cannot help and everything becomes a matter of opinion; not a position of enforced ignorance as such, but one in which the question of whether all views are equally true or equally false is a matter of taste, or perhaps rather "distasted with the salt of broken tears" (4.4.47). The *verba* of truth-telling and virtue and honor and knowledge are detached from the *res* that, in Troilus's estimation, had invested them with meaning—a condition that Troilus's vividly but imperfectly rhetorical presentation of his crisis (he conflates Ovid's Arachne and Ariadne in "Ariachne's broken woof" [5.2.159]) only tends to accentuate.[19] For one who, like Troilus, likes to regard himself as a simple soul courageously committed to the simple verities that make the world go round ("I am as true as truth's simplicity, / And simpler than the infancy of truth" [3.2.164–65]), it's all too much to bear. He flinches, and in place of his amatory self-image, he starts to conceive of himself as an agent of quasi-heroic revenge: "As much as I do Cressid love, / So much by weight I hate her Diomed. / That sleeve is mine that he'll bear in his helm. / Were it a casque composed by Vulcan's skill, / My sword should bite it" (5.2.174–78).

When, shortly thereafter, Pandarus hands Troilus a letter from Cressida, he casts it aside: "Words, words, mere words, no matter from the heart" (5.4.107). Petrarch is forsaken along with Cressida. Shakespeare, however, has other outcomes in mind. Irate though Troilus might be, he and Diomedes do little more than chase one another around ineffectually in what might easily look like a farce. Then the defenseless Hector is slaughtered and his corpse dragged indecorously across the field of battle, and Diomedes is forgotten. It is Troilus who reports the loss to the Trojans, announcing that "Hector is dead. There is no more to say" (5.11.22). A powerfully respectful claim, but an exaggeration: he carries on for nine further lines before resolving that "hope of revenge shall hide our inward woe" (5.11.31). In Chaucer, Achilles makes short work of the ardent young Trojan; Shakespeare is not so explicit, but things are poised to end as badly for Troilus as they do for most stage revengers of the 1590s and 1600s. This note of terminal bathos, and of deferral, is confirmed by Pandarus and his contagious diseases. The picture is bleak. Like the play's original audiences at the Inns of Court, we are left to make of it what we will.

On most measures, *Othello* is a more successful work of art than *Troilus and Cressida*. It is certainly a tighter and more emotionally immersive tragedy, and has enjoyed a vastly higher profile in the theater and the classroom than what is, in my estimation, Shakespeare's most intellectually demanding play. The collisions between Othello and Desdemona ("Why, what are thou?" [4.2.34]) will always arouse more pity and fear than the spectacle of Troilus's voyeuristically clenched anguish. What both works have in common is subject matter. Love in a military climate, where the delusions and trials of the lovers stand in synecdochical relation to the delusions and trials of societies whose fixation on public virtues (*honestas*, *decorum*, heroism, glory, the rest) leaves truth, and value more generally, indistinguishable from opinion. The differences between the two plays are real enough, but are those of style and design; especially, the pattern of characterization within the design. For all the duplicity and shortsightedness on display in *Troilus and Cressida*, the characters' motives are seldom either secret or obscure. In *Othello*, by contrast, nobody—not even the ruthlessly discerning Iago—fully understands why they feel and behave as they do. If *Troilus and Cressida* is a study in the corrosive inadequacy of heroic-chivalric honor, then *Othello* is a study in the harmful effects of *honestas* in the round.

Shakespeare's skill with beginnings is further in evidence. *Othello* opens not with the choric paradoxes of *Troilus and Cressida*, but actually in medias res. The scene is an urban street at nighttime. In the dark, two men are arguing. The first man appears to have just been informed of something disagreeable by the second: "Tush, never tell me." He continues: "I take it much unkindly / That thou, Iago, who has had my purse / As if the strings were thine, shouldst know of this." This Iago, probably wearing a military uniform, responds with a spirited self-vindication: "'Sblood [i.e., God's blood], but you'll not hear me. If ever I did dream / Of such a matter, abhor me" (1.1.1–4). In addition to the different choices of second person pronoun (the first man addresses Iago with the informal "thou," Iago addresses him with the formal "you"), the first man's suggestion that Iago has been in his pay affirms that the relationship between them is transactional. One of service. But we are given no clue as to what "this," what *res* ("such a matter"), has so exercised Iago and the man to whom he seems tied.

Rather than have someone explain, Shakespeare has the unnamed man change tack: "Thou told'st me / Thou didst hold him in thy hate" (1.1.5–6). Iago replies with an assurance that this is, in fact, the case: "Despise me / If I do not" (1.1.7–8). To support the point, he details exactly why he so dislikes this third, unnamed, man. Iago is a solider who believes himself to have been unjustly passed over for promotion—despite arranging for representations on his behalf from "three great ones of this city." It is the senior military officer who refused this promotion that he so lavishly hates—the more so as he refused it on account of his "own pride and purposes," and speaks "with a bombast circumstance / Horribly stuffed with epithets of war." The senior officer preferred a different sort of candidate: "One Michael Cassio, a Florentine," who "never set squadron in the field / Nor the division of a battle knows / More than a spinster—unless the bookish theoric / Wherein the toged consuls can propose / As masterly as he. Mere prattle without practice / Is all his soldiership." Although the officer has with "his eyes . . . seen the proof" of Iago's skill and valor, it is as nothing: he only cares for cosmetic appeal in his subordinates, not military prowess. So it is that Cassio "must his lieutenant be / And I, God bless the mark, his Moorship's ancient!" (1.1.19–32)—"ancient," as in the "ancient Pistoll" of the *Henry IV* plays and *Henry V*, is another term for ensign or standard-bearer, a significantly lower rank than that of lieutenant.

The critique of those who mistake *verba* for *res* is unambiguous. But Iago's words also index one of what will soon emerge as the many imponderables of his character: in attacking the superficiality of his superior officer's judgment, Iago's own judgment is unrelentingly superficial. We are given chapter and verse on Michael Cassio's background and shortcomings, but of the one who prefers him over Iago we are told only that he answers to his "own pride and purposes," that his delivery can be over-orotund, and that he is imperceptive. We are not even told his name, and have to make do with a sneering neologism that, more likely than not, suggests that he is the possessor of darker skin than the two men we are observing: "his Moorship." (In early modern English, "Moor" is an exonym for the inhabitants of Islamic North Africa west of Egypt; what we now think of as the Maghreb, and what was then more commonly referred to as "Barbary.") Nor have we been given any idea as to why the unnamed man to whom Iago answers is so exercised by his dislike of this officer. Perhaps Shakespeare's initial audiences would have inferred that "his Moorship" should be regarded as a diabolical creature akin to Aaron in *Titus Andronicus* or Ithamore in Marlowe's *Jew of Malta*; if we did not now know the story of *Othello* so well, perhaps we would infer the same.[20]

Shakespeare will in due course turn all such inferences on their head. But first, he makes his audiences wait. Rather than offering up new information about the object of the two confederates' enmity, he has Iago push on. The other man says and does little, other than to confirm that he is a long way out of his depth.

Insisting that he sticks with "the Moor" (1.1.39) not from love or loyalty or service, Iago declares that "I follow him to serve my turn upon him" (1.1.41). Thus begins one of the most darkly vertiginous speeches that Shakespeare wrote, in which Iago's "I" and "my" are simultaneously destabilized and made the center of the action that is about to unfold before us; in which Iago, at once an actor and a playwright, shows himself to be the impersonator of the self that he has forged as his own. Disdaining those "duteous and knee-crooking knave[s]" who wear themselves out for their masters' ease (1.1.44), he professes himself one of those who throw "but shows of service on their lords," and who "do well thrive by them" (1.1.51–52). He continues:

> For, sir,
> It is as sure as you are Roderigo [finally, the other man has a name],
> Were I the Moor, I would not be Iago.
> In following him I follow but myself:

Heaven is my judge, not I for love and duty
But seeming so, for my peculiar end,
For when my outward action doth demonstrate
The native act and figure of my heart
In complement extern, 'tis not long after
But I will wear my heart upon my sleeve
For daws to peck at: I am not what I am. (1.1.54–64)

At first glance, one might mistake this for a declaration of stage villainy; a Richard Gloucester confiding in his offstage audience that he has the wherewithal to smile, and murder while he smiles. Iago reiterates that he only follows "the Moor" to his own ends, and that any displays of "love and duty" that Roderigo might observe will be but "seeming." And yet, it is not just that Iago follows "the Moor" to his own ends. What he discloses is that "in following him I follow but myself"—leaving his listeners to infer that this self is less enabled by subterfuge and self-conscious pretense than it is defined by it. Iago likes to make much of his hardheaded Machiavellianism (or Machiavel-ism): his commitment to doing whatever is necessary to line his own pockets and to make life miserable for "the Moor." But this speech shows him to be a character as attracted to posturing—to a species of moral vanity—as any of those he disdains. Despite his professions of Machiavellianism, the ends are immaterial. The means are all. Without them, without being able to revel in the practices of pretense and deceit, he would be obliged to make plain his motives and inner disposition, which would in its turn lead to his destruction.

Why? Because he lives in a world governed by the nostrums of Ciceronian-humanist *honestas* and *decorum*, within which self-knowledge is measured by an individual's capacity to perform—to inhabit—one socially sanctioned *persona* or another. He sees as clearly as, say, Shakespeare that this is an inadequate way of proceeding, but is bound to it. Bound to it in angry opposition, but bound to it even so. Iago knows what he isn't, and is untroubled by these shortcomings. But he is reduced to sophistry in order to avoid a confrontation with the truth that who and what he is eludes him. A character like Edmund in *King Lear* might be guilty of, in Bacon's terms, simulation (pretending to be what one is not) or dissimulation (pretending not to be what one is).[21] For Iago, however, pretense is not a choice designed to cover his tracks or advance his interests. Instead, and at the most fundamental level, it is the only way in which he can make the *res* and the *verba* of his identity cohere. Like Brutus and Claudius and Hamlet before him, Iago struggles to move beyond the reality that he is constrained to representations—to the *personae*—in the effort to understand himself. The best he can do is to adopt *personae* that take pretense as both their form and their substance. "I am not what I am" is a striking enough proclamation in the mouth of the cross-dressed Viola in *Twelfth Night*, but things are yet more performative here.[22] Iago gives out that he is in touch with his that within which passes show, but—unlike Viola—he is dissembling; the claim has no more weight than his later efforts to account for his actions by posing as an agent of hell (1.3.402–3, 2.3.345–48).[23]

All of this may conceivably be intended to dazzle (thereby to blind) Roderigo, but is much more elaborate than it needs to be for Iago to keep his interlocutor-employer where he needs him. Part of the explanation is that Iago speaks for our benefit: disclosing to us something of his character, and of the *dianoia* through which it makes itself known. Not a matter of the "motiveless malignity" over which Coleridge and innumerable others have wrung their hands, but of humanist selfhood in its most decayed, and most revealing, form.[24] Iago also sets the tone for *Othello's* preoccupation with selfhood as existential role-play, with the failures of privacy that transform the humanistic pursuit of self-knowledge into tragic self-alienation. And yet, something more integral than this is going on—integral, that is, to the moral-dramatic economy of the play. Iago reveals something of himself in this scene precisely *because* Roderigo is an uncomprehending nonentity, because he, Iago, needs the illusion of dialogue with others as a mirror in which to behold himself, but has no stomach for what non-illusory versions of such dialogues might reveal. It is for this reason that he follows the examples of earlier villains like Aaron and Richard Gloucester, and soliloquizes directly to the audience, whereas Othello's soliloquies are those of someone addressing, or conversing with, himself. In the uneasiness and half-admiring consternation of those who cannot answer back, Iago sees all that he needs to, and in so doing affirms something that outdoes even Pandarus: the fact of complicity rather than the threat of contagion.[25]

Ciceronian convention regards virtue as social. By contrast, vice— particularly those forms of it that depend on dissembling or calculated dishonesty—is understood as a species of individualism, the expression of a refusal or inability to cohere with the rationally ordered model of civic life.[26] What Iago sees so clearly is that vice is inherently social too—and that it remains so whether its authors, victims, and critics like it or not. For him, it is not reason and virtue and love that provide the basis for the *personae* and the communities of which they are a part, but appetite and self-interest alongside the capacity for delusion and deceit. Thus armed, he is well-set to exploit the weaknesses of a society that is jealous of its "honesty" above all else.

But we should not get too far ahead of ourselves. Other than by missing the point, how does Roderigo react to Iago's partial self-disclosure? With a further attack on "the Moor," this time studded with overtly racist bluster: "the thicklips" (1.1.65) will need great good luck to prevail against Iago's scheming intelligence. In Iago's response, we receive our first clue as to what Roderigo had been told just before the play began: "Call up her father, / Rouse him, make after him, poison his delight" (1.1.66–67). We do not know who this woman might be, but it is a reasonable guess that Roderigo and "the Moor" both desire her—and, as Roderigo is so aggrieved, that her affections do not tend toward him. Further, that if she has come to an understanding with Roderigo's rival, she has done so without her father's knowledge or consent.

So it proves. The father, whose name is Brabantio, is awoken from his sleep. Iago is crassly confrontational: "Zounds, sir, you're robbed . . . Even now, now, very now, an old black ram / Is tupping your white ewe!" (1.1.85–88). Taken aback and angry, Brabantio is further unimpressed when Roderigo introduces himself: "I have charged thee not to haunt about my doors: / In honest plainness thou hast heard me say / My daughter is not for thee" (1.1.95–97). "Honest plainness" connotes not only what he regards as the simplicity and dignity of his speech (in contrast to the words with which he is now being assailed), but the rhetorical category of the *causa honesta*—in which one defends something unquestionably worthy of defense.[27] In this case, a daughter's honor and desires; one might recall that, in a world that largely confined women to the household, chastity and temperance were the only decisively feminine forms of *honestas*. On the face of it then, things look bad for Roderigo. In reality, they have been deftly stage-managed by Iago, whose vulgarity ("I am one, sir, that comes to tell you your daughter and the Moor are now making the beast with two backs" [1.1.114–15]) not only makes Roderigo's respectfully genteel circumlocution sound more creditable, but borrows some of this credit for itself. Brabantio duly allows them to impart to him the claim that his daughter has eloped with "the Moor" (still unnamed, but now "lascivious," to say nothing of "an extravagant and wheeling stranger / Of here and everywhere" [1.1.124, 134–35]), and is aghast to discover that she is not asleep in her bed.

This is not a conventionally tragic playworld. Forgoing depth of characterization—Aristotelian *ethos*—Shakespeare presents everyone as a type, even when they have a name and a backstory. Roderigo is a high-born dolt; Iago a cunning subordinate who resents his status but does not know how to exist without it; Brabantio is the crossed father of Roman and Shakespearean comedy; his daughter is the willfully passionate creature of the same plays; Iago's senior officer is essentially a void until he is figured as a sexually appetitive, and all but animalistic, African outsider. In the case of this senior officer, such a characterization fits easily enough with Iago's earlier complaint that he lacks judgment, as it does also with the feats of arms that, presumably, raised him up the ranks. But it is harder to square with Iago's later declaration that, in the forthcoming "Cyprus wars," "Another of his fathom they have none / To lead their business": not just an impassioned warrior, then, but a strategist and battlefield commander. Mindful that this discrepancy puts him in a spot (and unwilling publicly to testify against the man on whom his own livelihood rests), Iago departs. On his way out, he makes another show of calculating prudence for the benefit of Roderigo, and also perhaps for himself: "For necessity of present life / I must show out a flag and sign of love, / Which is indeed but sign" (1.1.148–55). "Sign" here connotes something between an act of pretense and a necessarily defective copy.[28]

One cannot avoid the suspicion that the way things are in this version of Venice takes second place to the ways in which they seem—can be *made* to seem—to be. This is why, with the partial exception of Iago, Shakespeare takes such a long time to reveal the details of his protagonists' identities and grievances. Who they are matters less than their status within the plots through which they can be defined by Iago, by themselves, and by their onstage audiences more generally. Perhaps, by their offstage audiences too.

The impression is confirmed and complicated over the course of the next several scenes. Although we learn the names of Othello and Desdemona (Othello remains nothing more specific than "the Moor" until the Duke addresses him directly at 1.3.49), their energies are devoted to the business not of defining their individuality but of making themselves look like types that differ from those on which Brabantio tries to insist. This undertaking is hard to second-guess: if Brabantio were to have prevailed in his argument that Desdemona had been enchanted by Othello, the consequences would have been severe. By presenting themselves as embodiments of nobly contemplative love—Abelard and Heloise after rather than before—they can more effectively move the Duke and the remainder of their senatorial audience than would have been the case if they had sought truly to describe their feelings for one another, to say nothing of the circumstances in which these feelings first arose. That they do so with carefully polished artlessness (Othello's "Rude am I in my speech / And little blest with the soft turn of phrase" [1.3.82–83], Desdemona's "let me find a charter in your voice / T'assist my simpleness" [1.3.246–47]) is clinching.[29] But it would be wrong to charge them with either disingenuousness or factitiousness, and not just because the design of Othello's remarks so closely follows that recommended in the handbooks of forensic oratory: the rhetoric of decorously sexless love is at the heart of their self-conception as a romantic pair. As we shall see in greater detail below, Othello and Desdemona seem genuinely to believe what they are saying, and go on doing so until Iago engrafts a very different sort of idealization within Othello's mind.

Once Desdemona has obtained her father's consent for the fait accompli of her match with Othello—along with the Duke's permission to join her new husband on campaign against the Ottomans in Cyprus—act 1 ends with a soliloquy from Iago. Other than adducing another reason for his hatred of Othello (the suspicion that Othello has had illicit sex with his wife), Iago shares his plan for a work of "double knavery" (1.3.393): injuring both Othello and Cassio by insinuating to Othello that Cassio is "too familiar" (1.3.395) with Desdemona.

Act 2 translates the principals from Venice to Cyprus. There is a richly comic—and all but celebratory—playfulness to these scenes as Othello and Desdemona are reunited and the Ottoman attack is thwarted by the weather.[30] In the combat of wits between Desdemona and Iago, Desdemona's confidence and sense of security enable her to affirm that despite her good humor, she worries that Othello's ship might not make it: "I do beguile / The thing I am by seeming otherwise" (2.1.122–23). She is, she teases Iago, a more complicated creature than he might assume.

The festive atmosphere continues, even as Iago manipulates Cassio into drunken disgrace. But it is here that *Othello* begins to immerse us in the teleology of suffering, just as *Romeo and Juliet* changes its complexion with the death of Mercutio. Reflecting on his brawl with Montano and subsequent loss of rank, Cassio declares that he is wounded "past all surgery": "Reputation, reputation, reputation! O, I have lost my reputation, I have lost the immortal part of myself—and what remains is bestial" (2.3.256, 258–60). In prose comparable to that of the tavern scenes in the *Henry IV* plays, Shakespeare shows us Cassio losing all perspective, and exposing the fault lines between the Ciceronian and Christian worldviews that sixteenth- and early seventeenth-century humanists went out of their way to ignore. As it is one's soul rather than one's reputation that is the immortal part of one's being in all forms of Christian doctrine (as well as that which confers the powers of rationality that provide for elevation over the rest of the created world), Cassio's words can sound like hyperbole.[31] So they are. And yet, within the Ciceronian worldview, *honestas* (honor) is the most important criterion against which one's moral standing is to be measured, and remains so after one's death (recall Antony on Brutus as "an honorable man"). As Ulysses so skillfully reminds Achilles in *Troilus and Cressida*, being honorable depends on being regarded as honorable in public. If one's honorable identity (or, in Cassio's terms, "reputation") is to survive one's death, such discussions need to continue, which, if one's honorableness is sufficiently renowned (or celebrated, or famous), they will. And, as even works of Christian humanism like Petrarch's *Trionfi* (within which fame triumphs over death, time triumphs over fame, and the divine triumphs over all things temporal) tend to reveal, the Roman and Christian positions on enduring identity are at root incompatible: one belongs to worldly remembrance, the other to the life eternal.[32] In other words, the confusion here does not belong to Cassio alone. It is just that, in his overwrought condition, he reveals that which more cautious—more disciplined—considerations of the topic tended to obscure.

The tension is further exposed in the competing notions of "honesty" with which *Othello* is obsessed. Not just in the paradoxical form of "honest Iago," but in the honesty that Roderigo, Brabantio, Desdemona, Othello, and Venice itself all at various points think of as their own. The topic gave rise to what might still be the best piece of critical writing about the play, William Empson's "Honest in *Othello*." Though his focus lies elsewhere, Empson's freewheeling luminosity does not overlook the tensions that inhere in *honestas*. Writing of Othello's "why should honour outlive honesty?" (5.2.242)—the rhetorical question that he poses after discovering that he has killed Desdemona unjustly—Empson reflects that "the question indeed so sums up the play that it involves nearly all of both words; it seems finally to shatter the concept of honesty whose connecting links the play has patiently removed." This is because the question with which *Othello* is concerned differs from that to which Othello, with decorous resignation, thinks he knows the answer. Not whether "honour" should be allowed to outlive "honesty" (Othello is still alive; Desdemona, like Emilia, is not) but whether "honesty" can be detached from honor, and from the humanists' discourse of virtuous publicity, at all. It is relatively uncomplicated to trace a history of *honestas* as it loses its Roman connotations and evolves into the quality of integrity, truth-telling, and plain dealing. Initially underwritten by faith or signs of grace, this kind of independence gradually became seen as its own reward; by the time one gets to the end of the seventeenth century, it starts to predominate. By contrast, what grips the Shakespeare of *Othello* is the prospect that the integrity and sense of identity that one might seek to fix through one's honesty is merely another *persona*: a fiction contrived to ward off fears of existential uncertainty that, in denying its own fictionality, causes us further to estrange ourselves from ourselves and from those around us.[33]

The best case in point is provided by returning to the ways in which Othello and Desdemona conceive of themselves as lovers, and as husband and wife. They have no interest in the Petrarchan role-play that is the element in which Troilus and (sometimes) Cressida try to swim, but their self-identification is every bit as idealized, every bit as outside-in, every bit as deformed by conventionality. Othello's opening claim is that "She loved me for the dangers I had passed / And I loved her that she did pity them" (1.3.168–69). A little later, Desdemona delivers herself of the view that after hearing Othello tell his story, "I saw Othello's visage in his mind, / And to his honours and his valiant parts / Did I my soul and fortunes consecrate" (1.3.253–55). *Consecrate*, note—not commit, or dedicate, or devote. Even as they figure the bond between them as coextensive with Othello's martial *honestas*, they present it as something sacralizing: not merely unsullied by their bodily desires, but actively transcending— possibly even redeeming—their corporeal state. Although such a view might offer a faintly ludicrous affirmation of what Anne Carson calls "the tactics of imagination" through which we negotiate the complexities of erotic desire, expressing it serves them well.[34] This is because they, like Brabantio, the Duke, and the members of the Senate, see only one alternative. In Othello's words, he desires Desdemona's company "not / To please the palate of my appetite, / Nor to comply with heat . . . But to be free and bounteous to her mind" (1.3.262–64, 266). He means to reassure his audience that taking Desdemona to Cyprus will not lead to any diminution of his military rigor (a beautiful domestication of the Mars and Venus topos made familiar by Botticelli: he will no more slacken in the Venetian interest than he will "Let housewives make a skillet of my helm" [1.3.273]).[35] Transparent pietism, but all find it easier to stomach than the dynamics of erotic love—in the world of *honestas* and *decorum* just as much as that of Christian temperance, sexual desire and activity are regarded with unease. Their instinctive, and frequently uncontrollable, qualities threaten the rationality and virtuous sociability that are supposed to set humankind apart from the remainder of animal life. And if sex is bad enough (the beast with two backs; goats and monkeys), the fear of interracial sex and of one's civilized-elevated portion of humankind being dragged closer to the animals through intercourse with a barbarian is even worse (the old black ram tupping the white ewe; you'll have your nephews neigh to you; and so on). Best to avert one's gaze, or to train it to see things in the appropriate ideological light.

Except that it is isn't. Doing so defaces our sense of what we are, and leaves a blind spot with which the likes of Iago are free to do their worst. Othello plays courteously with some lines of Terence in declaring, once reunited with Desdemona on Cyprus, that "if it were now to die / 'Twere now to be most happy" (2.1.187–88), and likewise borrows from classical mythology (in which Eros / Cupid was the first deity to emerge from the primordial matter of Chaos) in the attempt to make sense of his feelings: "Perdition catch my soul, / But I do love thee! and when I love thee not / Chaos is come again" (3.1.90–92).[36] Desdemona shares his conviction that, as a husband and a man, he is a class apart: "My noble Moor / Is of true mind, and made of no such baseness / As jealous creatures are" (3.4.26–28). We get nearer to the truth of the matter once Iago has opened up the spaces behind this loftily dispassionate masquerade: it is not the thought that Cassio has enjoyed the pleasures of Desdemona's conversation that drives Othello to distraction.

Grappling with the enormity of what Iago has led him to, Othello volunteers the opinions that "I had rather be a toad / . . . Than keep a corner in the thing I love / For others' uses" (3.3.274–77) and that "I had been happy if the general camp, / Pioneers and all, had tasted her sweet body, / So I had nothing known" (3.3.348–50). Then, when he has resolved to kill her for having hurt his reputation ("cuckold me!" [4.1.196]), he declares that "I'll not expostulate with her, lest her body and beauty unprovide my mind again" (4.1.201–3).[37] That "again" is telling, and takes us to the core of their relationship: he lacks now, as he has previously, the discursive wherewithal to account for the physical yearning that he feels for Desdemona and her beauty. Unable to distract himself from this appetitive reality with fictions of being "free and bounteous to her mind," he allows himself to be led toward the belief that he has been a victim of erotic intoxication; that, furthermore, this intoxication has unsettled his mind to the extent that he has allowed his wife to dishonor his name through her dalliance with Cassio. In a neat paradox, Shakespeare has Othello insist that the time for talking is over in the same breath that he confirms that, with the exception perhaps of some getting-to-know-you storytelling, talking had never really been their thing. The proximity of all this to *Troilus and Cressida* (as also to *Measure for Measure* and *All's Well*) is unmistakable, but nor is it very far removed from the depravity that we more readily associate with John Webster: "Damne her, that body of hers."[38] As for Desdemona, it is only through glancing at the path not taken, and that she could not by then hope to take, that she is briefly able to pierce the idealizations through which—to the end—she conceives of herself and her love for Othello: with Emilia, she ruefully agrees that "This Lodovico is a proper [i.e., handsome, comely] man" (4.3.34).[39]

It therefore seems fitting that when Iago furnishes Othello with the report of Cassio's confession to reinforce the evidence of the handkerchief—thereby confirming Othello's impression of Desdemona's guilt—it leads to Othello's physical collapse. According to the stage direction at 4.1.43 he "falls in a trance," and Iago glosses a little later on that he has "fallen into an epilepsy" (4.1.50). This seizure is not in Shakespeare's source: "Un capitano moro," one of the short stories that comprise Cinthio's *Hecatommithi*. Instead, it is likely to come from a hint that Shakespeare found in Seneca's *Hercules Furens*, a work that, as Robert Miola and Curtis Perry have shown, serves as a template for *Othello* more generally. Hercules prides himself on a rational self-control that shades into hubris, and when madness descends on him (leading him to kill his wife and children), he exhibits many of the same symptoms as the swooning Othello.[40] At the very least, the parallel is suggestive. What we can say with more certainty is that the purpose of Othello's collapse relates closely to the infirmities with which Shakespeare invests his Julius Caesar. In that play, we are prompted to notice the discrepancy between what Caesar is and what Brutus, Cassius, and the other *optimates* need him to be if they are to justify their aristocratic coup. In *Othello*, we are prompted to notice the discrepancy between corporeal reality and fantasies of control—fantasies of absolute love or absolute corruption. Just as Othello's body has an integrity and a frailty that are impervious to the *honestas* through which he refracts himself and the world at large, so the feelings that he shares with Desdemona have little to do with the notions of honor, decorousness, modesty, obedience, and so on that—on Iago's account—her sexual appetites have led her to violate.

It follows that although, in Cinthio, the Othello figure has the Iago figure batter the Desdemona figure to death with a sock full of wet sand before pulling a ceiling down upon her to cover up the crime, Shakespeare has Othello kill her himself, taking exquisite care not to "scar that whiter skin of hers than snow / And smooth as monumental alabaster" (5.2.4–5). Accordingly, what almost deters Othello is not moral deliberation, but a reminder of their intimacy: the "smell" of her and of her "breath" (5.2.15, 16). He cannot bring himself to disfigure or destroy that which has come to mean so much to him, even as he has resolved to extinguish the "light" that animates it. Doing so would bring him dangerously close to admitting that he is about to kill the woman he loves on account of the rage, upset, and urge to vengeance that burn within him. Dangerously close to admitting that, far from being the wronged but steadfast embodiment of impersonal *honestas*, he is the slave of his passions—a version of the lascivious and all but bestial African outsider with whom Iago sought to frighten Brabantio in act 1.

Forgetting his stated desire to "chop her into messes" (4.1.197), he first claims to himself that he has to kill her lest she dishonor others the way she has dishonored him: "Yet she must die, else she'll betray more men" (5.2.6). Then he presents himself as the agent of "Justice" (5.2.17), giving Desdemona her adulteress's due. Finally, and in response to Desdemona's protestations of innocence, he berates her for trying to make "me call what I intend to do / A murder, which I thought a sacrifice" (5.3.64–65). It is unclear whether he has in mind a sacrifice that he will have to make (i.e., giving up the body and beauty to which he is wedded) or whether he means to sacrifice Desdemona's soul (about which he has been solicitous in giving her the chance to pray) to preserve his image of her monumental alabaster. But in either case, his intent in speaking thus is the same, and is akin to that of Brutus in insisting that he and his fellow conspirators "be sacrificers, not butchers" in assassinating Caesar, or Lucius and Titus in imagining the vindictive slaughter of Alarbus as food for the "sacrificing fire" of "Roman rites." Like the well-tempered revenger imagined in Seneca's *De ira* (who seeks vengeance not with condign anger, but because it is what he ought—on balance and morally speaking—to do), they want to see themselves as acting from principle, not the dictates of appetite or emotional disturbance.[41] Constrained as Othello is to the language and assumptions of *honestas*, of virtue as the expression of decorously and autonomously masculine vigor, he cannot conceive of himself in terms other than the ones he does. No matter that his stated motives are confused and self-contradictory. No matter that they are far removed from emotional realities that he cannot begin to confront, much less to acknowledge. He needs to be able to tell himself that he is behaving in a way that is both honorable and honest, and so he does: "I did proceed upon just grounds / To this extremity" (5.2.136–37).

Othello's world comes crashing down not on account of killing Desdemona, but because, once Iago's duplicity becomes apparent, he recognizes that he will be seen as having acted dishonorably for killing her without good reason. (Emphatically not, we might note, instances of *peripeteia* and *anagnorisis* on the lines advanced by most exponents of Aristotelian

tragic poetics.) As honor is a social virtue dependent on the good opinion of one's peers, his actions mean that he has become dishonorable; as
becoming dishonorable has stripped from him the *personae* that represent his entire sense of self, the situation is literally one of life and death.
Rather than reflect on the aspects of his character and thought that
allowed things to take this course, he prefers the easier path of attacking
Iago as a devil: someone he thought of as a loyal friend and servant was, in
fact, an agent of Satan. As a trusting and courageous and unblinking sort
of fellow, Othello suggests that he was powerless to do other than he did.

The scene is set for his magnificent final monologue, which culmi-
nates in a stage-managed death to rival that of Cleopatra, and in which
he pretends to a privacy—with himself and his audience alike—that he is
quite unable to attain. In relating "these unlucky deeds," his listeners must
"nothing extenuate, / Nor set down aught in malice." They must instead
speak "Of one that loved not wisely, but too well; / Of one not easily jealous,
but, being wrought, / Perplexed in the extreme." One who, thus perplexed,
"threw a pearl away / richer than all his tribe." Above all, one who had
"done the state some service," and who—just as he had protected Venice by
cutting the throat of a "malignant and turbanned Turk" at Aleppo—now
chooses to safeguard it by ending his own life with the aid of a concealed
dagger (5.2.336–54).

Much might be said of these lines, and I want only to highlight three
features of them here. First, "these unlucky deeds." Othello not only writes
off what has happened to bad luck. He also disassociates himself from
what has happened: *these* deeds rather than *my* deeds. Second, Othello
treats Desdemona as if she were a treasured possession that he has carelessly cast aside, just as Brabantio earlier accused him of having "stolen"
(1.3.61) her. In the Heideggerian language through which I discussed
Hamlet in the previous chapter, she is a thing, given significance as an
object through the estimation—honorable, rational, and so on—of a masculine subject. Third, he mourns not for Desdemona herself, but for the
predicament in which killing her has left him: not only unable to perform
any more services for the Venetian state, but a threat to the serenity of that
peculiar, part-republican and part-imperialist, political entity. Or rather,
only one more service. That is, killing himself in a way that accentuates
both his own *honestas* (calmness, courage, and decorousness at the instant
of his greatest defeat and humiliation) and, by implication, the *honestas* of
the polity that raised him up to such heights. Cassio and Lodovico are glad
to accede, the former declaring that suicide was the always the likeliest
outcome for one so "great of heart" (5.2.359), and the latter directing Iago

to "Look on the tragic loading of this bed: / This is thy work" (5.3.361–62). The tragedy of Othello and Desdemona, on his account, was written by Iago; it is a drama that is now over and in which Lodovico, like Venetian society as a whole, had no part to play.

T. S. Eliot's assessment of Othello's final remarks has regularly been condemned by critics eager to assert their generosity of spirit as a corrective to Eliot's mandarin desiccation. But Eliot gets it almost exactly right: Othello "is endeavouring to escape reality, he has ceased to think about Desdemona, and is thinking about himself. . . . Othello succeeds in turning himself into a pathetic figure, by adopting an *aesthetic* rather than a moral attitude, dramatizing himself against his environment. He takes in the spectator, but the human motive is primarily to take in himself."[42] Eliot slips only by overlooking that in the humanistic space of *Othello*, the moral *is* the aesthetic: a matter of decorous performativity, of staying in the character written for you by the social virtues delineated in Cicero's *De officiis* and elaborated by its commentators. Shakespeare's point is not to damn Othello, but to portray him as a victim of the habits of thought that he has had to master to make his way; the victim of a culture in which playing yourself through actorly *personae* is the guarantor of virtue and identity, and in which the only *personae* that count are those defined by a masculinity that exists in a condition of near total denial about its emotional and instinctive dispositions.

Even Iago is no exception. He sees through both the *personae* of his social superiors and—to borrow an adjective from Kimberlé Crenshaw—the intersectional dynamics of race, gender, class, and politics on which their privileged status depends. But he is unable to escape these intersectional dynamics as they plot the horizon of his own selfhood, and he makes his way by fashioning *personae* of his own.[43] Ones defined not by *honestas* but by its antonym, *turpitudo*—depravity, shamefulness, duplicity, cunning. To put it another way, he replaces the concord fictions of humanist conversation with discord fictions that better suit his comprehension of himself and the world. It is not then any coincidence that his fall comes about through a form of moral obliviousness that closely parallels that of Othello: underestimating and misunderstanding his wife. It simply never occurs to him that, when confronted with the reality of his scheming against Othello and Desdemona, Emilia would tell the truth about his deeds out of loyalty and love to her former mistress.

Like the youths belittled by Hector in *Troilus and Cressida*, women are excluded from humanistic moral philosophy on the grounds that, although they could attain a measure of mastery in ethics and oeconomics, they lack the emotional self-control to do the same within the political sphere.[44] For all Desdemona's bravery in seeking to make a life with Othello without first obtaining her father's permission, and for all the steadfastness with which she clings to the ideal of this life in the face of Othello's abuse, it is through Emilia that the mores of the humanistic order are most directly challenged.[45] Not by her arguing that women are the equal of men as agents of rationality, but through her claim that male professions of rational agency—and with it, the purportedly God-given sovereignty to govern themselves and others—are self-serving make believe:

> Let husbands know
> Their wives have sense like them: they see, and smell,
> And have their palates both for sweet and sour
> As husbands have. What is it that they do
> When they change us for others? Is it sport?
> I think it is. And doth affection breed it?
> I think it doth. Is't frailty that thus errs?
> It is so too. And have we not affections?
> Desires for sport? and frailty, as men have?
> Then let them use us well: else let them know,
> The ills we do, their ills instruct us so. (4.3.92–102)

Emilia enjoys the chance to shock. There is nevertheless more to her remarks than an outspoken defense of female adultery. She emphasizes that what binds humankind together is not *honestas* and *decorum* but attributes such as taste ("palates"), passion ("affection"), "frailty," and the desire for sexual pleasure ("sport"). *Honestas* not only fails to prevent amorous straying, but encourages it by providing it with a veil of respectability. Better to be candid about who and what we are—about our common "frailty"—than to distort ourselves in obedience to a body of specious doctrine that denigrates and excludes most of that which makes us human. She shares her husband's impatience with the conventional *personae*, but unlike him is free from the urge to bind herself to the *personae* of the Machiavel and demonic plotter in their stead. Alas, the clarity of vision that she shares with Cressida (perhaps also with Cassandra and Andromache) does her no good. If only she hadn't, out of an eagerness to please, passed Iago that handkerchief (in Cinthio, Iago steals it himself). The love she feels as a wife collides with the love she has come to feel for Desdemona, and the collision leads to her demise.

At the end of *Othello*, one thing at least is clear. In both its principal aspects, *honestas* has been damaged beyond repair.

As honor, it has been shown to depend on the performance of *verba* with no corresponding *res*. Falstaff phrased it well when abut an English battlefield some years earlier: "What is honour? A word. What is in that word 'honour'? What is that 'honour'? Air." Likewise the title character of Jonson's *Sejanus* (a play in which Shakespeare performed shortly before writing *Othello*), who assures one of his confederates that "The coarsest act / Done to my service I can so requite / As all the world shall style it honourable."[46]

As honesty, *honestas* has been undermined by the dramatic realities of Othello, Iago, Desdemona, and Cassio: if you do not know who or what you are, you cannot be true to yourself. Staying in character might be enough for the kinds of audience found in the eyes of a lover—or among parents or leaders or friends or fellow soldiers—but it prevents you from recognizing and exploring the truth of what it is that you desire. Ultimately, the role-playing imperative means that your feelings, even those feelings in which you believe yourself to be most invested, are in a position to play you false. The pity of it.

CHAPTER FIVE

Beyond This Ignorant Present

MACBETH

ALTHOUGH *OTHELLO* LEAVES THE NOSTRUMS of honor, decorum, and performative selfhood in ruins, Shakespeare's starkest engagement with the *theatrum mundi*—the notion that "all the world's a stage, / And all the men and women merely players"—takes place in a landscape that could scarcely differ more than it does from Venetian Cyprus. A Scottish king laments the turn that events have taken: "Life's but a walking shadow, a poor player, / That struts and frets his hour upon the stage, / And then is heard no more. It is a tale / Told by an idiot, full of sound and fury / Signifying nothing" (*Macbeth*, 5.5.23–27).[1] In *Macbeth*, Shakespeare continues to wrestle with the problem that he had first brought into focus in *Hamlet*: how to understand yourself and the world around you if the only media (words, pictures, ideas) through which you can do so are representative. Learned fictions that—on the basis of convention, diktat, or habit—we employ as heuristics through which to comprehend life as we experience it, but whose heuristic status we generally contrive to forget or ignore in the interests of seeing things as we need to. Or, perhaps, as we feel we need to.

It seems fitting then that *Macbeth*, like *Hamlet* before it, begins on a note of indeterminacy. The first words we hear pose a question that does not receive a satisfactory answer: "When shall we three meet again?" They are spoken by one of three Weird Sisters, beings apparently possessed of the gift of prophecy. If it is curious that, being possessed of prophetic insight, she should have to ask, the two remaining sisters seem just as unsure. Several "whens" later, the nearest they get to an answer is "ere the set of sun" (1.1.1–5). We are pitched headlong into a playworld whose principal concerns include time, temporality, foresight, spectacle, and verbal legerdemain; the scene is set with what Emrys Jones calls "masterful abruptness."[2]

And as a good deal of recent criticism has affirmed, questions of time and temporality lead us right to the heart of what makes *Macbeth* such a powerful work of art: issues of history, prophecy, chronology (dramatic and historical), memory, succession (of events and of monarchs), eternity, and sempiternity preoccupy the play from first to last. In what follows, my focus is narrower—at least at the outset. I want further to explore Frank Kermode's proposition that *Macbeth* dramatizes the tension between two different temporalities: one secular and historical, the other sacred and transcendent.[3] Both, in the final analysis, are cast by Shakespeare as attempts to impose order where only confusion and contingency are to be found. Both emerge as the tools of a dramatis personae who, despite their best efforts to convince themselves otherwise, are innocent of little other than the future.

———

Let's start with a closer examination of life as "a walking shadow, a poor player." Shortly after a cry of women is heard offstage, Seyton enters to share with Macbeth the news that "The Queen, my lord, is dead." Thus Macbeth:

> She should have died hereafter;
> There would have been time for such a word.
> Tomorrow, and tomorrow, and tomorrow,
> Creeps in this petty pace from day to day,
> To the last syllable of recorded time;
> And all our yesterdays have lighted fools
> The way to dusty death. Out, out, brief candle,
> Life's but a walking shadow, a poor player,
> That struts and frets his hour upon the stage,
> And then is heard no more. It is a tale
> Told by an idiot, full of sound and fury
> Signifying nothing. (5.5.16–27)

Although much has been written about all of these lines, their extraordinary density of sense and reference leaves them far from exhausted. Take "dusty death." This is normally glossed with reference to the familiar words of the Order for the Burial of the Dead as canonized in the Book of Common Prayer, itself absorbing numerous passages of scripture: "Earth to earth, ashes to ashes, dust to dust, in sure and certain hope of resurrection to eternal life, through our Lord Jesus Christ . . ."[4] A reasonable enough interpretation, but one that quickly becomes strained: however else Macbeth's sentiments on learning of his wife's demise might be comprehended, they cannot intelligibly be described as Christian. The key here is found in his deployment of the *theatrum mundi* topos. As discussed at various points above, this topos usually depended on the notion of God making meaningful the drama of human activity by observing it from his position beyond the created world. That is, from *outside* the finite orders of time and space, on the immutable and immaterial plane of eternity. This plane existed before the creation of the physical cosmos, just as it will continue to exist after the apocalypse. In the words of one early modern authority, the eternal "is neither before, nor after. For eternitie is an entire being at once altogether, without any proceeding . . . Time therefore cannot accord with eternitie, nor be eternall, seeing eternall hath no processe."[5] And yet, for Macbeth, there is nothing beyond "the last syllable of recorded time."[6] Which is to say, no further state to which humankind might aspire after human history has run its course. Without a divine spectator to pass judgment on the good, the bad, and the virtuous in human affairs, life as Macbeth sees it is a meaningless farce. The end of days is literally terminal, not the point at which humankind leaves behind the dust, blood, and frustrations of terrestrial existence for an afterlife of beatitude or damnation.

How to resolve the conflict between "dusty death" as a Christian formulation and its place within a speech that is opposed to the fundamentals of Christian theology? One answer might be to say that although it would be excessive to label "dusty death" as purposefully Christian, the commonplace association of dust and death means that the question should not give us too much pause. Hamlet, for example, imagines Alexander the Great and Julius Caesar turned to dust and clay without worrying questions of eschatological nicety.[7] Or one might follow Lewis Theobald and other editors of the play in emending "dusty" to "dusky," thereby aligning the phrase more closely with the language of light, darkness, and shadows that surrounds it.[8]

The problem is a difficult one, but it can be resolved without recourse to special pleading or the textual editor's crystal ball. Specifically, by reading *Macbeth* alongside a well-known text from beyond the Christian tradition: Horace's *Odes*. Although Horace is not generally seen as Shakespeare's sort of thing—too decorous, too studied, too closely identified with Ben Jonson—*Macbeth* indicates that Shakespeare's engagement with his writings was no mere vestige of his years spent being drilled in a sixteenth-century grammar school.[9] Here is Ode 4.7:

Diffugere nives, redeunt iam gramina campis
      arboribusque comae;
mutat terra vices et decrescentia ripas
      flumina praetereunt.
Gratia cum Nymphis geminisque sororibus audet
      ducere nuda choros.
immortalia ne speres, monet annus et almum
      quae rapit hora diem.
frigora mitescunt Zephyris, ver proterit aestas
      interitura, simul
pomifer autumnus fruges effuderit; et mox
      bruma recurrit iners.
damna tamen celeres reparant caelestia lunae:
      nos ubi decidimus
quo pius Aeneas, quo Tullus dives et Ancus,
      pulvis et umbra sumus.
quis scit an adiciant hodiernae crastina summae
      tempora di superi?
cuncta manus avidas fugient heredis, amico
      quae dederis animo.
cum semel occideris et de te splendida Minos
      fecerit arbitria,
non, Torquate, genus, non te facundia, non te
      restituet pietas.
infernis neque enim tenebris Diana pudicum
      liberat Hippolytum,
nec Lethaea valet Theseus abrumpere caro
      vincula Pirithoo.

The snow has fled away; now grass is returning to the fields, and leaves to the trees. The earth is changing its seasons; the rivers subside and flow between their banks; the Grace along with the Nymphs and her twin sisters ventures to lead the dances naked. You should not hope for immortality: that is the message of the year and the hour that steals away the kindly day. The cold grows mild under the zephyrs; spring is trodden under foot by summer, which is doomed to die as soon as apple-bearing autumn pours forth its crops, and soon lifeless winter comes hurrying back. Yet the quickly changing moons recoup their losses in the sky; we, when we have gone down to the same place as dutiful Aeneas, as rich Tullus and Ancus, are dust and shadow. Who knows whether the gods above will add tomorrow's time to the total of today? Only what you have given to your own dear self will escape the greedy hands of your heir. Once you have died and Minos has pronounced his solemn verdict, neither high birth, nor eloquence, Torquatus, nor piety will bring you back; neither does Diana set Hippolytus free from the infernal darkness, for all his purity, nor has Theseus the power to break the fetters of Lethe that bind Pirithous, however much he loves him.][10]

April may or may not be the cruelest month, but the advent of spring reminds us that even as the seasons roll on in cyclical time, human life answers to a clock that is linear and finite. There is a sort of afterlife, yes, but it is drained of color, vibrancy, strength, and understanding—an ersatz version of life on earth. In all senses that matter, death is the end. In the words of the edition of Horace that Shakespeare is most likely to have used, the poem serves as an invitation "to live life merrily."[11]

In brief, my suggestion is that Shakespeare found in *pulvis et umbra sumus* ("we are dust and shadows") the starting point for "dusty death" in close proximity to the notion of life as a "walking shadow." Add in Horace's emphasis on the uncertainties of how and whether "tomorrow's time" (*crastina summae tempora*) will come to pass, to say nothing of the vexed business of succession and inheritance, and the ode's pertinence to *Macbeth* begins to look overwhelming.

Before taking this Horatian line of inquiry any further, I should address the status of *Macbeth* as a humanistic work of art: at first glance, it would be hard to dissent from the view that Shakespeare's supernaturally framed rendition of medieval Scotland is more gothic than classicizing. But the truth is that the Scottish play is every bit as humanistic, and every bit as preoccupied with the heritage of ancient Rome, as the other tragedies we have discussed so far. One of Macbeth's most obviously Roman moments comes when he compares his "genius" to that of Mark Antony (3.1.50–51).[12] Another occurs as he imagines himself creeping up to murder the sleeping Duncan in the fashion of Tarquin approaching Lucrece (2.1.54–56).[13] Yet another comes as the odds further lengthen on him being able to defeat Malcolm and Macduff, and shows him not only thinking about ancient Rome, but doing so with a distinctly Erasmian accent: "Why should I play the Roman fool, and die / On mine own sword?" (5.8.1–2). The Roman, and particularly Stoic, valorization of suicide as means of asserting one's autonomy and nobility in the face of defeat was well known, but Macbeth is unconvinced. As Plutarch and Shakespeare both understood, a supporting character like Eros (on whom, more in chapter 7 below) can end it all without too much ado. But to figures such as Brutus or Antony, habituated to seeing their postures of virtue or valor—of *honestas*—favorably reflected back at them in the reactions of others, suicide is less viable: by dying, one deprives oneself of the chance to behold one's virtuosity. Confusion, much of it rather histrionic, ensues. Even when suicide succeeds, as it does for Othello, the triumph is superficial: an act of courageous violence with which to paper over the gaps between the *res* of what one has become and the *verba* of how one would like to be remembered. Macbeth has no need to see himself validated in the eyes of others—at least, in the eyes of anyone other than the woman who has just died. Nor is grandstanding folly his thing. He resolves to fight on.[14]

Of course, Macbeth's "Roman fool" need have no more to do with Seneca than the "epicures" at 5.3.8 presuppose Shakespeare's close engagement with Lucretius, or the "augures" at 3.4.22 presuppose his study of premonitory birds in Cicero's *Of Divination*: all are staples of the Erasmian and post-Erasmian humanism of England and Northern Europe.[15] But if we head deeper into the play, a different picture emerges. One in which we find Shakespeare working hard to fuse together Horace and Seneca to his own dramatic ends—ends that, as usual, relate to indeterminacy and to the ways in which even the grandest human beings seek to negotiate their experience of it.

Stumbling into a funk of dissatisfaction at the news that the rebel army is afoot and ten thousand strong, Macbeth declares that "I have lived long enough: my way of life / Is fallen into the sere, the yellow leaf, / And that which should accompany old age, / As honour, love, obedience, troops of friends, / I must not look to have" (5.3.22–26). Baldwin plausibly sees in Macbeth's "way of life" and his descent into the colorful detritus of autumn an echo of Horace's *Epistles* (1.7), and of Lambinus's commentary on them.[16] Paul Hammond further observes that Macbeth mangles Horace's *Art of Poetry* in transposing onto old age the characteristics— "honour, love, obedience, troops of friends"—that Horace associates with life in its middle-aged masculine prime: Macbeth's "weariness" makes him realize that "he cannot even expect to enjoy the normal rewards of middle age. . . . his life has not merely 'fall'n into the sere,' it has fallen outside the regular path of human development, outside our normal understanding of time."[17] What is more, the Horatianism of these lines is engrafted onto another prominent strand of the humanistic tradition: the likeness of Seneca's Hercules. Although Seneca is not the structural influence on *Macbeth* that he is on *Othello* (or *Titus Andronicus* and *Hamlet*), scholars have long been aware that themes and *sententiae* from his tragedies are a conspicuous feature of the play. Here, they are part of Macbeth's effort to ironize, thereby to detach himself from, the likenesses through which he knows that his subjects regard him, but through which he has no interest in regarding himself.[18] A few lines later, his thoughts are again fashioned from echoes of Horace, interwoven with Seneca and Virgil. Discussing his wife's miserably afflicted condition, he entreats her doctor to offer her some "some sweet oblivious antidote" (5.3.43), a remedy that recalls those sought in the *Odes*, the *Aeneid*, and by Seneca's Hercules.[19]

This mingling of classical source material is at one level just another exercise in early modern literary-rhetorical convention—according to which, as we have seen, one makes one's compositions eloquent and authoritative by constructing them as bricolages of eloquent and authoritative quotations gathered up from the writing of others. On another level, we might further wish to see in it a deliberate stylistic playfulness. The sheer difficulty of understanding what it is that Macbeth is talking about (hard enough in print and at leisure; surely all but impossible in the early seventeenth-century theater, even in the best seats) recruits Horace for a sort of Gongorism—what Stephen Orgel calls Shakespeare's "poetics of incomprehensibility."[20] In so doing, and whether deliberately or not, Shakespeare offers a rejoinder to the assiduously transparent style that Jonson modeled after Horace and claimed for his own.[21] Shakespeare also ensures that any attempts to update his verse in the interests of easy comprehension, such as those in William Davenant's adaptation of *Macbeth* (first produced in 1663–64, but not printed until a decade later), are bound to go horribly wrong: "She should have Di'd hereafter, / I brought Her here, to see my Victimes, not to Die. / To Morrow, to Morrow, and to Morrow, / Creeps in a stealing pace from Day to Day, / To the last Minute of Recorded Time: / And all our Yesterdays have lighted Fools / To their Eternal Homes . . ."[22]

And yet the crux here is not *how* Shakespeare's Macbeth speaks as he does, but *why*. He does not seek to fashion himself an identity defined by *honestas* and *decorum*, or even one defined by *turpitudo* like Iago. Instead, he cleaves to his heavily citational manner of discourse because it enables him to shield his regal self-image from the threat of contamination by his horrific deeds. Consider the euphemisms through which he conceives of death as "surcease" (1.7.4), and murder as "this terrible feat" (1.7.82) or "this bloody business" (2.1.48), or the frequency with which he turns to rhetorical redescription—the figure of *paradiastole*. In one particularly good example, he hears a voice accusing him not of having killed the sleeping Duncan, but of having killed sleep itself (2.2.36–44). It is of course easier to think about murdering an abstract noun than one's king and houseguest, but what is of greatest moment here is that the act of rhetorical personification, or *prosopopoeia*, that makes this thought possible depends on a fusion of Ovid and Seneca.[23] Similarly, when Macbeth fixates on the blood coating his hands later in the scene, the note he strikes is Senecan: "Will all great Neptune's ocean wash this blood / Clean from my hand?" (2.2.61–62) adapts *Hercules Furens* (where Hercules realizes that he has killed his children), as also perhaps *Phaedra* (where Hippolytus weighs the consequences of sleeping with his stepmother).[24] It is not that Macbeth wants to imitate Seneca's troubled heroes in a version of what humanist educators discussed as *ethopoeia*, but that exerting himself in the style of Hercules allows him to evade questions of conscience and responsibility while affecting to be consumed by them.[25] The same thing happens when he declares that on account of his having contracted to give the "eternal jewel" of his soul to Satan ("the common enemy of man"), his planned murders of Banquo and Fleance will be the work of "fate"—not of himself or his hired assassins (3.1.67–71).[26] Suffice it to say that throughout this drama of equivocation, it is not only the high-toned Ross whose speech is "too nice" (4.3.174).

Without laboring the point about the humanistic fabric of *Macbeth* any further, I hope it can be agreed that there is nothing implausible about finding Horace's *Odes* in Macbeth's "dusty death" and the lines that surround it. In what follows, I want further to explore the possibility that the Roman points of reference in *Macbeth* are more than just a grammar-school boy turned actor turned playwright proving himself adept at the higher name dropping—that they do serious dramatic work. Through them, Shakespeare shows Macbeth not only attempting to rid himself of the *personae* (and with them the entire apparatus of the moral code based on *honestas* and *decorum*), but attempting to anchor his identity at a point beyond the contingencies of historical time. As Macbeth recruits the murderers who will kill Banquo, he riffs on the Tacitean notion of the *arcana imperii* (the necessary secrets of successful statecraft), telling them that in seeking their "assistance" he is "Masking the business from the common eye, / For sundry weighty reasons" (3.1.126–28).[27] But the point holds for

Macbeth's conduct more generally. The *personae* that, in their different ways, so preoccupy Hamlet and Claudius and Othello and Iago are of no interest to him as anything other than a mask—a device with which to win the freedom to pursue a kingly identity that signifies precisely because, in virtue of being invested with something like divinity, it cannot be witnessed by the common eye.

———

Emrys Jones seems to have been the first to notice that a quibble on "shadow" (for the early moderns, it could connote both an actor and a shadow as we understand the term) leads Shakespeare to Seneca in continuing Macbeth's reflections on time and the human condition.[28] For Seneca, writing in opposition to the doctrine of the *personae* advanced by Cicero, the well-regulated theater of the world was in reality the "farce of human life" (*humanae vitae mimus*)—an exercise in sustained pretense within which we are assigned roles that we "play so badly" that we resemble actors "strutting" vainly on the stage. It therefore behooves all those who would live meaningful existences—up to and including kings and other rulers—to move past the appearances of things, and to turn their attention toward the inner dispositions of their lives and of the world around them. Macbeth, needless to add, does not dwell on Seneca's recommendations for meaningful living. Confronted by the death of the one person whose opinion—and opinion of him—he cares about, he is engrossed in the *humanae vitae mimus* alone. All kinds of human life, and not just the public manifestations of it that Seneca affects to scorn, take the form of a "tale / Told by an idiot, full of sound and fury / Signifying nothing."[29]

Macbeth's words are also a repudiation of the carpe diem ethos that Horace so artfully refines in Ode 4.7. Alongside his insistence that "the last syllable of recorded time" will mark the end of everything, Macbeth's elaboration of *pulvis et umbra sumus* strongly suggests a belief that historical temporality is the be-all, just as it will prove to be the end-all.[30] And yet rather than find in this awareness a prompt to take pleasure in what he can while he can, he is moved to disdain.

The difficult thing to remember is that, at this point in the action, Macbeth (on the strength of the Weird Sisters' prophecies) believes that he will prevail in his confrontation with Malcolm, Macduff, and the forces at their command: his disregard for human affairs, in other words, is *not* caused by fears of an imminent defeat rendering void his gains, or by the suspicion that holding on to these gains would be more trouble than they are worth.

Instead, he struggles with the stirrings of a realization that the cynosure of his ambition has been a false light. Although kingship had promised much, his experience of it has been no more yielding than being the Thane of Glamis or of Cawdor, a successful warrior-general, or any other of the *personae* that he might have seen fit to make his own. If anything, the more elevated position is the harder to bear because, after forcing his way not just to the top of the Scottish social and political hierarchy, but to the doorstep of the absolute, there is no other place to which he can aspire.

And yet Macbeth clings on to his elevated status, not least because it provides him with a vantage from which to pass judgment on the *humanae vitae mimus* as if he were not fully a part of it himself. Things only begin to change when, a couple of lines later, an anonymous messenger arrives with the news that Birnham Wood appears to be on the move (5.5.33–34). Hearing this, Macbeth suspects that he has been the victim of a diabolical ruse through the medium of the third apparition summoned by the Weird Sisters in act 4 scene 1: perhaps there are supernatural— albeit satanic—spectators outside the *theatrum mundi* after all. He resolves to abandon his strong defensive position in the castle to confront his foes in open battle in the belief that if what the messenger "avouches does appear / There is nor flying hence nor tarrying here." If he is forced to fight for the crown without the certain assurance of his victory, then he will do so with millenarian brio: "I 'gin to be aweary of the sun, / And wish th'estate o'th'world were now undone." Mindful of his dignity as a warrior king, he reasons that "At least we'll die with harness [i.e., armor] on our back" (5.5.46–51). Although the guile and ruthlessness with which Macbeth seized and consolidated his power are akin to those that Machiavelli attributes to Cesare Borgia, Macbeth's strategic intelligence now deserts him. His physical bravery remains steadfast, but he is helpless and then hopeless before a not desperately cunning ruse de guerre of Malcolm's devising.

In trying to comprehend this moment, we must turn again to the relationship between historical time (in which human beings live their lives on earth) and eternity (divine, and outside the orders of time and space within which the human drama is played out).

Crucially, the prophecies by which Macbeth sets such store depend on the Weird Sisters being able, by some means and in some measure, to step outside the temporal order of things and gain a vantage on events that have not yet taken place. Banquo understands as much when he entreats the Weird Sisters to "look into the seeds of time" (1.3.58) in order to reveal the secrets of his future; by the same token, Macbeth later urges them not to scruple over "the treasure / Of Nature's germen" (4.1.57–58) in responding to his equally pressing set of queries. These "seeds" of time and nature are not an accident of Shakespeare's fertile imagination, but are offshoots of the theological doctrine of the *rationes seminales* (usually translated as "seeds of reason" or "seminal principles"). The *rationes seminales* have their origin in Stoic physics, and became a staple of Platonic thought through the influence of Plotinus's *Enneads*. Most importantly for *Macbeth*, they are also a prominent feature of Augustine's writings. For Augustine, the *rationes seminales* are the universal principles or causes on account of which the created world can develop and grow in time—a sort of ontological DNA that determines the limits of all that a particular entity can become. In Spenser's Garden of Adonis, they appear as "the first seminary / Of all things, that are borne to live and dye, / According to their kynds," and as Timothy Bright observes, they endure "till the end of all things."[31] They are also accessible to demons, who have the freedom to use their knowledge of them in seeking to corrupt humankind.[32] The extent of this freedom was open to debate (could demons do any more than anticipate that which God had already ordained?), but in reading *Macbeth*, the main point is uncontentious: by accessing the "seeds of nature" as Banquo and Macbeth suggest, the Weird Sisters could be taken to have prophesied with reasonable accuracy events that had not yet occurred.

How do the *rationes seminales* relate to the problems of time with which *Macbeth* is so concerned? One curiosity of the play's approach to the question is suggested by the excitement of Macbeth's initial response to the Weird Sisters. Having learned that he has in fact become Thane of Cawdor, he imagines their words as "happy prologues to the swelling act / Of the imperial theme" (1.3.130–31). Taking a more positive approach to the *theatrum mundi* topos than the one he will adopt in responding to the news of his wife's death, he praises the Weird Sisters' prophecies for playing a role *within* the worldly drama of which he sees himself as the protagonist, albeit one—that of the Prologue—that affects to extra-dramatic status: they are both of and not of the play that he is acting out. So, although prophecy (and with it the *rationes seminales*) needs to transcend the conditions of historical temporality, the version of it imagined in *Macbeth* does not do so by venturing onto the eternal plane from which God simultaneously beholds all that ever was, is, and will be—that which, through the mediation of the Holy Ghost, informs the prophecies contained in the books of Daniel and Revelation.[33]

A distinction noticed by Frank Kermode helps to make sense of this apparent conundrum: although the idea of historical time (*saeculum* or *tempus*) is clear enough, there was more than one kind of temporal transcendence available to early moderns. On the one hand, there was the *nunc-stans* or ever-abiding present inhabited by God the creator—that which we usually understand by "eternity." On the other, there was what late medieval theologians described as the *aevum* ("age" or "aeon").[34]

The *aevum* was an intermediate temporal order devised in response to a theological problem that arose as Aristotle's writings were recovered within the Western—which is to say, Latin—tradition in the twelfth and thirteenth centuries. How to synthesize the doctrine of the eternity of the physical universe as propounded by Aristotle with the Augustinian conviction that only the *nunc-stans* of God the creator can be thought of as eternal? The answer was to elaborate a category that enabled some parts of creation, such as the stars, to be conceived of as existing beyond the constraints of secular temporality. As a name and an idea, the *aevum* owed something to Cicero's *Dream of Scipio*. Specifically, to the *aevo sempiterno* ("perpetual age") from which the spirit of Scipio Africanus prophesies his grandson's future career, and from which it is possible to observe the entirety of the well-regulated cosmos.[35] But whatever its origins, the *aevum* belonged at a midpoint between time and eternity: it connoted an immortal and immutable kind of existence, but only within the universe framed by God's *nunc-stans*. Perpetual or sempiternal rather than eternal, it was a creation of the first day's work that would continue beyond the eschatological end point of the apocalypse, within which the historical order of things—the *saeculum*—would be consumed. The definition offered by the Oxford philosopher John Case is helpfully summative:

> Time is the measure of things that have a beginning and an end; *Aevum* is the measure of things that have a beginning but that lack an end; Eternity is called the measure of things that have neither beginning nor end.[36]

Although I have not been able to identify any early modern diagrams that show how and where the *aevum* was taken to fit in, the great Warburg scholar D. P. Walker took it upon himself to design one of his own.[37] It is reproduced in figure 7, and lays out transparently (or as transparently as possible) that which makes the *aevum* distinctive within the cosmogony of Christian belief.

As a medium with a beginning but no end, the *aevum* provided an ideal home for beings such as angels, which were taken to be immortal, but created and therefore less than fully divine. Many, including Dante, took the view that it was also the condition of hell.[38] Moreover, the *aevum*

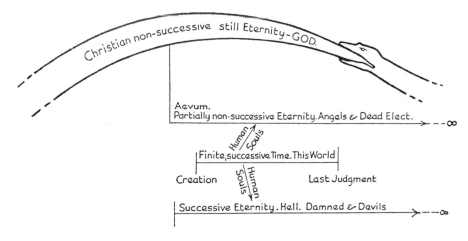

FIGURE 7. D. P. Walker, "Eternity and the Afterlife," *Journal of the Warburg and Courtauld Institutes* 27 (1964): 245.

proved useful in bestowing the dignity and immortality of a perfect species on a range of worldly phenomena: on the institutions of the law and the church, on peoples or nations, on empires, but most of all on kings. Some of this can look like an intermixture of special pleading and prestidigitatory excess, and not only in retrospect: Montaigne, for example, scoffs at the "mystical basis" on which legal authority seeks to establish itself. The fact is that such ideas were taken seriously. Here is Kantorowicz quoting the sixteenth-century lawyer Edmund Plowden on the doctrine (what Kantorowicz calls the "mystic fiction") of the king's two bodies:

> For the King has in him two Bodies, *viz.*, a Body natural, and a Body politic. His Body natural (if it be considered in itself) is a Body mortal, subject to all Infirmities that come by Nature or Accident, to the Imbecility of Infancy or old Age, and to the like Defects that happen to the natural Bodies of other People. But his Body politic is a Body that cannot be seen or handled, consisting of Policy and Government, and constituted for the Direction of the People, and the Management of the public weal, and this Body is utterly void of Infancy, and old Age, and other natural Defects and Imbecilities, which the Body natural is subject to, and for this Cause, what the King does in his Body politic, cannot be invalidated or frustrated by any Disability in his natural Body.[39]

Because the body politic exists in the sacred dimension of the *aevum* rather than in the fallen and finite world of secular history, it bestows mystical powers on the monarchs who assume it. If not quite able to recuperate

or purge defects in the body natural (sometimes known as the body temporal), the body politic (on this account a *corpus mysticum*) operates
autonomously of such shortcomings, and is unencumbered by them. It
can also endow the monarch with a kind of prescience that shades into
the prophetic. After Malcolm extols his ally and role model, the English
king Edward the Confessor, for his miraculous facility in curing "the Evil"
(i.e., the King's Evil, or scrofula), he adds that "With this strange virtue /
He hath a heavenly gift of prophecy, / And sundry blessings hang about his
throne / That speak him full of grace" (4.3.146–48, 156–59).[40]

Even so, the aspect of sacred kingship that most seized Shakespeare's
imagination in writing *Macbeth* is that—in virtue of its extra-temporal
perfection—the body politic purports to be anything but another *persona*,
or socially sanctioned form of identity. It defines who a monarch *is* rather
than a part that he fits himself out to play. Macbeth, we might recall, is relatively untroubled by the circumstances of his ascent to the throne, whereas
Lady Macbeth cannot wash her hands frequently enough to attain even
the semblance of equanimity—she may previously have been the gin in his
tonic, and was certainly his equal in the craft of rhetorical redescription,
but is now excluded from the benefits of the *corpus mysticum*. Comple-
menting the sacred status of the body politic, the monarch's body natural
equips him with the capacity to sow seeds of a less elevated sort in order to
attain dynastic perpetuity; or, as Kantorowicz puts it, to ensure "the unin-
terrupted line of royal bodies natural."[41] This is why Macbeth is haunted
by the prospect of Banquo's heirs "stretch[ing] out to th' crack of doom"
(4.1.116)—that is, until the various seismic and meteorological distur-
bances that, according to Revelation 11:19, will follow the sounding of the
seventh and final trumpet. His own want of heirs works to undermine not
only the amalgamation of bodies natural and politic within himself, but
also his sense that the body politic has the capacity to recuperate the mortal present. Moreover, it further cuts him off from his wife, who—whether
or not she has literally "given suck" (1.7.54) in the past—appears unable
now to have children. Unlike the aged Elizabeth I, it is not impossible that
Macbeth might live to perpetuate his line, but he seems unable to do so
with the woman he loves.

I know of no work that explicitly places the *rationes seminales* within
the *aevum*—but Spenser's Garden of Adonis comes close to it, Augustine
hints at something of the sort, and the two concepts are at the very least
suggestively compatible: the *rationes seminales* are to be found within the
temporal world, but are not of it.[42] As Kantorowicz remarks, the "*aevum*
was habitat of the Ideas, *Logoi*, or Prototypes, as well as of the 'Angels' of

alexandrianized Christian philosophy."[43] What can be ventured with more certainty is that *Macbeth* returns over and again to the kind of timelessness that is enjoyed by the *rationes seminales* and within the *aevum*; and, vitally, that it returns over and again both to the *appeal* of such timelessness, and to the costs that this appeal extorts as its due.

Consider the way in which Macbeth begins his first soliloquy:

If it were done, when 'tis done, then 'twere well
It were done quickly. If th'assassination
Could trammel up the consequence, and catch
With his surcease, success: that but this blow
Might be the be-all and end-all, here,
But here, upon this bank and shoal of time,
We'd jump the life to come. But in these cases,
We still have judgement here, that we but teach
Bloody instructions, which being taught, return
To plague th'inventor. (1.7.1–10)

These lines do not lend themselves to paraphrase. Superficially, they resemble something that Shakespeare's Richard Gloucester might have uttered while plotting his rise to power: the Machiavellian discourse of how best to bend fortune to the dictates of one's will. In reality, something far more interesting is going on. Macbeth imagines himself able to connect the past, the present, and future. Contemplating the murder of Duncan, he sees his future self looking back on a deed accomplished expeditiously, and uses this vision to guide his conduct in the historical world from which he has briefly absented himself. "Be-all and end-all" is odd (if something has come to an end, it can no longer lay claim to the condition of being), but Macbeth's sense is unambiguous. If the act of killing Duncan could be accomplished without discovery by others, then the benefits that would accrue would be worth any potential costs in the afterlife. The verb to "jump" here means to "risk" or to "hazard."[44] In saying so, Macbeth concedes that terrestrial living, washed along by the currents of linear temporality, is not all there is.

And yet it is not the fear of being judged harshly *sub specie aeternitatis* that holds his attention. Instead, he is drawn to a less demanding key: the moralizing wisdom common to the Bible and the tradition of revenge tragedy, which insists that even the most ingeniously executed crimes will rebound on their authors. Although the tide may turn and Macbeth may lose the opportunity to kill Duncan with comparative ease, the risks of exposure and of "judgement here" are just too high.[45] On the face of it, a textbook formulation. Conventional moral philosophy drew on the writings of Aristotle and Cicero to describe a polychronic instant in which memory, foresight, and present understanding merge to inform one's decision-making. The virtue of prudence involved stepping back from one's current predicament, allowing one's reason to look forward in light of the past, thereby furnishing oneself with the wherewithal to govern, and to control, the dictates of impulse and appetite. Francis Bacon encapsulates this view neatly. "*The Affection beholdeth meerely the present; Reason beholdeth the future, and summe of time.* And therefore, the *Present*, filling the *Imagination* more; *Reason* is commonly vanquished; But after that force of *Eloquence* and *Perswasion*, hath made thinges *future*, and *remote*, appeare as *present*, than uppon the revolt of the Imagination, Reason prevayleth."[46] Macbeth's reason does indeed behold the future and with it the limited "sum" of time. It then presents him with a vivid image of what the consequences of killing Duncan would be, making "thinges *future*, and *remote*, appeare as *present*." He resolves to stay the hand of violence.

Almost immediately, he encounters Lady Macbeth. After a few minutes in her company, his resolution wavers: the prospect of possessing now that which the Weird Sisters have prophesied for the hereafter is just too tempting. Although Lady Macbeth imputes cowardice and effeminacy to the suggestion that Duncan be spared, it is her insistence that true manliness would know no constraints of "time and place" (1.7.51) that is decisive. The question now becomes one of whether or not their plan will work, and once Lady Macbeth reassures him that it will, he has his mission. As they part company, Macbeth settles his nerves with the injunction that his wife should play her part in things by "mock[ing] the time with fairest show" (1.7.82). Husband and wife are united in the yearning to be transported "beyond / This ignorant present" and to "feel now / The future in an instant" (1.5.56–58). No matter the cost, they will make tangible that which could otherwise only be enjoyed as a thought experiment.

Returning now to the way in which Macbeth responds to his wife's death, we can see that it is precisely a vantage outside the temporal order to which, in imagining the progress of human history until the "last syllable of recorded time," he lays claim—for himself as a human being standing as the temporal embodiment of the monarchical *corpus mysticum*. By professing to observe the tomorrows and pretense through which the human drama has been and will continue to be measured, he seeks to place himself beyond the secular mode of temporality. And it is the gesture that counts: the details of belonging to the *aevum* do not concern him. As Kermode has proposed, it may be that Macbeth's "tomorrow, and tomorrow, and tomorrow" recalls the repeated "tomorrow and tomorrow" (*cras et cras*) from which Augustine so devoutly, and so frustratedly, wishes to escape in completing his conversion to Christianity, but Horace's "Diffugere nives" (to which Augustine himself may well owe a debt) provides us with a better intertext for understanding what is at stake.[47] Far from desiring that tomorrow and with it salvation should come about as soon as possible, Macbeth shares the view of Horace's narrator that it is a sign of typically human folly to worry about what may or may not come to pass. And yet rather than thrust himself into the distractions of the worldly present in the standard carpe diem manner—or even to condemn them in the fashion of a satirist—Macbeth tries to absent himself from time, and from history, altogether.

So, Macbeth makes a show to himself of his temporal detachment; doing so tends to validate both his body politic and the qualities of transcendence that it is supposed to confer. Things, however, are even more complicated than such a summary can allow. Without question, the posture that Macbeth adopts depends on his sense that a king, in virtue of being touched by divinity, is set apart from the *theatrum mundi*. What is remarkable is that there is nothing remotely glorifying or celebratory in what he says. Shakespeare instead has him hold fast to kingship in desperation, and sublimated fear: it is the only thing that allows him to go beyond the constraints of the masquerade of a life "signifying nothing." Part of this desperation is caused by his need to deny the needily impatient ambition that drove him to "jump" all and murder Duncan, but perhaps the greater part of it arises from the loss of his lover, confidant, and conspirator. It is a truism, and possibly just true, that the Macbeths are Shakespeare's only happily married couple. As his wife is gradually destroyed by the burden of what she has helped her husband to accomplish, it is this happiness—this mutually contented trust—from which Macbeth is gradually distanced, and of which Siward informs him that he is now bereft. As to acknowledge any of this, even by disowning it, would be to acknowledge the claims and perhaps the precedence of his body natural, he dismisses human affairs altogether: a medium unsuited to the long perspectives of a king. It is the last and greatest expression of his impulse to loftily evasive euphemism. If the body politic cannot be construed as a force for recuperation or redemption, then it can at least provide him with a temporal dimension from which to renounce the pain and performative historicity that would otherwise be his lot.

Of the many ironies with which Shakespeare infuses this moment, the most immediate is that in pushing aside the eternal plane by which he earlier on appeared to set such store, Macbeth collapses the frame-work within which the *aevum*, and with it the idea of sacred kingship to which he clings, is made possible. The universe he imagines is more akin to that of Lucretius, who holds that the material universe is mortal, and that its inevitable demise has no special significance. Time here does not have an existence of its own, and is merely an accident arising from matter in motion as perceived by human beings. Matter itself is eternal, and there is nothing (i.e., only the void) beyond it—no heavenly *aeternitas* and no sempiternal *aevum* from which to behold the past, present, and future development of the universe.[48] Indeed, Lucretius's *On the Nature of Things* makes for a powerful tool with which to read this part of *Macbeth*. It illuminates the ways in which Macbeth's understanding of the *theatrum mundi* work against his confidence that he is, or could be, in a position to foresee the human drama shamming onward to "the last syl-lable of recorded time." Even as he assumes an extra-temporal position from which to disdain the histrionic folly of the human condition, Mac-beth is himself a human being constrained to fret (though, at this point in the action, probably not to strut) on the stage of history.[49]

In any case, rather than finding in his desacralized cosmos a prompt to pursue the tranquility of the Epicureans, Macbeth regards it as the state of being against which he can, and must, define himself. If he belonged to it himself, his regal status would be no more meaningful than the remainder of human affairs—another version of the player king topos in Erasmus's "Tragicus Rex." That is, an emblem of the uncomfortable truth that, in the words of the epilogue to *All's Well*, "The King's a beggar, now the play is done."[50] Or, in the words of Hamlet while confounding Rosencrantz and Guildenstern by riddling on the two-bodies doctrine, an affirmation that "the King is a thing . . . of nothing."[51] The report that Birnham Wood is advancing toward Dunsinane, and with it the realization that he too is heading inconsequentially toward the apocalypse, hits Macbeth hard. The end cannot come soon enough.

———

That *Macbeth* is a topical play—one that engages with the discourses sur-rounding the early Jacobean regime—has been well attested. For instance, Lady Macbeth's instruction that her husband should "beguile the time" by "look[ing] like the innocent flower" while "be[ing] the serpent under't" recalls not just proverbial wisdom about snakes in the grass, but a medal struck to celebrate the unmasking of the 1605 Gunpowder Plot (see

FIGURE 8. Copper medal celebrating the unmasking of the 1605
Gunpowder Plot. Rijksmuseum, Amsterdam.

figure 8). On the obverse are embossed a serpent, an arrangement of roses
and lilies, and the inscription, "The concealed one is exposed" (*Detectus
qui latuit*).[52]

A more integral example is suggested by a playlet staged for James VI /
I outside St. John's College, Oxford in the summer of 1605. Matthew
Gwinne's *Tres Sybillae* consists of three sybils (dressed as nymphs) who
rehearse their prophecy that Banquo's heirs will have empire without
end, and who now repeat this prophecy for the benefit of Banquo's regal
descendent, James. Despite James's principled dismissal of prophecy, he
was by all accounts delighted. Gwinne adapted the same parts of Holinshed on which Shakespeare would lean in *Macbeth*, and although we do
not know whether Shakespeare encountered Gwinne's work directly, it
seems overwhelmingly likely that *Macbeth*'s emphasis on the Stuart line
of succession owes something to Gwinne's triumph.[53] Whatever its origins, the calculated topicality of offering James an image of his lineal—or,

rather, curvilineal—virtue interlocked with that of Edward the Confessor, the last English monarch before the succession crisis that precipitated
the Norman Conquest, shows that Shakespeare understood the force of
James's newly British interpretation of monarchy. But as critics as different as Harry Berger, David Norbrook, David Kastan, and John Kerrigan
have argued, to scratch the surface of this image is to see that Shakespeare
was no cheerleader for either the Jacobean ideology or the philosophies
and theologies that underpinned it.[54]

The dumb show pageant of Fleance's descendants in act 4 scene 1 is
pivotal. Shakespeare borrows many details of the Weird Sisters' prophecies from Holinshed, but this pageant seems to have been his invention
alone. And, as Kantorowicz remarks, it was designed to maintain "the fic-
titious oneness of the predecessors with potential successors, all of whom
were present and incorporated in the actual incumbent of the [monarchi-
cal] dignity."[55] Which is to say that, as the body politic (perpetual, transcendent, sacred) accommodates itself to the different bodies natural in
the order of patrilineal succession, so a particular king can claim a sort of
communion with those who have worn and will wear the crown before and
after him: his legitimacy and dignity are duly burnished, as is his capacity
to claim a fusion between his temporal and extra-temporal selves.

Macbeth is presented with the likenesses of eight kings, alongside the
ghost of their ultimate progenitor, Banquo. They are the handiwork of
the "masters," or magical assistants, that answer to the Weird Sisters, and
that have direct or indirect access to the *rationes seminales*. (Akin, perhaps, to the "spirits / That tend on mortal thoughts" summoned by Lady
Macbeth at 1.5.40–41).[56] Midway through, Macbeth worries where the
line of succession might end, only for it to conclude with the eighth and
final Stuart monarch of Scotland to have reigned before James VI. This
eighth monarch ought by rights to have been Mary, Queen of Scots, but
as James no more wished to be reminded of his difficult mother than did
his new English subjects, Shakespeare's decision to switch her out for a
king seems prudent—a maneuver that echoes his departure from Holinshed in not having Macbeth conspire with Banquo to kill Duncan. In any
case, this fictionalized eighth monarch carries a prophetic "glass." As Macbeth explains, this "glass / . . . shows me many more; and some I see / That
twofold balls and treble scepters carry" (4.1.118–20). A little like Milton's
Adam after discovering that his line will be extinguished in the Flood ("oh
visions ill foreseen!"), Macbeth is perturbed at this "horrible sight," a feeling exacerbated by Banquo's ghost gesturing at the line of kings as "his"
(4.1.121, 123).[57] It is hard to say exactly what this prophetic vision might

have entailed when *Macbeth* was first performed, but the stage glass can be counted on to have shown some representation or other of an enthroned and appropriately dignified James, especially if—as seems plausible—the play was staged at court.[58]

The Weird Sisters' pageant comprises an act of union between a fictionalized past and the political realities of the Jacobean present, but it is not the only instance of *Macbeth* taking pains to portray the Jacobean ideology, and James himself, in a favorable light. Once Macduff has safely dispatched Macbeth and returned to the stage carrying the "usurper's cursed head," he waxes lyrical about having redeemed Scotland from tyranny: "the time," he claims, "is free" (5.9.21). The new king, Malcolm, responds in a similar vein. He assures his new subjects that "We shall not spend a large expense of time / Before we reckon with your several loves," then declares that his "thanes and kinsmen" will "henceforth be earls"—a move of decided Anglicization that no doubt reflects his period at the court of Edward the Confessor. Malcolm continues that all remaining exiles should now be called home and "planted newly with the time," before concluding with the promise that "what needful else / That calls upon us, by the grace of grace, / We will perform in measure, time, and place" (5.9.26–39). The past, present, and future of historical time are redeemed in virtue of Malcolm's legitimacy as the eldest son of the murdered Duncan—in virtue, that is, of Malcolm's kingship holding a place both in the *saeculum*, and the perpetual-mystical space of the royal *aevum*. Order is restored, and if there is any difficulty in reconciling Malcolm's succession with James's line having been founded by Fleance (whose whereabouts are unclear after his escape from Macbeth's assassins), then the play stays silent about it.

The fact remains that *Macbeth*'s discourse of legitimacy is anything but straightforward. Macbeth is a murderer and a tyrant, to be sure, but it is not until he is safely dead and his successor is poised to assume power that Macduff calls him a "usurper." Malcolm had been Duncan's nominated heir (or Tanist) under the Scottish system of elective monarchy, and when Malcolm and his brother fled (in what was believed to be complicit guilt) after their father's killing, the Scottish nobility simply elected another king in Malcolm's place: Macbeth. So it is that although Macbeth is reflexively discussed as a "tyrant" by Malcolm and Macduff, even Malcolm is moved to concede that their success will depend on a kind of "revolt" (5.4.12).[59] Perhaps this is why Milton, when contemplating a tragedy of his own on the subject of Macbeth, proposed "beginning at the arrivall of Malcolm at Mackduffe."[60] In any event, when Malcolm's largely English army prevails against the forces commanded by the king of Scotland, he needs a better story. He does not know the truth about his father's murder, does not want to look like one of the two foreign-aligned rebels who sought to overturn his father's rule at the beginning of the play, and may yet need to behave in a way that his enemies could label tyrannical. In short, he would like to avoid offering any hostages to fortune. As the Scots, English, Irish, and Welsh would come to discover forty years or so after *Macbeth* was first performed, the line between regicide and tyrannicide is a fine one.

Shakespeare's Macbeth is thus recast as a usurper, not because his election was illegitimate or because he murdered Duncan, but because he has interfered with what is now implied to be the naturally patrilineal succession of the crown from father to eldest son. Malcolm is duly acclaimed king by the surviving thanes of Scotland, and informs them that their traditional ranks will be harmonized with those of the English feudal structure. The thanes may not realize the significance of this moment, but their successors will owe their status to Malcolm and his royal descendants, not the other way around. In due course—as Holinshed, Hector Boece, George Buchanan, and their various readers were well aware—Malcolm would abolish Tanistry, and institute the prerogative of primogeniture that would crown the infant James VI in 1567.[61] It is just that hereditary monarchy and the power that goes with it are that which Macbeth has so violently desired for himself.

That there is more in common between Malcolm and Macbeth than Malcolm and Macduff would prefer to admit is suggested by one of the most perplexing scenes of the play. It is one that is often cut or abbreviated in performance, but that—as Sally Mapstone has shown—lies at the center of the historiographical tradition on which *Macbeth* draws via Holinshed.[62] In it, Malcolm pretends to be lecherous, avaricious, and devoid of all the "king-becoming graces" (4.3.91) in claiming that he would be an even worse monarch than Macbeth. By so doing, he intends to test Macduff's commitment to the right, and with it his opposition to Macbeth's rule. (Malcolm suspects Macduff because although he claims to have turned against Macbeth, he did not take the precaution of bringing his wife and children with him when he fled to England.) Once Macduff's bona fides have been established to Malcolm's satisfaction, the would-be king comes clean about his stratagem, and declares that that Macduff should

> Here abjure
> The taints and blames I laid upon myself,
> For strangers to my nature. I am yet
> Unknown to woman, never was forsworn,

Scarcely have coveted what was mine own,
At no time broke my faith, would not betray
The devil to his fellow, and delight
No less in truth than life. My first false speaking
Was this upon myself. (4.3.123–31)

Putting to one side some of the less explicable vices that Malcolm attributes to Macbeth (lechery and avarice? Not on the evidence presented
in *Macbeth*), there are problems here. Malcolm notes at the beginning of
the scene that "This tyrant, whose sole name blisters our tongues, / Was
once thought honest" (4.3.12–13). As in *Othello*, "honest" does double duty:
someone who is both honorable and who has, or seems to have, the virtues
of inner truthfulness and plain dealing. Malcolm's point, of course, is that
Macbeth is *not* honest: that he has only ever pretended to be so while seeking to advance his own nefarious ends. And yet he, Malcolm, has just put
on a consummate show of simulation and dissimulation to test the mettle
of a possible ally in his pursuit of the Scottish crown. He insists that "My
first false speaking / Was this upon myself," but how can we or Macduff
be sure? Be sure, that is, that he hasn't spoken in this manner before and
won't do so again if he feels the need? If we can't be sure, how can we
know that he is not, like Macbeth (on Malcolm's own account), a self-
serving counterfeit? If, in line with the doctrine of the *arcana imperii*, we
go along with Malcolm's stratagem and accept that saying one thing and
meaning another can be an effective way of seizing and exercising the powers of the crown, should we conclude that Macbeth is not such a reprehensible piece of work after all? And if Malcolm's dishonesty (qua misleading
statements uttered by his body natural) is licensed by the demands of his
body politic, why might the same not be true of Macbeth? Once Malcolm
has finished explaining himself, Macduff is nonplussed: "Such welcome and
unwelcome things at once / 'Tis hard to reconcile" (4.3.138–39). Understand-
ably so. In this play of twos and threes and deeds doubly redoubled, in
which moral and epistemological clarity always shade into ambiguity (fair
is foul and foul is fair), nothing is as simple as Malcolm wants to suggest.
We either take his word for it, or we don't.

There has been no shortage of fine scholarship examining Shakespeare's skeptical attitude to sacred kingship. Following Kantorowicz's
lead, most of this has concentrated on *Richard II* and the later history
plays, though the ease with which Claudius (a regicide, fratricide, and
usurper) fends off Laertes's rebellion by invoking the "divinity" that "doth
hedge a king" (4.5.123) has also given pause. Rather than sermonizing on

behalf of the divine right of kings or agitating for rebellion, Shakespeare invites his audiences to observe that sacred kingship is a fiction—which a character like Richard II can use to console himself as his actual power ebbs away, and which a character like Claudius can use to pull the wool over his subjects' eyes. In other words, Shakespeare treats sacred kingship as a principle of aesthetic order, not one whose origins lie in theological or politico-theological truth. *Macbeth*, I would suggest, is another case in point. In it, Shakespeare explores the language and assumptions of the belief that a king's body politic exists beyond the confines of historical time. What is more, he invites us to acknowledge the dangers of mistaking an aesthetic doctrine for one that represents some version or other of politico-theological truth—not least in opening the door to the sort of monarchical absolutism that would become a common feature of seventeenth- and eighteenth-century political life.[63] Whatever kingly virtues and shortcomings Malcolm and Macbeth might possess, and wherever their legitimacy might be said to reside, their institutional bodies do not allow them to transcend the "times" that their bodies natural aim to dominate, and perhaps to "seed."

A comparison may help better to illuminate what is at stake here. Writing of the emphasis found within neoclassical dramatic theory on the Aristotelian unity of time, David Riggs makes the compelling argument that it was a response to a universe—material and intellectual—that was no longer anthropocentric and finite; confronted with a vision of reality that exceeded settled definition, dramatists refined their poetics in order to impose as much orderliness and control as they could.[64] Of course, Shakespeare could respect the unity of time when he wanted to, especially when making the contrivances of comic resolution one of his dramatic subjects: take *A Midsummer Night's Dream* or *The Tempest*. It is just that when writing tragedy, he found, in the unities, a form of representative curtailment that led to the distortion of the world as he saw it; a disjunction between lived experience and the elegantly patterned words of the playwright's art; an expression of a pseudo-mimetic rationalism that, though superficially appealing, was inimical to tragic mimesis. As the Aristotelian unity of time for Shakespearean tragedy in general, so the *aevum* as it is scrutinized in *Macbeth*. It is a fiction that has been allowed to harden into received opinion for three interconnected reasons: 1) to dignify and legitimate the office of the monarch; 2) to give the impression that there is a divinely ordained order to things; and 3) to give the impression that the human mind is equal to comprehending even the most abstruse features of this order.

Shakespeare has vanishingly little in common with the doyen of English legal historians, F. W. Maitland, but Maitland's verdict on the *corpus mysticum* as described by Plowden is one that the author of *Macbeth* would have had no difficulty in endorsing: "I do not know where to look in the whole series of our law books for so marvellous a display of metaphysical—or we might say metaphysiological—nonsense."[65] Maitland wrote as a theorist as well as an historian of the law, and was determined to draw attention to the errors that ensue when the *verba* through which a subject is habitually discussed are unthinkingly conflated with its *res*.[66] Shakespeare, by contrast, sees in the ideology of sacred kingship a specimen of the delusionality from which tragedy can be woven. Macbeth and Malcolm are drawn to the political theology of the king's two bodies for what it enables them to say about both themselves and their capacity to rule. Macbeth is destroyed by the historicity that he had thought himself to have left behind when assuming the dignity of the Scottish crown; Malcolm and the future that he so contentedly maps out after Macbeth's death are left to the discretion of the audience.

To cast this thought a little differently, Malcolm's plans for an all-hail hereafter close the play on a note of temporal and narrative open-endedness.[67] Like *Romeo and Juliet, Hamlet*, and *Othello*, we are presented with order in some measure restored. Like *Romeo and Juliet, Hamlet*, and *Othello*, we are left to wonder whether this restoration of order will prove meaningful or enduring; whether Malcolm's vision of the Scottish polity will be any more fruitful than the one outlined by Duncan after his foes were vanquished in act 1. This note of terminal ambiguity has a more specific aspect too. To doubt the sufficiency of Malcolm's speechifying is to suspect that matters may not, in the fulness of time, work out as he intends: that history might have other ideas. In a tragedy where both the crisis and its ostensible resolution are brought about by the conviction that a particular—highly privileged—human being can transcend the constraints of history and mortality, we are prompted to reflect that the *saeculum* and the *saeculum* alone is the measure of human achievement, living, and dying. And that, despite the ingenuity and ardency with which we frame our temporal-mortal existences with notions like eternity and the *aevum*, this will very likely remain the case for as long as human beings are around to worry the question. Northrop Frye is apt: "The basis of the tragic vision is being in time, the sense of the one-directional quality of life, where everything happens once and for all, where every act brings unavoidable and fateful consequences, and where all experience vanishes, not simply into the past, but into nothingness, annihilation."[68] In *Macbeth*, tragedy comprises not only the mimetic representation of being in time, but of our various attempts to go beyond it. To go beyond, that is, a shifting present that is always and necessarily ignorant not just of that which is to come, but of the circumstantiality and flux that, as it were, make it tick.

As a coda of sorts, some broader reflections on *Macbeth*'s engagement with the philosophy, theology, and politics of time. We might, with perfect justice, reflect that the play, especially in its title character's demystification of the apocalypse, conforms with Reinhart Koselleck's theory that it "was only when Christian eschatology shed its constant expectation of the imminent arrival of doomsday that a temporality could be revealed that would be open for the new and without limit."[69] And yet in Macbeth's response to his wife's demise he does not abandon the notion of an *eschaton* so much as strip it of its conventional significance. Pocock's more nuanced account of the same conceptual shift makes for a better fit. For him, Christian apocalypticism paradoxically ends up as "a powerful instrument of secularization, a means of drawing the redemptive process back into that dimension of social time from which Augustine had sought to separate it, and of depicting it [i.e., redemption] as the extension or the transformation of existing secular processes."[70] Although neither Macbeth nor *Macbeth* by any means disavow the framework employed by Christian thinkers to make sense of historical time, they provide us with a model of secular historicity—or, in Peter Brooks's terms, a plot—more than capable of accommodating the human belief, and the human need to believe, in ideas like providence.[71]

Such considerations strike me as having a good deal of value, but I am not at all sure that they go far enough in acknowledging the force of that which Shakespeare explores in *Macbeth*. He could not have guessed that James VI / I's eldest son would die in 1612, that his second son would be executed for treason in 1649, that the regnant branch of the Stuart family would be eclipsed in childless misery in 1714, or that its claims would be shattered once and for all at Culloden in 1746. Nor would he have sought to: as a poet, he took no interest in the vatic affirmations of Virgilian epic and its Christianizing Renaissance appropriators. What he grasped was that the best claim to perpetuity—or to any form of escape from "this bank and shoal of time"—does not belong to one royal dynasty or another, or to the institution of the monarchy. It belongs instead to the durable pigment of works like *Macbeth*. As Milton (adapting another of Horace's odes) understood well, Shakespeare's writings assume the most enduring kind of vitality by constructing "a live-long monument" to their author in the minds of his readers and auditors. By, that is, winning themselves enduring fame. Not necessarily the kind of thing in which the speaker of Sonnet 55 seeks to entangle the fair youth (his poetry, he insists, will abide in "the eyes of all posterity / That wear this world out to the ending doom"), but one that guarantees a hereafter extending far beyond the poet's historical moment.[72]

According to one of the most frequently repeated commonplaces of the sixteenth and seventeenth centuries, truth is the daughter of time; Erasmus likewise dilates on the theme that "time reveals all"—sooner or later, history brings everything to light.[73] Shakespeare, who would put the sentiment that "time shall unfold what plighted cunning hides" into the mouth of the banished Cordelia, viewed things differently.[74] Scotland and its rulers are no wiser or clearer sighted at the end of *Macbeth* than they are at its beginning. Historiography is always a negotiation between the imperatives of the present and what can be retrieved of the past, and is as such in thrall to the contingency and mutability of temporal phenomena. If Macbeth needs to be cast as a usurper—or if Mary, Queen of Scots, needs to become a man—then so be it. Discerning the truth of history or politics, and perhaps of anything human at all, depends on being willing and able to think through the cultivated though far from perfect atemporality of art. Testing the limits of that discernment, and of the truths that it can reveal, is the province of tragedy.

CHAPTER SIX

Against Nature

KING LEAR

One animal alone has been given the capacity for sorrow.

—PLINY, *NATURAL HISTORY*

THERE IS A SENSE in which *Macbeth* and *King Lear* are, if not exactly a diptych, then companion pieces. One dramatizes the struggles of an ambitious man to recuperate his existence by assuming a monarchical body politic; the other the struggles of a monarch to lead a meaningful life within his body natural after abdicating from the dignity and responsibilities of the crown. One glorifies the *rationes seminales*—the "seeds of time" and "the treasure / Of Nature's germen"—as the guarantor of prophetic truth; the other entreats the "all-shaking thunder" to "Crack nature's moulds, all germens spill at once / That make ingrateful man!" (3.2.6, 8–9). One summons "the great doom's image" in order capture the bloody horror of a regicide, before worrying at the implications and true significance of the apocalypse, the "last syllable of recorded time"; the other goes no further than employing the notion of "the promised end" (or its "image") in order to process an experience of overwhelming devastation and loss (5.2.262–63).

As *King Lear* begins, its title character is in a pinch. He is nearly eighty years old. He is tired, widowed, and knows that his body natural has failed to provide him with the key to dynastic perpetuity—that is, with a son to whom his kingdom can be bequeathed. The problem he faces is how, after his death, to prevent his lands from descending into civil war as his three daughters and their husbands fight to claim the lion's share for themselves. (Compare the plot of the originary Elizabethan tragedy, Sackville and Norton's *Gorboduc*.) Weakened as Lear is, however, he still has the powers bestowed by his body politic, and he resolves to use them so "that future strife / May be prevented now" (1.1.43–44). He will divide his kingdom into three parts, each to be ruled over by one of his three daughters and her spouse: the western and southwestern portions to his eldest daughter, married to the Duke of Cornwall; the northern portions to his second daughter, married to the Duke of Albany (i.e., Scotland); the remainder (central and southeastern England) to his youngest daughter, as yet unmarried but sought after by the King of France and the Duke of Burgundy. Through this settlement, Lear will also make a prominent display of his generosity, or what in a more humanistic idiom might be thought of as his munificence. As such, he will pass the power and dignity of the crown onto the next generation, but will also be in a position, for as long as he lives, to make use of his natural authority as a father and bene-factor to keep the peace between the siblings as a sort of arbiter-referee.[1]

Despite the conviction with which the monarchical *corpus mysticum* seems to have been imagined as a marker of a divine anointment from which one could not simply opt out, and despite the warning of James VI / I that a divided kingdom is a weakened kingdom, Lear's plan is not obviously fool-ish. Shakespeare could, for instance, have read in Montaigne of Charles V's abdications as Holy Roman Emperor (in favor of his brother) and King of Spain (in favor of his son), and retirement to a secluded monastery for the remainder of his days. Montaigne describes Charles as the very model of wisdom in giving up his kingly offices once age and infirmity prevented him from discharging their duties in full.[2]

Still, although Lear's stratagem is in no sense destined to fail, it leads to events that are far worse than those it seeks to forestall. This outcome has two points of origin, neither of which has anything to do with divine right theory. First, Lear's clear preference for his youngest daughter, Cordelia—in keeping with the Lear story as preserved by Geoffrey of Monmouth and Holin-shed, but distinctly at odds with the situation in two other of Shakespeare's sources, the anonymous play *King Leir* and the brief retelling of the Lear story in Spenser's *Faerie Queene* (both of which have the old king insisting that his three daughters be treated equally).[3] Shakespeare's Lear describes Cordelia as "our joy" (1.1.82), and informs her that "a third more opulent than your sisters" (1.1.86) is hers for the asking. Remarkably, he does so in earshot of his two elder daughters, Goneril and Regan. What is more, once he and Cordelia have fallen out, he declares (again so that all three daughters can hear) that "I loved her most" and that he had "thought to set my rest / On her kind nursery" (1.1.124–25). Which is to say that he had planned to live out his days, post-abdication, with Cordelia rather than Goneril or Regan.

This being the case, it would not be a stretch to infer that if Cordelia and her husband (be he Burgundy or France) were to have exploited the wealth of her territories at the expense of those possessed by her sisters, she would have had his support; and, further still, that Lear wanted to pass his kingdom in its entirety to Cordelia, but that he was prevented from doing so by her inexperience, her unmarried status, and his awareness that her sisters already had—through their marriages—strong power bases of their own. In short, although Lear makes a point of telling Regan that "'To thee and thine hereditary ever / Remain this ample third of our fair kingdom, / No less in space, validity and pleasure / Than that conferred on Goneril" (1.1.79–81), he expends no effort in pretending that their "thirds" are the equal of the wealthy and fertile portion being conferred on Cordelia.[4] Goneril and Regan are neither stupid nor oblivious to their self-interest. The implications of what Lear sought to accomplish are not lost on them.

But on their own, the old king's maneuverings in favor of Cordelia need not have led to disaster. Resentment from Goneril and Regan, yes, and no doubt conflict of one kind or another arising from this resentment—but not disaster, and probably not tragedy. For that to come about, a second point of origin is required. It takes the form of the medium through which Lear elects to settle on his children their new territories. Announcing that "'tis our far intent / To shake all cares and business from our age, / Conferring them on younger strengths, while we / Unburdened crawl toward death" (1.1.37–40), Lear demands (blurring the lines between the first-person pronoun and the majestic plural to which he will remain attached until the end of act 2) that his daughters should "Tell me . . . Which of you shall we say doth love us most, / That we our largest bounty may extend / Where nature doth with merit challenge" (1.1.48, 51–53). Of course, he knows exactly where he wishes to extend his bounty, on the grounds both of "merit" and of his "natural" affections as a father. In the play's opening lines, Kent and Gloucester seem only to have been informed that the kingdom is to be divided between Goneril and Regan (hence, perhaps, Cordelia's intended match with a foreign ruler), but Lear has already gone as far as to offer Cordelia's share of the kingdom to one and possibly both of her suitors as a dowry (1.1.195–98). Even so, he resolves to put his daughters through the motions of a love contest, and to do so in the presence of his assembled court. He does not tell us why, but his reasons are not far to seek. Partly to give himself a cover of legitimacy for his decision to give Cordelia the richest part of his kingdom. Partly to manage the pain involved in detaching himself from his body politic: by making himself the center of attention, thereby assuaging his sense of unease both at abdicating his crown and at having just avowed his waning potency (he is not, as we in the audience will shortly discover, much given to expressions of weakness or doubt). Mainly, to goad Goneril and Regan into declarations of filial love that will make it harder for them to go against his paternal judgment if, with only the resources of his body natural to support him, he were to take Cordelia's side in some future dispute.

Goneril and Regan are experienced in the ways of courtly living, and are unfazed by that which Lear demands of them. The former makes good use of the inexpressibility topos to insist that she loves him "more than word can wield the matter" (1.1.55)—before carrying on for another thirty breathless feet. The latter follows up with what might be paraphrased as "me too, but more so." That is, with the "outdoing" topos that was as much a staple of panegyric, and of epideictic rhetoric more generally, as the inexpressibility topos.[5] They lay it on thick. Lear is gratified, maybe half overlooking that what he has asked for and received is performance art.

Cordelia certainly fails to recognize it as such. After Goneril has said her piece: "What shall Cordelia speak? Love, and be silent" (1.1.62). After Regan has said hers: "Then poor Cordelia, / And yet not so, since I am sure my love's / More ponderous than my tongue" (1.1.77–79). There is pride here (like her father—and Edgar in the guise of Poor Tom—she is unembarrassed about regarding herself in the third person), and another outing for the inexpressibility topos. But for the most part Cordelia is stuck. As becomes clear in the following exchange with Lear (1.1.86–121), the mutual misunderstandings of which are the crucible from which the rest of the play will emerge, she cannot find a way of fitting *verba* to the *res* of her true feelings—cannot, that is, find a way of representing those feelings that does not have recourse to her inability to express them in words. In any case, and unable or unwilling to acknowledge that bodying forth emotional verity is not what is being demanded of her, she is affronted that her inability to translate the weighty matter of her feelings into words could be construed as anything other than an index of her integrity.

So, rather than offering up the ingenuous, unadorned, and even girlish sentiments that Lear anticipates (as he reveals to Kent at 1.1.130, he knows well her habit of "plain" speaking), she decides to stand on principle: to confront her father rather than to help steer him away from his excesses in the face of the "hereditary ever" with which he has failed to invest his kingdom. When asked what she has to say of her love, she is harshly deflationary. "Nothing, my lord." Incredulous, Lear seeks confirmation of what he has heard. Once he has it, he reassures himself of his own authority with the proverbial saw that "nothing will come of nothing" (in fact, Cordelia's "nothing" is a something from which rather a lot will eventuate), and urges her to "speak again."[6] So she does: "Unhappy that I am, I cannot heave / My heart into my mouth." Had she left things there then the situation might have been rescued. But she can no more hold her peace than can the disaffected Prince of *Hamlet*'s opening act. Nor does she have the least notion of how much is at stake in the role that Lear has asked her to play. "I love your majesty / According to my bond, no more nor less." By "bond" she suggests the affection by which children are bound to their fathers (an idea summoned by Edmund at 2.1.47–48): a tie that is natural, incontrovertible, and to Cordelia the only thing that matters.[7] But "bond" also carries the charge of something contractual or coldly trans-actional. Something that one does against one's desires from a sense of duty or obligation, in the expectation of material gain, or because one is forced—in bondage—so to do.[8] All told, and whether she means to or not, Cordelia cuts closer to the bone than Lear can tolerate.

Confronted with a favored daughter who not only refuses to play his game, but who publicly crosses him in condemning it, Lear's vision nar-rows into minatory forbearance: "Mend your speech a little / Lest you may mar your fortunes." Rather than insist that her love is not transactional and that she cannot conceive of it in such terms, Cordelia uses her father's logic to retaliate: "Good my lord, / You have begot me, bred me, loved me. I / Return those duties back as are right fit, / Obey you, love you and most honour you." Although the parallels between begetting and obedi-ence, breeding and loving, loving and honoring are imprecise at best, her purpose is to express herself in the language of public reciprocity, and of *decorum*—not that of the pseudo-emotionality that Lear has by now con-vinced himself that he needs to hear to validate his plans for his "joy" and the future of his kingdom. She concludes by rebuking what she regards as the hypocrisy of Goneril and Regan (as if they, Lear, or anyone else at court interpret their words literally): "Why have my sisters husbands, if they say / They love you all?" For her part, she will give "That lord whose hand must take my plight" half of her love, half of her "care and duty." In concluding, Cordelia declares that she could never marry if, "like my sisters," she professed "to love my father all." If a kingdom is divisible, then why not the love of a pious young woman?

Just as Cordelia fails to come to Lear's aid by mitigating the folly of the love-contest, so Lear now fails to recognize the fear, incomprehension, innocence, and wounded *amour propre* that shape his youngest and least worldly daughter's responses, all of which are exacerbated by the vulner-ability of her position on the threshold of a future with one of the two continental princes waiting somewhere just offstage. Rather than pausing to think about what they ought to say, father and daughter both speak as they feel—with scant regard for the consequences, or for considering that their emotions might be playing them false.

LEAR: But goes thy heart with this?
CORDELIA: Ay, my good lord.
LEAR: So young and so untender?
CORDELIA: So young, my lord, and true.
LEAR: Well, let it be so. Thy truth then be thy dower,
    For by the sacred radiance of the sun,
    The mysteries of Hecate and the night,
    By all the operation of the orbs
    From whom we do exist and cease to be,
    Here I disclaim all my paternal care,
    Propinquity and property of blood,
    And as a strange to my heart and me
    Hold thee from this for ever. The barbarous Scythian
    Or he that makes his generation messes
    To gorge his appetite, shall to my bosom
    Be as well neighboured, pitied and relieved,
    As thou my sometime daughter.

From being the favored child, heir to the richest part of the kingdom and key to Lear's plans for the future, Cordelia is disowned and disparaged. Swearing by the pagan deities Apollo and Hecate, as also by the natural motions of the heavens, Lear proclaims her monstrosity and avows that he will have nothing more to do with her. His severity feels excessive, even vindictive: he would, it seems reasonable to infer, treat the "barbarous Scythian" sympathetically because he, Lear, identifies with the Scythian's antipathetic treatment of "his generation."[9] He is both wounded (forgetting that he has instigated a courtly game, he seems genuinely hurt by her refusal to perform) and frustrated at being unable to negotiate the succession as he had intended. The feelings of impotence attendant on the last of these things no doubt act as a further spur to his anger. That all of this plays out in the gaze of the court cannot help. Shame compounds shame compounds shame. You cross me, I erase you. And yet, he can no more erase Cordelia than he can erase himself: in banishing the daughter he loves, he has set in motion a tragedy of agency in which he and those dearest to him will be obliged to confront the limits of that which is, and is not, in their power to understand or control.

Kent intervenes on Cordelia's behalf, but is cut off by Lear at his most peremptory: "Come not between the dragon and his wrath!" (1.1.123). For Shakespeare, dragons were emblematically splenetic in their anger, the more so because their activities were unchecked by social obligation.[10] Lear wants it to be clear that he means it and that he is still a king. He now calls for France and Burgundy to be brought on stage. But before they can arrive, he settles on Goneril and Regan that which was going to be Cordelia's, telling their husbands that "with my two daughters' dowers," they should "digest this third." He continues that "I do invest you jointly with my power, / Pre-eminence and all the large effects / That troop with majesty." Other than a retinue of a hundred knights, Lear will keep no more than "The name, and all th'addition to a king: the sway, / Revenue, execution of the rest, / Beloved sons, be yours; which to confirm, / This coronet part between you" (1.1.131–39). In other words, although Lear passes on to his successors the powers that had been conferred on him by his body politic, he wants to retain its exterior likeness: to be addressed and treated as if he were a king, and to continue dressing like one. The coronet that Lear invites Cornwall and Albany to share was presumably intended for Cordelia, and should not be confused with the crown that he continues to wear.

In Lear's anger and desire to spite Cordelia as fully as possible, he has blundered. Kent again attempts an intervention, avowing that "to plainness honor's bound / When majesty falls to folly," and insisting to Lear that he should "reserve thy state / And in thy best consideration check / This hideous rashness" (1.1.149–52). Kent's choice of "thy" rather than the formal "your" is less bold than an instance of provocative lèse-majesté. As, a little later, is his scoffing at Lear's swearing by Apollo. Perhaps Kent reasons that his only hope of getting through to the king is to shock him through extreme plainness of speech; perhaps, in his own incredulity and anger at the love-contest and its outcome, he loses the plot where a cooler-headed courtier would have found an excuse to distract or adjourn.[11] Either way, he fails to change Lear's mind, and promptly finds himself banished. Unlike Cordelia, he exits immediately.

This is the point at which Gloucester ushers in Cordelia's rival suitors. Lear is courtesy itself in addressing the two men, and leans into the chance further to humiliate his youngest daughter. Absent Cordelia's dowry, Burgundy demurs as gracefully as he can, then withdraws. Lear encourages France to do the same: "Avert your liking a more worthier way / Than on a wretch whom nature is ashamed / Almost t'acknowledge hers" (1.1.212–14). Before coming to a view, France asserts his kingly independence by

demanding to know what it is that Cordelia has done to invalidate the
commendations that Lear had previously lavished upon her:

> This is most strange,
> That she who even but now was your best object,
> The argument of your praise, balm of your age,
> The best, the dearest, should in this trice of time
> Commit a thing so monstrous, to dismantle
> So many folds of favour. Sure her offence
> Must be of such unnatural degree
> That monsters it, or your fore-vouched affection
> Fall into taint[.] (1.1.214–22)

Cordelia seizes the chance to interject. Perhaps Lear hesitates under the
force of France's questioning, or perhaps she simply makes haste to speak
up while she still can.

> I yet beseech your majesty,
> If for I want that glib and oily art
> To speak and purpose not—since what I well intend,
> I'll do't before I speak—that you make known
> It is no vicious blot, murder, or foulness,
> No unchaste action of dishonoured step,
> That hath deprived me of your favour,
> But even for want of that for which I am richer,
> A still soliciting eye and such a tongue
> That I am glad I have not—though not to have it
> Hath lost me in your liking. (1.1.225–34)

Her syntax is disjointed: she is rattled. She nevertheless plays a weak
hand well, and puts on a display of integrity, courage, and virtuous simplicity for the French king to admire. Although her rhetoric is neither
"glib" nor "oily," it by no means wants for art. Her repetition of the "liking" that Lear had urged France to bestow elsewhere is a particularly
deft touch.

Lear brushes Cordelia aside with more opprobrium ("better thou /
Hadst not been born than not to have pleased me better"), but her real
audience is enchanted. France professes himself astonished that her fault
is no more than "a tardiness in nature, / Which often leaves the history
unspoke / That it intends to do." That being the case, and as Burgundy does
not wish to take her hand, he proposes to make her his queen—and does so
with a courtly-poetical flourish that riffs on the opening of Shakespeare's
Sonnet 116: "Love's not love / When it is mingled with regards that stands

/ Aloof from th'entire point." No need for British territory, opulent or otherwise, when "she is herself a dowry" (1.1.237–43).

Certain now of her place and status, Cordelia recovers control of her syntax, and condescends flawlessly to Burgundy ("Since that respect and fortunes are his love, / I shall not be his wife" [1.1.250–51]). Once Lear has stormed offstage in the company of Burgundy, insulting France not only with abuse of his queen and the withholding of his "benison," but with the informal pronoun ("Thou hast her, France; let her be thine, for we / Have no such daughter" [1.1.264–65]), she gives her sisters similarly measured treatment: "I know what you are / And like a sister am most loath to call / Your faults as they are named." *Like* a sister is positively wintry. Goneril and Regan are in no mood to listen, and respond that Cordelia should "Prescribe not us our duty." She should instead "study" how best to "content" her new master: "You have obedience scanted, / And well are worth the want that you have wanted" (1.1.278–81). Cordelia counters with a burst of rhyming sententiousness ("Time shall unfold what plighted cunning hides, / Who covert faults at last with shame derides"), before departing with France to her new life (1.1.282–83).

Still this extraordinary opening scene is not over. Goneril and Regan remain—maybe alone, maybe in the company of unspecified court functionaries. They address one another in prose and with a formality that suggests wariness ("you," "sister"), but also grasp the need to act as confederates. In brief, they know that they have been lucky, and that they must tread carefully lest their luck should run out. Goneril observes that Lear "has always loved our sister most, and with what poor judgement he hath now cast her off appears too grossly." Regan nods that although "the infirmity of his age" has made things worse, "he hath ever but slenderly known himself" (1.1.292–95). The ill-governed temper that has unexpectedly raised them up could pull them down again if they cannot contrive to keep it under control: "If our father carry authority with such disposition as he bears, this last surrender of his will but offend us" (1.1.305–7). Thus phrased, their problem admits a clear solution: to ensure that whatever their father has in mind with the "name, and all th'addition to a king," it should be stripped of all "authority." For Goneril and Regan to enjoy security in their new positions, Lear must be reduced to playing at majesty—a condition in which his "disposition" need be no more consequential than the bad temper of an infant in need of a nap.

———◆———

I have discussed the opening scene at such length because it exposes so much of the substance from which *King Lear* is made. Not a microcosm as such, but very much more than a prelude. Opinions may differ on whether the love contest proceeds in a manner that satisfies the canons of Aristotelian probability (it seems to me that it does, and that Shakespeare writes from a Tolstoyan awareness that each unhappy family is unhappy in its own way), but one thing is unambiguous: none of it is necessary. Had Lear come up with another medium through which to reveal the division of his kingdom to his daughters and the court at large, had Cordelia recognized what Lear was trying to accomplish, had either of them slipped the shackles of self-righteousness to consider for a moment the vulnerabilities of the other's position, had Kent or perhaps Gloucester found the wherewithal to mitigate or divert their monarch's anger, then everything might have been different. And although Shakespeare would have had no time for the comedic ending imposed upon the play by Nahum Tate and approved by Samuel Johnson, the possibility that things will resolve themselves happily is one with which he toys throughout: in the Lear story as it is told in his sources—Geoffrey, Holinshed, Spenser, *King Leir*—Lear is restored to the throne and is succeeded by Cordelia. It is only after Cordelia has reigned for many years that things go awry. She is deposed by her nephews—the children that Shakespeare does not allow Goneril and Regan—and commits suicide in response. The deaths of Cordelia and Lear would have been the more shattering to the play's earliest audiences because they were so unexpected. As Swinburne puts it with fitting convolution, "the doom even of Desdemona seems as much less morally intolerable as it is more logically inevitable than the doom of Cordelia." With a persistence that can easily be mistaken for cruelty, Shakespeare ensures that this unexpectedness remains front and center; over and again comic or tragicomic resolution is implied, only to be withheld—and finally dashed. The potency of accidental judgments, casual slaughters, forced causes, and purposes mistook is as current in Shakespeare's rendering of early Iron Age Britain as in his Denmark of the High Middle Ages.[12]

Thinking further about the interactions between Lear and Cordelia, one could do a lot with an idea discussed at various points in the previous five chapters: that although humanistic moral philosophy relies on a cultivated form of moral vanity, moral vanity has no need of humanistic moral philosophy in order to flourish. By the same token, much could be said about the frequently paralogistic distance between *res* and *verba*. That is, about people pretending—to themselves and to others—to love, to honor, to obey, and to understand. Throughout the play, words seem unmoored from that which they purport, or might intelligently be construed, to represent; there is less distance than might be imagined between the courtly ingratiations of Goneril and Regan and Lear's towering insanity, or between either of these performances and the disguises assumed by Edgar and Kent. All are held together not by reason or representational content, but by patterns of words—or, in the case of Lear's extremities on the heath, by patterns of voiced sounds alone. Creatively sententious though the protagonists' speech often is, in the final analysis the coherence of what they have to say, like its effectiveness, is a matter of aesthetics.[13]

Following Stanley Cavell, one might go further and read the opening scene as an allegory of the ways in which human beings avoid the challenges of love by fixating on unobtainable forms of "knowledge." For Cavell, writing of Lear himself, each of the protagonists is engaged in an "attempt to avoid recognition, the shame of exposure, the threat of self-revelation."[14] Hence the role-playing, disguise, deceit, and disingenuousness: nobody in the play wants to accept themselves as they are or to make themselves vulnerable in the way that is demanded when acknowledging the deep reciprocity of love. Well, nearly nobody. The exception who proves the rule is Cordelia: "All her words are words of love; to love is all she knows how to do. That is her problem, and at the cause [*sic*] of the tragedy of *King Lear*."[15]

There is more than the kernel of insight here. Cavell sees, as very few critics of the play have been able to do, that the characters of *King Lear* not only do not know what they are doing or why they are doing it, but also seek to insulate themselves against any possibility of acknowledging that this is the case. His Cordelia should nevertheless give us pause. Cavell regards her not as a character with agency and freedom and uncertainties and a dramatic reality of her own, but as a symbol—intruded from outside the play—of that which is missing from her father and the remainder of the dramatis personae. And because her father never learns, never convinces himself of the need to accept the challenges of "presentness" and of loving in the world (rather than on some ideal plane where "knowledge" of love, being loved, etc. might be possible), her fate is to be sacrificed: "In Cordelia's death there is hope, because it shows the gods more just—more than we had hoped or wished . . . [it] means that *every* falsehood, every refusal of acknowledgment, will be tracked down."[16] Cavell's Cordelia is emblematic, even unto the gallows. A sort of semi-secular Christ without the passion.

I do not take the view that Cordelia is an emblem, and nor can I find the slightest hint of solace or hope or redemption in her execution. Wrenching in itself, and for how we watch it destroy what remains of her father. Nahum Tate and Samuel Johnson get that much right. What is more, once we notice that Cavell attempts to explain this suffering away by making it symbolic, we start to notice that similar strategies frame his entire approach to the play: the eye-gouging of Gloucester is a good case in point, with much ado about blindness and insight, "spiritual" implication in the crime, and so on, but precious little about the act and its authors. One might go on, but rather than dwelling on whether or not Cavell can really mean what he says about *King Lear*, I want to draw attention to the credo that led him to positions so at odds with the experience of the play: "If all we had to go on were the way the world goes, we would lose the concept of justice altogether; and then human life would become unbearable."[17] Consider likewise his belief that he understands what "full sensitivity and manliness" and "mature womanliness" comprise. His philosophical enquiries have taken him beyond mere historicity, and have allowed him to formulate firm views about what he calls our "common human nature" and the kinds of flourishing that it can permit. These views do not appear to have room for the "poor naked wretches" (3.4.28) invoked by Lear, but they allow Cavell to envision tragedy as the realm of the "extraordinary and the unnatural"—as also to contend that tragedy is so often misunderstood because "we no longer know what is ordinary and natural." "We," that is, who belong to a modern age obsessed with knowing rather than accepting, with detachment-through-objectification rather than the quest to inhabit the world as healthily as we can.[18]

Although the plight of humankind in the modern age is a topic on which thoughtful people are apt to disagree, it is easy to see the appeal of what Cavell proposes. Shakespearean tragedy as he conceives of it provides us with a depiction of our nostalgia for a sense of belonging that, paradoxically, we may not previously have attained. The study of Shakespearean tragedy is thereby cast as a medium through which we can discern the orders of justice and nature (and of natural justice) that are obscured by our immersion in everyday living; as such, literary criticism becomes a site of philosophical-moral-political critique, and possible recuperation.

The problem with all of this is simple but insuperable: certainties about the "ordinary and natural" condition of humankind make for an exceptionally poor vantage from which to explore *King Lear*—a play in which nature and its derivatives are anything but sources of stability, justice, or universality. Within it, invocations of the natural are instead dramatized—in the mouth of Edmund every bit as much as those of Lear, Gloucester, Edgar, and Albany—as desperate attempts to assert meaning and order when grappling with the vicissitudes, and then the horror, of "the way the world goes." For the remainder of this chapter, I put the case that *King Lear* makes it difficult to regard "nature" as anything other than a series of competing fictions through which Shakespeare's protagonists, often at great cost, seek to hold onto their illusions of understanding and control. After Lear abdicates the dignities of his body politic, he finds that his body natural is the site of questions that he can neither answer nor evade.

Shakespeare's sources do a lot with nature and naturalness. The aging Leir, for instance, speaks of the duties owed him by his daughters according to "nature's sacred law." A little later, Cordella insists that because nothing "can stop the course of nature's sacred power," her love for her father is elemental: "As easy is it for foure-footed beasts, / To stay themselves upon the liquid ayre / . . . As easy is it for the slimy Fish, / To live and thrive without the helpe of water: / . . . As I am able to forget my father."[19] Holinshed's Cordeilla likewise makes much of her love for her "naturall father"—who in due course takes exception to "the unkindnesse, or . . . the unnaturalnesse which he found in his two [other] daughters."[20] As usual though, Shakespeare has no interest in emulation. Instead, he expands the dramatic role given to ideas of nature and naturalness yet further, and does so by—*by*, not while—turning the screw on them interrogatively.[21] Shakespeare's tragedies are always more textured than the materials from which he drew in creating them, but even by his own standards *King Lear* is special: tragic *dianoia* has seldom if ever been weightier or more penetrating than it is here.

Lear first mentions nature when declaring—disingenuously, as we have seen—that he will divide his kingdom "where nature doth with merit challenge," with "challenge" here meaning something like "claim as its due." (Note that "nature" is only witnessed by the 1623 folio edition of text; the earlier quartos read "where merit doth most challenge it"—the "it" in question being Lear's "bounty.")[22] This paternal affection is echoed in the filial "bond" to which Cordelia pins her courage, but is quickly superseded by another sense of nature. Not of the feeling proper to a parent or child, but the principle of order according to which the physical universe coheres: "By all the operation of the orbs / From whom we do exist and cease to be, / Here I disclaim all my paternal care" (1.1.112–14). In traditional cosmogony, the universe consisted of eight concentric spheres or orbs (see figure 9); their motions in the night sky were held to be a source of transcendent harmony, along with considerable day-to-day influence (the matter of astrology) on life in the sublunary space of planet Earth.[23] In

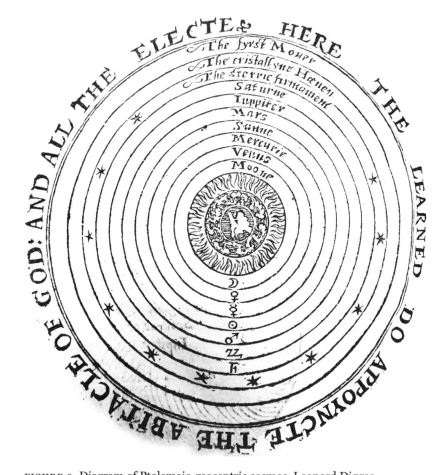

FIGURE 9. Diagram of Ptolemaic-geocentric cosmos. Leonard Digges,
A Prognostication Everlasting [London, 1596], sig. B2v. Rare Book Division,
Department of Rare Books and Special Collections, Princeton University Library.

speaking thus, Lear means to summon a dreadful solemnity, but he succeeds only in undermining the basis of his claims. Not simply in swearing
by nature to go against that which, by nature, is his station ("propinquity
and property of blood"), but by calling into question the adequacy of the
natural as a standard against which to measure virtuous living: the very
existence of "barbarous Scythians," like that of cruel daughters, suggests
that natural ordination does not do the work that Lear demands of it. Is
his disavowal of Cordelia itself an unnatural act akin to those of hungry
Scythian parents? Or is it legitimated by Cordelia's alleged transgressions
of natural writ? If Cordelia's transgressions are indeed transgressions,
what imperative condemns them while permitting the self-confessed

transgressions of her father? Does Lear, in virtue of the *corpus mysticum* of which he has not yet fully divested himself, believe that—even as a father—he exists outside the order of nature? Substantial though they are, all such questions are left up in the air.

The tacit admission that nature offers order without hard-and-fast law is on one level unremarkable. Perhaps even a little old-fashioned. After Aristotle, nature had generally been understood as being governed by rules rather than laws—which is to say, by an order that applied only *most* of the time. Nature (*physis* or *natura*) did what it did regularly rather than inexorably, and sometimes missed the mark: permitting babies born with six fingers, the existence of monstrous peoples, and so on. Monstrosity was not therefore nature in abeyance, but nature acting in error. It was beyond the scope of those things that could be classified as knowledge, and— like the miracles performed by the Christian God—there was no need to take account of it in formulating one's account of the natural.[24]

Although this version of nature had elasticity and epistemic modesty to recommend it, it offered a less than fully stable foundation for systems of natural justice, morality, or theology: if you are going to succeed with versions of the argument from design, you need to be able to show both that such a design exists, and that it corresponds with the theory of law, morals, or religion that you are seeking to promulgate. If that natural design is weakened by the existence of monsters and other inexplicable oddities, then it—and any argument based on it—will need to find buttresses elsewhere. In convention, say, or in the authority of tradition. Scholastic theories of natural law of the sort refined by Thomas Aquinas and Richard Hooker are a good example. But it is a short step from these sophistications to the belief that nature exists in virtue of its ability to affirm the truths of your legal, moral, or theological doctrine—a move that has all the costs and benefits that accrue to discursive circularity, and that in due course weakens the capacity of nature to validate anything at all. So it was that by the early seventeenth century, the Aristotelian version of nature was under attack. On the one hand, from Christian—and particularly Protestant— natural philosophers, who took the view that permitting nature the capacity to err was a slight against both the power and competence of God the creator. On the other, from proto-scientists like Francis Bacon who, very roughly speaking, argued that if a theory of nature excludes as monstrous those phenomena that it cannot explain, then it is a bad theory and should be replaced with a better one. By the end of the seventeenth century, nature had duly been reconfigured to exclude irregularity. It was frequently asserted that nature and human nature were governed by unbending laws, and that these laws were the only true basis on which to establish systems not only of science, but of justice, morality, politics, religion, and philosophy.[25]

Unlike the tragedy to which he lends his name, the Lear of acts 1 and 2 gives none of this a moment's thought. Instead, he grasps at whatever cudgels come to hand so as to wound those who frustrate him. Mainly, his daughters. His treatment of Cordelia we have seen. Once Goneril objects to the conduct and number of the knights in his train, she does little better: "Degenerate bastard" (1.4.245), "Ingratitude . . . / More hideous when thou show'st thee in a child / Than the sea-monster" (1.4.251–53). Albany attempts to calm things down, but Lear resists:

> Hear, Nature, hear, dear goddess, hear:
> Suspend thy purpose if thou didst intend
> To make this creature fruitful.
> Into her womb convey sterility,
> Dry up in her the organs of increase,
> And from her derogate body never spring
> A babe to honour her. If she must teem,
> Create her child of spleen, that it may live
> And be a thwart disnatured torment to her . . .
>   that she may feel,
> How sharper than a serpent's tooth it is
> To have a thankless child. (1.4.267–81)

Nature is now a goddess, and Lear entreats her assistance in wreaking vengeance on Goneril for her unnatural cruelty. A change of tack, to be sure, but not at first glance an especially startling one: personifications of Nature were a familiar feature of the verbal and visual arts from late antiquity through to the early seventeenth century, and depict her governing the operations of the created world (in Christian versions, as the viceregent of God—or, as Robert Chester imagines it at the beginning of *Love's Martyr*, his hylarchic "handmaid"). A good example comes from the "Mutabilitie Cantos" that would be added to the six completed books of the *Faerie Queene*. Spenser has Dame Nature (who appears "With goodly port and gracious Majesty; / Being far greater and more tall of stature / Then any of the gods or Powers on high") adjudicate between the competing claims of Mutabilitie and Jove to be acclaimed the dominant power in the universe; after hearing them out, she rules in favor of Jove. Crucially, Nature herself, and not what Spenser calls her "Sergeant (that is *Order*)," is the agent here.[26] With this distinction in mind, we can see that there is a telling change of emphasis in

Lear's words: rather than continuing to brandish natural "order" as a standard from which Goneril—like Cordelia before her—has fallen, Lear appeals to personified Nature to go *against* the orderly progression of the natural world; rather as, in a more playful cast of mind, the speaker of Sonnet 20 supposes that Nature created the fair youth as a woman, but fell in love with her handiwork and therefore went against "nature" by adding a penis so that she and other females could receive pleasure from it/him/her/them. In short, Nature should visit sterility on one who, by Lear's reckoning, is undeserving either of motherhood or the "hereditary ever" of dynastic succession. And if sterility is too much to ask for, Nature might at least curse Goneril with "disnatured" children who will "torment" her.

Two features of this change of emphasis are especially noteworthy. First, Lear treats Nature in a fashion that by the early seventeenth century was bordering on the archaic. As Katharine Park has demonstrated, personifications of Nature had by this time lost much of the power and authority with which they had been invested in the long Middle Ages. Instead, Nature was treated as an emblem of fertility and generativity; most frequently, cast in the likeness of a lactating woman (see figure 10). While Nature personified became grist to the allegorists' mill, the authority that had previously been hers was now the province of the newly afforced order according to which nature—which is to say, the entirety of the created world—goes about its business.[27] Lear opts for the older understanding of Nature not because he is advanced in years, but because doing so allows him to square the circle with which he had struggled in banishing Cordelia: he can lash out in vindictive anger at his daughters' refusal of their "natural" duties to him while simultaneously disavowing his own "natural" duties to them as a father. On this account, nature is not a set of more or less inexorable laws or rules, but is whatever the Goddess Nature can be persuaded to make it. This leads to the second crucial feature of Lear's remarks. The monstrous is not now a part of the natural world to be comprehended, howsoever obscurely, within notions of the natural, but is something positively *un*natural, "disnatured." Now that he has resigned his own kingly powers, he appeals to Nature as an absolute monarch—able to decree what does and does not have a place within her realm, and to do so without the encroachment of law or convention. *Rex* (well, *regina*), not *lex*; will, not reason. By recruiting her services, Lear can cast that which causes him pain not merely as aberrant, but as having no place within the design to which human and animal life belongs.

Once Goneril and Regan have made good on their plan to neutralize the threat of their father's caprice by reducing and then eliminating his

FIGURE 10. Cesare Ripa, *Iconologia* (Padua, 1618), 362. Marquand Library of Art and Archaeology, Princeton University.

train of knights ("What need one?" [2.2.452]), Lear's rage is intense. Complaining that their refusal to allow "nature more than nature needs" means that "Man's life is cheap as beast's" (2.2.455–56), he denounces them as "unnatural hags" (2.2.467). The intuition that, absent his body politic, he is impotent to do his daughters real harm serves as an intensifier: "I will do such things—/ What they are yet I know not, but they shall be / The terrors of the earth!" (2.2.469–71). The distance between the words in which he expresses his anger and the deeds to which his anger might lead is both obvious and pathetic. But *pathos* should not distract us either from the confusion of what he says (is humankind a part of nature or not? If not, or if that which most confers humanity is "more than nature needs," why does it matter that Goneril and Regan are "unnatural"?), or from the malice—at once vindictive and self-regarding—that animates it. The boundary between nature and the impassioned clay of human nature is one with which he will remain preoccupied for the duration of the play.

After leaving Goneril and Regan, Lear ventures out in the company of the Fool. The weather is atrocious and the landscape barren: "For many miles about / There's scarce a bush" (2.2.491–92). He is grandly unhinged. Not content with anthropomorphizing the elements, the storm raging around him leads him to the pathetic fallacy: "Blow winds and crack your cheeks!" (3.2.1). Torrential rains should continue until they have "drenched our steeples, drowned the cocks," while in lieu of oaks to cleave, the lightning is invited to "Singe my white head" (3.2.3, 6). Finally, he entreats the storm—through the medium of its thunder—to "Strike flat the thick rotundity o'the world, / Crack nature's moulds, all germens spill at once / That make ingrateful man!" (3.2.7–9). He figures the elements not as the province of the gods or some other supernatural force, but as an expression of his own disarray—of his continuing anger at the ingratitude displayed now by all three of his daughters, and at his continuing inability to do anything about it. If Lear cannot bring about their destruction, then the storm, acting as Lear's agent, should destroy those parts of the natural order that provide for the continued existence of humankind.

Real eloquence, with more than a hint of Seneca's Hercules.[28] The fact remains that Lear has given up on even the pretense of coherence: he gives voice to his vexed will, and his vexed will alone. Delusionality is not far away, and all the Fool can think to say in response is that Lear should swallow his pride and seek refuge with his daughters before the weather gets worse. Lear isn't interested, and instead turns his ire on the "rain, wind, thunder, fire" (3.2.15) for allying themselves with Goneril and Regan: "I call you servile ministers / That will with two pernicious daughters join / Your high-engendered battles 'gainst a head / So old and white as this" (3.2.21–24). His reference to two rather than three "pernicious daughters" is one of the only occasions between banishing Cordelia and reuniting with her at the end of act 4 that Lear shows an outward awareness of his youngest daughter's existence.[29] But his anthropomorphizing egoism is otherwise inviolate. Things are, at the most deeply felt level, all about him. All about the distance between the actuality of his body natural and the absolute fictions to which he had become habituated in his body politic.

Two scenes later, Edgar (in disguise as Poor Tom) emerges on the heath to join Lear, the Fool, and Kent (in disguise as Caius). The old king cannot bring himself to take shelter in the "hovel" that his companions have found for him. Edgar catches Lear's attention as one who must have been "brought . . . to this pass" by his daughters. Kent assures him that Edgar has no daughters, and Lear responds, "Death, traitor! Nothing could have subdued nature / To such a lowness but his unkind daughters" (3.4.63, 69–70). By "nature," Lear here refers to something like Edgar's inherent human dignity, but he is projecting his own predicament on his new acquaintance. No doubt he views this as his prerogative: the "traitor" with which he rebukes Kent may or may not qualify as self-conscious hyperbole, but indicates that the singularity of kingship endures. Either way, Lear's emphasis on humanity effaced by nakedness and incoherence marks a shift of focus from nature in general (as an expression of the troubled relationship between a father and his ungrateful daughters) to human nature in particular.

After Edgar has identified himself as a fallen courtier beset with a litany of fabricated vices (lust and duplicity chief among them) that recall the sins to which Malcolm pretends in testing Macduff's commitment to the cause, Lear finds himself sympathetic—and that he has been given pause for thought:

> Is man no more than this? Consider him well. Thou ow'st the worm no silk, the beast no hide, the sheep no wool, the cat no perfume. Ha? Here's three on's us are sophisticated; thou art the thing itself. Unaccommodated man is no more but such a poor, bare, forked animal as thou art. (3.4.101–6)

The shift to prose signals not just Lear's engagement with someone whom he perceives to be of lower social status, but his sense that he is cutting through the dignities through which he usually apprehends and addresses the world. Edgar, says Lear, is not "sophisticated"—an adjective that, in the early seventeenth century, was a recent arrival to the English lexicon. To borrow some helpful definitions from the *Oxford English Dictionary*: not "adulterated," not altered from or deprived of "primitive simplicity or naturalness," not "falsified in a greater or lesser degree."[30] It is thus that Edgar is "the thing itself." He is a vision of humankind in its essential bestiality: crude, but premoral and therefore blameless.[31] The rub, of course, is that Edgar is anything but crude. He is instead a sketch of crude simplicity executed according to his judgment of what a cultivated specimen like Lear or Kent might expect the "the thing itself" to resemble. A kind of strategic pastoral, devised perhaps with Lucretian and Ciceronian accounts of primitive humanity—finding what shelter it can in a hostile landscape, not yet fully furnished with clothing, language, and the verbal arts—in mind.[32]

Gloucester arrives. Rather than responding to Lear's observations, Edgar resumes his incantatory nonsense. Then, in response to a question from the father who has recently disowned him, he pushes his Poor Tom act to the limit ("that in the fury of his heart, when the foul fiend rages, eats cow-dung for salads" [3.4.127–28]). Strategic pastoral becomes elaborate grotesque; Edgar is determined not to be recognized, and succeeds. It is a commonplace to assert that the juxtaposition of Lear and the Fool is supposed to make us think twice about where madness and sanity or wisdom and folly can be said to inhere. But Edgar-as-Poor Tom prompts a question that is darker by far: if our ordering notions of sanity and insanity depend on discourses that are in the final analysis fictional—if the madman and the sage both give voice to visions of the world that veer between the counterfeit and the delusional—how can we speak of psycho-cognitive health at all?

Turning away from the apparently insignificant wretch, Gloucester bids Lear escape the "tyrannous night" with him, and return to Goneril and Regan. Lear stalls: "First let me talk with this philosopher . . . I'll talk a word with this same learned Theban" (3.4.147, 150, 153). Does Lear suppose that natural man will have a deeper insight into the nature of things than a sophisticate like him? Does he intuit that Edgar is more than he seems? Is he just prevaricating, unable to countenance the indignity of seeking shelter either with his daughters or in a hovel? Does this mark the point at which he takes leave of his senses? What does Thebes have to do with anything (just over twenty lines later, Lear will refer to Edgar as "his Athenian" [3.4.176])? Answers have been as various as they are inconclusive.[33] The direction of dramatic travel can be discerned with more confidence. Lear asks that his philosopher *sauvage* tell him about "the cause of thunder" (3.4.151), but Edgar is unwilling to be drawn (he remains keen to deflect his father's potentially unmasking attention by staying in character). Lear himself then loses interest: the nature of nature or of humankind in its natural condition is only of value to him to the extent that it reflects his grievances against Goneril and Regan. These can better be expressed by giving them a mock trial in absentia, and once Lear and his party have found an unspecified source of shelter, that is what— with the assistance of Edgar, Kent, and the Fool—he proceeds to do. For Edgar, the performance of naturalness now becomes more transparently bookish, as when he recites a list of dogs from a popular hunting manual (3.6.63–70).[34] Lear, meanwhile, is still harping on his daughters' cruelty: "Is there any cause in nature that make these hard hearts?" (3.6.73–74). His question is of course rhetorical, and means to affirms the *un*naturalness of their conduct toward him. But there is something else here too: a desperation to avoid the undertow of Larkin's coastal shelf—to avoid the recognition that he is himself a natural being and that he might, as such, be a part of the problem.

As the play moves toward its dreadful conclusion, Lear's attitude shows signs that it might be changing. When next he appears on stage, by which time he has traveled from the west country to the southeast coast, he has begun to conceive of himself as a sort of natural man—one, furthermore, engaged in bitter self-mockery by wearing a crown of flowers rather than the crown of state. Edgar, obliged to break off from sermonizing his father in the aftermath of his deception on the cliffs of Dover, exclaims (rather tactlessly, given Gloucester's blindness), "O thou side-piercing sight!"—to which Lear responds, "Nature's above art in that respect" (4.6.85–86). Lear implies that the reality of his situation is more piteous than the "art" of its floral counterfeit, but his words have a fuller import that only gradually becomes clear.

Most fundamentally, he suggests that his body natural is as unsophisticated as that acknowledged by Edgar's Poor Tom: sharing bonds of community with mice, birds, "the small gilded fly" (4.6.111), even polecats. This community is held together not by the purportedly civilizing power of ordered speech, but by appetite—whether for "toasted cheese" (4.6.89) or sexual pleasure. Though superficially similar, this idea is radically distinct from Lear's earlier insistence that he would become "comrade with the wolf and owl" (2.2.399) in asserting his independence of Goneril and her demeaning requests: one seeks a metaphor for dignity and predatory strength cast into the shadows; the other reflects a crisis about who and what Lear, and the human species to which he belongs, might be said to comprise. Simply put, Lear now sees his body politic as so much magical thinking. Fit only for prompting and receiving flattery and other fictions that worked to obscure his embodied humanity: "They told me I was everything; 'tis a lie, I am not ague-proof" (4.6.103–4). The discrepancy between what he now seems to be and what he once thought he was is the true source of the pity that his "natural" appearance now provokes. Hence his mordant fastidiousness when Gloucester, failing to grasp the significance of what Lear has been saying or his own contribution to this discrepancy (through his flattery as well as his adultery), seeks to kiss Lear's hand: "Let me wipe it first, it smells of mortality" (4.6.129). When Gloucester remains oblivious, Lear makes use of a motif lifted from English folk plays to spell out that the exercise of monarchical power is a matter of farm dogs barking at beggars: "The great image of authority: a dog's obeyed in office" (4.6.154–55).[35] No sense here that the natural condition of human beings is any sort of basis from which to derive political or ethical order; kingship is an "office," not an identity conferred by blood-lines and a body politic. Humankind, for all its ontological pride, differs but in degree from the nonrational animals.

And yet this acknowledgment is imperfect at best. Lear will in short order fantasize about how animals are subservient to his pursuit of ven-geance. He begins with a reassertion of human exceptionalism in a deploy-ment of the *theatrum mundi* topos that alludes to Pliny while recalling Macbeth's tale told by an idiot, full of sound and fury: "When we are born we cry that we are come / To this great stage of fools" (4.6.178–79).[36] As if newborns are in a position to judge.[37] Lear's "we" nevertheless serves as an acknowledgment of his own share in humanity's common lot, even as he claims to observe its dynamics in the round. But as animals cannot mean-ingfully be regarded as foolish, it also excludes the human condition from the animality to which, with some prompting from Edgar and Montaigne, Lear has just made so much. Pushing to one side any question of resigna-tion or apathy, Lear proposes to enlist the natural world—harnessed by human art and ingenuity—against those who have crossed him: "It were a delicate stratagem to shoe / A troop of horse with felt . . . / And when I have stolen upon these son-in-laws, / Then kill, kill, kill, kill, kill, kill!" (4.6.180–84). The ruse de guerre is less "delicate" than fanciful; its sole purpose is to provide an outlet for Lear's tenuously suppressed anger. The fact that one of his targets is already dead underscores that the true object of his attention lies elsewhere.

The reasons for his anger at his daughters need not be re-rehearsed, but to their number we can add what Lear has revealed of his attitudes to women and their sexuality. In men, sexual appetite is simply a part of what it means to be human, and is to be viewed with tolerant understand-ing wherever possible. In women, by contrast, it is rank monstrosity:

> Down from the waist they are centaurs, though women all above. But to the girdle do the gods inherit, beneath is all the fiend's: there's hell, there's darkness, there is the sulphurous pit, burning, scalding, stench, consumption! (4.6.121–25)

In scripting these lines, Shakespeare draws on authorities ranging from Horace and Ovid to Samuel Harsnett.[38] Lear offers no view as to whether the feminine monstrosity that so unsettles him exists within the natural order or in contravention of it, but such questions matter less than his disclosure of the deep psychosexual wounds that he carries around. In *Troilus and Cressida* and *Othello*, the delusions of lovers stand duty for, and illuminate, the delusions of the broader moral orders to which the protagonists belong. But here more even than in the prurient misogyny of Thersites and Iago, Shakespeare presents us with disgust at the physical fact of female sexuality, and—in virtue of the discrepancy between their "sulphurous pit[s]" and the decorous speech and behavior through which women conduct themselves—the status of women as hypocritical beings. Did Lear's queen (who must have been very much younger than him) come to die early because, Leontes-like, he had her punished for an act of real or perceived infidelity? Because she contracted a venereal disease that she passed on to him? We can only surmise, but he feels able to make a point to Regan by imagining her mother's tomb "Sepulchuring an adultress" (2.2.321), and such a scenario would certainly help to make sense of his otherwise puzzling conflation of sexual appetite with the betrayal that he believes his daughters to have visited upon him.[39] Notions of nature and naturalness, now shorn of all maternal personification, are at the point little more than an instrument with which to dignify his arabesque of revenge.

But these ideas, limited and distorting though they may be, also have a more fundamental role. By redefining female sexuality as something to be excluded from his normative ideals of nature and of femininity, Lear establishes the framework within which his reconciliation with Cordelia will take place: she becomes for him a figure of sexless, almost beatific, compassion.

As Cordelia prepares to set eyes on her father again, she entreats the "kind gods" to "Cure this great breach in his abused nature; / Th'untuned and jarring sense, O, wind up / Of this child-changed father" (4.7.14–17). From what she has heard, she infers that Goneril and Regan have separated this father-king from his natural condition, and transformed him into a needy child. At least her courtiers have taken pains to dress him as a king while he has slept. Their reunion is tentative, gentle, shot through with love and forgiveness: "Sir, do you know me?" (4.7.48); "Pray do not mock me. / I am a foolish, fond old man, / . . . And to deal plainly, / I fear that I am not in my perfect mind. / . . . Do not laugh at me, / For, as I am a man, I think this lady / To be my child Cordelia" (4.7.59–69). If Cordelia, now a queen herself, cannot quite bring herself to concede that she has had a role to play in the catastrophes that have befallen Albion and its erstwhile king, she is tender in dismissing Lear's profession of guilt: "No cause, no cause" (4.7.75). They exit, to stroll together offstage.

If *King Lear* were a different sort of play, it might come to an end at or around this point. As it is, the cadence of this recognition scene is as deceptive as anything in Bach or Beethoven or Wagner: when next we hear from the royal father and daughter, they are Edmund's prisoners. Cordelia sounds out of her depth, a little like Romeo after the killing of Mercutio: "We are not the first / Who with best meaning have incurred the worst" (5.3.3–4).[40] She nevertheless wants to confront her treacherous siblings in person. By contrast, after trying and failing to undo the effects of his abdication with the aid of French troops, Lear has seen enough. To be close to Cordelia is at this late stage of his life all he can desire—no matter that Cordelia has a future and a husband; no matter that the kingdom lapse into tyranny and misgovernment. The wrathful dragon now figures his daughter (a wife and queen and military commander) and himself as embodiments of natural innocence: songbirds who, though confined to prison, will find more than enough to enjoy by inhabiting their own virtuosity.[41] This conceit has obvious limits, so he also suggests that they will be able to take pleasure in the human comedy they observe through the bars of their cage, amusing themselves in trying to explain "the mystery of things / As if we were God's spies" (5.3.16–17). Once again, the shadow cast by Lear's *corpus mysticum* is long. Lear visualizes the two of them removed from "the great stage of fools," and observing the *theatrum mundi* from some point outside it: birdcage as *aevum*. Confused, frightened, and full of compassion for her father's doting phantasmagoria, Cordelia weeps. Lear now finds a different natural simile with which to express his desire that, in their imprisonment, he and Cordelia should remain united: "He that parts us shall bring a brand from heaven, / And fire us hence like foxes" (5.3.22–23). They will be harder to separate than it is to dislodge a fox from its burrow.[42] Lorna Hutson has written well of *King Lear* as a play about those "for whom the right time never comes," and one can only imagine Cordelia's rising dread as she listens to these shockingly untimely sentiments: in her father's words, she hears her future contracting before her.[43] Their only chance of escaping the plot laid for them by Edmund and Goneril—meeting their opponents face-to-face and enjoying the "form of justice" (3.7.25) that prevents Cornwall and Regan from killing Gloucester—has gone. The instant is captured with the appalled sympathy that comprises so much of Shakespeare's tragic stock-in-trade.

We in the audience are made to wait for more than two hundred agonizing lines to find out what has happened—one of Shakespeare's few essays in what Barthes calls "proairetic" plotting, and the more striking because the overarching structure of *King Lear* is so very un-suspenseful (none of the "will he or won't he?" with which we are sometimes caught up after Hamlet's interview with the Ghost).[44] Shakespeare teases us with the overcome Gentleman entering to share the news of Goneril and Regan having died ("O, she's dead!" [5.3.223]), before Albany eventually recalls the "Great thing of us forgot" (5.3.235) and the dying Edmund sends his reprieve. Then the anticipation is over, to devastating effect. Lear enters, cradling Cordelia's body in a bleak travesty of the pietà: not Mary holding the soon-to-be-resurrected Christ, but a father holding his hanged daughter; a former king holding what had until moments earlier been his last chance at dynastic succession; a foolish, fond, old man holding the mortal remains of the only person who could forgive him. The experience is wrenching, and yet the dramatic cadence is again deceptive: there is more. Albany, Edgar, and Kent each attempt to impose consolations of religious, tragic, and autobiographical order—only to emphasize that we in the audience are disconsolate. Or are we? Lear now abandons any lingering suggestion of human animality, crying out in rage and pain, "No, no, no life! / Why should a dog, a horse, a rat have life / And thou no breath at all?" (5.3.304–6). Human nature and nature in general are now things apart, distinct in kind rather than merely in degree. Perhaps this special status permits redemption, or physical recovery? The Folio version of the text makes the possibility explicit: "Do you see this? Look on her: look, her lips, / Look there, look there!" (5.3.309–10). Does Shakespeare's plot provide Cordelia with a future after all? No. Or, rather: no, no, no, no, no. Lear dies in the misbegotten hope of a restoration that Shakespeare's tragic vision forbids. Beholding him, we may not howl, but it is hard not to weep.

———

Viewed from here, the willingness of characters like Gloucester, Kent, and Albany to invoke nature and naturalness as a means of delegitimating that which they find reprehensible might tend further to support the notion that, in *King Lear*, "nature" is just a word. Something that exists to satisfy the analogical imperative—the urge to comprehend the human condition through representations and likenesses that are, more often than not, misleading.

A few examples. Gloucester attacks Edgar as "Unnatural, detested, brutish villain—worse than brutish!" (1.2.76–77), even as he appears to acknowledge a gap between our ideas of natural order—what he calls "the wisdom of Nature"—and natural phenomena themselves, such as "these late eclipses in the sun and moon" (1.2.103–6). Edmund, by Gloucester's reckoning, is a "loyal and natural boy" (2.1.84), the treatment of Lear by Regan and Cornwall is "unnatural dealing" (3.3.2), and Lear himself is a "ruined piece of nature" (4.6.130); likewise, he appeals to "the sparks of nature" after his eyes are gouged out (3.7.85–86). Oswald, on Kent's account, is "disclaimed" by "nature," and is instead the handiwork of a "tailor" (2.2.53); Lear's sorrows are "unnatural" (3.1.34), and his condition of internal exile means that "oppressed nature sleeps" (3.6.94). But as Albany rails against his wife for driving Lear away, it is he who offers the most vivid case in point:

> O Goneril,
> You are not worth the dust which the rude wind
> Blows in your face. I fear your disposition;
> That nature which contemns its origin
> Cannot be bordered certain in itself.

One who will abandon the natural bonds of filial love and duty will, Albany suggests, do anything.

Goneril is bored by her husband's homiletic outrage (she would rather be concentrating on the "woman's services" she might offer Edmund), and tells him to stop: "No more, the text is foolish." But Albany has only been warming up and cannot now be silenced:

> Wisdom and goodness to the vile seem vile;
> Filths savour but themselves. What have you done?
> Tigers, not daughters, what have you performed?
> A father, and a gracious aged man
> Whose reverence even the head-lugged bear would lick,
> Most barbarous, most degenerate, have you madded.
> Could my good brother suffer you to do it?
> A man, a prince, by him so benefitted?
> If that the heavens do not their visible spirits
> Send quickly down to tame these vile offences,
> It will come:
> Humanity must perforce prey on itself,
> Like monsters of the deep. (4.2.30–51)[45]

Goneril's treatment of her father is unnatural because it more resembles the behavior of tigers and bears than human beings: "barbarous," "degenerate." She has, in short, abused her position in the order of things, and thereby risks bringing the entirety of that order into disarray. If "the heavens" do not dispatch avenging angels ("their visible spirits") to "tame these vile offences," then worse really will come to worst: "Humanity must perforce prey on itself, / Like monsters of the deep."

The shape of the argument is familiar from Ulysses's great speech on "degree" in *Troilus and Cressida*. Go against the hierarchy of nature and everything valuable in human life will lapse into decay and corruption. For Ulysses, this fallen state assumes the form of "an universal wolf," that, "doubly seconded with will and power, / Must make perforce an universal prey / And last eat himself up" (*Troilus and Cressida*, 1.3.121–24).[46] For Albany, the image of appetitive chaos is less distinct, and will only come to pass in the absence of divine retribution for human sins. Still, his "monsters of the deep" were very likely animated by a passage on the politics of marine life in Olaus Magnus's history of the Scandinavian and Arctic north—a work for which Shakespeare had also found a use when writing *Hamlet*. Magnus assimilates the natural history compiled by Albert the Great (itself borrowing heavily from Aristotle's *History of Animals*) to attest the existence of a frightful beast named the "swamfisck," the "hahanc," or perhaps the "ahunus." In extremis, he notes, this deep-sea animal "sustains itself by feeding upon its own flesh."[47] Sensationally unpleasant, indistinct, and quite possibly a fabrication of the naturalist's art, the *swamfisck* (or *hahanc*, or *ahunus*) suits Shakespeare's purpose perfectly. Through it, Albany lays bare that which Ulysses's better-managed eloquence tends to obscure. Namely, that although it may be well and good to assert that going against the natural order of things leads to moral collapse, saying so not only presupposes a knowledge of this natural order. It also presupposes that certain creatures have the freedom to act *outside* the pattern or design that shapes every other part of the universe: be they self-consciously fictional grotesques (Ulysses's "universal wolf"), indistinct specimens of natural history (Albany's "monsters of the deep"), or blessed with the attributes of rational, linguistic, social, and bipedal elevation (humankind).[48]

The problem that Shakespeare saw so clearly runs as follows. If human deeds are not limited by nature in the way that those of a dog, a horse, a rat, a wolf, a fox, or a songbird are, what possible use can nature (or analogies with the natural world) have in determining how to govern human behavior, and in assessing the differences between right and wrong? The question is not one that Albany asks, much less seeks to answer. He simply needs to have it that Goneril is unnaturally "degenerate," just as he needs his creature of the deep to be an emblem of monstrosity—and so for him they are. That both might in themselves be a part of nature, and of a natural order operating according to a design that differs from the one he has in mind, does not occur to him. Instead, the monstrosity that he attributes to Goneril and the *swamfisck* is defined in opposition to the sorts of thing he believes nature should be doing; that of which he disapproves is ipso facto beyond the organic pale. Like the Lear of the first several scenes, he cleaves to a notion—an ideology—of naturalness that is somewhere between indifferent and impervious to the experience of the world.

If the utterances of Albany alongside those of Lear, Gloucester, and Kent were all we had to go on, we might therefore conclude that "nature" in *King Lear* has no more weight than the telescopic chorography that Edgar—glancing at Seneca's *Phoenician Women*—conjures for Gloucester as he tries to convince him that they are standing atop the cliffs of Dover (4.5.11–24).[49] Something we describe or invoke so that our moral and physical worlds might more fully cohere.

Before going any further, however, we must acknowledge another vision of nature and natural order in the play—one that in some lights the drama might seem to validate, if not to endorse. It is articulated in a soliloquy delivered by the "natural" (which is to say, illegitimate because conceived and born out of wedlock) son of Gloucester, Edmund:

> Thou, Nature, art my goddess; to thy law
> My services are bound. Wherefore should I
> Stand in the plague of custom, and permit
> The curiosity of nations to deprive me?
> For that I am some twelve or fourteen moonshines
> Lag of a brother? Why bastard? Wherefore base?
> When my dimensions are as well compact,
> My mind as generous and my shape as true
> As honest madam's issue? Why brand they us
> With base? With baseness, bastardy? Base, base?
> Who in the lusty stealth of nature take
> More composition and fierce quality
> Than doth within a dull stale tired bed
> Go to the creating of a whole tribe of fops
> Got 'tween a sleep and wake. Well, then,
> Legitimate Edgar, I must have your land.
> Our father's love is to the bastard Edmund
> As to the legitimate. Fine word, "legitimate"!
> Well, my legitimate, if this letter speed
> And my invention thrive, Edmund the base
> Shall top the legitimate. I grow, I prosper:
> Now gods, stand up for bastards! (1.2.1–22)

The first scene of the play is over, along with its displays of duplicity, pride, confusion, impetuosity, and strained decorum. The stage now clear,

Edmund's verse—mistakenly set as prose in the 1608 quarto—is a blast of stunning lucidity. The more so because when we in the audience last saw him, Edmund was obliged to endure his father's crassly jocular proclamations of the "good sport at his making" (1.1.22). Just as in the soliloquy that opens *Richard III*, there is something sympathetic, and perhaps deliberately seductive, in the performance of intelligence, charisma, and outsiderly frankness.

The substance of Edmund's words is on the face of it no less impressive. He has a philosophy that appears better to cohere with the world than the ones evinced by Lear and his father, and he also has a plan. Rather than regarding nature as an expression of the normative ideals articulated within moral philosophy, or regarding human nature as distinct from that of other animals, he views the natural order as essentially unitary: bound together not by reason or virtue or providential design, but a "law" (not, note, a rule) of "lusty stealth." Which is to say, by the pursuit and attainment of bodily pleasure unencumbered by that which received opinion might have to say on the matter. ("Stealth" here does not connote secret or furtive dealings, but the act or practice of stealing: Edmund has in mind acts of appetitive lawlessness that include, but are by no means limited to, the kind of furtive liaison on which he will later embark with Goneril.)[50] As such, and as William Elton has established in detail, Edmund follows the tenets of Renaissance libertinism, themselves something between an amplification and a distortion of the Epicureanism recorded in Lucretius's *On the Nature of Things*.[51] Edmund suggests that his "law" follows nature; his "nature" no more follows a customary legal or moral code than he does. This is because it is only through the customary fictions of naturalness that Edmund, despite his manifest qualities of person and mind, has been tarred with "baseness" and "bastardy"—only through them that he has been deprived of his birthright. And all because his parents refused to constrain themselves to the motions of nuptial duty during the procreative act, and instead took the liberty of having fun. Edgar's mother, the Countess of Gloucester (like Lear's queen, absent from the play) may have been an "honest madam," but "honesty" here carries the charge of which Shakespeare makes so much in *Othello*: honor, or socially sanctioned virtue, as folded up within the taffeta of Ciceronian-humanist *honestas*. Precisely the "plague of custom"—masquerading as naturalness and integrity—against which Edmund so purposefully aligns himself; precisely that which, in the wholly natural pursuit of an evening's sport, his father had chosen to disregard. By undermining his "legitimate" half-brother, Edmund proposes to advance himself through establishing a bond between father and son that is primal, not merely customary. The thing itself, so to speak.

When Edmund soliloquizes again, slightly less than a hundred lines later, he underscores his impatience with the purportedly "natural" account of humankind to which his father subscribes, and according to which he has contrived to have Edgar condemned. Amplifying Cassius's insistence that "the fault, dear Brutus, is not in our stars / But in ourselves," he holds that such doctrines are a way of denying our responsibility for actions whose outcomes we find it difficult to square with our self-image: "As if we were villains on necessity, fools by heavenly compulsion, knaves, thieves and treachers by spherical predominance; drunkards, liars and adulterers by an enforced obedience of planetary influence." It is, in short, "an admirable evasion of whoremaster man, to lay his goatish disposition on the charge of a star" (1.2.121–28).[52]

For all the energy we expend in contriving accounts of nature that cohere with the demands and exigencies of moral living, the fact for Edmund remains unambiguous. We are animals, driven by our appetites for pleasure and gain, and can therefore do as we please; or, rather, can *only* do as we please. Edmund's advantage, as he sees it, is that his intelligent asperity permits him to acknowledge the reality of this situation while everyone else is in denial. But Shakespeare wants us to notice that his vision is less perfect than he believes. Consider his insistence that Edgar's "nature is so far from doing harms / That he suspects none," and that he is therefore one "on whose foolish honesty / My practices ride easy" (1.2.178–80). Edgar's commitment to the ideology of nature articulated by his father and Lear may have blinded him to things as they really are, but it takes Edmund in too. Edmund is so content to scorn Edgar's witlessly conventional piety that he forgets that, like everyone else, Edgar is motivated by his appetites—his desire for pleasure, place, possessions, and security. His "nature" is at root the same as his brother's. So it is that once Edmund has been vanquished by Edgar, there is deep irony in Shakespeare's decision to have the hardheaded brother adopt the egoistic complacencies of the pious one: "Some good I mean to do, / Despite of mine own nature" (5.3.241–42). As if the facility for seeing and making sense of things through the lens of one's appetites had been a monstrosity particular to him, and not a characteristic of humankind as a whole. The final exchange between the two brothers calls to mind Edmund's dismissal of Edgar earlier in the play: "Pat . . . like the catastrophe of the old comedy" (1.2.134). Except that *King Lear* is no comedy. Even in death, Edmund remains a stranger to the good as conventionally defined. Nature and the gods, if they exist and are paying attention, do nothing to help. Cordelia is hanged.

A similar sort of picture emerges from Edmund's entanglements with Lear's daughters. Regan is his equal in boldness and cruelty, but only Goneril matches him for disdain at the distance between the truth of the human condition and the way in which it is played out in Albion. She aggravates her father with exquisitely calibrated hypocrisy (his knights need to go because they are guilty of "Epicurism and lust" [1.4.235]), proposes to switch gender roles in her marriage to Albany ("giv[ing] the distaff / Into my husband's hands" [4.2.17–18]), initiates a relationship with Edmund as a "woman" to his "man" (something Lawrentian here), and is quick to realize that she and her sister must join forces if they are to defeat the French invaders (5.1.29–31). And yet Albany's strictures about monsters of the deep coming to prey upon themselves in the absence of divine retribution seem justified: Goneril poisons Regan and then, her amorous scheming with Edmund exposed, stabs herself. Edmund fares little better.

What are we to infer from all this? Not, I think, that Edmund, Goneril, and Regan (and with them Cornwall) fall because their ambitions and deeds are reprehensible, or even because they underestimate their opponents: the play offers us no reason to conclude that virtue has triumphed; in their final remarks, Edgar and Albany *are* distinctly feeble. The clue comes at the beginning of Edmund's great soliloquy: "Thou, Nature, art my goddess; to thy law / My services are bound." Rigorously minimalist though Edmund's vision of nature might be in comparison to that of Lear, Kent, Gloucester, and Edgar, it too is an exercise in anthropocentrism and rationalistic overreach—hubris, even.

In claiming to have "bound" his services to Nature, Edmund makes the tacit suggestion that he could have acted otherwise: that he has the power to behave *un*naturally, but that he has actively chosen to obey. If so, the substance of his natural law (unchecked appetite, etc.) is either in error, or can lay no claims to being legally binding. If Edmund recognizes this problem, he ignores it—just as he ignores the collision between the authority of his goddess and her laws. As we have seen, Lear's "dear goddess" is an absolute monarch, to whom nature and natural law are subservient. But Edmund admits no distance between Nature and "her" law. He is an unlikely proponent of constitutional monarchy, and one might well wonder what is going on. The short answer is that he seeks to upend traditional notions not only of natural order, but of the Goddess Nature: rather than doing away with her in the name of the materialistic-appetitive rigor to which he regards himself as wedded, he remakes her to spite the dull conventionality of his father and brother. It is as if Spenser's Mutabilitie had been transposed onto his Dame Nature. But Edmund is too impressed with his own subversive brio. In the heat of his opposition to the "plague of custom" that has in his view held him back unjustly, he does not pause to think. Had he done so, he might have had occasion to reflect that he binds not just himself to natural law, but his Goddess too: she is bound to *his* understanding of how it is that the natural world functions. So much for the prerogatives, and mysteries, of divinity. So much for professions of obedience. In a sense very far removed from that advanced in the Book of Common Prayer, he treats service to his chosen deity as perfect freedom.

Except that Edmund is no more free than are Claudius and Iago. His vision of nature, every bit as much as those advanced by Lear et al., is an exercise in delusion: a projection onto the world of an order whose primary function is to legitimate his ambitions and calm his fears. It is not hard to imagine Edmund and Goneril triumphant. Regan, Lear, and Cordelia are dead; Gloucester and Edgar might as well be. Only the preachifying Albany stands between them and dominion over the reunified kingdom, and they finish him off without much ado. Dynastic perpetuity is theirs for the taking. They fail—their careful plotting fails—for the same reason that Romeo and Juliet come to die. Contingency and bad luck: a letter goes astray. Even a penetratingly unencumbered mind like Edmund's needs to believe that the nature of things is comprehensible, and he strives to make it so through fictions of order. These fictions, as unfortunately for him as for Lear and Cordelia, have no place for the sheer randomness— what might be thought of as the good and back luck—that shapes so much of the way the world goes. Like Claudius and Iago, Edmund can see the limitations and contradictions in the ideologies of others, but cannot do so for those to which he has himself become attached. He thought he was writing his own story, a snarlingly dark comedy in which he strikes it rich at the expense of the misapprehensions to which most of the rest of the dramatis personae are attached. But after Edgar overcomes him, he finds himself little more than a supporting character in a tragedy of incomprehension and incommensurable loss. In Albany's judgment, Edmund's death is "but a trifle here" (5.3.294). Few would dissent.

———◆———

Although it is perfectly possible, and even likely, that Shakespeare had read Montaigne's *Essais* in John Florio's translation (the first edition of which was published in 1603) by the time he sat down to write *King Lear*,

I have no idea whether this was in fact the case.[53] Nor, for the purposes of this chapter, do I think the question matters very much. What is important is that at least one passage of Montaigne provides us with a brilliant intertext through which better to understand the discourse of nature as a feature of Shakespeare's tragic *dianoia*.

In the longest of his essays, the "Apology for Raymond Sebond," Montaigne reflects on whether the principles of nature are knowable. After noting the religious zeal with which Aristotelian doctrines of nature were revered in early modern culture, Montaigne remarks that he can for his part see no more reason to believe in Aristotle's theories than in those of anyone else:

> I know not why I should or might not, as soon, & as easily accept, either *Platoes Ideas,* or *Epicurus* his Atomes and indivisible things, or the fulnes and emptines of *Leucippus* and *Democritus,* or the water of *Thales,* or of *Anaximanders* infinitie of nature, or the aire of *Diogenes,* or the numbers or proportion of *Pythagoras,* or the infinitie of *Parmenides,* or the single-one of *Musaeus,* or the water and fire of *Apollodorus,* or the similarie and resembling parts of *Anaxagoras,* or the discord and concord of *Empedocles,* or the fire of *Heraclitus,* or any other opinion (of this infinit confusion of opinions & sentences, which this goodly humane reason, by hir certaintie and clear-sighted vigilancie brings forth in what soever it medleth withal) as I should of *Aristotles* conceit, touching this subject of the principles of naturall things[.][54]

For Montaigne, although we must strive to follow nature as best we can, natural knowledge is something that for the most part eludes us; too often, we attempt to hide from this truth by surrendering our judgment to plausible opinions dressed up in the garb of institutional or cultural authority. Montaigne enjoys his authorly persona as one with the freedom to say the unsayable, but his remarks here are at root conventional. In Ian Maclean's neat summary, most early modern accounts of the subject took the view that "nature in the form of external reality is thus paradoxically both self-evident and hidden; its reality is not questioned, but the ability of man's mind to capture it either fully or accurately either through the senses or through the intellect can be doubted."[55]

King Lear extends this liberty about as far as it can go. For Shakespeare, *all* theories and media that purport to explain or depict nature, no matter how compelling or elegant or subtle or seductive they might be, tend toward the "confusion of opinions and sentences" that "goodly humane reason, by hir certaintie and clear-sighted vigilancie brings forth in what soever it medleth withal."[56] The competing visions of nature within *King Lear* are each dramatized as expressions of the human desire for order, for rationality, for knowledge, for security, for control. As the natural world, and the human condition within it, are phenomena that defy human powers of analysis, these visions are fictions—heuristics through which to apprehend that which would otherwise exceed our cognitive reach. Crucially, however, their proponents (to reiterate: Edmund as well as Edgar, Gloucester, and Lear) refuse to acknowledge them as such, and insist on their authority as templates for ethical, political, philosophical, and psychologically healthy living. Their views of themselves and of those around them are thereby distorted. Calamity ensues.

By translating calamity into tragedy, Shakespeare enables his audiences to do two interrelated and unusually valuable things. First, to see such events more distinctly and in a broader perspective: *catharsis* as clarification. Second, to explore the possibility that calamity might, in being seen more clearly, be something that humankind can work to ameliorate, if not to avoid.

A little earlier in the "Apology," Montaigne slightly misconstrues a line of Plato in writing of the similarity between poets and those who would construct systematic philosophies of nature: "nature is nothing but an aenigmaticall poesie," and attempts to explain it have little more than interpretative ingenuity to recommend them. Poets may esteem themselves as creatorly rivals to God, but their fuller significance lies in giving natural philosophers the license to dream up explanatory fictions of their own.[57]

Shakespeare takes a different view. The benefit of poetry, especially in the guise of tragic drama, emerges from its capacity to depict human beings as creatures whose peace of mind depends on being able to tell themselves stories of one kind or another. Not, that is, from the resolutions of Aristotelian tragic plotting, but from an awareness that the world in general—and the human condition in particular—can most usefully be understood through a heuristic medium that acknowledges its own fictionality. More even than the capacity for sorrow, it is the fictive capacity that distinguishes human beings from lions, tigers, bears, horses, foxes, cats, dogs, mice, and songbirds. Some of our fictions are concepts like "nature": words desperately in search of, or determined to hold on to, a settled sense of meaning. Others are plays like *King Lear*, in which Shakespeare does not simply reject the distinction between art and nature, but emphasizes that nature as something understood by the human mind *is* a work of artifice, and of human artifice at that.

By the time the play comes to an end there is—just as in *Hamlet* and *Macbeth*—little sense that things will be different once the action is over.

In Edgar and Albany, the platitudinous inherit the earth. As we behold them shuffling away from the enormity of what they have just witnessed, it is clear that misprision, calamity, and suffering are going nowhere. *King Lear* abides as a means through which we might, in time, accommodate ourselves to this indisputably human state of affairs: by accepting that we can neither comprehend nor intuit that which we discuss as "nature"; that the incomprehensibility of what we discuss as "nature" makes it an abysmally bad guide to the governance of human affairs; that we must look to ourselves, to the anxieties and blind spots and compensatory yearnings for order that we find it so tough to acknowledge, if we are to find a way in which we might flourish.

CHAPTER SEVEN

Romans, Egyptians, and Crocodiles

ANTONY AND CLEOPATRA

IN *MACBETH* AND *King Lear*, Shakespeare is preoccupied with sacred kingship: with the small number of individuals possessed of a "body politic" and not just the "body natural" common to all human beings; with the prospect of an identity anchored not in the historicity of everyday living and dying, but in the perpetuity of the *aevum*—a temporal dimension with a beginning but no end. *Macbeth* exposes the body politic as a delusion. *King Lear*, ruthlessly, does the same for the body natural. Both are cast as examples of the unacknowledged fictions to which we cleave in our desperation for things to make sense.

In *Antony and Cleopatra*, Shakespeare continues to puzzle at the constellation to which these fictions of order, stability, and perpetuity belong. As we have seen, the *aevum* was not only the home of the monarch's body politic: it also accommodated the angels, and served to bestow the dignity and immortality of a perfect species on the institutions of the church and the law. What is more, it did the same for the institution of empire. Macbeth's identification of the crown with "the imperial theme" is no accident. And just as sacred kingship had its origins in the deification of Julius Caesar (*divus Julius*) and his adopted son Augustus (in whose reign and within whose territories Christ had chosen to come into the world), so the notion of empire without end was decisively Roman. Virgil's *Aeneid* hymns the *imperium sine fine* of the Augustan settlement, and it was the Augustan ideal of universal monarchy that the Holy Roman Emperor, Charles V, translated into the political realm of sixteenth-century Europe:

a political entity unchecked by the constraints of time or geography, affirmed by Christian belief, and able to maintain a universal peace. Although the Roman genealogy of these ideals made them a helpful counterweight to the comparably universalizing claims of the Ottoman sultan, Süleyman the Magnificent, they did not long survive Charles's abdications of 1554–56. By this time, however, they had already been appropriated by other European monarchs. They were, for instance, particularly appealing to Henry VIII in his battles with the papacy. In 1533, Henry's government declared that "this realm of England is an Empire" in which the Pope's writ was of secondary significance, and in due course the dual roles of post-Reformation English kingship—temporal and spiritual supremacy—reinforced this imperial self-image. Neither Elizabeth I nor her successor, James VI / I, had anything like the military or territorial footprint of Charles V, but they (especially James) took pains to fashion themselves as rulers with divinely sanctioned *imperium* over the four nations of the British Isles; an *imperium* that might become more than aspirationally Augustan if, by the grace of God, it were to extend its reach beyond the northeastern corner of the Atlantic Ocean.[1]

Although Shakespeare saw in Rome a vehicle through which to dramatize some of the political, cultural, and social dynamics of early modern London, he never evinced the least interest in London (or England, or Britain) as a new Rome. *Troilus and Cressida* dismisses the Trojan foundation myths by which Geoffrey of Monmouth, Holinshed, and countless others set such store. *Titus Andronicus* and *Julius Caesar* subject to withering critique Roman claims to virtue, along with the Roman moral exceptionalism of which the humanist mainstream was so enamored. In *Antony and Cleopatra*, he nonetheless turns in earnest to the moment in history that saw the emergence not just of the Roman empire, but of the Roman empire as the guarantor of what Shakespeare's Octavius prophesies as a "time of universal peace" (4.6.5). That is, to the emergence of an ideology through which imperial conquest and dominion, in the early seventeenth century as at the beginning of the Common Era, was both glorified and legitimated.

————◆————

The scene on Pompey's galley is an excellent place to begin. A peace deal having been brokered between Pompey and the three rulers (Octavius Caesar, Antony, and Lepidus) to whom leadership of Rome had passed after the murder of Julius Caesar and the defeat of the senatorial faction

led by Brutus and Cassius, Pompey arranges a celebration aboard his flag-
ship. In the source from which Shakespeare worked, North's translation
of Plutarch's life of Antony, this gathering is noteworthy in two respects.
First, the assertion that Pompey and his guests "fell to be merie with Antonius love unto Cleopatra" in the middle of the feast. Plutarch does not
spell it out, but we infer that Roman masculinity finds something gratifying in the image of itself at play with exotic beauty; that there is pleasure
to be found in telling stories of one's amorous slips, because doing so
affirms that—like Julius Caesar, who had also been Cleopatra's lover—one
has the capacity to rise again at will. Second, Pompey's refusal to heed the
advice of his lieutenant, Menas, and to assassinate the triumvirs while they
are distracted with drink and festivity. After pondering for a moment or
two the prospect of a quick and easy path to power, Pompey dismisses it
as beneath his dignity. Shakespeare retains the Plutarchan outline of the
evening's events, but offers a much more detailed depiction of the moment
that Menas would have Pompey exploit; there is nothing of the kind in the
earlier Cleopatra plays by Jodelle, Garnier (subsequently translated into
English by Mary Sidney Herbert), Cinthio, and Samuel Daniel.[2]

Perhaps the most celebrated feature of Shakespeare's depiction is the
exchange between Lepidus and Antony on what the Nile crocodile is "like."
Wine has been taken. Antony is feeling the effects, and Lepidus is getting pitifully drunk. The conversation settles on Egypt, whence Antony
has recently returned and which neither Lepidus nor Octavius has visited. We first hear Antony providing a complex answer to a question about
measuring the level of the Nile and about the agricultural benefits of its
flood.[3] Lepidus then moves on to Egyptian "serpents," and asks for confirmation of the Ovidian commonplace that they are "bred . . . of your mud
by the operation of your sun" (2.7.17–27).[4] Lepidus's "your" is supposed
to indicate the condition of belonging to a group (i.e., the class of things
Egyptian), but sounds like a tactless deployment of the second person
genitive.[5] Antony has recently reasserted his allegiance to Rome by marrying Octavia, sister of Octavius, and does not want to have Egypt insinuated
as in some sense "his" by someone he has long regarded as an irritating
lightweight.[6] The more so because Lepidus's language so closely resembles
that in which Antony himself contrasted Egypt and Rome when ignoring
Octavius's messenger at the beginning of play: unlike "the wide arch / Of
the ranged empire," in Egypt "Our dungy earth alike / Feeds beast as man"
(1.1.34–35, 36–37).

Lepidus now asks about pyramids (which he botches as "pyramises"
[2.7.35]) and, after receiving no answer from Antony, fixes on crocodiles:

"What manner o' thing is your crocodile?" (2.7.41). In response, Antony switches to prose to articulate something between displeasure and disdain. Lepidus fails to notice; in an aside, Octavius cannot conceal his incredulity at the fact; Antony reassures Octavius that Lepidus is drunk enough to swallow anything. The exchange demands to be quoted in full:

> ANTONY It is shaped, sir, like itself, and it is as broad as it hath breadth.
> It is just so high as it is, and moves with it own organs. It lives
> by that which nourisheth it, and the elements once out of it, it
> transmigrates.
> LEPIDUS What colour is it of?
> ANTONY Of it own colour too.
> LEPIDUS 'Tis a strange serpent.
> ANTONY 'Tis so, and the tears of it are wet.
> CAESAR Will this description satisfy him?
> ANTONY With the health that Pompey gives him, else he is a very
> epicure. (2.7.42–53)

Antony insults Lepidus with flagrant tautologies and conveys no information about the crocodile other than the facetiously exotic claim—again, derived from Ovid—that it "transmigrates" after death, and an affirmation that its proverbially deceptive tears are "wet."[7]

Octavius takes no interest in the substance of what has been said, and the conversation is abandoned to more revelry. Before long, Lepidus has to be carried offstage, and Octavius declares that he has seen, drunk, said, and heard enough: "Our graver business / Frowns at this levity . . . / What needs more words? Good night" (2.7.120–21, 125). The onboard celebration concludes. Octavius, Antony, and Pompey return to shore.

What of the crocodile? Why, other than using it to put dramatic flesh on the bones of the unspoken discord between the triumvirs, does Shakespeare bother with it? As Janet Adelman notes, it is an animal whose appearance has "all the complexity of the historical tradition." She continues to observe that "what we do with so mutable a beast must be left to our critical discretion."[8] To take one prominent point of reference, we might look to Book 5 of Spenser's *Faerie Queene*, where crocodiles can emblematize guile, tyranny, lust, cruelty, hypocrisy, justice, uxoriousness, forcefulness, providential foresight, dynastic fecundity (Empson memorably suggests that Britomart "copulates with the crocodile and thus produces the English Monarchy"), and even the sun.[9] Or we might recall that authors since Cicero had suggested that the ancient Egyptians invested crocodiles with a dizzying range of meanings of their own, many of them divine.[10]

But critical discretion demands that we go further than noting the variety of crocodile lore and symbolism. For instance, Quintilian advises that logical games like paradoxes can help to remind the would-be orator that he should attend to every detail of his words. One of these involves an Egyptian crocodile that promises to return a son to his mother if the mother can correctly state what it will do with her son. She responds that the crocodile will not return her son to her, and, although the answer is truthful, the crocodile refuses to honor its word on the grounds that returning the child would give the lie to the mother's utterance.[11] *Crocodilites*, or the crocodile's argument, would retain its place in writing on logic and rhetoric throughout the early modern period, and testified to the importance of keeping your wits both trained and about you.[12] There is no struggle to hear an echo of it in the way that Antony treats Lepidus's drunken witlessness.

The play itself provides us with several further clues. For example, if we believe Cleopatra's own account of the matter, Antony imagines her as his "serpent of old Nile" (1.5.26). Serpent here not only denotes a snake like the asp, but also the category of lethally dangerous animals of which the crocodile is the bulkiest representative.[13] Like Lepidus's "strange serpent," Antony's term of endearment functions as a synecdoche in which the whole is made to speak for the part. But as the residue of Revelation 12:9 (in which Satan the tempter is an "old serpent") might suggest, nothing here is uncomplicated: Antony also toys with the notion that Cleopatra has beguiled him into breaking his marriage vows and neglecting his "Roman thought[s]" (1.2.88).[14] On a less anxious tack, Antony might well have something (or someone) other than an actual crocodile in mind when describing a being that can only be understood in relation to itself. Just as Plutarch's Antony makes much of the posture that he and Cleopatra are nonpareil, so his Shakespearean incarnation appears to share the view of Cleopatra's incomparability expressed by Enobarbus; by the end of the play, this "lass unparalleled" (5.2.315) even wins herself a transmigration of sorts.[15]

Perhaps so, but we should be careful not to overlook what would have been the least contestable meaning of the crocodile lore suggested by Antony's serpentine characterization of Cleopatra: along with the pyramids and the Nile, crocodiles stood for Egypt in its entirety.[16] As such, their representations became a ready emblem for the corruptions associated with the ancient Egyptian way of life. A good example comes from the expanded editions of Cesare Ripa's compendious *Iconologia* that appeared after 1613. Building on the account given in Valeriano's popular *Hieroglyphica*, Ripa used the crocodile to represent *lussuria*, or what Florio translates as the

FIGURE 11. Cesare Ripa, *Iconologia*, (Padua, 1618), 315. Marquand Library of Art and Archaeology, Princeton University.

family of vices that include "*luxurie, letcherie, lust, superfluitie and excesse in carnall pleasures, riot, and ranknesse*."[17] Ripa's emblem (see figure 11), shows a woman of decidedly Cleopatran bearing—an almost entirely nude female figure, covered only with a scarf; she might pass for an Africanized version of Raphael's *La Fornarina* or Piero di Cosimo's fantastic portrait of Simonetta Vespucci—holding Venus's bird, the dove, and sitting on top of a crocodile.[18]

Although I will revisit nearly all these contexts in the pages that follow, I want to approach the crocodile that Shakespeare scripts for Lepidus and Antony from a different perspective; one that will, I hope, help further to unpack the significance of the galley scene. Viewed from here, the crocodile that Antony does so little to describe reveals some essential but frequently overlooked truths about the rift between the Roman and Egyptian worldviews of which the play appears to make so much; about the ways in which Antony and Cleopatra fashion their image as lovers; and about Rome's lack of interest in Egypt as anything other than a screen on which to project conflicting versions of itself. The central point, I take it, is that everybody on Pompey's galley takes an interest in crocodiles not out of curiosity and/or wonder, but because they are a token whose currency has been predetermined by the value assigned to it within the moral and political economy of Rome.

———————

First, a step or two backward. As Erasmus rushed to prepare his parallel-text Greek and Latin edition of the New Testament in late 1515, he realized that it would need to be prefaced with a defense of his critical procedures. When the edition was published in 1516, this preface took the form of a short work titled the "Methodus." By the time of a heavily revised second edition in 1519, Erasmus had been able to write something more substantial. This was the *Ratio verae theologiae* ("True System of Theology"), in which he outlined a new theological curriculum and mode of study. It was nothing short of a manifesto, and took the place of the "Methodus" in all further editions of his text; it was also frequently reprinted in its own right.[19]

One of the core arguments of the *Ratio* is that the niceties of scholastic logic are worth less than the disciplines of grammar and rhetoric when attempting scriptural exegesis and hermeneutics. Noble though their truth-telling intentions may initially have been, the scholastics had come to distort sacred scripture by imposing on it patterns of philosophical and theological order that it could not be said to support—and had likewise come to distort biblical study by insisting on their way of doing things. In advancing this case, Erasmus settles on an eye-catching example:

> But I ask you, what will you divide or define or infer if you do not know the essence and the nature of the things you are discussing? How will it help you to have constructed a syllogism in the form of *celarent* or *baroco* when you dispute about a crocodile, if you do not know what kind of tree or animal a crocodile is? These things are not, in fact, learned so much from Aristotle's eight books of *Physics* . . . as from his extremely erudite commentaries on animals . . . from the books of Theophrastus *On Plants, On Winds, On Precious Stones*, from Pliny, from Macrobius and Athanaeus, from Dioscorides, from the *Natural Questions* of Seneca and other writers of this sort.[20]

"Celarent" and "baroco" are two of the mnemonics with which students were taught to recall the configurations into which logical syllogisms could be arranged.[21] In referring to them here, Erasmus suggests that syllogistic is at once trivial and hopelessly abstract. What is more, its refusal to engage with the historical world mean that its formulations are tautologous, unavoidably circular—devoid of content, and lacking any purpose other than propagating the cultural authority of the scholastic theologians who professed them.[22] Syllogistic habits of mind therefore prevented the clergyman from keeping in view the true *scopus* (the goal or unifying principle) of biblical study, and damaged his ability to guide his congregation toward Christ. Just as one keen to visualize crocodiles could not hope to do so through the operations of scholastic logic and should instead turn to books of natural history, so the would-be servant of the Holy Ghost should commit himself to the rewarding labors of grammar and philology.

Erasmus was, as his suggested crocodilian readings might imply, an enthusiastic natural historian: his writings are shot through with discussions of animal life, which usually lean on Aristotle and Pliny (who, in describing creatures not ordinarily encountered in Greece or Rome, were themselves often dependent on earlier writers such as Herodotus). Crocodiles, in the *Ratio* and elsewhere, are fine exemplars of the rule.[23] He must therefore have felt himself on solid ground when turning his fire on the scholastic approach to the Bible: the protocols of natural historical inquiry could help to demonstrate the absurdity of generalizing from inadequate data. And on one level, he was successful. The *Ratio* highlights, with only a hint of polemic triumphalism, the misguidedness of tackling scriptural questions armed with scholastic logic alone.

The catch is that Erasmus's stated authorities are unreliable. Their accounts of crocodilian physiology and behavior barely exceed educated guesswork, and owe as much to folkloric tradition (crocodile tears and so forth) as to empirical rigor. And as late as the second half of the sixteenth century, little had changed. Because even the most up-to-date zoologists had not been able to examine living specimens of the crocodile, they were dependent on book learning (and, occasionally, the taxidermist's art) in trying to account for it. Consider the almost comically misguided representation of an encounter between a crocodile and a hippopotamus (figure 12) included in the fourth book of Conrad Gesner's *Historia animalium*. Gesner insists that his illustration replicates a detail from the reliefs decorating the base of the first- or second-century sculpture known as the Vatican Nile, but it seems clear that neither he nor his immediate source, the well-traveled Pierre Belon, had seen this work for themselves.[24] Elsewhere, Gesner's authorities enabled him to capture the physical form of a crocodile with more accuracy (figure 13).

FIGURE 12. Conrad Gesner, *Conradi Gesneri medici Tigurini Historiae animalium liber IIII: Qui est de piscium & aquatilium animantium natura* (Zürich, 1558), 494. Rare Book Division, Department of Rare Books and Special Collections, Princeton University Library.

FIGURE 13. Conrad Gesner, *Conradi Gesneri medici Tigurini Historiae animalium liber IIII: Qui est de piscium & aquatilium animantium natura* (Zürich, 1558), 361. Rare Book Division, Department of Rare Books and Special Collections, Princeton University Library.

When writing his popular English-language natural histories in the early seventeenth century, Edward Topsell followed Gesner's lead in more ways than one. Although he claimed to "have seene a Crocodile in England brought out of Egypt dead, and killed with a Musket," he was perfectly content to reproduce that which he had read about crocodiles in the

Historia animalium.[25] A similar disconnection can be found in English accounts of encounters with crocodilians in the wild. George Sandys explored Egypt in person, but offered a first-hand account that depends almost entirely on received humanist wisdom: if he saw crocodiles as he says he did, then he did so through the lens of what his reading had conditioned him to expect.[26] The temptation to fall back on one's reading as a mode of observation is further illuminated by an English adventurer who happened to catch and kill a Mexican crocodile (or caiman, or alligator) in October 1567. He had no had recourse to learned expedients, and instead turned to everyday analogues in describing it: "23 foote by the rule, headed like a hogge, in bodie like a serpent, full of scales as broad as a sawcer, his taile long and full of knots, as bigge as a fawcon shotte [i.e., a small cannonball], he hath foure legges, his feete have long nailes like unto a dragon."[27] Like a pig, a snake, and a dragon—and very large. Job Hortop did not know what to make of what he had seen, and hoped that his readers would be excited to find themselves in a similar position. Although Hortop, Sandys, Topsell, and Gesner differ markedly from one another as writers, all of them embrace the rhetoric of semi-familiarizing visuality in seeking to bring their accounts of exotic fauna to life.

That the early moderns regarded crocodiles less as objects of natural inquiry than as spectacles or oddities is something that Shakespeare understood well. When Romeo dilates at length on the apothecary from whom he will procure the poison with which to relieve his heartbreak, he notes that "in his needy shop a tortoise hung, / An alligator stuffed, and other skins / Of ill-shaped fishes." From which we infer that, after perhaps being alerted to them by an aside in Thomas Nashe's splendidly titled *Have With You to Saffron Waldon*, Shakespeare knew of the crocodiles and crocodile skins that adorned many a *Wunderkammer*, or cabinet of curiosities (see figure 14).[28] Crocodile tears are another Shakespearean commonplace, while the outlandish cast of Hamlet's grief for the dead Ophelia finds expression in his vow to "eat a crocodile" despite the impenetrable toughness of its hide.[29]

Returning now to *Antony and Cleopatra*, we are in a position to see that the crocodiles evoked there are distinctive not as a site in which Shakespeare could dramatize the humanistic and para-humanistic habits of conjecture, commonplace, and exotic tale-telling. Rather, the play resembles Erasmus's *Ratio* in turning to that which lies behind the all but infinite variety with which, since antiquity, crocodilian life had been comprehended in the Greco-Latin West: for the Shakespeare of *Antony and Cleopatra* as for Erasmus, the fact that crocodiles exceed discursive convention means

that they can be used to indict the arts of language for their representational poverty. The difference between Shakespeare and Erasmus is that, for
Erasmus, the crocodile exposes the logic-chopping abstraction of scholastic theory, whereas for Shakespeare it exposes the treacherously unstable
foundations of the humanist rhetoric that Erasmus held dear.

So, as we observe Antony belittle Lepidus on Pompey's galley, the point
is not simply that Lepidus is drunkenly oblivious enough for Antony to get
away with behaving disrespectfully toward him. Nor are we invited to ponder some larger point about the inconsequentiality of conventional language, maybe to conclude—with the denizens of the Lagado academy in
Gulliver's Travels—that things in themselves are the only truly significant
mode of discourse.[30] Instead, we find Shakespeare leading us to the heart
of Roman rhetorical culture. Specifically, to an interrogation of its insistence on the visual qualities of successful rhetorical performance. In due
course, we are led to the conclusion that this insistent visuality leads to an
engagement with the world that, in its disregard for the bonds between *res*
and *verba*, is as self-serving as it is superficial.

For the Romans and their humanist heirs, the most effective way for
the orator to accomplish his ends is for him to make his audience "see" the
things (people, places, objects, events, etc.) that he wants to discuss.[31]
As discussed in connection with *Hamlet* in chapter 3, the rhetorical term
of art associated with this visually compelling intensity is *enargeia*. Cicero
and Quintilian insist on its importance, and their ideas resonate through
the rhetoric manuals of the sixteenth century—Erasmus's *De copia* prominent among them.[32] Quintilian gives a characteristically lucid account of
what is at stake. *Enargeia* occurs when

> the images through which things absent are represented to the mind
> appear so distinctly that we seem to see them with our eyes and to have
> them actually before us.

Just as the orator who wants to make his audience feel a particular emotion needs to ensure that he feels that emotion himself as he speaks, so
Quintilian insists that "the man who can best conceive such images" in his
own mind will be able to accomplish *enargeia* most powerfully—which is
to say, with the greatest amount of persuasive heft.[33]

It is easy to discern how this rhetorical method works well for "things
absent" that are known or that can readily be imagined from an audience's

FIGURE 14. Ferrante Imperato, *Dell'historia naturale* (Naples, 1599), sig. a3v–4r. Rare Book Division, Department of Rare Books and Special Collections, Princeton University Library.

reading or everyday experience. It is also easy to see how *enargeia* was at the heart of poetics as the early moderns understood it: the poet's powers of imagination made him supremely well-qualified to conjure up the vivid images that the rhetorical tradition demands. As Philip Sidney puts it, "to a man that had never seen an elephant or a rhinoceros, who should tell him most exquisitely all their shapes, colour, bigness, and particular marks . . . might well make the hearer able to repeat, as it were by rote, all he had heard, yet should never satisfy his inward conceit with being witness to itself of a true lively knowledge." It is this "inward conceit" of "true lively knowledge" that, for Sidney and his kind, both defines good poetry and means that it should be envisaged, after Horace, as a "speaking picture."[34] Mere descriptions, howsoever copious, will "never satisfy" that which successfully mimetic art can deliver: the experience of being a "witness" to the events or phenomena in question. (We might recall that a facility in making the members of a theatrical audience "see" action that is reported from offstage—rather than performed onstage before them—is one of the more distinctive features of Shakespeare's dramatic craft; and that, as Lorna Hutson has suggested, this craft owes much to Shakespeare's immersion in the rhetorical tradition.)[35]

But as forceful a technique as *enargeia* may be, Sidney's account of it suggests a possible limitation: the representation of objects, like rhinoceroses and elephants and crocodiles, that are unknown to the audience one seeks to move. As rhetorical success depends on being able to harness and manipulate the "visions" of an audience, the rhetorical handbooks' answer is plain: an unknown entity must be accommodated to an audience's frame of reference if it is to be "seen" in the desired fashion. Here, the most obvious and important medium is the class of metaphorical language—particularly the simile. The orator could turn to poetic writing as a storehouse of figures and tropes to be used in generating *enargeia*, and as a lesson in how to generate figures and tropes of his own.[36] He might also quote or adapt or allude to authoritative works of either history or poetry to help his audience form a likeness of an unfamiliar object; or, if this does not quite suit his purpose, he might exploit proverbs, *sententiae*, and popular wisdom both to uphold and to amplify the picture he is trying to present. A final set of maneuvers was discussed as the "topic of testimony" and comprised some of the early modern rhetorician's favorite stocks-in-trade. For example, rather than conjuring an image of a far-flung place like Egypt *ex novo*, an early modern English orator could present it in familiar, and hopefully compelling, terms through the pictures of it sketched by authorities like Herodotus and Pliny.[37]

As such, *enargeia* reasserts something fundamental about Shakespeare's understanding of rhetoric, as manifested both in *Antony and Cleopatra* and in general: if the effective rhetorician needs to be able to move the ignorant and what Demetrius disparages as "the common liar" (1.1.61), then the veracity of his utterances can only be an incidental virtue. His goal is victory rather than the pursuit of truth, and he must say whatever he needs to if he is to take his audience with him. If his audience has never seen Egypt but must be persuaded to form a view of it pursuant to some imperative or other of Roman policy, then persuade it he shall—no matter that this view be fictional or sensationalistic. "Behold and see" (1.1.13), declares Philo as the play begins. But he only does so after establishing the moral framework within which Antony—"The triple pillar of the world transformed / Into a strumpet's fool"—should be regarded (1.1.12–13). The injunction to "see," as if it were an appeal to objectivity rather than an affirmation of an observer's particular and invariably moralized viewpoint, occurs with startling frequency throughout *Antony and Cleopatra*. And yet at no point in the play is observation anything other than a normative activity. As Octavius puts it to Lepidus, "You may see . . . and henceforth know, / It is not Caesar's natural vice to hate / Our great competitor" (1.4.1–3).[38] Even without the example of *King Lear*, Octavius's deployment of that vexed adjective "natural" would sound like a mixture of irony and disingenuousness—an attempt to enjoin virtuous stability where it does not exist. What *is* his natural vice? And what of the ones that he may or may not prefer to call unnatural, and that might include the politicking duplicity that will in due course constrain Lepidus to the sidelines? The force of his comment is to insist on the magnanimity with which he would like to be regarded.

The same dynamics animate the exchange over the crocodile on Pompey's galley. It is not just that Antony cannot be bothered going through the motions in bringing the unfamiliar reptile to life for Lepidus's benefit, but that not even Antony evinces an interest in the reality of crocodiles or of life in Egypt more generally. He is only concerned with what such things mean to him—which, as we are reminded over and again when we first see him and Cleopatra interact ("Let Rome in Tiber melt" [1.1.34]), lends itself to a summary of the least demanding sort. Egypt is appealing because it is not the Rome in which he rose to power and in which, on account of being repeatedly outmatched by Octavius, he no longer feels comfortable. Antony has seen crocodiles in the flesh, to be sure. But they have to him been an alien curiosity in which he takes no interest as anything more than an analog of the Cleopatra whom, he likes to pretend, has used her boundless "cunning" (1.2.152) to entrap him. One piece of touristic exotica with which to explain another. The crocodiles on Pompey's galley thus do duty for all inhabitants of Egypt. They are entities defined by what Antony and his fellow Romans need them to be; they exist only through commonplaces, and the tautologies with which Erasmus had indicted the scholastic theologians. Shakespeare's point is that appearances, and plausibility, are everything within the Roman worldview that the humanists claimed as their own. Things as they really are, or might really be, are simply not pertinent provided one's account of them is vivid enough to hold an audience's attention. The ends accomplished, what needs more words?

———

From here, an inquiry into the meaning and significance of Antony's crocodile might proceed in several different directions.

Toward, for instance, a further confirmation of Shakespeare's conviction that rhetorical discourse is a strictly instrumental affair. For Cicero, Quintilian, and Erasmus, only the virtuous man (the *vir bonus*) could fully attain the quality of eloquence, but for "pragmatic" late humanists such as the unfortunate Petrus Ramus and Shakespeare's admirer Gabriel Harvey, rhetorical virtuosity was open to anyone who perfected the skills of the art.[39] Shakespeare moves briskly along the path cleared by Ramus and Harvey, but carries on where they draw to a halt. They took the cultivation of pragmatic humanism to be a good and desirable thing; Shakespeare grants the value of exposing the bedrock on which rhetorical proficiency rests, but depicts such pragmatism as an index of the dangerous ambivalence encouraged by rhetorical culture. In *Antony and Cleopatra*, the scope and cynosure of *Romanitas* is neither virtue nor clear-sightedly Machiavellian statecraft. It is instead the pursuit and priggishly hypocritical maintenance of power.

Recall that as two of the triumvirs deride the loss of judgment in the third, we in the audience see all three men as a sort of inset play through the contemptuously sober eyes of Menas. Menas discerns a chance to remove them from the scene and for Pompey to rule in their place. Pompey disapproves. Not of the plan itself, but of Menas's decision to involve him in it: "Ah, this thou shouldst have done / And not have spoken on't. In me 'tis villainy; / In thee't had been good service" (2.7.74–76). Now that Menas has told him about it, he feels bound to order its abandonment. Menas is appalled that his master should be so feebly seduced by his own self-image as an honorable Roman, and abandons him to his fate—which, as Menas intuits ("Pompey doth this day laugh away his fortune" [2.6.106–7]), is to be betrayed by Octavius and finally murdered. By urging Pompey to act when presented with the chance, Menas is not dramatized as a figure of treachery, but as one who—like Hubert in *King John*—has more courage and clarity of vision than the man he serves. Everything other than power politics takes the form of delusion (in which the Romans reassure themselves of their better natures) or disguise (in which they attempt to convince their victims of the same).

Still, if we are fully to understand how it is that the instrumentality of rhetoric matters to *Antony and Cleopatra*, it is necessary to look more closely at what the exchange on Pompey's galley discloses about the mutual standing of Rome and Egypt. If crocodiles are of no interest to Antony, Octavius, or Lepidus as anything other than tokens of imperial power, what status do they—and Cleopatra, and Egypt, and the purportedly Egyptian-pharaonic way of life—have within the dramaturgy of the play as a whole?

The opening scenes offer much with which to help us to address this family of questions. Take what looks to be the definitively Egyptian lovemaking with which Antony and Cleopatra make themselves known: hedonistic, passionate, unguarded and therefore the more sincere, and so on. As many critics of the play have noticed, there is something more than slightly histrionic about all of this. To Cleopatra's boast that she can limit the degree to which she is loved, Antony responds with the grandiose—and oddly biblical—assertion that "Then must thou needs find out new heaven, new earth" (1.1.17).[40] Once they have a Roman audience in Octavius's anonymous messenger, matters get stagier still—particularly as Cleopatra affects possessive jealousy at Antony's responsibilities to Fulvia and Octavius. We nonetheless indulge them and resist the prurient moralizing with which Philo, one of Antony's soldiers, frames the action. They act out the paradoxes and excesses of a poem like Donne's "Good Morrow" not in mannered self-indulgence, but because they have no alternative: they are middle-aged lovers doing whatever they can to negate the painful realities of time and their past lives.[41] As they have histories that are more complex and freighted than most others in their position, so their compensatory efforts are all the more ostentatious. "Excellent falsehood!" (1.1.41) indeed. Bumping up against mortality, self-awareness is overridden by the compulsion to act.

Shakespeare's emotional subtlety notwithstanding, the vital point here is that the "huge archetypal characters" into which Antony and Cleopatra transform themselves are no less Roman than the message from Octavius that they choose to neglect: the models for their transformation are Venus and Mars, the paradigmatically *Roman* gods of love and war. When Isis is mentioned in this connection, she does not express native Egyptian mystery, but is typologically consumed within Roman mythology—just as Antony's Hercules is the eastward looking face of his Mars.[42]

Consider likewise the habitually mutable, highly metaphorical, and frequently immoderate modes of discourse that characterize life in and around the play's depiction of Cleopatra's court. These are exemplifications of the "Asiatic" style of oratory that, as Plutarch observes, had long been Antony's own: "He used a manner of phrase in his speeche, called Asiatik . . . and [it] was much like to his manners and life: for it was full of ostentation, foolishe braverie, and vaine ambition." It is this "manner of phrase" that Shakespeare so powerfully contrasts to Brutus's clipped reasonableness in *Julius Caesar*, a fact that gives the lie to any suggestion that the "Asiatic" mode may be sympathetic to poetic or creative mindsets (remember Cinna the Poet). Rather, "Asianism" denotes a rhetorical style more elaborate—more concerned with wordplay and its affective force— than the Atticism preferred by Octavius and Brutus. Indeed, it is no exaggeration to say that if the "Asiatic" style had not existed, it would have been necessary to invent it as a foil to the compressed brevity championed by the Atticists: that is, precisely because the Attic style could not always be trusted to move an audience appropriately. (As Brutus finds to his cost.) Unadorned masculine virtue may have been its own reward, but was taking no chances; even when failing to achieve the ends of persuasion, it could pat itself on the back for eschewing the florid effeminacy of the Eastern peoples over whom, in its imperial mode, it proposed to exercise dominion.[43]

There is no better example of the "Asiatic" style than Enobarbus's set-piece description of how Cleopatra "pursed up" Antony's "heart upon the river of Cydnus" (2.2.197). In making comprehensible Cleopatra's unfamiliar allure, the otherwise plainspoken Enobarbus deploys the full range of simile, metaphor, testimony, paradox, and hyperbole at his disposal: the Ovidian conceit that Cleopatra "makes hungry / Where most she satisfies" (2.2.247–48) is a good case in point.[44]

So, although Cleopatra's appearance is boldly Venereal, it is never other than a deliberate self-presentation: she is not a goddess and knows she is not a goddess, but has taken pains to make herself look like one.[45] As such, she becomes both a work of artifice and an artificer. A sort of Pygmalion, Galatea, and Venus rolled into one; and, as Plutarch's tribute to her linguistic and rhetorical virtuosity suggests, one who is very good with words.[46] She is also well aware of what her Roman audience—Enobarbus, Antony, and beyond—*expect* to "see and behold" from her. It is her decision to appear at Cydnus *as if* she were a Roman fantasy of Venus ("O'erpicturing that Venus where we see / The fancy outwork nature" [2.2.210–11]) that allows Enobarbus to recreate her image so powerfully and vividly: his words are a kind of ekphrasis.[47] As, perhaps, is the definitively visual-theatrical performance with which she decides to die: Charmian is told to "Go fetch / My best attires . . . I am again for Cydnus / To meet Mark Antony" (5.2.226–28). The one exception to her rule of keeping Roman expectations in mind is that, on Octavius's account, she appeared "In th'habiliments of the goddess Isis" (3.6.17) when she and Antony publicly asserted their dominion over the eastern portion of the empire. But this, as Octavius explains, is another exercise in political theater, in this case accommodated to the needs of a non-Roman audience: a quasi-pharaonic masquerade, carefully fitted to the "common showplace where they exercise" (3.6.12). Octavius's uncharacteristically open rage at this turn of events arises from his awareness that, although he understands the power of giving an audience what they think they want as a means of controlling them, he does not have the performative flair of Antony, much less that of Antony's Egyptian lover and ally. He fears that he has, for once, been outmaneuvered.

All of which is to suggest that despite the commonplaces of critical tradition, *Antony and Cleopatra* does not depict a world in which there is a collision between Roman and Egyptian mores, tastes, or systems of belief. Nor does it depict one in which competing Roman and Egyptian ideologies bleed into one another as if they were no more fixed than the shapes in the clouds. To state the case as baldly as possible, this is because Egypt as seen in *Antony and Cleopatra* is a conjuring trick in which the Egyptians themselves, led by their Hellenistic-pharaonic queen, have no choice but to participate: it is only ever through the Roman imagination that we are allowed to behold Cleopatra, crocodiles, pyramids, or the mud of the Nile. What Shakespeare's drama anatomizes is not a conflict between Egypt and Rome, but one between two different versions of *Romanitas*, two different models through which the nascent Roman empire might make sense of itself. On the one hand, the epic impersonality of the Augustan age as imagined by Virgil; on the other, the violence and witty sensuousness of Ovid's *Amores*, where "Mars doth rage abroad without all pity, / And Venus rules in her Aeneas Citty."[48] Both visions project themselves as the one true representation of Rome, both owe their sense of their own coherence to an order that is at root aesthetic, and both are concomitantly unprepared to acknowledge any struggle for precedence with the other. Neither has the slightest interest in the reality—or in distorting the reality—of life in Egypt. For Shakespeare's Romans, it is a given the territories of Northeastern Africa exist only in virtue of their place within the Roman worldview.

We know how this story ends. Furthermore, and as many students of *Antony and Cleopatra* have noted, the place of Egypt within the play is readily compatible with the postcolonial discourse of "othering." Such readings are especially apt in relation to what would become the Augustan assertion of Roman *imperium* as a masculine redemption through domination of the feminine, degenerate, and luxurious East; the Ovidian Egypt projected throughout *Antony and Cleopatra* likewise chimes well with Said's claim that orientalism is a "citationary" mode of discourse.[49] But the postcolonial fit is imperfect: Shakespeare does not depict Egypt as "other" or subaltern, but as invisible. Or, rather, he depicts it as a culture and a polity rendered invisible by the chasm between *verba* and *res*, by the parochialism and indifference to truth of Roman politics and rhetoric. It is one with Antony's crocodile. Such enforced invisibility is a precondition of remaking conquered cultures in forms, more often than not "othered" forms, palatable to their colonizers; remakings that, as they are intended to, work to estrange conquered cultures from themselves (the unhappy paradox of Welshness and *Cymreictod* alike). The fact remains that Shakespeare's concern is to analyze the origins of this invisibility in Roman culture, not to explore its consequences once the action of the play concludes. The peculiar burden of his Cleopatra is to understand that she, and the realm for which she would win political autonomy, can only be apprehended through her enemies' habits of thought and speech.

———◆———

There are few things more Roman, or more in keeping with humanist notions of civic order, than Cleopatra's awareness that she must perform herself if she is to accomplish her desired ends. As discussed at various points above, the key text here is Cicero's *De officiis*, within which Cicero propounds the view that to discover one's true self is to discover the various parts that one has been fitted to play within the well-ordered drama of human life. These parts were defined by the social virtues of honor (*honestas*) and seemliness or propriety (*decorum*), and were known as *personae*. *Personae* were the masks worn by Roman actors to make their characters known on the stage; by extension they came to stand both for onstage characters as a whole, and for the actors who played them. Despite the externality of one's *personae*, their dependence on the natural force of one's disposition, reaffirmed by the rational and therefore naturally human qualities of *honestas* and *decorum*, meant that they comprised one's truest identity. Furthermore, and as these theatrical metaphors imply, such identities were far from singular. *Decorum* demands that one behave differently in different situations, making it necessary to adopt *personae* that differ according to the contexts in which one has to operate.[50]

It is Antony's failure to maintain the integrity of his martial *persona* in doting on Cleopatra that so vexes Octavius. That he should have conducted himself differently in the arms of an extramarital lover need not, in itself, have been a cause for concern; the more so as their affair had taken place in Egypt. The problem is that, under the influence of Cleopatra, he allowed this amatory *persona* to predominate, thereby neglecting the *decorum* with which he should, in conformity with the Roman ideology, have governed himself and his affairs—together with the honor (*honestas*) that decorous actions accrue. What is more, Octavius's commitment to *personae*, *honestas*, and *decorum* is one that Antony the Roman appears to share. Yes, he and Cleopatra can joke about "play[ing] one scene / Of excellent dissembling, and let[ting] it look / Like perfect honour" (1.3.79–81), but for Antony, *honestas* is an identity: it connotes being "the best of men; / Whose virtue and whose general graces speak / That which none else can utter" (2.2.136–38). A *homo honestissimus* of this sort is one who can perfectly play the lover, the fighter, or the dutiful husband as circumstances demand; one who, after the examples of Aeneas (and Julius Caesar), is prepared to forsake the love of an African queen for the greater glory of his *patria*. Tellingly, Octavius venerates Antony's martial accomplishments in the Alps, "so *like* a soldier" (1.4.71, my emphasis). Similitude is not imitation or pretense or "dissembling," but is a form of obeisance to a higher and more virtuous form of reality—one that, in the eyes of Octavius, Antony has allowed himself to besmirch in Egypt. The definitive instance of this comes in Cleopatra's reminiscence of joyous times in Antony's company: "I drunk him to his bed, / Then put my tires and mantles on him, whilst / I wore his sword Philippan" (2.5.21–23). Cleopatra enjoys her playfully cross-dressed tribute to Venus disarming the love-enfeebled Mars, and though we only have her word for it, it isn't hard to imagine that Antony might himself have enjoyed his part in the spectacle too.[51] And yet, for the Caesarian ideal of Rome for which Antony fought and killed at Philippi, their activities comprise the world turned upside down—like Vulcan in the versions of the Venus and Mars story preserved by Homer and Ovid,

Octavius views righting things as his unglamorous duty.[52] So it is that when Cleopatra expresses her relief that Antony has been able to escape "the world's great snare" (4.8.18) as arranged by Octavius, she nods to the finely woven net (*rete*) and snare (*laqueus*) of which Ovid's Vulcan makes use in exposing his wife and her lover; of course, it soon becomes clear that neither Antony nor Cleopatra has been able to do any such thing.

The Roman emphasis on the maintenance of *decorum* is also that which allows Octavius's characterizations of Cleopatra to differ so radically from one another: as the agent of Antony's corruption, she is a "whore" (3.6.68); as the ruler of territories whose value he would like to emphasize, she is his "dear queen" (5.2.184); as his captive, he is quite content to drag her through the streets of Rome as an exemplar of what happens to those who resist Roman dominion. We find the same plurality in Horace's ode on Cleopatra, where she is here a "deadly monster" (*fatale monstrum*) fueled by drink and lasciviousness, and there an exemplar of bravery, nobility, and dignity in defeat.[53] Although the *personae* through which Octavius and Horace apprehend her change from context to context, there is no contradiction here. They have no interest in apprehending her as she "really" is or might be: people are their *personae* and are as such inherently plural. The only constant is that the vigorously upright Roman male should at all times be able to control the ways in which he shows his face to the world.

This is why, when Antony disgraces himself at Actium by turning to follow the fleeing Cleopatra "like a doting mallard" (mating season on the Avon translated to the Ionian Sea), Scarus asserts that he "never saw an action of such shame. / Experience, manhood, honour, ne'er before / Did violate so itself" (3.10.20, 22–24). In most treatments of Antony and Cleopatra's story, it is this loss of moral and martial identity that simultaneously leads to the lovers' downfall and invests it with the force of tragedy. In the words of Fulke Greville, describing his own ill-fated play on the subject, Antony and Cleopatra "according to their irregular passions in foreaking empire to follow sensuality, were sacrificed in the fire."[54]

To get a sense of how little Shakespeare has in common with this tradition, we need only look more closely at his Antony. Far from being an impulsive creature of passion or the warrior-simpleton of Dryden's *All for Love*, he emerges in the aftermath of Actium as the only character in *Antony and Cleopatra* able to cast his gaze beyond the Roman attachment to displays of visual, rhetorical, and sociopolitical order.[55] Having suffered a military catastrophe and believing himself to have been betrayed by Cleopatra, he can no longer make any *persona* (warrior, general, lover,

husband) retain its form: "thou yet behold'st me?" (4.14.1), he wonders
of his follower Eros, only to insist that there is no stable Antony for his
follower to behold. In place of the quintessential Roman, he recognizes a
protean being figured by the shapes in the clouds:

> That which is now a horse, even with a thought
> The rack dislimns and makes it indistinct
> As water is in water . . .
> My good knave Eros, now thy captain is
> Even such a body. Here I am Antony,
> Yet cannot hold this visible shape, my knave. (4.14.9–14)

The language is a culminating echo of the play's obsession with verbs of transformation (becoming, making, melting, etc.); crucially, it also echoes the
ideas about creativity that, for many Renaissance theorists of the visual
and poetic arts, clustered around the "image made by chance" to which
Hamlet nods when obliging Polonius to detect the shapes of a weasel, a
whale, and a camel in the clouds. Here, the ability to "see" the likenesses of
things in the clouds reveals the powerfully projective imagination required
by all true artists. Antony inverts this usage by transfiguring the clouds not
to create something new, but to reveal how his formerly distinct self-image
has been unpainted from within by his appetites and errors of judgment.[56]

Selfhood could not be cast in terms less in thrall to humanist notions
of *Romanitas* than this. Still, it might be better to think of nephologi-
cal selfhood as a deliberately anti-Caesarian model of selfhood, and not
an anti-Roman one tout court—his words represent a sort of accelerated
Ovidianism, unchecked by the least semblance of *decorum* or mytho-
graphic order. Either way, Antony is disconcerted by the self-image he
has imagined and retreats from it into that most Roman of safe spaces:
the terminal dignity of suicide. Except, of course, that he has now closed
himself off from this too. Having had some of his thunder stolen by Eros's
nerveless self-slaughter, he bungles it—like Brutus before him, he is peril-
ously close to Macbeth's "Roman fool." Beholding the scene, an anonymous
guard falls back on the pseudo-apocalyptic coping mechanism employed
by Kent, Edgar, and Albany toward the end of *King Lear*: "Time is at his
period" (4.14.108). In fact, history continues apace. Another guard, Derce-
tus, makes off with Antony's sword so that Octavius can learn of his rival's
death, and then Cleopatra joins the dying Antony in striking the Ovidian
pose that Antony's stature had been so great that he alone could overcome
himself. No matter that this pose has remarkably little in common with his
suicide attempt as we have just seen it play out.[57]

Undeterred, Antony and Cleopatra come together in ensuring that, in death, he is regarded in the grandest Roman style. Antony hastens to misconstrue Virgil in dreaming that he and Cleopatra might outdo Dido and Aeneas in the splendor of their afterlife (4.14.52–55). Cleopatra, far more accomplished at this sort of thing, chooses to elaborate on her earlier vision of Antony as Hercules ("His legs bestrid the ocean" [5.2.81; cf., e.g., 1.3.85]), before declaring that he is "nature's piece 'gainst fancy" (5.2.98)— that is, a work of natural virtuosity that surpasses even her own ingenuity at Cydnus, where Enobarbus tells us that "the fancy outwork[ed] nature" (2.2.211).[58] But rather than paying tribute to the essential Antony or pre-paring herself for bittersweet reminiscences about the sunlight on the garden, Cleopatra's purpose in speaking thus is to set the scene for her final performance, within which "nature" as she portrays it will be sub-sumed within the demands of her art. As soon as she determines that the coldly pragmatic Octavius will not be swayed like Caesar and Antony had before him (when he first addresses her court, he does not even recognize which of Egyptian women before him is queen: to one who sees everything in the dry light of *imperium*, one curiously dressed female inhabitant of a recently conquered territory looks very much like another), she puts her plan into motion.

Once again, she is Venus to Antony's Mars. After misdirecting Octa-vius and attiring herself in the costume in which she originally aroused Antony's desire, she readies herself for an afterlife of marmoreal constancy (5.2.239)—and, although this vision is slightly upset by her crown falling "awry" in the act of dying (5.2.317), Charmian is on hand to straighten things out. Above all, Cleopatra's goal at this point in the action is "to keep decorum" (5.2.17), even to the point of hyperbole: "Husband, I come!" (5.2.286), she proclaims, despite knowing that Antony's Roman marriage to Octavia had not been annulled at the time of his death.

Writing amid the gathering storm of the 1930s, Walter Benjamin argued that fascism aestheticizes politics, that all such aestheticizations lead to war, and that communism responds to the threat by politicizing aesthetics. In the case of Cleopatra, we see that military defeat can lead to the aestheticization of politics too.[59] She arranges things so that a heavily idealized likeness of amorous fixity becomes a way in which to frustrate, and perhaps to repudiate, the success of her political-imperial rival. Octa-vius sees at once that the demands of her *decorum* have prevailed over his, and, as it would not be magnanimous of him to pretend otherwise (one of the reasons he was glad to have captured Cleopatra was that it gave an opportunity for "the world [to] see / His nobleness well acted"

[5.2.43–44]), he gives orders that she and Antony be buried together: "No grave upon the earth shall clip in it / A pair so famous. High events as these / Strike those that make them, and their story is / No less in pity than his glory which / Brought them to be lamented" (5.2.358–62). The downfall of Antony and Cleopatra elicits his quasi-tragic "pity," but his principal concern is to ensure that such feelings do not interfere with the expression of his "glory" as their conqueror. Presumably, Octavius has no plans to discuss Antony's funerary arrangements with his sister.

One further feature of the play's closing scene: tempting though it can be to see something mystical in Cleopatra's final transformation ("I am fire and air!" [5.2.288]), she does not transmigrate from one sort of being into another, as Julius Caesar does at the end of the *Metamorphoses*. Such a reading may have the virtue of echoing Antony's crocodile and the mutable clouds with which he traces his dissolution, but thoroughly misconstrues Cleopatra's artfully realized goal of seeing Octavius "unpolicied" (5.2.307). She is playing a political game, by rigorously political rules. Before *Antony and Cleopatra* begins, she reigned as a client queen. In Antony, and in Antony's Roman legions, she sees a chance for autonomy not by resisting imperial rule, but by winning power over the entire Roman Empire at Antony's side. The irony, and the constraint, of her position is that she can maintain it only by presenting Antony with a vision of herself, and of Egypt, that matches his transcultured Roman fantasies of what she and her country are supposed to be; fantasies that, when he is not hiding from them, Antony is happy to reciprocate. Cleopatra's situation is further complicated by the fact that she and Antony fall in love with one another, and do so through the media of their phantasmagoric self-presentations as Mars and Venus—media that may have started out as a form of parodically mimetic desire, but whose real value lies in reassuring them that they are more than "dull, sublunary lovers." Unfortunately for them both, Antony proves unable to match this serious play to the part of the military leader who must take the fight to Octavius. And yet, rather than turning this failing into a morality tale along the lines sketched by Antony's rivals, Shakespeare focuses our attention on Rome's power to determine the conditions in which Egypt, and the class of things Egyptian, can be taken to signify anything at all.[60]

Cleopatra, like Antony some of the time, realizes that she is acting—not least when taunting her lover that he does not know the real her (3.13.162), or when imagining herself obliged to watch her part taken by a child actor who will "boy my greatness / I'th' posture of a whore" (5.2.219–20).[61] Within a world of pretended or contingent virtue, deliberate pretense might even become a virtue in itself—the more so when set against the complacent self-regard of Roman civic order. But Cleopatra knows she has never had any choice in the matter. As she finds herself cornered by Octavius, her circumstances change only in degree: the space in which her royal and amatory *personae* are free to express themselves is diminished, not distorted. She is equal to the challenge. By figuring Antony's delights as "dolphin-like" (5.2.87, 88), she even alludes to the prophetic representation of Actium on Aeneas's shield in book 8 of the *Aeneid* (the same shield depicts the fate that Cleopatra escapes through suicide). We are left to infer that Antony rather than Octavius is the ideal Roman and that Cleopatra offers a proleptic repudiation of the Augustan propaganda with which Virgil would attempt to dignify Octavius's rule.[62] It seems more than coincidental that, according to the Plinian lore repeated by Erasmus and Topsell, dolphins were the mortal enemies of the crocodile.[63] Octavius claims the eastern empire by force of arms, but Cleopatra intuits that posterity might well be hers.

———

Aeneas's shield has no crocodiles on it, but in the historical aftermath of Antony and Cleopatra's defeat, crocodiles were not far from the thoughts of the Roman authorities: as the emblem of a conquered nation, a crocodile chained to a palm tree appeared on a great many coins. One of these (figure 15) was minted in present-day Turkey and is inscribed "Aegypto capta"—a phrase that requires no elaboration. Another was minted in southern Gaul and was taken to have borne the inscription "Colligavit nemo," or "never before bound" (figure 16).[64] This numismatic tradition in due course became the basis for a famous sixteenth-century emblem (figure 17), first printed in Claude Paradin's *Devises heroïques* (1557). Paradin's work was translated into English in 1591, and seems to have crossed Shakespeare's desk around the time he cowrote *Pericles*—the play that was entered into the register of the Stationers' Company at the same time as *Antony and Cleopatra* in 1608 (albeit that *Antony and Cleopatra* would have to wait until the 1623 folio to begin its career in print). In Paradin's gloss, Octavius used the chained crocodile

> to signifie that none before him did ever subdue Egypt, and triumphed over it. For the Crocodile representeth Egipt, which is to be found onely in the river Nilus, by the commodie whereof all Egypt is made fruitfull.

Besides the Crocodile is fastened to the Palme tree, that thereby the beholders might be admonished that the godly Prince Augustus triumphed over all Egypt, by getting of which victorie and peace, he was recreated and refreshed, as a drie and thirstie ground is with a showre of raine. Finally, this simbole signifieth that Augustus got the victorie, and prevailed against Antonius, and Cleopatra of famous memorie.[65]

Paradin deftly encapsulates the cultural and political dynamics to which Egypt is subject after the defeat of Cleopatra.[66] They are dynamics that Cleopatra grasps well: rather than allowing herself to be taken to Rome in triumph, she would prefer to be abandoned to "Nilus' mud," or for Octavius to "make / My country's high pyramides my gibbet / And hang me up in chains!" (5.2.57, 58–61). A little later, she flatters Octavius that on account of his victory, she and her fellow Egyptians are "Your scutcheons and your signs of conquest," who "shall / Hang in what place you please" (5.2.134–35). Octavius has no need to confirm or deny his dominance and demurs respectfully.

In bringing this chapter toward a conclusion, I want to propose that in these lines as in the exchange about crocodiles on Pompey's galley, Paradin's emblem provides us with an illuminating point of reference— one, moreover, that Shakespeare might very plausibly have had in mind. Like Cleopatra, the crocodile represents Egypt as the Romans see it. Like Cleopatra, the reality of its existence is of no more interest to the Romans than, say, Caliban is to Trinculo: a piece of subjugated exotica with which to advertise, and to advance, a project of imperial domination.[67] Deprived of his chance to bring Cleopatra to Rome as an emblem of his victory in the East (the historical Octavius apparently displayed a sculpture-effigy of the dead Cleopatra in his triumphal procession), Shakespeare's Octavius is not cast down.[68] Although the crocodile is not as potent a public relations symbol as the captive Cleopatra would have been, it will do the job perfectly well.

Most urgently for Octavius, the unfamiliarity of crocodiles—and the emblematic meanings with which, in lieu of solid observational data, they were invested—aided him in his goal of asserting victory over the luxuriously feminine corruptions of the East. On this reckoning, the peace would not have been disturbed if only Antony had not succumbed to the sensual disorder of the Egyptian worldview. But Shakespeare's insistence on competing visions of *Romanitas* makes clear what, in victory, his Octavius so assiduously seeks to disguise: the conflict between Octavius and Antony and Cleopatra

FIGURE 15. Silver denarius of Octavian (28–27 BCE), minted in Pergamum. Yale University Art Gallery.

FIGURE 16. Bronze denarius of Augustus (9–3 BCE), minted in Nîmes. Münzkabinett, Staatlichen Museen zu Berlin.

Colligauit nemo.

Hitherto no man hath conquered me.

There is vfed to this day certaine brafen
money with the image of Auguftus Cæfar on
it, vpon the one fide wherof is the portraiture

FIGURE 17. Claude Paradin, *The Heroicall Devises of M. Claude Paradin Canon of Beauieu*, trans. P. S. (London, 1591), 81. Rare Book Division, Department of Rare Books and Special Collections, Princeton University Library.

is a civil war, not one of imperial conquest. At Actium as at Philippi, one Rome—one vision of Roman *imperium*—triumphs over another.

Ultimately, the play's center of political gravity is not a vindication of Ovid against Virgil any more than it is an acknowledgment of the eggs that must be broken before one can rejoice in the omelet of universal empire. Shakespeare instead nudges us into the orbit of Tacitean skepticism about the virtues of imperialism, of imperialists, and of the quasi-divine rule to which Cleopatra, Octavius, and *divus Julius* all in their different ways aspired. Here, according to Tacitus, is the Caledonian leader Calgacus, about to do battle with (and be routed by) the Roman legions at the battle of Mons Graupius in present-day Scotland. As Calgacus sees it, the Romans are the

> robbers of the world . . . If the enemy bee rich, they seeke to winne wealth: if poore, they are content to gaine glory: whom not the east, not the west hath satisfyed: the onely men of all memory that seeke out all places, be they wealthy or poore, with like ardent affection. To take away by main force, to kill and to spoile, falsely they terme Empire and government: when all is waste as a wildernesse, that they call peace [*ubi solitudinem faciunt, pacem appellant*].[69]

The speech is likely of Tacitus's own invention. It nevertheless serves as an eloquent counterpoint to the history of Agricola's British conquests (the Caledonians lost at Mons Graupius, but would never be subjugated by Rome), and helps to make the case for liberty against imperial despotism and corruption as, in Tacitus's view, they had developed in the century and a half after Philippi.

Tacitus was valued in the last decade of the sixteenth century and first decades of the seventeenth as both an anatomist of authoritarian corruption and a champion of liberty: for instance, his Calgacus is put to strong use in the indictment of Roman imperialism offered in book 1 of a dialogue on the Roman military published in 1599 by the Anglo-Italian legal writer Alberico Gentili—a work that may have left a trace on Shakespeare's *Henry V*. And yet although one may also discern the impact of Taciteanism elsewhere in Shakespeare, it is impossible to say whether he had direct knowledge of Tacitus's works.[70] What can be said with complete certainty is that juxtaposing the *Agricola* with *Antony and Cleopatra* brings much into focus. Neither Octavius nor Antony / Cleopatra would have found anything to admire in Calgacus's angry eloquence: both sides consider possession of the "world" in its entirety to be their right. They differ only in the ways in which they theorize conquest and dominion, and in their assessment of who should be in charge. Or, to revisit the comparison between Virgil and Ovid, they differ in the fictions through which they seek to dignify their will to rule. The universal peace of the Virgilian-Augustan *imperium sine fine* prevails, but the audience is left to surmise that it is no less appetitive than its Ovidian rival—and that, in its devotion to the propagation of disinterestedly natural virtue, it is the more mendacious ideology by far.

Shakespeare lets us decide for ourselves how all of this might reflect on the *imperium* that the English crown (buttressed by the theory of sacred monarchy) began to assert as its right in the sixteenth and early seventeenth centuries—and invites us to do so by attending to the stylized modes of representation through which the protagonists of *Antony and Cleopatra* regard themselves and their milieux. These modes of representation lead to the elisions, distortions, and delusions that are the stuff of Shakespearean tragedy. Just as importantly, they draw attention to the uncomfortable truth that despite its rhetoric of transhistorical grandeur, the Roman imperial moment was anything but *sine fine*. In the case of the Latin West, it expired more than a millennium before Shakespeare's arrival at grammar school. To the extent that it survived the ruins of time, it did so in the words of writers like Virgil, Ovid, Plutarch, Cicero, Horace, and the rest. The self-same words that had not only allowed the Romans to misrepresent themselves to themselves, but that had been so far from winning eternal or sempiternal fame that, from the *trecento* onward, they had to be birthed anew by the humanist champions of cultural Renaissance. (The partial exception to this rule is Virgil, whose medieval prestige meant that the humanists had less to rebirth him than to refocus attention on the full significance—as they saw it—of his works.)[71] Shakespeare chafed against the humanists' precepts and example, but learned from them more than the skills of *copia* and affective flair. Although he understood that nothing human can lay claim to immortality, he embraced the possibility that it is through art that we can best step outside the vicissitudes of time, history, politics, and happenstance; of other people, and of ourselves.

As the machinery of the Augustan order moves into place at the end of *Antony and Cleopatra*, the part-tragic and part-historical irony is that the "pair so famous" have died not of necessity, but because the fictions around which they chose to pattern their world prevented them from matching those around which Octavius patterns his. As Octavius and Cleopatra face off, both in their different ways acknowledge the gulf between *res* and *verba* in the discourse of empire. The true incomparability of Cleopatra is that, as she contemplates her death, she recognizes that she is bound to *verba* alone—and finds solace in the possibility that, after all, this might be enough.

CHAPTER EIGHT

A Kind of Nothing

CORIOLANUS

FOR THE PAST SEVEN CHAPTERS or so, I have put the case that Shake-speare wants us to notice the failures of his tragic protagonists to arrive at adequate definitions of who and what they are. Despite the intensity with which his characters cleave to certain ideas of themselves and of the human condition, self-knowledge is cast as a near impossibility when the media through which it can be attained are, in one sense or another, fictional. That is, when human beings are the subjects of an inquiry that demands they also transform themselves into its objects, and when the only available means of transformation to objecthood are provided by the normative discourses of religion, philosophy, poetry, sociopolitical tradition, and so on.

Viewed from here, the denouement of *Antony and Cleopatra* can seem awkwardly pat: too resolutory to resolve. On the page as much as the stage, we are invited to feel that the art with which Cleopatra thwarts Octavius's celebratory scheming is a sort of balm; that the representa-tion of Antony and Cleopatra as idealized lovers confers an identity, and a meaningfulness, that the lived reality of their relationship could not; that although Antony and Cleopatra were prevented from fully realiz-ing their love by a historical moment whose *res* was hostile to them, they might fully become themselves through the longevity, if not the transcen-dence, of well-wrought *verba*. It is one thing to arrive at dramatic resolu-tion through the self-conscious artifice of a statue, like that of Hermione in *The Winter's Tale*, coming to life. Quite another to suggest that such resolution can be found in the translation of life to statuary. Or to put it another way, it is one thing for a play like *Macbeth* or *King Lear* to imply that tragic art is the best—perhaps the only—way in which to go beyond the contingency and historicity of everyday existence, but quite another for a character in such a tragedy to claim this artistic prerogative for the terminal self-presentation in which she seeks to enclose herself and her beloved. Are we to infer that if only Juliet, Othello, and Macbeth had paid more attention to the ways in which posterity would regard them and their predeceased spouses, then all would have been well? Even to ask the question is to take note that the goalposts have moved.

In the final scenes of *Hamlet, Othello, Macbeth,* and *King Lear,* restorations of order are staged to illuminate the centrality of our need for moral, political, and conventionally tragic fictions in which to believe. In *Antony and Cleopatra,* we are left with two competing models of imperial order, both of which are at root aesthetic (one Virgilian in tenor, the other Ovidian), but neither of which is presented as obviously invalid or deluded on this account—even if we are prompted to conclude that the Virgilian-Augustan model is unpleasantly mendacious and lacking in a certain flair. Having set the play up, every bit as much as the earlier tragedies, as a study of the inescapability of temporal living, of the indeterminacy at the heart of the human experience that human beings try so very hard to deny, Shakespeare allows Cleopatra a way out that is unavailable even to fabulists as gifted as Goneril, Edmund, and Edgar. He allows Antony, ostensibly an exploration of Roman idealism collapsing under the weight of its own contradictions, to be turned into a metatheatrical prop by Cleopatra and her grudging stagehand, Octavius.

Should *Antony and Cleopatra* be thought of as a grandiose tragicomedy? Possibly. But a better way of framing the question is to say that it traffics in Shakespeare's deep and enduring preoccupation with the collision between that which his tragic vision allowed him to apprehend, and the designs through he was able to represent these apprehensions. In *King Lear,* he stretched the representative powers of tragedy—its ability to imitate the human capacity for delusionality, and the kinds of action to which this delusionality leads—to their breaking point. His vision of a universe disnatured, and of humankind unable to come to terms with who, what, and where it is (let alone how and why it might have come into existence) avoids nihilistic despair only in virtue of its status as a work of tragic art—a something rather than a nothing; a medium that provides the ironized space in which we can, to the best of our limited ability, come to terms with the challenges and confinements of the human condition. As indeterminacy and our habitual responses to it are Shakespeare's subject, neatly resolved endings are no more pertinent than statements of the "natural" order of ethical, familial, or political relations. It takes no great leap of ingenuity to understand why it was that Tate and Johnson had such problems with *Lear*, but the play is a triumph: an astonishingly bold assertion of art's invigorating exactitude in the face of life at its most confounding. And yet, as it must be, the triumph is an uneasy one. Has it been too easily attained? Is the imposition of aesthetic order through the mimesis of plot, character, deep thought, and the rest just another all-purpose consolation of the sort grasped at by Edgar, Albany, and Kent? If it does escape the lure of consolation, howsoever construed, can it really be said to go far enough? Does art need to do something more transformative if its claims to potency and truth-telling—to invigoration through imitation—are to stand up?

In writing *Antony and Cleopatra*, Shakespeare bent in a different direction. Now, it is not just *his* art that has the power to make human experience comprehensible. Antony's attempt to fashion himself and Cleopatra as Aeneas and Dido might be a confused mess, but Shakespeare permits—glories in—Cleopatra's no less fanciful reconfiguration of their story as we have seen it unfold. Licensed by the knowledge that she is acting to frustrate Octavius, Cleopatra produces an imitation of reality that she knows to be a decorous fiction, but that she invites her various audiences to regard as if it were the truth. It is as if the deception on the cliffs of Dover were as soothing as Edgar would like it to be.

Once he had finished *Antony and Cleopatra*, Shakespeare seems to have realized that, as a tragic playwright, he had gone too far. That, having taken pains to depict a world constrained to ignorance of itself by performativity, he had given Cleopatra's fictioneering too much of a pass. Moreover, he seems to have realized that by doing so, he not only weakened his censure of the purportedly heroic virtue through which Octavius (and after him the innumerable later champions of *imperium sine fine*) had sought to dignify the institutions of conquest, dominion, suppression, and self-enrichment; he also threatened to cut himself off from the moral clarity—the openness to the ways in which humankind seeks to disguise its finitude and self-incomprehension—to which tragedy as he conceived it had given him access. In short, the triumph of political aesthetics that Shakespeare grants Cleopatra is extraordinarily hard to reconcile with that which, for Shakespeare, had made tragic art worthwhile. Before too much longer, this irreconcilability would lead him in the direction of his so-called "late" plays, within which imaginative-imitative "art" really does come to outwork, if not "nature," then the tragic apprehension of the way things are.

For now, it might suffice to say that in the aftermath of *Antony and Cleopatra*, Shakespeare had not yet made the decision to leave tragedy behind. Instead, his attention seems to have been caught by a passage in Plutarch's life of Antony. Reflecting on his feelings of isolation and betrayal after Actium, the disconsolate general shuns human society and in so doing compares himself to "Timon Misanthropus the Athenian":

> Antonius, he forsook the citie and companie of his frendes . . . saying that he would lead Timons life, because he had the like wrong offered him, that was affure offered unto Timon: and that for the unthanke-fulnes of those he had done good unto, and whom he tooke to be his frendes, he was angry with all men, and would trust no man.[1]

Plutarch's Antony gets over it, and returns to the sociable comforts of Cleopatra's palace. Shakespeare, by contrast, found occasion to pause.

It is easy to see why. How better to expose the ethics of Ciceronian-humanist peer review than to write about someone who—after bringing himself low through ostentatious displays of liberality—came to spurn both civility and civic life? The more so if this character were to make much of the need to be *seen* spurning the self-deceiving complacencies of the *polis* in order to affirm that, in withdrawing from his fellow human beings, he had chosen the correct path?

But from the perspective of a book such as this one, *Timon of Athens* is a problem. Its moral economy makes no more allowance for the transformations of Cleopatran stagecraft than does *Macbeth*, but if it qualifies as a tragedy, it is not one that sits easily with the remainder of Shakespeare's tragic oeuvre. When assembling the 1623 folio, even Heminges and Condell seem to have been unsure what to do with it. It was eventually inserted with the tragedies, but is titled *The Life of Timon of Athens*, not *The Tragedy of Timon of Athens* on the model of all the other tragedies printed in that volume. Critics have likewise observed that *Timon* has more in common with the satiric than the tragic tradition.[2] And it is indisputable that satire, always a miscellaneous form of writing (I am never absolutely sure whether it is a genre or a mode), fits *Timon* even better than *Troilus and Cressida*—the more so if one takes *Timon* to be in dialogue with city comedies like Ben Jonson's *Volpone*, and the same author's brilliant but commercially unsuccessful experiment in tragic satire, *Sejanus*.[3]

How to proceed? Aristotle's *Poetics* can help. As discussed in chapter 1, there are for Aristotle three core components to tragic drama: plot (*muthos*), character (*ethos*), and thought (*dianoia*). A great tragedy should have a share in all three, as Shakespeare's otherwise not-very-Aristotelian tragedies assuredly do. Crucially, however, Aristotle makes it clear that the interplay of *muthos*, *ethos*, and *dianoia* is a feature of only the *best* tragedics. In designating a work of drama a tragedy, *ethos* and *dianoia* are desirable but less than essential—the only indispensable item is a plot of the appropriate kind. The best kinds of tragic plot have complex features like scenes of reversal (*peripeteia*) and recognition (*anagnorisis*), but again the generic bar is low. Anything will do, as long as it respects the canons of probability and necessity in imitating a "high, complete action," and tends to the arousal of pity and fear in its audiences.

Keeping the *Poetics* in mind, we can make three broad observations about *Timon*. First, that it takes no interest in the deep characterization of *ethos* (most if not all of the dramatis personae, like the Poet and the Painter, appear to be emblems or types). Next, that its plot develops as a not-very-complicated reworking of the *de casibus* arc familiar from post-Boethian depictions of Fortune's wheel: a man rises to greatness, mistakenly regards his high station as an expression of his virtuosity or right, and as the wheel turns is brought low. Finally, that in the thinking-through-words with which its characters speak, *Timon* more than stands comparison with Shakespeare's earlier tragedies: much of the language emerges from an engagement with Seneca's sententious Latin, and some of it, particularly Timon's invective once he has left Athenian society behind, would not be out of place in acts 3 and 4 of *King Lear*.[4]

All of which is to say that although *Timon* can legitimately be regarded as a tragedy, it is not a tragedy of the same sort—the same quality—as Shakespeare's others. A further passage of Aristotle, this time from the opening portion of his *Politics*, brings the problem into sharper relief. According to Aristotle, human beings always exist as a part in relation to the whole, and are as such naturally sociopolitical animals. It follows that one "who refuses to enter into social relations, or who has no need to do so because he is self-sufficient, must either be a beast or a god."[5] Whether or not he knew Aristotle's text, Shakespeare would have had no more difficulty with such sentiments than the generality of humanist moral philosophers. In *Timon*, he must have been intrigued by the prospect of writing a character who abjures this model by placing himself outside the social and political orders to which he belongs—first as their supreme benefactor, then as their cave-dwelling critic and enemy.

But what Shakespeare seems to have discovered while writing *Timon* in collaboration with his younger colleague, Thomas Middleton, is that Timon did not offer enough grist for his mill. If he was going to write a tragedy about an antisocial soul suffering from delusions of autarchy, he would need to settle upon a protagonist of greater depth and complexity as its focal point; someone who gave him what he needed further to explore the interpenetrations of *ethos* and *muthos* that animate his other tragic plays. Someone who distances himself from the political and social whole of which he is a part, yes. Perhaps even someone alienated from this whole in a spirit, or a self-conceit, of heroic individualism. Ultimately though, he required a character who, while not necessarily introspective in the manner of a Hamlet or a Macbeth, could struggle with at least a little of the truth that his being is ineradicably dependent on its relations with others, and that his sense of self cannot therefore aspire to a fixity that transcends the conditions in which those around him are constrained to exist. In a word, Shakespeare's attention was drawn to that warrior general of early republican Rome, Caius Martius Coriolanus. At various points in the tragedy that bears his name, he is accused by an enemy of regarding the Roman populace as if he "were a god . . . not a man of their infirmity" (3.1.82–83); told by his mother that he has "imitate[d] the graces of the gods" (5.3.150); and described by his elderly friend and ally, Menenius, as comparable to a "dragon" (5.4.13) and a "horse" (5.4.17)—as well as one who, in a line that recasts Seneca's *De providentia* in Old Testament phraseology, "wants nothing of a god but eternity and a heaven to throne in" (5.4.23–24).[6] Even so, and although the central figure of *Coriolanus* does not understand himself any better than most of Shakespeare's other tragic protagonists, by the time he meets his end, he has been obliged to confront the conditions of his humanity head-on.

———

Shakespeare first mentions "Coriolanus" in *Titus Andronicus*, most likely remembering him from Livy's *Ab urbe condita* ("From the founding of the city"—usually translated as *The History of Rome*)—a text familiar from his schooldays, and soon to become the starting point for his *Lucrece*. A messenger enters to inform the emperor and empress, Saturninus and Tamora, that a foreign army led by one of Titus's sons is on its way to attack them:

> The Goths have gathered head, and with a power
> Of high-resolved men bent to the spoil
> They hither march amain under conduct
> Of Lucius, son to old Andronicus,
> Who threats in course of this revenge to do
> As much as ever Coriolanus did.[7]

Whoever this Coriolanus might have been, his name is one that Shakespeare's first Romans recognize as an emblem of martial implacability.

Saturninus is suitably alarmed; the messenger's allusion is not unpacked any further.

Nearly two decades later, Shakespeare found himself with much more to say. In addition to Livy, he had now read Plutarch, whose life of Coriolanus is paired with that of Alcibiades, to which Shakespeare had turned in preparing *Timon*. According to Plutarch, Coriolanus lost his father early and was brought up by his mother with an intensity and rigor intended to overcome this handicap. In short, and in Thomas North's translation, he was raised "to become an honest man, and to excell in vertue above the common sorte."[8]

As we saw in *Troilus and Cressida* and *Othello*, being "honest" in this sense means having a share in the *honestas* (honor) that is conferred when one is seen by one's peers to behave in a manner that reflects the qualities of seemliness and propriety (*decorum*). For Cicero and his humanist imitators and adaptors, *honestas* was the cornerstone of moral philosophy and personal identity alike; later, the English "honesty" would begin to change its meaning, coming to acquire the senses of truthfulness, integrity, and plain dealing with which we usually now associate it. From *Julius Caesar* onward, Shakespeare was interested in the slippages, overlaps, and ambiguities that arose from this process of semantic evolution: in whether it is possible to be honest (modern sense) without seeing oneself acknowledged as such by one's peers. *Coriolanus* does not fixate on honesty with the same obsessiveness as *Othello*, but in it Shakespeare remains preoccupied with the question of how and where virtue can be said to subsist—whether it should be understood as an individual or a collective phenomenon, and whether it should be regarded as contingent or absolute.

A version of the question also interested Plutarch. Having noted the ambition of Coriolanus's mother that her son should "excell in vertue," he remarks that "in those dayes, vallientnes was honoured in Rome above all other vertues: which they called *Virtus*, by the name of vertue selfe, as including in that generall name, all other speciall vertues besides. So that *Virtus* in Latin, was asmuche as valliantnes." Although the Latin *virtus* is usually taken to represent the condition of conventionally vigorous manliness in the round (courage, steadfastness, strength, generosity, magnanimity, good character, etc.), Plutarch suggests that in the early Roman republic it was taken to connote military bravery alone—the capacity for unbending courage on the field of battle.[9]

This insistence on the martial quality of virtue helps to explain an apparent discrepancy in Coriolanus's character as Plutarch depicts it. Although Caius Martius was brought up to be "honest" (which is to say, well-regarded by his peers) he had difficulty socializing, even as an adult: "He was so chollericke and impacient, that he would yeld to no living creature: which made him churlishe, uncivill, and altogether unfit for any man's conversation." All would have been lost but for the facts that "he was never overcome with pleasure, nor money," and would "endure easely all manner of paynes and travailles." Seeing this fortitude, his fellow citizens no longer lamented his ornery incivility, but "commended his stowtnes and temperancie." In Plutarch's telling, many thus saw in Coriolanus a want of moral education with which to temper his natural disposition; indeed, Plutarch himself reflects that "to saye truely, the greatest benefit that learning bringeth men unto, is this: that it teacheth men that be rude and rough of nature, by compasse and rule of reason, to be civill and curteous, and to like better the meane state, then the higher."[10] What Plutarch leaves between the lines is the suggestion that it was less a failure of educational practice than of educational culture that led to Coriolanus being Coriolanus. A society in which, as Shakespeare's Cominius puts it, "valour is the chiefest virtue" (2.2.82) is one with little use for the civilizing benefits of learning or, say, Ciceronian eloquence. Those who performed feats of arms were regarded as virtuous because they advanced the political and territorial claims of Rome; they were as such invested with *honestas*; this *honestas* did not simply affirm their virtuous identities, but affirmed them as something distinctively Roman, and thereby encouraged future feats of arms on behalf of the *patria*. Plutarch's interlinear insight, consonant with his more general belief that the Romans would benefit from a dose of Hellenic educational wisdom (*paideia*), is that it is a short step from this perspective to the assertion that anything unrelated to the performance of valor should ipso facto be regarded with suspicion—not inherently un-Roman, perhaps, but reeking of weakness, cowardice, femininity, servility, self-interest, and the willingness to temporize.[11]

Why then should a fatherless Roman youth, determined to win honor and glory for himself and his family, bother with books, tutors, decorous speech, and moral self-cultivation? A more likely course by far is that which, on Plutarch's account, was pursued by the boy who would become Coriolanus: he "beganne from his Childehood to geve him self to handle weapons, and daylie dyd exercise him selfe therein . . . he dyd so exercise his bodie to hardnes, and all kynde of activitie, that he was very swift in ronning, strong in wrestling, and mightie in griping, so that no man could ever cast him." What is more, he learned to match inner implacability to physical toughness: "He esteemed armour to no purpose, unles one were naturally armed within . . . [and] never yelded to any payne or toylc he tooke upon him." Anyone can go through the motions of courtesy and civility—the kind of thing calculated to win applause from whatever audience one happens to be addressing. Doing so costs little, and is of little intrinsic value. The true Roman, by contrast, rises above ingratiation and politesse. (Plutarch concedes that Coriolanus could on occasion make use of an "eloquent tongue," but only when absolutely necessary.) Through self-discipline in the service of the republic, he becomes a model of upright constancy, and through valor wins for himself the rewards of virtue and honor: an identity that will endure. It is this proposition—and with it the prospect that the life and death of Coriolanus might serve as a lens through which further to expose the delusionality at the heart of the Roman worldview—that Shakespeare took as the starting point for his final essay in tragic drama.[12]

From the outset, *Coriolanus* sets out its stall as the most clamorous of Shakespeare's tragedies: "Before we proceed any further, hear me speak" (1.1.1). A protest is afoot. The Roman people (*populares*) are hungry and aggrieved, and blame the grain-hoarding of the *optimates*—their patrician overlords—for their plight. One of them in particular: "You know Caius Martius is chief enemy to the people . . . Let us kill him and we'll have corn at our own price" (1.1.6–7, 9–10)—presumably because if they kill him, the other patricians will be panicked or otherwise worried into meeting their demands. This Martius is "a very dog to the commonalty" (1.1.26), and although he may have done certain unspecified "services" to Rome (1.1.27), his motivation is impure: "he pays himself with being proud" (1.1.30–31) in the pursuit of fame and glory.[13] An unsparing judgment, but one of the spokesmen for the crowd insists that "what he hath done famously, he did it to that end. Though soft-conscienced men can be content to say that it was for his country, he did it to please his mother, and to be partly proud—which he is, even to the altitude of his virtue" (1.1.33–36). This pride may be a fault of his "nature" and therefore not strictly speaking a "vice" (1.1.37), but his more volitional "faults" are so numerous that they "tire in repetition" (1.1.41). In sum, he should be put to death.

Before the members of the crowd can act, they are interrupted by the arrival of "Worthy Menenius Agrippa," who "hath always loved the people" (1.1.46–47). The patrician Menenius calms them down with an effective, though not unmannered, rendering of Aesop's fable of the belly: the patricians are the stomach of the state, and may therefore seem to get more than their fair share of grain; but without the stomach and its digestive capacities, the remainder of the body politic could not hope for nutrition or vitality. Having won the good will and agreement of his audience, Menenius concludes by teasing the second citizen-speaker that he is "the great toe of this assembly . . . For that, being one o'th' lowest, basest, poorest / Of this most wide rebellion, thou goes foremost." (1.1.150–53).[14] The joke goes over well. If not total victory, then close enough.

Enter the aforementioned Martius, who immediately shows that he shares none of Menenius's willingness to mollify: "What's the matter, you dissentious rogues, / That, rubbing the poor itch of your opinion, / Make yourselves scabs?" Even this fails to undo Menenius's work, and the second citizen offers a half line of wry humor in response, "We have ever your good word" (1.1.159–61). Martius fails to see the funny side, and thunders that "He that will give good words to thee will flatter / Beneath abhorring" (1.1.162–63)—and continues to insist that, rather than being ruled by their bestial appetites, the "rabble" (1.1.213) should be grateful for the patricians' duty of care; or, failing that, frightened into submission. As it is, Martius reports to his great displeasure that, in response to the popular unrest, the Roman government has sought to placate the people with "Five tribunes to defend their vulgar wisdoms, / Of their own choice" (1.1.210–11).

Before the citizens can respond either to Martius's words or the way in which he has delivered them, a messenger enters with the news that the Volscians have taken up arms against Rome. Martius—who, we now learn, is a soldier—is delighted and agrees to help lead the fight. Principally because it will provide him with the chance to pit himself against one of the few people he regards as his peer: the Volscian general, Aufidius. Making rather an ungainly attempt at the modesty topos, Martius declares that "I sin in envying his nobility, / And were I anything but what I am, / I would wish me only he" (1.1.225–27).[15] His disdain for the majority of his fellow human beings is reaffirmed, and the prospect of heroic combat is introduced. But what is of greatest moment here is his confident belief that he knows what he and Aufidius *are*.

Once Martius and the other patricians have settled on a plan of action and departed, the citizens "steal away" to leave Sicinius and Brutus, two of the newly appointed tribunes, alone on stage. "Was ever a man so proud as this Martius?" (1.1.247), wonders Sicinius, and Brutus agrees that there was not. It is, Brutus suggests, his pridefulness that makes "fame" that at "which he aims" (1.1.258), and that might also make him a difficult subordinate to the Roman Consul, Cominius. Neither tribune voices concern at the disregard that Martius appears to have for those they represent, and they depart to see how things play out.

The battle begins with Roman troops wilting before the Volscian assault. Martius is incensed, and with ruthlessness of word and deed rouses his troops to drive the Volscians back to Corioles. He then pursues his enemies inside the city walls, only to find that his men have thought better of following him in, and that the gates have been shut behind him. Close of play for a lesser warrior, but Martius fights on, survives, and eventually inspires a great Roman victory in the sack of Corioles. Still, the day is not won. Martius hastens to assist the other wing of the Roman army, where "the man of my soul's hate, Aufidius" (1.5.10) is causing Cominius problems. Finally, Martius gets his wish for single combat: "Let the first budger die the other's slave, / And the gods doom him after" (1.8.5–6). Blows and further invective are exchanged, before "certain Volces" infuriate Aufidius by coming to his aid: "Officious and not valiant, you have shamed me" (1.8.15). Martius fights on, and although he is on the front foot, their encounter is inconclusive. Aufidius resolves that the next time he and Martius meet, he will not be bound by "honour": "For where / I thought to crush him in an equal force, / True sword to sword, I'll poach at him some way. / Or wrath or craft may get him" (1.10.14–16). Exactly what this implies for Aufidius's "nobility," or for Martius's conception of his nobility as a mirror of his own, remains to be seen.

Martius's valor and military success are given fulsome acknowledgment. He refuses money and spoil as beneath his dignity, but accepts a new name (or cognomen): "for what he did before Corioles," Caius Martius becomes, with "all th'applause and clamour of the host, / Martius Caius Coriolanus!" (1.9.62–64). Martius again displays modesty ("I will go wash. / And when my face is fair, you shall perceive / Whether I blush or no" [1.9.66-68]); he also begs a favor of Cominius that will display his magnanimity. When in Corioles, he had taken shelter in the house of a "poor man" who "used me kindly." When this man shed tears at being taken prisoner by the Romans, Martius felt "pity" for him, but then caught sight of Aufidius and departed in a rage—leaving his host imprisoned. Could Cominius free him now? Cominius readily agrees, and all Martius need do is to reveal the prisoner's name. He cannot: "By Jupiter, forgot! / I am weary; yea, my memory is tired" (1.9.81–90). Martius retires to seek refreshment and treatment for his wounds in the company of Cominius, and the matter is not raised again.

In Plutarch, the comparable scene features "an olde friend and hoste of mine, an honest wealthie man," reduced after the defeat of the Volscians to living as "a poore prisoner in the handes of his enemies." Rather than seeking his release, Plutarch's Martius merely requests that he not be "solde as a slave." There is no suggestion that Martius abandons his friend to pursue Aufidius, that the friend's name is forgotten, or that Martius's request is in any way frustrated.[16] As ever, Shakespeare twists his source material to a purpose. In this case, to two interconnected purposes. First, to suggest that there is something performative about Martius's request and Cominius's willingness to grant it. Martius's valorous exploits have gained him a new name, rich in *honestas*; if some lowly Volscian loses his freedom because his insignificant name has slipped Martius's mind, it is no great matter; what is important is that Martius and Cominius have made a gesture of magnanimity such that they and their citizen-soldiers can affirm their identities—their *personae*—as virtuously noble Romans. Second, Shakespeare reveals that Martius is a more passionate creature than his unbendingly upright self-image can readily allow—one moved by "pity" for the poor nameless Volscian prisoner and then by "wrath" for Aufidius (far from coincidentally, the same emotion that Aufidius, at 1.10.16, hopes will bring Martius down). Cominius takes the invocation of these emotions to be a rhetorical ploy ("O, well begged!" [1.9.86]), as maybe it is; but the suggestion of an emotional disposition at odds with the ideal of steadfast Roman valor is unmistakable.

———

Martius, Cominius, and their troops now return to Rome. They are greeted with a mixture of delight, surprise, and relief. Martius, carried aloft, is cheered above everyone: "Welcome to Rome, renowned Coriolanus" (2.1.161, 162). After reuniting with his mother (Volumnia), his wife (Virgilia), and the aged Menenius, he proceeds toward the capitol; his mother is particularly delighted with his successes, and notes that there is now only "one thing wanting" for her maternal ambitions to be realized— which, she adds, she believes that "our Rome will cast upon thee." That is, the Consulship. It is clearly not the first time that she has raised the subject, and Martius sounds a note of caution in response: "I had rather be their servant in my way, / Than sway with them in theirs" (2.1.195–96, 198–99). Despite interruptions from Brutus the tribune and Martius's refusal to hear himself praised (or, as he phrases it, "to hear my nothings monstered" [2.2.75]), Cominius offers a vivid depiction of Martius's long record of achievement on behalf of the republic—including a prominent hand in the defeat of Tarquin, Rome's last king—and draws particular attention to Martius's conviction that valiant-virtuous-noble deeds are their own reward. Martius reenters, and Menenius tells him that "The senate, Coriolanus, are well pleased / To make thee consul." Martius affirms, diffidently enough, that "I do owe them still my life and services," to which Menenius responds that "it then remains that you speak to the people" (2.2.130–33). A Consul cannot be appointed by the Senate alone, and must also obtain the consent of the populace at large—especially now that they have formal representation through the tribunate. In Martius's case, doing so would not only involve seeking their acclamation—their "voice"—through decorously chosen words, but displaying to them the wounds he had received in Corioles, and elsewhere, in advancing the cause of Roman greatness.

Martius stumbles, and begs leave to "o'erleap that custom" (2.2.135). The supplicant is a "part / That I shall blush in acting" (2.2.143–44). Sounding as rhetorically bereft as Cordelia before her expectant father, he insists that "I cannot bring / My tongue to such a pace" (2.3.49–50)—cannot pretend to care one way or another what the great unwashed might think of him, much less bring himself to seek their favor. Supplication is a mode of address that Martius associates with the weakness of plebeian have-nots. He, by contrast, regards himself as a being whose existence is measured out in dignity, nobility, austerity, and valor: one with the courage and strength to speak plainly, and from the heart. (Shakespeare's starting point for this scene was Plutarch, but in the corresponding portion of his copy of Livy, we might note that one sixteenth-century reader—likely the schoolmaster and playwright Nicholas Udall—depicted Martius-Coriolanus as if he were a king on his throne. See figure 18.)[17] Still, Menenius's arguments prevail over Martius's blend of *amour propre* and anxiety, and, wearing the customary "gown of humility," the proud soldier puts in a competent shift with five unnamed citizens. All seems set fair, but once Martius has left them, the citizens begin to reconsider. He did not reveal his wounds to them. His manner was peremptory—scornful, perhaps. The tribunes Brutus and Sicinius have all they need to work with, and have soon persuaded the citizens to "revoke" their "sudden approbation" (2.3.247–48).

In passing on this news to Martius, Brutus and Sicinius do all they reasonably can to provoke him. Martius considers himself wronged not only by those whom he disdains, but by those before whom he had diminished himself (as he sees himself) in pursuit of political office. Righteous indignation overcomes his horror of self-exposure in public, and he cannot stop talking—despite the best efforts of Menenius and Cominius (no doubt reflecting that although "valour is the chiefest virtue," discretion has

FIGURE 18. Marginal depiction of Coriolanus as if he were enthroned. Livy, *T. Livii Patavini Latinae historiae principis decades tres* (Basel, 1549), 46. National Gallery of Art Library, Washington DC (PA6452.A2 1549).

its uses too) to move him along. By extending suffrage to the plebeian mass of the citizenry,

> we debase
> The nature of our seats, and make the rabble
> Call our cares fears, which will in time
> Break ope the locks o'the' Senate and bring in
> The crows to peck the eagles. (3.1.136–40)

After another thirty or so lines of noisily intemperate verbosity, the tribunes have heard enough to seek his arrest: Martius has shown himself to be an enemy of the republic. Mindful that Martius will not be an easy catch, the tribunes' assistants (the *aediles*) take the precaution of approaching with the aid of a mob. Martius resists, and the tribunes find themselves with another pretext to have him executed for treason. Eventually, Martius is prevailed upon to retire to his home, and Menenius again does solid rhetorical work in calming the enflamed *populares*; it is agreed that Martius should stand trial rather than face immediate execution.

Nevertheless, persuading Martius to submit himself to trial proves to be anything but straightforward. It also provides the occasion for the central scene of *Coriolanus* as a tragedy of selfhood and vexed identity.

Menenius and a group of senators join with Martius's mother, Volumnia, in the effort to make Martius see that he must present himself to the tribunes and people with a show of repentance, and humility. Addressing Volumnia, he comes straight to the point:

> Why did you wish me milder? Would you have me
> False to my nature? Rather say I play
> The man I am. (3.2.15–17)

If he were to appear before the hated "rabble" in milder guise, he would be lying—pretending to sentiments that are not in fact his own, and adulterating his fiercely virtuous "nature." The prospect of doing so is so demeaning that he would prefer to say that he is and has always been playing at—performing, imitating—the virtuous-valiant Roman warrior that he knows himself to *be*. Hyperbole, but his words recall his earlier relief at being informed that he could remove the "gown of humility" ("That I'll straight do, and, knowing myself again, / Repair to th' Senate-house" [2.3.145–46]), just as they foreshadow his later insistence that, in addressing the plebs, he would cease "to honour mine own truth / And by my body's action teach my mind / A most inherent baseness" (3.2.122–24). But there is more than a hint of self-negating paradox here: if he lived in a world in which he was limited to performative versions of identity, how would he be able to recognize the authentic self ("the man I am") that he threatens merely to "play"? If, as he says he does, he knows himself to be a model of virtuous constancy, and if the masses are as irremediably weak and ignorant and capricious as he believes them to be, how could appearing to them one way or another have the least bearing on his dignity or moral self-image?

Volumnia is unimpressed by her son's attempts to justify himself, and delivers him a lesson in the fundamentals of Roman *honestas* that would not seem out of place in the mouth of Shakespeare's Lucrece (who would have been about Volumnia's age had she not chosen death before dishonor after her mistreatment by Tarquin). Either way, and after a string of Shakespearean women including Emilia, Lady Macbeth, Goneril, and Cleopatra have in their different ways emphasized the inadequacy of humanist moral philosophy, it is striking that, in *Coriolanus*, it falls to a woman to serve as the ultimate protector of an order based on the virtues of performative masculinity; if Brutus had taken his wife into his confidence when attempting to think through his aristocratic revolt against Caesar, perhaps Portia would have been another case in point.[10] Volumnia begins by telling Martius that "you might have been enough the man you are / With striving less to be so," before adding that they would not be in this mess if "you had not showed them how ye were disposed / Ere they lacked power to cross you" (3.2.20–21, 23–24)—if, that is, he had not revealed his true disposition until the consulship was safely his. Menenius now returns to make it clear that Martius must "repent" of what he said to the tribunes, and when Martius refuses ("I cannot do it to the gods, / Must I do't to them?"), his mother bluntly urges him to grow up. He is "too absolute," and failing to think clearly: as by his own account "Honour and policy, like unsevered friends, / I'th'war do grow together," why should it be any less honorable "to seem / The same you are not" when in the midst of a political crisis? In response, Martius can only muster a surly "Why force you this?" that Volumnia forcefully shoves aside:

> Because that now it lies you on to speak
> To th'people, not by your own instruction,
> Nor by th'matter which your heart prompts you,
> But with such words that are but roted in
> Your tongue, though but bastards and syllables
> Of no allowance to your bosom's truth.
> Now, this no more dishonours you at all
> Than to take in a town with gentle words,
> Which else would put you to your fortune and
> The hazard of much blood.
> I would dissemble with my nature where
> My fortunes and my friends at stake required
> I should do so in honour.

As, she concludes, would "your wife, your son, these senators, the nobles." If he continues on his current path, he will forfeit the "loves" that would serve as the "safeguard / Of what that want might ruin" (3.2.40–70). And all because his moral vanity cannot bear the thought of going through the motions of repentance and humility in front of the plebs. Martius grasps the import of what she says, and no doubt has a grudging respect for the way in which she has said it: no supplication or entreaty here, but the maternal lash. The voice of true nobility. After a further wobble or two, he resolves to do as she has demanded. He will address the tribunes and people, and "mountebank their loves, / Cog their hearts from them and come home beloved"; he will "return consul / Or never trust to what my tongue can do / I'th' way of flattery further" (3.2.133–38).

In one of the least suspenseful developments in all of Shakespeare, Martius's self-control and ability to submit himself to the demands of rhetorical *decorum* prove unequal to the task. Although he begins equably, he is stung by the accusation that he is "a traitor to the people" (3.3.65), and launches into another tantrum of wounded self-righteousness: "the fires i'th' lowest hell" should "fold in the people!" (3.3.67). Victory being theirs, the tribunes are willing to consent that Martius should be banished and not thrown to his death from the Tarpeian rock. Martius, impotent against the force of popular justice, proclaims that the masses, mercurial and fearful and unable to defend themselves, are unworthy of the true *Romanitas* that he sees himself as embodying: "I banish you" (3.3.122). Which is to say, you can't banish me because *I* banish *you.*

———

Reflecting on the last two scenes in act 3, it is tempting to conclude that Martius is unable to live up to the rhetorical and political expectations of his mother, Menenius, and Cominius because he regards the *personae* as something that are singular and absolute, and not something that should be changed depending on the circumstances in which one is obliged to speak and act. He prides himself on being a soldier of patrician birth and unbending courage, and if he were to say or do anything out of keeping with this identity, it would deface his sense of who and what he is; it may fit the debased sense of *honestas* that governs plebeian life to seek favor or approval or advancement through ingratiation or displays of humility, but is out of the question for someone of his stature. One might also, with Gail Kern Paster, take the related view that Martius illustrates a broader tension within the Roman republican project, at least as it was idealized by Cicero. Like *Julius Caesar, Coriolanus* "enact[s] a central urban paradox: the social mandate for heroic self-sacrifice collides with the heroic mandate for self-realization conceived in civic terms."[19] The valorous individualism on which Martius's military heroism (and with it Roman security) relies is at odds with the social virtues that make for peaceful and prosperous living within the urban and suburban spaces of Rome.

But as valuable as such interpretations are, they seem to me to miss the full force of what Shakespeare is up to. For Martius, the plebs are not plebs because of the things they say and do; rather, the things they say and do are an expression of the fact that they are plebs. Likewise, and putting to one side hyperbole about his "mind" being led to a "most inherent baseness" by the pretense of humility, Martius takes the Aristotelian view that, irrespective of what he says and does (and of what others might say about him), he is bound to remain the man he "is," that his "nature" is bound to remain his "nature," that his "own truth" is bound to remain his "own truth."[20] It is just that he has come to know himself through a particular notion of virtue (one predicated of martial valor and constancy), and that doing or saying things that are at odds with this notion of virtue risks undermining what he thinks he knows of himself. If he succeeds in performing what he regards as servility, how can he be sure that he's not fundamentally servile himself? In exploring this question further, we can usefully turn to William Cornwallis's short text, the *Discourses Upon Seneca the Tragedian*.

Cornwallis ruminates on some lines taken from Seneca's *Hercules furens*, where Amphitryon observes that the world around him has become one in which "Crime that succeeds and prospers is given the name of virtue; [and in which] the good submit to the wicked."[21] Cornwallis begins by proposing that, this being the case, one who is "yet sober"—that is, "not drunke" with the "partiall affections" of "wealth and want"—is invariably moved to "shun the society of the world."[22] Turning to "vertue" a few pages later, he dilates on Seneca's currency in early seventeenth-century England: "Seemings are now sought, beings thought superfluous; the labour of most men now adayes is not to obtaine trueths, but opinions warrant." The dangers of this situation are most acute for those in public office, who run the risk of losing all powers of discrimination, and with them any possibility of a meaningful existence:

so miserable are the minds as well as the fortunes of the vulgar, that no action of greatness passeth without commendation: doth he meane to catch the people in his cappe, and makes courtesie intrap their simple understandings, they avow him to be humilitie itselfe. Doth pride and a selfe-opinion make him looke bigge? He carrieth himselfe like a Prince, to whose place it belongeth not to lose of his height, by declining to familiaritie: doth he spend? Hee reckons not his owne estate, so he may supplie the wants of others: doth he save? 'Tis nobly done, not to undo his posteritie: Loves he warres? Magnanimitie and fortitude shines in him; is it peace? No common-wealths men are so worthie as the preservers of peace: In a word, doth hee what he will, hee doth vertuously; let him get prosperitie, and get it how he can, he shall not want vertue, for—*prosperum ac foelix scelus / Virtus vocatur.*[23]

If you look the part and succeed in the tasks of winning and retaining power, people will be happy to embrace you. The rub is that the cost of such success is non-negligible: the habit of superficiality will erode and eventually efface your humanity.

Cornwallis is as such a useful test case for the prominence of Stoicism in the 1590s and first decade or so of the 1600s. An earlier generation of humanists viewed the nostrums of Ciceronian moral philosophy with more or less untroubled confidence: *honestas, decorum,* and socially anchored versions of both virtue and selfhood. But by the end of a century whose final decades, especially in France and the Low Countries, had been racked by political and religious strife, Ciceronian humanism—central though it remained to the discourses of moral philosophy—had lost its ability to reassure. One alternative was provided by Seneca's Stoicism, a body of thought that emerged not from republican idealism, but from seeking a way in which to live meaningfully amid the corruption and vicissitudes of Nero's imperial court. It offered a model of individual integrity that, particularly when paired with Christian notions of faith and inward grace, was appealing to a world in which social living could no longer be thought of as innately virtuous.[24]

Coriolanus is a play in which Seneca's tragedies have left many fewer traces than can be detected in *Titus, Hamlet, Othello, Macbeth,* and *Lear*—but a growing body of scholarship makes the persuasive claim that its conception is nonetheless importantly Senecan.[25] Although Martius could hardly be mistaken for the Brutus of *Julius Caesar,* his conviction that the kind of virtue he has trained himself to embody exists independently of everyday life is strikingly close to the Stoic ideals of autonomy and constancy. Martius and the Stoics both disavow any belief that, to borrow a phrase from Cornwallis, the "society of the world" could be the source of virtue that it is within Ciceronian moral philosophy: *honestas* and *decorum* depend on the opinions of others, and these opinions—easily swayed as they are by self-interest and the colors of rhetoric—are indifferent to truth. Martius differs from the Stoics only in the conviction that he is set apart by bravery and military prowess, not philosophically rigorous self-mastery.

The ease and zeal with which the citizenry changes its mind about Martius's elevation to the Consulship, like the calculating duplicity with which the *optimates* and tribunes are prepared to advance their respective interests, might be seen to bear out the truth of Cornwallis's Senecan extrapolations. And yet as we might expect from the author responsible for Brutus as a study in Stoic delusionality, Shakespeare was not content to leave things there. In one of the best readings of *Coriolanus* known to me, Geoffrey Miles discusses the play as a collision between two competing notions of Roman order: on the one hand, the constancy involved in acquiring and maintaining *honestas*; on the other, the inner constancy of Stoic individualism. As Miles puts it, *Coriolanus* sets these two notions "against each other, and shows how the internal self-contradictions of the ideal [of constancy], when it is pushed to its limits, come close to destroying Rome."[26] This is surely right, but we need to go further still. What captures the attention of Shakespeare the tragedian is less the dynamics of Roman moral and political life than the opportunity provided by these dynamics for probing away at the unacknowledged fictions to which human beings are drawn when seeking stability, order, and meaning. In this case, for revealing that despite Martius's assertions of virtue and nobility anchored in something more integral than the opinions of others, he is just as confined to the wilderness of mirrors as Brutus was before him—just as confined to projections and distorted reflections in the attempt to make sense of who and what he is.

———

Once he has left Rome, Martius makes for the Volscian city of Antium with a mind to defect. Disguised, he finds his way to the home of Aufidius, who is hosting a dinner party for the Volscian leaders on the eve of launching a campaign against the Roman territories—intending to take advantage of the tensions between patricians and plebeians that have weakened the Roman position. Unmasking himself before Aufidius, Martius is nonplussed that his mighty opposite fails to recognize him: "If, Tullus, / Not yet thou knowest me, and seeing me dost not / Think me for the man I am, necessity / Commands me to name myself" (4.5.56–59). After giving him several more chances to guess ("Knowest me thou yet?" [4.5.65]), Martius reveals all—the origins of the name Coriolanus (4.5.70), the circumstances of his departure from Rome, his desire "to be full quit of those my banishers" (4.5.85) in order to vindicate his name, and his willingness to fight for the Volscians against their old foe. Now that he knows who the oddly dressed stranger is, Aufidius is delighted—enraptured, even, at the spectacle and the idea. "But that I see thee here / Thou noble thing, more dances my rapt heart / Than when I first my wedded mistress saw / Bestride my threshold" (4.5.117–20). Quite what it is that gets Aufidius so excited, or so determined to perform excitement, is an open question—but he and his new guest proceed to meet the Volscian leaders, and at Martius's urging they agree not simply to strike at Roman territory, but at Rome itself. When next we hear from Aufidius, he is anything but enraptured. Martius's willingness to fight at the head of the Volscian troops has been a boon for his cause in overcoming Rome, but is of greater value in presenting him with an opportunity to overcome a personal enemy: "When, Caius, Rome is thine, / Thou art poor'st of all; then shortly thou art mine" (4.7.56–57).

Aufidius's inability to recognize Martius at first glance must have stung, the more so as Aufidius rhapsodizes so fluently on Martius once his mysterious visitor has disclosed his name, and with it the likeness of all that Martius the nobly unbending warrior-hero represents.[27] Martius values himself for what he believes himself to *be*, and not on account of the ways in which others see and refer to him. He believes that the virtues inherent to that self exist independently of Roman or Volscian approval, and can be expressed wherever he is given the opportunity to act. So it is that, in Cominius's telling, Martius has divested his identity of its *Romanitas*:

> Yet one time he did call me by my name.
> I urged our old acquaintance and the drops
> That we had bled together. "Coriolanus"
> He would not answer to, forbade all names.
> He was a kind of nothing, titleless,
> Till he had forged himself a name o'th' fire
> Of burning Rome. (5.1.10–14)

There are contradictions here. What of his desire to vindicate the name Coriolanus ("only that name remains") as outlined to Aufidius (4.5.75)? Does his determination to forge "a name o'th' fire / Of burning Rome" not suggest that there remains something fundamentally dependent in his relationship to the Roman state as an authority that, to be defied, must first be acknowledged? As usual, any doubts or concerns vanish within what, for Martius, is the universal solvent: the determination to act with dignified and decisive violence. A determination that is all the more powerful for being animated by the desire for vengeance—not only against the little people in their foolishness and caprice, but also "our dastard nobles" in their craven weak-spiritedness (4.5.77). *Our* dastard nobles, note.

Aufidius also regards his identity as in large measure independent of Volscian and Roman posturing, shrugging in the aftermath of military defeat that "I would I were a Roman, for I cannot, / Being a Volsce, be that I am" (1.10.4–5). The arc of his story will affirm that he is every bit as deluded as Martius in this belief, but unlike Martius he has the where-withal to notice comparable sorts of delusionality in others. In particular, Aufidius sees that whatever Martius might have to say to the contrary, it is not the condition of being a valorous warrior that matters to him, but the condition of being a valorously *Roman* warrior. As such, Martius can never truly commit himself to the Volscian cause. Aufidius will bide his time until using the knowledge to bring Martius down.

Unstoppable though Martius's appears to be at the head of the Vols-cian army, his family and fellow patricians have seen him coming. Quickly acknowledging that the negotiating skills of Cominius and Menenius are going to be no more fruitful than expecting the Roman troops to stand firm (what price now declarations that *virtus* and military valor are the same thing), they dispatch Martius's mother, wife, and son to intercept him. The prompt, perhaps, comes from Martius's insistence that, on account of his new allegiance and duty of vengeance, "wife, mother, child, I know not" (5.2.81). As they approach him, he reinforces his commitment to the way in which he now believes he should construe the man he is: "Out, affection! / All bond and privilege of nature break!" (5.3.24–25). If he had paused to reflect, he would have recognized that his cause is already lost: "affection" here signifies "love," and one as attached as Martius is to who and what he *is* can no more shirk such a feeling than he can wriggle free of a "bond" that he takes to be natural.[28] Instead, he ploughs on and is subjected to an elaborate assault on the emotions that he has just tried to banish. First, and despite his approach to Rome at the head of a conquering army, his wife curtsies to him. Then his mother bows "As if Olympus to a molehill should / In supplication nod." Finally, his "young boy" looks at his him with "an aspect of intercession" to which "Great Nature cries 'Deny not'" (5.3.30–32). In response, Martius offers one of the starkest instances of *paradiastole* (the figure of rhetorical redescription) in a play that is full of them: loving "affec-tion" becomes "instinct," and as instinct is an unworthy guide for a warrior who considers himself defined by his constancy, austerity, nobility, and the rest, he will ignore it.[29] Instead, he will "stand / As if a man were author of himself / And knew no other kin" (5.3.35–37).

Martius's "as if" is staggering from one who has so often proclaimed himself unable to speak or act if not from the "heart." Through it, he admits—to himself, to us, to anyone onstage who can hear him—that he has committed himself to an identity that he knows to be inauthentic. But even this reversal is less striking than the one involved in his suggestion that one's identity is a matter of choice; the man he is, we infer, is less important than the one he has come to feel that he ought to be. Furthermore, the man Martius now feels he ought to be is defined by his capacity to seem decorously Volscian to Aufidius and his other new allies. It is, in other words, a *persona* that provides him with the freedom to pursue vengeance against the Romans who either banished him or made themselves complicit in his banishment. He also reveals to his wife an inkling that it is not only his new identity that can be thought of in such terms: "Like a dull actor now, / I have forgot my part and I am out, / Even to full disgrace" (5.3.40–42). The histrionic framework of the *personae* is clear, and is reaffirmed by the suggestion of being "out"—a theatrical and oratorical adverb that describes the condition of forgetting one's lines.[30] Although, in his turmoil, he makes an inapposite choice of simile (it is not that he has forgotten his Roman part, but that he refuses now to perform it), we are supposed to hear in these words more than just a register of his discomfort at having to reject the affections and entreaties of those he loves. There is also recognition—a wary and strictly partial *anagnorisis*—that he might have been playing the man he is all along.

Forced further to confront the self-alienation of being allied to the Volscians by his pleasure at kissing Virgilia, Martius next turns to his "most noble mother," and kneels before her as an expression of his "deep duty" (5.3.49, 51)—as also, we may surmise, to assuage with an appropriately self-effacing gesture the pain he feels at the circumstances of their meeting. She tells him to stand up. But rather than admonishing her son for getting himself and Rome into such a mess, she does something that he does not expect: kneels before him as a supplicant.[31] This brilliantly passive-aggressive maneuver shatters Martius's sense of natural order: "What's this? / Your knees to me? . . . then let the mutinous winds / Strike the proud cedars 'gainst the fiery sun, / Murdering impossibility to make / What cannot be slight work" (5.3.56–62). That, at this of all instants, his mother should approach him with a carrot rather than her habitual stick is so shocking to him that anything seems possible.

As it happens, and exactly as Volumnia intends, the only transformation her actions bring about is a reversion, for Martius, to a simulacrum of the status quo ante. And because, as Volumnia realizes, this simulacrum can never hope to attain the qualities of the original fabrication—in striving for the marmoreal grandeur of Rome, it is constrained to grisaille—Martius's reversion will lead now to his death.

Once Martius has been forced to acknowledge the virtues of chaste Valeria (who may have been his childhood nurse) and to receive his son, Volumnia turns the screw: "Even he, your wife, this lady and myself / Are suitors to you" (5.3.77–78). Martius begins to flail. "I beseech you, peace!" (5.3.78), "tell me not / Wherein I seem unnatural. Desire not / T'allay my rages and revenges with / Your colder reasons" (5.3.83–86). But even this outburst is evasive: it is not Volumnia's "colder reasons" with which he is being forced to contend, but his own feelings of shame and compassion; compounded, no doubt, by fear at what might happen if he were to cast off his Volscian *persona*, and also perhaps by the awareness that he has hitherto presented vengeance as more a grim duty than a matter of condign rage. Volumnia, regardless, insists on being heard and launches a full assault on his self-consciousness as a son, a father, and a Roman: "Thou shalt no sooner / March to assault thy country than to tread . . . on thy mother's womb / That brought thee to this world" (5.3.122–24), "say my request's unjust / And spurn me back. But, if it be not so, / Thou are not honest and the gods will plague thee / That thou restrain'st me from the duty which / To a mother's part belongs" (5.3.164–68). When Martius, who appears to have misplaced the power of speech, fails to respond, she and her retinue sink again to their knees. Then, rising to depart, a final stab: "This fellow had a Volscian to his mother" (5.3.178). *This fellow.* At last, Martius admits to his supplicants and himself what was already plain. He has cracked, his vindictive ardor dissipated along with his obligation to seek the counsel of the Volscian military hierarchy: "O, mother, mother! What have you done?" Without pausing for an answer, he looks to spread the blame for his predicament yet more broadly: "Behold, the heavens do ope, / The gods look down and this unnatural scene / They laugh at" (5.3.183–85). As in *King Lear*, the *theatrum mundi* is employed as a mechanism for coping with a situation of undeniable desperation. "You have won a happy victory to Rome / But for your son, believe it, O, believe it / Most dangerously you have with him prevailed" (5.3.186–88). Volumnia hardly needs to be told, and as one who believes that a son's "good report" (1.3.20)—that is, his honor and reputation—overmatch any pull of maternal affection, she has already priced in her loss. Rome, the ideals of Roman dignity and autonomy and glory, come first. Martius served all of these superbly for a while, but now that he has ceased to do so, he is not merely expendable. He is dead to her. Hereafter, Volumnia is silent. Her grave business accomplished, she has nothing further to say.

Martius now turns to the watching Aufidius for confirmation that anyone in his position would have agreed to Volumnia's terms. Aufidius is

noncommittal: "I was moved withal" (5.3.194). A few lines later, he con-
fides to the audience what he really thinks: "I am glad thou hast set thy
mercy and thy honour / At difference in thee. Out of that I'll work / Myself
a former fortune" (5.3.200–202). By acknowledging the indelible truth of
his emotional bond to his family members, Martius has tarnished his *honestas* as a Volscian. Martius may try to make the best of it by presenting
himself as a peacemaker who has nonetheless won the Volscians more territory and spoil than might otherwise have been expected, but his fate is
sealed. It only remains to be seen what combination of carefully stage-
managed "wrath" and "craft" Aufidius will use to finish him.

Aufidius sends a letter to "the lords" of Antium (5.6.1), timed to arrive
before his return from Rome; in it, he lays out his accusations of Martius's
treachery. As he explains to one of his coconspirators, "my pretext to strike
at him admits / A good construction." Having "raised him" and "pawned /
Mine honour for his truth," he not only found himself treated as a "follower,
not partner" on account of Martius's insatiable pride, but was in due course
betrayed at the gates of Rome: "At a few drops of woman's rheum, which
are / As cheap as lies, he sold the blood and labour / Of our great action"
(5.6.19–48). But mindful that Martius will most likely give a strong account
of his conduct in Rome (and its advantages to the Volscians), Aufidius is
taking no chances. In addition to sending the letter, he and his confederates prepare themselves as an extrajudicial kill squad. It is a reminder that
the key term here is "pretext": Aufidius does not care very much one way
or the other about the crimes of which he accuses Martius. He merely wants
to ensure his rival's defeat and death, both in recompense for his earlier
losses in "equal force," and to ensure that he, Aufidius, returns to his station
as the valorous leader-hero of the Volscian armed forces.

In a Shakespearean invention (Plutarch has Martius giving as good
as he gets), Aufidius's ruthless clarity once in Antium is juxtaposed with
Martius's confusion. When Martius objects that Aufidius fails to address
him as "Coriolanus," Aufidius (like the tribunes before him, doing all he
can to goad Martius into some self-incriminating fit of pride) fires back,
"Ay, Martius, Caius Martius. Dost thou think / I'll grace thee with that
robbery, thy stolen name / 'Coriolanus' in Corioles?" (5.6.90–92).[32] In the
view that Aufidius now proclaims, the name was taken from the Volscian
city of Corioles by Roman force of arms, and when Martius was presented
with the chance to help the Volscians win recompense for this indignity,
a show of Roman tears led him to break his new oaths of allegiance in a
fashion altogether lacking in *virtus*, howsoever construed: confronted by
a handful of lachrymose womenfolk, "he whined and roared away your

victory" (5.6.100) as little more than a "boy of tears" (5.6.103). Martius has no right to a cognomen—an identity—that is an affront to his Volscian hosts, and that honors a valor to which he has no legitimate claim.

Martius is outraged. Despite the best efforts of an unnamed Volscian lord to have him hold his peace, he rails himself into exactly the position that Aufidius wants him: "If you have writ your annals true, 'tis there / That, like an eagle in a dovecote, I / Fluttered your Volscians in Corioles. / Alone I did it." (5.6.114–17). Forgetting not just that the name "Coriolanus" is an expression of Roman *honestas* that the Volscians might be disinclined to respect, but that he is speaking before an audience of those that he had vanquished at Corioles, Martius asserts his masculinity and valor—his honor as a man and a soldier—as forcefully as he can. In another instance of *paradiastole*, Aufidius now reworks Martius's great victory as a work of "blind fortune" (5.6.118), of which Martius has the effrontery to brag before his Volscian audience. Instantly, Aufidius's coconspirators cry out "let him die for't!" and the people are ready to join in: "Tear him to pieces." The one who slaughtered their sons, daughters, cousins, and fathers must pay the ultimate price. Another lord intervenes, but to no avail. "Kill, kill, kill, kill, kill him!" (5.6.119, 120, 131). Once Martius has been hacked and stabbed and bludgeoned to death, Aufidius stands exultantly over, maybe on, his corpse. The lords see exactly what has happened, and chastise Aufidius accordingly: "O Tullus!" says one, to which another adds "thou has done a deed whereat valour will weep" (5.6.133, 134). But perhaps most remarkable is what happens next. Once the patricians have resolved to treat Martius's body with respect, they draw a veil over what has happened. Rather than punish Aufidius and his confederates, they suggest that Martius's "impatience / Takes from Aufidius a great part of blame." Time to move on and "make the best of it" (5.6.146–48). Even Aufidius finds himself, not unlike Antony before the corpse of Brutus, able to profess "sorrow" (5.6.14) and a sort of magnanimity: despite the sufferings Martius brought to Antium and Corioles, he should be mourned as a great man and granted "a noble memory" (5.6.155). As Aufidius has already proposed, "our virtues / Lie in th'interpretation of the time" (4.7.49–50), and what once is praiseworthy will on another occasion attract blame. We infer that when the Volscian annals to which Martius has alluded come to be written, they will be a work of politic circumspection.

Plutarch also records that the dead body of Martius was treated with respect, but does so to demonstrate that Martius's "murder was not generally consented unto, of the most parte of the Volsces." He goes on to narrate that Martius was mourned in Rome, and that as the Volscians faced various military challenges over the years ahead (culminating in their defeat and utter subjugation to Rome), "Martius being dead, the whole state of the Volsces hartely wished him alive again."[33] The Shakespeare of *Coriolanus* pushes this historiographical capaciousness aside, and likewise eschews the restorations of order affected by Fortinbras, Malcolm, Albany, and Edgar—along, of course, with the differently calibrated restitution offered by Cleopatra. What we are left with is a tableau of Volscian Realpolitik, in which virtue and honor are not a matter of valor, but of what the Volscians decide to call virtuous and honorable. In which truth and justice are no more current than they are in the Rome that will in short order crush them, and in which the fictions through which people apprehend the world only become problematic when they threaten to become singular or fixed—when, that is, they become delusions.

Above all, what Shakespeare's Romans and Volscians share is a worldview in which social living is a matter of compromises, contingency, and performativity, and in which the *constantia* of the valorous warrior is a no more effectual means of arriving at autonomy than that of the Stoic philosopher. Everyone is bound to a form of role playing that, even in the self-consciously disingenuous form espoused by Aufidius, either ignores or distorts the emotional realities of life as they experience it. Appetite in all its forms is dismissed as barbarous. The virtuous man seeks advancement, conquest, glory, or love not for the pleasure or satisfaction it might bring, but for *honestas*—honor, the true guarantor of one's identity. In perhaps the most extreme example of the kind, the homoerotic desire strongly implied in Aufidius's idealization of Martius's physical magnificence ("let me twine / Mine arms about that body" [4.5.108–9]) is quite literally unthinkable, and so goes unthought—until it is in due course sublimated into the humiliations visited upon Martius as Aufidius bestrides him at the instant of his death.[34] But we might also list fear, anxiety, and the willingness to change one's mind, all of which the patricians use to smear the plebs—thereby pretending to themselves that they, governed as they are by valor and the rationally defined canons of *honestas* and *decorum*, are cut from different cloth. Even Martius's desire for revenge on his fellow Romans is presented in Senecan fashion as less an act of impulsive intensity than something that, on balance, Martius believes he must pursue (with his habitual steadfastness) if he is to vindicate the dignity of his name.[35]

It is fitting that after Martius's final confrontation with his mother, his demise is incidental: he has no grandly tragic final words like those of Othello and Hamlet; no pathetic ones along the lines of those scripted for Julius Caesar and King Lear. Aufidius does not even bother to frame the violence of his death in sacrificial terms, as Brutus does before and after the extrajudicial killing of Caesar. The representational excesses of Martius's depictions both as a paragon of martial valor and an arrogant traitor to the common good seem, as he is killed, wholly beside the point. What remains is a sort of tragic bathos, in which the possibility that *res* and *verba* might meaningfully be brought together is unceremoniously dismissed. To put this a little differently, by the end of *Coriolanus*, *catharsis*-as-clarity-of-vision discloses little or nothing that can be invigorated by the truth-telling capacities of tragic drama. In retelling this story of early republican Rome, the degree to which Shakespeare has become appalled by the human condition threatens, and perhaps more than threatens, to overcome his powers of imaginative sympathy—to say nothing of the representational ironies of his tragic art. E. K. Chambers was guessing when he suggested that Shakespeare suffered a nervous or emotional collapse around the time he wrote *Timon of Athens* and *Coriolanus*, but it isn't hard to see his point.[36]

———

What can be said with more confidence is that Shakespeare the poet-playwright required his powers of imaginative sympathy, like the representational ironies of his art, to be fully in harness—and that, after *Coriolanus*, he no longer felt this to be the case when writing tragedy. Tragedies in the Shakespearean mold continued to be written, to be sure, but they were the work of younger men like John Webster and Thomas Middleton, as well as (with *Coriolanus* in mind) the Ben Jonson of *Catiline*. Nearly a decade after writing *Julius Caesar*, Shakespeare himself was ready to try something else. The peculiar demands of tragedy as Shakespeare wrote it—the way in which he wove together the threads of *muthos*, *ethos*, and *dianoia*—had drawn him toward the political dimension of moral philosophy. It is at the center of all his Roman plays, and is only slightly less prominent in *Hamlet*, *Macbeth*, *Lear*, and *Troilus and Cressida*; his characters collide with others, and are obliged to seek self-understanding, on an irrefutably political stage. As such, and as we have seen, conflicts of political theory are an inescapable feature of the plays: from the blurred lines between elective and primogeniture monarchy in *Hamlet*, to the contested nature of divine right kingship in *Macbeth*, to whether kingdoms can legitimately be divided in *Lear*, to the full-scale collisions between monarchy, republicanism, and empire evinced in *Julius Caesar*, *Antony and Cleopatra*, and *Coriolanus*.

Fertile territory, as a good deal of fine criticism has affirmed over the past several decades. The problem is that Shakespeare seems to have regarded political theory as a matter of bad faith and magical thinking. *Coriolanus* brings this into focus with particularly disquieting clarity. Plebeians, tribunes, and patricians are all in it for themselves; all convince themselves that they are acting on principle, even when engaging in self-conscious simulation or dissimulation; all invent pretexts to shirk responsibility (and with it the need to reevaluate their favored ideologies) when things go wrong. For Machiavelli, the story of Coriolanus encapsulates that which made Rome great: despite itself, the republic is forced into a form of post-monarchical mixed governance in which the patricians and populace both have a share; the balance between the two factions prevents the corruption, and with it the weakening, of civic life. Shakespeare takes a different view, captured well by Eric Nelson. The "fundamental conviction" of *Coriolanus* is that "the whole question of the best regime," the debate about how to arrive at the Ciceronian *optimus status reipublicae* with which sixteenth-century political thought was preoccupied, "is a red herring." This is because, for Shakespeare, political ideology "is not concerned with value, but with interest. It provides a patina of legitimacy for actions that would otherwise be clear for what they are: naked attempts to advance the interests of specific political actors."[37]

Shakespeare regarded the Roman project, even in the earliest days of the republic, as one of warfare and conquest and expansion. At the point of the Romans' clash with the Volscians (which, it should be recalled, had begun under Tarquinian rule), they were no more than a local power. But over the centuries ahead, their republic would grow to encompass first the Italian peninsula, then most of the Mediterranean and European world; the tensions in Rome's internal affairs were eased by riches and glory arising from the conflict they sought with others; its status as a monarchy, a republic, or (in the Augustan formulation) an *imperium* masquerading as a republic was a matter of political cosmetics—behind one decorous facade or another, the desire, unchanging and immutable, to win and hold onto as much territory and wealth as possible. Part of the task accomplished by Virgil in the *Aeneid* was to reconfigure Roman history along imperial lines. If Rome had been an empire all along, then what might otherwise look like the Augustan revolution could be redescribed (*paradiastole* again) as a story of continuity and renewal.[38] Shakespeare agreed that there was never any falling off from a condition of republican virtue, but his vision of Rome and its origins—from the Trojan adulterations of

Troilus and Cressida to Octavius's culminating victory over Antony and Cleopatra—was anything but celebratory.

In his *Of the City of God*, Augustine writes well of Roman *libido dominandi* ("lust for dominance"). Although I can find nothing in *Coriolanus* or any other Shakespearean text to suggest that he shared Augustine's conviction that things would be better if only people turned their attention to community, via the church, in the person of God the Son, he would have been in agreement with the outline of Augustine's diagnosis—and may even have been familiar with it, though it should be noted that cognate notions can be found in Livy, in Tacitus, and in Senecan tragedy. (Augustine himself elaborated the idea from one of Sallust's epigrammatic asides.) Although their *libido* made the Romans rich and spread their dominion far and wide, their successes had the paradoxical effect of binding them to lusts, and to a desire for possession, that could never be fulfilled. And, as they were unable to acknowledge this state of affairs, it also bound them to spurious notions of who and what they were; in due course, these notions further alienated them from their humanity and from the prospect of true freedom. Augustine's theology furnishes him with firm views as to how all of this came about (in a word: sin) and how it might now be redeemed. The normative and the descriptive are one. By contrast, Shakespeare's tragedies are content to pose questions while insisting that any answers to them must be able to take full account of the human propensity for creating fictions of order through which to regulate their lives—a propensity that, to gauge from the history plays of the 1590s, to say nothing of *Hamlet* and *Macbeth*, he took to be no less in evidence after Constantine made Christianity the official religion of Rome than it was before.[39]

Returning to *Coriolanus*, we can see that although Aufidius, Menenius, and the tribunes may be guilty of disingenuousness (of pretending to believe in the truth of the positions they espouse), what interests Shakespeare here as in all his tragedies is the way in which fictions of order and legitimacy lead to delusionality, to the misplaced belief that one understands things as they really are. Claudius, Iago, Macbeth, Lady Macbeth, Edmund, Goneril, and even Octavius are as keen as Aufidius and Volumnia to congratulate themselves on their uncluttered perspicuity, but Shakespeare reveals them to be as much the prisoners of their beliefs— of the rationalistic hubris that tells them they have it all worked out—as those they seek to manipulate and push aside.

Politics, then, provided Shakespeare with a more than serviceable framework within which to depict characters who can only make sense of themselves through representative media that are inherently distorting.

But by the time he had finished *Coriolanus*, his insistence on political theory as smoke, mirrors, and wishful thinking was threatening to flatten his characters out; to make them the servants of plots that were driven by some strikingly disillusioned ideas, and not the mimetic verve of his tragedies at their best and most distinctive. No remotely intelligent student of *Cymbeline*, *The Winter's Tale*, or *The Tempest* could suggest that they are apolitical works, but in the romances that ended up being Shakespeare's final single-authored plays, there is a change of focus from the *polis* to the family (that is, to the oeconomic part of moral philosophy) as the forum within which plot and character are played out. In *Romeo and Juliet* and to some extent in *Othello*, Shakespeare found in the household all he needed to fire his tragic imagination; in the later plays, a version of the household—and with it the possibility of redemption through familial-feminine love—provided him with the occasion to write drama of a markedly different kind. As a tragedian, his work was done.

Tragedy and Truth

IN COMING TO THE END OF A BOOK about Shakespeare's tragic drama, there is a case to be made for following Shakespeare's own example and simply stopping; stopping, that is, rather than venturing something summative on the significance of that which has gone before. But as criticism has many fewer prerogatives than art, drawing a line after *Coriolanus* will not do. Shakespeare's tragic plays have more in common with one another than violence, high mortality rates, and the rhetorical heft with which their protagonists for the most part make themselves heard. A book like this one ought to be able to say where this commonality is to be found.

The challenge is that these common features are less than obvious. Indeed, if we regard the plays in formal terms, Shakespearean tragedy scarcely seems to exist at all. There is no template from which Shakespeare worked in writing his tragic dramas, and no tragic paradigm or ideology that he set out to validate through his art; nor does he write his way toward any such template or ideological paradigm. At times, it can seem that his tragedies actively resist generic classification, and not just in so-called "problem" cases like *Troilus and Cressida*. What we find instead is a series of experiments. These draw on many models of what tragedy might be said to comprise: from Aristotelian poetics to Marlowe's mighty line; from Boethius, Boccaccio, and the *de casibus* tradition to domestic tragedies like *Arden of Faversham*; from the broad brushstrokes of Horace and Evanthius to the self-conscious intricacies of Kyd's *Spanish Tragedy*; from the grandeur of Senecan rhetoric to the blood-soaked revengers of the popular stage; from Italianate tragicomedy to biblical tragedies of unsparingly Protestant design; from Sackville and Norton's *Gorboduc* to Jonson's *Sejanus*. And so on. Crucially, Shakespeare found in these and other models not guides, but a series of starting points, just like those he found in innumerable non-tragic sources ranging from Cicero and Ovid and Plautus to Roger Ascham and Thomas Nashe. All enabled him to modify, refine, and make new not just his tragic practice, but his sense of what tragedy might be able to accomplish. That this sense changes over the course of his career is one of the things that makes his tragic drama so hard to categorize.

What binds the plays together as a family, if not a genre or subgenre of their own, is their author's preoccupation with tragic plotting. Specifically, his preoccupation with how best to devise tragic plots that operate as a principle of aesthetic order while simultaneously reflecting the disorder, the contingency and happenstance and extra-ordinariness, that are fundamental to the human experience as Shakespeare apprehended it. For Shakespeare, the imitation of action prescribed in treatises like Philip Sidney's *Defence of Poetry* is less mimesis than rationalizing make-believe. The Aristotelian unities are expressions of the delusional conviction that the world and the place of humankind within it are coherent, or at least that they are coherent to the philosophically and/or morally elect. A blindfold as well as a straitjacket. In their refusal to acknowledge or respect the indeterminacy of things, such doctrines might find a place as the subject matter of tragic art, but cannot be allowed to stand as its frame.

Shakespeare's alertness to delusion and delusionality in all their forms—to the unacknowledged fictions that we embrace in our hunger for meaning—led him toward the two most distinctive features of his tragic plays. To borrow again from Aristotle (not because Shakespeare's tragedies are particularly Aristotelian, but because the *Poetics* provides us with a set of powerful heuristics through which to interpret them), the first of these features involves Shakespeare's profoundly and disconcertingly interpenetrative arrangement of plot and characterization. Despite the sincere and deeply felt claims of a Hamlet or a Gloucester, the sufferings that befall Shakespeare's dramatis personae have nothing to do with fate, fortune, nature, destiny, providence, or any voice from above; they emerge instead from the collisions between his protagonists' words, deeds, desires, and choices. Shakespeare depicts these collisions with a ruthless and occasionally terrifying disinterestedness.

So it is that Horatio's "accidental judgments" and "purposes mistook" are the result not only of narrowness of discernment (a failure, say, to compute what might happen in the aftermath of killing someone to whom one is tied by blood or obligation or a vow), but of defective self-knowledge. They arise from the self-alienation that, in Shakespeare's tragic vision, inheres in any attempt to profess a fixed comprehension of what one is—any attempt to insist on one's selfhood as settled and singular rather than something that, by virtue of continually *happening*, continually differs from itself. Shakespeare makes much of the contingency that shapes the construction of identity through the *personae* of Ciceronian and humanist orthodoxy, as also through the Stoic, Machiavellian, and Christian notions of selfhood that sought to supplant them. But it is not the fact of fashioning an identity through which to make sense of oneself that holds Shakespeare's attention: it is for him a given that everyone to a greater or lesser extent performs themselves, and that much of what we regard as our identities is therefore imitative. Rather, he uses his tragic protagonists to explore as fully as he can the human need to pretend that identity is not, at its core, a temporal phenomenon. The need to avoid, that is, the painful recognition that human life is shaped not just by mortality, but by the processes of historical change; that because one becomes different in the very instant of acknowledging something new about oneself, self-knowledge is always partial, always belated; that the powers and responsibilities of subjecthood prevent us from making ourselves into the objects with which we might anchor our presence in the world.

The deep immersiveness with which Shakespeare lays open his characters' yearnings and self-deceit has much to do with the second most distinctive feature of his tragedies: their *dianoia*, or the way in which, from Juliet onward, he has his characters articulate their thoughts and feelings. Leaving behind the ostentatious citationality of *Titus Andronicus*, Shakespeare found a way in which to capture the kinesthesis of minds talking to—and sometimes about—themselves in forms of language that are infused both with sententious eloquence and intelligently humanistic learning. Doing so was more than a demonstration of his virtuosity: the close relationship between *dianoia* and depth of characterization makes *dianoia* an integral part of his tragic designs. His characters fail to understand themselves and their predicaments precisely *because* they speak so well. Because speaking well offers them a kind of reassurance that they do, in fact, know what they are talking about—not despite the habitually paralogistic quality of their speech, but because its suasive force depends on paralogism of one sort or another. The distance between their fine-sounding *verba* and the *res* of who, what, and where they are makes them strangers to themselves. In its turn, this self-alienation drives the tragic plots on which Shakespeare expended so much ingenuity.

Shakespeare's cardinal responsibility in writing any work of stage drama was to his playing company—to the Lord Chamberlain's Men, and from

1603 onward, to the King's Men. It had to be something that he and his fellows had the wherewithal to perform, and that was likely to appeal to their audiences "from the most able, to him who can but spell." Building on Martha Nussbaum's suggestion that *catharsis* should be understood not as purgation or purification but as clarification, I have put the case that Shakespeare's tragedies also try to make their audiences think. In particular, to make them think about the status of human thought as an ineradicably emotional phenomenon that is far from being the province of an unblinking and dispassionate rationality. The Shakespeare of the tragedies goes beyond the familiar claim that reason is the slave of the passions, and asks us to infer that reason as we tend to discuss it is the *invention* of the passions—of our desperate need to feel that we understand, or have the capacity to understand, our earthly lot. In so doing, he does not imply that the mental phenomenon represented by the word "reason" (something like "the power of intelligence through which human beings process the world") does not exist, but that reason as generally understood is a heuristic—a fiction that the human mind has settled upon in the attempt to explain itself to itself. And to explain itself to itself in a way that satisfies its desire to be able to say that it comprehends things, it needs to diminish and occasionally to deny the role of the emotions in its work.

Iris Murdoch offers a useful way in which to take this claim further. Deliberating on the malaise that she took to have overcome cultural and intellectual life in the decade and a half after the end of World War II, she reflects that "we are not isolated free choosers, monarchs of all we survey, but benighted creatures sunk in a reality whose nature we are constantly and overwhelmingly tempted to deform by fantasy." The most prominent and persistent of these fantasies is the conviction that we have grasped the meaning of life: perhaps the pursuit of political or economic equality, perhaps the pursuit of eternal beatitude through obedience to God the creator, perhaps the pursuit of sexual pleasure or self-determination, perhaps the pursuit of a racially or ethnically homogenous society, perhaps the pursuit of *eudaimonia*, perhaps something else altogether. For Murdoch, although each of these pursuits may involve struggles and even anguish, all depend on the "dream-like facility" with which meaning is imposed by our unavoidable subjectivity—by our need to transform things unknown into objects that we can comprehend, organize, and in some measure thereby control. If we are to understand anything of the human condition as it truly is, "what we require is a renewed sense of the difficulty and complexity of the moral life and the opacity of persons." Murdoch concludes by agreeing with Simone Weil that as "morality" is "a matter of attention, not of will," what is needed above all else is "a new vocabulary of attention."[1]

Shakespeare's tragedies are an effort to provide something very close to this vocabulary of attention. Where they differ from what Murdoch envisages is in their awareness that such vocabularies can never hope to be either "new" or transparent. Instead, Shakespeare depicts the human condition as for better or worse wedded to the linguistic, cultural, and discursive traditions within which people learn to think and speak. The kind of attentiveness that his tragedies afford us involves an acceptance both that this is the case, and that we are bound to representative media in contemplating ourselves or anything else at all. The crucial distinction is not thus between the plain sense of things and a vision of reality deformed by fantasy, but between fictions of order that acknowledge themselves as such, and those that insist on their truth value. Whether the "things" we encounter are human, animal, vegetable, mineral, or notional; whether they are simple or complex; whether they are conditions like those we call bliss, pain, and hunger; whether they are conditions we can only imagine, like death—all need to be translated into objecthood if we are to think about them. These translations depend on the language and assumptions through which our minds process the world; and because that world is not fully intelligible to human beings, these translations obscure as much as they reveal.

To some theological and philosophical mindsets, I imagine that to discuss Shakespeare's tragedies in these terms is to veer off into relativistic nihilism—to force these transcendent celebrations of human complexity into the barren postmodern terrain within which truth, virtue, and beauty are laughed to scorn. Shakespeare strikes me more as a temperamental skeptic than a relativist (one who inclines to the view that all beliefs are equally false, not equally true), but put this to one side. Rather than "truth" of the absolutist sort promulgated by a Plato, an Augustine, a Kant, or a Hegel, Shakespeare's tragedies traffic in something of greater humility and, in my view, courage. Not hard-and-fast answers about the nature of things or the fundamentals of being alive, or even an illustration of the difficulties that we face in arriving at such hard-and-fast answers, but the space in which to recognize and reflect upon the imponderables of the human condition—and of the ways in which we are equipped to respond to them. That space is a property of the Kierkegaardian irony with which Shakespeare wrote. Within it, we are prompted to move beyond the muddled habits of imitation and pretense through which we understand ourselves as objects; or, rather, to move beyond some of the muddle and acknowledge that it is only through habits of imitation and pretense that we are able to think, and to think critically, at all. Through such an acknowledgment, and with it an acceptance that we cannot know ourselves or our environments as they "really" are, comes the realization that we can understand something of ourselves as actors, as intelligent creatures who *do* things; who have the capacity—the freedom—to *choose* what they do, even as the choices open to them are often grim; and whose actions, whether the work of their hands or their mouths, have consequences for themselves and for those around them. It is the failure of such acknowledgment under the pressure of desire, fear, conceit, expectation, or ideological conviction that is the engine of all Shakespeare's tragic plots.

Against the grain of a tragic tradition that begins with Aeschylus, the sufferings to which these plots give rise do not make Shakespeare's protagonists better, wiser, or more insightful people. Even as they approach their deaths, their energies are spent on hiding from the recognition that they cannot bring that which they feel they know into harmony with that which they know they feel; in some cases, on obscuring the suspicion that that which they feel they know they feel does not have a great deal in common with the reality of their emotional dispositions.

Shakespeare does not tell us what to do with that which his tragic irony allows us to observe. Again, art as he wrote it is not philosophy or theology—its power to describe and depict the human condition depends on the deliberate eschewal of didacticism; on not making the kinds of assertion and argument that are familiar from theological and philosophical tradition. This is more than a matter of Shakespeare's restlessness of mind, or the confidence with which he is willing to cede interpretative agency to his spectators and readers. He rather insists on our freedom to interpret his tragic art for ourselves, on our responsibility to think about— to think our way behind—the categories and convictions through which we encounter and habitually evade the world. This freedom affirms the truth of an existence that is not fully susceptible to rational analysis, and that is regularly deformed by the fictions of objecthood through which human beings are bound to conceive of it.

Shakespeare would not, I suspect, have had the least difficulty in endorsing Gorgias's view that tragedy is a form of art in which "the deceiver is more just than the non-deceiver, and the deceived is wiser than the undeceived."

ACKNOWLEDGMENTS

I BEGAN WRITING THIS BOOK SHORTLY after moving to Princeton in the summer of 2018, and have been fortunate in the preparedness of my new colleagues and students to help me. Particular thanks to Josh Billings, Zahid Chaudhary, Bradin Cormack, Jeff Dolven, Sophie Gee, Tony Grafton, Russ Leo, Alexander Nehamas, Bailey Sincox, Nigel Smith, Vance Smith, Susan Stewart, and—above all—to the graduate students who took my courses on early modern tragedy in the fall semesters of 2019 and 2021. Lunchtime seminars at the Society of Fellows and English Department were welcome chances to expand, as also to tighten up, some of my thinking. At the Firestone Library, John Logan and his colleagues were unstintingly helpful, most notably when the coronavirus pandemic of 2020–2022 prevented me from getting into the stacks in person; in the Special Collections reading room, Brianna Cregle, AnnaLee Pauls, and Gabriel Swift went above and beyond as I rushed to take photographs in the summer of 2023.

Further afield, I presented work in progress to audiences at Columbia University, the Université de Fribourg, the University of St. Andrews, and the University of Sydney. I am grateful for the invitations to speak, and for being put through my paces with warmth and astuteness.

A range of old friends and new made the time to read parts of this book as it was being written. Their learning, wit, sensitivity, and preparedness to repeat things until I understood them helped me to fashion a much less imperfect piece of work than would otherwise have been the case. Laura Ashe, Rebecca Bushnell, Kristine Haugen, Giulio Pertile, Nam Rao, Matt Rickard, Will Theodorou, and Pasquale Toscano each read two or more chapters with generous severity. Beci Carver, Indira Ghose, David Kastan, and Seth Lerer did the same for virtually the entire manuscript. After he read my last book, the late David Bevington was the first to suggest to me that I should address Shakespearean tragedy tout ensemble; although by the time I completed my earliest chapters it was no longer possible to seek his counsel, I have written with him—and readers like him—in mind.

For ideas or advice or references or encouragement (in several cases, for all four), thanks to Armand D'Angour, Harriet Archer, Branka Arsić, Dan Blank, Jan Bloemendal, Claire Bourne, the late Paul Cantor, Chris Crosbie, Nan Da, Raine Daston, Nat Din-Kariuki, Daniel Dorogusker, James Dowthwaite, Moti Feingold, Kantik Ghosh, Rudolph Glitz, Julián Jiménez

Heffernan, Blair Hoxby, Vanessa Lim, Jan Machielsen, Nick McDowell, Edward Mendelson, Subha Mukherjee, Vanita Neelakanta, Eric Nelson, Curtis Perry, John-Mark Philo, Will Poole, Neil Rhodes, Lauren Robertson, Sanna-Mai Sabers, Kilian Schindler, Liam Semler, Devani Singh, Quentin Skinner, Tiffany Stern, Alan Stewart, Leah Whittington, Jessica Wolfe, and Andrew Zurcher. To those whose contributions I've forgotten: apologies in addition to thanks.

Princeton University Press have again made things easy. The professionalism and commitment to the cause of my editor, Anne Savarese, are remarkable; later on, Kathleen Cioffi guided me through the production process with patient expertise. Lachlan Brooks's copyediting proved to be a matter of delicacy and precision, and I am greatly in her debt. Although single-blind peer review very much is what it is, I was also lucky in my anonymous readers, and am grateful to them for the sympathy and intelligence (and enthusiasm) they brought to their charge.

But for the tireless attentions of Max and Oscar Lewis, this book would probably have been completed two to three years ago; crucially though, writing it would have been a lot less fun. Without Sarah Rivett's support, writing it would not have been possible at all.

R.L.
Stone Harbor
August 2023

NOTES

Introduction

1. James Baldwin, "The Artist's Struggle for Integrity," in *The Cross of Redemption: Uncollected Writings*, ed. Randall Kenan (New York, 2010), 50–58, here 51.

2. James Baldwin, "This Nettle, Danger . . . ," in *Collected Essays*, ed. Toni Morrison (New York, 1998), 687–91, here 687.

3. James Baldwin, "The Creative Process," in *Collected Essays*, ed. Toni Morrison (New York, 1998), 669–72, here 669, 671.

4. Frank Kermode, *The Sense of an Ending: Studies in the Theory of Fiction*, 2nd ed. (New York, 2000), 64. As Kermode will go on (ibid., 105–6) to explain, the urge to bring together "reality" and "justice" in this sense is at root Yeatsian.

5. Joel B. Altman, *The Tudor Play of Mind: Rhetorical Enquiry and the Development of Elizabethan Drama* (Berkeley and Los Angeles, 1978), 6. See further Neil Rhodes, "The Controversial Plot: Declamation and the Concept of the Problem Play," *Modern Language Review* 95 (2000): 609–22; and, for more on the structural patterns of the plays, see Emrys Jones, *Scenic Form in Shakespeare* (Oxford, 1971); Mark Rose, *Shakespearean Design* (Cambridge, MA, 1972).

6. Helen Vendler, *The Art of Shakespeare's Sonnets* (Cambridge, MA, 1997), 2. Emphases are Vendler's.

7. For useful introductions to humanism as I understand it, see Paul Oskar Kristeller, "Humanism," in *The Cambridge History of Renaissance Philosophy*, ed. Charles B. Schmitt, Quentin Skinner, and Jill Kraye (Cambridge, UK, 1988), 113–37; Charles G. Nauert, *Humanism and the Culture of Renaissance Europe*, 2nd ed. (Cambridge, UK, 2006).

8. For related discussion, see Stephen Orgel, *Wit's Treasury: Renaissance England and the Classics* (Philadelphia, 2021), 136–39.

9. Stephen Orgel, "The Poetics of Incomprehensibility," *Shakespeare Quarterly* 42 (1991): 431–37. On Shakespeare's Latin, see J. W. Binns, "Shakespeare's Latin Citations: The Editorial Problem," *Shakespeare Survey* 35 (1982): 119–28. On Pythagoras and the transmigration of souls, see *As You Like It*, ed. Juliet Dusinberre (London, 2006), 3.2.172–73; *Twelfth Night, or What You Will*, ed. Keir Elam (London, 2008), 4.2.49–55.

10. Although I am impatient with the notion of modernity (when has anyone *not* believed themselves to be living in modern times?), I make do with "early modern," along with "Elizabethan" and "Jacobean," as the least imperfect of the chronological shorthands available. For a more sympathetic account of periodization and its limitations, see Margreta de Grazia, *Four Shakespearean Period Pieces* (Chicago, 2021), chap. 3. See also Frank Kermode, *History and Value* (Oxford, 1988), 117–27.

11. Lukas Erne, *Shakespeare as Literary Dramatist* (Cambridge, UK, 2003), esp. 136–39, 177–83, 230–41. See further David Scott Kastan, *Shakespeare and the Book* (Cambridge, UK, 2001); Patrick Cheney, *Shakespeare's Literary Authorship*

(Cambridge, UK, 2008), 203–33; Lukas Erne, *Shakespeare and the Book Trade* (Cambridge, UK, 2013); Claire M. L. Bourne, *Typographies of Performance in Early Modern England* (Oxford, 2020), 1–31.

12. Bourne, *Typographies of Performance*, 243.

13. On the early modern theatrical scene, the conscientious and overwhelmingly accurate studies of E. K. Chambers (*The Elizabethan Stage*, 4 vols. [Oxford, 1923]) and Gerald Eades Bentley (*The Jacobean and Caroline Stage*, 7 vols. [Oxford, 1941–68]) have yet to be surpassed. But see also W. W. Greg, *Dramatic Documents from the Elizabethan Playhouses: Stage Plots: Actors' Parts: Prompt Books*, 2 vols. (Oxford 1931); Andrew Gurr, *The Shakespearean Stage, 1574–1642*, 4th ed. (Cambridge, UK, 2009); Tiffany Stern, *Documents of Performance in Early Modern England* (Cambridge, UK, 2009). On the claim about Oxbridge performances of *Hamlet*, see Paul Menzer, *The Hamlets: Cues, Qs, and Remembered Texts* (Newark, DE, 2008), 163–66. For visual depictions of the theater, see R. A. Foakes, *Illustrations of the English Stage, 1580–1642* (Stanford, CA, 1985). The Peacham sketch is discussed in chapter 2 below.

14. On which, see Bernice W. Kliman, "At Sea about *Hamlet* at Sea: A Detective Story," *Shakespeare Quarterly* 62 (2011): 180–204.

15. On the post-1660 invention of Shakespearean tradition, see Michael Dobson, *The Making of the National Poet: Shakespeare, Adaptation and Authorship, 1660–1769* (Oxford, 1994); Emma Depledge, *Shakespeare's Rise to Cultural Prominence: Politics, Print and Alteration, 1642–1700* (Cambridge, UK, 2018).

16. Fulke Greville, "A Dedication to Sir Philip Sidney," chap. 18, in *The Prose Works of Fulke Greville, Lord Brooke*, ed. John Gouws (Oxford, 1986), 134. Greville enjoins his reader to "behold these acts upon their true stage . . . that stage whereon himself is an actor, even the state he lives in" (ibid., 135).

17. On the changing status of playwrights, see Gerald Eades Bentley, *The Profession of Dramatist in Shakespeare's Time, 1590–1642* (Princeton, NJ, 1971), esp. 38–61. See also Bart van Es, *Shakespeare in Company* (Oxford, 2013), esp. chaps. 1–3.

18. William Shakespeare, *Troilus and Cressida*, ed. David Bevington (London, 2001), 145 ("A Never Writer to an Ever Reader. News").

19. Francesco Robortello, *In librum Aristotelis de arte poetica explicationes* (Florence, 1548), 58. Translation, slightly modified, from Bernard Weinberg, *A History of Literary Criticism in the Italian Renaissance*, 2 vols. (Chicago, 1961), 1:393. Robortello adapts Aristotle's suggestion that a tragedy is still a tragedy even without being performed in public by actors (*Poetics*, 1450b).

Chapter 1: Tragedy, History, Irony

1. Thomas Rymer, *A Short View of Tragedy*, in *William Shakespeare: The Critical Heritage*, 6 vols., ed. Brian Vickers (London, 1974–81), 2:18; dedication to Nahum Tate's *The History of King Lear*, in ibid., 1:295. For related discussion, see Dobson, *Making of the National Poet*; Jean I. Marsden, *The Re-Imagined Text: Shakespeare, Adaptation, and Eighteenth-Century Literary Theory* (Lexington, KY, 1995); Robert D. Hume, "Before the Bard: 'Shakespeare' in Early Eighteenth-Century London," *ELH* 64 (1997): 41–75; Michael Caines, *Shakespeare and the Eighteenth Century* (Oxford, 2013). See further Paul D. Cannan, *The Emergence of Dramatic Criticism in England, from Jonson to Pope* (New York, 2006).

2. "Preface" to Samuel Johnson, *Plays of William Shakespeare*, in *William Shakespeare: The Critical Heritage*, ed. Vickers, 5:45, 48.

3. For this and the next two paragraphs, see Michelle Gellrich [Zerba], *Tragedy and Theory: The Problem of Conflict since Aristotle* (Princeton, NJ, 1988); Julian Young, *The Philosophy of Tragedy: From Plato to Žižek* (Cambridge, UK, 2013); Joshua Billings, *Genealogy of the Tragic: Greek Tragedy and German Philosophy* (Princeton, NJ, 2014); Edward Pechter, "Shakespearean Tragedy: The Romantic Inheritance," in *The Oxford Handbook of Shakespearean Tragedy*, ed. Michael Neill and David Schalkwyk (Oxford, 2016), 54–70. See also Miriam Leonard, *Tragic Modernities* (Cambridge, MA, 2015).

4. Jean-Pierre Vernant and Pierre Vidal-Naquet, *Myth and Tragedy in Ancient Greece* (New York, 1990), 186.

5. Bernard Williams, *Shame and Necessity* (Berkeley and Los Angeles, 1993), 163–64. For a comparable reading of tragedy against philosophical absolutism, see Robert B. Pippin, *Philosophy by Other Means: The Arts in Philosophy and Philosophy in the Arts* (Chicago, 2021), 19–38.

6. V. S. Naipaul, *A Bend in the River* (New York, 1979), 92. Cf. Kiernan Ryan, *Shakespearean Tragedy* (London, 2021), where it is proposed that "Shakespeare's creation of protagonists who cannot come to terms with their world" prophesies a future of "freedom, equality and justice" (xiv).

7. On the difficulties of defining tragedy, see, e.g., Alastair Fowler, *Kinds of Literature: An Introduction to the Theory of Genres and Modes* (Oxford, 1982), 39–40, 55–56. And, in very different keys, see Terry Eagleton, *Sweet Violence: The Idea of the Tragic* (Oxford, 2003), 1–22; William Marx, *The Tomb of Oedipus: Why Greek Tragedies Were Not Tragic*, trans. Nicholas Elliott (London, 2022). See also Rosalie Colie, *The Resources of Kind: Genre Theory in the Renaissance*, ed. Barbara Lewalski (Berkeley and Los Angeles, 1973), 1–31.

8. Erasmus, *Parabolae sive similia*, in *The Collected Works of Erasmus*, ed. R.A.B. Mynors, Robert D. Sider, J. K. Sowards, Craig R. Thompson, et al., 86 vols. (Toronto, 1974-), 23:159. Erasmus paraphrases a line from Plutarch's "On Exile" (Plutarch, *Moralia*, 599b).

9. Stephen Booth, *King Lear, Macbeth, Indefinition, and Tragedy* (New Haven, CT, 1983), 84–86. See also Gellrich [Zerba], *Tragedy and Theory*, passim. As Raymond Williams, a critic whose preoccupations and approach are far removed from those of Booth, rightly observes: if we think of the tragic "as a theory about a single and permanent kind of fact, we can end only with the metaphysical conclusions that are built into any such assumption" (*Modern Tragedy*, ed. Pamela McCallum [Peterborough, Ontario, 2006], 69).

10. *A Warning for Fair Women: A Critical Edition*, ed. Charles Dale Cannon (The Hague, 1975), 97–99 (Induction, 1–89). On tragedy as understood by the early moderns, the best introductions include Madeleine Doran, *Endeavors of Art: A Study of Form in Elizabethan Drama* (Madison, WI, 1954), 101–47; Daniel Javitch, "The Emergence of Poetic Genre Theory in the Sixteenth Century," *Modern Language Quarterly* 59 (1998): 139–69; Timothy J. Reiss, "Renaissance Theatre and the Theory of Tragedy," in *The Cambridge History of Literary Criticism*, vol. 3, *The Renaissance*, ed. Glyn P. Norton (Cambridge, UK, 1999), 229–47. See also Howard B. Norland, *Neoclassical Tragedy in Elizabethan England* (Newark, DE, 2009); Blair Hoxby, *What*

Was Tragedy? Theory and the Early Modern Canon (Oxford, 2015), 8–14, 57–108; Russ Leo, *Tragedy as Philosophy in the Reformation World* (Oxford, 2019), 3–42; *A Cultural History of Tragedy*, vol. 3, *A Cultural History of Tragedy in the Early Modern Age*, ed. Rebecca Bushnell et al. (London, 2020).

11. For purple patches, see Horace, *Ars poetica*, 14–16. "Buskins" were the high laced boots worn by ancient Greek tragic actors; figuratively, they signify anything executed in a tragic manner. See George Puttenham, *The Art of English Poesy: A Critical Edition*, ed. Frank Whigham and Wayne Rebhorn (Ithaca, NY, 2007), 123 (1.15).

12. The title page to the 1599 first printing of *A Warning for Fair Women* advertises that "it hathe been lately diverse times acted by the right Honourable, the Lord Chamberlaine his Servantes." On the possible allusion to Shakespeare, cf. *King Henry IV, Part 2*, ed. James C. Bulman (London, 2016), 2.1.42–43 ("How now, whose mare's dead? What's the matter?"). *A Warning* has at least one other Shakespearean echo: "Yonder she sits to light this obscure street / Like a bright diamond worne in some darke place" (107 [ii.344]) pastiches Romeo's rapture at his first sight of Juliet (*Romeo and Juliet*, ed. René Weis [London, 2012], 1.5.44–45).

13. See, e.g., Philip Sidney, *Defence of Poetry*, in *Miscellaneous Prose of Sir Philip Sidney*, ed. Katherine Duncan-Jones and Jan van Dorsten (Oxford, 1973), 114–16; Puttenham, *The Art of English Poesy*, 115–16 (1.11), 121–24 (1.14–15); William Scott, *The Model of Poesy*, ed. Gavin Alexander (Cambridge, UK, 2013), 22–24. Although William Webbe measures comedy and tragedy against one another, he also divides dramatic poetry into the "comical, tragical, historical" schema (William Webbe, *A Discourse of English Poetry (1586)*, ed. Sonia Hernández-Santano [Cambridge, UK, 2016], 88–89); cf. the similar account in John Florio, *Florios Second Frutes* (London, 1591), 23.

14. Francis Meres, *Palladis Tamia, Wits Treasury* (London, 1598), fol. 282r. Meres categorizes the history plays with which we are familiar as tragedies—as do the title pages of the earliest printed editions of, e.g., *Richard II* and *Richard III*. More on the relationship between tragedy and history below.

15. Philip Stubbes, *The Anatomie of Abuses*, ed. Margaret Jane Kidnie (Tempe, AZ, 2002), 202. See also Stephen Gosson, *Plays Confuted in Five Actions* (London, 1582), sig. C5r-v.

16. Thomas Kyd, *The Spanish Tragedy*, ed. J. R. Mulryne, 2nd ed. (London, 1989), 108 (4.2.155–61); Kyd's "*Tragedia Cothurnata*, fitting kings" tips the hat to Ovid, *Tristia*, 2.553–54. John Webster, "To the Reader," *The White Devil*, in *The Works of John Webster*, ed. David Gunby, David Carnegie, and Antony Hammond, 3 vols. (Cambridge, UK, 1995), 1:140. See also Jonson's introductory remarks to his *Sejanus* (1603) where (although admitting his disregard for the Aristotelian unities), he claims that "in truth of argument, dignity of persons, gravity and height of elocution, fulness and frequency of sentence, I have discharged the other offices of a tragic writer" ("To the Readers," *Sejanus*, in *The Cambridge Edition of the Works of Ben Jonson*, ed. David Bevington, Martin Butler, Ian Donaldson, et al., 7 vols. [Cambridge, UK, 2012], 2:213–14).

17. Horace, *Ars poetica*, 89–100. Translation from *Ancient Literary Criticism: The Principal Texts in New Translations*, ed. and trans. D. A. Russell and Michael Winterbottom (Oxford, 1972), 281–82.

18. Evanthius, "De fabula," 4.2, in Donatus, *Aeli Donati Commentum Terenti*, ed. Paul Wessner, 3 vols. (Leipzig, 1902–8), 1:21. See Henry Ansgar Kelly, *Ideas and Forms of Tragedy from Aristotle to the Middle Ages* (Cambridge, UK, 1993), esp. 5–15;

Robert Miola, *Shakespeare and Classical Comedy: The Influence of Plautus and Terence* (Oxford, 1994), 170–74.

19. Evanthius, "Excerpta de comoedia," 5.1, in Donatus, *Aeli Donati Commentum Terenti*, ed. Wessner, 1:22. Hamlet reminds the visiting players of "the purpose of playing, whose end, both at the first and now, was and is to hold as 'twere the mirror up to nature; to show virtue her feature, scorn her own image, and the very age and body of the time his form and pressure" (*Hamlet*, ed. Harold Jenkins [London, 1982], 3.2.19–24). See further Rhodri Lewis, *Hamlet and the Vision of Darkness* (Princeton, NJ, 2017), 200–205; Baxter Hathaway, *The Age of Criticism: The Late Renaissance in Italy* (Ithaca, NY, 1962), esp. 3–5, 16–18, 35, 39–40, 76–77, 144–46, 331–32, 343–44, 447–48; Rayna Kalas, *Frame, Glass, Verse: The Technology of Poetic Invention in the English Renaissance* (Ithaca, NY, 2007), 106–32.

20. Evanthius, "De fabula," 4.5 and "Excerpta de comoedia," 7.1–4, in Donatus, *Aeli Donati Commentum Terenti*, ed. Wessner, 1:22, 27–28. On the prolonged influence of Donatus and Evanthius on dramatic theory, see the thick detail of T. W. Baldwin, *Shakspere's Five-Act Structure* (Urbana, IL, 1947), esp. chaps. 2, 4–5, 10–14. On sixteenth-century dramatic plotting, see also Marvin T. Herrick, *Comic Theory in the Sixteenth Century* (Urbana, IL, 1950), 26–31, 89–129. Scott's *Model of Poesy*, 76–77 is good on the close comparability of "the formal parts in general" in comedies and tragedies.

21. Boethius, *De consolatione*, 1.pr.1, 2.pr.2, 3.pr.6, 3.pr.7; the relationship between providence, fate, chance, and fortune is treated at length in book 4. Although *meretricula* is a diminutive of *meretrix*, I take the two terms here—as in, e.g., Quintilian, *Institutio oratoria*, 11.3.74—to signify the same thing.

22. See Kelly, *Ideas and Forms of Tragedy*, 68–78, 126–30, 170–75.

23. For an overview of the ways in which latinized Greek—and especially Euripidean—tragedy influenced sixteenth-century vernacular playwrights, see Tanya Pollard, *Greek Tragic Women on Shakespearean Stages* (Oxford, 2017). Much more on Seneca in the chapters to come.

24. Thomas Elyot, *A Critical Edition of Sir Thomas Elyot's The Boke Named the Governour*, ed. Donald W. Rude (New York, 1992), 48 (1.10); [Thomas Lodge], [*A Defence of Poetry, Music, and Stage Plays*], (London, 1579), 36; Webbe, *Discourse*, 88; Greville, "Dedication to Sir Philip Sidney," chap. 18, in *Prose Works of Fulke Greville*, 133; Christopher Marlowe, "Prologue" to *Tamburlaine the Great, Part 1*, in *The Complete Works of Christopher Marlowe*, ed. Roma Gill et al., 5 vols. (Oxford, 1987–98), 5:6. See Henry Ansgar Kelly, *Chaucerian Tragedy* (Cambridge, UK, 1997); Rebecca W. Bushnell, *Tragedies of Tyrants: Political Thought and Theater in the English Renaissance* (Ithaca, NY, 1990); Paul Budra, *A Mirror for Magistrates and the de casibus Tradition* (Toronto, 2000). On Greville, see Jonathan Dollimore, *Radical Tragedy: Religion, Ideology and Power in the Drama of Shakespeare and His Contemporaries*, 3rd ed. (Basingstoke, UK, 2004), 83–86, 120–33.

25. Aristotle, *Poetics*, 1449b. Translation, slightly modified, from *Ancient Literary Criticism*, ed. and trans. Russell and Winterbottom, 97. For introductions to the *Poetics*, see Stephen Halliwell, *Aristotle's Poetics*, 2nd ed. (London, 1998) and Martha Nussbaum, *The Fragility of Goodness: Luck and Ethics in Greek Tragedy and Philosophy*, 2nd ed. (Cambridge, UK, 2001), 378–94.

26. Aristotle, *Poetics*, 1449b–1450b.

27. Ibid., 1453a.

28. But for a good example of replicating confusion, see the conflicting opinions on tragic endings articulated by Julius Caesar Scaliger: *Poetices libri septem: Sieben Bucher über die Dichtkunst*, ed. Luc Deitz, Gregor Vogt-Spira, and Manfred Fuhrmann, 6 vols. (Stuttgart, 1994–2011), 1:132 (1.6, where tragedies must have a "miserable ending" [*exitus infelix*]), and 3:26 (3.96 [usually cited as 3.97], where the fact of a plot representing "horrible things" [*res atroces*] is enough to permit a less gloomy denouement).

29. Herman's Latin is translated in *Medieval Literary Theory and Criticism c. 1100 to c. 1375*, ed. and trans. A. J. Minnis, A. B. Scott, and David Wallace (Oxford, 1988), 277–313. See further Henry Ansgar Kelly, "Aristotle-Averroes-Alemannus on Tragedy: The Influence of the *Poetics* on the Latin Middle Ages," *Viator* 10 (1979): 161–209; Donalee Dox, *The Idea of the Theater in Latin Christian Thought: Augustine to the Fourteenth Century* (Ann Arbor, MI, 2004), 95–124. On Aristotelian tragedy and forensic-inferential logic, see Kathy Eden, *Poetic and Legal Fiction in the Aristotelian Tradition* (Princeton, NJ, 1986), 7–24, 112–75; Terence Cave, *Recognitions: A Study in Poetics* (Oxford, 1988), esp. 72–78. On the reception of the *Poetics* more broadly, see Weinberg, *History of Literary Criticism*, 1:349–634; Luc Deitz, " 'Aristoteles imperator noster . . .'? J. C. Scaliger and Aristotle on Poetic Theory," *International Journal of the Classical Tradition* 2 (1995): 54–67; Brigitte Kappl, *Die Poetik des Aristoteles in der Dichtungstheorie des Cinquecento* (Berlin and New York, 2006). See also Donald V. Stump, "Sidney's Concept of Tragedy in the *Apology* and in the *Arcadia*," *Studies in Philology* 79 (1982): 41–61.

30. See Leo, *Tragedy as Philosophy* (on tragedy and theology); Hoxby, *What Was Tragedy?* (on the long genealogy of neoclassicism). See also Kristine Louise Haugen, "The Birth of Tragedy in the Cinquecento: Humanism and Literary History," *Journal of the History of Ideas* 72 (2011): 351–70; Micha Lazarus, "Tragedy at Wittenberg: Sophocles in Reformation Europe," *Renaissance Quarterly* 73 (2020): 33–77.

31. Roger Ascham, *The Scholemaster (1570)*, ed. Lawrence V. Ryan (Ithaca, NY, 1967), 139. Note that Ascham uses Evanthius's terminology for the first and second sections of a play. See further Thomas Watson, *A Humanist's "Trew Imitation": Thomas Watson's Absalom: A Critical Edition and Translation*, ed. John Hazel Smith (Urbana, IL, 1964); George Buchanan, *Tragedies*, ed. P. Sharratt and P. G. Walsh (Edinburgh, 1983), 21–94. On *tragoedia sacra*, see Leo, *Tragedy as Philosophy*, 29–31.

32. Sidney, *Defence*, in *Miscellaneous Prose*, 113, 114–15; a little later, Sidney claims that "the tragedies of Buchanan do justly bring forth a divine admiration" (116). See Thomas Norton and Thomas Sackville, *Gorboduc*, ed. Harriet Archer and Paul Frazer (Manchester, forthcoming).

33. For a plausible account of the ways in which the *Poetics* might have exerted an indirect influence on Shakespeare, see Sarah Dewar-Watson, *Shakespeare's Poetics: Aristotle and the Anglo-Italian Renaissance Genres* (London, 2018). See also Donald V. Stump, "Greek and Shakespearean Tragedy: Four Indirect Routes from Athens to London," in *Hamartia: The Concept of Error in the Western Tradition*, ed. Donald V. Stump et al. (New York, 1983), 211–46.

34. On Polonius's theatrical currency, see Lewis, *Hamlet and the Vision of Darkness*, 181–82; Louisa George Clubb, *Italian Drama in Shakespeare's Time* (New Haven, CT, 1989), 186–87, 249–80.

35. William Shakespeare, *King Henry IV, Part 1*, ed. David Scott Kastan (London, 2002), 2.4.374–84 (here 2.4.376). Through Falstaff, Shakespeare mocks both older tragedies like Thomas Preston's 1569 *Cambyses* (cf. Thomas Preston, *A Critical Edition of Thomas Preston's Cambises*, ed. Robert C. Johnson [Salzburg, 1975], 77 [ll. 530–34], 105–10 [ll. 1030–1126]), and newer ones like Kyd's *Soliman and Perseda* (see the list of parallels in William Shakespeare, *The First Part of King Henry the Fourth*, ed. R. P. Cowl and A. E. Morgan [London, 1914], 97–98).

36. The next three paragraphs draw from Anne Barton, *Shakespeare and the Idea of the Play* (London, 1962), 83–86.

37. William Shakespeare, *King Henry VI, Part 2*, ed. Ronald Knowles (London, 1999), 3.2.194; William Shakespeare, *King Richard III*, ed. James R. Siemon (London, 2009), 4.4.7. Cf. similar usages in William Shakespeare, *Titus Andronicus*, ed. Jonathan Bate (London, 1995), 2.2.265, 4.1.47; and, although the lines in question are not likely to be Shakespeare's work, *King Henry VI, Part 1*, ed. Edward Burns (London, 2000), 1.4.76.

38. William Shakespeare, *King Henry VI, Part 3*, ed. John D. Cox and Eric Rasmussen (London, 2001), 2.3.25–28.

39. My phraseology borrows from Jaques in *As You Like It*, 2.7.140–67. On theatrical metaphors of the world, see Ernst Robert Curtius, *European Literature and the Latin Middle Ages*, trans. Willard R. Trask (New York, 1953), 138–44; Lynda G. Christian, *Theatrum Mundi: The History of an Idea* (New York, 1987); *"If Then the World a Theatre Present . . .": Revisions of the Theatrum Mundi Metaphor in Early Modern England*, ed. Björn Quiring (Berlin, 2014). On the possibility of human spectatorship within the *theatrum mundi*, see Ann Blair, *The Theater of Nature: Jean Bodin and Renaissance Science* (Princeton, NJ, 1997), 153–59. According to one tradition, the Globe took the Latin tag *totus mundus agit histrionem* ("the whole world plays the actor") as its motto; see Tiffany Stern, "Was *totus mundus agit histrionem* Ever the Motto of the Globe Theatre?," *Theatre Notebook* 51 (1997): 122–27.

40. William Shakespeare, *King Henry V*, ed. T. W. Craik (London, 1995), 1.2.105–7 ("Edward the Black Prince, / Who on the French ground played a tragedy, / Making defeat on the full power of France"); William Shakespeare, *Othello*, ed. E.A.J. Honigmann (London, 1997), 5.2.361–62 ("Look on the tragic loading of this bed: / This is thy work").

41. William Shakespeare, *King Lear*, ed. R. A. Foakes (London, 1997), 5.3.230–31.

42. On the challenges of *King Lear*'s ending, see Booth, *King Lear, Macbeth, Indefinition, and Tragedy*, 5–11; Claire McEachern, *Believing in Shakespeare: Studies in Longing* (Cambridge, UK, 2018), 253–75.

43. On the apocalyptic features of the play, see Kristen Poole, "Poetic Creation in an Apocalyptic Age: *King Lear* and the Making and the Unmaking of the World," in *The Cambridge Companion to Shakespeare and Religion*, ed. Hannibal Hamlin (Cambridge, UK, 2019), 234–51.

44. On "overliving," see Emily Wilson, *Mocked by Death: Tragic Overliving from Sophocles to Milton* (Baltimore, 2004), 113–28.

45. Toward the end of chapter 9 and in chapter 24, Aristotle conceives of wonder or awe (*thaumaston*) as related to the feelings of fear and pity to which tragedy should lead (*Poetics*, 1452a, 1460a); cf. the place of "wonder" in his *Rhetoric*, 1371a–b, 1404b and *Metaphysics*, 982b. See Marvin T. Herrick, "Some Neglected Sources of

Admiratio," Modern Language Notes 62 (1947): 222–26; J. V. Cunningham, "Aught of Woe or Wonder" and "Wonder," in *The Collected Essays of J. V. Cunningham* (Chicago, 1976), 9–29, 53–96; T. G. Bishop, *Shakespeare and the Theatre of Wonder* (Cambridge, UK, 1996), 17–41. Elsewhere in the play (e.g., at 1.2.192, 1.2.235, 3.2.317–21), "wonder," "admiration," and "amazement" are in this sense virtually synonymous. For more on the discourse of "wonder" (and its ambivalence) in the early modern world, see Lorraine Daston and Katharine Park, *Wonders and the Order of Nature, 1150–1750* (New York, 1998), esp. chaps. 3 and 8.

46. William Shakespeare, *Hamlet: The Texts of 1603 and 1623*, ed. Ann Thompson and Neil Taylor (London, 2006), 171 (17.113–14, 120–21).

47. For a comparable use of "forced," see Hamlet's description of the contrived sighs that go along with conventional mourning: "Windy suspiration of forc'd breath" (1.2.79). See also "indirect and forced courses" (*Othello*, 1.3.111), and "forced baseness" (*The Winter's Tale*, ed. John Pitcher [London, 2010], 2.3.77).

48. On *Hamlet's* refusals of narrative-tragic closure, see Michael Neill, *Issues of Death: Mortality and Identity in English Renaissance Tragedy* (Oxford, 1997), 237–42.

49. Aristotle, *Poetics*, 1454a–b; Horace, *Ars poetica*, 191–92.

50. "Preface" to Johnson's edition of the *Plays*, in *William Shakespeare: The Critical Heritage*, ed. Vickers, 5:48.

51. George Steiner, *The Death of Tragedy*, 2nd ed. (New Haven, CT, 1996), xii–xiii, 8.

52. Cave, *Recognitions*, 275–76.

53. "The Christian Tragic Hero," in W. H. Auden, *The Complete Works*, vol. 2, *Prose, 1939–1948*, ed. Edward Mendelson (Princeton, NJ, 2002), 258–61, here 258.

54. J.G.A. Pocock, *The Machiavellian Moment: Florentine Political Thought and the Atlantic Republican Tradition* (Princeton, NJ, 1975), 6.

55. For later Aristotelians, "chance" was a more or less permissible feature of comic plotting. See Cave, *Recognitions*, 59–60.

56. Aristotle, *Poetics*, 1452a. Translation, slightly modified, from *Ancient Literary Criticism*, ed. Russell and Winterbottom, 103.

57. Aristotle, *Poetics*, 1456a. Translation from *Ancient Literary Criticism*, ed. Russell and Winterbottom, 116.

58. Aristotle, *Poetics*, 1460a; the maxim about preferring probable impossibilities to improbable possibilities is repeated in the following chapter (1461b). Translation from *Ancient Literary Criticism*, ed. Russell and Winterbottom, 125–26.

59. Aristotle, *Poetics*, 1460b. Translation from *Ancient Literary Criticism*, ed. Russell and Winterbottom, 128.

60. See Lorna Hutson's *The Invention of Suspicion: Law and Mimesis in Shakespeare and Renaissance Drama* (Oxford, 2007) and *Circumstantial Shakespeare* (Oxford, 2015); Quentin Skinner, *Forensic Shakespeare* (Oxford, 2014). But as both Skinner and Hutson make plain, other aspects of the rhetorical tradition—including some of the techniques used to test the probability of a proposition—did help Shakespeare to structure individual scenes.

61. Cf. Bacon's complaint in the *Cogitata et visa* that the opinions of Aristotle, and of the ancient Greek philosophers more generally, "have what is proper to a dramatic plot (*fabula*): a neat roundedness foreign to a narration of fact" (translation, slightly

modified, from Benjamin Farrington, *The Philosophy of Francis Bacon: An Essay on Its Development from 1603 to 1609 with New Translations of Fundamental Texts* [Liverpool, 1964], 84–85).

62. Roland Barthes, *S / Z*, trans. Richard Miller (Oxford, 1990), 18–20. Cf. Barthes's claim that "of all readings, that of tragedy is the most perverse: I take pleasure in hearing myself tell a story *whose end I know*: I know and I don't know, I act toward myself as though I did not know: I know perfectly well Oedipus will be unmasked, that Danton will be guillotined, *but all the same*" (Roland Barthes, *The Pleasure of the Text*, trans. Richard Miller [New York, 1975], 47–48). Altman, *Tudor Play of Mind*, 64–106.

63. "Preface" to Johnson's edition of the *Plays*, in *William Shakespeare: The Critical Heritage*, ed. Vickers, 5:47.

64. Thomas Rymer, *The Tragedies of the Last Age*, in *William Shakespeare: The Critical Heritage*, ed. Vickers, 1:162. See the detailed discussion of these points in Hoxby, *What Was Tragedy?*, 258–93. For more on plot and the neoclassicists, see David Riggs, "Plot and Episode in Early Neoclassical Criticism," *Renaissance Drama* 6 (1973): 149–75. If there is a contradiction between criticizing Shakespeare for overdone historicity while attacking him for anachronism (mechanical clocks in ancient Rome, Trojan heroes citing Aristotle, etc.), it does not seem to have occurred to the eighteenth century; see de Grazia, *Four Shakespearean Period Pieces*, 23–59.

65. "Preface" to Johnson's edition of the *Plays*, in *William Shakespeare: The Critical Heritage*, ed. Vickers, 5:49.

66. See Peter Brooks, *Reading for the Plot: Design and Intention in Narrative* (New York, 1984), 6–7.

67. Although I suspect that Benjamin's distinction between tragedy (dramatizing myths; largely ancient) and *Trauerspiel* (dramatizing history; distinctively modern) cannot hold, one could from his perspective regard Shakespearean tragedy as *trauerspielartig*. See Walter Benjamin, *The Origin of German Tragic Drama*, trans. John Osborne (London, 1998), 57–158.

68. Lodovico Castelvetro, *Castelvetro on the Art of Poetry: An Abridged Translation of Lodovico Castelvetro's Poetica d'Aristotele Vulgarizzata et Sposta*, ed. and trans. Andrew Bongiorno (Binghamton, NY, 1984), 64–72 (3.4), 161–75 (3.14); Aristotle, *Poetics*, 1450a (translation, slightly modified, from *Ancient Literary Criticism*, ed. Russell and Winterbottom, 99). See Edward Burns, *Character: Acting and Being on the Pre-Modern Stage* (Basingstoke, UK, 1990); and, with different emphasis, Christy Desmet, *Reading Shakespeare's Characters: Rhetoric, Ethics, and Identity* (Amherst, MA, 1992); John E. Curran, Jr., *Character and the Individual Personality in English Renaissance Drama* (Newark, DE, 2014); McEachern, *Believing in Shakespeare*, 183–224. On Shakespeare and the growth of character criticism, see Deidre Shauna Lynch, *The Economy of Character: Novels, Market Culture, and the Business of Inner Meaning* (Chicago, 1998), 133–41.

69. Thomas Cooper, *Thesaurus linguae Romanae & Britannicae* (London, 1565), s.vv. "Mos, moris" and "Persona, persónae" ("The qualitie or state whereby one man differeth from an other . . . Also a person or personage: a man or woman: a visour like a mans face . . . A personage or parte in a play"). On Theophrastan characters, see Jacques Bos, "Individuality and Inwardness in the Literary Character Sketches

of the Seventeenth Century," *Journal of the Warburg and Courtauld Institutes* 61 (1998): 142–57; Christy Desmet, "The Persistence of Character," *Shakespeare Studies* 34 (2006): 46–55. On early modern plays having "persons," see Hoxby, *What Was Tragedy?*, 48–51, 69–72, 75–79. On *prosopa / personae* as deployed in ancient theater, see David Wiles, *The Masks of Menander: Sign and Meaning in Greek and Roman Performance* (Cambridge, UK, 1991).

70. On the importance of Burbage to Shakespeare's characterization, see Gurr, *Shakespearean Stage*, 117–22. On the need for early modern actors to do more than speak well, see B. L. Joseph, *Elizabethan Acting* (London, 1951), esp. 60–82; David Bevington, *Action and Eloquence* (Cambridge, MA, 1984), 67–98; David Wiles, *The Players' Advice to Hamlet: The Rhetorical Acting Method from the Renaissance to the Enlightenment* (Cambridge, UK, 2020), chaps. 3 and 4.

71. Aristotle, *Poetics*, 1450b.

72. Henry James, "The Art of Fiction," in *The Critical Muse: Selected Literary Criticism*, ed. Roger Gard (Harmondsworth, UK, 1987), 186–206, here 196–97.

73. T. S. Eliot, "Shakespeare and the Stoicism of Seneca," in *Selected Essays*, 2nd ed. (London, 1934), 126–40, here 131.

74. On tragic selfhood and identity being "continuously situated by linguistic acts," see John Kerrigan, *Revenge Tragedy: Aeschylus to Armageddon* (Oxford, 1996), 354–67.

75. Ralph Waldo Emerson, "Experience," in *The Complete Essays and Other Writings*, ed. Brooks Atkinson (New York, 1950), 342–64, here 344. On transcending conventional discourse, see Emerson's essays on "Nature" and "The Poet." See further Sharon Cameron, *Impersonality: Seven Essays* (Chicago, 2007), 53–78.

76. On Stanley Cavell's Shakespeare, see esp. chapter 6 below.

77. Aristotle, *Poetics*, 1456a–b. Translation from *Ancient Literary Criticism*, ed. Russell and Winterbottom, 116. Note that in chapter 6 of the *Poetics*, Aristotle construes *dianoia* in narrower terms. See further, e.g., Aristotle, *Rhetoric*, 1403a–b.

78. Charlton T. Lewis and Charles Short, *A Latin Dictionary* (Oxford, 1879), s.v. "sententia," esp. II.B. For *dianoia* as *sententia* see, e.g., Robortello, *Explicationes*, 57, 64–66, 68–69; Scaliger, *Poetices*, 3:28 (3.96, usually cited as 3.97); Daniel Heinsius, *De tragica constitutione* (Leiden, 1611), 178–98 (chap. 16). Although doing so may bolster the case that *pathos* was the determinate feature of tragedy as the early moderns understood it, there is no warrant for translating *dianoia / sententia* as "sentiments"; cf. Hoxby, *What Was Tragedy?*, 69–72, 79–84.

79. See G. K. Hunter, "The Marking of *Sententiae* in Elizabethan Printed Plays, Poems, and Romances," *The Library* 6 (1951): 171–88; Marjorie Donker, *Shakespeare's Proverbial Themes: A Rhetorical Context for the Sententia as Res* (Westport, CT, 1992), 1–21; Mary Thomas Crane, *Framing Authority: Sayings, Self, and Society in Sixteenth-Century England* (Princeton, NJ, 1993), esp. chaps. 1–2; Ann Moss, *Printed Commonplace Books and the Structuring of Renaissance Thought* (Oxford, 1996). On Harvey, see Tania Demetriou, "How Gabriel Harvey Read Tragedy," *Renaissance Studies* 35 (2021): 757–87.

80. Zachary Lesser and Peter Stallybrass, "The First Literary *Hamlet* and the Commonplacing of Professional Plays," *Shakespeare Quarterly* 59 (2008): 371–420; Carla Suthren, "Translating Commonplace Marks in Gascoigne and Kinwelmersh's *Jocasta*," *Translation and Literature* 29 (2020): 59–84.

81. On the *insigne verbum*, see Erasmus, *De copia*, 1.8, 1.9 and *De ratione studii*, in *Collected Works*, ed. Mynors et al., 24:302, 303, 670. On the apian metaphor, see Seneca the Younger, *Epistulae morales*, 84; Thomas Greene, *The Light in Troy: Imitation and Discovery in Renaissance Poetry* (New Haven, CT, 1982), 72–80; Colin Burrow, *Imitating Authors: Plato to Futurity* (Oxford, 2019), 108–10, 145–46, 152–53. For Montaigne, see *The Complete Essays*, ed. and trans. M. A. Screech (Harmondsworth, UK, 1991), 166 (1.26, "On Educating Children"); cf. 155–56 (1.25, "On Schoolmasters' Learning").

82. On the centrality of being able to conceal one's rhetorical art, see, e.g., Quintilian, *Institutio oratoria*, 1.11.3, 2.5.7.

83. On the *vir bonus*, see, e.g., Quintilian, *Institutio oratoria*, 12.1.1–45. See further Richard A. Lanham, *The Motives of Eloquence: Literary Rhetoric in the Renaissance* (New Haven, CT, 1976), 1–35; Anthony Grafton and Lisa Jardine, *From Humanism to the Humanities: Education and the Liberal Arts in Fifteenth- and Sixteenth-Century Europe* (London, 1986), 184–200; Brian Vickers, *In Defence of Rhetoric* (Oxford, 1988), 39–43, 167–69, 351–52.

84. Pseudo-Longinus, *On the Sublime*, 1.3–4, 7.1–4; Lewis, *Hamlet and the Vision of Darkness*, 313–14. See further Robert Duran, *The Theory of the Sublime from Longinus to Kant* (Cambridge, UK, 2015).

85. Patrick Cheney, *English Authorship and the Early Modern Sublime: Spenser, Marlowe, Shakespeare, Jonson* (Cambridge, UK, 2018), esp. chaps. 4 and 5.

86. See Scaliger, *Poetices*, 1:132 (1.6) and Castelvetro, *Art of Poetry*, 56 (3.1); Castelvetro probably had in mind Aristotle's *Rhetoric*, 1383a. Webster, *Duchess of Malfi*, 4.2.7, 10, in *The Works of John Webster*, ed. Gunby et al., 1:539. On early modern approaches to *catharsis*, see Hathaway, *Age of Criticism*, 205–300; Hoxby, *What Was Tragedy?*, 62–68. On the eighteenth century and after, see Billings, *Genealogy of the Tragic*, 24–26, 36–37, 101–3, and *passim*. On Brecht, see, e.g., Bertolt Brecht, *Brecht on Theatre: The Development of an Aesthetic*, ed. and trans. John Willett (London, 1964), 78, 87, 181.

87. Nussbaum, *Fragility of Goodness*, 391. See also Alexander Nehamas, "Pity and Fear in the *Rhetoric* and the *Poetics*," in *Essays on Aristotle's Poetics*, ed. Amélie Oksenberg Rorty (Princeton, NJ, 1992), 291–314, here 303–8; Jonathan Lear, "Katharsis," in *Essays on Aristotle's Poetics*, ed. Amélie Oksenberg Rorty (Princeton, NJ, 1992), 315–40.

88. Williams, *Shame and Necessity*, 164; Pippin, *Philosophy by Other Means*, 25.

89. "Preface" to Johnson's edition of the *Plays*, in *William Shakespeare: The Critical Heritage*, ed. Vickers, 5:47. For Williams, see note 5 above.

90. Of the introductions to irony, the most useful to me have been Norman Knox, *The Word Irony and Its Context, 1500–1755* (Durham, NC, 1961); D. C. Muecke, *The Compass of Irony* (London, 1969); Wayne C. Booth, *A Rhetoric of Irony* (Chicago, 1974); Dilwyn Knox, *Ironia: Medieval and Renaissance Ideas on Irony* (Leiden, 1989); Joseph A. Dane, *The Critical Mythology of Irony* (Athens, GA, 1991); Paul de Man, "The Concept of Irony," in *Aesthetic Ideology*, ed. Andrzej Warminski (Minneapolis, 1996), 163–84; Jonathan Lear, *A Case for Irony* (Cambridge, MA, 2011). On *King Lear* and structural irony, see William R. Elton, *King Lear and the Gods*, 2nd ed. (Lexington, KY, 1988), 328–34.

91. Søren Kierkegaard, *The Concept of Irony, with Continual Reference to Socrates*, ed. and trans. Howard V. Hong and Edna H. Hong (Princeton, NJ, 1989), 26, 254, 259, 261, 271; Søren Kierkegaard, *Concluding Unscientific Postscript to the Philosophical*

Crumbs, ed. and trans. Alastair Hannay (Cambridge, UK, 2009), 422; Lear, *Case for Irony*, 31. Cf. G.W.F. Hegel, *Aesthetics: Lectures on Fine Art*, ed. and trans. T. M. Knox, 2 vols. (Oxford, 1975), 1:64–69. For the "Hegelian fool," see Søren Kierkegaard, *Kierkegaard's Journals and Notebooks*, ed. Niels Jørgen Cappelørn, Alastair Hannay, Bruce H. Kirmmse, George Pattison, Jon Stewart, et al., 11 vols. (Princeton, NJ, 2007–2020), 8:29. See further Michael Strawser, *Both / And: Reading Kierkegaard from Irony to Edification* (New York, 2003).

92. John Milton, "On Shakespeare," in *The Complete Shorter Poems*, ed. John Carey, 2nd ed. (London, 1997), 127.

93. As quoted in Plutarch, *Moralia*, 348d (also in Plutarch's *How the Young Man Should Study Poetry*, 1 = *Moralia*, 15d). Translation from *Ancient Literary Criticism*, ed. Russell and Winterbottom, 6. Heinsius uses Gorgias's line as the epigraph to his *De tragica constitutione* (sig. A5r).

94. Rowan Williams, *The Tragic Imagination* (Oxford, 2016), 3.

95. William Shakespeare, *Measure for Measure*, ed. A. R. Braunmuller and Robert Watson (London, 2019), 2.2.120–26.

96. On "glassy essence," see J. V. Cunningham, "Idea as Structure: *The Phoenix and Turtle*," in *Collected Essays*, 196–209, esp. 197–200; Herbert Grabes, *The Mutable Glass: Mirror-Imagery in Titles and Texts of the Middle Ages and English Renaissance*, trans. Gordon Collier (Cambridge, UK, 1982), 218–20; Maurice A. Hunt, *Shakespeare's Speculative Art* (New York, 2011), 16–18, 206–7. On "carnal reason," see, e.g., Jean Calvin, *Institutes of the Christian Religion*, ed. John T. McNeill and trans. Ford Lewis Battles, 2 vols. (Philadelphia, 1960), 1:199 (1.16).

97. *Macbeth*, 5.5.23; much more on these lines in chapter 5 below.

98. Martin Heidegger, "The Age of the World Picture," in *The Question Concerning Technology, and Other Essays*, ed. and trans. William Lovitt (New York, 1977), 115–54, here 130. For a reading of the early modern proscenium stage as a Heideggerian frame, see Margreta de Grazia, "World Pictures, Modern Periods, and the Early Stage," in *A New History of Early English Drama*, ed. John D. Cox and David Scott Kastan (New York, 1997), 7–21, here 19–21.

99. See Walter S. Gibson, *Pieter Bruegel the Elder: Two Studies* ([Lawrence, KS], 1991), 53–86; Elke Oberthaler, Sabine Pénot, Manfred Sellink, and Ron Spronk, with Alice Hoppe-Harnoncourt, *Bruegel: The Master* (London, 2018), 162–67; Anna Pawlak, "The Imaginarium of Death: Pieter Bruegel's *The Triumph of Death*," in *Pieter Bruegel the Elder and Religion*, ed. Bertram Kaschek, Jürgen Müller, and Jessica Buskirk (Leiden, 2018), 134–58. On early modern mousetraps, see Lewis, *Hamlet and the Vision of Darkness*, 70–72. For an excellent account of early modern tragedy and the visual art of the danse macabre and Triumph of Death, see Neill, *Issues of Death*, 51–101.

100. Revelation 20:13. Gibson, *Pieter Bruegel the Elder*, 60. On Bruegel and Heidegger, see Joseph Leo Koerner, *Bosch & Bruegel: From Enemy Painting to Everyday Life* (Princeton, NJ, 2016), 274–87, esp. 279–80.

101. Kermode, *Sense of an Ending*, 82. On Shakespeare and the *theatrum mundi*, see also Richard Wilson, *Worldly Shakespeare: The Theatre of Our Good Will* (Edinburgh, 2016), 32–52.

102. For a Hegelian take on humankind as subject and object in Shakespearean tragedy, cf. Paul Kottman, "What is Shakespearean Tragedy?," in *Oxford Handbook of Shakespearean Tragedy*, ed. Neill and Schalkwyk, 3–18.

Chapter 2: Early Experiments

1. *Humanist Tragedies*, ed. and trans. Gary R. Grund (Cambridge, MA, 2011), vii. See further Marvin T. Herrick, *Italian Tragedy in the Renaissance* (Urbana, IL, 1965); Salvatore Di Maria, *The Italian Tragedy in the Renaissance: Cultural Realities and Theatrical Innovations* (Lewisburg, PA, 2002). See also Cinthio (Giambattista Giraldi) and Daniel Javitch, "Discourse or Letter on the Composition of Comedies and Tragedies," *Renaissance Drama* 39 (2011): 207–55.

2. See related discussion in Clubb, *Italian Drama in Shakespeare's Time*, 1–26.

3. On sixteenth-century English tragedy and the ways in which Marlowe and Kyd changed it, see, e.g., Martin Wiggins, *Shakespeare and the Drama of His Time* (Oxford, 2000), 32–52; Goran Stanivukovic and John H. Cameron, *Tragedies of the English Renaissance: An Introduction* (Edinburgh, 2018), esp. 36–74.

4. Doran, *Endeavors of Art*, 116–47.

5. See related discussion in see Pascale Aebischer, "Vampires, Cannibals and Victim-Revengers: Watching Shakespearean Tragedy through Horror Film," *Shakespeare Jahrbuch* 143 (2007): 119–31.

6. "To the Reader" in Edward Ravenscroft, *Titus Andronicus, or The Rape of Lavinia . . . A Tragedy*, in *William Shakespeare: The Critical Heritage*, ed. Vickers, 1:205.

7. Ben Jonson, *Bartholomew Fair*, in *The Cambridge Edition of the Works of Ben Jonson*, ed. Bevington et al., 4:280 (Induction, 79–80).

8. On Peacham's sketch as reflective of carefully structured plotting, see Kerrigan, *Revenge Tragedy*, 195–200. On comedic borrowings, see Hutson, *Invention of Suspicion*, 92–103; Adele Scafuro, "Roman Comedy and Renaissance Revenge Drama: *Titus Andronicus* as Exemplary Text," in *Ancient Comedy and Reception: Essays in Honor of Jeffrey Henderson*, ed. S. Douglas Olson (Berlin, 2014), 537–64; Misha Teramura, "Black Comedy: Shakespeare, Terence, and *Titus Andronicus*," *ELH* 84 (2018): 877–908. For a view of *Titus Andronicus* as a tragedy unified by the character of Titus himself, see Ruth Nevo, "Tragic Form in *Titus Andronicus*," in *Further Studies in English Literature*, ed. A. A. Mendilow (Jerusalem, 1973), 1–18.

9. On the sketch, see Foakes, *Illustrations of the English Stage*, 48–51; Shakespeare, *Titus Andronicus*, ed. Bate, 38–43; Shakespeare, *Titus Andronicus*, ed. Eugene M. Waith (Oxford, 1984), 20–27; Richard Levin, "The Longleat Manuscript and *Titus Andronicus*," *Shakespeare Quarterly* 53 (2002): 323–40. For the very plausible suggestion that Peacham identifies Aaron with the Vice figure of the medieval mystery plays, see Christopher Crosbie, "The Longleat Manuscript Reconsidered: Shakespeare and the Sword of Lath," *English Literary Renaissance* 44 (2014): 221–40; relatedly, Misha Teramura ("Black Comedy," 892) suggests that Aaron's appearance resembles that of the cunning slave figure in Roman New Comedy.

10. On the Virgilian traces deployed by Shakespeare and Peele (or Peele and Shakespeare) in act 1, see Heather James, *Shakespeare's Troy: Drama, Politics, and the Translation of Empire* (Cambridge, UK, 1997), 42–84, esp. 49–64. For "empire without end" (*imperium sine fine*), see Virgil, *Aeneid*, 1.279. On the Roman disavowal of human sacrifice as a practice fit only for Gauls and Carthaginians, see Celia E. Schultz, "The Romans and Ritual Murder," *Journal of the American Academy of Religion* 78 (2010): 520–28.

11. For more on the *personae*, see notes 51–56 below.

12. Ovid, *Amores*, 1.8.41–42, as translated in Marlowe, *Complete Works*, 1:24. On *Titus* and Ovid, see Robert Miola, *Shakespeare's Rome* (Cambridge, UK, 1983), 59–75; Jonathan Bate, *Shakespeare and Ovid* (Oxford, 1993), 101–17; Colin Burrow, *Shakespeare and Classical Antiquity* (Oxford, 2013), 105–14.

13. The starting point for *contaminatio* is Terence's *Andria* (Preface, lines 15–16); see Greene, *Light in Troy*, 39–40, 156–69. On the Senecan features of *Titus*, see Burrow, *Shakespeare and Classical Antiquity*, 165–66, 183–85; Robert Miola, *Shakespeare and Classical Tragedy: The Influence of Seneca* (Oxford, 1992), 13–31; Curtis Perry, *Shakespeare and Senecan Tragedy* (Cambridge, UK, 2020), esp. 26–27, 201–12. On the Euripidean ones, see Pollard, *Greek Tragic Women*, 99–110; Emrys Jones, *The Origins of Shakespeare* (Oxford, 1977), 85–107; Penelope Meyers Usher, "Greek Sacrifice in Shakespeare's Rome: *Titus Andronicus* and *Iphigenia in Aulis*," in *Rethinking Shakespeare Source Study*, ed. Dennis Britton and Melissa Walter (New York and London, 2018), 206–24. See, more generally, Pramit Chaudhuri, "Classical Quotation in *Titus Andronicus*," *ELH* 81 (2014): 787–810; Michael Neill, "The Designs of *Titus Andronicus*," in *The Oxford Handbook of Shakespearean Tragedy*, ed. Neill and Schalkwyk, 339–57.

14. On the Senecan and Ovidian resonances of the scene in the woods, see Mike Pincombe, "Classical and Contemporary Sources of the 'Gloomy Woods' of *Titus Andronicus*: Ovid, Seneca, Spenser," in *Shakespearean Continuities: Essays in Honour of E.A.J. Honigmann*, ed. John Batchelor, Tom Cain, and Claire Lamont (London, 1997), 40–55. *Arden of Faversham*, ed. Martin White and Tom Lockwood, 2nd ed. (London, 2007), esp. Arden's dream at 6.5–31. On *Titus* and hunting, see Miola, *Shakespeare and Classical Tragedy*, 17–18; Richard Marienstras, *Le proche et le lointain: Sur Shakespeare, le drame élisabéthain et l'idéologie anglaise aux XVIe et XVIIe siècles* (Paris, 1981), 65–74; Edward Berry, *Shakespeare and the Hunt: A Cultural and Social Study* (Cambridge, UK, 2001), 70–86. On the rituals of dismemberment after the hunt, see George Gascoigne, *The Noble Arte of Venerie or Hunting* (London, 1575), 127–35; John Cummins, *The Hound and the Hawk: The Art of Medieval Hunting* (London, 1998), 41–44. For the biblical injunction that those who hunt by guile will perish in their own devices, see Ecclesiastes 10:8; cf., e.g., Psalms 7:15, 91:15, 46:7–8, 67:6, and Ecclesiasticus 27:25–27.

15. Berry, *Shakespeare and the Hunt*, 79–80. On Shakespeare's critique of hunting rituals, see Lewis, *Hamlet and the Vision of Darkness*, 80–92.

16. Seneca, *Thyestes*, 491–507. On the *Phaedra*, see A. J. Boyle, *Tragic Seneca: An Essay in the Theatrical Tradition* (London, 1997), 57–67, here 57; Walter Burkert, *Homo Necans: The Anthropology of Ancient Greek Sacrificial Ritual and Myth*, trans. Peter Bing (Berkeley and Los Angeles, 1983), 103–9; C.A.J. Littlewood, *Self-Representation and Illusion in Senecan Tragedy* (Oxford, 2004), 269–301. On Shakespeare's knowledge of the *Phaedra*, see, e.g., *Titus Andronicus*, 1.1.635 and 4.1.81–82 (cf. *Phaedra*, 1180 and 671–72); William Shakespeare, *A Midsummer Night's Dream*, ed. Sukanta Chaudhuri (London, 2017), 4.1.102–26 (cf. *Phaedra*, 1–53).

17. On the anti-Black prejudices that frame the Andronici's depiction of Aaron, see Noémie Ndiaye, *Scripts of Blackness: Early Modern Performance Culture and the Making of Race* (Philadelphia, 2022), 40–45.

18. Lawrence Danson, "The Device of Wonder: *Titus Andronicus* and Revenge Tragedies," *Texas Studies in Literature and Language* 16 (1974): 27–43; Vernon Guy Dickson,

"'A Pattern, Precedent, and Lively Warrant': Emulation, Rhetoric, and Cruel Propriety in *Titus Andronicus*," *Renaissance Quarterly* 62 (2009): 376–409.

19. Seneca, *Thyestes*, 195–96.

20. Ascham, *Scholemaster*, 115; cf., e.g., Cicero, *De oratore*, 3.61. On the increasingly unstable relationship between *res* and *verba* in the early modern period, see Terence Cave, *The Cornucopian Text: Problems of Writing in the French Renaissance* (Oxford, 1979), 3–34; *Res et Verba in der Renaissance*, ed. Eckhard Kessler and Ian Maclean (Wiesbaden, 2002).

21. For an outstanding entrée into the place of *Titus* within the political crises of the 1590s, see Paulina Kewes, "'I Ask Your Voice and Your Suffrages': The Bogus Rome of Peele and Shakespeare's *Titus Andronicus*," *The Review of Politics* 78 (2016): 551–70; on the political currency of *Titus*, see Helmer Helmers, "The Politics of Mobility: Shakespeare's *Titus Andronicus*, Jan Vos's *Aran en Titus*, and the Poetics of Empire," in *Politics and Aesthetics in European Baroque and Classicist Tragedy*, ed. Jan Bloemendal and Nigel Smith (Leiden, 2016), 344–72. Cf. Peter Lake, *Hamlet's Choice: Religion and Resistance in Shakespeare's Revenge Tragedies* (New Haven, CT, 2020), 17–70. For Cecil, see Henry Peacham the Younger, *The Compleat Gentleman* (London, 1622), 45 (chap. 6); and, on the importance of Ciceronianism to Cecil's worldview, see Norman Jones, *Governing by Virtue: Lord Burghley and the Management of Elizabethan England* (Oxford, 2015), chaps. 2–3. For the origins of the commonplace, see Pliny, *Natural History*, Pr.22–23; "The Godly Feast" (*Convivium religiosum*) in Erasmus, *Collected Works*, ed. Mynors et al., 39:184.

22. For Horace on the kinds of violence that can be staged and those that should only be reported, see *Ars poetica*, 179–88. On Shakespeare's evocation of offstage ("unscene") action, see Lorna Hutson, "The Play in the Mind's Eye," in *The Places of Early Modern Criticism*, ed. Gavin Alexander, Emma Gilby, and Alexander Marr (Oxford, 2021), 97–111.

23. Brooke's *Romeus and Juliet* quoted from Geoffrey Bullough, *Narrative and Dramatic Sources of Shakespeare*, 8 vols. (London, 1957–75), 1:286. For an insightful comparison of the prefatory sonnets by Shakespeare and Brooke—as well as a discussion of *Romeo and Juliet* to which I am more generally in debt—see Emma Smith, *This Is Shakespeare* (London, 2019), 67–81.

24. On the uses to which Shakespeare put sonnets—and amatory verse in general—within the play, see Hester Lees-Jeffries, "Body Language: Making Love in Lyric in *Romeo and Juliet*," *Review of English Studies* 74 (2023): 237–53.

25. Susan Snyder, *The Comic Matrix of Shakespeare's Tragedies: Romeo and Juliet, Hamlet, Othello, and King Lear* (Princeton, NJ, 1979), 56–70, here 66. On *thesis* and *hypothesis*, see Aphthonius, *Progymnasmata*, 15, in *Progymnasmata: Greek Textbooks on Prose Composition and Rhetoric*, ed. and trans. George A. Kennedy (Atlanta, GA, 2003), 120–24. On Milton's copy of the 1623 folio, discovered recently in the collections of the Free Library of Philadelphia, see Claire M. L. Bourne and Jason Scott-Warren, "'Thy Unvalued Booke': John Milton's Copy of the Shakespeare First Folio," *Milton Quarterly* 56 (2022): 1–85.

26. Altman, *The Tudor Play of Mind*, 267–82, here 270–71 (italics in the original). See also Jones, *The Origins of Shakespeare*, 196–206; Philip Edwards, "Thrusting Elysium into Hell: The Originality of *The Spanish Tragedy*," in *The Elizabethan Theatre XI*, ed. A. L. Magnusson and C. E. McGee (Port Credit, Ontario, 1990), 117–32.

27. On the plot of *Romeo and Juliet* as structured around contingencies and their interrogation rather than tragic necessity, see Hutson, *Circumstantial Shakespeare*, 36–69. For an insistence on tragic necessity (of a Hegelian rather than an Aristotelian stamp), see Paul Kottman, "Defying the Stars: Tragic Love as the Struggle for Freedom in *Romeo and Juliet*," *Shakespeare Quarterly* 63 (2012): 1–38.

28. Marlowe, *Complete Works*, 1:61.

29. On domestic tragedy, see Viviana Comensoli, *Household Business: Domestic Plays of Early Modern England* (Toronto, 1996); Catherine Richardson, *Domestic Life and Domestic Tragedy in Early Modern England: The Material Life of the Household* (Manchester, 2006); Emma Whipday, *Shakespeare's Domestic Tragedies: Violence in the Early Modern Home* (Cambridge, UK, 2019); Richard McCabe, "Tragedy, or the Fall of Middle-Class Men," in *Literature, Learning, and Social Hierarchy in Early Modern Europe*, ed. Neil Kenny (Oxford, 2022), 219–38. On *Romeo and Juliet* as a domestic tragedy, see Lynette Hunter and Peter Lichtenfels, *Negotiating Shakespeare's Language in Romeo and Juliet: Reading Strategies from Criticism, Editing and the Theatre* (Farnham, UK, 2009), 27–28, 88–89, 114–15.

30. Mercutio teases Romeo for his ardent Petrarchanism at 2.4.37–45.

31. For laughing Jove, see Ovid, *Ars amatoria*, 1.633. On Juliet's Ovidian characteristics, see Heather James, *Ovid and the Liberty of Speech in Shakespeare's England* (Cambridge, UK, 2021), 101–39. For other Ovidian features of the play, and for the suggestion that its structure follows that of Phaëthon's ill-fated journey in *Metamorphoses* 2, see Bate, *Shakespeare and Ovid*, 176–80; I do not understand why Bate thinks that Juliet's invocation of laughing Jove is "supremely out of control" (180).

32. This might be the point at which to remember that Shakespeare would not have written Juliet the way he did if he hadn't had confidence in the skills of the boy actor—likely Robert Gough—playing her for the newly formed Lord Chamberlain's Men. For possible impacts of the Lord Chamberlain's Men on Shakespeare's writing practices, see van Es, *Shakespeare in Company*, chaps. 4–7.

33. Cf. *Richard III*, 1.1.1–13 (beginning "Now is the winter of our discontent / Made glorious summer by this son of York"). When confronted with what he thinks is Juliet's corpse, Romeo will also personify Death as an amorous rival (5.3.102–5).

34. These forensic enquiries closely follow the advice of the rhetoric handbooks for establishing a "conjectural cause." See Hutson, *Circumstantial Shakespeare*, 55–60; Skinner, *Forensic Shakespeare*, 8, 53–54, 271–74; T. W. Baldwin, *William Shakspere's Small Latine & Lesse Greeke*, 2 vols. (Urbana, IL, 1944), 2:76–80.

35. Scaliger, *Poetices*, 3:31–32 (3.96, usually cited as 3.97).

36. *Characters of Shakespear's Plays* (1817), in *The Selected Writings of William Hazlitt*, ed. Duncan Wu, 9 vols. (London, 1998), 1:107.

37. On imputations of textual corruption, see E. K. Chambers, *William Shakespeare: A Study of Facts and Problems*, 2 vols. (Oxford, 1930), 1:398–99.

38. On the language of the play, see Burrow, *Shakespeare and Classical Antiquity*, 216–17.

39. See Jones, *Scenic Form*, 106–13.

40. On conventional representations of Caesar, see Nigel Mortimer, *Medieval and Early Modern Portrayals of Julius Caesar: The Transmission of an Idea* (Oxford, 2020), esp. 599–632. On Higgins's 1587 additions, see Paulina Kewes, "Romans in the Mirror," in *A Mirror for Magistrates in Context*, ed. Harriet Archer and Andrew

Hadfield (Cambridge, UK, 2016), 126–46; Harriet Archer, *Unperfect Histories: The Mirror for Magistrates, 1559–1610* (Oxford, 2017), 110–38. For "Caesar's thrasonical brag," see *As You Like It*, 5.2.30.

41. "Die tragedy vom ersten keyser Julio Caesare mitt ohngefahr 15 personen sehen gar artlich agieren" (Thomas Platter, *Beschreibung der Reisen durch Frankreich, Spanien, England und die Niederlande, 1595–1600*, ed. Rut Keiser, 2 vols. [Basel and Stuttgart, 1968], 2:791; although the translation is not always reliable, see also Thomas Platter, *Thomas Platter's Travels in England, 1599*, ed. and trans. Clare Williams [London, 1937]). Note that in one of the earliest English appreciations of the play, Leonard Digges relates that audiences were "ravish'd" to "wonder" not by Caesar or his assassination, but by the quarrel between Brutus and Cassius in act 4, scene 3 (Leonard Digges, "Uppon Master William Shakespeare, the Deceased Author," in *William Shakespeare: The Critical Heritage*, ed. Vickers, 1:25).

42. Petrarch, *The Canzoniere or Rerum vulgarium fragmenta*, ed. and trans. Mark Musa (Bloomington and Indianapolis, 1996), 280–81. Thomas Wyatt, *The Complete Poems*, ed. R. A. Rebholz, 2nd ed. (London, 1997), 77. On *Julius Caesar* and hunting, see Berry, *Shakespeare and the Hunt*, 86–94.

43. Cummins, *Hound and the Hawk*, 41.

44. Gascoigne, *Noble Arte*, 34–37, 132–35, 242; Cummins, *Hound and the Hawk*, 44–46.

45. Plutarch, "Julius Caesar," in Bullough, *Narrative and Dramatic Sources*, 5:86 (cf. the slightly less gory account of the assassination in Plutarch's life of Brutus: ibid., 5:102). *The Tragedy of Caesar's Revenge*, ed. F. S. Boas ([London], 1911), act 3, scene 8 (ll. 1693–1739) (also in Bullough, *Narrative and Dramatic Sources*, 5:204–5).

46. On blooding, see Berry, *Shakespeare and the Hunt*, 39–41, 89–90.

47. Gascoigne's translation of Bouchet's "Complainte" is Gascoigne, *Noble Arte*, 136–40. The reference of Antony's "lethe" is clear enough: the venous blood of the dead Caesar. But its sense is obscure. It may simply adapt the common understanding of Lethe as a river in Hades that the dead must cross; this usually connotes forgetting, but could conceivably connote death itself, particularly if we heed the conjecture of the *OED* (s.v. "Lethe," n. 2) that it carries the charge of the Latin *letum* (sometimes spelled *lethum*)—meaning "death." Perhaps so, but the Lethe of Hades slackens the metaphorical economy that otherwise governs Antony's attempt to make us behold Caesar the hunted hart. Alert to the problem, Edward Capell proposed that "lethe" was a term-of-art "us'd by hunters, to signify the blood shed by a deer at its fall" (William Shakespeare, *A New Variorum Edition of Shakespeare: The Tragedy of Julius Caesar*, ed. H. H. Furness [Philadelphia, 1913], 155). This usage sounds plausible; although I can find no evidence to support it, note that the Middle English verb "letheren" designates the act of becoming "covered (with blood or sweat)" (Hans Kurath, Sherman M. Kuhn, and Robert E. Lewis, *Middle English Dictionary* [Ann Arbor, MI, 1952–2001], s.v. "letheren," v).

48. *OED*, s.v. "havoc," n. 1, v. 1; Roger B. Manning, *Hunters and Poachers: A Social and Cultural History of Unlawful Hunting in England, 1485–1640* (Oxford, 1993), 47–49, 139–40, 161–62, 210, 215; Adrian Poole, "Dogs, War and Loyalty in Shakespeare," *Shakespearean International Yearbook* 11 (2011): 92–94. For comparable Shakespearean usages, see *Hamlet*, 5.2.369; *Coriolanus*, ed. Peter Holland (London, 2013), 3.1.276–77.

49. On *Julius Caesar* and ideals of *Romanitas*, see Miola, *Shakespeare's Rome*, 76–115; Warren Chernaik, *The Myth of Rome in Shakespeare and His Contemporaries* (Cambridge, UK, 2011), 79–92. On Plutarch's dissatisfaction with these ideals (and its impact on Shakespeare), see Burrow, *Shakespeare and Classical Antiquity*, 202–39.

50. See, e.g., Cicero, *De officiis*, 1.104, 3.68; Cicero, *Tusculan Disputations*, 2.18.40–41.

51. Cicero, *De officiis*, 1.11–16, 1.21–22, 1.93–151, 3.43; also Cicero, *Tusculan Disputations*, 2.58–59. On the centrality of the *De officiis* to the humanist project, see Grafton and Jardine, *Humanism to the Humanities*, 2–3, 19–23; Lawrence Manley, *Convention, 1500–1750* (Cambridge, MA, 1980), 106–33; Howard Jones, *Master Tully: Cicero in Tudor England* (Nieuwkoop, Netherlands, 1998), esp. 42–46, 132–42; James Hankins, *Virtue Politics: Soulcraft and Statecraft in Renaissance Italy* (Cambridge, MA, 2019), 41–48. On *personae* and Ciceronian moral philosophy, see Timothy J. Reiss, *Mirages of the Selfe: Patterns of Personhood in Ancient and Early Modern Europe* (Stanford, CA, 2003), 120–38. On modes of obtaining self-knowledge, see Eliza Gregory Wilkins, *"Know Thyself" in Greek and Latin Literature* (Chicago, 1917), 78–88. See further Rolf Soellner, *Shakespeare's Patterns of Self-Knowledge* ([Columbus, OH], 1972), esp. 3–40.

52. On Shakespeare and the *De officiis*, see Baldwin, *William Shakspere's Small Latine and Lesse Greeke*, 2:578–616; Lewis, *Hamlet and the Vision of Darkness*, 19–34; Geoffrey Miles, *Shakespeare and the Constant Romans* (Oxford, 1996), 18–37.

53. Cf. the way in which Ulysses maneuvers Achilles into the field in *Troilus and Cressida*, 3.3.116–21.

54. For Cicero on constancy, see *De officiis*, 1.120–21, 125–26.

55. Cicero, *De officiis*, 1.107. As Cicero explains at 1.101, reason governs appetite, and is the faculty that determines how we should and should not behave.

56. On rhetoric and the play's account of political ideology, see David Colclough, "Talking to the Animals: Persuasion, Counsel and Their Discontents in *Julius Caesar*," in *Shakespeare and Early Modern Political Thought*, ed. David Armitage, Conal Condren, and Andrew Fitzmaurice (Cambridge, UK, 2009), 217–33; Markku Peltonen, "Popularity and the Art of Rhetoric: *Julius Caesar* in Context," in *Shakespeare and the Politics of Commoners: Digesting the New Social History*, ed. Chris Fitter (Oxford, 2017), 163–79.

57. Puttenham, *The Art of English Poesy*, 259 (3.16); see also Scott, *Model of Poesy*, 67. For Shakespeare's standard approach to Caesar, see *Richard III*, 3.1.84–88; *Love's Labour's Lost*, ed. H. R. Woudhuysen (London, 1998), 4.1.68–70; *Henry IV, Part 2*, 2.2.123–24, 4.2.41–42; *As You Like It*, 5.2.30–31. Also cf. *Cymbeline*, ed. Valerie Wayne (London, 2017), 3.1.24; and, for Caesar the conqueror, *Henry V*, 5.0.26–28. Thomas Kyd, *Cornelia*, in *Robert Garnier in Elizabethan England: Mary Sidney Herbert's Antonius and Thomas Kyd's Cornelia*, ed. and trans. Marie-Alice Belle and Line Cottegnies (Cambridge, UK, 2017), 250 (4.2.147, 149). On the proverbiality of *veni, vidi, vici*, see Morris Palmer Tilley, *A Dictionary of Proverbs in England in the Sixteenth and Seventeenth Centuries* (Ann Arbor, MI, 1950), 112 (C540). Plutarch's text is Bullough, *Narrative and Dramatic Sources*, 5:81. On Shakespeare's unusual depiction of Caesar in *Julius Caesar*, see Bushnell, *Tragedies of Tyrants*, 143–53; Mortimer, *Medieval and Early Modern Portrayals*, 608–14; Pasquale Toscano, "Pity, Singular Disability, and the Makings of Shakespearean Tragedy in *Julius Caesar*," *SEL: Studies*

in English Literature, 1500–1800 61 (2021): 203–40. For another instance of Shakespeare transposing Lucan's Pompey onto his own Caesar, see Jones, *The Origins of Shakespeare*, 274–75.

58. Brutus's soliloquy telescopes the discussion between Suffolk, York, the Cardinal, and Queen Margaret in *Henry VI, Part 2*, 3.1.223–80, where they justify to themselves their determination that Gloucester must die.

59. Aristotle, *Nicomachean Ethics*, 1059b (on the inadequacy of honor as a measure of virtuous living), 1147a (on the unsuitability of histrionic metaphors for virtuous living).

60. Cf. Milton, *Paradise Regained*, 4.300, 308, in *Complete Shorter Poems*, ed. Carey, 497, where Milton echoes Cicero (*De finibus*, 3.1) to imagine the "Stoic" employing "subtle shifts conviction to evade."

61. For the *Praise of Folly* on Stoic self-deceit, see Erasmus, *Collected Works*, ed. Mynors et al., 27:90, 97, 104. See further Jill Kraye, "Moral Philosophy," in *Cambridge History of Renaissance Philosophy*, ed. Schmitt et al., 301–86, here 360–74; Christopher Brooke, *Philosophic Pride: Stoicism and Political Thought from Lipsius to Rousseau* (Princeton, NJ, 2012). On the performative character of Brutus's Stoicism, see Paul A. Cantor, *Shakespeare's Roman Trilogy: The Twilight of the Ancient World* (Chicago, 2017), 43–45.

62. Note that although Plutarch admits the possibility that Strato helped Brutus kill himself, his own view is that Brutus acted alone (Bullough, *Narrative and Dramatic Sources*, 5:131).

63. Erasmus, *Praise of Folly*, in *Collected Works*, ed. Mynors et al., 27:98–99. On Holbein's marginal illustration, see Erika Betty Goodman Michael, "The Drawings by Hans Holbein the Younger for Erasmus' *Praise of Folly*" (PhD diss., University of Washington, 1981), 71, 222–29; Yona Pinson, *The Fools' Journey: A Myth of Obsession in Northern Renaissance Art* (Turnhout, Belgium, 2008), 13–17.

64. Plutarch, "Brutus," in Bullough, *Narrative and Dramatic Sources*, 5:122.

Chapter 3: Things, Things, Things

1. Bill Brown, "Thing Theory," in *Things*, ed. Bill Brown (Chicago, 2004), 1–22; Bill Brown, *Other Things* (Chicago, 2017), esp. 17–48. See further Martin Heidegger, "The Thing," in *Poetry, Language, Thought*, ed. and trans. Albert Hofstadter (New York, 1971), 161–85.

2. On *Hamlet* and "things," see Lewis, *Hamlet and the Vision of Darkness*, 38–39. On generic-deictic "your," see Kathleen M. Wales, "Generic 'Your' and Jacobean Drama: The Rise and Fall of a Pronominal Usage," *English Studies* 66 (1985): 7–24. On the philosophy shared between Hamlet and Horatio, cf. Andrew Hui, "Horatio's Philosophy in *Hamlet*," *Renaissance Drama* 41 (2013): 151–71. I do not believe that the folio text of *Hamlet* is Shakespeare's (or anyone else's) "revision" of the second quarto; the arguments are complicated and often arcane, but see Lewis, *Hamlet and the Vision of Darkness*, xvii–xix.

3. William Empson, *Some Versions of Pastoral* (New York, 1974), 5.

4. On *enargeia*, see Lewis, *Hamlet and the Vision of Darkness*, 224–26; Heinrich F. Plett, *Enargeia in Classical Antiquity and the Early Modern Age: The Aesthetics of Evidence* (Leiden, 2012); chapter 7 below, notes 31–37. The more usual sort of

theatrical ghost is memorably described in the "Induction" to *A Warning for Fair Women*: after the discovery of some crime or other, "a filthie whining ghost / Lapt in some fowle sheet, or a leather pelch, / Comes skreaming like a pigge halfe stickt, / And cries, *Vindicta*, revenge, revenge" (*Warning for Fair Women*, ed. Cannon, 98). On the dramatically innovative qualities of Shakespeare's Ghost, see Lewis, *Hamlet and the Vision of Darkness*, 147–48; E. Pearlman, "Shakespeare at Work: The Invention of the Ghost," in *Hamlet: New Critical Essays*, ed. Arthur F. Kinney (New York, 2002), 71–84. On the opening scene of the play more generally, see Frank Kermode, *Shakespeare's Language* (London, 2000), 97–100.

5. Cf. Cassius's assertion that the prodigies preceding the killing of Caesar were "strange eruptions" (*Julius Caesar*, 1.3.78).

6. Armado writes Jaquenetta: "*Thus dost thou hear the Nemean lion roar / 'Gainst thee, thou lamb, that standest as his prey. / Submissive fall his princely feet before, / And from forage will incline to play*" (*Love's Labour's Lost*, 4.1.87–90).

7. Of the huge literature on early modern ghosts, see Keith Thomas, *Religion and the Decline of Magic: Studies in Popular Beliefs in Sixteenth- and Seventeenth-Century England* (London, 1971), 701–34; Peter Marshall, *Beliefs and the Dead in Reformation England* (Oxford, 2002), 232–64; Stuart Clark, *Vanities of the Eye: Vision in Early Modern European Culture* (Oxford, 2007), 204–35; Pierre Kapitaniak, *Spectres, ombres et fantômes. Discours et représentations dramatiques en Angleterre, 1576-1642* (Paris, 2008), 41–150; Euan Cameron, "Angels, Demons, and Everything in Between: Spiritual Beings in Early Modern Europe," in *Angels of Light?: Sanctity and the Discernment of Spirits in the Early Modern Period*, ed. Clare Copeland and Jan Machielsen (Leiden, 2013), 17–52. Of the no less sizeable literature on ghosts and the Ghost, see Lewis, *Hamlet and the Vision of Darkness*, 206–14; Kapitaniak, *Spectres, ombres et fantômes*, 610–80; Stephen Greenblatt, *Hamlet in Purgatory* (Princeton, NJ, 2001). On Purgatory, see Jacques Le Goff, *The Birth of Purgatory*, trans. Arthur Goldhammer (Chicago, 1984), esp. 79–82, 177–81, 243–44, 293–94; Jean-Claude Schmitt, *Ghosts in the Middle Ages: The Living and the Dead in Medieval Society*, trans. Teresa Lavender Fagan (Chicago, 1998). On Scot's insistence that ghosts are natural rather than supernatural phenomena, see Stuart Clark, *Thinking with Demons: The Idea of Witchcraft in Early Modern Europe* (Oxford, 1999), 211–12, 249–50; Philip C. Almond, *England's First Demonologist: Reginald Scot and the "Discoverie of Witchcraft"* (London, 2011), esp. 177–86. On the ability of ghosts to make themselves visible to one person and not another, see Ludwig Lavater, *Of Ghostes and Spirites Walking by Nyght (1572)*, ed. John Dover Wilson and May Yardley (Oxford, 1929), 89–90 (1.19); Reginald Scot, *The Discoverie of Witchcraft* (London, 1584), 535. Lady Macbeth's phrase is *Macbeth*, 1.5.49.

8. Peter McCullough, "Christmas at Elsinore," *Essays in Criticism* 58 (2008): 311, 313. See also Roland Mushat Frye, *The Renaissance Hamlet: Issues and Responses in 1600* (Princeton, NJ, 1984), 14–28.

9. John Gee, *New Shreds Out of the Old Snare* (London, 1624), 20.

10. Lewis, *Hamlet and the Vision of Darkness*, 75–78, 124–26.

11. Ibid., 214–19.

12. W. W. Greg, "Hamlet's Hallucination," *Modern Language Review* 12 (1917): 393–421; John Dover Wilson, *What Happens in Hamlet?*, 3rd ed. (Cambridge, UK, 1951), chap. 1 and *passim*; Stanley Cavell, *Disowning Knowledge in Seven Plays of*

Shakespeare, 2nd ed. (Cambridge, UK, 2003), 179–91. See further Kerrigan, *Revenge Tragedy*, 78–79; Lewis, *Hamlet and the Vision of Darkness*, 227–30; Gabriel Josipovici, *Hamlet: Fold on Fold* (New Haven, CT, 2016), 143–45.

13. See, e.g., Harry Levin, *The Question of Hamlet* (London, 1959), 3; A. D. Nuttall, *Shakespeare the Thinker* (New Haven, CT, 2007), 200–201.

14. Lewis, *Hamlet and the Vision of Darkness*, 219–26; Rhodri Lewis, "Shakespeare's Clouds and the Image Made by Chance," *Essays in Criticism* 62 (2012): 1–24; H. W. Janson, "The 'Image Made by Chance' in Renaissance Thought," in *De Artibus Opuscula XL: Essays in Honor of Erwin Panofsky*, 2 vols., ed. Millard Meiss (New York, 1961), 1:254–66. See further Hubert Damisch, *Théorie du nuage: Pour une histoire de la peinture* (Paris, 1972), chap. 1; E. H. Gombrich, *Art and Illusion: A Study in the Psychology of Pictorial Representation*, 6th ed. (London, 2002), 154–69.

15. On *Hamlet* as a rejection of mimetic mirroring, see Pauline Kiernan, *Shakespeare's Theory of Drama* (Cambridge, UK, 1996), 116–26; Alison Thorne, *Vision and Rhetoric in Shakespeare: Looking through Language* (Basingstoke, UK, 2002), 121–26. On the inescapability of verbal artifice within the play, see Richard A. Lanham, *The Motives of Eloquence: Literary Rhetoric in the Renaissance* (New Haven, CT, 1976), 129–43.

16. William Shakespeare, *Hamlet: The Texts of 1603 and 1623*, ed. Ann Taylor and Neil Thompson (London, 2006), 92 (7.110). See David Scott Kastan, *A Will to Believe: Shakespeare and Religion* (Oxford, 2014), 136–39; Margreta de Grazia, "Soliloquies and Wages in the Age of Emergent Consciousness," *Textual Practice* 9 (1995): 73–75.

17. *OED*, s.v. "question," n. 2a; Wilson, *Art of Rhetoric*, 45–46 (bk. 1). See Skinner, *Forensic Shakespeare*, 21–25, 55–58; Burrow, *Shakespeare and Classical Antiquity*, 42. On arguing both sides of the question more generally, see Quentin Skinner, "Moral Ambiguity and the Renaissance Art of Eloquence," *Essays in Criticism* 44 (1994): 267–91. My discussion of the fourth soliloquy draws from Lewis, *Hamlet and the Vision of Darkness*, 266–79.

18. There are too many competing interpretations to précis here, but see the overview in Shakespeare, *Hamlet*, ed. Jenkins, 484–89. For more recent engagements with the soliloquy, see Margreta de Grazia, *"Hamlet" without Hamlet* (Cambridge, UK, 2007), 199–201; Douglas Bruster, *To Be or Not to Be* (London, 2007).

19. On the soliloquies as self-address, see James Hirsh, *Shakespeare and the History of Soliloquies* (Madison, NJ, 2003), chaps. 5 and 6 (though note Hirsh's belief that the fourth soliloquy is "feigned"); Brian Cummings, *Mortal Thoughts: Religion, Secularity and Identity in Shakespeare and Early Modern Culture* (Oxford, 2013), 170–75.

20. Aristotle, *On Interpretation*, 16b19–25. On "to be, or not to be" and the history of logic, see further Frye, *Renaissance Hamlet*, 188–89; Leon Howard, *The Logic of Hamlet's Soliloquies* (Lone Pine, CA, 1964), esp. 17–22.

21. Aristotle, *On Interpretation*, 16a9–18.

22. Cicero, *Tusculan Disputations*, 1.13–14, in *Those Fyve Questions, Which Marke Tullye Cicero, Disputed in his Manor of Tusculanum*, trans. John Dolman (London, 1561), sig. B7v.

23. *Doctor Faustus*, 1.12 (i.e., 1.1.12), in Marlowe, *Complete Works*, 2:4 (I have emended the garbled "*Oncaymaeon*"). Sextus Empiricus, *Against the Logicians*, ed. and trans. Richard Bett (Cambridge, UK, 2005), 15–16 (1.65–67).

E.A.J. Honigmann ("To Be or Not to Be," in *In Arden: Editing Shakespeare. Essays in Honour of Richard Proudfoot*, ed. Gordon McMullan and Ann Thompson [London, 2003], 209–10) suggests that Hamlet enters reading the *Tusculan Disputations*; Vanessa Lim (" 'To Be or Not to Be': Hamlet's Humanistic *Quaestio*," *Review of English Studies* 70 [2019]: 640–58) suggests that Hamlet's personal commonplace book is a more likely candidate, and that he is looking up entries under the heading for "death."

24. Sidney, *Miscellaneous Prose*, 83. On black as the academic color, see Barbara Everett, *Young Hamlet: Essays on Shakespeare's Tragedies* (Oxford, 1989), 18.

25. Seneca, *Epistulae*, 85.5–9. On the commonplaces from which the thread of the soliloquy is spun, see Shakespeare, *Hamlet*, ed. Jenkins, 489–90; Jones, *The Origins of Shakespeare*, 11–12; Sayre N. Greenfield, "Quoting *Hamlet* in the Early Seventeenth Century," *Modern Philology* 105 (2008): 525–31; Peter Stallybrass, "Against Thinking," *PMLA* 122 (2007): 1581–82.

26. See, e.g., Boethius, *De consolatione*, 1.pr.3, 1.met.4, 1.met.5, 2.met.1, 2.pr.2. Cf. Horace, *Odes*, 1.35; Cicero, *De officiis*, 2.19; Seneca, *Epistulae*, 107.8. On this increasing prominence of this image for sixteenth-century writers and visual artists, see Frederick Kiefer, *Fortune and Elizabethan Tragedy* (San Marino, CA, 1983), 204–17; Florence Buttay-Jutier, *Fortuna: Usages politiques d'une allégorie morale à la renaissance* (Paris, 2008), 87–162.

27. Cicero, *Those Fyve Questions*, trans. Dolman, sig. G6r–v (*Tusculan Disputations*, 1.97–98). For the original of Socrates's death speech, see Plato, *Apology*, 40c–41d. Seneca, *Phaedra*, 93; *Edward II*, 23.65–66 (i.e., 5.6.65–66) in Marlowe, *Complete Works*, 3:87. See further Baldwin, *Small Latine & Lesse Greek*, 2:601–10; Miles, *Shakespeare and the Constant Romans*, 20–27.

28. Aristotle, *Poetics*, 1460b.

29. Aristotle, *Sophistical Refutations*, 165b24–169b17 (here 169b1–2). Another of Aristotle's instances of paralogism, which makes an appearance in *Hamlet* (5.1.134) and which will play a central role in *Macbeth*, is "equivocation." For the warning about style in representing *ethos* and *dianoia*, see *Poetics*, 1460b (translation from *Ancient Literary Criticism*, ed. Russell and Winterbottom, 126). For Shakespeare's interest in the dramatic usefulness of the logical tradition, see Katrin Ettenhuber, *The Logical Renaissance: Literature, Cognition, and Argument, 1479–1630* (Oxford, 2023), chap. 6.

30. Zachary Lesser, *Hamlet After Q1: An Uncanny History of the Shakespearean Text* (Philadelphia, 2015), 195–206.

31. Aristotle, *Poetics*, 1455a, 1460a (translation from *Ancient Literary Criticism*, ed. Russell and Winterbottom, 126). See the illuminating discussion in Cave, *Recognitions*, 39–43, 75–77, 282–92.

32. Hutson, *Invention of Suspicion*, esp. 306–12; Hutson, *Circumstantial Shakespeare*, chap. 1. See also Benedict Robinson, *Passion's Fictions from Shakespeare to Richardson: Literature and the Sciences of the Soul and Mind* (Oxford, 2021), 222–25.

33. On Claudius's soliloquy, see Lewis, *Hamlet and the Vision of Darkness*, 106–11; Martin Dodsworth, *Hamlet Closely Observed* (London, 1985), 178–87; Ramie Targoff, "The Performance of Prayer: Sincerity and Theatricality in Early Modern England," *Representations* 60 (1997): 49–69, esp. 49–50, 61–65.

34. George Herbert, "Prayer (I)," in *The English Poems*, ed. Helen Wilcox (Cambridge, UK, 2007), 178 (1.3).

35. On the play's patterns of doubling, see Frank Kermode, *Forms of Attention: Botticelli and Hamlet* (Chicago, 1985), 33–64.

36. Cf. Niccolò Machiavelli, *Machiavelli's The Prince: An Elizabethan Translation*, ed. Hardin Craig (Chapel Hill, NC, 1944), 115 (chap. 25). See further Pocock, *Machiavellian Moment*, 36–44.

37. On Hamlet's problems with the memory of his father, see Lewis, *Hamlet and the Vision of Darkness*, chap. 3. For a reassertion of the line that Hamlet's difficulties here arise from a collision between the values of his humanist education and the filial imperative to vengeance, see Judith Owens, *Emotional Settings in Early Modern Pedagogical Culture* (Cham, 2020), chaps. 6 and 7.

38. *2 Tamburlaine*, in Marlowe, *Complete Works*, 5:129–30 (4.1.148–60). Compare similar formulations in ibid., 5:41, 52 (*1 Tamburlaine*, 3.3.44; 4.2.32); 5:91, 104, 135, 137, 145 (*2 Tamburlaine*, 1.3.60–64, 2.4.80; 4.3.24; 4.3.99; 5.1.185).

39. Francis Bacon, *Advancement of Learning*, in *The Oxford Francis Bacon*, eds. Michael Kiernan, Graham Rees, Alan Stewart, Maria Wakely, et al., 15 vols. (Oxford, 1996–), 4:22.

40. Snyder, *Comic Matrix*, 91.

41. This paragraph tries to condense what seem to me the most salient features of Dasein as they are developed across the nearly four hundred closely argued pages of Martin Heidegger, *Being and Time: A Translation of Sein und Zeit*, trans. Joan Stambaugh (Albany, NY, 1996). For a suggestive reading of *Sein und Zeit* as a "tragic" work ("affirming life as it is revealed against the horizon of death") see Jahan Ramazani, "Heidegger and the Theory of Tragedy," *The Centennial Review* 32 (1988): 103–29. On the possible importance of *Hamlet* to Heidegger, see Andrew Cutrofello, *All for Nothing: Hamlet's Negativity* (Cambridge, MA, 2014), 205–25.

42. Heidegger, *Being and Time*, 152 (1.5; 162).

Chapter 4: Being, Wrought

1. Ovid, *Amores*, 1.9.1. Cf., e.g., Petrarch, *Canzoniere*, ed. Musa, 116–18 (21); Edmund Spenser, *Amoretti*, 57, in *The Yale Edition of the Shorter Poems of Edmund Spenser*, ed. William A. Oram (New Haven, CT, 1989), 634; John Donne, "Love's War," in *The Complete Poems of John Donne*, ed. Robin Robbins (London, 2010), 320–25. In a different key, see also the back-and-forth between Helena and Parolles in *All's Well That Ends Well*, ed. Suzanne Gossett and Helen Wilcox (London, 2019), 1.1.110–63: "Is there no military policy how virgins might blow up men?"

2. "Preface" to Dryden's *Troilus and Cressida, or Truth Found Too Late* [1679], in *William Shakespeare: The Critical Heritage*, ed. Vickers, 1:215.

3. On beginning in medias res, see Horace, *Ars poetica*, 147–50. Of those proposing to write tragedies on historical subjects, Sidney's *Defence* insists that they "must not (as Horace saith) begin *ab ovo*, but they must come to the principal point of that one action which they will represent" (Sidney, *Miscellaneous Prose*, 114).

4. See Jessica Wolfe, *Homer and the Question of Strife from Erasmus to Hobbes* (Toronto, 2015), 299–304. On the play's ironic subversions more generally, see

Rosalie L. Colie, *Shakespeare's Living Art* (Princeton, NJ, 1974), 317–50. *Ludovico Ariosto's Orlando Furioso: Translated into English Heroical Verse by Sir John Harington (1591)*, ed. Robert McNulty (Oxford, 1972), 403 (35.24). On Ariosto, see Colin Burrow, *Epic Romance: Homer to Milton* (Oxford, 1993), chap. 4. On Aeneas, see Craig Kallendorf, *The Other Virgil: "Pessimistic" Readings of the Aeneid in Early Modern Culture* (Oxford, 2007).

5. Edmund Spenser, *The Faerie Queene*, ed. A. C. Hamilton et al. (London, 2001), 249 (2.10.9–13). See further James, *Shakespeare's Troy*, 85–118; Arthur B. Ferguson, *Utter Antiquity: Perceptions of Prehistory in Renaissance England* (Durham, NC, 1993); Laura Ashe, "Holinshed and Mythic History," in *The Oxford Handbook of Holinshed's Chronicles*, ed. Felicity Heal, Ian Archer, and Paulina Kewes (Oxford, 2013), 153–70.

6. Shakespeare, *Troilus and Cressida*, ed. Bevington, 375–97; Bullough, *Narrative and Dramatic Sources*, 6:83–221; Robert Kimbrough, *Shakespeare's Troilus & Cressida and Its Setting* (Cambridge, MA, 1964), chap. 3.

7. Note that the play is likely to have been written for an audience of lawyers and law students. See William R. Elton, *Shakespeare's Troilus and Cressida and the Inns of Court Revels* (Aldershot, UK, 2000), esp. 76–116. On the play's engagement with ideals of "constancy" more generally, see John Kerrigan, *Shakespeare's Binding Language* (Oxford, 2016), 256–89.

8. In addition to Elton's monograph, the following paragraphs draw on Kimbrough, *Shakespeare's Troilus & Cressida*, 138–49; Colie, *Shakespeare's Living Art*, 320–22; William R. Elton, "Shakespeare's Ulysses and the Problem of Value," *Shakespeare Studies* 2 (1966): 95–111; Robert Grudin, "The Soul of State: Ulyssean Irony in *Troilus and Cressida*," *Anglia* 93 (1975): 55–69; David Norbrook, "Rhetoric, Ideology, and the Elizabethan World Picture," in *Renaissance Rhetoric*, ed. Peter Mack (Basingstoke, UK, 1994), 140–64.

9. Cicero, *De re publica*, 6.17–18. Shakespeare also leans on the astronomy of the *Dream of Scipio* in *The Merchant of Venice*, ed. John Drakakis (London, 2010), 5.1.60–65. See further Baldwin, *Small Latine & Lesse Greeke*, 2:599–600. On the Chain of Being, see Elyot, *Boke*, ed. Rude, 16–18 (1.1); Blair, *Theater of Nature*, 126–42; Edward P. Mahoney, "Metaphysical Foundations of the Hierarchy of Being According to Some Late Medieval and Renaissance Philosophers," in *Philosophies of Existence, Ancient and Medieval*, ed. Parviz Morewedge (New York, 1982), 165–257; Marion L. Kuntz and Paul G. Kuntz, *Jacob's Ladder and the Tree of Life: Concepts of Hierarchy and the Great Chain of Being* (New York, 1987), esp. section 4. On the status of the sun as a "planet" (the preeminent one at that), see Edward Grant, *Planets, Stars, and Orbs: The Medieval Cosmos, 1200–1687* (Cambridge, UK, 1994), 226–27, 231–33, 311, 413–19, and esp. 451–59.

10. On justice as the rational midpoint between privation and excess, see Aristotle, *Nicomachean Ethics*, 1129a–1138b, esp. 1133b–1134a. On the intermediate quality of virtue, see also, e.g., Cicero, *De officiis*, 1.89, 1.130, 1.140, 2.59–60.

11. Aristotle, *Nicomachean Ethics*, 1095a. For useful discussions of humanist moral philosophy and the place of politics within it, see Bevington's extensive notes in the Arden Third Series edition of *Troilus*; Kraye, "Moral Philosophy"; Rolf Soellner, "Prudence and the Price of Helen: The Debate of the Trojans in *Troilus and Cressida*," *Shakespeare Quarterly* 20 (1969): 255–63; Ian Maclean, *The Renaissance*

Notion of Woman: A Study of the Fortunes of Scholasticism and Medical Science in European Intellectual Life (Cambridge, UK, 1980), 48–67; Anna Becker, *Gendering the Renaissance Commonwealth* (Cambridge, UK, 2020), chap. 1. For some recent commentary, see Burrow, *Shakespeare and Classical Antiquity*, 25–27; de Grazia, *Four Shakespearean Period Pieces*, 23–29. On litotes, see Puttenham, *The Art of English Poesy*, 269 (3.17); Richard Sherry, *A Treatise of Schemes & Tropes* (London, 1550), sig. D7r; Baldwin, *Small Latine & Lesse Greeke*, 2:157–58.

12. Juvenal, *Satires*, 1.30–32. On *Troilus and Cressida* and satire, see Alvin Kernan, *The Cankered Muse: Satire of the English Renaissance* (New Haven, CT, 1959), 194–98; Hester Lees-Jeffries, "Tragedy and the Satiric Voice," in *The Oxford Handbook of Shakespearean Tragedy*, ed. Neill and Schalkwyk, 250–66. Satire is almost as resistant to settled definition as tragedy; for intelligent ways into the subject, see Dustin Griffin, *Satire: A Critical Reintroduction* (Lexington, KY, 1994) and Jonathan Greenberg, *The Cambridge Introduction to Satire* (Cambridge, UK, 2019). On early modern satire, see (in addition to Kernan), James S. Baumlin, "The Generic Contexts of Elizabethan Satire," in *Renaissance Genres*, ed. Barbara Lewalski (Cambridge, MA, 1986), 444–67; Angela J. Wheeler, *English Verse Satire from Donne to Dryden* (Heidelberg, 1992). On Cressida, see the excellent reading in Holly A. Crocker, *The Matter of Virtue: Women's Ethical Action from Chaucer to Shakespeare* (Philadelphia, 2019), 99–107. For Thersites's starting point, see Horace, *Satires*, 1.3.107–8: "Nam fuit ante Helenam cunnus taeterrima belli / causa" ("even before Helen's time, cunts were the cause of the most terrible wars"). On *contaminatio*, see chapter 2, note 13 above.

13. Erasmus, *Adagia* (*Thersitae facies*, "The look of Thersites"), in *Collected Works*, ed. Mynors et al., 36:48 (4.3.80). Sidney, *Defence*, in *Miscellaneous Prose*, 95. On *Troilus and Cressida* as an intervention in the so-called "poetomachia," see James P. Bednarz, *Shakespeare and the Poets' War* (New York, 2001), 19–52.

14. Sidney, *Defence*, in *Miscellaneous Prose*, 96.

15. See chapter 1, note 87.

16. Burrow, *Shakespeare and Classical Antiquity*, 155–59.

17. On memory, recollection, and the *ars memoriae*, see Lewis, *Hamlet and the Vision of Darkness*, 134–38, 151–62.

18. "The process or faculty of reasoning; reasoned argument or thought; reason, rationality" (*OED*, s.v. "reason," n. 1). See further Lewis, *Hamlet and the Vision of Darkness*, 130–35. Shakespeare, *Hamlet*, 1.2.150–51. Cf. Desdemona's "If e'er my will did trespass 'gainst his love / Either in discourse of thought or actual deed" (*Othello*, 4.2.154–55).

19. The myth of Arachne is related in Ovid, *Metamorphoses*, 6.1–145; for Ariadne (who betrayed her father and her country by providing the thread that allowed Theseus to escape the Labyrinth, and who was betrayed by Theseus in her turn), see Ovid, *Heroides*, 10. See further Elizabeth Freund, "'Ariachne's Broken Woof': The Rhetoric of Citation in *Troilus and Cressida*," in *Shakespeare and the Question of Theory*, ed. Geoffrey Hartmann and Patricia Parker (New York, 1985), 19–35. On the central importance of "opinion" in the play, see Frank Kermode, "Opinion in *Troilus and Cressida*," *Critical Quarterly* 54 (2012): 88–102.

20. See *OED*, s.v. "Moor," n. 2; "Blackamoor / Moor," in Nandini Das, João Vincente Melo, Haig Z. Smith, and Lauren Woking, *Keywords of Identity, Race, and Human Mobility in Early Modern England* (Amsterdam, 2021), 40–50. Of the now

sizeable literature on *Othello* and race, see Ndiaye, *Scripts of Blackness*, 55–63; Mary Floyd-Wilson, *English Ethnicity and Race in Early Modern Drama* (Cambridge, UK, 2003), 132–60; Emily Bartels, *Speaking of the Moor, from Alcazar to Othello* (Philadelphia, 2008); Ian Smith, "Seeing Blackness: Reading Race in *Othello*," in *The Oxford Handbook of Shakespearean Tragedy*, ed. Neill and Schalkwyk, 405–20; Patricia Akhimie, *Shakespeare and the Cultivation of Difference: Race and Conduct in the Early Modern World* (London, 2018), 49–82; *The Cambridge Companion to Shakespeare and Race*, ed. Ayanna Thompson (Cambridge, UK, 2021), esp. the essays by Ambereen Dadabhoy, Carol Mejia LaPerle, Matthew Dimmock, and Adrian Lester. See also Ato Quayson, *Tragedy and Postcolonial Literature* (Cambridge, UK, 2021), 44–82.

21. Francis Bacon, "Of Simulation and Dissimulation," in *The Oxford Francis Bacon*, ed. Kiernan et al., 15:20–23. On strategies of deliberate "seeming," see further Perez Zagorin, *Ways of Lying: Dissimulation, Persecution, and Conformity in Early Modern Europe* (Cambridge, MA, 1990); Richard Tuck, *Philosophy and Government, 1572–1651* (Cambridge, UK, 1993), chap. 3.

22. Shakespeare, *Twelfth Night*, 3.1.139.

23. Diabolism is also the straw at which Othello clutches when trying to rationalize the existence of phenomena—in particular, Desdemona's apparent adultery—that he finds painful or otherwise disagreeable. See, e.g., 3.3.481, 4.1.6–8, 4.1.43, 4.1.239, 4.1.243, 5.2.283–84, 5.2.298–99. After the disgrace of his drunken brawl with Montano, Cassio finds the "devil" in the "invisible spirit of wine" (2.3.278–79; cf. 2.3.303–4).

24. Samuel Taylor Coleridge, *Coleridge's Criticism of Shakespeare: A Selection*, ed. R. A. Foakes (London, 1989), 113.

25. The best account of Iago's troubled selfhood is Joel B. Altman, *The Improbability of Othello: Rhetorical Anthropology and Shakespearean Selfhood* (Chicago, 2010), chap. 5 and *passim*. See also Janet Adelman, "Iago's Alter Ego: Race as Projection in *Othello*," *Shakespeare Quarterly* 48 (1997): 125–44. On the challenges of our relationship with Iago, see Marjorie Garber, "'Vassal Actors': The Role of the Audience in Shakespearean Tragedy," *Renaissance Drama* 9 (1978): 71–89, esp. 79–80.

26. Cicero, *De officiis*, 3.60–72.

27. See Skinner, *Forensic Shakespeare*, 69–73.

28. *OED*, s.v. "sign," n. 1e, 8.

29. On the deft rhetorical design of Othello's speech, see Skinner, *Forensic Shakespeare*, 117–24. On the costs and benefits accrued by Othello's rhetorical proficiency, see Catherine Nicholson, "*Othello* and the Geography of Persuasion," *English Literary Renaissance* 40 (2010): 56–87.

30. On the comedic features of the play, see Snyder, *Comic Matrix*, 70–90; Jones, *Scenic Form*, 117–51.

31. See Katharine Park, "The Organic Soul," in *The Cambridge History of Renaissance Philosophy*, ed. Charles B. Schmitt, Quentin Skinner, and Jill Kraye (Cambridge, UK, 1988), 464–84; Eckhard Kessler, "The Intellective Soul," in *The Cambridge History of Renaissance Philosophy*, ed. Charles B. Schmitt, Quentin Skinner, and Jill Kraye (Cambridge, UK, 1988), 485–534; Richard W. Serjeantson, "The Soul," in *The Oxford Handbook of Philosophy in Early Modern Europe*, ed. Desmond Clarke and Catherine Wilson (Oxford, 2011), 119–41. On human exceptionality, see Kraye, "Moral Philosophy," 306–16.

32. See Philip Hardie, *Rumour and Renown: Representations of Fama in Western Literature* (Cambridge, UK, 2012); Gianni Guastella, *Word of Mouth: Fama and Its Personifications in Art and Literature from Ancient Rome to the Middle Ages* (Oxford, 2017), esp. chaps. 7 and 8.

33. William Empson, *The Structure of Complex Words* (London, 1951), 218–49, here 228. *OED*, s.v. "honesty," 1a-c, 2, 3a, 3d. See further Jennifer Richards, *Rhetoric and Courtliness in Early Modern Literature* (Cambridge, UK, 2003), chaps. 1 and 4; Keith Thomas, *The Ends of Life: Roads to Fulfillment in Early Modern England* (Oxford, 2009), chap. 5; Phil Withington, "Honestas," in *Early Modern Theatricality*, ed. Henry S. Turner (Oxford, 2013), 516–33.

34. Anne Carson, *Eros the Bittersweet: An Essay* (Princeton, NJ, 1986), 69.

35. On Venus disarming Mars (just as Hercules was said to have been disarmed by Omphale), see Lucretius, *On the Nature of Things*, 1.29–40; William Shakespeare, *Venus and Adonis*, ll. 97–114, in *Shakespeare's Poems: Venus and Adonis, The Rape of Lucrece, and the Shorter Poems*, ed. Katherine Duncan-Jones and H. R. Woudhuysen (London, 2007), 141–43; Edgar Wind, *Pagan Mysteries in the Renaissance* (New Haven, CT, 1958), 84–88.

36. On love (or Love) emerging from Chaos, see Natali Conti, *Mythologiae*, ed. John Mulryan and Stephen Brown, 2 vols. (Tempe, AZ, 2006), 1:331 (4.14); Edmund Spenser, "An Hymne in Honour of Love," in *Shorter Poems*, ed. Oram et al., 694–95 (ll. 57–91). Terence, *Eunuchus*, 551–52. See further Baldwin, *Shakspere's Five-Act Structure*, 556–57; as Baldwin notes, this passage of Terence is reproduced in Nicholas Udall, *Flowers or Eloquent Phrases of the Latine Speach, Gathered out of all the Sixe Comoedies of Terence* (London, 1575), sig. H6r; Udall's work was first published in 1533, and frequently reprinted thereafter.

37. On the particular disgrace of cuckoldry in early modern England, see Thomas, *Ends of Life*, 166–68.

38. Webster, *The Duchess of Malfi*, 4.1.118, in *The Works of John Webster*, ed. Gunby, Carnegie, and Hammond, 1:538.

39. The Arden Third Series editor, E.A.J. Honigmann, gives these lines to Emilia on the basis that "for Desdemona to praise Lodovico at this point seems out of character" (291). This intervention is without textual or interpretative warrant. It is not discussed in Honigmann's *The Texts of Othello and Shakespearean Revision* (London, 1996).

40. Miola, *Shakespeare and Classical Tragedy*, 124–42; Perry, *Shakespeare and Senecan Tragedy*, 231–65. See further Rolf Soellner, "The Madness of Hercules and the Elizabethans," *Comparative Literature* 10 (1958): 309–23; Stephanie Moss, "Transformation and Degeneration: the Paracelsan / Galenic Body in *Othello*," in *Disease, Diagnosis, and Cure on the Early Modern Stage*, ed. Stephanie Moss and Kaara L. Peterson (Aldershot, UK, 2004), 151–70.

41. Seneca, *De ira*, 1.12.1–5.

42. Eliot, "Shakespeare and the Stoicism of Seneca," 130–31 (the emphasis is Eliot's). See further Christopher Ricks, *Along Heroic Lines* (Oxford, 2021), 84–105.

43. On *Othello* and intersectionality, see Smith, *This Is Shakespeare*, 218–19. See also Ndiaye, *Scripts of Blackness*, 57–63; Ania Loomba, *Shakespeare, Race, and Colonialism* (Oxford, 2002), 91–111.

44. See note 11 above.

45. See Carol Thomas Neely, "Women and Men in *Othello*," in *The Woman's Part: Feminist Criticism of Shakespeare*, ed. Carolyn Ruth Swift Lenz, Gayle Greene, and Carol Thomas Neely (Urbana, IL, 1980), 211–39.

46. Shakespeare, *Henry IV, Part 1*, 5.1.133–35. Ben Jonson, *Sejanus*, 1.327–29, in *The Cambridge Edition of the Works of Ben Jonson*, ed. Bevington et al., 2:253–54. On Shakespeare and the studiously Tacitean *Sejanus*, see John-Mark Philo, "Ben Jonson's *Sejanus* and Shakespeare's *Othello*: Two Plays Performed by the King's Men in 1603," *Shakespeare Survey* 75 (2022): 122–36.

Chapter 5: Beyond This Ignorant Present

1. This chapter draws from (and frequently adapts) Rhodri Lewis, "Polychronic *Macbeth*," *Modern Philology* 117 (2020): 323–46.

2. Jones, *Scenic Form*, 195.

3. Kermode, *Sense of an Ending*, 83–89. On *Macbeth* and the discourses of times and temporality, see, e.g., David Scott Kastan, *Shakespeare and the Shapes of Time* (Hanover, NH, 1982), 91–101; Luisa Guj, "*Macbeth* and the Seeds of Time," *Shakespeare Studies* 18 (1986): 175–88; Donald W. Foster, "Macbeth's War on Time," *English Literary Renaissance* 16 (1986): 319–42; Brian Richardson, "'Hours Dreadful and Things Strange': Inversions of Chronology and Causality in *Macbeth*," *Philological Quarterly* 68 (1989): 283–94; Tzachi Zamir, *Double Vision: Moral Philosophy and Shakespearean Drama* (Princeton, NJ, 2007), 92–111; Kristen Poole, *Supernatural Environments in Shakespeare's England* (Cambridge, UK, 2011), 156–67; Rebecca Bushnell, *Tragic Time in Drama, Films, and Video Games* (London, 2016), 12–21; Julián Jiménez Heffernan, "'Beyond This ignorant present': The Poverty of Historicism in *Macbeth*," *Palgrave Communications* 2 (2016): no. 16054, https://doi.org/10.1057/palcomms.2016.54.

4. *The Book of Common Prayer: The Texts of 1549, 1559, and 1662*, ed. Brian Cummings (Oxford, 2011), 82–83 (1549), 172 (1559). Cf., e.g., Genesis 3.19; Psalms 22.15; Ecclesiastes 3.20. See further Daniel Swift, *Shakespeare's Common Prayers: The Book of Common Prayer and the Elizabethan Age* (Oxford, 2012), 54–58, 161–89, 193–246; Hannibal Hamlin, *The Bible in Shakespeare* (Oxford, 2013), 271–304.

5. Pierre de La Primaudaye, *The Third Volume of the French Academie, Contayning a Notable Description of the Whole World, and of all the Principall Parts and Contents Thereof*, trans. Richard Dolman (London, 1601), 8–9 (chap. 2). The key discussion of why the distinction between temporality and eternity mattered to the early moderns remains Pocock, *Machiavellian Moment*, 3–80.

6. Macbeth's phrase may be an ironic appropriation of what Nicholas Ridley, like many Protestant polemicists, referred to derisively as "the doctrine of the last sillable, which is that transubstanciation is done by miracle in an instaunt, at the sounde of the last sillable (*um*) in this sentence, *Hoc est corpus meum*" (Nicholas Ridley, *A Brief Declaracion of the Lordes Supper* [Emden, 1555], sig. C7v).

7. *Hamlet*, 5.1.203–6. See further Tilley, *Dictionary*, A119; R. W. Dent, *Proverbial Language in English Drama Exclusive of Shakespeare, 1495–1616* (Berkeley and Los Angeles, 1984), E30, M253.

8. William Shakespeare, *A New Variorum Edition of Shakespeare: Macbeth*, ed. Howard Horace Furness (New York, 1963), 334.

9. In *Titus Andronicus* (4.2.20–24), Chiron half recognizes Horace's Ode 1.22 on account of its place in the humanistic curriculum. Cf., e.g., Shakespeare, *Love's Labour's Lost*, 4.2.101; *Timon of Athens*, ed. Anthony B. Dawson and Gretchen E. Minton (London, 2008), 1.2.28. To the best of my knowledge, the only sustained attempt to relate Horace to Shakespeare is Baldwin, *Small Latine & Lesse Greeke*, 2:497–525. But see Stuart Gillespie, *Shakespeare's Books* (London, 2001), 259–68; Jonathan Bate, *How the Classics Made Shakespeare* (Princeton, NJ, 2019), chap. 9. On Jonson, see Victoria Moul, *Jonson, Horace and the Classical Tradition* (Cambridge, UK, 2010).

10. Horace, *Odes*, 4.7. Translation, slightly altered, from Horace, *Odes and Epodes*, ed. and trans. Niall Rudd (Cambridge, MA, 2004), 239, 241. A. E. Housman called this ode "the most beautiful poem in ancient literature" (Grant Richards, *Housman, 1897–1936* [London, 1941], 289), but its fame seems to postdate the early modern period. Note that the *Odes* did not appear in printed English translation until five years after Shakespeare's death.

11. "Veris adventu, & aequa moriendi conditione proposita, invitat ad hilariter vivendum" (Horace, *Q. Horatius Flaccus, ex fide, atque auctoritate decem librorum manu scriptorum, opera*, ed. Denys Lambin [Lyon, 1561], 369). On the importance of this edition, see Baldwin, *Small Latine & Lesse Greeke*, 2:500–13.

12. For the origins of this conceit in Plutarch's *Parallel Lives*, see Bullough, *Narrative and Dramatic Sources*, 5:280.

13. Cf. *Lucrece*, ll. 302–434, esp. 412–13, where Tarquin (his desire enflamed by the sight of Lucrece's naked breasts) "like a foul usurper went about / From this fair throne to heave the owner out" (*Shakespeare's Poems*, ed. Duncan-Jones and Woudhuysen, 264–75). On the importance of Livy—whence Shakespeare derived the tale of Tarquin and Lucrece—to *Macbeth*, see John-Mark Philo, "Shakespeare's *Macbeth* and Livy's Legendary Rome," *Review of English Studies* 67 (2015): 250–74.

14. For this kind of Roman suicide, the *loci classici* are Seneca, *Epistles*, 70 and 77 (but cf. 24, where suicide is condemned as a whim), and Plutarch, *Life of Cato the Younger*, 67–72. Shakespeare, *Julius Caesar*, 5.5.45–51; *Antony and Cleopatra*, 4.14.73–142. For Plutarch, see Bullough, *Narrative and Dramatic Sources*, 5:131 (Brutus), 5:309–10 (Antony). See also Erasmus, *Praise of Folly*, in *Collected Works*, ed. Mynors et al., 27:105. On Shakespeare's wider critique of Roman suicide-doctrine, see Drew Daniel, *Joy of the Worm: Suicide and Pleasure in Early Modern English Literature* (Chicago, 2022), 61–93.

15. On Macbeth's "epicures," see Mary Floyd-Wilson, "English Epicures and Scottish Witches," *Shakespeare Quarterly* 57 (2006): 131–61; on premonitory birds, see Jerzy Linderski, "Cicero and Roman Divination" and "Watching the Birds," in *Roman Questions: Selected Papers, 1958–1993* (Stuttgart, 1994), 458–84 and 485–95.

16. Baldwin, *Small Latine & Lesse Greeke*, 2:517–19. Baldwin highlights Lambinus's elaboration of Horace's "vitae via" as Shakespeare's likely prompt. Also cf. Horace, *Odes*, 1.18.

17. Paul Hammond, "Macbeth and the Ages of Man," *Notes and Queries* 36 (1989): 332–33; cf. Horace, *Art of Poetry*, 166–68. On the ages of humankind—usually seven in number and notably riffed in Jaques's "all the world's a stage" speech—see John Erskine Hankins, *Backgrounds of Shakespeare's Thought* (Hamden, CT, 1978), 61–67; J. A. Burrow, *The Ages of Man: A Study in Medieval Writing and Thought* (Oxford, 1988), chaps. 1–2.

18. On Hercules, see Burrow, *Shakespeare and Classical Antiquity*, 189–90, and cf. Seneca, *Hercules Furens*, 1259–61. The literature on Seneca and *Macbeth* is large. See, e.g., Inga-Stina Ewbank, "The Fiend-Like Queen: A Note on *Macbeth* and Seneca's *Medea*," *Shakespeare Survey* 19 (1967): 82–94; Gordon Braden, "Senecan Tragedy and the Renaissance," *Illinois Classical Studies* 9 (1984): 277–92; Charles Martindale and Michelle Martindale, *Shakespeare and the Uses of Antiquity* (London, 1990), 15–19, 36–41, 177–78; Miola, *Shakespeare and Classical Tragedy*, 92–121; Yves Peyré, "'Confusion Now Hath Made His Masterpiece': Senecan Resonances in *Macbeth*," in *Shakespeare and the Classics*, ed. Charles Martindale and A. B. Taylor (Cambridge, UK, 2004), 141–55.

19. Horace, *Odes*, 2.7.21; Virgil, *Aeneid*, 6.714–15; Seneca, *Hercules Furens*, 1077–81. See Baldwin, *Small Latine & Lesse Greeke*, 2:471.

20. Orgel, "Poetics of Incomprehensibility."

21. See, e.g., the uses to which Horace is put in Jonson's prefatory remarks to Jonson, *Sejanus* (*The Cambridge Edition of the Works of Ben Jonson*, ed. Bevington et al., 2:213).

22. William Shakespeare, *Macbeth, A Tragœdy. With all the Alterations, Amendments, Additions, and New Songs*, [ed. William Davenant] (London, 1674), 61.

23. On *paradiastole*, see Quentin Skinner, *From Humanism to Hobbes: Studies in Rhetoric and Politics* (Cambridge, UK, 2018), 89–117. Although it is a commonplace that *paradiastole* is the figure through which vice is transformed into virtue (and vice versa), for a formulation (borrowed from 2 Corinthians 11:14) that seems peculiarly applicable to *Macbeth*, see Joannes Susenbrotus, *Epitome troporum ac schematum* (London, 1562), 46: through *paradiastole*, "Satan can be transformed into an angel of light" (*Satanas transfiguratur in Angelum luds*). Ovid, *Metamorphoses*, 11.723–26; Seneca, *Hercules Furens*, 1065–81.

24. Seneca, *Hercules Furens*, 1323–29; *Phaedra*, 725–28. See Martindale and Martindale, *Shakespeare and the Uses of Antiquity*, 17–19. Cf. Miola, *Shakespeare and Classical Tragedy*, 112–17; Burrow, *Shakespeare and Classical Antiquity*, 189–90.

25. On *ethopoeia*, see Aphthonius, *Progymnasmata*, 11, in *Progymnasmata*, ed. and trans. Kennedy, 116. See further Baldwin, *Small Latine & Lesse Greeke*, 2:193–94; Lynn Enterline, *Shakespeare's Schoolroom: Rhetoric, Discipline, Emotion* (Philadelphia, 2012), 126–28, 137–39.

26. At 4.1.82–83, he will similarly imagine himself "tak[ing] a bond of fate." Also cf. his "bond" at 3.2.50. See further Kerrigan, *Shakespeare's Binding Language*, 318–21.

27. On *arcana imperii*, see Tuck, *Philosophy and Government*, 31–136; Ernst H. Kantorowicz, "Mysteries of State: An Absolutist Concept and Its Late Mediaeval Origins," *Harvard Theological Review* 48 (1955): 65–91; Carlo Ginzburg, "High and Low: The Theme of Forbidden Knowledge in the Sixteenth and Seventeenth Centuries," *Past & Present* 73 (1976): 28–41; Alan T. Bradford, "Stuart Absolutism and the 'Utility' of Tacitus," *Huntington Library Quarterly* 46 (1983): 127–55.

28. Jones, *The Origins of Shakespeare*, 278–82. On the double sense of "shadow," see, e.g., Shakespeare, *Midsummer Night's Dream*, 5.1.210, 5.1.413. See further *OED*, s.v. "shadow," n. 6b.

29. "Hic humanae vitae mimus, qui nobis partes quas male agamus adsignat. Ille, qui in scaena latus incedit et haec resupinus . . ." (Seneca, *Epistles*, 80.7). As discussed

in Jones, *The Origins of Shakespeare*, 278–79, Erasmus's "Tragicus Rex" makes much of Seneca in this regard; see Erasmus, *Adages*, in *Collected Works*, ed. Mynors et al., 33:276 (2.5.78). On strutting, see Cooper, *Thesaurus*, s.v. "incedo." Cf. the "great stage of fools" of which Lear "preaches" to Gloucester (*King Lear*, 4.6.179).

30. Petrarch's Sonnet 294 adapts the same line of Horace to similar ends (Petrarch, *Canzoniere*, ed. Musa, 414).

31. On prophecy and the transcendence of historical time, see Pocock, *Machiavellian Moment*, 32–33, 43–49. Cf. Augustine's remarks on prophecy, foresight, and expectation in *Confessions*, 11.18–20. Spenser, *Faerie Queene*, ed. Hamilton et al., 346 (3.6.30); Timothy Bright, *A Treatise of Melancholie* (London, 1586), 34. See Hankins, *Backgrounds*, 34–38; Maryanne Cline Horowitz, *Seeds of Virtue and Knowledge* (Princeton, NJ, 1998), esp. 49–52; W. C. Curry, *Shakespeare's Philosophical Patterns* (Baton Rouge, 1937), 30–49. Also cf. Shakespeare, *King Lear*, 3.2.8; *Winter's Tale*, 4.4.484. Augustine, *On the Literal Meaning of Genesis*, 6.14.25–6.19.27 and *On the Trinity*, 3.8; Gerald P. Boersma, "The *Rationes Seminales* in Augustine's Theology of Creation," *Nova et Vetera* 18 (2020): 413–41. On Spenser, see further James Nohrnberg, *The Analogy of The Faerie Queene* (Princeton, NJ, 1976), esp. 534–68; Richard A. McCabe, *The Pillars of Eternity: Time and Providence in The Faerie Queene* (Dublin, 1989), 140–44.

32. In the words of a 1603 treatise on the plague, "the devil gathereth of the first seeds of nature, and applyeth them to some matter, and so can produce strange effects . . . but how farre he can proceede in nature it is hard to judge" (Henry Holland, *Spirituall Preservatives Against the Pestilence* [London, 1603], 61). Cf. Thomas Nashe, *Pierce Pennilesse*, in *The Works of Thomas Nashe*, ed. R. B. McKerrow and F. P. Wilson, 5 vols. (Oxford, 1966), 1:228.

33. Cf. the pre-Christian Soothsayer in *Antony and Cleopatra*, whose powers rest on his claim that "In nature's infinite book of secrecy / A little I can read" (Shakespeare, *Antony and Cleopatra*, 1.2.10–11).

34. For introductions to the *aevum*, see Kermode, *Sense of an Ending*, 69–74; Ernst H. Kantorowicz, *The King's Two Bodies: A Study in Mediaeval Political Theology* (Princeton, NJ, 1957), 274–83, 314–42; the essays by Henryk Anzulewicz, Pasquale Porro, Olivier Boulnois, Constantino Esposito, and Paolo Ponzio in *The Medieval Concept of Time: Studies on the Scholastic Debate and its Reception in Early Modern Philosophy*, ed. Pasquale Porro (Leiden, 2001).

35. Cicero, *De re publica*, 6.13.

36. John Case, *Ancilla philosophiae, seu epitome in octo libros Physicorum Aristotelis* (Frankfurt, 1600), 74. Quoted in translation here from Michael Edwards, *Time and the Science of the Soul in Early Modern Philosophy* (Leiden, 2013), 16.

37. D. P. Walker, "Eternity and the Afterlife," *Journal of the Warburg and Courtauld Institutes* 27 (1964): 245.

38. Dante Alighieri, *The Divine Comedy of Dante Alighieri*, ed. and trans. Robert M. Durlin et al., 3 vols. (Oxford, 1996–2011), 1:43 (3.7–8).

39. Kantorowicz, *King's Two Bodies*, 7. See also Henry Turner, *The Corporate Commonwealth: Pluralism and Political Fictions in England, 1516–1651* (Chicago, 2016), esp. 1–32; Paul Raffield, "Time, Equity, and the Artifice of English Law: Reflections on *The King's Two Bodies*," *Law, Culture, and the Humanities* 13 (2017): 36–45. On

Plowden (who, in his still unprinted manuscript work of 1567, "A Treatise of Succession," wrote a comprehensive account of the two bodies theory that was apparently unknown to Kantorowicz), see Alan Cromartie, *The Constitutionalist Revolution: An Essay on the History of England, 1450–1642* (Cambridge, UK, 2006), 80–114; Lorna Hutson, "On the Knees of the Body Politic," *Representations* 152 (2020): 25–54; Lorna Hutson, *England's Insular Imagining: The Elizabethan Erasure of Scotland* (Cambridge, UK, 2023), 154–87. For Montaigne, see "On Experience," *Essays*, ed. and trans. Screech, 1216 (3.13). For more on the body politic and anthropomorphic imaginings of the polity, see Leonard Barkan, *Nature's Work of Art: The Human Body as Image of the World* (New Haven, CT, 1975), chap. 2. On the ludicrousness of the *corpus mysticum*, see the remarks of F. W. Maitland quoted below.

40. See Jennifer R. Rust, *The Body in Mystery: The Political Theology of the Corpus Mysticum in the Literature of Reformation England* (Evanston, IL, 2014), esp. 3–28. On scrofula, see Kantorowicz, *King's Two Bodies*, 252–53; Marc Bloch, *The Royal Touch: Sacred Monarchy and Scrofula in England and France*, trans. J. E. Anderson (London, 1973), esp. 23–27.

41. Kantorowicz, *King's Two Bodies*, 316.

42. Augustine, *On the Literal Meaning of Genesis*, 6.14.25, where the *rationes seminales* are created within the six days' work, but where they possess a version of timelessness on account of being brought into physical actuality only at the appropriate time (*quod tempori congruat*). On Spenser and the *aevum*, see Kermode, *Sense of an Ending*, 75–80; McCabe, *Pillars of Eternity*, 36–38, 133–36.

43. Kantorowicz, *King's Two Bodies*, 84.

44. See *OED*, s.v. "jump," v. II.11. Cf. Shakespeare, *Cymbeline*, ed. Valerie Wayne (London, 2017), 5.4.153 ("jump the after-enquiry on your own peril").

45. On crimes rebounding on their authors, see Lewis, *Hamlet and the Vision of Darkness*, 90–91. On the right time to do something—*kairos* or *occasio*—see Joanne Paul, "The Use of *Kairos* in Renaissance Political Philosophy," *Renaissance Quarterly* 67 (2014): 43–78.

46. Francis Bacon, *Advancement of Learning*, in *The Oxford Francis Bacon*, ed. Kiernan et al., 4:128–29. See also Aristotle, *On the Soul*, 433b5–7; Cicero, *On Invention*, 2.53.160 (discussing the virtue of prudence).

47. Augustine, *Confessions*, 8.12. Kermode, *Sense of an Ending*, 84–85.

48. Lucretius, *On the Nature of Things*, 1.459–63 (on time), and 5.91–415 (on the universe and its mortality). See further the useful discussion in James I. Porter, "Lucretius and the Poetics of Void," in *Le jardin romain: Épicurisme et poésie à Rome*, ed. Annick Monet (Villeneuve-d'Ascq, France, 2003), 197–226.

49. See *OED*, s.v. "fret," v. 1.9a: "To distress oneself with constant thoughts of regret or discontent; to vex oneself, chafe, worry." On Macbeth's delivery, see John Kerrigan, *Shakespeare's Originality* (Oxford, 2018), 60–61.

50. Erasmus, *Adages*, in *Collected Works*, ed. Mynors et al., 33:276 (2.5.78); Shakespeare, *All's Well That Ends Well*, 5.ep.1. See Jones, *Origins*, 278–82.

51. Shakespeare, *Hamlet*, 4.2.27, 29. See Turner, *Corporate Commonwealth*, 148–56.

52. On the medal, see Henry N. Paul, *The Royal Play of Macbeth* (New York, 1950), 227. The serpentine proverb is Tilley, *Dictionary*, S585. On *Macbeth* and its historical contexts, see Arthur F. Kinney, *Lies Like Truth: Shakespeare, Macbeth, and*

the Cultural Moment (Detroit, 2001); James Shapiro, *The Year of Lear: Shakespeare in 1606* (New York, 2015), esp. 181–200.

53. Gwinne's text is Bullough, *Narrative and Dramatic Sources*, 7:470–72. See Paul, *Royal Play*, 19–24; Daniel Blank, *Shakespeare and University Drama in Early Modern England* (Oxford, 2023), chap. 4. It is striking that on Simon Forman's account, the Weird Sisters as performed at the Globe in 1611 were "3 women feiries or Nimphes" (Shakespeare, *Macbeth*, ed. Clark and Mason, 337). James believed that the coming of Christ marked the end of the age of prophecy. See his *Basilikon Doron. Devided into Three Bookes* (Edinburgh, 1599), 68, 128–29.

54. Harry Berger, Jr., *Making Trifles of Terrors: Redistributing Complicities in Shakespeare*, ed. Peter Erickson (Stanford, CA, 1997), 70–97; David Norbrook, "*Macbeth* and the Politics of Historiography," in *Politics of Discourse: The Literature and History of Seventeenth-Century England*, eds. Kevin Sharpe and Steven N. Zwicker (Berkeley and Los Angeles, 1987), 78–116; David Scott Kastan, *Shakespeare After Theory* (New York and London, 1999), 151–67; John Kerrigan, *Archipelagic English* (Oxford, 2008), 91–114. See further Rebecca Lemon, "Sovereignty and Treason in *Macbeth*," in *Macbeth: New Critical Essays*, ed. Nick Moschovakis (New York, 2008), 73–87; Jane Rickard, *Writing the Monarch: Jonson, Donne, Shakespeare, and the Works of King James* (Cambridge, UK, 2015), 230–43.

55. Kantorowicz, *King's Two Bodies*, 387. Kantorowicz misremembers a "ghostly procession of Macbeth's predecessor kings"—rather, that is, than of James's. On the significance of the pageant, see the excellent account in William C. Carroll, "Spectacle, Representation and Lineage in *Macbeth* 4.1," *Shakespeare Survey* 67 (2014): 345–71.

56. On this usage of "masters," see Spenser, *Faerie Queene*, ed. Hamilton et al., 362 (3.8.4); *Tempest*, 5.1.36–41.

57. On this sort of "glass," see Spenser, *Faerie Queene*, ed. Hamilton et al., 304–5 (3.2.18–21); Shakespeare, *Measure for Measure*, 2.2.98–103. Cf. the skeptical counterblast in Scot, *Discoverie*, 260–61 (12.17), 315–17 (13.19). Parenthetical quotation from John Milton, *Paradise Lost*, ed. Alastair Fowler, 2nd ed. (London, 1997), 638 (11.763).

58. See Tiffany Stern, *Making Shakespeare: The Pressures of Stage and Page* (London, 2004), 32–33. Perhaps because *Macbeth* is a short play, Richard Dutton's *Shakespeare: Court Dramatist* (Oxford, 2016) has little to say about it. See further Stephen Orgel, "*Macbeth* and the Antic Round," *Shakespeare Survey* 52 (1999): 143–53.

59. Cf. Duncan's comparable use of the term at 1.2.2.

60. John Milton, "Ideas for Dramas," in *The Complete Works of John Milton*, vol. 11, *Manuscript Writings*, ed. William Poole (Oxford, 2019), 369.

61. On the preceding paragraph, see Norbrook, "*Macbeth* and the Politics of Historiography."

62. Sally Mapstone, "Shakespeare and Scottish Kingship: A Case History," in *The Rose and the Thistle: Essays on the Culture of Late Medieval and Renaissance Scotland*, ed. Sally Mapstone and Juliet Wood (East Linton, UK, 1998), 158–89. See also Hutson, *England's Insular Imagining*, 286–92. On the broader treatment of Macbeth within the Scottish historiographical tradition, see Benjamin Hudson, *Macbeth Before Shakespeare* (Oxford, 2023), 144–64.

63. In general, see David Womersley, *Divinity and State* (Oxford, 2010), 261–99; Lorna Hutson, "Not the King's Two Bodies: Reading the 'Body Politic' in Shakespeare's

Henry IV, Parts 1 and 2," in *Rhetoric and Law in Early Modern Europe,* ed. Victoria Kahn and Lorna Hutson (New Haven, CT, 2001), 166–98; Victoria Kahn, *The Future of Illusion: Political Theology and Early Modern Texts* (Chicago, 2014), 55–82. David Norbrook argues that the significance of Kantorowicz's two-bodies theory has been exaggerated, but grants that it had currency and prominence in the late Elizabethan and Jacobean years: see "The Emperor's New Body? *Richard II,* Ernst Kantorowicz, and the Politics of Shakespeare Criticism," *Textual Practice* 10 (1996): 329–57. On *Macbeth* and the critique of sacred kingship, see—with all the usual caveats about schematic Hegelianism— Franco Moretti, *Signs Taken for Wonders: Essays in the Sociology of Literary Forms,* trans. Susan Fischer, David Forgacs, and David Miller (New York, 1983), 56–72.

64. David Riggs, "The Artificial Day and the Infinite Universe," *The Journal of Medieval and Renaissance Studies* 5 (1975): 155–85.

65. F. W. Maitland, "The Crown as Corporation," in *State, Trust, and Corporation,* ed. David Runciman and Magnus Ryan (Cambridge, UK, 2003), 32–51, here 35.

66. "You will certainly read that the crown does this and the crown does that. As a matter of fact we know that the crown does nothing but lie in the Tower of London to be gazed at by sight-seers. No, the crown is a convenient cover for ignorance: it saves us from asking difficult questions . . . I do not deny that it is a convenient term, and you may have to use it; but I do say that you should never be content with it" (F. W. Maitland, *The Constitutional History of England* [Cambridge, UK, 1920], 418).

67. On which, see Kastan, *Shakespeare and the Shapes of Time,* 91–101; Booth, *Indefinition,* 90–94.

68. Northrop Frye, *Fools of Time: Studies in Shakespearean Tragedy* (Toronto, 1967), 3.

69. Reinhart Koselleck, *Futures Past: On the Semantics of Historical Time,* trans. Keith Tribe (New York, 2004), 232.

70. Pocock, *Machiavellian Moment,* 46.

71. Cf. Brooks, *Reading for the Plot,* 6–7.

72. Milton, *Shorter Poems,* ed. Carey, 127. Horace, *Odes,* 3.30. William Shakespeare, *Shakespeare's Sonnets,* ed. Katherine Duncan-Jones (London, 1997), 221 (55). Cf. Ben Jonson's more or less ingenuous praise that Shakespeare's works are "not of an age, but for all time!" (*William Shakespeare: The Critical Heritage,* ed. Vickers, 1:21).

73. See Fritz Saxl, "Veritas filia temporis," in *Philosophy and History: Essays Presented to Ernst Cassirer,* ed. Raymond Klibansky and H. J. Paton (Oxford, 1936), 197–222; Simona Cohen, *Transformations of Time and Temporality in Medieval and Renaissance Art* (Leiden, 2014), 245–304. Erasmus, *Adages,* in *Collected Works,* ed. Mynors et al., 33:198 (2.4.17, "Tempus omnia revelat").

74. Shakespeare, *King Lear,* 1.1.282. As Edmund expires midway through the play's long final scene, he echoes Cordelia's line: "What you have charged me with, that have I done, / And more, much more; the time will bring it out" (5.3.160–61). Maybe, maybe not. Once Lear returns with the dead Cordelia in his arms, not even Edgar cares.

Chapter 6: Against Nature

1. On the dynamics of the opening scene, see Richard Strier, *Resistant Structures: Particularity, Radicalism, and Renaissance Texts* (Berkeley and Los Angeles, 1997), 177–82; Ralph Berry, *Tragic Instance: The Sequence of Shakespeare's Tragedies*

(Newark, DE, 1999), 137–49; Arthur Kinney, *Shakespeare's Webs: Networks of Meaning in Renaissance Drama* (New York, 2004), 101–43. As the opening scene of the 1608 quarto edition of the play lacks several expressions of Lear's motivation (e.g., his hope "that future strife / May be prevented now") recorded in the 1623 folio, this is probably the place to state my belief that both versions of the text authoritatively and imperfectly witness the work as Shakespeare wrote it; I do not see a convincing case for authorial revision. Debates over the textual status of the play have taken on the quality of Jarndyce v. Jarndyce over the course of the past five decades, but see the judicious overview in William Shakespeare, *A New Variorum Edition of Shakespeare: King Lear*, ed Richard Knowles, 2 vols. (New York, 2020), 2:1042–1240, esp. 1174–1207. See further Peter Blayney, *The Texts of King Lear and Their Origins* (Cambridge, UK, 1982); *The Division of the Kingdoms: Shakespeare's Two Versions of King Lear*, eds. Gary Taylor and Michael Warren (Oxford, 1983). I quote from Foakes's Arden Third Series edition of the text.

2. James VI and I, *Political Writings*, ed. Johann P. Sommerville (Cambridge, UK, 1994), 42 (*Basilicon Doron*). Montaigne, *Essays*, 439 (2.8, "On the Affection of Fathers for Their Children"); for more on *Lear* and Montaigne, see note 53 below.

3. For Geoffrey and Holinshed, see Bullough, *Narrative and Dramatic Sources*, 7:311–12 and 317. "But [King Leyr] had no issue male him to succeed, / But three faire daughters, which were well uptrained, / In all that seemed fitt for kingly seed: / Mongst whom his realme he equally decreed / To have divided" (Spenser, *Faerie Queene*, ed. Hamilton et al., 252 [2.10.27]). For *King Leir*, printed in 1605 but written (most likely) in the earlier 1590s, see Bullough, *Narrative and Dramatic Sources*, 7:337–401. See further Richard Knowles, "How Shakespeare Knew *King Leir*," *Shakespeare Survey* 55 (2002): 12–35, esp. 14–16; Meredith Anne Skura, "Dragon Fathers and Unnatural Children: Warring Generations in *King Lear* and Its Sources," *Comparative Drama* 42 (2008): 123–34.

4. Regan is gifted her territories with significantly more autonomy than Goneril: "Thee and thine hereditary ever" versus "thine and Albany's issues" (1.1.66). As this means that *any* children she might bear would inherit, rather than just those fathered by Cornwall, perhaps Kent and Gloucester were correct in supposing that Lear "more affected the Duke of Albany than Cornwall" (1.1.1–2); then again, maybe we are to infer that Lear distrusts Goneril, and wants to prevent her abandoning her husband for another.

5. See Curtius, *European Literature*, 159–66.

6. Tilley, *Dictionary*, 505 (N285). On the philosophical idea *nihil ex nihilo fit* (traceable to Lucretius's *On the Nature of Things*, 1.149–266), see Elton, *Lear and the Gods*, 179–90. On the problem of nothingness and negative affirmation (nothing is not nothing so long as we can say "this is nothing"—the affirmative statement is itself a something), see Rosalie Colie, *Paradoxia Epidemica: The Renaissance Tradition of Paradox* (Princeton, NJ, 1966), 219–51.

7. Behind all such formulations lies the *vis naturae* between parents and their offspring described in Cicero, *De finibus*, 3.62–63; cf. the claims for nature as a source of other virtues at 4.16–18.

8. See Kerrigan, *Binding Language*, 347–53.

9. "Was never Scythia half so barbarous!" exclaims Chiron as Titus moves to sacrifice Alarbus (*Titus Andronicus*, 1.1.134). Cf., e.g., Marlowe, *Complete Works*, 5:48,

116–17 (*1 Tamburlaine*, 3.3.270–71; *2 Tamburlaine*, 3.4.19–22); Montaigne, *Essays*, 235 (1.31, "On the Cannibals"). Montaigne draws chiefly from Herodotus, *Histories*, chap. 4 and Pliny, *Natural History*, 4.88, 6.50, 7.9. See further Aristotle, *Nicomachean Ethics*, 1148b19–24. Aristotle regards Scythian cannibalism—and infant cannibalism—as exemplary deviations from the natural order.

10. For Shakespearean dragons, see William Shakespeare, *King John*, ed. Jesse M. Lander and J.I.M. Tobin (London, 2018), 2.1.68; *Richard III*, 5.3.350; *Coriolanus*, 4.1.30, 4.6.23, 5.3.12–13.

11. On Kent, see Ivan Lupić, *Subjects of Advice: Drama and Counsel from More to Shakespeare* (Philadelphia, 2019), 141–65.

12. Algernon Charles Swinburne, *A Study of Shakespeare* (London, 1880), 176. On the comedic inheritance that Shakespeare assimilates within *Lear*'s design, see Snyder, *Comic Matrix*, 137–79; Booth, *Indefinition*, 59–78; Miola, *Shakespeare and Classical Comedy*, 187–201. On *Lear* and the conventions of pastoral romance, see also Leo Salingar, *Dramatic Form in Shakespeare and the Jacobeans* (Cambridge, UK, 1986), 91–106.

13. See related discussion in Paul Hammond, *The Strangeness of Tragedy* (Oxford, 2009), 160–80.

14. Cavell, *Disowning Knowledge*, 58. For fuller reflections on Cavell's account of *King Lear*, see Richard Strier, "The Judgment of the Critics that Makes Us Tremble: 'Distributing Complicities' in Recent Criticism of *King Lear*," in *Shakespeare and Judgment*, ed. Kevin Curran (Edinburgh, 2017), 215–34; Nicholas Luke, "Avoidance as Love: Evading Cavell on Dover Cliff," *Modern Philology* 117 (2020): 445–69.

15. Cavell, *Disowning Knowledge*, 63.

16. Ibid., 80. Emphasis Cavell's.

17. Ibid., 80–81.

18. Ibid., 65, 80, 121.

19. *King Leir*, ll. 898, 1264–74, in Bullough, *Narrative and Dramatic Sources*, 7:359, 368.

20. Bullough, *Narrative and Dramatic Sources*, 7:317, 318.

21. The literature on *Lear* and the discourse of nature is huge, and occasionally partisan. Some of the more useful studies include Empson, *Structure of Complex Words*, 125–57; Elton, *Lear and the Gods*; Dollimore, *Radical Tragedy*, 189–203; John F. Danby, *Shakespeare's Doctrine of Nature: A Study of King Lear* (London, 1961); Laurence Berns, "Gratitude, Nature, and Piety in *King Lear*," *Interpretation* 3 (1972): 27–51; Mark A. McDonald, *Shakespeare's King Lear and The Tempest: The Discovery of Nature and the Recovery of Natural Right* (Lanham, MD, 2004); Paul A. Cantor, "Nature and Convention in *King Lear*," in *Poets, Princes, and Private Citizens: Literary Alternatives to Postmodern Politics*, ed. Joseph M. Knippenberg and Peter Augustine Lawler (Lanham, MD, 1996), 213–34; Paul A. Cantor, "The Cause of Thunder: Nature and Justice in *King Lear*," in *King Lear: New Critical Essays*, ed. Jeffrey Kahan (New York and London, 2008), 231–52; Seth Lobis, "Sympathy and Antipathy in *King Lear*," in *Sympathy in Transformation*, ed. Roman Alexander Barton, Alexander Klaudies, and Thomas Micklich (Berlin, 2018), 89–107. Although it does not discuss *Lear* at length, see also Charlotte Scott, *Shakespeare's Nature: From Cultivation to Culture* (Oxford, 2014).

22. Shakespeare, *King Lear*, ed. Knowles, 1:45–46.

23. On the doctrine of the spheres, see Grant, *Planets, Stars, and Orbs*, 440–51; W.G.L. Randles, *The Unmaking of the Medieval Christian Cosmos: From Solid Heavens to Boundless Aether, 1500–1750* (Aldershot, UK, 1999). See further Hankins, *Backgrounds*, 17–34, 190–92; Clarence J. Glacken, *Traces on the Rhodian Shore: Nature and Culture in Western Thought from Ancient Times to the End of the Eighteenth Century* (Berkeley and Los Angeles, 1967), esp. 429–60.

24. Daston and Park, *Wonders and the Order of Nature*, chap. 3; Robert M. Grant, *Miracle and Natural Law in Graeco Roman and Early Christian Thought* (Amsterdam, 1952). For an overview of "nature" in its various senses from the pre-Socratics to modern English, see C. S. Lewis, *Studies in Words* (Cambridge, UK, 1960), 24–74.

25. See Manley, *Convention*, 15–66, 90–136; Hankins, *Backgrounds*, 192–200; Peter Harrison, *The Bible, Protestantism, and the Rise of Natural Science* (Cambridge, UK, 1998), esp. 34–63; J. R. Milton, "Laws of Nature," in *The Cambridge History of Seventeenth-Century Philosophy*, ed. Daniel Garber and Michael Ayers, 2 vols. (Cambridge, 1998), 1:680–701; *Natural Laws and Laws of Nature in Early Modern Europe*, ed. Lorraine Daston and Michael Stolleis (Farnham, UK, 2008), esp. the essays by Catherine Wilson, Ian Maclean, Sachiko Kusukawa, and Friedrich Steinle; Lorraine Daston, *Rules: A Short History of What We Live By* (Princeton, NJ, 2022), 212–37. On Bacon, see further Sophie Weeks, "Francis Bacon and the Art-Nature Distinction," *Ambix* 54 (2007): 117–45.

26. Spenser, *Faerie Queene*, ed. Hamilton et al., 701–11 (7.7), quotations from 702 (7.7.5) and 701 (7.7.4). Robert Chester, *Loves Martyr: Or, Rosalins Complaint* (London, 1601), 2. See Curtius, *European Literature*, 106–27; George D. Economou, *The Goddess Natura in Medieval Literature* (Cambridge, MA, 1972); Mechthild Modersohn, *Natura als Göttin im Mittelalter: Ikonographische Studien zu Darstellungen der personifizierten Natur* (Berlin, 1997). On Spenser, see further Kellie Robertson, *Nature Speaks: Medieval Literature and Aristotelian Philosophy* (Philadelphia, 2017), 326–32.

27. Katharine Park, "Nature in Person: Medieval and Renaissance Allegories and Emblems," in *The Moral Authority of Nature*, ed. Lorraine Daston and Fernando Vidal (Chicago, 2004), 50–73. See further Wolfgang Kemp, *Natura: Ikonographische Studien zur Geschichte und Verbreitung einer Allegorie* (Tübingen, 1973).

28. Cf. Seneca, *Hercules Furens*, ll. 1202–5. Burrow (*Shakespeare and Classical Antiquity*, 199–200) hears a purposeful echo of Seneca's *Hippolytus*, ll. 671–83. On Shakespeare's debts to Seneca in *King Lear* (to his Oedipus as much as his Hercules), see Miola, *Shakespeare and Classical Tragedy*, 143–74; Burrow, *Shakespeare and Classical Antiquity*, 195–201; Perry, *Shakespeare and Senecan Tragedy*, chap. 5.

29. The other occasion comes at 2.2.401–4, where he says that he would rather seek shelter with the now-detested Goneril than "the hot-blooded France, that dowerless took / Our youngest born."

30. *OED*, s.v. "sophisticated," adj., 1, 2a, 3a.

31. For the ideas on which Lear draws here, see Elton, *Lear and the Gods*, 190–97; Laurie Shannon, *The Unaccommodated Animal: Cosmopolity in Shakespearean Locales* (Chicago, 2013), chap. 3.

32. Lucretius, *On the Nature of Things*, 5.925–1010, 1028–90; Cicero, *De inventione*, 1.2–3; Pliny, *Natural History*, 7.1–3. On the early modern currency of these ideas, see, e.g., George Buchanan, *A Dialogue on the Law of Kingship Among the*

Scots: A Critical Edition of George Buchanan's De Iure Regni apud Scotus Dialogus, ed. and trans. Roger A. Mason and Martin S. Smith (Aldershot, UK, 2004), 14–21. Cf. Aristotle, *Parts of Animals,* 687a–b. On Edgar's self-presentation as Poor Tom more generally, see Giulio Pertile, "*King Lear* and the Uses of Mortification," *Shakespeare Quarterly* 67 (2016): 319–43.

33. See Shakespeare, *King Lear,* ed. Knowles, 1:572–74.

34. Cf., e.g., [Juliana Berners], *Hawking, Hunting, Fouling, and Fishing . . . A Work Right Pleasant and Profitable for All Estates,* ed. William Gryndall (London, 1596), sig. G2r. Much of Edgar's Poor Tom routine is drawn from the frauds described in Samuel Harsnett's *Declaration of Egregious Popish Impostures.* See Kenneth Muir, "Samuel Harsnett and *King Lear,*" *Review of English Studies* 2 (1951): 11–21; F. W. Brownlow, *Shakespeare, Harsnett, and the Devils of Denham* (Newark, DE, 1993), esp. 110–31.

35. See Robert Weimann, *Shakespeare and the Popular Tradition in the Theater: Studies in the Social Dimension of Dramatic Form and Function,* ed. Robert Schwartz (Baltimore, 1978), 40.

36. In the translation of Philemon Holland, Pliny wonders whether Nature "hath done the part of a kind mother, or a hard and cruell step-dame" in relation to humankind: "Man alone, poore wretch, she hath laid all naked upon the bare earth, even on his birthday, to cry and wraule presently from the very first houre that he is borne into this world" (*The Historie of the World, Commonlie Called the Naturall Historie of C. Plinius Secundus,* trans. Philemon Holland [London, 1603], 152; i.e., *Natural History,* 7.2).

37. When it becomes apparent that all is not going to go to plan, Lear wonders of the Fool, "Dost thou call me fool, boy?" To which the Fool responds, "All thy other titles thou hast given away; that thou wast born with" (1.4.141–43).

38. Horace, *Ars poetica,* ll. 3–4; Ovid, *Metamorphoses,* 12.210–537; Harsnett, *Declaration,* chaps. 12 and 18, in Brownlow, *Shakespeare, Harsnett, and the Devils of Denham,* 248–53, 287–88. See further Bate, *Shakespeare and Ovid,* 194; Muir, "Samuel Harsnett and *King Lear,*" 21.

39. See related discussion in Janet Adelman, *Suffocating Mothers: Fantasies of Maternal Origin in Shakespeare's Plays* (New York and London, 1992), 103–29; Coppélia Kahn, "The Absent Mother in *King Lear,*" in *Rewriting the Renaissance: The Discourses of Sexual Difference in Early Modern Europe,* ed. Margaret Ferguson, Maureen Quilligan, and Nancy Vickers (Chicago, 1986), 33–49.

40. "I thought it all for the best" (Shakespeare, *Romeo and Juliet,* 3.1.106).

41. Cf. Shakespeare, *Henry VI, Part 3,* 4.6.11–15, where Henry—preferring cloistered living to the burdens of rule—describes his imprisonment as "such a pleasure as encaged birds / Conceive."

42. Shakespeare's imagination was often drawn to the process of extracting foxes from their holes—the term of art for which is "unkennelling." See, e.g., Shakespeare, *Hamlet,* 3.2.81; *All's Well,* 3.6.98–100; *The Merry Wives of Windsor,* ed. Giorgio Melchiori (London, 2000), 3.3.150. See further Lewis, *Hamlet and the Vision of Darkness,* 66–68.

43. Hutson, *Circumstantial Shakespeare,* 96–101, here 100.

44. On Barthes, see chapter 1, 62. On the structure of *Lear,* see Jones, *Scenic Form,* 152–94.

45. Only 4.2.30–32 is witnessed by both the quarto and folio editions of the text; the meat of Albany's attack is witnessed by the quarto alone.

46. See chapter 4, notes 8–9.

47. Olaus Magnus, *Historia de gentibus septentrionalibus*, ed. and trans. Peter Foote, Peter Fisher, and Humphrey Higgens, 3 vols. (London, 1996–98), 3:1090 (21.8). See Rhodri Lewis, "Shakespeare, Olaus Magnus, and Monsters of the Deep," *Notes and Queries* 65 (2018): 76–81; and, on Magnus's *Historia* and *Hamlet*, Julie Maxwell, "Counter-Reformation Versions of Saxo: A New Source for *Hamlet*?," *Renaissance Quarterly* 57 (2004): 518–60.

48. On human exceptionality, see Kraye, "Moral Philosophy," 306–16; Hankins, *Backgrounds*, 146–214; Paul Oskar Kristeller, *Studies in Renaissance Thought and Letters* (Rome, 1956), 279–86.

49. Seneca, *Phoenician Women*, ll. 67–73 (cf. 22–25, 114–18). Edgar's remarks may also parody the trope (common to Stoicism, Platonism, and Epicureanism) of seeking consolation through the "view from above"—on which, see Pierre Hadot, *Philosophy as a Way of Life*, ed. Arnold I. Davidson and trans. Michael Chase (Oxford, 1995), 238–50.

50. *OED*, s.v. "stealth," 1–2. Cf. Shakespeare, *Timon of Athens*, 3.4.26–27 ("I know that my lord hath spend of Timon's wealth, / And now ingratitude makes it worse than stealth"), though note that the lines in question are probably the work of Shakespeare's coauthor, Thomas Middleton.

51. Elton, *Lear and the Gods*, 115–46, esp. 125–35. Cf. the two different theories of natural origins sketched by Francis Bacon in his *Wisdom of the Ancients*: one holds that nature is the work of a divine creator, the other that it emerges from the material "seeds of things" (*rerum semina*) mixed randomly together (*De sapientia veterum* [London, 1609], 17–18 [fable 6, "Pan"]).

52. Shakespeare, *Julius Caesar*, 1.2.139–40.

53. Of the extensive literature on the question, see Salingar, *Dramatic Form*, 107–39; Peter Mack, *Reading and Rhetoric in Montaigne and Shakespeare* (London, 2010), 158–68; William Hamlin, *Montaigne's English Journey: Reading the "Essays" in Shakespeare's Day* (Oxford, 2013), esp. 110–28; Colin Burrow, "Montaignian Moments: Shakespeare and the *Essays*," in *Montaigne in Transit: Essays in Honor of Ian Maclean*, ed. Neil Kenny, Richard Scholar, and Wes Williams (Cambridge, UK, 2016), 233–46; Peter G. Platt, *Shakespeare's Essays: Sampling Montaigne from Hamlet to The Tempest* (Edinburgh, 2020), 109–28; Alison Calhoun, "Feeling Indifference: Flaying Narratives in Montaigne and Shakespeare," in *Shakespeare and Montaigne*, eds. Lars Engle, Patrick Gray, and William Hamlin (Edinburgh, 2021), 180–97, esp. 187–95. On Florio's translation more generally, see Warren Boutcher, *The School of Montaigne in Early Modern Europe*, 2 vols. (Oxford, 2017), esp. 2:189–271.

54. Michel Eyquem, Seigneur de Montaigne, *The Essayes or Morall, Politike and Militarie Discourses of Lo: Michaell de Montaigne*, trans. John Florio (London, 1603), 313 (2.12); see also Montaigne, *Essays*, 606.

55. Ian Maclean, *Logic, Signs, and Nature in the Renaissance: The Case of Learned Medicine* (Cambridge, UK, 2002), 236.

56. For "clear-sighted vigilancie," Montaigne's French original simply has *clairvoyance*, or clear-sightedness; Florio's "vigilancie" emphasizes the hint of self-congratulatory attentiveness and acuity.

57. Montaigne, *Essayes*, trans. Florio, 311 (2.12); see also Montaigne, *Essays*, 602. Cf. Plato, *Second Alcibiades*, 147b–c.

Chapter 7: Romans, Egyptians, and Crocodiles

1. See Kantorowicz, *King's Two Bodies*, esp. 292–302; Frances Yates, *Astraea: The Imperial Theme in the Sixteenth Century* (London, 1975), esp. chaps. 1–2; Anthony Pagden, *Lords of All the World: Ideologies of Empire in Spain, Britain and France c. 1500–c. 1800* (Cambridge, UK, 1995), chaps. 1–2; David Armitage, *The Ideological Origins of the British Empire* (Cambridge, UK, 2000), chap. 2. See further Kerrigan, *Archipelagic English*, 49–54; Frank Kermode, *The Classic: Literary Images of Permanence and Change* (New York, 1975), 49–80. Quotations from Virgil, *Aeneid*, 1.279; *The Tudor Constitution: Documents and Commentary*, ed. G. R. Elton (Cambridge, UK, 1968), 344.

2. For the sources and analogues of *Antony and Cleopatra*, see Bullough, *Narrative and Dramatic Sources*, 5:215–449; Plutarch's account of the scene on Pompey's galley is at 279. On the other Cleopatra plays—and on their possible relations to Shakespeare's text—see Yasmin Arshad, *Imagining Cleopatra: Performing Gender and Power in Early Modern England* (London, 2019). Although *Antony and Cleopatra* refers to "Caesar," I use "Octavius" to avoid any confusion with Julius Caesar; throughout this chapter, I draw from Rhodri Lewis, "Romans, Egyptians, and Crocodiles," *Shakespeare Quarterly* 68 (2017): 320–50.

3. On the early modern fascination with Africa's rivers and their tendency to flood, see Kim F. Hall, *Things of Darkness: Economies of Race and Gender in Early Modern England* (Ithaca, NY, 1996), 26–28, 156–57.

4. See Ovid, *Metamorphoses*, 1.422–37. Cf., e.g., Spenser, *Faerie Queene*, 1.1.21; Donne, "Satyre 4," in *Complete Poems*, 399 (ll. 18–19).

5. Cf., e.g., "your four negatives make your two affirmatives," in Shakespeare, *Twelfth Night*, 5.1.19; and see further Wales, "Generic 'Your' and Jacobean Drama."

6. On Antony's disregard for "This . . . slight unmeritable man," see Shakespeare, *Julius Caesar*, 4.1.12–40.

7. Ovid, *Metamorphoses*, 15.143–75. See further Leonard Barkan, *The Gods Made Flesh: Metamorphosis and the Pursuit of Paganism* (New Haven, CT, 1986), 86–87. On crocodile tears, see Tilley, *Dictionary*, 129 (C831).

8. Janet Adelman, *The Common Liar: An Essay on Antony and Cleopatra* (New Haven, CT, 1973), 61, 62.

9. Spenser, *Faerie Queene*, 5.7.6–16. William Empson, "Paradoxes in *The Faerie Queene* V and VI," in *The Strengths of the Shrew: Essays, Memoirs, and Reviews*, ed. John Haffenden (Sheffield, UK, 1995), 111–116, here 112. See further Jane Aptekar, *Icons of Justice: Iconography and Thematic Imagination in Book V of The Faerie Queene* (New York, 1969), 87–107.

10. See, e.g., Cicero, *Tusculan Disputations*, 5.78–79; Cicero, *De natura deorum*, 1.29.82, 3.19.47–48; Plutarch, *Moralia*, 381b–c ("Isis and Osiris"), 976a–c ("On the Intelligence of Animals"); Juvenal, *Satires*, 15.1–2, 9–11; [Laurence Humphrey], *The Nobles or of Nobilitye. The Original Nature, Dutyes, Right, and Christian Institucion Thereof* (London, 1563), sig. m8v. See further Hans Gossen and August Steier, "Krokodile und Eidechsen," in *Realencyclopädie der classischen Altertumswissenschaft*, ed. A. F. von Pauly, Georg Wissowa, et al., 1st ser. (Stuttgart, 1893–1980), vol. 11.2: cols. 1947–70.

11. Quintilian, *Institutio oratoriae*, 1.10.5–6.

12. See, e.g., Erasmus, *Praise of Folly* and *Ecclesiastes* (book 2), in *Collected Works*, 27:96–97 (*Praise of Folly*), 68:687–88 (*Ecclesiastes*); Thomas Wilson, *The Rule of Reason, Conteinying the Arte of Logique*, ed. Richard S. Sprague (Northridge, CA, 1972), 210–11. See further E. J. Ashworth, *Language and Logic in the Post-Medieval Period* (Dordrecht, Netherlands, 1974), 114–15.

13. As Topsell puts it, "By Serpents we understand . . . all venomous Beasts, whether creeping without legges, as Adders and Snakes, or with legges, as Crocodiles and Lizards, or more neerely compacted bodies, as Toades, Spiders and Bees" (Edward Topsell, *The Historie of Serpents* [London, 1608], 10).

14. Henry Peacham the Younger would later emblematize Satan as a crocodile: see his *Minerva Britanna, or A Garden of Heroical Devises* (London, 1612), 154.

15. "For they made an order betwene them, which they called Amimetobion (as much to say, no life comparable and matcheable with it) one feasting ech other by turnes, and in cost, exceeding all measure and reason" (Bullough, *Narrative and Dramatic Sources*, 5:275, cf. also 5:305). On Enobarbus, see discussion at notes 44–47 below. On the crocodilian aspect of Cleopatra's final transmigration-metamorphosis, see further Neill, *Issues of Death*, 321–22; Eric S. Mallin, *Godless Shakespeare* (London, 2007), 112–14.

16. See Spencer J. Weinreich, "Thinking with Crocodiles: An Iconic Animal at the Intersection of Early Modern Religion and Natural Philosophy," *Early Science and Medicine* 20 (2015): 213–15.

17. Cesare Ripa, *Iconologia*, 2 vols. (Siena, 1613), 2:15; Pierio Valeriano Bolzani, *Hieroglyphica sive de sacris Aegyptiorum literis commentarii* (Basel, 1556), fols. 205v–8r (book 29). John Florio, *Queen Anna's New World of Words, or Dictionarie of the Italian and English Tongues* (London, 1611), s.v., "lussúria."

18. On the dove as symbol of Venereal lust, see Giovanni Boccaccio, *Genealogy of the Pagan Gods*, ed. and trans. Jon Solomon, 2 vols. (Cambridge, MA, 2011–17), 1:392 (3.22); Vincenzo Cartari, *Vincenzo Cartari's Images of the Gods of the Ancients: The First Italian Mythography*, ed. and trans. John Mulryan (Tempe, AZ, 2012), 408 (section 15, "Venus"). Immediately before deciding to part ways with him, Enobarbus compares Antony to a dove (3.13.202).

19. On the *Ratio*, see Marjorie O'Rourke Boyle, *Erasmus on Language and Method in Theology* (Toronto, 1977), 59–127; Jean-Claude Margolin, "Ex philologo theologus? Philologus et theologus? Réflexions autour de la *Ratio verae theologiae*," *Rinascimento* 48 (2008): 197–228.

20. Erasmus, *Ratio verae theologiae*, in *Complete Works*, 41:502–3.

21. On syllogistic mnemonics, see Wilson, *Rule of Reason*, 66–68; Grafton and Jardine, *Humanism to the Humanities*, 10–13; Ashworth, *Language and Logic*, 232–39.

22. Cf., e.g., Erasmus, *Praise of Folly*, in *Collected Works*, 27:129, 133–34.

23. Cf., e.g., Erasmus, *Collected Works*, 23:233–34, 250 (*Parabolae*); 31:7; 32:270; 33:8, 222; 35:195, 206 (*Adagia*); 40:629, 1038–40, 1042 (*Colloquia*). Of his sources, see Aristotle, *History of Animals*, 503a1–14, 558a15–24, 612a21–24; Aristotle, *Parts of Animals*, 660b26–34, 690b18–691a6, 691a28–691b27; Pliny, *Natural History*, 8.37–38; Herodotus, *Histories*, 2.68–70. Also cf. Solinus, *The Excellent and Pleasant Work . . . Polyhistor*, trans. Arthur Golding (London, 1587), sigs. U2r–X2r (ch. 44).

See further Debra Hawhee, *Rhetoric in Tooth and Claw: Animals, Language, Sensation* (Chicago, 2016), 133–59.

24. Conrad Gesner, *Conradi Gesneri medici Tigurini Historiae animalium liber IIII: Qui est de piscium & aquatilium animantium natura* (Zürich, 1558), 494. Cf. Pierre Belon, *L'histoire naturelle des estranges poissons marins* (Paris, 1551), fol. 50r; Pierre Belon, *De aquatilibus, libri duo* (Paris, 1553), 25. See further Molly Swetnam-Burland, "Egypt Embodied: The Vatican Nile," *American Journal of Archaeology* 113 (2009): 445–46; and, on the rhetoric of visuality, see François Hartog, *The Mirror of Herodotus: The Representation of the Other in the Writing of History*, trans. Janet Lloyd (Berkeley and Los Angeles, 1988), 248–58.

25. Topsell, *Historie of Serpents*, 126–40, esp. 128. See further Joan Barclay Lloyd, *African Animals in Renaissance Literature and Art* (Oxford, 1971), 103–10. In an earlier work, Topsell reproduced Gesner's depiction of the encounter between the crocodile and the hippo: see Edward Topsell, *The Historie of Foure-Footed Beastes* (London, 1607), 328.

26. George Sandys, *A Relation of a Journey Began An: Dom: 1610* (London, 1615), 100–101.

27. Job Hortop, *The Travailes of an English Man* (London, 1591), 12.

28. Shakespeare, *Romeo and Juliet*, 5.1.37, 42–44. Nashe satirizes his enemy Gabriel Harvey as having dissected a rat, "and after hangd her over his head in his studie, instead of an Apothecaries Crocodile, or dride *Alligatur*" (Nashe, *Have with You to Saffron-Walden*, in *The Works of Thomas Nashe*, 3:67). Cf., e.g., Thomas Coryate, *Coryats Crudities* (London, 1611), 147–48. On *Wunderkammern*, see Weinreich, "Thinking with Crocodiles," esp. 227–37; Daston and Park, *Wonders and the Order of Nature*, 84–86.

29. Shakespeare, *Hamlet*, 5.1.271. On crocodile tears, cf. *King John*, 4.3.107–8; *Henry VI, Part 2*, 3.1.226–27; *Othello*, 4.1.245.

30. Cf. James P. Hammersmith, "The Serpent of Old Nile," *Interpretations* 14 (1982): 11–16; John Gillies, *Shakespeare and the Geography of Difference* (Cambridge, UK, 1994), 121–22.

31. See Vickers, *In Defence of Rhetoric*, 72–80; Wayne Rebhorn, *The Emperor of Men's Minds: Literature and the Renaissance Discourse of Rhetoric* (Ithaca, NY, 1995), esp. 2–79.

32. Of classical sources, see Cicero, *Academica*, 2.6.17; Cicero, *De oratore*, 3.202; Cicero, *Topica*, 26.97; Cicero, *Partitiones oratoriae*, 6.19–20; *Rhetorica ad Herennium*, 4.39.51, 4.55.68–69; Quintilian, *Institutio oratoria*, 4.2.63–65, 6.2.29–35, 8.3.61–72, 9.2.40–41. Of early modern ones, see, e.g., Erasmus, *Collected Works*, 24:577–89 (*De copia*, 2.5); Sherry, *Treatise*, sig. E1v; Thomas Wilson, *The Art of Rhetoric*, ed. Peter E. Medine (University Park, PA, 1994), 203–5 (book 3); Henry Peacham the Elder, *The Garden of Eloquence* (London, 1577), sig. O2r. See further Plett, *Enargeia*; Cave, *Cornucopian Text*, 27–34, 102–11.

33. Quintilian, *Institutio oratoria*, 6.2.29–30.

34. *Defence of Poetry*, in Sidney, *Miscellaneous Prose*, 85, 80. For the origins of the *ut pictura poesis* ("as painting is, so is poetry") topos, see Horace, *Art of Poetry*, 361. See further Lucy Gent, *Picture and Poetry, 1560–1620* (Leamington Spa, UK, 1981), esp. 38–65; Leonard Barkan, *Mute Poetry, Speaking Pictures* (Princeton, NJ, 2013).

35. Hutson, "The Play in the Mind's Eye."

36. See, e.g., Quintilian, *Institutio oratoria*, 8.3.72, 8.6.19–20; Sherry, *Treatise*, sig. C4v. See further Quentin Skinner, *Reason and Rhetoric in the Philosophy of Hobbes* (Cambridge, UK, 1996), 182–88.

37. See, e.g., Wilson, *Rule of Reason*, 121–22. See further Richard W. Serjeantson, "Testimony: The Artless Proof," in *Renaissance Figures of Speech*, ed. Sylvia Adamson, Gavin Alexander, and Katrin Ettenhuber (Cambridge, UK, 2007), 181–94. On received representations of Egypt, see Simon Schama, *Landscape and Memory* (New York, 1995), 268–308. See further Brian Curran, *The Egyptian Renaissance: The Afterlife of Ancient Egypt in Early Modern Italy* (Chicago, 2007).

38. Cf., e.g., 1.2.140, 148; 1.3.2, 62, 65; 2.7.91 (in jest); 3.3.41–42; 3.11.30; 4.3.23–29; 4.4.9, 16–17; 4.14.7; 4.15.64; 5.1.35, 73–77; 5.2.34, 43, 149. Antony's flimsy "Would I had never seen her!" (1.2.159) is especially telling: characters see what they are disposed to see.

39. See Grafton and Jardine, *Humanism to the Humanities*, 184–200. On the orator as *vir bonus*, see chapter 1, note 83.

40. Both 2 Peter 3:13 and Revelation 21:1 have versions of "a new heaven, and a new earth."

41. "Let maps to others, worlds on worlds have shown; / Let us possess our world: each hath one, and is one" (Donne, *Complete Poems*, 198).

42. Quotation from Iggy Pop, "Caesar Lives," *Classics Ireland* 2 (1995): 94. See Raymond B. Waddington, "Antony and Cleopatra: 'What Venus Did with Mars,'" *Shakespeare Studies* 2 (1966): 210–27. For a digest of some other Roman parts inhabited by Antony and Cleopatra, see further Miola, *Shakespeare's Rome*, 119–33.

43. Bullough, *Narrative and Dramatic Sources*, 5:255. On the "Asiatic" and Attic styles, see Cicero's *Brutus*, 50–53 and *Orator*, 20–32, 230–31. See also Quintilian, *Institutio oratoria*, 12.10.1–25; Erasmus, *Collected Works*, 24:299–301 (*De copia*, 1.4–6); Richard Sherry, *A Treatise of the Figures of Grammer and Rhetorike* (London, 1555), fol. 10r; Ulrich von Wilamowitz-Möllendorff, "Asianismus und Atticismus," *Hermes* 35 (1900): 1–52. On Asianism in *Antony and Cleopatra*, see the excellent account in Colie, *Shakespeare's Living Art*, 168–207.

44. See Adelman, *Common Liar*, 113–22; Thorne, *Vision and Rhetoric*, 166–97. On the conceit, cf. Ovid, *Metamorphoses*, 3.466.

45. See Barkan, *Gods Made Flesh*, 228–29.

46. Bullough, *Narrative and Dramatic Sources*, 5:275.

47. Sylvester's translation of du Bartas has "*Apelles Venus*, which allur'd well-neere / As many Loves, as *Venus* self had heere: / Are proofes enough that learned Painting can / Can [*sic*] Goddesse-like another Nature frame" (Guillaume de Salluste du Bartas, *The Divine Weeks and Works of Guillaume de Saluste, Sieur du Bartas*, ed. Susan Snyder, trans. Josuah Sylvester [Oxford, 1979], 1:286 [week 1, day 6], cf. 1:124–25 [week 1, day 1], 1:257 [week 1, day 5]).

48. Quotation from Ovid, *Amores*, 1.8.41–42, as translated in Marlowe, *Complete Works*, 1:24. On the Ovidian features of the play, see Bate, *Shakespeare and Ovid*, 203–14; Adelman, *Common Liar*, 131–49. See further Paul A. Cantor, "*Antony and Cleopatra*: Empire, Globalization, and the Clash of Civilizations," in *Shakespeare and Politics*, ed. Bruce E. Altschuler and Michael A. Genovese (Boulder, CO, 2014), 65–83.

49. On *Antony and Cleopatra* and postcoloniality, see Gillies, *Shakespeare and the Geography of Difference*, 1–7, 25–34, 112–23; Loomba, *Shakespeare, Race, and Colonialism*, 112–34; Ania Loomba, *Gender, Race, Renaissance Drama* (Manchester, 1989), 119–41. Edward Said, *Orientalism* (London, 1978), 176–77.

50. Cicero, *De officiis*, 1.11–16, 21–22, 93–151; 3.43. Cf. Cicero, *Tusculan Disputations*, 2.58–59, and see further Curtis Perry, "After Decorum: Self-Performance and Political Liminality in *Antony and Cleopatra*," in *Antony and Cleopatra: A Critical Reader*, ed. Domenico Lovascio (London, 2020), 113–31.

51. On Venus's stylishly amorous subjugation of Mars, see Lucretius, *On the Nature of Things*, 1.29–40. Shakespeare treats the topic in *Venus and Adonis*, ll. 97–114, where Venus makes no mention of how her affair with Mars came to an end (*Shakespeare's Poems*, ed. Duncan-Jones and Woudhuysen, 141–43). See also *Othello*, 1.3.273, as discussed in chapter 4 above, note 35. Plutarch compares Antony to Hercules as disarmed by Omphale (Bullough, *Narrative and Dramatic Sources*, 5:319).

52. Homer, *Odyssey*, 8.266–328; Ovid, *Metamorphoses*, 4.171–89.

53. Horace, *Odes*, 1.37.

54. Greville, "Dedication to Sir Philip Sidney," chap. 14, in *Prose Works of Fulke Greville*, 93.

55. Dryden introduces his Antony as follows: "He's somewhat lewd, but a well-meaning mind; / Weeps much, fights little, but is wondrous kind" (*All for Love*, ed. N. J. Andrews [London, 1975], 43 [1.0.12–13]). On Shakespeare's refusal to moralize Antony, see further Chernaik, *Myth of Rome*, 140–64.

56. See Lewis, "Shakespeare's Clouds," 7–11. See further Janson, "The 'Image Made by Chance'"; Damisch, *Théorie du nuage*, chap. 1; Gombrich, *Art and Illusion*, 154–69.

57. For the origins of the line about only Antony overcoming Antony, see Ovid, *Metamorphoses*, 13.390. After helping Brutus to kill himself, Strato tells a similar lie ("Brutus only overcame himself"), only for it speedily to be exposed by Messala's questioning (Shakespeare, *Julius Caesar*, 5.5.57–66); for Macbeth's disparagement of suicide, see chapter 5 above, note 14. See further Daniel, *Joy of the Worm*, 69–76.

58. The passage of Virgil that Antony misconstrues is *Aeneid*, 6.467–74, where Dido refuses to receive Aeneas in the underworld.

59. Walter Benjamin, *The Work of Art in the Age of its Technical Reproducibility, and Other Writings on Media*, ed. and trans. Michael W. Jennings, Edmund Jephcott, et al. (Cambridge, MA, 2008), 41–42.

60. In Ovid's *Metamorphoses*, 15.843–51, Caesar undergoes "catasterism," becoming a star. Of Cleopatra's final performance, Curtis Perry ("After Decorum," 127–31) has gone as far as to suggest that it is an act of Stoic-Senecan resistance and self-determination. "Dull, sublunary lovers" is from Donne, "A Valediction Forbidding Mourning," in *Complete Poems*, 259 (l. 13).

61. Shakespeare must have been lucky in the quality of the adolescent male actor who played Cleopatra. See further Harry R. McCarthy, *Boy Actors in Early Modern England: Skill and Stagecraft in the Theatre* (Cambridge, UK, 2022), chap. 4.

62. Virgil, *Aeneid*, 8.626–731. See further Adelman, *Common Liar*, 71–73. See further David Quint, *Epic and Empire: Politics and Generic Form from Virgil to Milton* (Princeton, NJ, 1993), 21–48; Robert Alan Gurval, *Actium and Augustus: The Politics and Emotions of Civil War* (Ann Arbor, MI, 1995), 137–278.

63. Pliny, *Natural History*, 8.38; Erasmus, *Collected Works*, 33:8, 35:401–2 (*Adagia*), 39:181, 40:1038 (*Colloquia*); Topsell, *Historie of Serpents*, 129, 137. For a set-piece battle between dolphins and crocodiles at the mouth of the Nile (in which dolphins prevail), see Seneca, *Naturales quaestiones*, 4A.13–14.

64. In fact, the expansion of "Col Nem" to "Colligavit nemo" is an error: see Rubem Amaral Jr., "The Reverse of the *As* of Nîmes: An Emblematic Puzzle," in *The International Emblem: From Incunabula to Internet*, ed. Simon McKeown (Newcastle upon Tyne, 2010), 47–68; Pierre-François Puech, Bernard Puech, and Fernand Puech, "The 'As de Nîmes,' a Roman Coin and the Myth of Antony and Cleopatra: Octavian and Agrippa Victorious over Antony," *OMNI: Revue numismatique / Revista numismática* 8 (2014): 58–66. On the numismatic Cleopatra, see further John Cunnally, *Images of the Illustrious: The Numismatic Presence in the Renaissance* (Princeton, NJ, 1999), 18, 57, 64.

65. Claude Paradin, *The Heroicall Devises of M. Claudius Paradin Canon of Beauieu*, trans. P. S. (London, 1591), 82. On Paradin and *Pericles*, see William O. Scott, "Another 'Heroical Devise' in *Pericles*," *Shakespeare Quarterly* 20 (1969): 91–95; John Klause, "A Shakespearean Scene in *Pericles*, II," *Notes and Queries* 62 (2015): 578–83.

66. See Molly Swetnam-Burland, *Egypt in Italy: Visions of Egypt in Roman Imperial Culture* (Cambridge, UK, 2015), esp. 71–82.

67. On Trinculo and Caliban, see Shakespeare, *Tempest*, 2.2.27–32.

68. On Plutarch's account, "in [Octavius's] triumphe he caried Cleopatraes image, with an Aspicke byting of her arme" (Bullough, *Narrative and Dramatic Sources*, 5:316). On Renaissance claims to have recovered this statue, see Arshad, *Imagining Cleopatra*, 225–45; Leonard Barkan, *Unearthing the Past: Archaeology and Aesthetics in the Making of Renaissance Culture* (New Haven, CT, 1999), 233–47.

69. Tacitus, *The Ende of Nero and the Beginning of Galba: Fower Bookes of the Histories of Cornelius Tacitus. The Life of Agricola*, trans. Henry Savile (London, 1591), 255 (*Agricola*, 30–31). Cf. the unflattering depiction of Roman imperial habits in Tacitus's account of Boudica's uprising and death (like Cleopatra, suicide by poison after military defeat) in *The Annales of Cornelius Tacitus: The Description of Germanie*, trans. Richard Grenewey (London, 1598), 209–12 (*Annales*, 14.29–37).

70. Of the now extensive literature on the English vogue for Tacitus at the end of the sixteenth and beginning of the seventeenth centuries, see Bradford, "Stuart Absolutism"; Alexandra Gajda, "Tacitus and Political Thought in Early Modern Europe, c. 1530–1640," in *The Cambridge Companion to Tacitus*, ed. A. J. Woodman (Cambridge, UK, 2010), 253–68; Mordechai Feingold, "Scholarship and Politics: Henry Savile's Tacitus and the Essex Connection," *Review of English Studies* 67 (2016): 855–74; R. Malcolm Smuts, "Varieties of Tacitism," *Huntington Library Quarterly* 83 (2020): 441–65. Alberico Gentili, *The Wars of the Romans: A Critical Edition and Translation of De armis Romanis*, ed. Benedict Kingsbury and Benjamin Straumann, trans. David Lupher (Oxford, 2011), 116–17 (1.13); for the possible trace in *Henry V*, see Christopher N. Warren, "*Henry V*, Anachronism, and the History of International Law," in *The Oxford Handbook of English Law and Literature*, ed. Lorna Hutson (Oxford, 2017), 709–27. On other possible debts to Tacitus, see George R. Price, "Henry V and Germanicus," *Shakespeare Quarterly* 12 (1961): 57–60; David Womersley, "*3 Henry VI*: Shakespeare, Tacitus, and Parricide," *Notes and Queries* 32 (1985): 468–73; James

Shapiro, *1599: A Year in the Life of William Shakespeare* (London, 2005), 138–42; Herbert W. Benario, "Shakespeare's Debt to Tacitus' *Histories*," *Notes and Queries* 55 (2008): 202–5.

71. See Craig Kallendorf, "Virgil, Dante, and Empire in Italian Thought, 1300–1500," *Vergilius* 34 (1988): 44–69; Fabio Stok, "Virgil Between the Middle Ages and Renaissance," *International Journal of the Classical Tradition* 1 (1994): 15–22; Christopher Baswell, *Virgil in Medieval England: Figuring the Aeneid from the Twelfth Century to Chaucer* (Cambridge, UK, 1995); *The Virgilian Tradition: The First Fifteen Hundred Years*, eds. Jan Ziolkowski and Michael C. J. Putnam (New Haven, CT, 2008).

Chapter 8: A Kind of Nothing

1. Bullough, *Narrative and Dramatic Sources*, 5:304. It is impossible to say when exactly *Timon* was written, but my assumption is that it either postdates or was concurrent with *Antony and Cleopatra*, ca. 1607; see Shakespeare, *Timon of Athens*, ed. Dawson and Minton, 12–18.

2. On *Timon* and genre, see Shakespeare, *Timon of Athens*, ed. Dawson and Minton, 27–38; William W. E. Slights, "*Genera mixta* and *Timon of Athens*," *Studies in Philology* 74 (1977): 39–62; Robert Wilcher, "*Timon of Athens*: A Shakespearean Experiment," *Cahiers Élisabéthains* 34 (1988): 61–78; Lees-Jeffries, "Tragedy and the Satiric Voice." More generally, see Rolf Soellner, *Timon of Athens: Shakespeare's Pessimistic Tragedy* (Columbus, OH, 1979).

3. On *Troilus and Cressida* and satire, see chapter 4 above, note 12.

4. On *Timon* and Seneca, see John M. Wallace, "*Timon of Athens* and the Three Graces: Shakespeare's Senecan Study," *Modern Philology* 83 (1986): 349–63.

5. Aristotle, *Politics*, 1253a.

6. Cf. Seneca, *De providentia*, 1.5–6; Isaiah 57:15.

7. Shakespeare, *Titus Andronicus*, 4.4.62–67. Cf. Livy, *Ab urbe condita*, 2.39. On Shakespeare's knowledge of Livy, see Baldwin, *Small Latine & Lesse Greeke*, 2:564–68, 573–74; Baldwin, *On the Literary Genetics of Shakspere's Poems and Sonnets* (Urbana, IL, 1950), 97–106.

8. Bullough, *Narrative and Dramatic Sources*, 5:506. On Shakespeare's adaptations of Plutarch in *Coriolanus*, see Burrow, *Shakespeare and Classical Antiquity*, 226–39.

9. Bullough, *Narrative and Dramatic Sources*, 5:506. Cf. Lewis and Short, *Dictionary*, s.v. "virtus." See further Phyllis Rackin, "*Coriolanus*: Shakespeare's Anatomy of *virtus*," *Modern Language Quarterly* 13 (1983): 68–79.

10. Bullough, *Narrative and Dramatic Sources*, 5:506.

11. On Plutarch's attitude to Roman *mores*, see D. A. Russell, *Plutarch*, 2nd ed. (Bristol, 2001).

12. Bullough, *Narrative and Dramatic Sources*, 5:506–7, 5:543. Plutarch elsewhere relates that, to the Volscians, Coriolanus seemed "no lesse eloquent in tongue, then warlike in shew" (ibid., 5:531). On enduring identity, see further D. J. Gordon, "Name and Fame: Shakespeare's *Coriolanus*," in *The Renaissance Imagination: Essays and Lectures by D. J. Gordon*, ed. Stephen Orgel (Berkeley and Los Angeles, 1975), 203–19.

13. I refer to Shakespeare's protagonist as "Martius" rather than as "Coriolanus"—he is not awarded his cognomen until the end of act 1, claims to renounce it in act 5, and finally has it denied him by Aufidius.

14. On Menenius and the fable of the belly, see Barkan, *Nature's Work of Art*, 95–109; Zvi Jagendorf, "*Coriolanus*: Body Politic and Private Parts," *Shakespeare Quarterly* 41 (1990): 455–69; Annabel Patterson, *Fables of Power: Aesopian Writing and Political History* (Durham, NC, 1991), 111–56; Eric Nelson, *The Greek Tradition in Republican Thought* (Cambridge, UK, 2004), 49–52, 96. On the rhetorical utility of fables (citing the example of Menenius), see Wilson, *Art of Rhetoric*, 221–22 (book 3).

15. On the modesty topos, see Curtius, *European Literature*, 83–85.

16. Bullough, *Narrative and Dramatic Sources*, 5:515.

17. See related discussion in Leah Whittington, *Renaissance Suppliants: Poetry, Antiquity, Reconciliation* (Oxford, 2016), 137–60. On Martius's deliberate refusal of civic eloquence, as opposed to his inability to perform it, see Cathy Shrank, "Civility and the City in *Coriolanus*," *Shakespeare Quarterly* 54 (2003): 406–23. See also Michael West and Myron Silberstein, "The Controversial Eloquence of Shakespeare's Coriolanus—an Anti-Ciceronian Orator?," *Modern Philology* 102 (2005): 307–31.

18. On Volumnia's severity, see Adelman, *Suffocating Mothers*, 146–64; Coppélia Kahn, *Roman Shakespeare: Warriors, Wounds and Women* (London, 1997), 144–59.

19. Gail Kern Paster, *The Idea of the City in the Age of Shakespeare* (Athens, GA, 1985), 58.

20. Cf. Aristotle, *Nicomachean Ethics*, 1059b, where the inadequacy of honor as a criterion of virtue—precisely because it depends on the opinions of others—is suggested.

21. "Prosperum ac felix scelus / virtus vocatur; sontibus parent boni" (Seneca, *Hercules Furens*, 251–52). Cf. Jonson, *Catiline*, in *Works*, ed. Bevington et al., 4:99 (3.3.15–16); John Marston, *The Malcontent*, ed. Simon Trussler and William Naismith (London, 1987), 5.3.87–88.

22. William Cornwallis, *Discourses Upon Seneca the Tragedian* (London, 1601), sig. B2r.

23. Ibid., sigs. B4v, B5r–v.

24. See Tuck, *Philosophy and Government*, chaps. 1–2; Gilles D. Monsarrat, *Light from the Porch: Stoicism and English Renaissance Literature* (Paris, 1984), chaps. 1–5; J.H.M. Salmon, "Stoicism and the Roman Example: Seneca and Tacitus in Jacobean England," *Journal of the History of Ideas* 50 (1989): 199–225; Geoff Baldwin, "Individual and Self in the Late Renaissance," *The Historical Journal* 44 (2001): 341–64.

25. See, e.g., Perry, *Shakespeare and Senecan Tragedy*, 152–86; John M. Wallace, "The Senecan Context of *Coriolanus*," *Modern Philology* 90 (1993): 465–78; Robert N. Watson, "Coriolanus and 'The Common Part,'" *Shakespeare Survey* 69 (2016): 181–97.

26. Miles, *Shakespeare and the Constant Romans*, 149–68, here 149.

27. On Martius being more impressively vivid in description than in dramatic reality, see Katharine A. Craik, "Staging Rhetorical Vividness in *Coriolanus*," *Shakespeare Studies* 47 (2019): 143–68.

28. *OED*, s.v. "affection," n. 2a–b. Cf., e.g., William Shakespeare, *Much Ado About Nothing*, ed. Claire McEachern (London, 2006), 2.1.338–39, 2.3.123, 3.1.42, and *passim*.

29. On *paradiastole*, see Skinner, *Humanism to Hobbes*, 89–117; David Colclough, "'Slippery Turns': Rhetoric and Politics in Shakespeare's *Coriolanus*," *Global Intellectual History* 5 (2020): 295–309.

30. On this use of "out," cf. Shakespeare, *Love's Labour's Lost*, 5.2.152, 165, 173; *As You Like It*, 4.1.69, 75.

31. On which, see Whittington, *Renaissance Suppliants*, 153–59.

32. Cf. the tribunes addressing him as Martius at 3.1.212.

33. Bullough, *Narrative and Dramatic Sources*, 5:544.

34. See Jonathan Goldberg, "The Anus in *Coriolanus*," in *Historicism, Psychoanalysis and Early Modern Culture*, ed. Carla Mazzio and Douglas Trevor (London, 2000), 260–71.

35. Cf. Seneca, *De ira*, 1.12.1–5.

36. Chambers, *William Shakespeare*, 1:481–83.

37. Niccolò Machiavelli, *Discourses on Livy*, ed. and trans. Harvey Mansfield and Nathan Tarcov (Chicago, 1996), 24 (1.7). Eric Nelson, "Shakespeare and the Best State of a Commonwealth," in *Shakespeare and Early Modern Political Thought*, ed. David Armitage, Conal Condren, and Andrew Fitzmaurice (Cambridge, UK, 2009), 253–70, here 269. Cicero, *De legibus*, 1.15. Of the many accounts of *Coriolanus* and politics, the following are particularly useful: Anne Barton, "Livy, Machiavelli, and Shakespeare's *Coriolanus*," *Shakespeare Survey* 38 (1985): 115–30; James Kuzner, "Unbuilding the City: *Coriolanus* and the Birth of Republican Rome," *Shakespeare Quarterly* 58 (2007): 174–99; Oliver Arnold, *The Third Citizen: Shakespeare's Theater and the Early Modern House of Commons* (Baltimore, 2007), 179–214; Paul Cantor, *Shakespeare's Rome: Republic and Empire*, 2nd ed. (Chicago, 2017), 55–126; David Norbrook, "Rehearsing the Plebeians: *Coriolanus* and the Reading of Roman History," in *Shakespeare and the Politics of Commoners: Digesting the New Social History*, ed. Chris Fitter (Oxford, 2017), 180–216.

38. On this point, see James, *Shakespeare's Troy*, 13–14.

39. See Augustine, *Of the City of God*, 1.pr., and *passim*; Sallust, *Catiline's War*, 2.2. On Shakespeare and the *libido dominandi*, cf. Patrick Gray, *Shakespeare and the Fall of the Roman Republic: Selfhood, Stoicism and Civil War* (Edinburgh, 2019); Lee Oser, *Christian Humanism in Shakespeare: A Study in Religion and Literature* (Washington, DC, 2022).

Conclusion

1. "Against Dryness," in Iris Murdoch, *Existentialists and Mystics: Writings on Philosophy and Literature*, ed. Peter Conradi (London, 1997), 287–95, here 293. Cf. Simone Weil, *Gravity and Grace*, ed. Gustave Thibon, trans. Emma Crawford and Mario von der Ruhr (London, 2002), 116–22.

BIBLIOGRAPHY

ANONYMOUS PRIMARY SOURCES are listed alphabetically by title, excluding initial articles. Anthologies of primary texts and edited volumes of essays are listed alphabetically by title, and not under the names of their editors. Multiple works by the same author are arranged chronologically (oldest on top); multiple editions of the same text by Shakespeare are listed as a group, and are also arranged chronologically.

Primary Sources

Alighieri, Dante, *The Divine Comedy of Dante Alighieri*, ed. and trans. Robert M. Durling et al., 3 vols. (Oxford, 1996–2011).
Ancient Literary Criticism: The Principal Texts in New Translations, ed. and trans. D. A. Russell and Michael Winterbottom (Oxford, 1972).
Arden of Faversham, ed. Martin White and Tom Lockwood, 2nd ed. (London, 2007).
Ariosto, Lodovico, *Ludovico Ariosto's Orlando Furioso: Translated into English Heroical Verse by Sir John Harington (1591)*, ed. Robert McNulty (Oxford, 1972).
Aristotle, *Ethica Nicomachea*, ed. Ingram Bywater (Oxford, 1894).
———, *Categoriae et liber de interpretatione*, ed. Lorenzo Minio-Paluello (Oxford, 1949).
———, *Physica*, ed. W. D. Ross (Oxford, 1950).
———, *De anima*, ed. W. D. Ross (Oxford, 1956).
———, *Politica*, ed. W. D. Ross (Oxford, 1957).
———, *Metaphysica*, ed. Werner Jaeger (Oxford, 1957).
———, *Topica et Sophistici elenchi*, ed. W. D. Ross (Oxford, 1958).
———, *Ars rhetorica*, ed. W. D. Ross (Oxford, 1959).
———, *De arte poetica liber*, ed. Rudolf Kassel (Oxford, 1965).
———, *History of Animals*, ed. and trans. A. L. Peck and D. L. Balme, 3 vols. (Cambridge, MA, 1965–91).
———, *Parts of Animals. Movement of Animals. Progression of Animals*, ed. and trans. A. L. Peck and E. S. Forster, 2nd ed. (Cambridge, MA, 2014).
Ascham, Roger, *The Scholemaster (1570)*, ed. Lawrence V. Ryan (Ithaca, NY, 1967).
Auden, W. H., *The Complete Works*, vol. 2, *Prose, 1939–1948*, ed. Edward Mendelson (Princeton, NJ, 2002).
Augustine of Hippo, St., *De Genesi ad litteram*, ed. Joseph Zycha (Vienna, 1894).
———, *Confessiones*, ed. Martin Skutelle, Heiko Jürgens, and Wiebke Schaub (Stuttgart, 1969).
———, *De civitate Dei*, ed. Bernhard Dombart and Alphonse Kalb, 2 vols. (Stuttgart, 1981).
———, *De trinitate libri XV*, ed. W. J. Mountain and François Glorie (Turnhout, Belgium, 1968).

Bacon, Francis, *De sapientia veterum* (London, 1609).

——, *The Oxford Francis Bacon*, ed. Michael Kiernan, Graham Rees, Alan Stewart, Maria Wakely, et al., 15 vols. (Oxford, 1996–).

Baldwin, James, *Collected Essays*, ed. Toni Morrison (New York, 1998).

——, *The Cross of Redemption: Uncollected Writings*, ed. Randall Kenan (New York, 2010).

du Bartas, Guillaume de Salluste, *The Divine Weeks and Works of Guillaume de Saluste, Sieur du Bartas*, ed. Susan Snyder, trans. Josuah Sylvester, 2 vols. (Oxford, 1979).

Belon, Pierre, *L'histoire naturelle des estranges poissons marins* (Paris, 1551).

——, *De aquatilibus, libri duo* (Paris, 1553).

[Berners, Juliana], *Hawking, Hunting, Fouling, and Fishing . . . A Work Right Pleasant and Profitable for All Estates*, ed. William Gryndall (London, 1596).

Boccaccio, Giovanni, *Genealogy of the Pagan Gods*, ed. and trans. Jon Solomon, 2 vols. (Cambridge, MA, 2011–17).

Boethius, *De consolatione philosophiae. Opuscula theologica*, ed. Claudio Moreschini (Leipzig and Munich, 2005).

Bolzani, Pierio Valeriano, *Hieroglyphica sive de sacris Aegyptiorum literis commentarii* (Basel, 1556).

The Book of Common Prayer: The Texts of 1549, 1559, and 1662, ed. Brian Cummings (Oxford, 2011).

Bright, Timothy, *A Treatise of Melancholie* (London, 1586).

Buchanan, George, *Tragedies*, ed. P. Sharratt and P. G. Walsh (Edinburgh, 1983).

——, *A Dialogue on the Law of Kingship Among the Scots: A Critical Edition of George Buchanan's De Iure Regni apud Scotus Dialogus*, ed. and trans. Roger A. Mason and Martin S. Smith (Aldershot, UK, 2004).

Bullough, Geoffrey, *Narrative and Dramatic Sources of Shakespeare*, 8 vols. (London, 1957–75).

Calvin, Jean, *The Institutes of the Christian Religion*, ed. and trans. John T. McNeill and Ford Lewis Battles, 2 vols. (Philadelphia, 1960).

Cartari, Vincenzo, *Vincenzo Cartari's Images of the Gods of the Ancients: The First Italian Mythography*, ed. and trans. John Mulryan (Tempe, AZ, 2012).

Case, John, *Ancilla philosophiae, seu epitome in octo libros Physicorum Aristotelis* (Frankfurt, 1600).

Castelvetro, Lodovico, *Castelvetro on the Art of Poetry: An Abridged Translation of Lodovico Castelvetro's Poetica d'Aristotele Vulgarizzata et Sposta*, ed. and trans. Andrew Bongiorno (Binghamton, NY, 1984).

Chaucer, Geoffrey, *The Riverside Chaucer*, ed. Larry D. Benson et al., 3rd ed. (Boston, 1987).

Chester, Robert, *Loves Martyr: Or, Rosalins Complaint* (London, 1601).

Cicero, *Marcus Tullius Ciceroes Thre Bokes of Duties, to Marcus his Sonne*, trans. Nicholas Grimald (London, 1556).

——, *Those Fyve Questions, Which Marke Tullye Cicero, Disputed in his Manor of Tusculanum*, trans. John Dolman (London, 1561).

——, *Orationes*, ed. A. C. Clark and William Peterson, 6 vols. (Oxford, 1901–11).

——, *Rhetorica*, ed. A. S. Wilkins, 2 vols. (Oxford, 1902–3).

——, *Tusculanae disputationes*, ed. Otto Heine and Max Pohlenz, 2 vols. (Leipzig and Berlin, 1912–22).

——, *De natura deorum*, ed. Arthur Stanley Pease (Cambridge, MA, 1955).

——, *De divinatione. De fato*, ed. Remo Giomini (Leipzig, 1975).

——, *De officiis*, ed. Michael Winterbottom (Oxford, 1994).

——, *De re publica. De legibus. Cato major. De senectute. Laelius. De amicitia*, ed. J.G.F. Powell (Oxford, 2006).

Cinthio (Giambattista Giraldi), and Daniel Javitch, "Discourse or Letter on the Composition of Comedies and Tragedies," *Renaissance Drama* 39 (2011): 207–55.

Coleridge, Samuel Taylor, *Coleridge's Criticism of Shakespeare: A Selection*, ed. R. A. Foakes (London, 1989).

Conti, Natali, *Mythologiae*, ed. John Mulryan and Stephen Brown, 2 vols. (Tempe, AZ, 2006).

Cooper, Thomas, *Thesaurus linguae Romanae & Britannicae* (London, 1565).

Cornwallis, William, *Discourses Upon Seneca the Tragedian* (London, 1601).

——, *Essayes*, ed. Don Cameron Allen (Baltimore, 1946).

Coryate, Thomas, *Coryats Crudities* (London, 1611).

Digges, Leonard, *A Prognostication Everlasting* [London, 1596].

Donatus, *Aeli Donati Commentum Terenti*, ed. Paul Wessner, 3 vols. (Leipzig, 1902–8).

Donne, John, *The Complete Poems of John Donne*, ed. Robin Robbins (London, 2010).

Dryden, John, *All for Love*, ed. N. J. Andrews (London, 1975).

Elyot, Thomas, *A Critical Edition of Sir Thomas Elyot's The Boke Named the Governour*, ed. Donald W. Rude (New York, 1992).

Emerson, Ralph Waldo, *The Complete Essays and Other Writings*, ed. Brooks Atkinson (New York, 1950).

Erasmus, Desiderius, *Erasmi Roterodami μωρίας ἐγκώμιον. i.[e.] Stulticiae laus* (Basel, 1515).

——, *The Collected Works of Erasmus*, ed. R.A.B. Mynors, Robert D. Sider, J. K. Sowards, Craig R. Thompson, et al., 86 vols. (Toronto, 1974–).

Ficino, Marsilio, *Platonic Theology*, ed. and trans. Michael J. B. Allen, James Hankins, et al., 6 vols. (Cambridge, MA, 2002–6).

Florio, John, *Florios Second Frutes* (London, 1591).

——, *Queen Anna's New World of Words, or Dictionarie of the Italian and English Tongues* (London, 1611).

Garnier, Robert, *Robert Garnier in Elizabethan England: Mary Sidney Herbert's Antonius and Thomas Kyd's Cornelia*, ed. and trans. Marie-Alice Belle and Line Cottegnies (Cambridge, UK, 2017).

Gascoigne, George, *The Noble Arte of Venerie or Hunting* (London, 1575).

Gee, John, *New Shreds Out of the Old Snare* (London, 1624).

Gentili, Alberico, *The Wars of the Romans: A Critical Edition and Translation of De armis Romanis*, ed. Benedict Kingsbury and Benjamin Straumann, trans. David Lupher (Oxford, 2011).

Gesner, Conrad, *Conradi Gesneri medici Tigurini Historiae animalium liber IIII: Qui est de piscium & aquatilium animantium natura* (Zürich, 1558).

Gosson, Stephen, *Plays Confuted in Five Actions* (London, 1582).

Greville, Fulke, *The Prose Works of Fulke Greville, Lord Brooke*, ed. John Gouws (Oxford, 1986).

Hazlitt, William, *The Selected Writings of William Hazlitt*, ed. Duncan Wu, 9 vols. (London, 1998).

Hegel, G.W.F., *Aesthetics: Lectures on Fine Art*, ed. and trans. T. M. Knox, 2 vols. (Oxford, 1975).

Heidegger, Martin, *Poetry, Language, Thought*, ed. and trans. Albert Hofstadter (New York, 1971).

——, *The Question Concerning Technology, and Other Essays*, ed. and trans. William Lovitt (New York, 1977).

——, *Being and Time: A Translation of Sein und Zeit*, trans. Joan Stambaugh (Albany, NY, 1996).

Heinsius, Daniel, *De tragica constitutione* (Leiden, 1611).

Herbert, George, *The English Poems*, ed. Helen Wilcox (Cambridge, UK, 2007).

Herodotus, *Historiae, libri I-IV*, ed. N. G. Wilson (Oxford, 2015).

Holland, Henry, *Spirituall Preservatives Against the Pestilence* (London, 1603).

Homer, *Odyssea*, ed. M. L. West (Berlin, 2017).

Horace, *Q. Horatius Flaccus, ex fide, atque auctoritate decem librorum manu scriptorum, opera*, ed. Denys Lambin (Lyon, 1561).

——, *Opera*, ed. H. W. Garrod and E. C. Wickham (Oxford, 1912).

——, *Odes and Epodes*, ed. and trans. Niall Rudd (Cambridge, MA, 2004).

Hortop, Job, *The Travailes of an English Man* (London, 1591).

Humanist Tragedies, ed. and trans. Gary R. Grund (Cambridge, MA, 2011).

[Humphrey, Laurence], *The Nobles or of Nobilitye. The Original Nature, Dutyes, Right, and Christian Institucion Thereof* (London, 1563).

Imperato, Ferrante, *Dell'historia naturale* (Naples, 1599).

James VI and I, King, *Daemonologie, in Forme of a Dialogue* (Edinburgh, 1597).

——, *Basilikon Doron. Devided into Three Bookes* (Edinburgh, 1599).

——, *Political Writings*, ed. Johann P. Sommerville (Cambridge, UK, 1994).

Jonson, Ben, *The Cambridge Edition of the Works of Ben Jonson*, ed. David Bevington, Martin Butler, Ian Donaldson, et al., 7 vols. (Cambridge, UK, 2012).

Kierkegaard, Søren, *The Concept of Irony, with Continual Reference to Socrates*, ed. and trans. Howard V. Hong and Edna H. Hong (Princeton, NJ, 1989).

——, *Kierkegaard's Journals and Notebooks*, ed. Niels Jørgen Cappelørn, Alastair Hannay, Bruce H. Kirmmse, George Pattison, Jon Stewart, et al., 11 vols. (Princeton, NJ, 2007–20).

——, *Concluding Unscientific Postscript to the Philosophical Crumbs*, ed. and trans. Alastair Hannay (Cambridge, UK, 2009).

Kyd, Thomas, *The Spanish Tragedy*, ed. J. R. Mulryne, 2nd ed. (London, 1989).

La Primaudaye, Pierre de, *The Third Volume of the French Academie, Contayning Notable Description of the Whole World, and of All the Principall Parts and Contents Thereof*, trans. Richard Dolman (London, 1601).

Lavater, Ludwig, *Of Ghostes and Spirites Walking by Nyght (1572)*, ed. John Dover Wilson and May Yardley (Oxford, 1929).

Livy, *T. Livii Patavini Latinae historiae principis decades tres* (Basel, 1549).

[Lodge, Thomas], [*A Defence of Poetry, Music, and Stage Plays*], (London, 1579).

Lucretius, *De rerum natura*, ed. W.H.D. Rouse and Martin F. Smith (Cambridge, MA, 1982).

Machiavelli, Niccolò, *Machiavelli's The Prince: An Elizabethan Translation*, ed. Hardin Craig (Chapel Hill, NC, 1944).

———, *Discourses on Livy*, ed. and trans. Harvey Mansfield and Nathan Tarcov (Chicago, 1996).

Magnus, Olaus, *Historia de gentibus septentrionalibus*, ed. and trans. Peter Foote, Peter Fisher, and Humphrey Higgens, 3 vols. (London, 1996–98).

Marlowe, Christopher, *The Complete Works of Christopher Marlowe*, ed. Roma Gill et al., 5 vols. (Oxford, 1987–98).

Marston, John, *The Malcontent*, ed. Simon Trussler and William Naismith (London, 1987).

Medieval Literary Theory and Criticism c. 1100 to c. 1375, ed. and trans. A. J. Minnis, A. B. Scott, and David Wallace (Oxford, 1988).

Meres, Francis, *Palladis Tamia, Wits Treasury* (London, 1598).

Middleton, Thomas, *The Collected Works*, ed. John Lavagnino, Gary Taylor, et al. (Oxford, 2007).

Milton, John, *The Complete Shorter Poems*, ed. John Carey, 2nd ed. (London, 1997).

———, *Paradise Lost*, ed. Alastair Fowler, 2nd ed. (London, 1997).

———, *The Complete Works of John Milton*, vol. 11, *Manuscript Writings*, ed. William Poole (Oxford, 2019).

Montaigne, Michel Eyquem, Seigneur de, *The Essayes or Morall, Politike and Millitarie Discourses of Lo: Michaell de Montaigne*, trans. John Florio (London, 1603).

———, *The Complete Essays*, ed. and trans. M. A. Screech (Harmondsworth, UK, 1991).

Murdoch, Iris, *Existentialists and Mystics: Writings on Philosophy and Literature*, ed. Peter Conradi (London, 1997).

Naipaul, V. S., *A Bend in the River* (New York, 1979).

Nashe, Thomas, *The Works of Thomas Nashe*, ed. R. B. McKerrow and F. P. Wilson, 5 vols. (Oxford, 1966).

Norton, Thomas, and Thomas Sackville, *Gorboduc*, ed. Harriet Archer and Paul Frazer (Manchester, forthcoming).

Ovid, *Amores. Medicamina faciei femineae. Ars amatoria. Remedia amoris*, ed. Edward J. Kenney (Oxford, 1994).

———, *Metamorphoses*, ed. R. J. Tarrant (Oxford, 2004).

Paradin, Claude, *The Heroicall Devises of M. Claudius Paradin Canon of Beauieu*, trans. P. S. (London, 1591).

Peacham, Henry, the Elder, *The Garden of Eloquence* (London, 1577).

Peacham, Henry, the Younger, *Minerva Britanna, or A Garden of Heroical Devises* (London, 1612).

———, *The Compleat Gentleman* (London, 1622).

Persius and Juvenal, *Saturae*, ed. W. V. Clausen (Oxford, 1992).

Petrarch, *The Canzoniere or Rerum vulgarium fragmenta*, ed. and trans. Mark Musa (Bloomington and Indianapolis, 1996).

Plato, *Opera*, ed. John Burnet, 5 vols. (Oxford, 1900–1907).

———, *Opera. Tomus I: Euthyphro, Apologia, Crito, Phaedo, Cratylus, Theaetetus, Sophista, Politicus*, ed. E. A. Duke et al. (Oxford, 1995).

——, *Respublica*, ed. S. R. Slings (Oxford, 2003).

Platter, Thomas, *Thomas Platter's Travels in England, 1599*, ed. and trans. Clare Williams (London, 1937).

——, *Beschreibung der Reisen durch Frankreich, Spanien, England und die Niederlande, 1595–1600*, ed. Rut Keiser, 2 vols. (Basel and Stuttgart, 1968).

Plautus, *Comoediae*, ed. W. M. Lindsay, 2 vols. (Oxford, 1903).

Pliny the Elder, *The Historie of the World, Commonlie Called the Naturall Historie of C. Plinius Secundus*, trans. Philemon Holland (London, 1603).

——, *Naturalis historia*, ed. Ludwig von Jan and Karl Mayhoff, 6 vols. (Leipzig, 1892–1909).

Plutarch, *The Lives of the Noble Grecians and Romanes Compared Together*, trans. Jacques Amyot and Thomas North (London, 1579).

——, *The Philosophie, Commonlie Called, the Morals Written by the Learned Philosopher Plutarch of Chaeronea*, trans. Philemon Holland (London, 1603).

——, *Moralia*, ed. Curtius Hubert et al., 7 vols. (Leipzig, 1925–78).

——, *Vitae parallelae*, ed. Claes Lindskog and Konrat Ziegler, 4 vols. (Leipzig, 1960–73).

Preston, Thomas, *A Critical Edition of Thomas Preston's Cambises*, ed. Robert C. Johnson (Salzburg, 1975).

Progymnasmata: Greek Textbooks on Prose Composition and Rhetoric, ed. and trans. George A. Kennedy (Atlanta, GA, 2003).

Pseudo-Longinus, *Libellus de sublimitate*, ed. D. A. Russell (Oxford, 1968).

Puttenham, George, *The Art of English Poesy: A Critical Edition*, ed. Frank Whigham and Wayne Rebhorn (Ithaca, NY, 2007).

Quintilian, *Institutionis oratoriae libri duodecim*, ed. Michael Winterbottom, 2 vols. (Oxford, 1970).

Ridley, Nicholas, *A Brief Declaracion of the Lordes Supper* (Emden, 1555).

Ripa, Cesare, *Iconologia*, 2 vols. (Siena, 1613).

Robortello, Francesco, *In librum Aristotelis de arte poetica explicationes* (Florence, 1548).

Sallust, *Catilina. Iugurtha. Historiarum fragmenta selecta. Appendix Sallustiana*, ed. L. D. Reynolds (Oxford, 1991).

Sandys, George, *A Relation of a Journey Began An: Dom: 1610* (London, 1615).

Scaliger, Julius Caesar, *Poetices libri septem: Sieben Bucher über die Dichtkunst*, ed. Luc Deitz, Gregor Vogt-Spira, and Manfred Fuhrmann, 6 vols. (Stuttgart, 1994–2011).

Scot, Reginald, *The Discoverie of Witchcraft* (London, 1584).

Scott, William, *The Model of Poesy*, ed. Gavin Alexander (Cambridge, UK, 2013).

Seneca the Younger, *Epistulae morales*, ed. L. D. Reynolds, 2 vols. (Oxford, 1965).

——, *Dialogi*, ed. L. D. Reynolds (Oxford, 1977).

——, *Thyestes (1560)*, ed. Joost Daalder, trans. Jasper Heywood (London, 1982).

——, *Tragoediae*, ed. Otto Zwierlein (Oxford, 1986).

Sextus Empiricus, *Against the Logicians*, ed. and trans. Richard Bett (Cambridge, UK, 2005).

Shakespeare, William, *Mr. William Shakespeares Comedies, Histories, & Tragedies* (London, 1623).

——, *The First Folio of Shakespeare*, ed. Charlton Hinman and Peter Blayney, 2nd ed. (New York, 1996).

——, *All's Well That Ends Well*, ed. Suzanne Gossett and Helen Wilcox (London, 2019).

——, *Antony and Cleopatra*, ed. John Wilders (London, 1995).

——, *As You Like It*, ed. Juliet Dusinberre (London, 2006).

——, *Coriolanus*, ed. Peter Holland (London, 2013).

——, *Cymbeline*, ed. Valerie Wayne (London, 2017).

——, *A New Variorum Edition of Shakespeare: Hamlet*, ed. Horace Howard Furness, 2 vols. (Philadelphia, 1877).

——, *Hamlet*, ed. Harold Jenkins (London, 1982).

——, *Hamlet: The Texts of 1603 and 1623*, ed. Ann Thompson and Neil Taylor (London, 2006).

——, *A New Variorum Edition of Shakespeare: The Tragedy of Julius Caesar*, ed. H. H. Furness (Philadelphia, 1913).

——, *Julius Caesar*, ed. David Daniell (London, 1998).

——, *The First Part of King Henry the Fourth*, ed. R. P. Cowl and A. E. Morgan (London, 1914).

——, *King Henry IV, Part 1*, ed. David Scott Kastan (London, 2002).

——, *King Henry IV, Part 2*, ed. James C. Bulman (London, 2016).

——, *King Henry V*, ed. T. W. Craik (London, 1995).

——, *King Henry VI, Part 1*, ed. Edward Burns (London, 2000).

——, *King Henry VI, Part 2*, ed. Ronald Knowles (London, 1999).

——, *King Henry VI, Part 3*, ed. John D. Cox and Eric Rasmussen (London, 2001).

——, *King John*, ed. Jesse M. Lander and J.I.M. Tobin (London, 2018).

——, *King Lear*, ed. R. A. Foakes (London, 1997).

——, *A New Variorum Edition of Shakespeare: King Lear*, ed Richard Knowles, 2 vols. (New York, 2020).

——, *King Richard II*, ed. Charles R. Forker (London, 2002).

——, *King Richard III*, ed. James Siemon (London, 2009).

——, *Love's Labour's Lost*, ed. H. R. Woudhuysen (London, 1998).

——, *Macbeth, A Tragœdy. With all the Alterations, Amendments, Additions, and New Songs*, [ed. William Davenant] (London, 1674).

——, *A New Variorum Edition of Shakespeare: Macbeth*, ed. Howard Horace Furness (New York, 1963).

——, *Macbeth*, ed. Sandra Clark and Pamela Mason (London, 2015).

——, *Measure for Measure*, ed. A. R. Braunmuller and Robert Watson (London, 2019).

——, *The Merchant of Venice*, ed. John Drakakis (London, 2010).

——, *The Merry Wives of Windsor*, ed. Giorgio Melchiori (London, 2000).

——, *A Midsummer Night's Dream*, ed. Sukanta Chaudhuri (London, 2017).

——, *Much Ado About Nothing*, ed. Claire McEachern (London, 2006).

——, *Othello*, ed. E.A.J. Honigmann (London, 1997).

——, *Romeo and Juliet*, ed. René Weis (London, 2012).

——, *Shakespeare's Poems: Venus and Adonis, The Rape of Lucrece, and the Shorter Poems*, ed. Katherine Duncan-Jones and H. R. Woudhuysen (London, 2007).

——, *Shakespeare's Sonnets*, ed. Katherine Duncan-Jones (London, 2010).

——, *Sir Thomas More*, ed. John Jowett (London, 2011).

——, *The Taming of the Shrew*, ed. Barbara Hodgdon (London, 2010).

———, *The Tempest*, ed. Virginia Mason Vaughan and Alden T. Vaughan (London, 1999).

———, *Timon of Athens*, ed. Anthony B. Dawson and Gretchen E. Minton (London, 2008).

———, *Titus Andronicus*, ed. Jonathan Bate (London, 1995).

———, *Troilus and Cressida*, ed. David Bevington (London, 2001).

———, *Twelfth Night*, ed. Keir Elam (London, 2008).

———, *The Two Gentlemen of Verona*, ed. William C. Carroll (London, 2004).

———, *The Winter's Tale*, ed. John Pitcher (London, 2010).

Sherry, Richard, *A Treatise of Schemes & Tropes* (London, 1550).

———, *A Treatise of the Figures of Grammer and Rhetorike* (London, 1555).

Sidney, Philip, *Miscellaneous Prose of Sir Philip Sidney*, ed. Katherine Duncan-Jones and Jan van Dorsten (Oxford, 1973).

Solinus, *The Excellent and Pleasant Work . . . Polyhistor*, trans. Arthur Golding (London, 1587).

Spenser, Edmund, *The Yale Edition of the Shorter Poems of Edmund Spenser*, ed. William A. Oram (New Haven, CT, 1989).

———, *The Faerie Queene*, ed. A. C. Hamilton et al., 2nd ed. (London, 2001).

Stubbes, Philip, *The Anatomie of Abuses*, ed. Margaret Jane Kidnie (Tempe, AZ, 2002).

Susenbrotus, Joannes, *Epitome troporum ac schematum* (London, 1562).

Tactitus, *The Ende of Nero and the Beginning of Galba: Fower Bookes of the Histories of Cornelius Tacitus. The Life of Agricola*, ed. and trans. Henry Savile (Oxford, 1591).

———, *The Annales of Cornelius Tacitus: The Description of Germanie*, trans. Richard Grenewey (London, 1598).

———, *Annales*, ed. C. D. Fisher (Oxford, 1906).

———, *Historiae*, ed. C. D. Fisher (Oxford, 1911).

Terence, *Comoediae*, ed. Robert Kauer and Wallace M. Lindsay (Oxford, 1926).

The Three Parnassus Plays (1598–1601), ed. J. B. Leishman (London, 1949).

Three Turk Plays from Early Modern England, ed. Daniel Viktus (New York, 2000).

Topsell, Edward, *The Historie of Foure-Footed Beastes* (London, 1607).

———, *The Historie of Serpents* (London, 1608).

The Tragedy of Caesar's Revenge, ed. F. S. Boas ([London], 1911).

Tragicorum Graecorum fragmenta selecta, ed. James Diggle (Oxford, 1998).

The Tudor Constitution: Documents and Commentary, ed. G. R. Elton (Cambridge, UK, 1968).

Udall, Nicholas, *Flowers or Eloquent Phrases of the Latine Speach, Gathered out of all the Sixe Comedies of Terence* (London, 1575).

Virgil, *Opera*, ed. R.A.B. Mynors (Oxford, 1969).

A Warning for Fair Women: A Critical Edition, ed. Charles Dale Cannon (The Hague, 1975).

Watson, Thomas, *A Humanist's "Trew Imitation": Thomas Watson's Absalom; A Critical Edition and Translation*, ed. John Hazel Smith (Urbana, IL, 1964).

Webbe, William, *A Discourse of English Poetry (1586)*, ed. Sonia Hernández-Santano (Cambridge, UK, 2016).

Webster, John, *The Works of John Webster*, ed. David Gunby, David Carnegie, and Antony Hammond, 3 vols. (Cambridge, UK, 1995).

Weil, Simone, *Gravity and Grace*, ed. Gustave Thibon, trans. Emma Crawford and Mario von der Ruhr (London, 2002).

William Shakespeare: The Critical Heritage, ed. Brian Vickers, 6 vols. (London, 1974–81).

Wilson, Thomas, *The Rule of Reason, Conteinying the Arte of Logique*, ed. Richard S. Sprague (Northridge, CA, 1972).

——, *The Art of Rhetoric*, ed. Peter E. Medine (University Park, PA, 1994).

Wyatt, Thomas, *The Complete Poems*, ed. R. A. Rebholz, 2nd ed. (London, 1997).

Secondary Sources

Adelman, Janet, *The Common Liar: An Essay on Antony and Cleopatra* (New Haven, CT, 1973).

——, *Suffocating Mothers: Fantasies of Maternal Origin in Shakespeare's Plays* (New York and London, 1992).

——, "Iago's Alter Ego: Race as Projection in *Othello*," *Shakespeare Quarterly* 48 (1997): 125–44.

Aebischer, Pascale, "Vampires, Cannibals and Victim-Revengers: Watching Shakespearean Tragedy through Horror Film," *Shakespeare Jahrbuch* 143 (2007): 119–31.

Akhimie, Patricia, *Shakespeare and the Cultivation of Difference: Race and Conduct in the Early Modern World* (London, 2018).

Alexander, Gavin, "*Prosopopoeia*: The Speaking Figure," in *Renaissance Figures of Speech*, ed. Sylvia Adamson, Gavin Alexander, and Katrin Ettenhuber (Cambridge, UK, 2007), 97–114.

Almond, Philip C., *England's First Demonologist: Reginald Scot and the "Discoverie of Witchcraft"* (London, 2011).

Altman, Joel B., *The Tudor Play of Mind: Rhetorical Inquiry and the Development of Elizabethan Drama* (Berkeley and Los Angeles, 1978).

——, *The Improbability of Othello: Rhetorical Anthropology and Shakespearean Selfhood* (Chicago, 2010).

Amaral, Rubem, Jr., "The Reverse of the *As* of Nîmes: An Emblematic Puzzle," in *The International Emblem: From Incunabula to Internet*, ed. Simon McKeown (Newcastle upon Tyne, 2010), 47–68.

Aptekar, Jane, *Icons of Justice: Iconography and Thematic Imagination in Book V of The Faerie Queene* (New York, 1969).

Archer, Harriet, *Unperfect Histories: The Mirror for Magistrates, 1559–1610* (Oxford, 2017).

Armitage, David, *The Ideological Origins of the British Empire* (Cambridge, UK, 2000).

Arnold, Oliver, *The Third Citizen: Shakespeare's Theater and the Early Modern House of Commons* (Baltimore, 2007).

Arshad, Yasmin, *Imagining Cleopatra: Performing Gender and Power in Early Modern England* (London, 2019).

Ashe, Laura, "Holinshed and Mythic History," in *The Oxford Handbook of Holinshed's Chronicles*, ed. Felicity Heal, Ian Archer, and Paulina Kewes (Oxford, 2013), 153–70.

Ashworth, E. J., *Language and Logic in the Post-Medieval Period* (Dordrecht, Netherlands, 1974).

Astington, John, *Actors and Acting in Shakespeare's Time: The Art of Stage Playing* (Cambridge, UK, 2010).

Auerbach, Erich, *Mimesis: The Representation of Reality in Western Literature*, trans. Willard R. Trask (Princeton, NJ, 1953).

Baldwin, Geoff, "Individual and Self in the Late Renaissance," *The Historical Journal* 44 (2001): 341–64.

Baldwin, T. W., *William Shakspere's Small Latine & Lesse Greeke*, 2 vols. (Urbana, IL, 1944).

——, *Shakspere's Five-Act Structure* (Urbana, IL, 1947).

——, *On the Literary Genetics of Shakspere's Poems and Sonnets* (Urbana, IL, 1950).

Barish, Jonas, *The Antitheatrical Prejudice* (Berkeley and Los Angeles, 1981).

Barkan, Leonard, *Nature's Work of Art: The Human Body as Image of the World* (New Haven, CT, 1975).

——, *The Gods Made Flesh: Metamorphosis and the Pursuit of Paganism* (New Haven, CT, 1986).

——, *Unearthing the Past: Archaeology and Aesthetics in the Making of Renaissance Culture* (New Haven, CT, 1999).

——, *Mute Poetry, Speaking Pictures* (Princeton, NJ, 2013).

Bartels, Emily, *Speaking of the Moor, from Alcazar to Othello* (Philadelphia, 2008).

Barthes, Roland, *The Pleasure of the Text*, trans. Richard Miller (New York, 1975).

——, *S / Z*, trans. Richard Miller (Oxford, 1990).

Barton, Anne, *Shakespeare and the Idea of the Play* (London, 1962).

——, "Livy, Machiavelli, and Shakespeare's *Coriolanus*," *Shakespeare Survey* 38 (1985): 115–30.

Baswell, Christopher, *Virgil in Medieval England: Figuring the Aeneid from the Twelfth Century to Chaucer* (Cambridge, UK, 1995).

Bate, Jonathan, *Shakespeare and Ovid* (Oxford, 1993).

——, *How the Classics Made Shakespeare* (Princeton, NJ, 2019).

Baumlin, James S., "The Generic Contexts of Elizabethan Satire," in *Renaissance Genres*, ed. Barbara Lewalski (Cambridge, MA, 1986), 444–67.

Becker, Anna, *Gendering the Renaissance Commonwealth* (Cambridge, UK, 2020).

Bednarz, James P., *Shakespeare and the Poets' War* (New York, 2001).

Benario, Herbert W., "Shakespeare's Debt to Tacitus' *Histories*," *Notes and Queries* 55 (2008): 202–5.

Benjamin, Walter, *The Origin of German Tragic Drama*, trans. John Osborne (London, 1998).

——, *The Work of Art in the Age of its Technical Reproducibility, and Other Writings on Media*, ed. and trans. Michael W. Jennings, Edmund Jephcott, et al. (Cambridge, MA, 2008).

Bentley, Gerald Eades, *The Jacobean and Caroline Stage*, 7 vols. (Oxford, 1941–68).

——, *The Profession of Dramatist in Shakespeare's Time, 1590–1642* (Princeton, NJ, 1971).

——, *The Profession of Player in Shakespeare's Time* (Princeton, NJ, 1984).

Berger, Harry, Jr., *Making Trifles of Terrors: Redistributing Complicities in Shakespeare*, ed. Peter Erickson (Stanford, CA, 1997).

Berns, Laurence, "Gratitude, Nature, and Piety in *King Lear*," *Interpretation* 3 (1972): 27–51.

Berry, Edward, *Shakespeare and the Hunt: A Cultural and Social Study* (Cambridge, UK, 2001).

Berry, Ralph, *Tragic Instance: The Sequence of Shakespeare's Tragedies* (Newark, DE, 1999).

Bevington, David, *Action and Eloquence* (Cambridge, MA, 1984).

——, *Shakespeare's Ideas: More Things in Heaven and Earth* (Chichester, 2008).

——, *Murder Most Foul: Hamlet through the Ages* (Oxford, 2011).

Billings, Joshua, *Genealogy of the Tragic: Greek Tragedy and German Philosophy* (Princeton, NJ, 2014).

Binns, J. W., "Shakespeare's Latin Citations: The Editorial Problem," *Shakespeare Survey* 35 (1982): 119–28.

Bishop, T. G., *Shakespeare and the Theatre of Wonder* (Cambridge, UK, 1996).

Blair, Ann, *The Theater of Nature: Jean Bodin and Renaissance Science* (Princeton, NJ, 1997).

Blank, Daniel, *Shakespeare and University Drama in Early Modern England* (Oxford, 2023).

Blayney, Peter, *The Texts of King Lear and Their Origins* (Cambridge, UK, 1982).

Bloch, Marc, *The Royal Touch: Sacred Monarchy and Scrofula in England and France*, trans. J. E. Anderson (London, 1973).

Boersma, Gerald P., "The *Rationes Seminales* in Augustine's Theology of Creation," *Nova et Vetera* 18 (2020): 413–41.

Booth, Stephen, "On the Value of *Hamlet*," in *Reinterpretations of Elizabethan Drama*, ed. Norman Rabkin (New York, 1969), 137–76.

——, *King Lear, Macbeth, Indefinition, and Tragedy* (New Haven, CT, 1983).

Booth, Wayne C., *A Rhetoric of Irony* (Chicago, 1974).

Bos, Jacques, "Individuality and Inwardness in the Literary Character Sketches of the Seventeenth Century," *Journal of the Warburg and Courtauld Institutes* 61 (1998): 142–57.

Bourne, Claire M. L., *Typographies of Performance in Early Modern England* (Oxford, 2020).

Bourne, Claire M. L. and Jason Scott-Warren, " 'Thy Unvalued Booke': John Milton's Copy of the Shakespeare First Folio," *Milton Quarterly* 56 (2022): 1–85.

Boutcher, Warren, *The School of Montaigne in Early Modern Europe*, 2 vols. (Oxford, 2017).

Boyle, A. J., *Tragic Seneca: An Essay in the Theatrical Tradition* (London, 1997).

Boyle, Marjorie O'Rourke, *Erasmus on Language and Method in Theology* (Toronto, 1977).

Bradbrook, M. C., *The Rise of the Common Player* (Cambridge, MA, 1962).

Braden, Gordon, "Senecan Tragedy and the Renaissance," *Illinois Classical Studies* 9 (1984): 277–92.

——, *Renaissance Tragedy and the Senecan Tradition* (New Haven, CT, 1985).

Bradford, Alan T., "Stuart Absolutism and the 'Utility' of Tacitus," *Huntington Library Quarterly* 46 (1983): 127–55.

Bradley, A. C., *Shakespearean Tragedy: Lectures on Hamlet, Othello, King Lear, Macbeth*, 2nd ed. (London, 1905).

Brecht, Bertolt, *Brecht on Theatre: The Development of an Aesthetic*, ed. and trans. John Willett (London, 1964).

Brooke, Christopher, *Philosophic Pride: Stoicism and Political Thought from Lipsius to Rousseau* (Princeton, NJ, 2012).

Brooks, Peter, *Reading for the Plot: Design and Intention in Narrative* (New York, 1984).

Brown, Bill, "Thing Theory," in *Things*, ed. Bill Brown (Chicago, 2004), 1–22.

———, *Other Things* (Chicago, 2017).

Brownlow, F. W., *Shakespeare, Harsnett, and the Devils of Denham* (Newark, DE, 1993).

Bruster, Douglas, *To Be or Not to Be* (London, 2007).

Budra, Paul, *A Mirror for Magistrates and the de casibus Tradition* (Toronto, 2000).

Burkert, Walter, *Homo Necans: The Anthropology of Ancient Greek Sacrificial Ritual and Myth*, trans. Peter Bing (Berkeley and Los Angeles, 1983).

Burns, Edward, *Character: Acting and Being on the Pre-Modern Stage* (Basingstoke, UK, 1990).

Burrow, Colin, *Epic Romance: Homer to Milton* (Oxford, 1993).

———, *Shakespeare and Classical Antiquity* (Oxford, 2013).

———, "Montaignian Moments: Shakespeare and the *Essays*," in *Montaigne in Transit: Essays in Honor of Ian Maclean*, ed. Neil Kenny, Richard Scholar, and Wes Williams (Cambridge, UK, 2016), 233–46.

———, *Imitating Authors: Plato to Futurity* (Oxford, 2019).

Burrow, J. A., *The Ages of Man: A Study in Medieval Writing and Thought* (Oxford, 1988).

Bushnell, Rebecca, *Tragedies of Tyrants: Political Thought and Theater in the English Renaissance* (Ithaca, NY, 1990).

———, *A Culture of Teaching: Early Modern Humanism in Theory and Practice* (Ithaca, NY, 1996).

———, *Tragic Time in Drama, Films, and Video Games* (London, 2016).

Buttay-Jutier, Florence, *Fortuna: Usages politiques d'une allégorie morale à la renaissance* (Paris, 2008).

Caines, Michael, *Shakespeare and the Eighteenth Century* (Oxford, 2013).

Calhoun, Alison, "Feeling Indifference: Flaying Narratives in Montaigne and Shakespeare," in *Shakespeare and Montaigne*, ed. Lars Engle, Patrick Gray, and William Hamlin (Edinburgh, 2021), 180–97.

The Cambridge Companion to Renaissance Humanism, ed. Jill Kraye (Cambridge, UK, 1996).

The Cambridge Companion to Shakespeare and Race, ed. Ayanna Thompson (Cambridge, UK, 2021).

The Cambridge History of Literary Criticism, vol. 3, *The Renaissance*, ed. Glyn P. Norton (Cambridge, UK, 1999).

The Cambridge History of Renaissance Philosophy, ed. Charles B. Schmitt, Quentin Skinner, and Jill Kraye (Cambridge, UK, 1988).

Cameron, Euan, "Angels, Demons, and Everything in Between: Spiritual Beings in Early Modern Europe," in *Angels of Light?: Sanctity and the Discernment of Spirits in the Early Modern Period*, ed. Clare Copeland and Jan Machielsen (Leiden, 2013), 17–52.

Cameron, Sharon, *Impersonality: Seven Essays* (Chicago, 2007).

Cannan, Paul D., *The Emergence of Dramatic Criticism in England, from Jonson to Pope* (New York, 2006).

Cantor, Paul A., "Nature and Convention in *King Lear*," in *Poets, Princes, and Private Citizens: Literary Alternatives to Postmodern Politics*, ed. Joseph M. Knippenberg and Peter Augustine Lawler (Lanham, MD, 1996), 213–34.

———, "The Cause of Thunder: Nature and Justice in *King Lear*," in *King Lear: New Critical Essays*, ed. Jeffrey Kahan (New York and London, 2008), 231–52.

———, "*Antony and Cleopatra*. Empire, Globalization, and the Clash of Civilizations," in *Shakespeare and Politics*, ed. Bruce E. Altschuler and Michael A. Genovese (Boulder, CO, 2014), 65–83.

———, *Shakespeare's Roman Trilogy: The Twilight of the Ancient World* (Chicago, 2017).

———, *Shakespeare's Rome: Republic and Empire*, 2nd ed. (Chicago, 2017).

Carroll, William C., "Spectacle, Representation and Lineage in *Macbeth* 4.1," *Shakespeare Survey* 67 (2014): 345–71.

Carson, Anne, *Eros the Bittersweet: An Essay* (Princeton, NJ, 1986).

Cave, Terence, *The Cornucopian Text: Problems of Writing in the French Renaissance* (Oxford, 1979).

———, *Recognitions: A Study in Poetics* (Oxford, 1990).

Cavell, Stanley, *Disowning Knowledge in Seven Plays of Shakespeare*, 2nd ed. (Cambridge, UK, 2003).

Chambers, E. K., *The Elizabethan Stage*, 4 vols. (Oxford, 1923).

———, *William Shakespeare: A Study of Facts and Problems*, 2 vols. (Oxford, 1930).

Chaudhuri, Pramit, "Classical Quotation in *Titus Andronicus*," *ELH* 81 (2014): 787–810.

Cheney, Patrick, *Shakespeare's Literary Authorship* (Cambridge, UK, 2008).

———, *English Authorship and the Early Modern Sublime: Spenser, Marlowe, Shakespeare, Jonson* (Cambridge, UK, 2018).

Chernaik, Warren, *The Myth of Rome in Shakespeare and His Contemporaries* (Cambridge, UK, 2011).

Christian, Lynda G., *Theatrum Mundi: The History of an Idea* (New York, 1987).

Clark, Stuart, *Thinking with Demons: The Idea of Witchcraft in Early Modern Europe* (Oxford, 1999).

———, *Vanities of the Eye: Vision in Early Modern European Culture* (Oxford, 2007).

Clubb, Louise George, *Italian Drama in Shakespeare's Time* (New Haven, CT, 1989).

Cohen, Simona, *Transformations of Time and Temporality in Medieval and Renaissance Art* (Leiden, 2014).

Colclough, David, "Talking to the Animals: Persuasion, Counsel and Their Discontents in *Julius Caesar*," in *Shakespeare and Early Modern Political Thought*, ed. David Armitage, Conal Condren, and Andrew Fitzmaurice (Cambridge, UK, 2009), 217–33.

———, "'Slippery Turns': Rhetoric and Politics in Shakespeare's *Coriolanus*," *Global Intellectual History* 5 (2020): 295–309.

Colie, Rosalie L., *Paradoxia Epidemica: The Renaissance Tradition of Paradox* (Princeton, NJ, 1966).

———, *The Resources of Kind: Genre Theory in the Renaissance*, ed. Barbara Lewalski (Berkeley and Los Angeles, 1973).

———, *Shakespeare's Living Art* (Princeton, NJ, 1974).

Comensoli, Viviana, *Household Business: Domestic Plays of Early Modern England* (Toronto, 1996).

Craik, Katharine A., "Staging Rhetorical Vividness in *Coriolanus*," *Shakespeare Studies* 47 (2019): 143–68.

Crane, Mary Thomas, *Framing Authority: Sayings, Self, and Society in Sixteenth-Century England* (Princeton, NJ, 1993).

Crocker, Holly A., *The Matter of Virtue: Women's Ethical Action from Chaucer to Shakespeare* (Philadelphia, 2019).

Cromartie, Alan, *The Constitutionalist Revolution: An Essay on the History of England, 1450–1642* (Cambridge, UK, 2006).

Crosbie, Christopher, "The Longleat Manuscript Reconsidered: Shakespeare and the Sword of Lath," *English Literary Renaissance* 44 (2014): 221–40.

A Cultural History of Tragedy, ed. Rebecca Bushnell et al., 6 vols. (London, 2020).

Cummins, John, *The Hound and the Hawk: The Art of Medieval Hunting* (London, 1998).

Cummings, Brian, *Mortal Thoughts: Religion, Secularity and Identity in Shakespeare and Early Modern Culture* (Oxford, 2013).

Cunnally, John, *Images of the Illustrious: The Numismatic Presence in the Renaissance* (Princeton, NJ, 1999).

Cunningham, J. V., *The Collected Essays of J. V. Cunningham* (Chicago, 1976).

Curran, Brian, *The Egyptian Renaissance: The Afterlife of Ancient Egypt in Early Modern Italy* (Chicago, 2007).

Curran, John E., Jr., *Character and the Individual Personality in English Renaissance Drama* (Newark, DE, 2014).

Curry, W. C., *Shakespeare's Philosophical Patterns* (Baton Rouge, 1937).

Curtius, Ernst Robert, *European Literature and the Latin Middle Ages*, trans. Willard R. Trask (New York, 1953).

Cutrofello, Andrew, *All for Nothing: Hamlet's Negativity* (Cambridge, MA, 2014).

Damisch, Hubert, *Théorie du nuage: Pour une histoire de la peinture* (Paris, 1972).

Danby, John F., *Shakespeare's Doctrine of Nature: A Study of King Lear* (London, 1961).

Dane, Joseph A., *The Critical Mythology of Irony* (Athens, GA, 1991).

Daniel, Drew, *Joy of the Worm: Suicide and Pleasure in Early Modern English Literature* (Chicago, 2022).

Danson, Lawrence, "The Device of Wonder: *Titus Andronicus* and Revenge Tragedies," *Texas Studies in Literature and Language* 16 (1974): 27–43.

Das, Nandini, João Vincente Melo, Haig Z. Smith, and Lauren Woking, *Keywords of Identity, Race, and Human Mobility in Early Modern England* (Amsterdam, 2021).

Daston, Lorraine, *Rules: A Short History of What We Live By* (Princeton, NJ, 2022).

Daston, Lorraine, and Katharine Park, *Wonders and the Order of Nature, 1150–1750* (New York, 1998).

Deitz, Luc, " 'Aristoteles imperator noster . . .'? J. C. Scaliger and Aristotle on Poetic Theory," *International Journal of the Classical Tradition* 2 (1995): 54–67.

Demetriou, Tania, "How Gabriel Harvey Read Tragedy," *Renaissance Studies* 35 (2021): 757–87.

Dent, R. W., *Proverbial Language in English Drama Exclusive of Shakespeare, 1495–1616* (Berkeley and Los Angeles, 1984).

Depledge, Emma, *Shakespeare's Rise to Cultural Prominence: Politics, Print and Alteration, 1642–1700* (Cambridge, UK, 2018).

Desmet, Christy, *Reading Shakespeare's Characters: Rhetoric, Ethics, and Identity* (Amherst, MA, 1992).

———, "The Persistence of Character," *Shakespeare Studies* 34 (2006): 46–55.

Detienne, Marcel, and Jean-Pierre Vernant, *Cunning Intelligence in Greek Culture and Society*, trans. Janet Lloyd (Chicago, 1991).

Dewar-Watson, Sarah, *Shakespeare's Poetics: Aristotle and the Anglo-Italian Renaissance Genres* (London, 2018).

Dickson, Vernon Guy, " 'A Pattern, Precedent, and Lively Warrant': Emulation, Rhetoric, and Cruel Propriety in *Titus Andronicus*," *Renaissance Quarterly* 62 (2009): 376–409.

Di Maria, Salvatore, *The Italian Tragedy in the Renaissance: Cultural Realities and Theatrical Innovations* (Lewisburg, PA, 2002).

The Division of the Kingdoms: Shakespeare's Two Versions of King Lear, eds. Gary Taylor and Michael Warren (Oxford, 1983).

Dobson, Michael, *The Making of the National Poet: Shakespeare, Adaptation and Authorship, 1660–1769* (Oxford, 1994).

Dodsworth, Martin, *Hamlet Closely Observed* (London, 1985).

Dollimore, Jonathan, *Radical Tragedy: Religion, Ideology and Power in the Drama of Shakespeare and His Contemporaries*, 3rd ed. (Basingstoke, UK, 2004).

Donker, Marjorie, *Shakespeare's Proverbial Themes: A Rhetorical Context for the Sententia as Res* (Westport, CT, 1992).

Doran, Madeleine, *Endeavors of Art: A Study of Form in Elizabethan Drama* (Madison, WI, 1954).

Dox, Donalee, *The Idea of the Theater in Latin Christian Thought: Augustine to the Fourteenth Century* (Ann Arbor, MI, 2004).

Duran, Robert, *The Theory of the Sublime from Longinus to Kant* (Cambridge, UK, 2015).

Dutton, Richard, *Shakespeare: Court Dramatist* (Oxford, 2016).

Eagleton, Terry, *Sweet Violence: The Idea of the Tragic* (Oxford, 2003).

Economou, George D., *The Goddess Natura in Medieval Literature* (Cambridge, MA, 1972).

Eden, Kathy, *Poetic and Legal Fiction in the Aristotelian Tradition* (Princeton, NJ, 1986).

Edwards, Michael, *Time and the Science of the Soul in Early Modern Philosophy* (Leiden, 2013).

Edwards, Philip, "Thrusting Elysium into Hell: The Originality of *The Spanish Tragedy*," in *The Elizabethan Theatre XI*, ed. A. L. Magnusson and C. E. McGee (Port Credit, Ontario, 1990), 117–32.

Eliot, T. S., *Selected Essays*, 2nd ed. (London, 1934).

Elton, William R., "Shakespeare's Ulysses and the Problem of Value," *Shakespeare Studies* 2 (1966): 95–111.

———, *King Lear and the Gods*, 2nd ed. (Lexington, KY, 1988).

———, *Shakespeare's Troilus and Cressida and the Inns of Court Revels* (Aldershot, UK, 2000).

Empson, William, *The Structure of Complex Words* (London, 1951).

———, *Some Versions of Pastoral* (New York, 1974).

———, *The Strengths of the Shrew: Essays, Memoirs, and Reviews*, ed. John Haffenden (Sheffield, UK, 1995).

Enterline, Lynn, *Shakespeare's Schoolroom: Rhetoric, Discipline, Emotion* (Philadelphia, 2012).

Erne, Lukas, *Shakespeare as Literary Dramatist* (Cambridge, UK, 2003).

——, *Shakespeare and the Book Trade* (Cambridge, UK, 2013).

Essays on Aristotle's Poetics, ed. Amélie Oksenberg Rorty (Princeton, NJ, 1992).

Ettenhuber, Katrin, *The Logical Renaissance: Literature, Cognition, and Argument, 1479–1630* (Oxford, 2023).

Everett, Barbara, *Young Hamlet: Essays on Shakespeare's Tragedies* (Oxford, 1989).

Ewbank, Inga-Stina, "The Fiend-Like Queen: A Note on *Macbeth* and Seneca's *Medea*," *Shakespeare Survey* 19 (1967): 82–94.

Farrington, Benjamin, *The Philosophy of Francis Bacon: An Essay on Its Development from 1603 to 1609 with New Translations of Fundamental Texts* (Liverpool, 1964).

Feingold, Mordechai, "Scholarship and Politics: Henry Savile's Tacitus and the Essex Connection," *Review of English Studies* 67 (2016): 855–74.

Ferguson, Arthur B., *Utter Antiquity: Perceptions of Prehistory in Renaissance England* (Durham, NC, 1993).

Floyd-Wilson, Mary, *English Ethnicity and Race in Early Modern Drama* (Cambridge, UK, 2003).

——, "English Epicures and Scottish Witches," *Shakespeare Quarterly* 57 (2006): 131–61.

Foakes, R. A., *Illustrations of the English Stage, 1580–1642* (Stanford, CA, 1985).

Foster, Donald W., "Macbeth's War on Time," *English Literary Renaissance* 16 (1986): 319–42.

Fowler, Alastair, *Kinds of Literature: An Introduction to the Theory of Genres and Modes* (Oxford, 1982).

Freund, Elizabeth, "'Ariachne's Broken Woof': The Rhetoric of Citation in *Troilus and Cressida*," in *Shakespeare and the Question of Theory*, ed. Geoffrey Hartmann and Patricia Parker (New York, 1985), 19–35.

Frye, Northrop, *Fools of Time: Studies in Shakespearean Tragedy* (Toronto, 1967).

Frye, Roland Mushat, *The Renaissance Hamlet: Issues and Responses in 1600* (Princeton, NJ, 1984).

Gajda, Alexandra, "Tacitus and Political Thought in Early Modern Europe, c. 1530–1640," in *The Cambridge Companion to Tacitus*, ed. A. J. Woodman (Cambridge, UK, 2010), 253–68.

Garber, Marjorie, "'Vassal Actors': The Role of the Audience in Shakespearean Tragedy," *Renaissance Drama* 9 (1978): 71–89.

Gellrich [Zerba], Michelle, *Tragedy and Theory: The Problem of Conflict since Aristotle* (Princeton, NJ, 1988).

Gent, Lucy, *Picture and Poetry, 1560–1620* (Leamington Spa, UK, 1981).

Gibson, Walter S., *Pieter Bruegel the Elder: Two Studies* ([Lawrence, KS], 1991).

Gillespie, Stuart, *Shakespeare's Books* (London, 2001).

Gillies, John, *Shakespeare and the Geography of Difference* (Cambridge, UK, 1994).

Ginzburg, Carlo, "High and Low: The Theme of Forbidden Knowledge in the Sixteenth and Seventeenth Centuries," *Past & Present* 73 (1976): 28–41.

Glacken, Clarence J., *Traces on the Rhodian Shore: Nature and Culture in Western Thought from Ancient Times to the End of the Eighteenth Century* (Berkeley and Los Angeles, 1967).

Goldberg, Jonathan, "The Anus in *Coriolanus*," in *Historicism, Psychoanalysis and Early Modern Culture*, ed. Carla Mazzio and Douglas Trevor (London, 2000), 260–71.

Gombrich, E. H., *Art and Illusion: A Study in the Psychology of Pictorial Representation*, 6th ed. (London, 2002).

Gordon, D. J., *The Renaissance Imagination: Essays and Lectures by D. J. Gordon*, ed. Stephen Orgel (Berkeley and Los Angeles, 1975).

Gossen, Hans, and August Steier, "Krokodile und Eidechsen," in *Realencyclopädie der classischen Altertumswissenschaft*, ed. A. F. von Pauly, Georg Wissowa, et al., 1st ser. (Stuttgart, 1893–1980), vol. 11.2: cols. 1947–70.

Grabes, Herbert, *The Mutable Glass: Mirror-Imagery in Titles and Texts of the Middle Ages and English Renaissance*, trans. Gordon Collier (Cambridge, UK, 1982).

Grafton, Anthony, and Lisa Jardine, *From Humanism to the Humanities: Education and the Liberal Arts in Fifteenth- and Sixteenth-Century Europe* (London, 1986).

Grant, Edward, *Planets, Stars, and Orbs: The Medieval Cosmos, 1200–1687* (Cambridge, UK, 1994).

Grant, Robert M., *Miracle and Natural Law in Graeco-Roman and Early Christian Thought* (Amsterdam, 1952).

Gray, Patrick, *Shakespeare and the Fall of the Roman Republic: Selfhood, Stoicism and Civil War* (Edinburgh, 2019).

de Grazia, Margreta, "Soliloquies and Wages in the Age of Emergent Consciousness," *Textual Practice* 9 (1995): 67–92.

——, "World Pictures, Modern Periods, and the Early Stage," in *A New History of Early English Drama*, ed. John D. Cox and David Scott Kastan (New York, 1997).

——, *"Hamlet" without Hamlet* (Cambridge, UK, 2007).

——, *Four Shakespearean Period Pieces* (Chicago, 2021).

Greenberg, Jonathan, *The Cambridge Introduction to Satire* (Cambridge, UK, 2019).

Greenblatt, Stephen, *Hamlet in Purgatory* (Princeton, NJ, 2001).

Greene, Thomas, *The Light in Troy: Imitation and Discovery in Renaissance Poetry* (New Haven, CT, 1982).

Greenfield, Sayre N., "Quoting *Hamlet* in the Early Seventeenth Century," *Modern Philology* 105 (2008): 510–34.

Greg, W. W., "Hamlet's Hallucination," *Modern Language Review* 12 (1917): 393–421.

——, *Dramatic Documents from the Elizabethan Playhouses: Stage Plots: Actors' Parts: Prompt Books*, 2 vols. (Oxford 1931).

Grene, Nicholas, *Shakespeare's Tragic Imagination* (Basingstoke, UK, 1992).

Griffin, Dustin, *Satire: A Critical Reintroduction* (Lexington, KY, 1994).

Grundin, Robert, "The Soul of State: Ulyssean Irony in *Troilus and Cressida*," *Anglia* 93 (1975): 55–69.

Guastella, Gianni, *Word of Mouth: Fama and Its Personifications in Art and Literature from Ancient Rome to the Middle Ages* (Oxford, 2017).

Guj, Luisa, "*Macbeth* and the Seeds of Time," *Shakespeare Studies* 18 (1986): 175–88.

Gurr, Andrew, *The Shakespearean Stage, 1574–1642*, 4th ed. (Cambridge, UK, 2009).

Gurval, Robert Alan, *Actium and Augustus: The Politics and Emotions of Civil War* (Ann Arbor, MI, 1995).

Hadot, Pierre, *Philosophy as a Way of Life*, ed. Arnold I. Davidson, trans. Michael Chase (Oxford, 1995).

Hall, Kim F., *Things of Darkness: Economies of Race and Gender in Early Modern England* (Ithaca, NY, 1996).

Hallett, Charles A., and Elaine S. Hallett, *The Revenger's Madness: A Study of Revenge Tragedy Motifs* (Lincoln, NE, 1980).

Halliwell, Stephen, *Aristotle's Poetics*, 2nd ed. (London, 1998).

Hamlin, Hannibal, *The Bible in Shakespeare* (Oxford, 2013).

Hamlin, William, *Montaigne's English Journey: Reading the "Essays" in Shakespeare's Day* (Oxford, 2013).

Hammersmith, James P., "The Serpent of Old Nile," *Interpretations* 14 (1982): 11–16.

Hammond, Paul, "Macbeth and the Ages of Man," *Notes and Queries* 36 (1989): 332–33.

——, *The Strangeness of Tragedy* (Oxford, 2009).

Hankins, James, *Virtue Politics: Soulcraft and Statecraft in Renaissance Italy* (Cambridge, MA, 2019).

Hankins, John Erskine, *Backgrounds of Shakespeare's Thought* (Hamden, CT, 1978).

Hardie, Philip, *Rumour and Renown: Representations of Fama in Western Literature* (Cambridge, UK, 2012).

Harrison, Peter, *The Bible, Protestantism, and the Rise of Natural Science* (Cambridge, UK, 1998).

Hartog, François, *The Mirror of Herodotus: The Representation of the Other in the Writing of History*, trans. Janet Lloyd (Berkeley and Los Angeles, 1988).

Hathaway, Baxter, *The Age of Criticism: The Late Renaissance in Italy* (Ithaca, NY, 1962).

Haugen, Kristine Louise, "The Birth of Tragedy in the Cinquecento: Humanism and Literary History," *Journal of the History of Ideas* 72 (2011): 351–70.

Hawhee, Debra, *Rhetoric in Tooth and Claw: Animals, Language, Sensation* (Chicago, 2016).

Heffernan, Julián Jiménez, "'Beyond This Ignorant Present': The Poverty of Historicism in *Macbeth*," *Palgrave Communications* 2 (2016): no. 16054, https://doi.org/10.1057/palcomms.2016.54.

Helmers, Helmer, "The Politics of Mobility: Shakespeare's *Titus Andronicus*, Jan Vos's *Aran en Titus*, and the Poetics of Empire," in *Politics and Aesthetics in European Baroque and Classicist Tragedy*, ed. Jan Bloemendal and Nigel Smith (Leiden, 2016), 344–72.

Herrick, Marvin T., "Some Neglected Sources of *Admiratio*," *Modern Language Notes* 62 (1947): 222–26.

——, *Comic Theory in the Sixteenth Century* (Urbana, IL, 1950).

——, *Italian Tragedy in the Renaissance* (Urbana, IL, 1965).

Hirsh, James, *Shakespeare and the History of Soliloquies* (Madison, NJ, 2003).

Honigmann, E.A.J., *The Texts of Othello and Shakespearean Revision* (London, 1996).

——, "To Be or Not to Be," in *In Arden: Editing Shakespeare. Essays in Honour of Richard Proudfoot*, ed. Gordon McMullan and Ann Thompson (London, 2003), 209–10.

Horowitz, Maryanne Cline, *Seeds of Virtue and Knowledge* (Princeton, NJ, 1998).

Howard, Leon, *The Logic of Hamlet's Soliloquies* (Lone Pine, CA, 1964).

Hoxby, Blair, *What Was Tragedy? Theory and the Early Modern Canon* (Oxford, 2015).

Hudson, Benjamin, *Macbeth Before Shakespeare* (Oxford, 2023).

Hui, Andrew, "Horatio's Philosophy in *Hamlet*," *Renaissance Drama* 41 (2013): 151–71.

Hume, Robert D., "Before the Bard: 'Shakespeare' in Early Eighteenth-Century London," *ELH* 64 (1997): 41–75.

Hunt, Maurice A., *Shakespeare's Speculative Art* (New York, 2011).

Hunter, G. K., "The Marking of *Sententiae* in Elizabethan Printed Plays, Poems, and Romances," *The Library* 6 (1951): 171–88.

Hunter, Lynette and Peter Lichtenfels, *Negotiating Shakespeare's Language in Romeo and Juliet: Reading Strategies from Criticism, Editing and the Theatre* (Farnham, UK, 2009).

Hutson, Lorna, "Not the King's Two Bodies: Reading the 'Body Politic' in Shakespeare's *Henry IV*, Parts 1 and 2," in *Rhetoric and Law in Early Modern Europe*, ed. Victoria Kahn and Lorna Hutson (New Haven, CT, 2001), 166–98.

———, *The Invention of Suspicion: Law and Mimesis in Shakespeare and Renaissance Drama* (Oxford, 2007).

———, *Circumstantial Shakespeare* (Oxford, 2015).

———, "On the Knees of the Body Politic," *Representations* 152 (2020): 25–54.

———, "The Play in the Mind's Eye," in *The Places of Early Modern Criticism*, ed. Gavin Alexander, Emma Gilby, and Alexander Marr (Oxford, 2021), 97–111.

———, *England's Insular Imagining: The Elizabethan Erasure of Scotland* (Cambridge, UK, 2023).

"If Then the World a Theatre Present . . .": Revisions of the Theatrum Mundi Metaphor in Early Modern England, ed. Björn Quiring (Berlin, 2014).

Jagendorf, Zvi, "*Coriolanus*: Body Politic and Private Parts," *Shakespeare Quarterly* 41 (1990): 455–69.

James, Heather, *Shakespeare's Troy: Drama, Politics, and the Translation of Empire* (Cambridge, UK, 1997).

———, *Ovid and the Liberty of Speech in Shakespeare's England* (Cambridge, UK, 2021).

James, Henry, *The Critical Muse: Selected Literary Criticism*, ed. Roger Gard (Harmondsworth, UK, 1987).

Janson, H. W., "The 'Image Made by Chance' in Renaissance Thought," in *De Artibus Opuscula XL: Essays in Honor of Erwin Panofsky*, ed. Millard Meiss, vol. 1 (New York, 1961), 254–66.

Javitch, Daniel, "The Emergence of Poetic Genre Theory in the Sixteenth Century," *Modern Language Quarterly* 59 (1998): 139–69.

Jones, Emrys, *Scenic Form in Shakespeare* (Oxford, 1971).

———, *The Origins of Shakespeare* (Oxford, 1977).

Jones, Howard, *Master Tully: Cicero in Tudor England* (Nieuwkoop, Netherlands, 1998).

Jones, Norman, *Governing by Virtue: Lord Burghley and the Management of Elizabethan England* (Oxford, 2015).

Joseph, B. L., *Elizabethan Acting* (London, 1951).

Josipovici, Gabriel, *Hamlet: Fold on Fold* (New Haven, CT, 2016).

Kahn, Coppélia, "The Absent Mother in *King Lear*," in *Rewriting the Renaissance: The Discourses of Sexual Difference in Early Modern Europe*, ed. Margaret Ferguson, Maureen Quilligan, and Nancy Vickers (Chicago, 1986), 33–49.

———, *Roman Shakespeare: Warriors, Wounds and Women* (London, 1997).

Kahn, Victoria, *The Future of Illusion: Political Theology and Early Modern Texts* (Chicago, 2014).

Kalas, Rayna, *Frame, Glass, Verse: The Technology of Poetic Invention in the English Renaissance* (Ithaca, NY, 2007).

Kallendorf, Craig, "Virgil, Dante, and Empire in Italian Thought, 1300–1500," *Vergilius* 34 (1988): 44–69.

———, *The Other Virgil: "Pessimistic" Readings of the Aeneid in Early Modern Culture* (Oxford, 2007).

Kantorowicz, Ernst H., "Mysteries of State: An Absolutist Concept and Its Late Mediaeval Origins," *Harvard Theological Review* 48 (1955): 65–91.

———, *The King's Two Bodies: A Study in Mediaeval Political Theology* (Princeton, NJ, 1957).

Kapitaniak, Pierre, *Spectres, ombres et fantômes. Discours et représentations dramatiques en Angleterre, 1576–1642* (Paris, 2008).

Kappl, Brigitte, *Die Poetik des Aristoteles in der Dichtungstheorie des Cinquecento* (Berlin and New York, 2006).

Karim-Cooper, Farah, *Cosmetics in Shakespearean and Renaissance Drama* (Edinburgh, 2006).

Kastan, David Scott, *Shakespeare and the Shapes of Time* (Hanover, NH, 1982).

———, "'His Semblable His Mirror': *Hamlet* and the Imitation of Revenge," *Shakespeare Studies* 19 (1987): 111–24.

———, *Shakespeare After Theory* (New York and London, 1999).

———, *Shakespeare and the Book* (Cambridge, UK, 2001).

———, *A Will to Believe: Shakespeare and Religion* (Oxford, 2014).

Kelly, Henry Ansgar, "Aristotle-Averroes-Alemannus on Tragedy: The Influence of the *Poetics* on the Latin Middle Ages," *Viator* 10 (1979): 161–209.

———, *Ideas and Forms of Tragedy from Aristotle to the Middle Ages* (Cambridge, UK, 1993).

———, *Chaucerian Tragedy* (Cambridge, UK, 1997).

Kemp, Wolfgang, *Natura: Ikonographische Studien zur Geschichte und Verbreitung einer Allegorie* (Tübingen, 1973).

Kermode, Frank, *The Classic: Literary Images of Permanence and Change* (New York, 1975).

———, *Forms of Attention: Botticelli and Hamlet* (Chicago, 1985).

———, *History and Value* (Oxford, 1988).

———, *Shakespeare's Language* (London, 2000).

———, *The Sense of an Ending: Studies in the Theory of Fiction*, 2nd ed. (New York, 2000).

———, "Opinion in *Troilus and Cressida*," *Critical Quarterly* 54 (2012): 88–102.

Kernan, Alvin, *The Cankered Muse: Satire of the English Renaissance* (New Haven, CT, 1959).

Kerrigan, John, *Revenge Tragedy: Aeschylus to Armageddon* (Oxford, 1996).

———, *Archipelagic English* (Oxford, 2008).

———, *Shakespeare's Binding Language* (Oxford, 2016).

———, *Shakespeare's Originality* (Oxford, 2018).

Kessler, Eckhard, "The Intellective Soul," in *The Cambridge History of Renaissance Philosophy*, ed. Charles B. Schmitt, Quentin Skinner, and Jill Kraye (Cambridge, UK, 1988), 485–534.

Kewes, Paulina, "Romans in the Mirror," in *A Mirror for Magistrates in Context*, ed. Harriet Archer and Andrew Hadfield (Cambridge, UK, 2016), 126–46.

———, "'I Ask Your Voice and Your Suffrages'· The Bogus Rome of Peele and Shakespeare's *Titus Andronicus*," *The Review of Politics* 78 (2016): 551–70.

Kiefer, Frederick, *Fortune and Elizabethan Tragedy* (San Marino, CA, 1983).

Kiernan, Pauline, *Shakespeare's Theory of Drama* (Cambridge, UK, 1996).

Kimbrough, Robert, *Shakespeare's Troilus & Cressida and Its Setting* (Cambridge, MA, 1964).

Kinney, Arthur F., *Lies Like Truth: Shakespeare, Macbeth, and the Cultural Moment* (Detroit, 2001).

———, *Shakespeare's Webs: Networks of Meaning in Renaissance Drama* (New York, 2004).

Kiséry, András, *Hamlet's Moment: Drama and Political Knowledge in Early Modern England* (Oxford, 2016).

Klause, John, "A Shakespearean Scene in *Pericles*, II," *Notes and Queries* 62 (2015): 578–83.

Kliman, Bernice W., "At Sea about *Hamlet* at Sea: A Detective Story," *Shakespeare Quarterly* 62 (2011): 180–204.

Knowles, Richard, "How Shakespeare Knew *King Leir*," *Shakespeare Survey* 55 (2002): 12–35.

Knowles, Ronald, "Hamlet and Counter-Humanism", *Renaissance Quarterly* 52 (1999): 1046–69.

Knox, Dilwyn, *Ironia: Medieval and Renaissance Ideas on Irony* (Leiden, 1989).

Knox, Norman, *The Word Irony and Its Context, 1500–1755* (Durham, NC, 1961).

Koerner, Joseph Leo, *Bosch & Bruegel: From Enemy Painting to Everyday Life* (Princeton, NJ, 2016).

Koselleck, Reinhart, *Futures Past: On the Semantics of Historical Time*, trans. Keith Tribe (New York, 2004).

Kottman, Paul, "Defying the Stars: Tragic Love as the Struggle for Freedom in *Romeo and Juliet*," *Shakespeare Quarterly* 63 (2012): 1–38.

———, "What Is Shakespearean Tragedy?," in *The Oxford Handbook of Shakespearean Tragedy*, ed. Michael Neill and David Schalkwyk (Oxford, 2016), 3–18.

Kraye, Jill, "Moral Philosophy", in *The Cambridge History of Renaissance Philosophy*, ed. Charles B. Schmitt, Quentin Skinner, and Jill Kraye (Cambridge, UK, 1988), 303–86.

Kristeller, Paul Oskar, *Studies in Renaissance Thought and Letters* (Rome, 1956).

———, *Renaissance Thought and the Arts: Collected Essays* (Princeton, NJ, 1980).

———, "Humanism," in *The Cambridge History of Renaissance Philosophy*, ed. Charles B. Schmitt, Quentin Skinner, and Jill Kraye (Cambridge, UK, 1988), 113–37.

Kuntz, Marion L., and Paul G. Kuntz, *Jacob's Ladder and the Tree of Life: Concepts of Hierarchy and the Great Chain of Being* (New York, 1987).

Kurath, Hans, Sherman M. Kuhn, and Robert E. Lewis, *Middle English Dictionary* (Ann Arbor, MI, 1952–2001).

Kuzner, James, "Unbuilding the City: *Coriolanus* and the Birth of Republican Rome," *Shakespeare Quarterly* 58 (2007): 174–99.

Lake, Peter, *Hamlet's Choice: Religion and Resistance in Shakespeare's Revenge Tragedies* (New Haven, CT, 2020).

Lanham, Richard A., *The Motives of Eloquence: Literary Rhetoric in the Renaissance* (New Haven, CT, 1976).

Lazarus, Micha, "Tragedy at Wittenberg: Sophocles in Reformation Europe," *Renaissance Quarterly* 73 (2020): 33–77.

Lear, Jonathan, "Katharsis," in *Essays on Aristotle's Poetics*, ed. Amélie Oksenberg Rorty (Princeton, NJ, 1992), 315–40.

———, *A Case for Irony* (Cambridge, MA, 2011).

Lees-Jeffries, Hester, "Tragedy and the Satiric Voice," in *The Oxford Handbook of Shakespearean Tragedy*, ed. Michael Neill and David Schalkwyk (Oxford, 2016), 250–66.

———, "Body Language: Making Love in Lyric in *Romeo and Juliet*," *Review of English Studies* 74 (2023): 237–53.

Le Goff, Jacques, *The Birth of Purgatory*, trans. Arthur Goldhammer (Chicago, 1984).

Lemon, Rebecca, "Sovereignty and Treason in *Macbeth*," in *Macbeth: New Critical Essays*, ed. Nick Moschovakis (New York, 2008), 73–87.

Leo, Russ, *Tragedy as Philosophy in the Reformation World* (Oxford, 2019).

Leonard, Miriam, *Tragic Modernities* (Cambridge, MA, 2015).

Lesser, Zachary, *Hamlet After Q1: An Uncanny History of the Shakespearean Text* (Philadelphia, 2015).

Lesser, Zachary, and Peter Stallybrass, "The First Literary *Hamlet* and the Commonplacing of Professional Plays," *Shakespeare Quarterly* 59 (2008): 371–420.

Levin, Harry, *The Question of Hamlet* (London, 1959).

Levin, Richard, "The Longleat Manuscript and *Titus Andronicus*," *Shakespeare Quarterly* 53 (2002): 323–40.

Lewis, Charlton T., and Charles Short, *A Latin Dictionary* (Oxford, 1879).

Lewis, C. S., *Studies in Words* (Cambridge, UK, 1960).

Lewis, Rhodri, "Shakespeare's Clouds and the Image Made by Chance," *Essays in Criticism* 62 (2012): 1–24.

———, *Hamlet and the Vision of Darkness* (Princeton, NJ, 2017).

———, "Romans, Egyptians, and Crocodiles," *Shakespeare Quarterly* 68 (2017): 320–50.

———, "Shakespeare, Olaus Magnus, and Monsters of the Deep," *Notes and Queries* 65 (2018): 76–81.

———, "Polychronic *Macbeth*," *Modern Philology* 117 (2020): 323–46.

Lim, Vanessa, "'To Be or Not to Be': Hamlet's Humanistic *Quaestio*," *Review of English Studies* 70 (2019): 640–58.

Linderski, Jerzy, *Roman Questions: Selected Papers, 1958–1993* (Stuttgart, 1994).

Littlewood, C.A.J., *Self-Representation and Illusion in Senecan Tragedy* (Oxford, 2004).

Lloyd, Joan Barclay, *African Animals in Renaissance Literature and Art* (Oxford, 1971).

Lobis, Seth, "Sympathy and Antipathy in *King Lear*," in *Sympathy in Transformation*, ed. Roman Alexander Barton, Alexander Klaudies, and Thomas Micklich (Berlin, 2018), 89–107.

Loomba, Ania, *Gender, Race, Renaissance Drama* (Manchester, 1989).

———, *Shakespeare, Race, and Colonialism* (Oxford, 2002).

Luke, Nicholas, "Avoidance as Love: Evading Cavell on Dover Cliff," *Modern Philology* 117 (2020): 445–69.

Lupić, Ivan, *Subjects of Advice: Drama and Counsel from More to Shakespeare* (Philadelphia, 2019).

Lynch, Deidre Shauna, *The Economy of Character: Novels, Market Culture, and the Business of Inner Meaning* (Chicago, 1998).

Mack, Peter, *Reading and Rhetoric in Montaigne and Shakespeare* (London, 2010).

Maclean, Ian, *The Renaissance Notion of Woman: A Study of the Fortunes of Scholasticism and Medical Science in European Intellectual Life* (Cambridge, UK, 1980).

———, *Logic, Signs, and Nature in the Renaissance: The Case of Learned Medicine* (Cambridge, UK, 2002).

Mahoney, Edward P., "Metaphysical Foundations of the Hierarchy of Being According to Some Late Medieval and Renaissance Philosophers," in *Philosophies of Existence, Ancient and Medieval*, ed. Parviz Morewedge (New York, 1982), 165–257.

Maitland, F. W., *The Constitutional History of England* (Cambridge, UK, 1920).

———, *State, Trust, and Corporation*, ed. David Runciman and Magnus Ryan (Cambridge, UK, 2003).

Mallin, Eric S., *Godless Shakespeare* (London, 2007).

de Man, Paul, *Aesthetic Ideology*, ed. Andrzej Warminski (Minneapolis, 1996).

Manley, Lawrence, *Convention, 1500–1750* (Cambridge, MA, 1980).

Manning, Roger B., *Hunters and Poachers: A Social and Cultural History of Unlawful Hunting in England, 1485–1640* (Oxford, 1993).

Mapstone, Sally, "Shakespeare and Scottish Kingship: A Case History," in *The Rose and the Thistle: Essays on the Culture of Late Medieval and Renaissance Scotland*, ed. Sally Mapstone and Juliet Wood (East Linton, UK, 1998), 158–89.

Margolin, Jean-Claude, "Ex philologo theologus? Philologus et theologus? Réflexions autour de la *Ratio verae theologiae*," *Rinascimento* 48 (2008): 197–228.

Marienstras, Richard, *Le proche et le lointain: Sur Shakespeare, le drame élisabéthain et l'idéologie anglaise aux XVIe et XVIIe siècles* (Paris, 1981).

Marsden, Jean I., *The Re-Imagined Text: Shakespeare, Adaptation, and Eighteenth-Century Literary Theory* (Lexington, KY, 1995).

Marshall, Peter, *Beliefs and the Dead in Reformation England* (Oxford, 2002).

Martindale, Charles, and Michelle Martindale, *Shakespeare and the Uses of Antiquity* (London, 1990).

Marx, William, *The Tomb of Oedipus: Why Greek Tragedies Were Not Tragic*, trans. Nicholas Elliot (London, 2022).

Maxwell, Julie, "Counter-Reformation Versions of Saxo: A New Source for *Hamlet*?," *Renaissance Quarterly* 57 (2004): 518–60.

McCabe, Richard, *The Pillars of Eternity: Time and Providence in The Faerie Queene* (Dublin, 1989).

———, "Tragedy, or the Fall of Middle-Class Men," in *Literature, Learning, and Social Hierarchy in Early Modern Europe*, ed. Neil Kenny (Oxford, 2022), 219–38.

McCarthy, Harry R., *Boy Actors in Early Modern England: Skill and Stagecraft in the Theatre* (Cambridge, UK, 2022).

McCullough, Peter, "Christmas at Elsinore," *Essays in Criticism* 58 (2008): 311–32.

McDonald, Charles Osborne, *The Rhetoric of Tragedy: Form in Stuart Drama* ([Amherst, MA], 1966).

McDonald, Mark A., *Shakespeare's King Lear and The Tempest: The Discovery of Nature and the Recovery of Natural Right* (Lanham, MD, 2004).

McDonald, Russ, *Shakespeare and the Arts of Language* (Oxford, 2001).

McEachern, Claire, *Believing in Shakespeare: Studies in Longing* (Cambridge, UK, 2018).

The Medieval Concept of Time: Studies on the Scholastic Debate and its Reception in Early Modern Philosophy, ed. Pasquale Porro (Leiden, 2001).

Menzer, Paul, *The Hamlets: Cues, Qs, and Remembered Texts* (Newark, DE, 2008).

Mercer, Peter, *Hamlet and the Acting of Revenge* (Iowa City, 1984).

Michael, Erika Betty Goodman, "The Drawings by Hans Holbein the Younger for Erasmus' *Praise of Folly*" (PhD diss., University of Washington, 1981).

Miles, Geoffrey, *Shakespeare and the Constant Romans* (Oxford, 1996).

Milton, J. R., "Laws of Nature," in *The Cambridge History of Seventeenth-Century Philosophy*, ed. Daniel Garber and Michael Ayers, vol. 1 (Cambridge, UK, 1998), 680–701.

Miola, Robert, *Shakespeare's Rome* (Cambridge, UK, 1983).

——, *Shakespeare and Classical Tragedy: The Influence of Seneca* (Oxford, 1992).

——, *Shakespeare and Classical Comedy: The Influence of Plautus and Terence* (Oxford, 1994).

Modersohn, Mechthild, *Natura als Göttin im Mittelalter: Ikonographische Studien zu Darstellungen der personifizierten Nature* (Berlin, 1997).

Monsarrat, Gilles D., *Light from the Porch: Stoicism and English Renaissance Literature* (Paris, 1984).

Moretti, Franco, *Signs Taken for Wonders: Essays in the Sociology of Literary Forms*, trans. Susan Fisher, David Forgacs, and David Miller (New York, 1983).

Mortimer, Nigel, *Medieval and Early Modern Portrayals of Julius Caesar: The Transmission of an Idea* (Oxford, 2020).

Moss, Ann, *Printed Commonplace Books and the Structuring of Renaissance Thought* (Oxford, 1996).

Moss, Stephanie, "Transformation and Degeneration: The Paracelsan / Galenic Body in *Othello*," in *Disease, Diagnosis, and Cure on the Early Modern Stage*, ed. Stephanie Moss and Kaara L. Peterson (Aldershot, UK, 2004), 151–70.

Moul, Victoria, *Jonson, Horace and the Classical Tradition* (Cambridge, UK, 2010).

Muecke, D. C., *The Compass of Irony* (London, 1969).

Muir, Kenneth, "Samuel Harsnett and *King Lear*," *Review of English Studies* 2 (1951): 11–21.

Mukherji, Subha, *Law and Representation in Early Modern Drama* (Cambridge, UK, 2006).

Natural Laws and Laws of Nature in Early Modern Europe, ed. Lorraine Daston and Michael Stolleis (Farnham, UK, 2008).

Nauert, Charles G., *Humanism and the Culture of Renaissance Europe*, 2nd ed. (Cambridge, UK, 2006).

Ndiaye, Noémie, *Scripts of Blackness: Early Modern Performance Culture and the Making of Race* (Philadelphia, 2022).

Neely, Carol Thomas, "Women and Men in *Othello*," in *The Woman's Part: Feminist Criticism of Shakespeare*, ed. Carolyn Ruth Swift Lenz, Gayle Greene, and Carol Thomas Neely (Urbana, IL, 1980), 211–39.

Nehamas, Alexander, "Pity and Fear in the *Rhetoric* and the *Poetics*," in *Essays on Aristotle's Poetics*, ed. Amélie Oksenberg Rorty (Princeton, NJ, 1992), 291–314.

Neill, Michael, *Issues of Death: Mortality and Identity in English Renaissance Tragedy* (Oxford, 1997).

——, "The Designs of *Titus Andronicus*," in *The Oxford Handbook of Shakespearean Tragedy*, ed. Michael Neill and David Schalkwyk (Oxford, 2016), 339–57.

Nelson, Eric, *The Greek Tradition in Republican Thought* (Cambridge, UK, 2004).

——, "Shakespeare and the Best State of a Commonwealth," in *Shakespeare and Early Modern Political Thought*, ed. David Armitage, Conal Condren, and Andrew Fitzmaurice (Cambridge, UK, 2009), 253–70.

Nevo, Ruth, "Tragic Form in *Titus Andronicus*," in *Further Studies in English Literature*, ed. A. A. Mendilow (Jerusalem, 1973), 1–18.

Nicholson, Catherine, "*Othello* and the Geography of Persuasion," *English Literary Renaissance* 40 (2010): 56–87.

Nohrnberg, James, *The Analogy of The Faerie Queene* (Princeton, NJ, 1976).

Norbrook, David, "*Macbeth* and the Politics of Historiography," in *Politics of Discourse: The Literature and History of Seventeenth-Century England*, eds. Kevin Sharpe and Steven N. Zwicker (Berkeley and Los Angeles, 1987), 78–116.

——, "Rhetoric, Ideology, and the Elizabethan World Picture," in *Renaissance Rhetoric*, ed. Peter Mack (Basingstoke, UK, 1994), 140–64.

——, "The Emperor's New Body? *Richard II*, Ernst Kantorowicz, and the Politics of Shakespeare Criticism," *Textual Practice* 10 (1996): 329–57.

——, "Rehearsing the Plebeians: *Coriolanus* and the Reading of Roman History," in *Shakespeare and the Politics of Commoners: Digesting the New Social History*, ed. Chris Fitter (Oxford, 2017), 180–216.

Norland, Howard B., *Neoclassical Tragedy in Elizabethan England* (Newark, DE, 2009).

Nussbaum, Martha, *The Fragility of Goodness: Luck and Ethics in Greek Tragedy and Philosophy*, 2nd ed. (Cambridge, UK, 2001).

Nuttall, A. D., *Shakespeare the Thinker* (New Haven, CT, 2007).

Oberthaler, Elke, Sabine Pénot, Manfred Sellink, and Ron Spronk, with Alice Hoppe-Harnoncourt, *Bruegel: The Master* (London, 2018).

Orgel, Stephen, "The Poetics of Incomprehensibility," *Shakespeare Quarterly* 42 (1991): 431–37.

——, "*Macbeth* and the Antic Round," *Shakespeare Survey* 52 (1999): 143–53.

——, *Wit's Treasury: Renaissance England and the Classics* (Philadelphia, 2021).

Oser, Lee, *Christian Humanism in Shakespeare: A Study in Religion and Literature* (Washington, DC, 2022).

Owens, Judith, *Emotional Settings in Early Modern Pedagogical Culture* (Cham, 2020).

The Oxford Handbook of Shakespearean Tragedy, ed. Michael Neill and David Schalkwyk (Oxford, 2016).

Pagden, Anthony, *Lords of All the World: Ideologies of Empire in Spain, Britain and France c. 1500–c. 1800* (Cambridge, UK, 1995).

Palmer, Ada, *Reading Lucretius in the Renaissance* (Cambridge, MA, 2014).

Park, Katharine, "The Organic Soul," in *The Cambridge History of Renaissance Philosophy*, ed. Charles B. Schmitt, Quentin Skinner, and Jill Kraye (Cambridge, UK, 1988), 464–84.

———, "Nature in Person: Medieval and Renaissance Allegories and Emblems," in *The Moral Authority of Nature*, ed. Lorraine Daston and Fernando Vidal (Chicago, 2004), 50–73.

Parker, John, "Persona," in *Cultural Reformations: Medieval and Renaissance in Literary History*, ed. Brian Cummings and James Simpson (Oxford, 2010), 591–608.

Paster, Gail Kern, *The Idea of the City in the Age of Shakespeare* (Athens, GA, 1985).

Patterson, Annabel, *Fables of Power: Aesopian Writing and Political History* (Durham, NC, 1991).

Paul, Henry N., *The Royal Play of Macbeth* (New York, 1950).

Paul, Joanne, "The Use of *Kairos* in Renaissance Political Philosophy," *Renaissance Quarterly* 67 (2014): 43–78.

Pawlak, Anna, "The Imaginarium of Death: Pieter Bruegel's *The Triumph of Death*," in *Pieter Bruegel the Elder and Religion*, ed. Bertram Kaschek, Jürgen Müller, and Jessica Buskirk (Leiden, 2018).

Pearlman, E., "Shakespeare at Work: The Invention of the Ghost", in *Hamlet: New Critical Essays*, ed. Arthur F. Kinney (New York, 2002), 71–84.

Pechter, Edward, "Shakespearean Tragedy: The Romantic Inheritance," in *Oxford Handbook of Shakespearean Tragedy*, ed. Michael Neill and David Schalkwyk (Oxford, 2016), 54–70.

Peltonen, Markku, "Popularity and the Art of Rhetoric: *Julius Caesar* in Context," in *Shakespeare and the Politics of Commoners: Digesting the New Social History*, ed. Chris Fitter (Oxford, 2017), 163–79.

Perry, Curtis, *Shakespeare and Senecan Tragedy* (Cambridge, UK, 2020).

———, "After Decorum: Self-Performance and Political Liminality in *Antony and Cleopatra*," in *Antony and Cleopatra: A Critical Reader*, ed. Domenico Lovascio (London, 2020).

Pertile, Giulio, "*King Lear* and the Uses of Mortification," *Shakespeare Quarterly* 67 (2016): 319–43.

Peyré, Yves, " 'Confusion Now Hath Made His Masterpiece': Senecan Resonances in *Macbeth*," in *Shakespeare and the Classics*, ed. Charles Martindale and A. B. Taylor (Cambridge, UK, 2004), 141–55.

Philo, John-Mark, "Shakespeare's *Macbeth* and Livy's Legendary Rome," *Review of English Studies* 67 (2015): 250–74.

———, "Ben Jonson's *Sejanus* and Shakespeare's *Othello*: Two Plays Performed by the King's Men in 1603," *Shakespeare Survey* 75 (2022): 122–36.

Pincombe, Mike, "Classical and Contemporary Sources of the 'Gloomy Woods' of *Titus Andronicus*: Ovid, Seneca, Spenser," in *Shakespearean Continuities: Essays in Honour of E.A.J. Honigmann*, ed. John Batchelor, Tom Cain, and Claire Lamont (London, 1997), 40–55.

Pinson, Yona, *The Fools' Journey: A Myth of Obsession in Northern Renaissance Art* (Turnhout, Belgium, 2008).

Pippin, Robert B., *Philosophy by Other Means: The Arts in Philosophy and Philosophy in the Arts* (Chicago, 2021).

Platt, Peter G., *Shakespeare's Essays: Sampling Montaigne from Hamlet to The Tempest* (Edinburgh, 2020).

Plett, Heinrich F., *Enargeia in Classical Antiquity and the Early Modern Age: The Aesthetics of Evidence* (Leiden, 2012).

Pocock, J.G.A., *The Machiavellian Moment: Florentine Political Thought and the Atlantic Republican Tradition* (Princeton, NJ, 1975).

Pollard, Tanya, *Greek Tragic Women on Shakespearean Stages* (Oxford, 2017).

Poole, Adrian, "Dogs, War and Loyalty in Shakespeare," *The Shakespearean International Yearbook* 11 (2011): 89–111.

Poole, Kristen, *Supernatural Environments in Shakespeare's England: Spaces of Demonism, Divinity, and Drama* (Cambridge, UK, 2011).

———, "Poetic Creation in an Apocalyptic Age: *King Lear* and the Making and the Unmaking of the World," in *The Cambridge Companion to Shakespeare and Religion*, ed. Hannibal Hamlin (Cambridge, UK, 2019), 234–51.

Pop, Iggy, "Caesar Lives," *Classics Ireland* 2 (1995): 94–96.

Porter, James I., "Lucretius and the Poetics of Void," in *Le jardin romain: Épicurisme et poésie à Rome*, ed. Annick Monet (Villeneuve-d'Ascq, France, 2003), 197–226.

Price, George R., "Henry V and Germanicus," *Shakespeare Quarterly* 12 (1961): 57–60.

Puech, Pierre-François, Bernard Puech, and Fernand Puech, "The 'As de Nîmes,' a Roman Coin and the Myth of Antony and Cleopatra: Octavian and Agrippa Victorious over Antony," *OMNI: Revue numismatique / Revista numismática* 8 (2014): 58–66.

Quayson, Ato, *Tragedy and Postcolonial Literature* (Cambridge, UK, 2021).

Quint, David, *Epic and Empire: Politics and Generic Form from Virgil to Milton* (Princeton, NJ, 1993).

Rackin, Phyllis, "*Coriolanus*: Shakespeare's Anatomy of *Virtus*," *Modern Language Quarterly* 13 (1983): 68–79.

Raffield, Paul, "Time, Equity, and the Artifice of English Law: Reflections on *The King's Two Bodies*," *Law, Culture, and the Humanities* 13 (2017): 36–45.

Ramazani, Jahan, "Heidegger and the Theory of Tragedy," *The Centennial Review* 32 (1988): 103–29.

Randles, W.G.L., *The Unmaking of the Medieval Christian Cosmos: From Solid Heavens to Boundless Aether, 1500–1750* (Aldershot, UK, 1999).

Rebhorn, Wayne, *The Emperor of Men's Minds: Literature and the Renaissance Discourse of Rhetoric* (Ithaca, NY, 1995).

Reiss, Timothy J., "Renaissance Theatre and the Theory of Tragedy," in *Cambridge History of Literary Criticism*, vol. 3, *The Renaissance*, ed. Glyn P. Norton (Cambridge, UK, 1999), 229–47.

———, *Mirages of the Selfe: Patterns of Personhood in Ancient and Early Modern Europe* (Stanford, CA, 2003).

Renaissance Figures of Speech, ed. Sylvia Adamson, Gavin Alexander, and Katrin Ettenhuber (Cambridge, UK, 2007).

Res et Verba in der Renaissance, ed. Eckhard Kessler and Ian Maclean (Wiesbaden, 2002).

Rhodes, Neil, "The Controversial Plot: Declamation and the Concept of the Problem Play," *Modern Language Review* 95 (2000): 609–22.

Richards, Grant, *Housman, 1897–1936* (London, 1941).

Richards, Jennifer, *Rhetoric and Courtliness in Early Modern Literature* (Cambridge, UK, 2003).

Richardson, Brian, "'Hours Dreadful and Things Strange': Inversions of Chronology and Causality in *Macbeth*," *Philological Quarterly* 68 (1989): 283–94.

Richardson, Catherine, *Domestic Life and Domestic Tragedy in Early Modern England: The Material Life of the Household* (Manchester, 2006).

Rickard, Jane, *Writing the Monarch: Jonson, Donne, Shakespeare, and the Works of King James* (Cambridge, UK, 2015).

Ricks, Christopher, *Along Heroic Lines* (Oxford, 2021).

Riggs, David, "Plot and Episode in Early Neoclassical Criticism," *Renaissance Drama* 6 (1973): 149–75.

——, "The Artificial Day and the Infinite Universe," *The Journal of Medieval and Renaissance Studies* 5 (1975): 155–85.

Robertson, Kellie, *Nature Speaks: Medieval Literature and Aristotelian Philosophy* (Philadelphia, 2017).

Robinson, Benedict, *Passion's Fictions from Shakespeare to Richardson: Literature and the Sciences of the Soul and Mind* (Oxford, 2021).

Rose, Mark, *Shakespearean Design* (Cambridge, MA, 1972).

Russell, D. A., *Plutarch*, 2nd ed. (Bristol, 2001).

Rust, Jennifer R., *The Body in Mystery: The Political Theology of the Corpus Mysticum in the Literature of Reformation England* (Evanston, IL, 2014).

Ryan, Kiernan, *Shakespearean Tragedy* (London, 2021).

Said, Edward, *Orientalism* (London, 1978).

Salingar, Leo, *Dramatic Form in Shakespeare and the Jacobeans* (Cambridge, UK, 1986).

Salmon, J.H.M., "Stoicism and the Roman Example: Seneca and Tacitus in Jacobean England," *Journal of the History of Ideas* 50 (1989): 199–225.

Saxl, Fritz, "Veritas filia temporis," in *Philosophy and History: Essays Presented to Ernst Cassirer*, ed. Raymond Klibansky and H. J. Paton (Oxford, 1936), 197–222.

Scafuro, Adele, "Roman Comedy and Renaissance Revenge Drama: *Titus Andronicus* as Exemplary Text," in *Ancient Comedy and Reception: Essays in Honor of Jeffrey Henderson*, ed. S. Douglas Olson (Berlin, 2014), 537–64.

Schama, Simon, *Landscape and Memory* (New York, 1995).

Schmitt, Jean-Claude, *Ghosts in the Middle Ages: The Living and the Dead in Medieval Society*, trans. Teresa Lavender Fagan (Chicago, 1998).

Schoenbaum, Samuel, *William Shakespeare: A Documentary Life* (Oxford, 1975).

Schultz, Celia E., "The Romans and Ritual Murder," *Journal of the American Academy of Religion* 78 (2010): 516–41.

Scott, Charlotte, *Shakespeare's Nature: From Cultivation to Culture* (Oxford, 2014).

Scott, William O., "Another 'Heroical Devise' in *Pericles*," *Shakespeare Quarterly* 20 (1969): 91–95.

Serjeantson, Richard W., "Testimony and Proof in Early-Modern England," *Studies in the History and Philosophy of Science* 30 (1999): 195–236.

——, "Testimony: The Artless Proof," in *Renaissance Figures of Speech*, ed. Sylvia Adamson, Gavin Alexander, and Katrin Ettenhuber (Cambridge, UK, 2007), 181–94.

——, "The Soul," in *The Oxford Handbook of Philosophy in Early Modern Europe*, ed. Desmond Clarke and Catherine Wilson (Oxford, 2011), 119–41.

Shakespeare and Early Modern Political Thought, ed. David Armitage, Conal Condren, and Andrew Fitzmaurice (Cambridge, UK, 2009).

Shakespeare and the Politics of Commoners: Digesting the New Social History, ed. Chris Fitter (Oxford, 2017).

Shannon, Laurie, *The Unaccommodated Animal: Cosmopolity in Shakespearean Locales* (Chicago, 2013).

Shapiro, James, *1599: A Year in the Life of William Shakespeare* (London, 2005).

——, *The Year of Lear: Shakespeare in 1606* (New York, 2015).

Shrank, Cathy, "Civility and the City in *Coriolanus*," *Shakespeare Quarterly* 54 (2003): 406–23.

Skinner, Quentin, *The Foundations of Modern Political Thought*, 2 vols. (Cambridge, UK, 1978).

——, "Moral Ambiguity and the Renaissance Art of Eloquence", *Essays in Criticism* 44 (1994): 267–91.

——, *Reason and Rhetoric in the Philosophy of Hobbes* (Cambridge, UK, 1996).

——, *Visions of Politics*, 3 vols. (Cambridge, UK, 2002).

——, *Forensic Shakespeare* (Oxford, 2014).

——, *From Humanism to Hobbes: Studies in Rhetoric and Politics* (Cambridge, UK, 2018).

Skura, Meredith Anne, "Dragon Fathers and Unnatural Children: Warring Generations in *King Lear* and Its Sources," *Comparative Drama* 42 (2008): 121–48.

Slights, William W. E., "*Genera mixta* and *Timon of Athens*," *Studies in Philology* 74 (1977): 39–62.

Smith, Emma, *This Is Shakespeare* (London, 2019).

Smith, Ian, "Seeing Blackness: Reading Race in *Othello*," in *The Oxford Handbook of Shakespearean Tragedy*, ed. Michael Neill and David Schalkwyk (Oxford, 2016), 405–20.

Smuts, R. Malcolm, "Varieties of Tacitism," *Huntington Library Quarterly* 83 (2020): 441–65.

Snyder, Susan, *The Comic Matrix of Shakespeare's Tragedies: Romeo and Juliet, Hamlet, Othello, and King Lear* (Princeton, NJ, 1979).

Soellner, Rolf, "The Madness of Hercules and the Elizabethans," *Comparative Literature* 10 (1958): 309–23.

——, "Prudence and the Price of Helen: The Debate of the Trojans in *Troilus and Cressida*," *Shakespeare Quarterly* 20 (1969): 255–63.

——, *Shakespeare's Patterns of Self-Knowledge* ([Columbus, OH], 1972).

——, *Timon of Athens: Shakespeare's Pessimistic Tragedy* (Columbus, OH, 1979).

Stallybrass, Peter, "Against Thinking," *PMLA* 122 (2007): 1580–87.

Stanivukovic, Goran, and John H. Cameron, *Tragedies of the English Renaissance: An Introduction* (Edinburgh, 2018).

Steiner, George, *The Death of Tragedy*, 2nd ed. (New Haven, CT, 1996).

Stern, Tiffany, "Was *totus mundus agit histrionem* Ever the Motto of the Globe Theatre?," *Theatre Notebook* 51 (1997): 122–27.

——, *Making Shakespeare: The Pressures of Stage and Page* (London, 2004).

——, *Documents of Performance in Early Modern England* (Cambridge, UK, 2009).

Stewart, Alan, *Shakespeare's Letters* (Oxford, 2008).

Stok, Fabio, "Virgil Between the Middle Ages and Renaissance," *International Journal of the Classical Tradition* 1 (1994): 15–22.

Strawser, Michael, *Both / And: Reading Kierkegaard from Irony to Edification* (New York, 2003).

Strier, Richard, *Resistant Structures: Particularity, Radicalism, and Renaissance Texts* (Berkeley and Los Angeles, 1997).

——, "The Judgment of the Critics that Makes Us Tremble: 'Distributing Complicities' in Recent Criticism of *King Lear*," in *Shakespeare and Judgment*, ed. Kevin Curran (Edinburgh, 2017), 215–34.

Stump, Donald V., "Sidney's Concept of Tragedy in the *Apology* and in the *Arcadia*," *Studies in Philology* 79 (1982): 41–61.

——, "Greek and Shakespearean Tragedy: Four Indirect Routes from Athens to London," in *Hamartia: The Concept of Error in the Western Tradition*, ed. Donald V. Stump et al. (New York, 1983), 211–46.

Suthren, Carla, "Translating Commonplace Marks in Gascoigne and Kinwelmersh's *Jocasta*," *Translation and Literature* 29 (2020): 59–84.

Swetnam-Burland, Molly, "Egypt Embodied: The Vatican Nile," *American Journal of Archaeology* 113 (2009): 439–57.

——, *Egypt in Italy: Visions of Egypt in Roman Imperial Culture* (Cambridge, UK, 2015).

Swift, Daniel, *Shakespeare's Common Prayers: The Book of Common Prayer and the Elizabethan Age* (Oxford, 2012).

Swinburne, Algernon Charles, *A Study of Shakespeare* (London, 1880).

Targoff, Ramie, "The Performance of Prayer: Sincerity and Theatricality in Early Modern England," *Representations* 60 (1997): 49–69.

Teramura, Misha, "Black Comedy: Shakespeare, Terence, and *Titus Andronicus*," *ELH* 84 (2018): 877–908.

Thomas, Keith, *Religion and the Decline of Magic: Studies in Popular Beliefs in Sixteenth- and Seventeenth-Century England* (London, 1971).

——, *The Ends of Life: Roads to Fulfillment in Early Modern England* (Oxford, 2009).

Thorne, Alison, *Vision and Rhetoric in Shakespeare: Looking through Language* (Basingstoke, UK, 2000).

Tilley, Morris Palmer, *A Dictionary of Proverbs in England in the Sixteenth and Seventeenth Centuries* (Ann Arbor, MI, 1950).

Toscano, Pasquale, "Pity, Singular Disability, and the Makings of Shakespearean Tragedy in *Julius Caesar*," *SEL: Studies in English Literature, 1500–1800* 61 (2021): 203–40.

Tuck, Richard, *Philosophy and Government, 1572–1651* (Cambridge, UK, 1993).

Turner, Henry, *The Corporate Commonwealth: Pluralism and Political Fictions in England, 1516–1651* (Chicago, 2016).

Usher, Penelope Meyers, "Greek Sacrifice in Shakespeare's Rome: *Titus Andronicus* and *Iphigenia in Aulis*," in *Rethinking Shakespeare Source Study*, ed. Dennis Britton and Melissa Walter (New York and London, 2018), 206–24.

Van Es, Bart, *Shakespeare in Company* (Oxford, 2013).

Vendler, Helen, *The Art of Shakespeare's Sonnets* (Cambridge, MA, 1997).

Vernant, Jean-Pierre, and Pierre Vidal-Naquet, *Myth and Tragedy in Ancient Greece* (New York, 1990).

Vickers, Brian, *In Defence of Rhetoric* (Oxford, 1988).

The Virgilian Tradition: The First Fifteen Hundred Years, ed. Jan Ziolkowski and Michael C. J. Putnam (New Haven, CT, 2008).

Waddington, Raymond B., "Antony and Cleopatra: 'What Venus Did with Mars,'" *Shakespeare Studies* 2 (1966): 210–27.

Wales, Kathleen M., "Generic 'Your' and Jacobean Drama: The Rise and Fall of a Pronominal Usage," *English Studies* 66 (1985): 7–24.

Walker, D. P., "Eternity and the Afterlife," *Journal of the Warburg and Courtauld Institutes* 27 (1964): 241–50.

Wallace, John M., "*Timon of Athens* and the Three Graces: Shakespeare's Senecan Study," *Modern Philology* 83 (1986): 349–63.

———, "The Senecan Context of *Coriolanus*," *Modern Philology* 90 (1993): 465–78.

Warren, Christopher N., "*Henry V*, Anachronism, and the History of International Law," in *The Oxford Handbook of English Law and Literature*, ed. Lorna Hutson (Oxford, 2017), 709–27.

Watson, Robert N., "Coriolanus and 'The Common Part,'" *Shakespeare Survey* 69 (2016): 181–97.

Weeks, Sophie, "Francis Bacon and the Art-Nature Distinction," *Ambix* 54 (2007): 117–45.

Weimann, Robert, *Shakespeare and the Popular Tradition in the Theater: Studies in the Social Dimension of Dramatic Form and Function*, ed. Robert Schwartz (Baltimore, 1978).

———, *Author's Pen and Actor's Voice: Playing and Writing in Shakespeare's Theatre*, ed. Helen Higbee and William West (Cambridge, UK, 2000).

Weinberg, Bernard, *A History of Literary Criticism in the Italian Renaissance*, 2 vols. (Chicago, 1961).

Weinreich, Spencer J., "Thinking with Crocodiles: An Iconic Animal at the Intersection of Early Modern Religion and Natural Philosophy," *Early Science and Medicine* 20 (2015): 209–40.

West, Michael, and Myron Silberstein, "The Controversial Eloquence of Shakespeare's Coriolanus—an Anti-Ciceronian Orator?," *Modern Philology* 102 (2005): 307–31.

Wheeler, Angela J., *English Verse Satire from Donne to Dryden* (Heidelberg, 1992).

Whipday, Emma, *Shakespeare's Domestic Tragedies: Violence in the Early Modern Home* (Cambridge, UK, 2019).

Whittington, Leah, *Renaissance Suppliants: Poetry, Antiquity, Reconciliation* (Oxford, 2016).

Wiggins, Martin, *Shakespeare and the Drama of His Time* (Oxford, 2000).

Wilamowitz-Möllendorff, Ulrich von, "Asianismus und Atticismus," *Hermes* 35 (1900): 1–52.

Wilcher, Robert, "*Timon of Athens*: A Shakespearean Experiment," *Cahiers Élisabéthains* 34 (1988): 61–78.

Wilders, John, *The Lost Garden: A View of Shakespeare's English and Roman History Plays* (London, 1978).

Wiles, David, *The Masks of Menander: Sign and Meaning in Greek and Roman Performance* (Cambridge, UK, 1991).

———, *The Players' Advice to Hamlet: The Rhetorical Acting Method from the Renaissance to the Enlightenment* (Cambridge, UK, 2020).

Wilkins, Eliza Gregory, *"Know Thyself" in Greek and Latin Literature* (Chicago, 1917).

Williams, Bernard, *Shame and Necessity* (Berkeley and Los Angeles, 1993).

Williams, Raymond, *Modern Tragedy*, ed. Pamela McCallum (Peterborough, Ontario, 2006).

Williams, Rowan, *The Tragic Imagination* (Oxford, 2016).

Wilson, Emily, *Mocked by Death: Tragic Overliving from Sophocles to Milton* (Baltimore, 2004).

Wilson, John Dover, *What Happens in Hamlet?*, 3rd ed. (Cambridge, UK, 1951).

Wilson, Richard, *Worldly Shakespeare: The Theatre of Our Good Will* (Edinburgh, 2016).

Wind, Edgar, *Pagan Mysteries in the Renaissance* (New Haven, CT, 1958).

Withington, Phil, "Honestas," in *Early Modern Theatricality*, ed. Henry S. Turner (Oxford, 2013).

Wolfe, Jessica, *Homer and the Question of Strife from Erasmus to Hobbes* (Toronto, 2015).

Womersley, David, *"3 Henry VI*: Shakespeare, Tacitus, and Parricide," *Notes and Queries* 32 (1985): 468–73.

———, *Divinity and State* (Oxford, 2010).

Yates, Frances, *Astraea: The Imperial Theme in the Sixteenth Century* (London, 1975).

Young, Julian, *The Philosophy of Tragedy: From Plato to Žižek* (Cambridge, UK, 2013).

Zagorin, Perez, *Ways of Lying: Dissimulation, Persecution, and Conformity in Early Modern Europe* (Cambridge, MA, 1990).

Zamir, Tzachi, *Double Vision: Moral Philosophy and Shakespearean Drama* (Princeton, NJ, 2007).

INDEX

Ravenscroft, Edward, 61

recognition (*anagnorisis*), 23, 26, 34, 42, 44, 48, 51, 93, 114–15, 127, 157–58, 199, 210, 212–13, 260, 278, 289, 292

rhetoric, 4, 5, 24, 28, 30, 35, 44–46, 51, 68–72, 74, 80–81, 87, 99, 100, 108–21, 134–38, 139, 144, 150, 151–52, 168–69, 192, 196, 229, 234–44, 246, 268, 270, 272, 274, 277, 287, 310

Ridley, Nicholas, 322

Riggs, David, 185, 303, 328

Ripa, Cesare, 206, 229–30

Robortello, Francesco, 11–12, 24, 296, 304

Romanticism, 14–15, 17, 39, 49, 57

Romeo and Juliet (Shakespeare), 32, 36, 38, 43, 61, 72–81, 82, 83, 126, 153, 186, 213, 221, 234, 286, 298

Rousseau, Jean-Jacques, 64

Rose, the (theater), 9

Rymer, Thomas, 13, 36, 37

Said, Edward, 244, 338

Salingar, J. G., 64

Sallust, 285, 342

Sandys, George, 234

satire, 72, 127, 138–40, 141, 259

Schlegel, August Wilhelm, 14

Schlegel, Friedrich, 14

Schopenhauer, Arthur, 109

Scot, Reginald, 102, 103, 314

Scott, William, 24, 298, 299, 312

Seneca the Younger, 19, 22, 26, 27, 32, 36, 45, 46, 59–60, 64, 65, 66, 67, 68, 69, 71, 75–76, 85, 103, 111, 113, 122, 133–34, 156, 157, 167–68, 169, 170, 207, 217, 231, 260, 261, 273–75, 282, 285, 287, 305, 323, 339

Sextus Empiricus, 110

Shakespeare, William: as author, 1, 2, 6–7, 8–12, 28, 65, 187–88, 260, 287–88; career of, 11, 126–28, 169, 256–59, 286; education of, 6, 45, 69, 164–66, 169, 255. See also *individually listed poems and plays*; tragedy, Shakespearean

Sherry, Richard, 319, 336, 337

Sidney, Philip, 11, 24, 25–26, 28, 30, 110–11, 112, 114, 139, 140, 238, 288, 298, 300, 317, 319

Skinner, Quentin, 35, 294, 302, 310, 315, 320, 324, 337, 342

Snyder, Susan, 74, 121, 309, 317, 320, 330

Socrates, 49, 111, 316

Solinus, 335

Sophocles, 14, 15, 16, 22, 23, 32, 35

Sopranos, The, 7

Sonnets (Shakespeare), 5, 11, 127, 188, 196–97, 205, 328

Spenser, Edmund, 131, 172, 175, 190, 198, 204–05, 221, 228, 317, 321, 327, 329, 334

Steiner, George, 32, 51, 302

Stendhal (Marie-Henri Beyle), 41

Stoicism, 87, 90–91, 133–34, 135, 167, 172, 274–75, 282, 289

Stubbes, Philip, 19

Sublime, the, 46–48

Suckling, John, 8

suicide, 27, 73, 90, 91, 109, 113, 158, 167, 198, 247, 250, 270, 323

Süleyman the Magnificent (Ottoman Sultan), 226

Susenbrotus, Johannes, 324

Swan, the (theater), 9

Swinburne, Algernon Charles, 198

Tacitus, 169, 253–55, 285, 322

Tarantino, Quentin, 7

Terence, 20, 26, 155, 308

Tempest, The (Shakespeare), 185, 251, 286, 327, 339

Theobald, Lewis, 164

Theophrastan characters, 40, 303–04

thing theory, 96–97

thought in speech (*dianoia/sententia*), 23, 39, 44–46, 61, 71–72, 78–80, 82, 103–04, 111–14, 115-16, 149, 201, 222, 259–60, 283, 289. See also paralogism; rhetoric

Thucydides, 16

Timon of Athens (Shakespeare and Thomas Middleton), 2, 32, 259–61, 262, 283, 323, 333

Titus Andronicus (Shakespeare and George Peele), 2, 7, 9, 28, 46, 61–72, 78, 79, 81, 82, 83, 86, 92, 111, 121, 146, 157, 168, 226, 261–62, 274, 289, 301, 323, 329

Tolstoy, Leo, 41, 198

A NOTE ON THE TYPE

———◆———

THIS BOOK has been composed in Miller, a Scotch Roman typeface designed by Matthew Carter and first released by Font Bureau in 1997. It resembles Monticello, the typeface developed for The Papers of Thomas Jefferson in the 1940s by C. H. Griffith and P. J. Conkwright and reinterpreted in digital form by Carter in 2003.

Pleasant Jefferson ("P. J.") Conkwright (1905–1986) was Typographer at Princeton University Press from 1939 to 1970. He was an acclaimed book designer and AIGA Medalist.